D1228797

Alexander Hamilton

American Foreign Policy

COURTESY OF MUSEUM OF FINE ARTS,
BOSTON, BEQUEST OF R. C. WINTHROP

Alexander Hamilton

From a portrait by John Trumbull, painted near the end of Hamilton's life

"His judgement [was] intuitively great." (George Washington)

Alexander Hamilton & American Foreign Policy

A DESIGN FOR GREATNESS

by

Gilbert L. Lycan

UNIVERSITY OF OKLAHOMA PRESS
NORMAN

BOOKS BY GILBERT L. LYCAN

Bases of World Order (with others) (Richmond, 1945)
Inside Racing: Sports and Politics (co-author) (New York, 1961)
Twelve Major Turning Points in American History (Deland, Florida, 1968)

327.73
L981

International Standard Book Number: 0–8061–0880–0

Library of Congress Catalog Card Number: 69–16730

Copyright 1970 by the University of Oklahoma Press, Publishing Division of the University. *Composed and printed at Norman, Oklahoma, U.S.A., by the University of Oklahoma Press. First edition.*

To my mother
who first inspired me with a love for
history

2/17/71 U.OKLA.P. 8.20

Preface

AT THE BEGINNING of this work, which had its origin in a dissertation at Yale in the mid-thirties, it was my intention to be so completely objective that no reader could tell whether I am, at heart, a Hamiltonian or a Jeffersonian, a Federalist or a Republican. This approach became increasingly difficult, not merely because Hamilton is such a captivating figure, but primarily because many of the issues that faced Americans during the early national period are still with us in the twentieth century, and are still unsettled. How can one avoid taking sides?

The old argument concerning states' rights is still alive, though it is constantly shifting its ground. Democracy is still an experiment, and who can state with assurance whether our liberties will be enhanced or endangered by firmer governmental controls? We hope that Jefferson's faith in the perfectibility of man is well placed, but we are not certain of it. We hope that the common man is more adept at making choices than Hamilton thought, but the history of the human race during our lifetime gives reasons for doubt.

Hamilton's outgoing diplomacy, based on the idea of obtaining justice and protecting the national interests through peaceful negotiations backed up by military force, contrasts sharply with Jefferson's reliance on the strength of moral and economic forces and on his belief that formally established military power is likely to be dangerous and self-defeating for any liberty-loving people. No issue facing Americans in this era has been debated more keenly than this one, and there is no question fraught with graver consequence. Jefferson's favorite method in diplomacy, especially with Britain and Spain, was to marshal a formidable array of arguments to beat down the opponent, whereas Hamilton tried to build a firm peace with Britain and France by a policy of patience accompanied by steady and candid negotiations designed to create a general awareness of mutual international interests based on peace and commerce. He deplored Jefferson's practice of trying always to prove that America's position was lily-white and that the foreign government alone was guilty of treaty violations or other wrongs. The efficacy of these methods constitutes a crucial point in twentieth-century diplomacy, and one on which Americans remain sharply divided. An advocate of either view can support his position by referring to the experience of the 1790's, and any officer charged with the conduct of American foreign policy in our times should study the lives of Hamilton and Jefferson.

There was also a wide area of agreement between these two leaders. It will be illustrated in the following chapters that each was devoted to the republican form of government, where the will of the people is exercised through elected representatives. Each wished to see a free movement of commerce among nations, though neither fought for the abolition of all tariff restrictions. Both were sincere advocates of peace among nations, but they differed about the best methods of promoting peace. Both believed in the market economy propelled by private enterprise. Americans accept these principles today, usually without trying to analyze them, but we still argue, as did Hamilton and Jefferson, about points within this framework.

As this work progressed, it became obvious that Hamilton has had a bad press through the years. Jefferson and his admirers of the eighteenth century and later frequently misjudged Hamilton and imputed to the great Federalist ill motives that have no basis in fact. Writers of the twentieth century have tried to relate him to greedy self-seeking capitalists and conscienceless monopolists, whom Hamilton would never have countenanced. They have created a distorted image of Hamilton, and they have sought to explain away all Jefferson's weaknesses and mistakes. This distortion still runs deep in the American mind. Hamilton's name is well known, but his work, his plans, and his intentions remain less well known than those of some of the other leading men of his time. Much of Hamilton's important work, especially his policies toward Britain and France from 1790 to 1800, have never been clearly described.

Many of these distortions and omissions are dealt with in the pages that follow. It is my hope that in many instances I have been able to set the record straight. This book is, therefore, both an analysis of Hamilton's policies and a consideration of the place he holds in the literature of history. In the effort to arrive at a mature appraisal of him, I have consulted and cited a great many scholars and authors, living and dead.

Few men have lived as richly and served a nation as grandly as Hamilton did during his brief life. Coming from the West Indies to the mainland of North America as a youth seeking to complete his education, he was soon caught up in the momentous controversy between Britain and its American colonies. He chose sides early and threw all his energies into the fight for American independence. His high-spirited contribution during the Revolutionary War was the beginning, for he was convinced that liberty would be only an illusion if it was not accompanied by law and order emanating from the people and maintained by a firm national government.

Hamilton was not perfect in judgment or in behavior. He sometimes went to extremes, or was pushed to excessive positions by the excesses of his opponents. He was subject to moods of pessimism and gloom that momentarily dimmed his vision and confused his actions. Some of the derogatory statements he made about the common people—statements that were eagerly quoted and exaggerated by his enemies and detractors—were the products of passing moods. Temporary gloom was undoubtedly the reason for the great mistake he made in attacking John Adams during the presidential campaign of 1800.

In an effort to ensure a fuller understanding of the men and their policies, I have sometimes found it necessary to contrast the ideas of Hamilton with those of Jefferson or some other contemporary. At times I have pointed out that subsequent developments proved Hamilton—or Jefferson—wrong in certain points. I hope this will not mislead any reader into thinking that I am anti-Jefferson, or that I am inconsistent in speaking well of Hamilton for some actions and criticizing him adversely for others.

It was not Hamilton's custom to dodge an issue because it might be unpopular. He did not have the timidity—or was it prudence?—to send up trial balloons. He tackled issues straight on, though this approach often made him the recognized champion of an unpopular cause and sometimes forced him to differ sharply with his closest Federalist friends. His statesmanship represented a purity of purpose and a high level of ability that is rare in the history of the world. It is amazing to discover on how many issues he saw the correct answers when few others of the time could see them. His thinking was so rapid and so penetrating that he seldom found it necessary to alter his conclusions, though his steady devotion to the nation's welfare made it possible for him to change his position in the few instances where justice seemed to require it. Perhaps no other prominent American leader has shown a higher degree of consistency in his views throughout his lifetime.

Over the past number of years several works on Hamilton have appeared. The reaction of many Jefferson scholars has been an outcry against any attempt to present Hamilton in an objective manner and a concerted effort to preserve or re-establish the old, distorted image of Hamilton. Polemics are unnecessary. A valid judgment of Hamilton and his views must eventually be made. My only purpose is to present an accurate picture of him. I have constantly tried to avoid exaggerating his virtues or accomplishments. I have not consciously omitted any fact that, if known, might seem to reduce his stature as a political leader, and I have not consciously failed at any point to give full credit to the good works and good intentions of his contemporaries. In a sense this book is "pro-Hamilton," but in supporting my conclusions I have not deliberately selected some materials and omitted others in order to make Hamilton look good or his opponents weak.

There are voluminous sources for research on Hamilton; yet there are gaps that are not likely to be filled and interesting questions that are not likely to be answered. This book is based on source materials in the Library of Congress and elsewhere in the United States and on biographies and monographs. For British and French documents I relied on the photostats and transcripts in the Library of Congress and on several volumes of printed documents. In lieu of Spanish documents and of French and British documents that are not available in the United States, I used the rather large number of monographs by several able historians who used European archives in studying this period of American diplomacy.

It is a pleasure to recall the generosity with which a great many persons have assisted me in this work. Among others at the Library of Congress, St. George L. Sioussat and Grace Gardner Griffin showed a keen personal interest in the work and gave invaluable aid. My deep appreciation is extended to Alexander Hamilton, of New York, for granting me the use of the Special Collection of Hamilton Papers in the Library of Congress; to Henry Adams, curator of the Adams Papers of the Massachusetts Historical Society, and Stephen T. Riley, librarian of the society, for the transcriptions of Hamilton material that was not otherwise available and for other assistance while I was working in their fine collections; to Frank Monaghan, for transcripts of letters from the Jay Papers; to Christopher Crittenden and D. L. Corbitt, for facilitating my study of the papers of the Hamilton period preserved in the North Carolina Archives; to A. P. Nasatir, of San Diego State College, for useful criticism of my early treatment of Hamilton's Louisiana policy; to A. F. Gamber, of Stetson University, for reading the manuscript and helping me eliminate errors; to Eliot Allen, Byron H. Gibson, and William E. Taylor, of the Department of English of Stetson, for assistance in overcoming difficult points of grammar and construction; to William Hugh McEniry, formerly dean of Stetson University, for grants-in-aid and other forms of support; and to Noel R. Parsons, for preparing the index.

Special mention must be made of the kindness of Samuel Flagg Bemis, of Yale University, for his constant interest and encouragement through the years, and for his willingness to read an early draft of the manuscript and make useful suggestions.

Honesty compels me to add that I did not agree with all the suggestions made by my friends, and so I must accept responsibility for any unfortunate errors or misinterpretations that may appear in the book.

GILBERT L. LYCAN

Stetson University
Deland, Florida
January 24, 1969

Contents

Illustrations

Map

Abbreviations Used in Footnotes

Annals	*Annals of Congress.* 42 vols. Washington, 1834–56.
ASPFR	*American State Papers. Class I. Foreign Relations.* Ed. by Walter Lowrie *et al.* 6 vols. Washington, 1832–59.
AW	*The Works of John Adams.* Ed. by Charles Francis Adams. 10 vols. Boston, 1850–56.
Brant	Brant, Irving. *James Madison.* 6 vols. Indianapolis, 1941–61.
Brymner	Brymner, Douglas, ed. "Relations with the United States after the Peace of 1783," *Report on Canadian Archives, 1890.* Ottawa, 1891.
Farrand	Farrand, Max, ed. *The Records of the Federal Convention of 1787.* 4 vols. New Haven, 1927–37.
FCA	Foreign Correspondence, American, London. Henry Adams Transcripts, Library of Congress.
Gibbs	Gibbs, George, ed. *Memoirs of the Administrations of Washington and John Adams. Edited from the Papers of Oliver Wolcott.* 2 vols. New York, 1846.
HPLC	Hamilton Papers. Library of Congress. 109 vols.
HPSCLC	Hamilton Papers. Special Collection, Library of Congress. 4 boxes.
HWH	*The Works of Alexander Hamilton.* Ed. by John C. Hamilton. 7 vols. New York, 1850–51.
HWL	*The Works of Alexander Hamilton.* Ed. by Henry Cabot Lodge. 12 vols. New York, 1904.
JCC	*Journals of the Continental Congress, 1774–1789.* Ed. by W. C. Ford *et. al.* 34 vols. Washington, 1904–37.
JMW	*The Writings of James Monroe.* Ed. by Stanislaus Murray Hamilton. 7 vols. New York, 1898–1903.

JQAW	*The Writings of John Quincy Adams.* Ed. by W. C. Ford. 7 vols. New York, 1913–17.
JW	*The Writings of Thomas Jefferson.* Memorial Edition by A. A. Liscomb and A. E. Bergh. 20 vols. Washington, 1903–1904.
KC	*The Life and Correspondence of Rufus King.* Ed. by Charles R. King. 6 vols. New York, 1894–1900.
Malone	Malone, Dumas. *Jefferson and His Time.* 3 vols. Boston, 1948–62.
Mayo	Mayo, Bernard, ed. *Instructions to the British Ministers to the United States, 1791–1812.* Washington, 1941.
MDFR	Morris, Gouverneur. *Diary of the French Revolution.* Ed. by B. C. Davenport. 2 vols. New York, 1939.
MDL	*The Diary and Letters of Gouverneur Morris.* Ed. by Anne Cary Morris. 2 vols. New York, 1888.
MW	*The Writings of James Madison.* Ed. by Gaillard Hunt. 9 vols. New York, 1900–10.
PROFO	Public Record Office, Foreign Office, London. Transcripts in Library of Congress.
RDC	*Revolutionary Diplomatic Correspondence of the United States.* Ed. by Francis Wharton. 6 vols. Washington, 1889.
Richardson	Richardson, James D., ed. *A Compilation of the Messages and Papers of the Presidents.* 11 vols. Washington, 1896–1911.
SJC	*Secret Journals of the Acts and Proceedings of Congress from the First Meeting Thereof to the Dissolution of the Confederation.* 4 vols. Boston, 1821.
Steiner	Steiner, Bernard C. *Life and Correspondence of James McHenry.* Cleveland, 1907.
WW	*The Writings of George Washington.* Ed. by John C. Fitzpatrick. 39 vols. Washington, 1931–44.

Alexander Hamilton

American Foreign Policy

CHAPTER I

Political Ideas and Personal Ambitions

ALEXANDER HAMILTON lived through a period when grim reality forced American leaders to think. New forms of government had to be established, set in motion, and tested. A national character had to be developed, customs had to be formed, and policies leading into the future had to be determined. Clear thinking, no less than courageous action, was vital for the welfare of the nation.

The study of Hamilton's foreign policy must begin with a review of his political theories, for his foreign policy was, in many respects, quite inseparable from his ideas about government in general. American diplomacy during the early years was concerned chiefly with Britain, France, and Spain. Hamilton's admiration for the British form of government was partly responsible for his desire to establish a policy of friendship and close commercial relations with that nation. His dread of governmental disorders led him to look coldly upon revolutionary France when it entered the violent stage. His abhorrence of the despotism of the Bourbon monarchs of Spain went far toward shaping his concepts of the proper relations between the United States and that country.

It is not difficult to discover Hamilton's political ideas. His essays and other papers explain his thoughts on nearly every important act of government with which he was associated. The fact that some of the ideas he proposed in *The Federalist* essays proved unworkable, or undesirable, after he became secretary of the treasury has given rise to accusations of "contradictions and inconsistencies"[1] in his policies. Yet no man who gave his candid opinion on nearly every provision in the Constitution could have proved to be right in every judgment. In contrast to other American statesmen, Hamilton displayed few contradictions between his teachings and his actions. He thought carefully and explained his ideas clearly, for he

[1] Joseph Charles, *The Origins of the American Party System* (Williamsburg, 1956), 7–12.

was frequently trying to persuade others to his point of view. He held that every act must be in accord with sound principle. Therefore, he seldom changed his mind—and he was never given to opportunism.

Chapters I and II of this book summarize Hamilton's political principles throughout his life. Therefore, they chronologically overlap the subsequent chapters, which generally follow the sequence of events. This book is intended to be, not a deep philosophical analysis of Hamilton's politics, but rather an illustration of his practical views on the day-to-day affairs of government.

From the age of nineteen onward, Hamilton was constantly ready to declare himself on every important political issue of the times. His formal political essays, discussed at length below, are his best-known contributions. *The Federalist* essays,[2] explaining the Constitution and recommending its ratification, are the most famous, but no student of American history or government should overlook the influence of "A Full Vindication" (1774),[3] supporting the First Continental Congress; "Publius" (1778),[4] scathingly condemning corruption in public office; "The Continentalist" (1781 to 1782),[5] setting forth the inadequacies of the Articles of Confederation; "Letters from Phocion" (1784),[6] urging the people of New York to stop persecuting the Tories; "Pacificus" and others (1793 to 1798),[7] concerning diplomatic relations with France; and "Americanus" (1794),[8] trying to soften American animosity toward Great Britain; "Camillus" (1795 to 1796),[9] defending Jay's Treaty. His economic papers, which concerned banking, currency, manufacturing, and trade and probably made a great impact on American life, lie outside the scope of this book.

Hamilton was highly esteemed as an orator—one who could convince his hearers and could sometimes change the mind of a jury, a judge, or a stubborn opponent. In his speeches in the Constitutional Convention of 1787 he expressed his thoughts at their highest pitch in order to "tone up" the less nationalistic members. His influence on the writing of the Consti-

[2] *HWL*, XI–XII.

[3] *Ibid.*, I, 3–52. Apparently Hamilton was born in 1755, not 1757, and was therefore nineteen when he wrote this essay.

[4] *Ibid.*, 199–209.

[5] *Ibid.*, 243–87.

[6] *Ibid.*, IV, 230–90.

[7] *Ibid.*, 432–89.

[8] *Ibid.*, V, 74–96.

[9] *Ibid.*, V, 189–491; VI, 1–197.

tution is difficult to assess, but it was probably not major. However, his addresses before the New York State Ratification Convention at Poughkeepsie carried momentous weight.[10] At the beginning of the session only nineteen of the sixty-five delegates were believed to be in favor of accepting the federal Constitution. Through patience and moderation and with exquisite discourse that was incredibly convincing, Hamilton succeeded at last in winning over the floor leader of the opposition and enough additional delegates to obtain a favorable vote of thirty to twenty-seven. True, he was assisted by the flow of events in the nation while the New York convention was deliberating; but had it not been for Hamilton's astuteness, the body would have made an early adverse decision and adjourned.

Hamilton was quite positive that the satisfaction of man's political needs required a representative form of government, whether it be a republic, as in the United States, or a limited monarchy, as in England. His study of history taught him that despotism, which he called the "natural disease of monarchy," made it necessary for the people to "murder, expel, depose, or reduce" kings to a "nominal existence, and institute popular government." He was equally vehement in denouncing "pure democracy." When the New York convention was debating the federal Constitution in 1788, a delegate proposed that, "if it were practicable," pure democracy would be "the most perfect government." Again using his knowledge of history, Hamilton strongly opposed the idea. Reminding his readers of the disastrous effects of demagoguery in ancient Athens, he maintained that an assembly of the people in a democracy could become an "ungovernable mob." They could not really deliberate, he said, but were at the mercy of rival groups of clever speakers who swayed their emotions. In the end the people were "led blindly by one tyrant or by another." When acting directly, the people were weak, pitiable, and helpless. In happy contrast, "When the people act by their representatives they are commonly irresistible."[11]

From time to time throughout his life Hamilton saw fit to mention this subject. In his exuberant youthful essay "A Full Vindication," arguing for the colonial cause against British oppression, he said that a man is a slave if he is not "governed by the laws to which he has given his consent, either in person or by his representative."[12] During the Revolutionary

[10] Some of Hamilton's speeches at the convention are given in *ibid.*, II, 3–100.

[11] *Ibid.*, 22, 52.

[12] *Ibid.*, I, 5–6.

War he wrote to his friend Gouverneur Morris that "a representative democracy," in which the officials were "chosen really and not nominally by the people," would be "most likely to be happy, regular, and durable."[13] In his famous "Continentalist" essays, which Henry Cabot Lodge called "the public beginning of the movement for a new system of government," Hamilton said that the Continental Congress had escaped the pitfalls of demagoguery because every power was "exercised by representation, not in tumultuary assemblies of the collective body of the people."[14] In the Constitutional Convention he proposed that the members of the House of Representatives (but not those of the Senate) should be elected by the "free male citizens . . . all of whom, of the age of twenty-one years and upwards should be entitled to an equal vote."[15] When Charles Cotesworth Pinckney of South Carolina moved that the representatives be elected "in such manner as the Legislature of each state should direct," Hamilton replied that such an arrangement would "vitiate the plan" for a national government.[16]

Late in the convention, Dr. Hugh Williamson of North Carolina moved to increase the number of members of the House of Representatives. Hamilton supported the motion with "great earnestness and anxiety," asserting that the "popular branch . . . should be on a broad foundation" and that if the House was not enlarged the people's liberties would be endangered. The motion was lost for the day, but later a similar motion was adopted when Washington also gave it his support.[17]

The presidential election of 1800, resulting initially in a tie between Jefferson and Burr, gave rise to several suggestions for amending the Constitution. One proposal called for the election of presidential electors by a direct vote of the people, thus taking that power from the state legislatures. Hamilton favored the proposal, for he thought it was a "sound principle to let the federal government rest, as much as possible, *on the shoulders of the people*," and to reduce the prerogatives of state legislatures.[18]

[13] Hamilton to Gouverneur Morris, May 19, 1777, *ibid.*, IX, 72.

[14] *Ibid.*, I, 243n., 247.

[15] *Ibid.*, 351.

[16] *Ibid.*, 406; Charles C. Tansill (ed.), *Documents Illustrative of the Formation of the Union of the American States* (Washington, 1927), 252 (hereafter cited as *Documents Illustrative of the Formation of the Union*).

[17] Tansill, *Documents Illustrative of the Formation of the Union*, 694, 741.

[18] Hamilton to Gouverneur Morris, April 6, 1802, *HWL*, X, 431. Italics are in the original unless otherwise indicated.

The procedure that later developed in the United States by which the people go to the polls and mark their ballots in the course of each presidential election has had the effects Hamilton desired: it has reduced the significance of the state legislatures and increased the citizens' responsibility in national affairs.

Hamilton's respect for man's experience in the past constituted a definite phase of his developing attitude toward political affairs. It accounted for his avid interest in history. He knew less about political theory and philosophy than Adams and Jefferson did, and he spent far less time than they in speculative reading; but he had a surer grasp of history. In his *Federalist* essays, in his speeches on the Constitution, and even in his personal correspondence we can almost see ancient Greece living again. He made frequent references to Rome, the empire of Charlemagne, to the Holy Roman Empire, and to the nations of modern Europe. He was sometimes in error in his discourses on history—the books of his time were not noted for accuracy, and he had no time for original research—but in his sense of closeness to history and in his reliance upon history he stands well above most other American statesmen.

He did not look backward in the manner of a reactionary, but, believing that the rules of prudent personal and political conduct derive from the experience of mankind, he searched out the past to discover more certainly the path that had proved wisest.[19] This path he would map into the distance, unless it seemed clear that a different route would be better.

In the course of praising Jefferson, Benjamin O. Fowler, founder of *The Twentieth Century*, once wrote that Hamilton's attitude toward the past made him "timid and fearful."[20] That appraisal has an element of logic in it, but actually Hamilton was no less bold than his contemporaries. He simply dreaded theorizing. "Overdriven theory" palsied "the operations of . . . government and [rendered] all rational *practice* impossible."[21] Americans had no right to consider themselves "wiser or better than other men."[22] In "The Federalist," No. 20, written by Hamilton and Madison, experience was declared to be "the oracle of truth; and where its responses are unequivocal, they ought to be conclusive and sacred."[23] C. F. Dunbar,

19 "Federalist," No. 20, *ibid.*, XI, 158.

20 "Jefferson's Service to Civilization During the Founding of the Republic," *JW*, VII, *xix*.

21 Hamilton to William Smith, 1797, *HWL*, X, 225.

22 "Continentalist," No. 3, August 9, 1781, *ibid.*, I, 254.

23 *Ibid.*, XI, 158.

writing sympathetically of Hamilton, pointed out that he seldom went "beyond the range of already tried experiments, except when required to do so by the conditions of his task."[24]

There were many occasions when the conditions of Hamilton's tasks led him to assume that he had to act on the basis of prudent calculations rather than upon examples from history; and many times he found it necessary to refute as irrelevant his colleagues' allusions to history. He knew that man's past experience had no exact or complete parallel for the United States.

Hamilton sometimes sounded epigrammatical because of his practice of supporting his arguments by the use of maxims, which he assumed were drawn directly from history. The following examples are typical:

> Good or evil is seldom as great in the reality as in the prospect.
>
> It is more easy for the human mind to calculate the evils than the advantages of a measure.
>
> There is bigotry in politics as well as in religions, equally pernicious in both.
>
> Civil and religious liberty always go together.
>
> Violent and unjust measures commonly defeat their own purpose.
>
> Luxury indicates the declension of a state.[25]

Hamilton fully realized that the new nation was establishing precedents. In 1784, when protesting against American tendencies to violate the peace treaty with Britain, he admonished his fellow citizens: "Our governments, hitherto, have no habits. How important to the happiness, not of America alone, but of mankind, that they should acquire good ones."[26] His apprehensions regarding good political habits were acute during Washington's administration. Washington shared his apprehensions, but Jefferson was less concerned about them, assuming that future generations must steer their own course. Hamilton frequently called Jefferson's attention to the importance of setting good patterns for the future, as in an unheated communication in 1791 concerning a commercial treaty with France in which

[24] C. F. Dunbar, "Some Precedents Followed by Hamilton," *Quarterly Journal of Economics*, Vol. III (October, 1888), 35. See also Hamilton to William Smith, 1797, *HWL*, X, 225; Hamilton to General Greene, June 10, 1783, HPSCLC, Box 1. This collection, consisting of four boxes of Hamilton papers, had not previously been opened to the public. It was made available for this study through the kindness of Alexander Hamilton, of New York.

[25] *HWL*, IV, 338; *ibid.*, II, 59; *ibid.*, IV, 284; *ibid.*, I, 37; *ibid.*, VI, 245; *ibid.*, I, 22.

[26] "Letters from Phocion," No. 2, 1784, *ibid.*, IV, 288.

he pointed out that "inconvenient precedents are always embarrassing."[27] Not only would he read history; he would make history, too.

"No plan of government is well founded which does not regard man as a compound of selfish and virtuous passions," said Hamilton. By "selfish passions" he meant, first, one's own legitimate interests, which every man should pursue. In addition he included demagoguery and the abhorrent practices of dishonesty in business or in government, which he condemned as destructive of human character and public welfare. The "virtuous passions" with which he thought man to be endowed included love of one's country, devotion to public welfare and duty, generosity, and a number of character qualities which he categorized under one of his most-used terms: "liberal." To expect a man to be "wholly guided" by virtuous passions, he said, "would be as great an error as to suppose him wholly destitute of them."[28] This statement, written in 1796, is Hamilton's mature philosophy on the subject of the basic factors underlying men's actions—that is, that men are guided by selfish interests and by their virtues.

Historians have placed unduly heavy emphasis on Hamilton's view of financial interest as an influence in man's behavior. It is only half of the story. Beard was correct in stating that "Hamilton proceeded on the assumptions of national interest," but Beard also understood that Hamilton "was swayed throughout the period of formation of the Constitution by large policies of government—not by any personal interests so often ascribed to him."[29] Tugwell and Dorfman went so far as to say that Hamilton defined liberty in terms of "freedom to acquire and keep wealth" and that "Jefferson's weakness for political preferment was certainly matched by Hamilton's ambition for place and money." Nathan Schachner wrote that in 1780 Hamilton "dismissed idealism as a means of governing, and thereafter made wealth the sole support of government for mutual profit."[30] In a similar vein Carl Bridenbaugh, reviewing two books on Hamilton, referred to "Hamiltonian reliance on human greed," and Adrienne

[27] Cabinet Paper, January 11, 1791, *ibid.*, 347.

[28] Hamilton's draft of Washington's speech to Congress, December 7, 1796, *ibid.*, VIII, 220.

[29] Charles A. Beard, *The Idea of National Interest* (New York, 1934), 45; Charles A. Beard, *An Economic Interpretation of the Constitution of the United States* (New York, 1913), 114 (hereafter cited as *Economic Interpretation*).

[30] Rexford Guy Tugwell and Joseph Dorfman, "Alexander Hamilton: Nation-Maker," *Columbia University Quarterly*, Vol. XXIX (December, 1937), 224; *ibid.*, Vol. XXX (March, 1938), 71; Nathan Schachner, *Alexander Hamilton* (New York, 1946), 113.

Koch in an article following the Hamilton bicentennial celebrations also took up the old refrain that Hamilton was interested only in money and power.[31]

These criticisms miss the point. Hamilton abhorred "human greed." He was of the opinion that "when avarice takes the lead in a state, it is commonly the forerunner of its fall."[32] He "was not convinced that the rich were virtuous."[33] He spoke proudly in 1784 of the "law of inheritance" in New York, which made an "equal division among the children of the parents' property," and he predicted that the law would "soon melt down those great estates, which, if they continued, might favor the power of the few."[34] His plan for the Constitution in 1787 provided that no "title of nobility be granted by the United States, or by either of them."[35] He held that the rich must be made to pay taxes for their "luxuries," for there must be some way of "taxing their superior wealth."[36] As for poll taxes, he was opposed to them "without scruple," believing that it was the duty of government "to guard the least wealthy part of the community from oppression."[37]

Hamilton saw no grounds for basic conflict between commercial and agricultural interests: "They are so inseparably interwoven that one cannot be injured without injury nor benefited without benefit to the other."[38] Unlike Washington and Jefferson, he had little firsthand knowledge of agriculture, but he had much sympathy for farmers and their problems. Before the Revolution he pointed out that in all countries where freedom was unknown the farmer was "most oppressed."[39] He shared Jefferson's idea that those who cultivate the land should own it. During the Revolution he recommended "a small tax on uncultivated land" so that the proprietor would "cultivate it himself or . . . dispose of it to some person that would." Care should be taken to see that "too great a proportion of taxes"

[31] "Founding Fathers in Modern Dress" (reviews of Louis M. Hacker, *Alexander Hamilton in the American Tradition*; and Richard B. Morris, *Alexander Hamilton and the Founding of the Nation*), *The New York Times Book Review*, January 13, 1957, 1; "Hamilton and Power," *Yale Review*, Vol. XLVII (June, 1958), 537–51.

[32] "Publius," October 19, 1778, *HWL*, I, 200.

[33] Thomas P. Govan, "The Rich, the Well-born, and Alexander Hamilton," *Mississippi Valley Historical Review*, Vol. XXXVI (March, 1950), 676.

[34] "Letters from Phocion," No. 2, *HWL*, IV, 283.

[35] *Ibid.*, I, 364.

[36] "Continentalist," No. 6, July 4, 1782, *ibid.*, 283–84.

[37] "Federalist," No. 36, *ibid.*, XI, 283.

[38] "Continentalist," No. 6, July 4, 1782, *ibid.*, I, 281.

[39] "A Full Vindication," December 15, 1774, *ibid.*, 34.

should not fall "upon land, and upon the necessaries of life—the produce of that land," for such taxation would "oppress the poor."[40] In his "Report on Manufactures (December, 1791), he referred to farming as "a state most favorable to the freedom and independence of the human mind."[41] In Hamilton's draft of Washington's speech to Congress on December 7, 1796, he held forth on the same thought he had expressed in 1774: "Among the objects of labor and industry, agriculture, considered with reference either to individual or national welfare, is first in importance."[42]

Though often asserted by historians, it cannot be proved that Hamilton wanted the United States to be continuously ruled by the rich and well-born who, as Russell Kirk expressed it, "could keep their saddles and ride . . . like English squires."[43] Nor is it easy to follow Kirk's view that in recommending a centralized government and industrialization Hamilton lacked vision for not seeing that they would lead to leveling tendencies and the welfare state. Hamilton would have assumed that the industrial workers would act in accordance with their interests and that their interests would not be contradictory to those of the owner class and the nation at large. His fulminations against the French Revolution (see Chapter VIII) were directed at the irresponsible leaders, not at the rising masses.

It is unjust to try to cast Hamilton as a precursor of the hard-bitten American millionaires of the late nineteenth century. He could never have consorted with men of wealth like those who within two generations after his death were ruthlessly exploiting the country's natural resources and building monopolies that were endangering the life of the Republic. He would probably not have joined forces with William Jennings Bryan, but neither would he have supported Mark Hanna and William McKinley. He would have been shocked by the Republican position on the gold standard under 1896 conditions. His banking policy was to make financial credit more abundant, not to restrict it. Paper money, to be issued by the federal government, did not frighten him. During the war crisis of 1798, wishing to "keep the circulation full," he recommended the issuance of "treasury notes" with no mention of any metallic, or other, backing.[44]

[40] "Continentalist," No. 4, August 30, 1781, "Continentalist," No. 6, July 4, 1782, *ibid.*, 261 n., 278.

[41] *Ibid.*, IV, 74.

[42] *Ibid.*, VIII, 214.

[43] Russell Kirk, *The Conservative Mind* (Chicago, 1953), 69.

[44] Hamilton to Oliver Wolcott, August 22, 1798, *HWL*, X, 317.

In so far as he supported financial, commercial, and industrial enterprise, he did so with the thought that it would promote the general welfare, not personal or class welfare. Nor would he have opposed government ownership of some of the country's natural resources. His thoughts concerning mining are illustrative of this point. He assumed that mining would someday have great economic importance in America, where "nature had so richly impregnated the bowels of the earth." He stated that "all the precious metals should be absolutely the property of the Federal Government" and that the government should own a share in all other mines.[45]

This is not to say that Hamilton had no concern for money. Beard perhaps mildly exaggerated in saying that "an intense augmentation of his personal fortune was no consideration with him."[46] Hamilton had a moderate desire to accumulate wealth. In the various public offices he held, he was always persistent in seeing that he received his full salary, upon which he was quite dependent. It was largely for financial reasons that he resigned his position as secretary of the treasury in 1795. He "retired from office with clean, though empty, hands."[47] His devoted wife was of aristocratic lineage, and apparently he shared her desire to live in good style. Ford says, "He left the public service . . . because he was starved out," meaning simply that Hamilton's salary did not meet his needs. He was reported at the time to have told his friends that he was not worth more than "five hundred dollars in the world."[48]

Hamilton's son James A. Hamilton described a rather touching incident that took place soon after the Revolutionary War ended. Hamilton, Jay, and a few others who had gathered for dinner fell to discussing which was the better investment—land in the suburbs of New York City or rural land. Jay held to the former position, acted upon it, and grew rich. Hamilton "took the opposite view" and bought land in the northern part of the state. "The wild lands were purchased at a few cents the acre, but they were not settled very rapidly" and left Hamilton poor. From the same source comes the story that on one occasion the notorious French diplomat Talleyrand, who apparently appreciated in others the integrity which he himself lacked, saw the former secretary of the treasury working late at

45 "Continentalist," No. 6, July 4, 1782, *ibid.*, I, 285–86.

46 Beard, *Economic Interpretation*, 114.

47 Seth Ames (ed.), *Works of Fisher Ames* (Boston, 1854), II, 262.

48 Henry Jones Ford, *Alexander Hamilton* (New York, 1920), 258; Robert Irving Warshow, *Alexander Hamilton: First American Business Man* (New York, 1931), 185, citing "Custis in His Recollections of Washington."

night on a legal case and "remarked to a friend, 'I have beheld one of the wonders of the world. I have seen a man who has made the fortune of a nation laboring all night to support his family.' "[49]

Hamilton spoke often of the "virtuous passions" of men. Most of his essays in the public press would have made no sense at all had he not been appealing to the noble qualities of the minds of his contemporaries. He called out to "the true patriot who never fears to sacrifice popularity to what he believes to be the cause of the public good," and he asked his fellow Americans to "aspire to the glory of the greatest triumph which a people can gain, a triumph over prejudice."[50] He believed there were "some men" who would stand true to their duties in spite of economic distress or the temptations of wealth.[51]

Hamilton suffered from periods of mental depression and disappointment, and at such times he occasionally made extremely gloomy appraisals of the character and capabilities of his fellow creatures. At other times in the course of an argument he would state a point emphatically without the qualifications that were actually part of his thought. Some of his statements regarding "interest" are examples of generalizations expressed when time or circumstances made it difficult for him to give a full explanation of his views. In the Constitutional Convention of 1787 he set forth his most adversely critical estimate of man. He held that it was a mistake to rely upon "pure patriotism" and that if a man was to be brought to serve the public the government must "interest his passions in doing so."[52] In other words, Hamilton believed that the policies of government should be concerned with the economic welfare of the people. In the twentieth century this approach has come to be generally accepted—that is, when twentieth-century issues are under discussion. Proposals are made and supported because they will "stop deflation," "halt inflation," "stabilize industry," "bring 'parity prices' to the farmer," "help balance the budget," and so on. This is the standard approach of congressmen, journalists, and news commentators, who assume, as did Hamilton, that the nation should be governed in accordance with the economic interests of the people.

Hamilton proposed the founding of the First Bank of the United States on the grounds that it would serve the nation's interests and would attract

[49] James A. Hamilton, *Reminiscences* (New York, 1869), 7–8.
[50] "Camillus," No. 5, 1795, *HWL*, V, 234.
[51] "Federalist," No. 73, *ibid.*, XII, 219.
[52] *Ibid.*, I, 408–409.

to the federal government the support of financial leaders. For the same reasons he proposed that the federal government assume the debts the states had contracted during the Revolutionary War and pay off the national debt at its full face value, thereby making the people willing to lend their money again if circumstances should make it necessary.[53] He urged that measures be taken by the federal government to support commerce and win the favor of those engaged in trade.[54] He wished to see roads and canals constructed under federal authority to lessen the devotion of the people at large to their state governments.[55] In foreign policy he refused to accept the profuse fraternal protestations of Genêt and his compatriots in 1793 as anything more than a cloak for personal or nationalistic designs.[56] At times he dared to defy public clamor for measures of hostility by demanding a policy of peace with Great Britain and later with France, when he perceived that America's interest—"constant with honor," he always added—required peace.[57]

Hamilton was not a sufficiently thoroughgoing economic determinist to believe that people will always act according to their interests; he believed that they might not understand the issues at hand or might be diverted by their "passions" or "emotions," two words he used interchangeably. In one of his "Continentalist" essays (1781) he affirmed that it would always be "the true interest" of every state to "preserve the Union." Yet he anticipated that, in the absence of a stronger constitution, the "vanity and self-importance" of the states would be "very likely to overpower that motive" and lead to disunion.[58] Similarly, when recommending patience in diplomatic dealings with France in 1797, he implored, "God grant that the public interest may not be sacrificed at the shrine of irritation and mistaken pride."[59] In 1794, when war with Great Britain was threatening, he wrote to President Washington that "wars oftener proceed from angry and perverse passions, than from cool calculations of interest."[60]

[53] Hamilton to Oliver Wolcott, April 10, 1795, Wolcott Papers, Connecticut Historical Society, Hartford, VII.

[54] "Camillus," No. 28, 1795, *HWL*, VI, 74.

[55] Hamilton to Jonathan Dayton, 1799, *ibid.*, X, 331–34.

[56] "Pacificus," No. 4, July 10, 1793, *ibid.*, IV, 463–65; "Horatius," May, 1795, *ibid.*, V, 184.

[57] "Americanus," February 1, February 8, 1794, *ibid.*, 74–96; "Horatius," May, 1795, *ibid.*, 181–85; Hamilton to Washington, September 15, 1790, *ibid.*, IV, 331; "Camillus," No. 5, 1795, *ibid.*, V, 241; Hamilton to Wolcott, April 5, 1797, *ibid.*, X, 252.

[58] *Ibid.*, I, 254.

[59] Hamilton to William Smith, April 10, 1797, *ibid.*, X, 256.

[60] Hamilton to Washington, *ibid.*, V, 99.

In theory at least, Jefferson was more inclined than Hamilton to accept "pure patriotism" as a moving force among men. Jefferson used the word "corruption" to describe—or rather, to anathematize—the practice of supporting laws that would promote one's economic interests. After death removed Hamilton from the scene, Jefferson said many kind things about him, but he was unfair to Hamilton's memory in harking back repeatedly to the spurious "corruption" theme.[61] Hamilton admired the British government because of its order and efficiency, and he believed those qualities would have disappeared had the government not supported laws that advanced the economic welfare of the English people. Jefferson interpreted this attitude to mean that Hamilton admired the British government because it was corrupt.

The Jefferson scholar Saul K. Padover repeated the accusation and allowed it to pass unrebuked and unexplained.[62] Hamilton's "mind" revolted as quickly as Jefferson's against bribery, peculation, or other forms of malfeasance in office. He was scrupulously honest himself, as Jefferson freely admitted, and his ire blazed forth furiously against any public official who was not. When he heard that Samuel Chase, a member of the Continental Congress, had made personal profits from "the knowledge of secrets to which his office gave him access," he denounced him in the pages of the *New York Journal*, holding that the guilty congressman "ought to feel the utmost rigor of public resentment, and be detested as a traitor of the worst and most dangerous kind."[63] Hamilton's demand for honesty in public office was a frequent topic in his essays and in his private correspondence, and he gave much thought to methods of cultivating and maintaining this virtue.[64]

The word "passion" had a rather special meaning in the eighteenth century. The Federalist Theodore Sedgwick said that Madison's proposals of 1789 to invoke retaliatory measures against Britain's commerce were based on "passion."[65] Hamilton was convinced that those Americans in 1794 who seemed to want war with Britain were "under the influence of some of the strongest passions that can actuate human conduct," those passions being hatred for Britain and attachment to France.[66]

[61] *The Anas*, *JW*, I, 279.

[62] Saul K. Padover, *The Mind of Alexander Hamilton* (New York, 1958), 12.

[63] October 19, 1778, *HWL*, I, 201.

[64] Hamilton to William Short, September 1, 1790, *ibid.*, IV, 304.

[65] Brant, III, 310.

[66] Hamilton to Washington, April 14, 1794, *HWL*, V, 100.

He thought that he could see those sentiments in Jefferson and Madison as early as 1792, when he declared Jefferson to be "a man of profound ambition and violent passions."[67] Jefferson's biographer Dumas Malone commented that "Hamilton must have been looking in the glass,"[68] but Malone may not have understood Hamilton's full meaning. By "ambition," as Hamilton used the word there and elsewhere concerning his rival, he meant Jefferson's hope—in spite of all his disclaimers—of becoming president (though Hamilton may have been mistaken in his assumption that Jefferson consciously desired to be president). By "passions" Hamilton meant Jefferson's sentiments toward the European nations, which Hamilton believed endangered peace, and Jefferson's efforts to disrupt the financial plans of the Treasury Department by appealing to a low order of emotions among the people. Later Hamilton expressed this belief emphatically in asserting that "at the very moment" when the Jeffersonians "are eulogizing the reason of men, and profession to appeal only to that faculty, they are courting the strongest and most active passion of the human heart, vanity."[69] Hamilton's barb was too sharp, but he was undoubtedly sincere in speaking of Jefferson as a man actuated by "violent passions."

Hamilton deplored some of the passions of man.[70] Many times he warned his countrymen against inordinate national pride, which might lead the people too lightly to hazard war; a misdirected sense of honor, which could cause a nation to be quarrelsome; oversensitive jealousy, which might create unnecessary antipathies among the people and confusion within the councils of state; and infatuation for another nation, which could lead to inestimable loss or injury.[71]

Hamilton was deeply interested in man's basic traits. As Harold J. Laski has pointed out, he insisted that "the raw materials of an adequate theory must be found in human nature."[72] "Take man as we find him"[73] was the beginning of his solution to many a problem. He did not place man on a pedestal as Jefferson tried to do. In fact, Hamilton's grave appre-

[67] Hamilton to Col. Edward Carrington, May 26, 1792, *ibid.*, IX, 527, 535.

[68] Malone, II, 455.

[69] Hamilton to James A. Bayard, April, 1802, *HWL*, X, 433.

[70] "Letters from Phocion," No. 1, 1784, *ibid.*, IV, 233.

[71] "Camillus," No. 2, 1795, *ibid.*, V, 200–201; Hamilton to William Smith, April 10, 1797, *ibid.*, X, 256; "Camillus," No. 5, 1795, *ibid.*, V, 235–37; "Detector," 1798, *ibid.*, VI, 318–28.

[72] Harold J. Laski, *A Grammar of Politics* (New Haven, 1931), 140.

[73] Comment in the Constitutional Convention, June 22, 1787, *HWL*, I, 409.

hensions regarding man's character were a source of much unhappiness to him. Yet he spent half the labors of his life trying to induce his fellow Americans to follow their better impulses. Again and again until the end of his life, he reiterated that the way to happiness lay along the path of truth, honesty, and justice. He would never have accepted any public office had he not assumed that men would support him for patriotic reasons that would go beyond all considerations of selfish, personal interests.

"Men are governed by opinion," said Hamilton in 1780.[74] Throughout his adult life—from his college days, when he tried to "refute" the Tory "Farmer" and "vindicate" the Congress, to 1801, when he wrote eighteen editorials (totaling 127 pages in Lodge's edition of his works) attacking Jefferson's message to Congress of December 7, 1801, and later still, in 1803, when he defended the Louisiana Purchase—he spent much of his time and energies trying to cultivate, direct, and control public opinion.[75] He was primarily a "leader of the leaders";[76] yet he spent much of his time trying to guide and influence the public at large. Many of his essays in the press were addressed to the people—sometimes even to particular labor groups, as when he tried to persuade the carpenters of New York to oppose the post-Revolutionary War persecution of the Tories, warning them that if further large numbers of Tories were compelled to leave the city the demand for new homes would end.[77] He seldom tried to be clever, and he seldom tried to arouse his readers' emotions. Rather, calm reasoning was what he urged upon them. When he had a message for the people's hearts—as when he referred to national pride and the future greatness of the United States—he chose to direct it to their intellects. His writings were "better calculated to impress those who think than those who feel."[78]

His study of history persuaded him that all governments, even "the most despotic," were "in a great degree" dependent upon opinion; and he was sure that was "most peculiarly the case" in republics.[79] War should not

[74] Hamilton to James Duane, September 3, 1780, *ibid.*, 238.

[75] *Ibid.*, 3–177; *ibid.*, VIII, 246–73; *New York Evening Post*, March 11, March 21, July 5, 1803.

[76] Henry Cabot Lodge, *Alexander Hamilton* (Boston, 1882), 191.

[77] "Letters from Phocion," No. 1, 1784, *HWL*, IV, 245.

[78] Ford, *Alexander Hamilton*, 39.

[79] Speech on the Constitution, New York State Ratification Convention, June 21, 1788, *HWL*, II, 20.

be resorted to, even when the nation's leaders thought it would be good policy, unless the move would receive the "cheerful support of the people."[80]

Opinion abroad was also to be reckoned with. Hamilton urged the Continental Congress to pay Baron Friedrich von Steuben liberally for his services during the Revolution because it would hurt America's prestige abroad to "dismiss an old soldier empty and hungry."[81] Paying the foreign debt was necessary on grounds of honesty but was also a means of winning favorable attention abroad. However, he sharply corrected those persons who had said that maintaining financial credit abroad was more important than maintaining it at home. "The latter," he said, "is far the most important nursery of resource."[82]

The Federalist—that noble work by Hamilton, Madison, and Jay recommending ratification of the Constitution—was directed to the American people. It was "reserved to the people of this country," wrote Hamilton in the opening essay, to decide by "their conduct and example" whether "men are really capable . . . of establishing good government from reflection and choice" or whether they must forever "depend for their political constitutions on accident and force."[83] The words "reflection and choice" are the keystone of the structure of his lifelong public policy.

Hamilton won notable victories with his pen, though he lost several engagements, too. To his friend Fisher Ames he appeared a mighty Jove holding "his bolts in his talons."[84] For years his influence on public opinion was a force his opponents dared not overlook. Actually Jefferson, and other Republicans, frequently exaggerated Hamilton's influence both in and out of government by attributing to him alone many of the unpopular measures of the Federalist administration. It was in reference to his power in the public press that Jefferson called him a "colossus" and "an host within himself."[85]

Hamilton did not understand the people as well as Jefferson and Patrick Henry did, and that shortcoming was the source of some of his mistakes,

[80] Hamilton to Washington, September 15, 1790, *ibid.*, IV, 335.

[81] Hamilton to Washington, October 30, 1787, *ibid.*, IX, 426.

[82] Hamilton to Oliver Wolcott, April 10, 1795, Wolcott Papers, Connecticut Historical Society, Hartford, VII.

[83] *HWL*, XI, 3.

[84] Ames to Dwight Foster, January 4, 1796, Ames, *Works of Fisher Ames*, I, 183.

[85] Jefferson to Madison, September 21, 1795, *JW*, IX, 309–10.

such as the whisky tax and his support of the Alien and Sedition Acts. He did not trust an unguided people to find its own way. The Senate should be helpful in defending the people "against their own temporary errors and delusions." If the "interests of the people" should come to be "at variance with their inclinations," the elected officials should "withstand the temporary delusion, in order to give them time and opportunity for more cool and sedate reflections." Later the people might show their gratitude for the men "who had courage and magnanimity enough to serve them at the peril of their displeasure." The "true patriot" must stand ready "to sacrifice popularity to what he believes to be the cause of public good."[86] Hamilton detested politicians who were constantly concerned with "what will *please* [and] not what will *benefit* the people."[87]

Hamilton's frankness in expressing his ideas about the people sometimes proved injurious to his reputation. A man of strong opinions on many subjects, he was sometimes deficient in tact.[88] There were other men in public life who held the people in no higher esteem, but Hamilton was "apt to express what others had prudence enough to suppress."[89] His recurrent moods of depression led him to make statements so extreme that they were not at all representative of his general belief, as when, on November 11, 1794, stung deeply by the refusal of the western farmers to pay the whisky tax, he wrote to Washington that he had "learned to hold popular opinions of no value." In his chagrin at the fickleness of the people in their attitude toward revolutionary France, he observed that "plausible ideas are always enough for the multitude." It has been asserted, though not proved, that at a New York dinner he was once taunted into the assertion, "Your people, sir—your people is a great beast."[90]

His distrust of the people did not really go that far; otherwise he would not have toiled so long to cultivate the public mind. Such outbursts have been put to cruel use by unsympathetic critics. Senator George G. Vest,

[86] "Federalist," No. 63, *HWL*, XII, 137. This essay, by Hamilton or Madison, represents the thought of both men in 1788; "Federalist," No. 71, *ibid.*, 207; "Camillus," No. 5, 1795, *ibid.*, V, 234.

[87] Hamilton to Robert Morris, August 13, 1782, *ibid.*, IX, 273.

[88] Frank Monaghan, *John Jay, Defender of Liberty* (New York, 1935), 343.

[89] Octavius Pickering and C. W. Upham, *Life of Timothy Pickering* (Boston, 1867–73), III, 415.

[90] *HWL*, VI, 457; Hamilton to William Smith, April 5, 1797, *ibid.*, X, 254; Henry Adams, *History of the United States During the Administrations of Jefferson and Madison* (New York, 1889), I, 85.

while approving "Jefferson's Passports to Immortality," overreached the subject by claiming that "Hamilton had no sympathy with the people or popular government."[91] Some critics have gone still further. Early in his career William E. Dodd stated that "Hamilton . . . thought the people a great beast, which must be securely bound if one would live at peace and under a good government." Leland D. Baldwin charged that "the touchstone of Hamilton's life and policy was his fear of and loathing for the people."[92] A more crafty man than Hamilton would have foreseen that unguarded comments about the people's powers of discernment would be repaid in similar coin or worse. But historians should consider Hamilton's lifework before making their indictments. Theodore Roosevelt displayed a balanced view of the interactions between Hamilton and the people when he observed that the Federalists fell from power because they had not learned that the American way is to give the individual great power and trust him to use it well.[93]

Of Hamilton's ideas on constitutional questions, the distinguishing feature—and, indeed, the basic principle of the Federalist party—was that the national government should be strong and that power should be centered in the national executive. So much of Hamilton's life was devoted to assuring and increasing that power that it stands out as the dominant theme of his life. He was an outspoken advocate of law and order. In a letter to Robert Morris on August 13, 1782, he complained that in the government of the state of New York "there [was] no *order* that [had] a will of its own."[94] Nothing irked him quite as deeply as confusion in public affairs.[95] Mob violence he abhorred, even when perpetrated by his friends against his political opponents.[96] He never wavered in his belief that any people has the right to rebel against oppression and set up a new government, in the United States or France or elsewhere; but he insisted

[91] *JW*, XII, *xxv*; from the Senator's address to the Jefferson Club of St. Louis, October 31, 1895.

[92] William E. Dodd, *The Life of Nathaniel Macon* (Raleigh, 1903), 58; Leland D. Baldwin, *The Stream of American History* (New York, 1952), I, 304.

[93] Theodore Roosevelt, *Gouverneur Morris* (Boston, 1888), 138.

[94] Hamilton to Robert Morris, *HWL*, IX, 273.

[95] Roland J. Mulford, *The Political Theories of Alexander Hamilton* (Baltimore, 1903), 13.

[96] For Hamilton's defense of the Tory Dr. Myles Cooper, and for his strong complaints against the mob that destroyed James Rivington's press, see John C. Hamilton, *Life of Alexander Hamilton* (New York, 1834–40), I, 48–49.

that measures must be taken in an orderly manner without crime and irregular or unnecessary violence.[97]

His tendency to emphasize the importance of the executive may have arisen partly from his West Indies background, where, as Francis Wharton says, "the only authority to appeal to was executive, and where the action of such authority, to be effective, had to be quick and despotic."[98] This emphasis became more pronounced when he was vexed by the inefficiency of Congress during the Revolution, and even more so when he suffered continuous mortification because of the growing debility of Congress from the end of the war until the Constitutional Convention was called in 1787. There he reached his crescendo.

Hamilton knew that the energies of the nation were poorly directed during the war, and he was quick to lay the blame on the weakness of the "Confederation" and especially of the Continental Congress. While aide-de-camp to General Washington, from March 1, 1777, to April 30, 1781, he began corresponding with some of the nation's leaders on the subject. On February 13, 1778, in a letter to George Clinton, governor of New York, he deplored the "consequence of having a Congress despised at home and abroad." The "common force" could not be exerted in the war, and the "European negotiations" could not succeed unless an adequate national government was established. In one of his "Publius" letters he remarked that a member of Congress should "be regarded not only as a legislator, but as a founder of an empire."[99]

In the summer of 1780, Congressman James Duane of New York went to Washington's headquarters to discuss military affairs. Hamilton seized the opportunity to place before Duane his suggestions for reorganizing the government. Fortunately for history, Duane asked the young aide to put his thoughts in writing. The resulting letter, written on September 3, 1780, occupies twenty-seven pages in Lodge's edition of Hamilton's works.[100]

In the letter Hamilton emphasized that the desperate plight of the country required prompt, bold action. Lack of supplies and attention had reduced the army to a "mob." It was without clothing, without pay, without

[97] Hamilton to Washington, April, 1793, May 2, 1793, *HWL*, IV, 374, 386–87, 407.

[98] *RDC*, I, 261.

[99] Hamilton to Clinton, *HWL*, IX, 125; I, 206.

[100] Hamilton to Duane, *ibid.*, I, 213–39.

provisions, without morals, and without discipline and was "ripening for a dissolution." The "fundamental defect" was "a want of power in Congress," which had arisen from three causes: the jealousy of the states, which were trying to retain all the power; the timidity of Congress, which was rendering that body unwilling to assume "full power *to preserve the republic from harm*"; and, finally, the lack of authority vested in Congress. The "Confederation itself" required alteration, being, in its present state, "neither fit for war nor peace." Hamilton assumed that there was not enough spirit in Congress to lead it to assert its "discretionary powers" courageously; thus he believed it necessary to call immediately a "Convention of all the States" to draw up a new constitution. Congress should be empowered to levy and collect taxes, for "without certain revenues, a government can have no power." All military forces and operations should be under the control of Congress, which would also have authority over the navy, fortifications, commerce, diplomacy, finance, money, banks, and appropriations and would have the power to grant "bounties and premiums" to stimulate production and exports. He considered it necessary for the state legislatures to continue their control over "that part of the internal police which relates to the rights of property and life among individuals, and . . . internal taxes."

Despite these augmented powers, however, Congress should cease its efforts to exercise executive authority. Congress, properly a "deliberative corps, . . . forgets itself when it attempts to play the executive." He recommended the immediate appointment by Congress of "great officers of state" to head departments of foreign affairs, war, marine, finance, and trade. Hamilton was so sure of himself in this matter that he recommended General Philip J. Schuyler for the war department; General Alexander McDougall, for marine; and Robert Morris, for finance. Members of Congress need have no fear of finding themselves with nothing to do after the proposed appointments were made; "they would have precisely the same rights and powers as heretofore, happily disencumbered of the detail."

Congress was unwilling to adopt such an ambitious program, but that did not quell the clamorous young correspondent. Six weeks later he wrote to Isaac Sears, an enthusiastic patriot from New York: "All those who love their country ought to exert their influence in the states where they reside" to urge Congress "to take up this object with energy." The nation "must have a government with more power . . . a tax . . . a foreign loan . . . a bank."[101]

In 1781, Hamilton was not elated by the news that Maryland was about to ratify the Articles of Confederation, the last state to do so. This final accession, which brought rejoicing in Philadelphia and elsewhere, disturbed Hamilton, who believed that it might "make people believe that the Confederacy gives Congress power enough."[102]

The early part of the year 1781 was a dark period in the war. British armies under Cornwallis and the traitor Arnold were laying waste to Virginia, and much of the deeper South had been lost to the enemy. Hamilton looked beyond the battlefield to what he saw as the basic problem—the need for improving the national government. In his letter of April 30 to Robert Morris concerning financial affairs and the need for a national bank, he commented that " 'tis by introducing order into our finances—by restoring public credit—not by gaining battles, that we are finally to gain our object." A logical system should be established for the national debt, which he anticipated could be paid in full within twenty years "without at all encumbering the people." In the meantime, "a national debt, if it is not excessive, will be to us a national blessing. It will be a powerful cement of our Union."[103] A short time later Morris echoed this sentiment in a letter of his own to Nathaniel Appleton of Massachusetts: "A public debt supported by public revenue will prove the strongest cement to keep our confederacy together."[104]

Hoping to bring the public to his point of view, Hamilton published the first of his "Continentalist" essays on July 12, 1781. The series continued until July 4, 1782.[105] The chief aim of the "Continentalist" was to warn the nation about the dangers arising from the "want of power in Congress." He was convinced that there was hardly "a man of information in America" who would not "acknowledge" that the government did not have enough power for "a vigorous prosecution of the war" or for "a preservation of the union in peace." Yet there was a deplorable lack of "agreement in the modes of remedying the defect." His proposed remedy was to enlarge the powers of Congress "without delay." A Congress dependent

[101] Hamilton to Isaac Sears, October 12, 1780, *ibid.*, IX, 224.

[102] Hamilton to unnamed correspondent, February 7, 1781, *ibid.*, IX, 230.

[103] Hamilton to Robert Morris, *ibid.*, III, 343, 387.

[104] Merrill Jensen, *The New Nation: A History of the United States During the Confederation; 1781–1789* (New York, 1950), 46 (hereafter cited as *The New Nation*).

[105] *HWL*, I, 243–87.

upon the states could "neither have dignity, vigor, nor credit." From the beginning of the war, "vesting Congress with the power of regulating trade ought to have been a principal object of the Confederation." As in his private correspondence, Hamilton mentioned other powers that should be conferred upon Congress: control of the military, a share in the ore mines, the power to tax, and control of all "unlocated land."

He could see no danger that liberty might be suppressed by a powerful national government. He believed the real danger was "on the other side—that [the states would] be an overmatch for the common head." History was "full of examples where, in contests for liberty, a jealousy [for local authority] defeated the attempt to recover or preserve it." He wished to weaken the state constitutions, but he would not destroy them. He could see "their imperfection," but he believed that for some time they should aid "the common defense and the maintenance of order" and that they appeared to have "the seeds of improvement."

In the closing essay of the series, published on the anniversary of independence—not quite nine months after the surrender of Cornwallis at Yorktown—Hamilton tried to stir the national pride of his fellow Americans: "There is something noble and magnificent in the perspective of a great Federal Republic, closely linked in the pursuit of a common interest, tranquil and prosperous at home, respectable abroad." But he loathed the "diminutive and contemptible" sight of "petty states . . . jarring, jealous, and perverse."

CHAPTER II

Political Ideas and Personal Ambitions (Continued)

After the siege of Yorktown and the surrender of Cornwallis (see Chapter III), Hamilton undertook a diligent study of the law. He fancied that he had given up public service for private practice—or so, at least, he informed his friend, Colonel Richard K. Meade. He had married Elizabeth Schuyler, the daughter of General Philip Schuyler, in 1780, and in 1781 their first son, Philip, was born. He wrote that he sighed for nothing but the company of his "wife and . . . baby."[1]

The period of domestic life was to be brief. In May, 1782, he bowed to the urgent request of Robert Morris—who had been appointed superintendent of finance, as Hamilton had recommended to Congressman Duane—to serve as receiver of taxes for the state of New York. To some persons it must have seemed a grotesque joke to cast Hamilton in the role of taxgatherer under the feeble Confederation. Yet no position in the young republic could have enabled him to follow more directly his self-chosen task of strengthening the national government.

New York's Governor Clinton and a majority of the state legislators were opposed to granting more powers to Congress, and had slowed down their appropriations of funds and supplies; but Hamilton moved briskly forward. At his request he was allowed to appear before a committee representing both houses of the legislature. His plea brought a prompt appropriation of eighteen thousand pounds for the national government, though he wrote to Robert Morris that after deductions were made for goods previously delivered and other items the national treasury would probably not receive more than half that sum. At his instance the lawmakers also set up a "committee to devise . . . a more effectual system of taxation."[2] His most astonishing achievement was to induce the legisla-

[1] March, 1782, *HWL*, IX, 253.

[2] Hamilton to Robert Morris, July 22, 1782, *ibid.*, 264–65.

ture to pass a resolution he had drafted asking Congress to call for "a general convention of the states, specially authorized to revise and amend the confederation." The resolution declared that it was "the opinion of [the] Legislature" that "the want of sufficient power in Congress" was the "radical source" of most of the nation's "embarrassments."[3]

Hamilton must have regarded that resolution as a major accomplishment—and indeed it was, for it helped direct the thinking of the people toward the drafting of a new constitution. His personal correspondence shows that he was further gratified when the New York legislature appointed him a delegate to the Continental Congress, an appointment that was to prove highly significant. He wrote to one of his South Carolina friends, John Laurens, whom he had met while serving on Washington's staff, urging him also to accept an appointment to Congress. In a spirit of cheerfulness and exuberance rather unusual for him, he informed Laurens that favorable terms of peace were "upon the carpet" but that in order to make "independence a blessing" there remained the "herculean task" of placing the "Union on solid foundations." That would require "all the virtue and all the abilities of the country." He added, "We have fought side by side to make America free; let us hand in hand struggle to make her happy."[4] Unfortunately, young Laurens was killed in a skirmish with the British, probably before the letter reached him.

Hamilton took his seat in Congress on November 25, 1782, and soon joined in the discussions of financial affairs, foreign policy, and proposals for strengthening the national government. When Congress received Rhode Island's bold rejection of a provision allowing Congress to collect tariff revenues, Hamilton moved that a delegation be sent to that state to try to induce the legislature to change its decision. (At the moment it appeared that Rhode Island was alone in obstructing the provision.)

Congress passed Hamilton's motion, and he was appointed chairman of a committee to write a refutation of Rhode Island's arguments. The report of the committee was almost exclusively the work of Hamilton.[5] It evidently had the effect intended by Congress—surprisingly enough, for the report was not tactfully written. It displays much irritation and impatience, and is cast in a haughty, menacing tone not uncommon in Hamilton's private communications but rare in his state papers. The collection

[3] Resolution, July 21, 1782, *ibid.*, I, 291–95.
[4] August 15, 1782, *ibid.*, IX, 280–81.
[5] December 16, 1782, *ibid.*, II, 179–92.

of tariff within a state would not burden the state's commerce, Hamilton maintained, for the merchants would simply add the duty to the cost of the goods, and the consumer would have to pay it all. That argument was not fully consistent with Hamilton's treatment of the subject in his "Continentalist" essays, and it must have offended the state authorities to be told that it was "the reverse of a just position, that the duty would bear hardest on the most commercial states."

One of the objections Rhode Island had made was that the congressional proposal would "introduce into that and the other states, officers unknown and unaccountable to them, and was against the constitution of the state." If that view should prevail, Hamilton replied, his chief political aim was hardly more than a futile dream; but he would not agree that it was true. No state constitution should assume the right to name all state officers for the future. New needs might create demands for new state offices. The attempt by any state to prevent Congress from sending an officer into a state was violative of the Articles of Confederation—particularly Article IX, giving Congress power over the "post-office." If the state's position were correct, how could the national government appoint any officers at all?

The third objection raised by Rhode Island must have annoyed Hamilton most of all. It was that to grant the tariff revenues to Congress, "the expenditures of which they are not to be accountable to the States," would make Congress "independent of their constituents" and would be "repugnant to the liberty of the United States." Expressions like these grew out of the extreme states' rights sentiments rampant in Rhode Island, and they account for that state's later refusal to ratify the Constitution until every other state had done so.

The arguments presented by Hamilton and his colleagues, in combination with other influences, won out for the moment, and Rhode Island agreed to allow Congress to collect the tariff revenues. But on March 15, 1783, Hamilton's own state of New York dealt a heavy blow to his plans when the legislature, urged on by Governor Clinton, repealed its earlier agreement to the imposts. This new obstacle was not overcome until the Constitution was adopted and the new government set in motion. Yet New York's action may have been helpful to Hamilton's plan in the long run. The revenue obtained from the imposts, though a mere crutch for the weak government, might have given it enough support to draw the sting from the Federalist arguments, and the Constitutional Convention might have been postponed for several years longer.

On January 27, 1783, a resolution was introduced by Congressman James Wilson of Pennsylvania calling for congressional appointment of agents to reside in each state and collect for the national government the customs revenues which, it was hoped, the states would finally allow. Hamilton supported this resolution with so much energy that he frightened off some of the less resolute supporters. He made it clear that he was interested in more than the funds alone. He coveted for the nation the energizing effect of a body of national officers who were entirely free from state supervision. He was moving so rapidly toward national centralization that he outdistanced others who were still feeling their way in the same direction.

Before New York's action denying Congress the right to collect tariff, Hamilton kept up his well-aimed correspondence with Governor Clinton. He told the governor that every day proved "more and more the insufficiency of the Confederation," adding that adherents to that point of view were "increasing fast" and that "many of the most sensible men" had come to recognize the wisdom of the action of the New York legislature in recommending a constitutional convention. He was tactful enough to refer to New York lawmakers as "your Legislature."[6]

The connection between the powers of Congress and the hopes for meeting the nation's financial obligations in 1783 was obvious to many Americans besides Hamilton. Quite a number of influential persons were holding various forms of certificates of indebtedness that had been authorized by Congress. Both officers and soldiers of the Continental Army were in a dangerous mood because they had not been paid in the early months of 1783. Some of them had contracted debts which they could honor only when they received their pay. General Washington was convinced that if they were discharged before their accounts were settled several of them would soon be in jail.

Hamilton ventured onto a dangerous path when he began toying with the idea of encouraging the forces of the army and the nonmilitary creditors to induce the states to grant additional revenue to Congress. He hoped that this alliance might prove strong enough to persuade the states to allow Congress to collect the revenue. He incautiously mentioned the idea in a letter to Washington, which has led some historians of good repute,

[6] Hamilton to Clinton, January 12, 1783, *ibid.*, IX, 309.

including Adrienne Koch, to charge that Hamilton's intention was to use the power of the army to overthrow the government of the Confederation and establish the more efficient system he so ardently desired.[7] It is difficult to see how such a conclusion can be drawn from the documents produced by Hamilton or from his life and beliefs.

As Hamilton wrote to Washington, he saw that it might be difficult to "keep a *complaining* and *suffering army* within the bounds of moderation," but "this," he said, in a rather highhanded tone, "your Excellency's influence must effect."[8] Washington was in the difficult position of urging moderation upon an army that was near mutiny and at the same time insisting that the states and Congress meet the army's just demands. In replying to Hamilton, he referred to the seething resentment within the army and used sober language to urge his former aide to place the ominous facts squarely before the delegates from states that were obstructing or withholding revenue. They should be told that "if any disastrous consequences should follow, by reason of their delinquency . . . they must be answerable to God and their Country."[9]

In June, 1783, a segment of the army encamped near Philadelphia did mutiny. Three hundred soldiers surrounded the statehouse with rifles and bayonets and gave Congress only twenty minutes to meet their demands. The members of Congress departed in haste and disorder, but no one was injured. Hamilton was exasperated by the refusal of John Dickinson, president of Pennsylvania, to call out the state militia. Dickinson replied that the militia officers, including General Arthur St. Clair, agreed that the militia could not be relied on to serve against army troops as long as they committed no "outrage on person or property."[10] The troops finally withdrew, upon hearing that loyal forces were approaching. Congress made a partial payment to the men and promised the officers five years' pay after discharge. These steps, plus the wisdom and prestige of Washington and the basic good sense and patriotism of the soldiers, enabled the nation to pass safely through the crisis.

Hamilton believed that the country had been seriously injured by what he considered an insult to Congress, but the alarming helplessness of the

[7] Adrienne Koch, *Jefferson and Madison* (New York, 1950), 542.

[8] Hamilton to Washington, February 7, 1783, *HWL*, IX, 311.

[9] Washington to Hamilton, March 12, 1783, *WW*, XXVI, 217.

[10] Charles J. Stillé, *The Life and Times of John Dickinson, 1732–1808* (Philadelphia, 1891), 244–45.

nation's government and the inaction of the Pennsylvania authorities during the crisis were useful tonic for stimulating the growth of nationalism. The episode supplied the best single argument for the later decision to establish the seat of the national government in a federal district policed and governed by Congress.

Nearly every political event of this period reminded Hamilton of the need for strengthening the national government. In March, 1783, upon hearing of the terms of the peace with Britain, he wrote to Washington that in order to make "independence truly a blessing" there yet remained the task of "making solid establishments within to perpetuate [the] Union."[11]

In his reply Washington emphatically agreed, saying that no man in the nation was "more deeply impressed" with the need for reforming the Confederation. The "want of Powers in Congress" had prolonged the war and produced "half the perplexities" of his command and "almost the whole of the difficulties and distress of the Army." He saw possibilities of a bright future for the new nation but held that it required "not the second sight to see" that a continuation under a weak system of government would leave the country helpless before its European "enemies."[12]

This exchange and letters of a similar nature written during the succeeding four years reveal the basis for the close co-operation in which the two men worked for the remainder of Washington's life. Their mutual desire for a stronger central government was the bond that held them together. In their letters to one another each man seemed to be trying to express the same sentiment in language more cogent than the other's. Significantly, both men had suffered mental anguish during the war because of the weakness of the central authority, and both were shocked by the impotence of the Confederation. By 1787 both had arrived at approximately the same point in this aspect of their political philosophies.

During the latter part of Hamilton's brief service in Congress in 1783, he fought ahead on that front. He resented the general criticism by some persons of congressional inaction. Little should be expected, he said, of a Union "the constitutional imbecility of which must be apparent to every man of reflection." It was illogical to blame the members of Congress for "not doing what they have no means of doing." Everyone who had "the

[11] Hamilton to Washington, *HWL*, IX, 327.

[12] Washington to Hamilton, March 31, 1783, *WW*, XXVI, 276–77.

welfare of the community at heart" should impress upon the people the conviction that the nation, "to be happy, must have a stronger bond of Union and a Confederation capable of drawing forth the resources of the country."[13]

He tried to persuade Congress to commit itself to the need for a new instrument of government. On June 30, 1783, he offered a resolution carefully setting forth the weaknesses of the existing system. Congress did not pass the resolution, but it remains an important document, for it constitutes a clear summary of a subject that has often commanded the attention of students of American history. He described in some detail the major flaws in the national government as it was constituted under the Articles: no power over taxation and commerce, no authority to enforce treaties, no independent executive authority, no "Federal Judicature," inadequate "provisions for interior or exterior defense," and the rule that important measures could be enacted into law only after the affirmative vote of the representatives of nine states.[14]

After the rejection of the resolution Hamilton was discouraged and ready to return to New York. Congress had no power, nor enough spirit to ask for any, and people seemed unperturbed by the continuing deterioration of the nation's political affairs. By June, 1783, he was convinced that he could not serve the country's interests by remaining in Congress. "Experience must convince" the nation that its political "establishments [were] Utopian" before it would be willing to improve them.[15]

He returned to Albany, and in November, after British forces departed, he moved to New York City, where he resumed the practice of law. His attention was drawn to the controversy over the harsh treatment of the Tories in New York (see Chapter V), a situation that was further evidence, Hamilton believed, of the need for a stronger national government. He observed caustically that "discrimination bills, partial taxes, . . . and paper bubbles [were] the only dishes that [suited] the public palate."[16]

Though deeply engrossed in his law practice, he did not lose interest in politics. He realized that the new Society of the Cincinnati, an association of Revolutionary War officers, could help promote national unity,

[13] *HWL*, I, 327–31. It is not clear whether this undated paper is part of a speech, a letter, or an essay.

[14] *Ibid.*, 305–14. For a survey of Hamilton's work in Congress, see Broadus Mitchell, *Alexander Hamilton* (New York, 1957), I, 279–326.

[15] Hamilton to General Greene, June 10, 1783, HPSCLC, Box 1.

[16] Hamilton to Gouverneur Morris, April 7, 1784, *HWL*, IX, 403.

and he urged the members to use their influence for the cause.[17] During the middle 1780's, as Hamilton had predicted, more and more people came to realize that for an orderly society firmer governmental controls were necessary. Persons of wealth and ambition were the strongest advocates of such controls, but they alone could not have determined the nation's course. Many common people also came to believe that a stronger government was needed.

Shays's Rebellion, which erupted in Massachusetts in 1786, was interpreted by many as a warning signal of approaching anarchy. Shays and his followers tried to obstruct court actions ordering the seizure of debtors' property and to force the legislature to pass a law allowing debtors to discharge their obligations with paper money. Their failure to receive wide support from fellow sufferers, and the willingness of the Massachusetts militia to put down the rebellion, revealed the strength of American conservatism from which the new federalism drew its support.

Some American historians have held that Washington, Hamilton, and their Federalist friends exaggerated the need for a new government (a view powerfully reinforced by Merrill Jensen in *The New Nation*). But even if the dangers were not quite as alarming as some of the Founding Fathers believed, it is difficult to see how solutions to the nation's problems, foreign and domestic, could have been reached by a government with fewer powers than those provided by the Constitution.

Hamilton was appointed a delegate from New York to the Annapolis Convention, held in September, 1786, for the purpose of suggesting regulations for "commercial intercourse." The twelve delegates concluded that it was inexpedient to prepare a set of recommendations with "so partial and defective a representation," but their famous "Address," recommending a national convention, led to the Constitutional Convention in Philadelphia the following year. Hamilton was the principal author of the "Address," though other delegates were influential in toning down his high-pitched proposals. Even so, it was a rather bold instrument, calling for the appointment of "commissioners" to meet and "devise such further provisions as shall appear to them necessary to render the Constitution of the Federal Government *adequate to the exigencies of the Union*."[18]

[17] Hamilton, James Duane, and William Duer, as a New York committee, to the President of the Society of the Cincinnati in New Hampshire, November 1, 1786, HPSCLC, Box 1.

[18] *HWL*, I, 335–39.

It could hardly have escaped Hamilton's attention that when the Continental Congress gave its halfhearted approval to the Annapolis "Address" it asked the states to send representatives to Philadelphia for the "sole and express purpose of revising the Articles of Confederation."[19] When Hamilton arrived in Philadelphia to represent New York at the convention, he was impatient with fellow delegates who wished to be guided by the strict terms laid down by Congress. He deplored such timidity. "The States," he said, "sent us here to provide for the exigencies of the Union. . . . The great question is: What provision shall we make for the happiness of our Country."[20]

Taking a strong stand at the outset in favor of centralized government, Hamilton recommended that the president and members of the Senate serve for life or during good behavior and that the president have absolute veto power over the acts of Congress. The national government should appoint the governor of each state, and the governor should have veto power over all state legislation.[21] He was convinced that there could be no "good government" for the nation "so long as state sovereignties do, in any shape, exist" and, further, that "two sovereignties cannot coexist within the same limits." Later in the convention sessions he modified his views on state government.

Hamilton wanted a powerful Senate with a "permanent will" to give stability to the government. "Nothing but a permanent body," he said, "can check the imprudence of democracy." As long as senators were chosen by electors responsible to the people, he was confident that they would serve the interests of the people. In the same paragraph in which he spoke of the "imprudence of democracy," he urged that the new government should "go to the full length of republican principles."[22] A little later, in a reference to the death of Socrates, he asserted that if Athens had had a body like the United States Senate "popular liberty might then have escaped the indelible reproach of decreeing to the same citizens the hemlock on one day and statues on the next."[23]

[19] Resolution, February 21, 1787, *JCC*, XXXII, 74.

[20] Speech in the Convention, June 18, 1787, *HWL*, I, 382–83.

[21] "Propositions for a Constitution," June 18, 1787, and his speech on the same date, *ibid.*, 349, 387.

[22] *Ibid.*, 401–402.

[23] "Federalist," No. 63, *ibid.*, XII, 137. This essay, by Hamilton or Madison, certainly expresses Hamilton's view.

Hamilton knew he was in a minority at the convention, and he was also aware that the nation was not ready to accept his views. Nevertheless, hoping to draw the other delegates at least part way toward his position, he presented it candidly and forcefully. Referring to the growing debility of the Confederation, he saw "the Union dissolving, or already dissolved" and "evils operating in the states which must soon cure the people of their fondness for democracies."[24] He described with an amazing degree of prescience the conflicts that would arise between state and national authority.

By 1787, Hamilton had become known as an extreme advocate of centralization. Long tortured by the spectacle of a government too weak to rule at home or maintain respect abroad, he had even come to fear that the republican form of government was a mirage. As a thirsty man on a parched plain thinks not of a glass of water but of a mountain lake, so Hamilton adopted a position far more extreme than the one he had held in previous years. His radicalism at the convention injured his reputation and weakened his influence with the people, and it opened a breach through which his enemies never ceased to attack him. As Louis M. Hacker has pointed out, Hamilton's stand was "courageous, honest, and thoughtful, . . . but his political enemies always continued to misrepresent it."[25]

General Washington's esteem for Hamilton was not diminished by anything that was said at the convention. When adverse votes of the other New York delegates, Robert Yates and John Lansing, caused Hamilton to leave Philadelphia for a period, he wrote to Washington on July 3, 1787, that he found public opinion in New York moving definitely toward "a strong, well-mounted government." He urged Washington not to be swayed by "the supposed repugnance of the people to an efficient constitution." He cautiously pointed out that he had not compared his ideas with Washington's, but he was "persuaded" that the "genuineness of his representations" would be accepted as justification for the letter. He justified himself for speaking out by saying that he feared the convention might "let slip the golden opportunity of rescuing the American empire from disunion, anarchy, and misery."[26]

[24] *Ibid.*, I, 393. See also Louis M. Hacker, *Alexander Hamilton in the American Tradition* (New York, 1957), 105.

[25] Hacker, *Alexander Hamilton in the American Tradition*, 113.

[26] Hamilton to Washington, *HWL*, IX, 417–18.

It must have pleased the young man immensely when Washington replied: "I am sorry you went away—I wish you were back." As for the crucial problem facing the nation, Washington stated incisively: "The men who oppose a strong and energetic government are, in my opinion, narrow minded politicians, or are under the influence of local views."[27] Upon receiving this letter, Hamilton returned to the convention. Undoubtedly this shared attitude served to bind the two men more closely together.

As Hamilton listened to the views of other delegates, he, like others, modified his own views somewhat.[28] Later in his life he said that at the convention he gave up his idea of having the president serve for "good behaviour" and supported a convention proposal for a three-year presidential term. He also softened his attitude toward the states, though he held firmly to his conviction that the national government should be empowered to legislate directly upon the states, through the states, and upon the citizens.[29]

Many of the provisions finally agreed upon were not at all pleasing to Hamilton; yet he gave the Constitution his full support. He was convinced it was better than the only alternative at the time, the Articles of Confederation. The Constitution presented "a chance of good," and without it there was the prospect of "anarchy and convulsion."[30] He looked toward the day when a stronger instrument of government could be prepared, after the people had become accustomed to working together as a nation. As his friend Gouverneur Morris stated rather cynically a few years later, Hamilton accepted the Constitution because he believed that it would hold the nation "together for some time, and he knew that national sentiment is the offspring of national existence."[31]

From Hamilton's convention speech arose the accusation that he had proposed a monarchical form of government. His skepticism about the wisdom of the people and his ceaseless efforts to energize the national government made the accusation appear credible to many. Hamilton's life, works, and writings bear witness that the charge was based on mis-

[27] *WW*, XXIX, 245–46.

[28] William Anderson, "The Intention of the Framers: A Note on Constitutional Interpretation," *American Political Science Review*, XLIX (June, 1955), 342.

[29] Hamilton to Timothy Pickering, September 18, 1803, *HWL*, X, 447; "Federalist," No. 23, *ibid.*, XI, 183.

[30] Speech in the Convention, September 17, 1787, *ibid.*, I, 420.

[31] *MDL*, II, 524.

understanding or malice. During the Federalist period members of each party employed harsh language against their opponents—much stronger than the followers of either major political party would ordinarily use today—except to describe the adherents of a third party. "Monarchist," as it was used during and after the Revolution, had various meanings, all of them highly uncomplimentary. It was regularly used to describe any person who was deemed antirepublican or later opposed the French revolutionaries who had killed their monarch.[32]

"Democracy" was also used disparagingly during the early years of independence. At that time the word ordinarily connoted rule by a mob; this was Hamilton's interpretation of the word. In connection with a Massachusetts libel suit in 1789, one able lawyer calmly wrote to another: "One Whipple has sued Ben Russel for a paragraph which, he says, lost him the office. I admit it is actionable and slanderous to call a man a democrat."[33] Gouverneur Morris asserted that his own opposition to democracy grew out of his love for liberty.[34] In citing Hamilton's criticism of "democracy," his detractors have often overlooked the nature of semantics.

In his own time, Hamilton's political enemies even tried to convince the public that he advocated hereditary rule in the United States. They spread the rumor that he tried to induce the convention to ask Prince Frederick, Duke of York, to accept a crown. Not many months before Hamilton's death, he heard that Governor Clinton had been circulating the story. Hamilton wrote the governor a resolute letter of inquiry. A few letters were exchanged, after which the governor disavowed any belief that Hamilton had ever supported such a design.[35]

The persistence of this rumor and the significant role it played in relations with Great Britain and France make it essential to consider it in some detail. It would be hopeless to try to prove in absolute terms the falsity of the charge; and without definitive proof the human tendency is to believe or disbelieve it according to one's personal, political, or historical predilections. It can be demonstrated, however, that the story has little indeed to sustain it.

[32] Louise Burnham Dunbar, *A Study of "Monarchical" Tendencies in the United States from 1776 to 1801* (Urbana, 1922), 126.

[33] Ames to Christopher Gore, July 22, 1798, Ames, *Works of Fisher Ames*, I, 237.

[34] Daniel Walther, *Gouverneur Morris: Witness of Two Revolutions* (New York, 1934), 75.

[35] The Hamilton and Clinton letters with the enclosures can be found by consulting both the Lodge and the John C. Hamilton editions of Hamilton's works: *HWL*, X, 450–55; *HWH*, VI, 561–65.

In 1792, President Washington was deeply disturbed when Secretary of State Jefferson told him that his secretary of the treasury was being referred to as a monarchist. He promptly informed Hamilton about the charge.[36] The vociferous denials Hamilton made on this and other occasions are not themselves proof that the story was a fabrication, but one wonders how he could have denied the story to Washington if he had supported the idea at the convention, over which Washington had presided. A careful reading of the President's letter makes it clear that he was both pained and surprised by the charge against his trusted friend. Hamilton's reply to Washington was straightforward. He showed that the accusation had its origin in references he had made to the British government in 1787 and that it had been circulated by his political enemies in the intervening years.[37]

Accompanying that rumor was another more subtle one that Hamilton hoped to use his influence in the national government to draw more and more authority into hands of national leaders until the popular elements of the Constitution were destroyed and a monarchy was established. This oft-repeated accusation was a serious hindrance to Hamilton's efforts to guide American diplomacy, for it led many people to believe Hamilton too ready to see the British point of view. It has been ably refuted by some historians; others continue to give it credence (see Chapter XIX). Again, the evidence runs heavily against the verity of the charge.

Little weight should be given to statements by Hamilton's contemporaries, among them Thomas Jefferson and Gouverneur Morris, that he "avowed himself" a monarchist. Jefferson's *The Anas* (which S. E. Morison refers to as Jefferson's "private diary of fugitive political gossip"[38]) contains reports from a "Mr. Butler," Tench Coxe, and others that they or someone else heard Hamilton affirm his devotion to the monarchical form of government. Jefferson said that Hamilton was "bewitched and perverted by the British example," and he expressed indignation at Hamilton's state-

[36] Washington to Hamilton, July 29, 1792, *WW*, XXXII, 97–99. The President also included in this letter a report of the accusation he had heard in Virginia that Hamilton was muddling the nation's finances.

[37] Hamilton's reply was part of his long letter of August 18, 1792 (*HWL*, II, 427–72), sometimes referred to as "Hamilton's Defense of the Funding System." In his letter of May 26, 1792, to Colonel Edward Carrington, he declared: "I am affectionately attached to the republican theory. I desire above all things to see the equality of political rights, exclusive of all hereditary distinction, firmly established" (*ibid.*, IX, 533).

[38] Samuel Eliot Morison (ed.), *The Life and Letters of Harrison Gray Otis* (Boston, 1913), I, 97.

ment, made in his presence, that the British government was the best on earth. He also described John Adams' incisive protest that "an elective government will not do."[39] In 1811, almost seven years after Hamilton's death, Jefferson wrote that he did not agree with "Hamilton's plan" of having the chief officials of two branches of the government—the executive and the judiciary—hold their positions for "life" and that he was even more strongly opposed to the idea that these officials become "hereditary, as others desire."[40] Obviously Jefferson did not believe that Hamilton had desired hereditary rulers for the country, for he explicitly attributed that idea to "others."

Morris' allegations have sometimes been given greater credibility because Hamilton and Morris were leaders of the Federalist party, they were known to hold many views in common, and they were regarded as close friends. Actually, during Hamilton's later years their friendship was far from perfect.[41] Morris behaved generously in helping pay off Hamilton's debts after his death, but in the funeral oration (and later in his correspondence) he showed no reluctance to recite the worst of Hamilton's weaknesses and mistakes. Hamilton's disciple William Coleman was so angered by the oration that on the day after the funeral he called on Morris, seized Morris' draft of the address, threw it in the fire, and burned it.[42] The copy of the oration published by Coleman, parts of which have been quoted many times, probably differs greatly from what Morris actually said.[43]

Morris later wrote that Hamilton "never failed, on every occasion, to advocate the excellence of and avow his attachment to monarchical government."[44] By that phrase it seems clear that he was referring to Hamilton's desire for "energy in the executive"; many times in his letters to Morris he expressed his earnest desire to uphold and invigorate the Constitution.[45] In 1799, Morris wrote in his diary that Hamilton had urged him to take an active part in public affairs to help defeat "the Anti-Federalists" in

[39] *JW*, I, 324–25, 416–17.

[40] *Ibid.*, XII, 362.

[41] Roosevelt, *Gouverneur Morris*, 321.

[42] *MDL*, II, 456–58.

[43] William Coleman (ed.), *A Collection of the Facts and Documents Relative to the Death of Major-General Alexander Hamilton* (New York, 1804), 41–46 (hereafter cited as *The Death of Major-General Alexander Hamilton*).

[44] Morris to Robert Walsh, February 5, 1811, *MDL*, II, 526.

[45] Hamilton to Morris, May 19, 1777, *HWL*, IX, 71; January 10, 1801, *ibid.*, X, 409; February 27, 1802, *ibid.*, 425–26.

their attempt "to overthrow our Constitution."[46] Morris developed a practice of "quoting" Hamilton to prove his own ideas, and it is significant that, in 1804, Morris predicted that "at the rate things go on, the Constitution cannot last, and an unbalanced monarchy will be established on its ruins."[47]

Hamilton's praise of the British government as the "best on earth" should have alarmed no one. The Constitutional Convention was called because the government provided under the Articles had all but failed. In 1787 there were few Americans who would have characterized the government of the United States as "the best on earth." At the time of the Revolution, English democracy had centuries of healthful development behind it, and it was decidedly improved by the effects of the war. For more than a year before the adoption of the Declaration of Independence, Americans waged war for the "rights of Englishmen," and the loudest complaint in that immortal document is that Americans had been denied the justice to which they were entitled under English law. At the time of the writing of the Constitution, Jefferson observed that the "English constitution was acknowledged to be better than all which [had] preceded it."[48] Both John Adams and John Quincy Adams wanted the new American government to resemble that of the British.[49] In fact, the elder Adams looked upon the political developments of the British as one of the most notable accomplishments in the history of mankind. A few months before the convention assembled at Philadelphia, he described the British government as a monument to human intelligence as great as the "formation of languages" or as "the whole art of navigation and ship-building."[50] Upon the outbreak of the French Revolution in 1789, Lafayette sent word to President Washington that the French leaders were trying "to obtain for France a constitution nearly resembling that of England, which we regard as the most perfect model of government which is hitherto known."[51]

Hamilton specifically named the features of the British system which he regarded as essential for the harmony of a nation: "public strength"

[46] *MDL*, II, 379.

[47] Morris to Jonathan Dayton, January 7, 1804, *ibid.*, 453.

[48] Jefferson to John Adams, September 28, 1787, *JW*, VI, 321.

[49] Samuel Flagg Bemis, *John Quincy Adams and the Foundations of American Foreign Policy* (New York, 1949), 27–28.

[50] John Adams in an essay, "A Defense of the Constitutions," January, 1787, *AW*, IV, 358.

[51] John Trumbull, *Autobiography, Reminiscences, and Letters* (New York, 1841), 151.

and "individual security."[52] The former was seriously deficient in the United States, and he believed that the persecution of the Tories in violation of the treaty of 1783, as well as the paper-money and other prodebtor laws of various states, were signs that the latter had not yet been assured.[53]

In seeking to refute the "monarchist" charge, Hamilton frequently took the offensive. He warned the Constitutional Convention that too much democracy might cause the country to "*shoot into a monarchy*."[54] In his first *Federalist* essay he warned his readers that anyone desiring to set up a monarchy was more likely to cloak his design by a pretended "zeal for the rights of the people" than by "the forbidding appearance of zeal for the firmness and efficiency of government."[55] He was convinced that the subversion of the Constitution could come only "from convulsions and disorders, in consequence of the arts of popular demagogues."[56] After the arrival of Edmond Genêt, the first French minister, in 1793, Hamilton was genuinely fearful that the enthusiastic response of the American people might lead the country to "despotism." Before Napoleon became famous abroad, Hamilton described the manner in which the furor of a popular revolution could lead to a military dictatorship, and he correctly predicted that outcome in France.[57] Jefferson, on the other hand, was confidently asserting as late as 1800 that if "Bonaparte [declared] for Royalty" he would forthwith be assassinated.[58]

In the various collections of notes on the proceedings of the Constitutional Convention, Hamilton's doubts about the adequacy of the representative form of government were always expressed in tones of regret.[59] Many times then and later, proclaiming his devotion to the cause of liberty, he expressed a desire for a system embracing as much republicanism as possible without endangering the people's welfare.[60] That these avowals were substantially verified by his actions will be seen in later chapters.

52 Speech in the Constitutional Convention, June 18, 1787, *HWL*, I, 389.

53 The refusal of North Carolina to ratify the Constitution in 1788 "shows that, during the years 1782 to 1788, the spirit of particularism . . . had been growing stronger" (Dodd, *The Life of Nathaniel Macon*, 51). See also Hamilton's "Letters from Phocion," No. 1, 1784, *HWL*, IV, 243; Hamilton to Gouverneur Morris, March 21, 1784, *ibid.*, IX, 402.

54 *HWL*, I, 411.

55 *Ibid.*, XI, 6–7.

56 Hamilton to Washington, August 18, 1792, *ibid.*, II, 460.

57 "Americanus," No. 1, February 1, 1794, *ibid.*, V, 77.

58 Jefferson to Henry Innis, January 23, 1800, *JW*, X, 145.

59 See, for example, his speeches in the Constitutional Convention on June 22, 1787, and June 26, 1787, *HWL*, I, 410–11.

60 "Letters from Phocion," No. 1, 1784, *ibid.*, IV, 232–33.

Hamilton was fervent in his desire that every member of the convention should sign the Constitution; yet he was the only delegate from New York to do so.[61] His desperate and successful efforts to persuade the people of New York to ratify the Constitution, including *The Federalist* essays and the protracted struggle in the state convention at Poughkeepsie, were the culmination of a ten-year struggle to persuade his fellow countrymen to achieve a closer union.

As Washington's secretary of the treasury, Hamilton tried to direct the new government toward achieving the powers with which he believed it should have been endowed by the Constitution. He hoped to see this end achieved through amendments to the Constitution and frequent exercise of the "implied powers."[62] The recurrent accusation that he sought to make the government stronger than the Constitution[63] arose from his effort to make the Constitution stronger than it appeared to be in its original form. Only in connection with Hamilton's desire to see it strengthened can we interpret correctly his later lament that the Constitution was a "frail and worthless fabric."[64] It was not a monarchy that Hamilton sought but rather the growth of the nation's political institutions into the maturity they have attained in the twentieth century. Before concluding that his suggestions were dangerous, one should pause to consider the extent to which they have subsequently been adopted. Though many significant features of his program of 1787 have not been accepted, in some aspects the centralization of power has far exceeded his anticipation. For example, he was convinced that federal agencies would never find occasion to take control of agriculture.[65]

It is one of the ironies of history that Hamilton's opponents and critics succeeded in placing him on the defensive about his loyalty to the Constitution. As Hamilton frequently pointed out, the powerful group opposed to ratification in 1787 and 1788 was to become largely identifiable with Jefferson's Republican party of later years.[66] Historians have rarely censured those leaders for their stand. On the contrary, their opposition to

[61] Speech in the Constitutional Convention, September 17, 1787, *ibid.*, I, 419–20.

[62] See especially Hamilton to Washington, February 23, 1791, on "the Constitutionality of the Bank of the United States," *ibid.*, III, 445–93.

[63] B. O. Flower, *JW*, XII, *xxv*.

[64] Hamilton to Gouverneur Morris, February 27, 1802, *HWL*, X, 425.

[65] "Federalist," No. 17, *ibid.*, XI, 129.

[66] "Address to the Electors of the State of New York," 1801, *ibid.*, VIII, 230.

ratification has usually been viewed simply as a quaint and interesting sidelight.

When the Republican administration took office in 1801, some of its measures, such as lowering taxes, reducing the size of the armed forces, and recalling from abroad a large part of the diplomatic staff, made Hamilton apprehensive. In his correspondence and through the press he issued somber warnings.[67] In part it was a move in the well-known American political game of "viewing with alarm" in order to build up formidable opposition to the party in power. But the personal correspondence of the leading Federalists makes it clear that by 1804 Hamilton had come to consider the nation gravely imperiled by the enervating influence of the Republican administration on the one hand and by the possible secession of New England on the other.[68] He was vigorously opposed to the secession scheme. His final political service to his country, rendered on the day before the duel, was his stout assertion that "dismemberment of our empire will be a clear sacrifice of great positive advantages without any counterbalancing good."[69] His advice to his powerful friends, together with his dramatic death at the hands of a man who many believe (perhaps incorrectly) was in league with the conspirators, "doomed the movement toward New England secession."[70]

In Hamilton's public life, as in his private affairs, there were both flaws and virtues. He enjoyed exerting authority, and he grasped whatever power lay within his reach; yet power was not his ultimate goal. Nearly everything he did reflected the most ardent desire of his life: that future generations of Americans would look upon him as an honest, able statesman who guided well the infant nation and helped to clear the path it would travel toward its ultimate grandeur.[71] The durability of his fame will depend upon the verdict of history concerning the value of his work

[67] Hamilton to Rufus King, June 3, 1802, *ibid.*, X, 437–41; Hamilton to C. C. Pinckney, December 29, 1802, *ibid.*, 445–46; "Examination of Jefferson's Message to Congress of December 7, 1801" (series of eighteen essays published December 17, 1801–April 8, 1802), *ibid.*, VIII, 246–373.

[68] Robert Troup to Rufus King, April 9, 1802, *KC*, IV, 104.

[69] Hamilton to Theodore Sedgwick, July 10, 1804, *HWL*, X, 458.

[70] Henry Putnam Prentiss, *Timothy Pickering as the Leader of New England Federalism, 1800–1815* (Salem, 1934), 33. See also Schachner, *Alexander Hamilton*, 432.

[71] Ames, "A Sketch of the Character of Alexander Hamilton," *Works of Fisher Ames*, II, 256–64.

in advancing the cause of a firmer union, in establishing the financial credit of the federal government, and finally in helping to lay the foundations of a sound foreign policy, which is the subject of the following chapters.

CHAPTER III

Patriots, Tories, and Redcoats

THE American Revolution provided many examples of the tendency of a national crisis to bring able and enterprising men to the fore. A man of Hamilton's genius could scarcely have failed to achieve prominence under any circumstances, but there is no question that the conflict provided an ideal opportunity for him to display his talents and fulfill his ambitions. Few men were as intimately associated with the founding of the new nation.

In 1772, Hamilton left his home on the island of Nevis in the British West Indies and sailed to the colonies, landing at Boston. He went to New York City, and after working for an importing firm for two years, he enrolled at King's College (later Columbia University). The sensitive and impressionable youth readily grasped the momentous significance of the stream of events swirling about him. He saw the prerogatives of monarchy and empire being challenged in a vigorous new country willing to fight for its own interests. He promptly aligned himself with those who were determined to resist the oppressive acts of king and Parliament.

The conflicts of 1774 were not new to Hamilton. The Stamp Act and other commercial restrictions had evoked sharp resistance in the West Indies. Two of his closest boyhood friends, Edward Stevens and the Reverend Hugh Knox, had been loud in their condemnation of the restrictions, and in that period the West Indies "figured grandly in the world's affairs,"[1] and reactions of British citizens living there were too important to be ignored. It is not known precisely what Hamilton's views were on such issues when he left his island home, but the opinion once held that he was pro-British at the time seems incorrect.

Students at King's College were much given to debating, formally and informally. Hamilton quickly joined in the debates and was soon the out-

[1] Ford, *Alexander Hamilton*, 2, 19; Mitchell, *Alexander Hamilton*, I, 23.

standing advocate of American rights at the college. He wrote essays, published in *Holt's Journal*, defending the Boston Tea Party and commenting on related subjects. The essays gained him favorable attention, and on July 6 friends induced him to address a mass meeting in the "Fields" in New York City. Tradition has it that his fiery speech attracted more attention than any other part of the meeting.

Two months later the Continental Congress met at Philadelphia and quickly became the focus of disagreement. Hamilton approved the delegates' bold action of forming an "Association" to wage economic warfare against Britain, a position that placed him among the radicals of the day. One might assume that his youthfulness contributed to his outlook—he was but nineteen years old—but a study of his subsequent life reveals that he always stood for decisive action when he thought it was time to act.

The conservative Reverend Samuel Seabury, signing himself "A Westchester Farmer," published a pamphlet making a well-reasoned attack upon the actions of the Continental Congress. Seabury's analysis aroused consternation among the patriots. Hamilton replied to it in two much longer pamphlets, "A Full Vindication," and later, when the controversy grew more intense, "The Farmer Refuted." In addition to forcefully expressing Hamilton's ideas on government, the essays set forth his concept of the course that American "diplomacy" should take and his view of the nature of the bonds between Britain and the colonies.

Liberty, he held, is "the greatest of terrestrial blessings," and Americans would not allow the "rapacity" of Parliament to "extort that inestimable jewel from [them] without a manly and virtuous struggle." True, Americans were dependent upon the king of England; yet they were a "free people" and would put themselves to "any inconvenience" rather than be "victims" of the "lawless ambition" of Parliament. In the colonial charters Hamilton found repeated guaranties of liberty for Americans, and he found nothing to support the idea that Parliament could legally rule the new country. Yet, he held, whether or not it was stated in the charters, the colonists had an "inherent right" to "exercise a legislative power," a right "founded upon the rights of all men to freedom and happiness." Though vowing his allegiance to the king, he could see no grounds upon which "the inhabitants of Great Britain [had] a right to dispose of the lives and properties of the inhabitants of America." When the Westchester Farmer pointed out that not all Hamilton's claims could be verified in the colonial charters, the youthful pamphleteer produced an oft-quoted literary gem which must be quoted yet again:

> The sacred rights of mankind are not to be rummaged for among old parchments or musty records. They are written, as with a sunbeam, in the whole volume of human nature, by the hand of the Divinity itself, and can never be erased or obscured by mortal power.[2]

Hamilton warned Americans about the grave dangers of Parliament's "thirst" for power. Parliamentary rule in the colonies would be more "despotic" and "intolerable" than "absolute monarchy," for "most men are glad to remove any burdens off themselves and place them upon the necks of their neighbors." Hamilton sensed an "inveterate design to exterminate the liberties of America" and presented as one plausible motive for such action "a jealousy of [America's] dawning splendor." To tamely submit to Parliament—and specifically to fail to render aid to Massachusetts, which was being punished by the closing of the port of Boston and the subversion of her charter until the famous tea was paid for—would simply invite further injuries and final ruin. He supported the resolutions for economic resistance and retaliation adopted by Congress. The members of Congress were guardians who deserved public support for adopting measures of "justice and vigor" that had the "probability of success." Had they done otherwise, they might properly have been considered the "betrayers" of the people. Seabury and others who were clamoring against Congress did "nothing less than advise [Americans] to be slaves."

Hamilton was convinced that Britain would not stand against a resolute America. He lamented the "unnatural quarrel" and prayed for a "speedy reconciliation—a perpetual and mutually beneficial union." Surely Britain would not resort to the "madness" of trying to reduce the colonists "by fire and sword." But if such an unfortunate war should come about, America could raise a force of at least 500,000 fighting men (though not all of them in organized armies), thirty times as many men, he believed, as Britain could send into the conflict. A "certain enthusiasm in liberty" would move Americans to "acts of bravery and heroism." Blockades could not conquer the colonies, for they were too nearly self-sufficient economically; they could "live without trade of any kind." Moreover, Britain's European rivals would quickly take advantage of her in such a contest by

[2] *HWL*, I, 113.

rendering aid to the struggling colonies. He was sure France and Spain would send aid; otherwise, "causes must fail of their usual effects . . . princes and nations must cease to be ambitious and avaricious. And the French, from being a jealous, politic, and entertaining people, must be grown negligent, stupid, and inattentive to their own interests."

The succeeding years of struggle cured Hamilton of some of his exuberant optimism about the respective military forces of Britain and the United States and his facile assumptions about foreign aid. Yet he was trying to win support for a cause, and what advocate, in such a situation, fails to proclaim that his side is sure to win? He was essentially correct in his estimate of the potential strength of the new nation. What he failed to foresee was that great numbers of his fellow Americans would offer their lives and fortunes to help Britain suppress the rebellion. His appraisal of the sentiments of Britain's rivals was correct in principle, in that they were jealous of Britain and acted in their own interests; but he failed to predict the dangers inherent in accepting foreign aid, and, in order to present a strong case, he did not mention the reasons, which he may even then have seen, why foreign aid must be marked by fear, crosscurrents of jealousy, and reluctance on the part of the ally to render assistance when needed.

Hamilton was distressed by the discord within the empire. He already saw in outline the policy that was to be so important in his diplomacy of later years—that the welfare of both Britain and the United States would be promoted by friendly co-operation. By "kind treatment" Britain could secure American "attachment in the powerful bands of self-interest." This was the approach that "prudence and sound policy" called for. "In fifty or sixty years" the United States would be rich and powerful, with "a debt of gratitude to the parent state," if she had been treated properly in the meantime. "A perseverance in ill-treatment would naturally beget deep-rooted animosities in America that might never be eradicated, and might operate to the prejudice of the empire to the latest period."

There was a reassuring freedom from passion in Hamilton's essays. British acts were denounced as "unconstitutional, unjust, and tyrannical," but the young writer did not indulge in outbursts of hatred or demands for revenge. He did not try to be polite to Seabury, but his search for a wise national policy was marked by calm reasoning.

Hamilton's essays of 1774 and 1775 were long and rambling and were weakened by boyish repartee; yet they made good sense. They were permeated with the radical views of the period. Their salient points can also be found in the writings of James Wilson, Thomas Jefferson, John Adams, and others; but it must be remembered that Hamilton lived and wrote in New York, where opinion was deeply and often bitterly divided. His pamphlets were widely read and influenced many New Yorkers who would not have followed the writings of men in other colonies.

Massachusetts, with its vigilant minutemen, was close to Hamilton's thoughts. Indeed, the young patriot "heard" the shots fired at Concord Bridge and Bunker Hill. He had no direct part in Washington's victory at Boston—in which the general cleared the city of redcoats without an open battle—but the young college student was more and more caught up in the spirit of war. He began to study military subjects, particularly gunnery, and he and some of his classmates began drilling with the militia. In August, 1775, while under fire from a British warship, he joined with the militia and other members of the populace in removing twenty-one pieces of artillery from the Battery to keep it from falling into British hands. When the Provincial Congress of New York authorized a company of artillery in January, 1776, young Hamilton asked to be placed in command. The legislators must have been startled by such a request from one so young and so lacking in military experience; yet Colonel McDougall and other acquaintances recommended him so highly that he was permitted to appear before an examining board. The board, impressed by his spirit and intellect and by his knowledge of gunnery, appointed him captain of artillery on March 14, 1776.[3]

As yet Captain Hamilton had no company to command; it was his task to raise one. Incomplete records indicate that to recruit and outfit his thirty troops he spent the last of the money that had been intended to pay for his college education. In his eagerness he drilled the men so rigorously that he soon encountered severe discipline problems; but he worked hard, and soon his company was performing its exercises on the "Fields" of New York City with precision that added new luster to his growing reputation. At such performances the dashing young captain wore a brightly colored uniform and expensive shoes. Fortunately, Curtenius, his New York clothier, did not demand immediate payment for the "blue Shalloon" and "blue Strouds."[4]

[3] Schachner, *Alexander Hamilton*, 45; Mitchell, *Alexander Hamilton*, I, 80–84.
[4] Mitchell, *Alexander Hamilton*, I, 81.

Hamilton must have felt that his hour of opportunity had arrived. In 1769, as a boy of fourteen, he had written to his friend Edward Stevens, "I mean to prepare the way for futurity . . . I wish there was a war."[5] Then he was doubtless thinking of entering battle in the company of an organized, trained, and equipped force commanded by an established body of officers serving the well-ordered British government. Instead, the war, when it came, was a civil war, in which his job was to recruit and train men at the behest of the newly established government of a rebellious colony. What about supplies? What about money? Who were his friends, and who were his enemies? It was a perilous situation, but it offered him an unlimited field for proving his talents and for testing his ability to think clearly and to lay out and follow a consistent course when confronted with obstacles that baffled the irresolute and broke the spirits of the impatient. Rarely has enthusiasm for a cause been accompanied by so high a degree of constancy as that displayed by Hamilton during the extended ordeal of the Revolution.

The New York legislators displayed confidence in their young artillery captain. They met his requests for money and supplies and followed his recommendations for promotions for his men. On its part the company worked hard to build fortifications in a futile effort to save New York City and the lower Hudson River from the British. The records do not reveal exactly what part Hamilton played in the disastrous battle of Long Island, in August, 1776, but it is known that he joined in the retreat to Harlem Heights and on into New Jersey. The bitter experience was good training for him, and his steadfastness demonstrated that he was no sunshine patriot. He participated in the spirited engagements at Trenton and Princeton, and at some point during those winter months of retreats and hard fighting he first met General Washington.

The general soon realized the value of this young officer, who could face danger in the field with unconcern and who could think clearly and command effectively under fire. On March 1, 1777, Hamilton was appointed aide-de-camp to General Washington with the rank of lieutenant colonel. Washington needed an aide with literary ability who could write letters and prepare accurate reports.

The appointment placed Hamilton in a position to utilize his intellect and personality. General Washington assigned to him the preparation of

[5] Hamilton to Edward Stevens, November 11, 1769, *HWL*, IX, 38.

his most delicate and difficult papers. Washington's personality remained firmly imprinted upon them, but there is no question that the style improved under the hand of his new aide. The young colonel's personality also made him effective in delicate liaison assignments. Because of his remarkable aptitude for taking the comprehensive view of a complex situation and his clear understanding of Washington's strategy, he was soon busily engaged in working out agreements with French military leaders, undertaking missions to other American generals, and negotiating cartels with the enemy. For such assignments Washington conferred great authority upon him, and apparently he used that authority with prudence.

Hamilton's experiences on Washington's staff had an important influence on the development of his foreign policy. He became acquainted with some of the outstanding leaders of the United States, as well as with Lafayette and several other prominent French officers. He gained the favorable attention of Congress and the public through his courageous deeds, especially at the Battle of Monmouth, where he won high praise from Washington. Finally, since Washington shared his continuous interest in foreign policy and concern about the currents of diplomacy, his close relationship with the general gave his own views added weight.

Hamilton readily appreciated the significance of the alliance formed between the United States and France in 1778. From the time of his earliest public statements he had been favorably inclined toward France. There was French Huguenot blood in his ancestry, and he had spoken French since childhood—one reason Washington employed him so freely to confer with French officers. From the beginning of the conflict in 1775 it was to France above all other nations that Hamilton looked for assistance. He could not see how France could be so negligent of her interests as to forgo the opportunity to weaken the British Empire.

Early in the conflict Hamilton thought his prediction had proved correct when he saw the promptness with which France began funneling munitions to the colonies. Then French hesitation to negotiate a formal alliance forced him to reappraise his earlier conclusions. In July, 1777, he wrote to the Reverend Mr. Knox that he believed the French would extend whatever aid they deemed absolutely essential to maintain American independence but that they would do so "with as much convenience to themselves" as possible. He realized that they were trying to avoid outright war with Britain. He also saw that England was trying to avoid war with France and predicted that she "will not enter into one, till she is compelled to do it." He lamented, "It becomes extremely difficult" to draw France into the war,[6] and he felt strongly that Americans must not slacken their efforts in either the military or the diplomatic aspects of the struggle.

He deplored a growing lethargy among Americans in the pursuit of the war. In March and April, when he was making regular reports on the war to a New York legislative committee composed of Gouverneur Morris, Robert R. Livingston, and William Allison, he took the opportunity to do what he could to shake Americans out of that lethargy. In a letter written during a lull in the fighting, he expressed the belief that the enemy would undertake no further action until it received reinforcements, but he urged the committee not to give that statement any circulation. Many people, he said, could be spurred to action only "by the fear of immediate danger," and if they thought that the enemy would remain idle for six weeks, they "would think they had a right to doze away forty days at least."[7]

Later in 1777 the improved prospects of an alliance with France cheered Hamilton enormously. When writing to the legislative committee about military matters, even favorable news, Hamilton employed a rather matter-of-fact style. But his spirit became buoyant when he could report any favorable information or speculation about negotiations for the alliance. In his first letter to the legislators he commented on the British army's losses from desertions and its difficulties in foraging. He adopted a much livelier tone in reporting the "rumor" that Congress had received a letter from Benjamin Franklin indicating progress in his mission in France. In a letter written two days later, containing further military information, Hamilton gleefully reported that Franklin had written to his son-in-law, Richard Bache, describing relations with France as "in an excellent train" and war between France and Britain "as inevitable as death." Even when Hamilton had no news to report about the negotiations, he included a paragraph stating as much.[8] At no time did it occur to him that the compact was an "unnatural alliance," as Beveridge called it, even though it joined together "French Autocracy and American Liberty."[9] In spite of his anxiety about

[6] Hamilton to Knox, *ibid.*, 86.

[7] Hamilton to New York legislative committee, March 22, 1777, *ibid.*, 49.

[8] Hamilton to New York legislative committee, March 20 to April 28, 1777, *ibid.*, 45–59.

[9] Albert J. Beveridge, *Life of John Marshall* (Boston, 1916–19), II, 2.

the delays, Hamilton looked upon the alliance as a logical step by which France and the United States could mutually profit.

After the alliance was formally established in 1778, Hamilton was mortified to discover that many of his countrymen were inclined to relax and let France carry the burden of the war.[10] He still believed that a unified nation could quickly win it, but he deplored the lack of a sound monetary system, and he complained that nearly half the people of the state of New York were "more attached to Great Britain than to their liberty."[11] To his intimate friend John Laurens he bitterly commented that their countrymen had "the folly of the ass" and the "passiveness of the sheep in their compositions. . . . If we are saved France and Spain must save us."[12]

In his letters to French acquaintances he never tried to minimize the willingness of many Americans to lean heavily on their ally. He lamented it loudly but also reminded his correspondents that the war would be lost unless the French contributed mightily to the struggle. French money, as well as French military and naval strength, was necessary. He advised James Duane, a member of the Continental Congress, that the way to get money from the French was to tell them that without it the United States would have to "make terms with Great Britain." Characteristically, he added that such warnings would have to be made "with plainness and firmness, but with respect, and without petulance." He saw no likelihood that the United States would be abandoned by France, for the latter's "interest and honor" were "too deeply involved."[13]

As the military situation darkened in the early part of 1781, he was more than ever convinced that success depended upon French support.[14] Even in 1782, more than a year after the victory at Yorktown, Hamilton was begging Lafayette to use his influence to prevent the withdrawal of the French army. He believed that Great Britain was probably in such straitened circumstances that she would have to make peace; but peace was "necessary for America" also. He assured Lafayette that Americans were unanimous in their devotion to the alliance,[15] an exaggeration he believed

10 Hamilton to James Duane, September 3, 1780, *HWL*, I, 229.

11 "Continentalist" No. 3, August 9, 1781, *ibid.*, 255–56; Hamilton to Robert Morris, August 13, 1782, *ibid.*, IX, 277.

12 Hamilton to Lawrens, June 30, 1780, HPSCLC, Box 1.

13 Hamilton to Duane, September 3, 1780, *HWL*, I, 229–30.

14 Hamilton to unnamed correspondent, February 7, 1781, *ibid.*, IX, 231.

15 Hamilton to Lafayette, November 3, 1782, *ibid.*, 305.

justified by the urgent need to maintain the United States' new-won independence.

Throughout this period Hamilton did what he could to instill in American hearts a livelier spirit of resistance, and to combat any feeling of ill will toward France. In the fourth of his "Continentalist" essays he tried to place France in the best light possible. "Everything may be hoped from the generosity of France which her means will permit," he assured his readers, but added that France had "full employment for her revenues and credit in the prosecution of the war on her own part."[16]

The one sour note Hamilton encountered in his efforts to co-ordinate French and American military efforts was the persistent demands made by French military adventurers for high commissions in the Continental Army. Even before France had formally declared a state of hostilities, Hamilton was finding it a troublesome problem. Some of the applicants were lacking in ability and experience, and their language difficulties, their impatience, and their ignorance of American scarcities of money and supplies rendered most of them ineffective. He thought that their applications should be denied, but tactfully, so as not to weaken pro-American sentiment in France.[17]

The embarrassment he suffered from the importunities of overly ambitious Frenchmen was more than outweighed by the heartwarming friendships that he formed with a number of outstanding French officers. He developed an enduring comradely feeling with them, as shown by the long-continued fraternal correspondence with Lafayette and the evidence of good relations with Louis Marie, Vicomte de Noailles; Charles Hector, Comte d'Estaing; and General Louis Duportail.

Hamilton was convinced that the Continental Congress could not properly conduct the nation's foreign policy through committees appointed from its own membership, the procedure followed until 1781. He urged Congress to appoint a full-time secretary of foreign affairs.[18] His counsel in the matter coincided with that of the Chevalier de la Luzerne, the French minister in Philadelphia. In due time the office was established, and Robert R. Livingston was named secretary. Luzerne claimed credit for the creation of the office,[19] but Hamilton's words must have carried weight, too.

[16] August 30, 1781, *ibid.*, I, 266.
[17] Hamilton to William Duer, May 6, 1777, *ibid.*, IX, 63–65.
[18] Hamilton to Duane, September 3, 1780, *ibid.*, I, 225.
[19] Jensen, *The New Nation*, 56.

Through his father-in-law, General Schuyler, a powerful New York political leader and a member of Congress from 1778 to 1781, and others, Hamilton exerted considerable influence on Congress. He was fully aware of the fact and took pride in it, seeking to use it to awaken the legislators to other problems he believed urgent, primarily governmental and financial reforms.

To a correspondent whose name has been lost, he wrote that "the first step to reformation, as well in an administration as in an individual, is to be sensible of our faults. This begins to be our case." But, he added, in a pessimistic vein, "we are so accustomed to doing right by halves, and spoiling a good intention in the execution, that I always wait to see the end of our public arrangements before I venture to expect good or evil from them."[20]

He also believed that the nation's future was jeopardized by financial confusion. Six months before the Battle of Yorktown he wrote to Robert Morris that the restoration of "public credit" was essential for winning the war. "The game we play," as he called the contest with Great Britain, "is a sure game if we play it with skill."[21]

Throughout the war Hamilton maintained his keen interest in diplomacy. In the spring of 1777, following the winter victories at Trenton and Princeton, Hamilton thought that the "bustling aspect of European affairs" might cause the British forces in the United States to undertake some risky venture as a means of counterbalancing the anti-British diplomacy in Europe. At the time he was confident of American military superiority and evidently eager for the British to renew their efforts to take Philadelphia.[22] He was aware that Frederick the Great of Prussia was jealous of Great Britain, and he believed that Prussia's recent acquisition of Polish territory along the Baltic Sea would stimulate Frederick's interest in "commerce and navy" and cause him to frown upon German mercenaries joining the British army. Similarly, the widespread antipathy of Europeans toward Britain would, he felt, prevent the Russian government from granting aid to the British.[23]

Later in the war Hamilton received warnings from Lafayette about

[20] Hamilton to unknown correspondent, February 7, 1781, *HWL*, IX, 230.

[21] Hamilton to Robert Morris, April 30, 1781, *ibid.*, III, 343–83.

[22] Hamilton to the New York legislative committee, April 5, 1777, *ibid.*, IX, 51.

[23] Hamilton to Robert R. Livingston, June 28, 1777, *ibid., 80.* See also Zoltan Haraszti, *John Adams and the Prophets of Progress* (Cambridge, 1952), 99–100.

ominous developments in French and Spanish diplomacy that might rob the United States of some of the expected fruits of victory.[24] This news did not startle Hamilton, who had always assumed that France would generally follow the path of national interest—which he thought called for American independence. Moreover, he knew that throughout the war years, while the generals were testing their battle plans in North America, so were the diplomats going through their maneuvers in Europe.

Then he heard that mediation might be offered by Austria and Russia.[25] Later reports were even more disquieting. He learned from Lafayette and others that the Spaniards were jealous of the new nation's rising fortunes and might induce France to come to terms with Britain after all, under circumstances that might be severely disappointing to the United States.[26] Hamilton complained sharply upon hearing that Spain was entertaining irregular negotiations with the British in the midst of the struggle.[27] Of course, Hamilton had no means of distinguishing positively between rumor and fact, but it is interesting to note that he had a reasonably accurate picture of the currents of European diplomacy.

Hamilton was uneasy when he learned of the death of Empress Maria Theresa of Austria, who had been more or less favorably disposed to the United States, and the succession of her son, Joseph II, who appeared to be much less friendly. Hamilton noted that "among the potentates which we look upon as amicable, three of the principal ones are at a very advanced stage of life—King of Spain, the King of Prussia, and the Empress of Russia." He saw no certain means of predicting the attitudes of their successors. Americans had not sufficiently calculated such "contingencies," he said, "nor reflected that the death of a single prince, the change or caprice of a single minister, was capable of giving a new face to the whole system." He did not despair, for he could see that the basic interests of most European nations would be served by a reduction in British power. He still had confidence in his ability to foresee the long-term developments of European diplomacy, but he had misgivings about possible impulsive actions of new rulers and ministers—a rather far cry from the lofty optimism he had displayed in "The Farmer Refuted."[28]

[24] Lafayette to Hamilton, April 12, 1782, *HWH*, I, 277.

[25] "Continentalist," No. 3, August 9, 1781, *HWL*, I, 259.

[26] Lafayette to Hamilton, June 29, 1782, *HWH*, I, 283.

[27] Hamilton to Robert Morris, April 30, 1781, *HWL*, III, 358. See also Samuel F. Bemis, *The Hussey-Cumberland Mission and American Independence* (Princeton, 1931).

[28] "Continentalist," No. 3, August 9, 1781, *HWL*, I, 258–59.

Hamilton's wartime career changed course abruptly in 1781, when he resigned from Washington's personal staff. On February 16 he had a caustic verbal encounter with Washington during which the general accused him of disrespect. After his replacement had been arranged for, his resignation became formal on April 30. Since Hamilton's subsequent policies, both foreign and domestic, were profoundly influenced by his relations with Washington, this episode is particularly significant.

Hamilton reported his version of the incident in a letter to his father-in-law. In response to Washington's command, Hamilton was on his way to the general's office at headquarters when he happened to meet Lafayette in the hall. They spoke together briefly "on a matter of business." Then he hastened on toward Washington's office. He found the general standing at the head of the stairs, where, speaking in an angry tone, he accused Hamilton of disrespectfully keeping him waiting for ten minutes. Hamilton made a brief and rather haughty denial and added, "Since you have thought it necessary to tell me so, we part." Within an hour Washington tried to mend the breach, but Hamilton remained adamant, agreeing only to continue in his post until absent staff members returned to carry on the work.[29]

Hamilton's impounded discontent of several months had finally broken through the dam of self-restraint. He had found his desk job irksome and longed for an opportunity to command a force in battle. He had been with Washington for four years. His ability and devotion had won him wide acclaim; yet he felt that his efforts were building Washington's reputation at the expense of his own. He was still a lieutenant colonel, and he was afraid the war might end before he had a chance to raise his "character as a soldier above mediocrity."[30] He had repeatedly asked for a command "in the line," and Washington had indicated that he would grant the request in time. He had begun his career in the line early in 1776, and he was convinced that if he had continued as a field officer and refused to join Washington's staff he would have attained a higher rank.[31]

These attitudes reflect Hamilton's personal ambition—his critics have called it his "lust for glory"—which accompanied him throughout life. More, it reflects his pride. He disliked being another man's aide. He had refused to serve in that capacity under two other generals before accepting

29 Hamilton to Schuyler, February 18, 1781, *ibid.*, IX, 232–37. This letter contains a complete account of the incident.

30 Hamilton to Washington, November 22, 1780, *ibid.*, 226.

31 Hamilton to Washington, April 27, 1781, *ibid.*, 239.

Washington's invitation. His French officer friends had told him that such a position did not befit a man of his talents. Further, Hamilton relished the excitement of battle. Though in his adulthood he was never eager for war, once it came he wanted to take a leading role in it.

Before his resignation Hamilton had tried to persuade Congress to appoint him special commissioner to France to obtain further financial and military assistance. He had assumed that it would be a temporary task, followed by a high-ranking appointment in the army. Congress had refused to make the appointment, for reasons that are unclear.

Hamilton risked his future when he rejected Washington's conciliatory overtures. His father-in-law urged him not to leave the general's staff, arguing, with considerable flattery, that the French might regard the break as another division among their allies and lose confidence in them.[32] Fortunately, Washington's anger soon passed away, leaving undiminished his high regard for the younger man. Washington was not particularly slow to anger, and he had a no more forgiving spirit than other men had. In his correspondence there are outbursts of anger, distrust, and resentment—directed at Monroe, Jefferson, Dr. George Logan (for his unauthorized negotiations with France in 1798), and others. But for Hamilton, Washington had a particularly deep regard and a profound appreciation of his character and talents. Not long before the rupture he had written of Hamilton that he knew of "none whose soul [was] more firmly engaged in the cause, or who [exceeded] him in probity and sterling virtue."[33] Perhaps to demonstrate his continuing regard, three months after Hamilton's resignation Washington placed him in command of a battalion, at a time when it appeared certain that the army would soon be launching an attack on General Clinton in New York or on Cornwallis in Virginia. The appointment fulfilled the young colonel's most cherished dream.

Apparently Washington never fully explained his reaction to Hamilton's resignation, though he referred to it in a letter to Lafayette[34] and also talked with the French general about it. It appears that Washington did not blame Hamilton for the break and was fully aware of the tensions to which both men were subjected in those years of ordeal.[35]

[32] Philip Schuyler to Hamilton, February 25, 1781, HPLC.

[33] Washington to John Sullivan (of Congress), February 4, 1781, *WW*, XXI, 181.

[34] Washington to Lafayette, April 22, 1781, *ibid.*, 491.

[35] Detailed accounts of the episode may be found in Schachner, *Alexander Hamilton*, 120–32; Mitchell, *Alexander Hamilton*, I, 222–42; and J. C. Fitzpatrick, *George Washington Himself* (Indianapolis, 1933), 383–85.

Hamilton's resignation thus proved to further, not injure, his career. It made possible his brilliant military exploit at the Battle of Yorktown, where he led a successful charge against one of Cornwallis' most important fortifications. This victory gave Hamilton keen satisfaction. He wrote proudly to his young wife: "You will see the particulars in the Philadelphia papers."[36] It also added greatly to his national prestige. As Mitchell has aptly stated, "From the instant he mounted a redoubt in Cornwallis' lines America never lost sight of him."[37] Thus does a nation remember acts of valor, especially if those acts contribute to an immediate victory. The military reputation he established enabled Washington to obtain for him the rank of major general when war with France threatened in 1798.

After Yorktown most Americans believed that the war was over, or at least had entered a long period of stalemate. Until peace was firmly secured, however, it would be necessary for Washington to maintain a standing army to uphold the sovereignty of the new nation. But Hamilton realized that under such conditions military promotions would be few and large-scale battles rare. The profession of law again beckoned, and he discontinued active military duty to resume his studies, devoting to them the same energy he had dedicated to the cause of freedom. In May, 1782, he was appointed receiver of taxes for New York State, but in spite of the interruptions his official duties entailed, he was formally admitted to the bar in July of the same year.

He was to be still further delayed in taking up his profession. On July 22 the New York legislature named him a representative to the Continental Congress, and he took his seat on November 25. Appointments to Congress were not sought after at the time, and many prominent men were refusing to serve, giving as their reasons personal affairs or service in state governments, where the real power was being exercised. Yet it was an important period in Hamilton's life, as well as in the lives of other members of that Congress, notably James Madison and James Wilson. During his term Hamilton made valuable new acquaintances. Peace negotiations had become the nation's main interest, and Congress, though weak in many respects, had firm control of diplomacy. When Hamilton joined that body, he became one of the nation's foremost shapers of American foreign policy.

[36] Hamilton to Mrs. Hamilton, October 16, 1781, *HWL*, IX, 250.
[37] Mitchell, *Alexander Hamilton*, I, 249.

CHAPTER IV

The Confederation at Peace

THE SURRENDER of Cornwallis at Yorktown on October 19, 1781, brought a surge of rejoicing that swept the nation—contrasting sharply with the deep gloom of the previous months. At the end of May, Governor Thomas Jefferson of Virginia had written to General Washington in the gravest terms about the destructive and almost unimpeded maraudings of Cornwallis and Arnold in Virginia. He saw the state at the verge of ruin and urged the general to return to his "own Country" to help banish its woes,[1] if the total conditions of the war would permit him to do so. Washington's reply was prompt and sympathetic. He emphasized the importance of his operations around New York but observed that the ravages of the British were evidence of their design "to make as large seeming conquests as possible that they may urge the plea of *uti possidetis* in the proposed mediation" for peace.[2]

When the national celebrations died down after Yorktown and Americans had time to take stock of their situation, it was obvious that the country was in dire straits and desperately needed peace. The government's finances were a shambles. The president of the Continental Congress, Elias Boudinot, recorded that "when the messenger brought to Congress the news of [Cornwallis'] capitulation, it was necessary to furnish him with hard money for his expenses. There was not a sufficiency in the Treasury to do it, and the members of Congress, of which I was one, each paid a dollar to accomplish it."[3] The states had almost stopped sending funds to Congress. This condition continued to embarrass the nation's leaders—or at least some of them. Hamilton's motion, made several months later, that the states "be

[1] Jefferson to Washington, May 28, 1781, Julian Boyd *et al.* (eds.), *The Papers of Thomas Jefferson* (Princeton, 1952), VI, 32–33.

[2] Washington to Jefferson, June 8, 1781, *WW*, XXII, 189–90.

[3] George Adams Boyd, *Elias Boudinot, Patriot and Statesman, 1740–1821* (Princeton, 1952), 94.

called upon in the most earnest manner" to collect taxes and remit money to Congress was met by an attempt by Congressmen Bland and Mercer of Virginia to have the motion declared unconstitutional.[4] The failure of their motion did not mean that funds were forthcoming.

The soldiers' mutiny of 1783 was a further indication of the state of affairs. The British were still holding sections of American territory, including New York City, the most strategic spot on the Atlantic Coast, and Congress could send General Washington no funds or supplies to support a campaign to oust them. American envoys were engaged in peace negotiations with British representatives in Paris, but Congress protested that the peace commissioners did not send frequent dispatches; on one occasion during the negotiations five months passed with no word from them. Washington, with the army at Newburgh, New York, complained that Congress was leaving him in the dark about "the political and pecuniary state of . . . affairs."[5]

During the summer of 1782, when there was no peace treaty in sight, Hamilton became suspicious that the British were not really aiming at a reasonable peace with the United States. He accused them of trying to "conciliate in Europe and seduce in America" while making "economic arrangements [for] enlarging the credit of their government, and multiplying its resources."[6]

Hamilton saw further dangers for the new nation if France should withdraw her army. Just before taking his seat in Congress in 1782, he wrote to Lafayette that trade was "prodigiously cramped" and that the states were "in no humor for continuing exertions." He apologized for the "inertness" of his countrymen but felt that the ally must know that "if the war lasts it must be carried on by external succors."[7]

In Congress, James Madison shared Hamilton's concern about the debility of the government. The British were still holding on in New York, while the French, who had been seriously defeated in the West Indies, showed no signs of recovery.[8] One of the arguments used to persuade Rhode Island to allow Congress to collect duties on imports was that the nation still had "an enemy vigilant, intriguing, well acquainted with our defects and embarrass-

[4] *JCC*, May 2, May 5, 1783, XXIV, 325, 328.

[5] Washington to Hamilton, March 4, 1783, *WW*, XXVI, 185.

[6] Resolution, Legislature of New York, July 21, 1782, *HWL*, I, 292.

[7] Hamilton to Lafayette, November 3, 1782, *ibid.*, IX, 304.

[8] Brant, II, 253.

ments."[9] The French minister at Philadelphia, Luzerne, emphasized French defeats—or, as he expressed it, the unexpected success of the British—and warned the American government not to slacken its "efforts and preparations for an ensuing campaign."[10]

Hamilton's efforts as a member of Congress to strengthen the national government were closely related to his plans for foreign relations. In his resolution of June 30, 1783, he spoke of the need for a "Federal Judicature" to see that "local regulations of particular States" did not interfere with the implementation of the peace treaty with Britain, or treaties that might be entered into with other nations. He saw the need for "vesting in the United States a general superintendence of trade," for removing some of the restrictions on the treaty-making power included in the Articles of Confederation, and for giving Congress authority to make and enforce laws through which the United States could honor its obligations under international law.[11] The same sentiments reverberated from the headquarters of General Washington, for he, too, was concerned with both foreign and domestic affairs, as he made clear when he wrote that "unless Congress have powers competent to all *general* purposes, . . . the distresses we have encountered, the expense we have incurred, and the blood we have spilt in the course of an eight years war, will avail us nothing."[12]

As a member of Congress, Hamilton was in a position to exert a great deal of control over the nation's foreign policy. Article VI of the Articles of Confederation provided that "no state, without the consent of the United States in Congress assembled, shall send any embassy to, or receive any embassy from, or enter into any conference, agreement, alliance or treaty with any King, prince or state."[13] While the peace commissioners were at work—leisurely it seemed—in Paris, there was not much Congress could do but wait for the results of the negotiations. Waiting was frustrating and onerous.

In 1779, Congress had instructed John Adams to demand British recognition of American independence and the territory westward to the Mississippi and down that river to the northern boundary of Florida, which was to be designated as the thirty-first parallel. The cession of Canada and Nova

[9] December 16, 1782, *JCC*, XXIII, 803.
[10] *Ibid.*, XXIV, 5.
[11] *HWL*, I, 305–14.
[12] Washington to Hamilton, March 4, 1783, *WW*, XXVI, 188.
[13] Tansill, *Documents Illustrative of the Formation of the Union*, 29.

Scotia to the United States would be desirable.[14] In June, 1781, Congress entrusted the negotiations to a commission of five: Adams, Franklin, Jay, Henry Laurens, and Jefferson, with instructions, first, to obtain independence. On the other points they were to be guided by the French government. The instructions carried the following astounding directive: "You are to make the most candid and confidential communications, upon all subjects, to the Ministers of our generous ally the king of France; to undertake nothing in the negotiations for peace or truce, without their knowledge and concurrence."[15] This directive was considered a victory for Luzerne; but Congress would not have placed its emissaries under such restrictions had it not felt the acute need for continued French military and financial aid. Hamilton had recently written in a private letter, "God send that the negotiation abroad for money may succeed, for it is only this that can give success to our interior efforts."[16] Later that year the secretary of foreign affairs, Robert R. Livingston, instructed Franklin to do his best to borrow more money from France, saying that there had never been a time when money was "more necessary."[17]

Jefferson was unable to go to Paris in 1781, and Laurens did not arrive until after the negotiations were almost completed. It was Franklin who drew up a list of "necessary" terms for peace, including independence for the United States, a boundary settlement reducing Canada to her pre-1763 limits—which would push her back north of the Great Lakes and possibly confine her to the St. Lawrence Valley—and free use of the North Atlantic fishing areas. His "desirable" terms called for the cession of Canada, indemnity for towns destroyed in the war, a British apology for the mistreatment of her former colonies in America, and Anglo-American trade reciprocity.[18]

Thus the most important events of 1782 transpired not in the United States, but in Paris. John Jay's activities are well known: the brilliant, suspicious young commissioner refused to be bound by the instructions from Philadelphia and drew his colleagues into a full current of negotiations with the British, neglecting to confer with the French on all points. Though the French foreign minister, Charles Gravier, Comte de Vergennes, had

[14] *JCC*, XIV, 955–66.

[15] *Ibid.*, XX, 617.

[16] Hamilton to unnamed correspondent, February 7, 1781, *HWL*, IX, 231.

[17] Livingston to Franklin, November 26, 1781, *RDC*, V, 5.

[18] Much of the development of Franklin's ideas regarding the peace treaty can be traced through his "Journal of the Negotiations for Peace with Great Britain, from March 21 to July 1, 1782," John Bigelow (ed.), *The Works of Benjamin Franklin* (New York, 1904), IX, 248–372.

advised the Americans to proceed with discussions with the British representatives, he protested, mildly, when he was informed that a treaty of peace had been agreed upon. The French-American alliance was not breached, for the treaty was to go into effect only after terms of peace should be agreed upon between France and Britain, but the explicit instructions of the Continental Congress had been violated.

In the Treaty of Paris the United States obtained recognition of its independence; recognition of the Mississippi River as the western boundary of the new nation; and the "right" to fish on the Grand Bank and the "liberty" to fish in other areas. British forces would be withdrawn from the United States and would not carry away any public or private property, "Negroes," or valuable papers belonging to Americans; and "the navigation of the river Mississippi [would] forever remain free and open" to the citizens of both countries. The United States agreed that there was to be "no lawful impediment" to the collection of prewar debts; that there would be no further prosecution of the Tories in the United States; and that Congress was to "recommend" restitution of Tory or private British property that had been seized during the war.[19] The treaty terms constituted a splendid victory for the United States—probably far greater than that Congress had anticipated. Samuel Flagg Bemis, the noted historian of this period, believes that Congress would have accepted the Allegheny Mountains as the western boundary.[20]

The United States was fortunate in being represented by such an able delegation. The success of the negotiations was due, however, as much to favorable British predilections as to the diplomatic proficiency of Franklin and his colleagues. A number of Englishmen in high places desired a peace that would help wipe out the bitterness of war and open the way for friendly commercial relations at the very least, if not for some form of political partnership.

Charles James Fox, British secretary of foreign affairs when the negotiations opened, was in favor of an immediate recognition of American independence, hoping thereby to wean the new nation from its French compact. The Earl of Shelburne, soon to be promoted from the office of

[19] For a text of the treaty, see Hunter Miller (ed.), *Treaties and Other International Acts of the United States of America, 1776–1863* (Washington, 1933), II, 151–57 (hereafter cited as *Treaties*).

[20] Samuel Flagg Bemis, *A Diplomatic History of the United States* (4th ed., New York, 1955), 60.

secretary for home affairs to that of prime minister, opposed a hasty concession of independence. He desired, instead, to present peace terms so favorable that Americans would accept an "economic union" with the mother country. He detested the thought of political separation of the English-speaking peoples, considering it a "vicious and unnatural" step that "would gravely injure both societies." He believed that France was "jealous of American claims rather than partial to them"; therefore, he tried to "buy America out of the Bourbon camp." He also wanted to promote westward expansion across North America "as a joint Anglo-American enterprise," and he was convinced that voluntary "economic interdependence of Britain and America offered vast possibilities."[21]

Shelburne's liberal attitude toward the United States, as embodied in the treaty, helped cost him his position. Many Englishmen feared the possible results of a buildup of the American merchant marine, and wartime resentments still prevailed. Through the maneuverings of Fox and Lord North Parliament dismissed him from office early in 1783, but not until the peace settlement was so far advanced that a reversal of terms was virtually impossible.

No serious problems were encountered in working out the final wording of the treaty. Congress appointed a committee of three, Hamilton, Madison, and Richard Peters, to study it and report whether it should be ratified. Inadequate records of the committee's work indicate that a majority, Madison and Peters, recommended against ratifying the treaty, apparently on the grounds that it was not clearly written. Subsequent evidence makes it appear likely that Madison was displeased by the liberal treatment awarded debtors and Tories and by the absence of any schedule for British withdrawal from the military posts in the Old Northwest. Hamilton urged acceptance of the treaty. After further consideration the ratification of the "Preliminary Articles of Peace" was voted unanimously, and Congress proclaimed the treaty to be in effect on April 15, 1783.[22] Final ratification and proclamation of the treaty and the collateral agreements had to wait until early the following year.

Congress was so well pleased with the terms of the treaty that it was willing to ignore the disobedience of the envoys, at least in all public state-

[21] Vincent T. Harlow, *The Founding of the Second British Empire* (London, 1952), I, 299–311.

[22] A brief summary of the facts concerning the ratification and proclamation is given by Miller, *Treaties*, II, 104–107.

ments. Secretary Livingston, acting without instructions from Congress, gave the commissioners a "tremendous wigging" for their apparent "distrust" of the French government and for the secret article regarding the boundaries of Florida, which seemed to plant the seeds of future discord with Spain and to show preference for the British.[23] In his notes on the proceedings of the Continental Congress, Madison indicated that in the preliminary discussions several members expressed keen disappointment at "the separate and secret manner in which the Ministers had proceeded with respect to France and the confidential manner with respect to the British Ministers." They were particularly provoked at Jay, who had told the British negotiators of his distrust of the French before he had discussed the point with Franklin.[24] The secret article, which was not included in the final draft of the treaty, placed the northern boundary of East and West Florida at the junction of the Mississippi and the "Yassous" (Yazoo) rivers, provided Britain recovered the province from Spain, which had conquered it during the war and to which it was ceded by the terms of the treaty. If Spain continued to hold the province, the boundary would presumably be 166 miles farther south, at the thirty-first parallel.[25] Congress accepted Hamilton's motion that the contents of this article be communicated to the French and that the terms of the treaty of 1778 between the United States and France be scrupulously observed, but that the negotiators be publicly commended for their valuable work.[26]

Congress understood that the Paris representatives took an independent course because they suspected that Vergennes might trade off some of the United States' territorial or other gains in order to obtain more favorable peace terms for France. Congress had been warned repeatedly that some such exchange might be made. For instance, Francis Dana, while passing through western Europe on the way to assume his position as United States minister to Russia, had written from Berlin that Britain might seek peace on terms that would compromise American independence, adding that he believed such a proposal would "not meet with a very vigorous opposition" from France.[27]

[23] *RDC*, VI, 338–40; George Dangerfield, *Chancellor Robert R. Livingston of New York, 1746–1813* (New York, 1960), 175.
[24] *JCC*, XXV, 924.
[25] Miller, *Treaties*, II, 101.
[26] *JCC*, XXIV, 194.
[27] *RDC*, IV, 611–12.

On March 19, 1783, Hamilton, speaking in Congress, commented that he was well acquainted with John Jay, who frequently distrusted the motives of persons with whom he dealt, and added that his own knowledge of recent trends in European diplomacy and his respect for Jay's intelligence and character caused him to believe it entirely possible that the suspicions of French motives were well founded.[28]

Hamilton had his own reasons for being concerned about the devious ways of European diplomacy. Lafayette, who warmly cherished the interests of the United States, as well as his friendship with Hamilton, wrote to the latter from Paris in April, 1782, that he suspected there were secret Franco-British negotiations that might prove harmful to the United States. Two months later he warned his friend that Spanish plans to take Gibraltar might have harmful consequences, for "the Spaniards don't like America."[29] Hamilton soon learned to look askance at a great many European leaders. He told Congress that he assumed the French government had procrastinated in order to negotiate at length for their own interests. Yet he did not show bitterness toward France, assuming that each nation should look out for its own interests. Two months before the treaty arrived from Paris, he wrote to Governor Clinton of New York deploring the "uncertainty with respect to the negotiations." He added, "The duplicity and unsteadiness for which Lord Shelburne is remarkable will not justify any confidence in his intentions. . . . I suspect, too, the Spaniards and Dutch will have large demands."[30] His apprehensions were not quieted by the arrival of the first draft of the treaty. He was afraid there might be further delays because of the demands of Holland and "the hope in France of greater acquisitions in the East."[31]

When at length the treaty was presented to Congress, the members showed no great disappointment that it did not include other items they desired, though Livingston did express the view (which was not his alone) that he was "sorry that the commercial article [had been] stricken out."[32] The "commercial article" was a reference to the 1779 instructions to John Adams, in which Congress had expressed a desire for a close commercial treaty with Britain and instructed him to negotiate one if possible.[33]

[28] *Ibid.*, I, 260.

[29] Lafayette to Hamilton, *HWH*, I, 277, 283.

[30] Hamilton to Clinton, January 12, 1783, *HWL*, IX, 308–309.

[31] Hamilton to Washington, March 17, 1783, *ibid.*, 324.

[32] *RDC*, VI, 344.

[33] *JCC*, XIV, 955–66.

The revolutionary generation was not destined to see commercial relations between the two English-speaking countries placed on an even keel, which was to come about only after a number of false starts and reversals. In July, 1782, Congress moved to revoke Adams' instructions about the commercial treaty.[34] All the southern states and some of the northern ones voted for the revocation. Six months later a committee, of which Hamilton was the chairman, recommended that the peace envoys try to include in the treaty provisions allowing American citizens to carry on "direct commerce to all parts of the British dominions and possessions, in like manner as all parts of the United States may be opened to a direct commerce with British subjects."[35] The motion brought no immediate results but helped keep the issue alive. John Adams was as deeply interested in commerce with Britain as Hamilton was, and it was an important topic of his correspondence during the period. He did not appear to be personally offended when Congress told him to drop negotiations for a treaty of commerce (he always addressed Congress, or Livingston, with respect and moderation), but marshaled his strongest arguments to reverse the instructions. He reminded the members of Congress that, from the outset of the war, he had said the United States should not wish to weaken England beyond the point of acknowledging the colonies' independence, and he had always pointed out that the United States' proper interest in Europe was commercial, not political or diplomatic.[36]

Congress was influenced by Adams' reasoning. It was then that the committee led by Hamilton reported strongly in favor of renewing the instructions. It was ordered that the commissioners at Paris be authorized to "enter into a treaty of commerce between the United States and Great Britain, subject to the revisal of the contracting parties."[37]

There were no immediate results. Adams reported that British merchants and others were so busy formulating plans to injure American commerce, especially with the West Indies, that he could see little hope of an agreement "upon any regulation of commerce here."[38] He still saw a chance to negotiate such a treaty, provided that one man, not a committee, was sent to London to do so. "Long and bloody wars," he reasoned, might be the

[34] *RDC*, IV, 562.

[35] *JCC*, XIII, 838.

[36] Adams to Livingston, February 3, 1783, *RDC*, VI, 242–47.

[37] May 1, 1783, *JCC*, XXIV, 321.

[38] Adams to Livingston, June 23, 1783, *RDC*, VI, 501–506.

results of the failure to handle the subject "wisely."[39] Shelburne's earlier plan for commercial reciprocity between Britain and the United States still had some support in London. William Pitt offered a bill to that effect in 1783, but Parliament rejected it. It appeared to be a one-sided agreement in which Britain would give far more than she received, unless the United States would accept some form of limited political connection.[40] Two years later Adams was sent to London, but he found the British cold and surly and unwilling to negotiate seriously with him.

Apparently Congress did not comment at length on the fisheries article included in the treaty, though that provision was later to prove unsatisfactory, owing in part to the inclusion of the word "liberty" at one point instead of "right." The meager records preserved in the *Journals of the Continental Congress* indicate that during the previous two years the fisheries had been discussed far more often in Congress than the critical issues of independence and boundaries.

During this period Hamilton devoted himself to improving the system of conducting the nation's foreign affairs. Among other recommendations his committee urged the establishment of a "Department of Foreign Affairs,"[41] with the secretary to be "the head of the Diplomatic corps of the United States." The secretary was to make long-term plans for American diplomacy and, from time to time, lay them before Congress. The purposes behind the recommendations were to develop a more unified approach to diplomacy and to place more power and responsibility in the hands of the person in control. Livingston, as secretary of foreign affairs, was never quite sure where he stood vis-à-vis Congress or the ministers serving abroad, and he sometimes found Congress unintentionally working at cross purposes with him, a situation that was not to be resolved until the new government was set up under the Constitution.

Once peace was attained, Congress quickly altered its erstwhile somewhat dependent attitude toward the European nations. While the American government continued to seek financial aid, apprehensions grew that further treaties might embroil the young republic in European affairs. Francis Dana had gone to Russia to obtain recognition of the United States, membership in the Armed Neutrality (a group of northern European countries

[39] Adams to Livingston, June 27, 1783, *ibid.*, 506–507.

[40] Harlow, *The Founding of the Second British Empire*, I, 308–11, 434–51.

[41] May 8, 1783, *JCC*, XXIV, 334–35.

joined together to uphold principles of maritime warfare that were objectionable to Britain), and a commercial treaty with Russia. The Treaty of Paris placed these objectives in a different light. Hamilton and Madison offered a motion to instruct Dana that, since the commercial treaty had become less important to the United States, if he had not already "proceeded too far," he was to tell the Russians that such a treaty must be limited to fifteen years' duration and that any agreement he might make would be subject "to the revisal and approbation of Congress."[42] When it was first presented, the motion failed to pass because it included some extraneous material; but when resubmitted alone, it passed unanimously.

A similar situation arose with regard to the Netherlands. The Dutch appeared to be interested in contracting a treaty with the United States in support of the "small navy" nations' position on maritime warfare—that is, to limit the measures that a belligerent navy might take in connection with blockades and contraband, as the Armed Neutrality of 1780 had tried to do. Congress had previously been much interested in such a treaty, as evidenced by the Dana mission to Russia; but the restoration of peace brought about a different attitude on this subject, too. Since 1780 the influence of the Armed Neutrality, though not fully effective, had been helpful to the United States. America's pioneer diplomat Silas Deane observed that the Armed Neutrality had enabled Britain's European rivals to circumvent many of her efforts to obstruct the commerce of France and the Netherlands.[43] Those nations' support of the maritime rights of neutrals had inhibited Britain's naval warfare to the extent that there seemed to be an almost universal coalition against the British.[44] Moreover, in 1776 the Continental Congress had sanctioned similar principles, which had become part of the Treaty of Commerce with France in 1778.[45] It was obvious that the principles which those powers were advocating were likely to be the same ones that the United States would wish to prevail in future European wars.[46] But while the advantages of such a coalition might be considerable under certain circumstances, the risks involved seemed too great for the new nation to hazard. It should be recalled that the Netherlands' unwilling

[42] May 21, 22, 1783, *ibid.*, 348–57.

[43] Charles Isham (ed.), *The Deane Papers* (New York, 1890), IV, 206.

[44] James Brown Scott (ed.), *The Armed Neutralities of 1780 and 1800* (New York, 1918). The agreement of July 9, 1780, between Russia and Denmark is given on pages 299–304.

[45] Miller, *Treaties*, II, 3–27.

[46] John Bassett Moore, *A Digest of International Law* (Washington, 1906), VII, 558–83.

involvement in the war in 1780 resulted from her attempt to join the Armed Neutrality.[47] Who could tell how many years might elapse before the United States could hope to launch a naval fleet strong enough to check the proud Mistress of the Seas?

Congress was thus willing to tell the Dutch that the United States looked with favor upon the idea of extensive maritime rights for neutrals but would not contract to uphold such rights by force of arms.[48] Hamilton knew that the United States' position differed markedly from that of any European power. Europe and the United States each had, as he had stated a few years later, "a distinct set of interests."[49] He believed for many years that the new nation could enjoy a more or less "insulated situation."[50] Congress decided that the United States should stand aside from European politics and be prepared to attend to its interests as best it might after the nations of Europe, in any future conflict, had chosen sides. This approach to foreign policy, as enunciated later by Washington and Jefferson, constituted the essence of the neutrality tradition established during the first century of the nation's history.[51]

A latent desire to play the game of diplomacy without interference from any outside force had been gaining strength long before the Treaty of Paris opened the way for its outward expression. In wartime Congress had expressed a willingness to consider an alliance with the Netherlands only if it was "limited in its duration to the present war."[52] This spirit was obviously a concomitant to independence from Great Britain; but it was also stimulated by dissatisfaction with the alliance with France, caused largely by Luzerne's overreaching himself in his effort to guide Congress.[53] He spoke in fraternal endearing terms, but he went too far. In his first appearance before Congress he declared that the "treaties dictated by moderation have fixed upon a permanent base the union of France with the American republic."[54] Did Americans desire a union with France?

[47] Bemis, *The Diplomacy of the American Revolution* (New York, 1935), 162–63.

[48] June 12, 1783, *JCC*, XXIV, 394.

[49] "Federalist," No. 11, *HWL*, XI, 87.

[50] "Federalist," No. 8, *ibid.*, 58.

[51] Washington to Lafayette, August 11, 1790, *WW*, XXXI, 88; Jefferson to John Adams, September 28, 1787, *JW*, VI, 323; Jefferson to Dr. Joseph Priestley, January 29, 1804, *ibid.*, X, 446–47; Bemis, "The Background of Washington's Foreign Policy," *Yale Review*, Vol. XVI (January, 1927), 325.

[52] Instructions to John Adams, August 16, 1781, *RDC*, IV, 636.

[53] Jensen, *The New Nation*, 56.

[54] November 17, 1779, *JCC*, XV, 1280.

Some members of Congress felt uneasy about possible French designs on Louisiana and Canada,[55] even though in Article VI of the Treaty of Alliance France had promised not to try to acquire Canada or any part of the continent east of the Mississippi.[56] It was widely believed that France hoped Britain would deny Americans a share in the fisheries so that French fishermen would have no competition from the American fishermen. Apparently there were good grounds for suspicion.[57]

Hamilton was not greatly disturbed by any alleged French designs, but he was alarmed by the growing tendency of Americans to attach themselves too closely either to France, on the one hand, or Britain, on the other. While the nation was rejoicing at news that peace had been signed, he wrote to Washington about his concern over the "men in trust" who had "a hankering after British connection" and "others whose confidence in France savors of credulity." Faint foreshadowings of Washington's Farewell Address can be detected in Hamilton's next sentence: "The intrigues of the former and incautiousness of the latter may be both, though in different degrees, injurious to the American interests, and make it difficult for prudent men to steer a proper course."[58]

Clearly, he saw dangers involved in drawing too close to either nation, but, significantly, in "different degrees." He was far more fearful of Britain. He admitted that, as Jay thought, France might have delayed the peace for her own selfish reasons; but even if she had, her actions, as he told Congress, compared favorably with England's "illiberal policy." American ministers in Paris were "divided as to the policy of the court of France, but . . . they were all agreed in the necessity of being on the watch against Great Britain." He advised Congress to "survey the past cruelty and present duplicity" of Britain's councils. "Behold her watching every occasion and trying every project for dissolving the honorable ties which bind the United States to their ally, and then say on which side our resentments and jealousies ought to lie."[59] Speaking on the same subject a short time later, Hamilton warned against those Americans who seemed willing to be enslaved to "the policy even of our friends," but he deplored even more

55 Bernard Fay, *The Revolutionary Spirit in France and America* (New York, 1927), 121.

56 Miller, *Treaties*, II, 38.

57 Bemis, *The Diplomacy of the American Revolution*, 241.

58 Hamilton to Washington, March 17, 1783, *HWL*, IX, 324.

59 March 19, 1783, *RDC*, I, 258–61.

strongly "the overweening readiness" of others "to suspect every thing on that side, and to throw themselves into the bosom of our enemies."[60]

Henry Cabot Lodge, Hamilton's best-known biographer until the twentieth century, considered the two speeches proof that "Hamilton's natural inclination was toward France" rather than toward Britain.[61] Certainly it is obvious that in 1783, and for some years thereafter, he looked upon France much more favorably than he did Great Britain, influenced, as were others, by understandable wartime antipathies, appreciation for the assistance France had given the struggling young nation, and cordial personal relations with several French officers.

It is important to remember that General Washington shared Hamilton's attitudes toward Britain and France. Failure to do so leads to distortions of the lives of both statesmen. In this respect they are to be differentiated from several of their contemporaries in public life who, though sympathetic to the American cause, took no active part in the fighting and became notably pro-British soon after the close of the conflict.

While Hamilton was in Congress, he maintained an interesting correspondence with Washington, who was still with the army, pending the final peace settlement and the withdrawal of Britain's main forces. At Hamilton's suggestion Congress instructed Livingston to report fully to Washington about the progress of foreign affairs,[62] and in every manner Hamilton seemed intent on treating the general with deference and consideration. Washington was appreciative of these efforts, and the two men gradually came to regard each other, not as general and former aide, but as colleagues. Evidently the flare of tempers that had resulted in Hamilton's resignation from Washington's staff was forgotten. The similarity in their political ideas became more and more apparent. Washington came to see that the younger man had the stature of a statesman, and no doubt Hamilton concluded that not only his personal welfare but, more important, his program for the nation would be promoted most effectively through a close, affectionate connection with the man who had led the Continental Army to victory and had earned a claim to the bountiful public rewards a grateful nation might be expected to bestow upon its grandest hero.

Hamilton communicated to Washington as freely as security considera-

[60] *RDC*, I, 335.
[61] *HWL*, IV, 229n.
[62] *JCC*, XXIV, 142.

tions would permit about the progress of negotiations abroad and the domestic situation, especially the attitude of Congress toward the army. He did not hesitate to report untoward developments in Congress and in the various state governments, and he trusted the high-minded general not to blame him when he must serve as the bearer of unwelcome news. In reply to a sentiment expressed in such fashion, Washington assured his friend that he would think himself "obliged by a free communication of Sentiments." Each correspondent confided to the other his innermost feelings about vital issues of the day, exhibiting a rare degree of confidence in the other's integrity. Each observed that the peace treaty was more favorable than might have been expected; yet each was disturbed by the growing tendency in America to declaim against—or, as Washington said, to "carp at"—those parts of the treaty that fell short of what could be desired. Both were impressed by the seriousness of the tasks that lay ahead: of building a firm national government and planning a foreign policy that would render the new nation secure from exterior control. Measures must be taken, said Hamilton, "to prevent our being a ball in the hands of European powers, bandied against each other at their pleasure." The nation must be careful, said Washington, not to become "instruments in the hands of our enemies."[63] The growing collaboration and sympathy between Hamilton, with his powers of quick reasoning and sharp logic, and Washington, with his profound wisdom and firm judgment, augured well for the new republic. Each needed the other for the work that lay ahead, and the historian cannot present a clear picture of one of these statesmen without including the other. Their extraordinary contribution to the building of the nation was a joint contribution.

The United States soon learned that it was easier to negotiate a treaty than to implement it. The Treaty of Paris was a compromise, and it contained provisions that proved embarrassing to both nations. Subsequent violations by the signatories were by no means surprising. In its first review of the preliminary terms, Congress had realized that it would be difficult to comply with Article IV, which called for the collection of private debts; Article VI, which precluded further confiscation of Tory, or loyalist, property; and Article V, which required Congress to recommend to the states

[63] "Letters from Phocion," No. 1, 1784, *HWL*, IV, 240; Hamilton to Washington, March 24, March 25, 1783, and enclosure of same date, *ibid.*, IX, 327–31; Washington to Hamilton, March 4, March 31, and April 16, 1783, *WW*, XXVI, 185, 276–77, 326.

at least partial restoration of confiscated loyalist property. When Livingston relayed the peace terms to General Washington, he used a single sentence to paraphrase each article, except for Articles V and VI, which he enclosed in full for the general's "perusal, as they are likely to be the least satisfactory here."[64] Livingston asked Franklin and his colleagues to seek clarification and, if possible, amelioration of those articles.[65] The commissioners obediently placed the subject before David Hartley, the British representative in Paris, pointing out that American debtors had suffered such "heavy losses by the operations of British arms" that many of them could not possibly pay the debts immediately. They requested a delay of three years and the cancellation of all interest that had accrued during the war, arguing that Americans should not be expected to pay for delays "which were occasioned by the civil and military measures of Great Britain."[66] The effort failed.

Hamilton, in the meantime, boldly offered a resolution in Congress that the states "are hereby required to remove all obstructions" which might stand in the way of the collection of the debts or which might allow further confiscations. This provision appeared to be mandatory under the treaty. Then, in connection with the recommendation that the states restore some of the property previously confiscated, he called upon every state to consider the subject with the "spirit of moderation and liberality which ought ever to characterize the deliberations and measures of a free and enlightened nation."[67] His words were well chosen, clear, and emphatic. But Congress sought delay. Every member present except Hamilton voted to ask the committee of which he was chairman to make a further study of the subject.

The following day Livingston wrote to the peace commissioners that "the fifth and sixth articles . . . excite much ferment here." Everyone agreed, he reported, that it was a good treaty on the whole, but some persons were determined "to take only what they like and leave out what they disapprove." The "relaxation of government" was so great and "disorder," "uneasiness," "resentments," and "apprehensions" were so widespread among the people that he could not predict how the nation might finally resolve the problem of the debts and confiscated property.[68]

[64] Livingston to Washington, March 12, 1783, *RDC*, VI, 291.
[65] March 25, 1783, *ibid.*, 338.
[66] July 17, 1783, *ibid.*, 556–57.
[67] May 30, 1783, *JCC*, XXIV, 369–72.
[68] May 31, 1783, *RDC*, VI, 459.

Congress ratified the definitive treaty on January 14, 1784, and in the accompanying proclamation called upon all "good citizens of these states of every vocation and condition" to observe the terms of the agreement "with that good faith which is every man's surest guide." State legislatures were asked to take whatever action might be necessary to honor the provisions concerning debts and loyalists.[69] Unfortunately, the treaty was already being widely violated, and the violations continued, in spite of the command from Congress, which lacked the power to halt them.

The acrimonious controversy with Britain regarding the Old Northwest (the region between the Ohio and Mississippi rivers around the Great Lakes), a controversy that was to continue for a decade, might well have been prevented in 1783 by a Congress with more diplomatic experience—or even a more cautious one. The difficulty was clearly foreseen. After receiving the preliminary articles of peace, Livingston wrote to Franklin that he had "as yet discovered no inclination in the enemy to evacuate their posts." He urged Franklin to incorporate into the final treaty a statement "relative to the time and manner of evacuating these posts." He predicted that "without more precision and accuracy in this than we find in the provisional articles we shall soon be involved in new disputes with Great Britain."[70] Franklin and his colleagues proposed that the British agree to withdraw their forces from New York City and other seaboard areas within "three months after the signature of the definitive treaty, or sooner, if possible." That proposal was accepted; but when the envoys asked the British to agree to give up the northwestern posts as soon as Congress sent a garrison to occupy each point,[71] the British refused to do so.

Hamilton and Madison had separate plans for getting the British out of the Northwest. Madison's plan was to release British prisoners in gradual stages as the soldiers evacuated the posts. Undoubtedly his plan would have worked. Hamilton's plan was similar, but he wanted Congress to appoint General Washington to supervise the procedure. Congress refused to do so, and for that reason Hamilton voted against Madison's plan on the crucial ballot. Then, in a mood of parsimony, Congress decided to rid itself of the expense of feeding and sheltering the prisoners and ordered all of them released without demanding the simultaneous withdrawal

69 *Ibid.*, 756–57.
70 Livingston to Franklin, May 9, 1783, *ibid.*, 418.
71 Adams, Franklin, and Jay to Hartley, July 17, 1783, *ibid.*, 557.

of the British from the posts. Too late, Hamilton tried to stem the tide by bringing all his support to Madison's plan with only one slight modification; but at that time Congress was unable to obtain the support of enough states. The order for immediate release could not be rescinded, and the hour of opportunity passed.[72]

Article VII of the treaty pledged that in their withdrawal the British would not carry away any "Negroes"—meaning, of course, slaves. This provision led to a perplexing diplomatic squabble that was never clearly settled. During the war the British armies had usually operated in the areas where the most slaves were to be found—in the South and in the urban areas of the North. They had gathered up the slaves, especially in the South, as a military measure, to put them to work as laborers and also to deprive their owners of their services and thereby weaken the United States. Many Negroes, including several who had belonged to Thomas Jefferson, died of fever while in British hands. When the hostilities ended, Sir Guy Carleton, the British commander at New York, undertook to "emancipate" and remove a large number of Negroes from the country.

In accordance with a motion by Hamilton, Congress instructed the peace commissioners to remonstrate with Britain about this procedure.[73] In his instructions to the commissioners Livingston complained sharply and in considerable detail.[74] The instructions were followed, but in words that carried no sense of urgency or conviction.[75] The treaty provision was breached repeatedly, but no redress was forthcoming, then or at any later time.

The slavery clause was placed in the treaty at the suggestion of Henry Laurens, a peace commissioner who was also a South Carolina planter. Slavery was considered legal in all the states at the end of the war, but few American leaders at that time were willing to hold forth in favor of the institution. Hamilton's motion and protests were made solely for their diplomatic effect—a makeweight in the negotiations with the British. He disapproved of slavery. Later, when the federal Constitution was being debated before the New York convention, he would speak of the "situation of the Southern States" as "unfortunate" in that "a great part of their population as well as property" was made up of slaves. He did not like

[72] Brant, 281–83.

[73] May 26, 1783, *JCC*, XXIV, 363–64.

[74] May 28, 1783, *RDC*, VI, 453.

[75] Adams, Franklin, and Jay to Hartley, July 17, 1783, *ibid.*, 556.

the use of the word "property" in reference to human beings; he added, "They are men, though degraded to the condition of slavery."[76]

Hamilton was convinced that the United States should maintain a peacetime army and navy. He prepared for Congress a long report on the subject, and he left a sheaf of notes apparently used, or intended to be used, in a speech supporting the report. Writing as a representative of New York, he dispatched a long letter to Governer Clinton setting forth the ideas that various members of Congress had expressed on the subject.[77] Some of them believed that Article IX of the Articles of Confederation conferred on Congress the authority to raise land and naval forces only during time of war. Hamilton rejected that conclusion outright. The article itself mentioned no such limitation, and he could not see any logic in denying the national government the power to raise a regiment or equip a warship until a declaration of war was made or the country invaded.

He thought there should be a regular standing army of about five thousand men, including infantry, cavalry, artillerymen, and engineers. He was not in favor of building warships immediately, but he thought an agent of marine should be appointed to make plans and preparations for such construction. He recalled the words of Demosthenes: "The want of an army lost the liberty of Athens."

On the subject of military preparations as on many others, Hamilton's recommendations far exceeded the willingness of Congress to act. He had already displayed, as Wharton says, "administrative genius at its best."[78] He was extremely active in Congress and must have been greatly respected, but his colleagues were more ready to listen than to follow. He played a major role in laying down the principles that were to guide the nation's foreign policy for more than a century—policies that are sometimes erroneously assumed to have developed later, during Washington's administration—but he was usually frustrated in his proposals for specific action in such areas as establishing a standing army, collecting revenue, and strengthening the national government. He did not seek reappointment to Congress and apparently was relieved as the end of his term approached. The uncertain authority of Congress and the dilatoriness of several of its members aroused his disgust. He came to believe that Congress was no

[76] *HWL*, II, 14.
[77] Military Papers, *ibid.*, VI, 463–83; Hamilton to Clinton, October 3, 1783, *ibid.*, IX, 388–94.
[78] *RDC*, I, 258.

place for a man interested in promoting the public welfare to spend his time.[79] In July he left Princeton, where Congress had been meeting, and went to Albany to join his wife and son. In November, 1783, soon after the withdrawal of the British army, he moved to New York City to take up the practice of law. On that stage was played the next brilliant scene of his dramatic life.

79 Hamilton to General Greene, June 10, 1783, HPSCLC, Box 1.

CHAPTER V

Diplomacy Marks Time

AMERICAN diplomacy from 1784 to 1789 was a record of disappointment. The crux of the difficulty was the weakness of the national government. Under the Articles of Confederation Congress could not force Americans to obey its proclamation of January 14, 1784, calling for faithful observance of the peace treaty. The loyalists were made to suffer by state governments that looked with contempt upon the efforts of Congress to tell them how to treat "their own citizens." The nation had vast economic resources, but the spirit of particularism which was abroad in the land rendered it impossible for Congress to control commerce or to use foreign trade as a bargaining point in negotiating a commercial treaty with Great Britain. The nation's population, resources, and location enabled it to defy aggression by any other nation, but its political disunity was so enervating that within three years after the restoration of peace the nation was in imminent danger of losing the Southwest to Spain and the Northwest to Britain. Even Vermont, it was rumored, might pull away and join Canada.

Hamilton found the temper of the nation frustrating and a cause for apprehension. He was convinced that he knew the remedy for the nation's ills, but for years the current of opinions flowed against him. The people's attachment to their state governments precluded any movement to endow the national government with more authority.

Hamilton spent most of these years practicing law in New York City. The period of readjustment and development following the British evacuation brought a cascade of legal disputes for the New York bar to struggle with. Hamilton had a large share of the cases, and his prestige and personal fortune were in the ascendant.[1] It was a happy period in his life, except for those intervals when his attention was drawn to political affairs—state, national, and international.

[1] Schachner, *Alexander Hamilton*, 168–83; Mitchell, *Alexander Hamilton*, I, 327–55.

Postwar bitterness against the loyalists was intense in New York, and the legislature gave expression to the popular resentment by passing the Trespass Act, which gave patriots the right to collect damages from loyalists or British subjects who had occupied their property during the war. The law provided that damages could not be avoided on the grounds that the occupation was in accordance with "military orders."[2] Later generations of Americans, enjoying security and reflecting on the old adage that there are two sides to every argument, would stop thinking of the loyalists as traitors in the usual sense; but in 1784 the victors were not inclined to be lenient. Many of them viewed a loyalist as an accomplice of the invaders, and they recognized no mitigating circumstances.

Hamilton believed that the punishment of loyalists should cease with the war's end. They had already suffered greatly; in every state most of their property had been confiscated.[3] He wanted the Treaty of Paris observed and he thought the loyalists were no longer a danger to the nation and would become useful citizens provided they were treated with tolerance. George Washington, Patrick Henry, and many other leading Americans held the same view.

Hamilton viewed with dismay the furious attitude of the people and the intemperate acts of the legislature. He wrote to his friend Gouverneur Morris that the lawmakers of the state were neglecting the most important problems while "laboring to contrive methods to mortify and punish Tories and to explain away treaties." Morris had an unmatched sense of humor with an admixture of grimness and cynicism. Hamilton's style sometimes took on the same quality, as in this letter to Morris on the loyalist subject, in which he excused himself for not writing sooner on the grounds that "legislative folly has afforded so plentiful a harvest to us lawyers that we have scarcely a moment to spare from the substantial business of reaping." He later regretfully reported that "discrimination bills, partial taxes, schemes to engross public property in the hands of those who have present power, to banish the real wealth of the State" seemed to be the order of the day.[4]

A few months after Hamilton opened his law office in New York he found himself in an unequal contest on the loyalist question. A widow, Mrs. Elizabeth Rutgers, and her son had owned a brewery in New York.

[2] C. H. Van Tyne, *Loyalists in the American Revolution* (New York, 1929), 295.

[3] *Ibid.*, 268.

[4] Hamilton to Gouverneur Morris, March 21, April 7, 1784, *HWL*, IX, 399–403.

When the war erupted, her devotion to American independence caused her to leave the city before the British captured it in the summer of 1776. British military authorities leased the brewery to two British merchants, Benjamin Waddington and Evelyn Pierrepont. Mrs. Rutgers regained possession in 1783 and under the terms of the Trespass Act sued Waddington for four and a half years' rent. Hamilton agreed to serve as the attorney for the merchant. As usual throughout his life, he fought for what he thought was right, regardless of the heavy odds against him.

During the trial Hamilton argued that the treaty with Britain overruled the law of the New York legislature. The treaty provided that no new prosecutions were to be commenced against any persons for their part in the war, and he maintained that the treaty must be held supreme over state law. He argued from logical principles and cited great specialists in international law, among them Emmerich de Vattel, Hugo Grotius, and Jean Barbeyrac. He asserted that an award for the plaintiff would prove injurious to the "national character."[5] He especially emphasized the diplomatic aspect of the case—that the treaty should be observed to maintain the nation's honor and advance its welfare.

The case was tried in the Mayor's Court of New York City, presided over by Hamilton's friend James Duane. The public was intensely interested in the case and critical of Hamilton for representing the merchant. In making his decision, Duane, who was also willing to risk public censure, ruled in favor of Hamilton's contention that the treaty was supreme over the law of any state; but he found defects in the original British order, which, he ruled, placed the case outside the protection of the treaty. He instructed the jury to determine the amount of damages to be awarded the plaintiff, and Waddington was compelled to pay Mrs. Rutgers £791 13s. 4d. The courageous young attorney won the argument on principle, but his client lost the case. Later the legislature condemned the decision by a vote of twenty-five to nineteen and passed a resolution that Duane's decision, setting aside a law of the state in favor of the treaty on principles of international law, was "subversive of all law and good order."

Hamilton was not satisfied with his partial victory. Fully engrossed in the subject, he wanted a wider audience before which to expound it than the courtroom could give him. Characteristically, he resorted to the press. As Allan Nevins says, "Hamilton's fingers whenever he was in a tight place

[5] Schachner, *Alexander Hamilton*, 175–78; Mitchell, *Alexander Hamilton*, I, 340–45.

always itched for the pen."[6] He published two thick pamphlets under the name "Phocion,"[7] appealing to the people to pause and reflect on the dangers of violating the treaty. The main points were presented in the first essay, which was answered by several journalists, among them Isaac Ledyard, who signed himself "Mentor." In his refutation Hamilton could do little but restate his earlier arguments. This he did at great length, and with some tedium.

His purpose was to convince the public; therefore, he was careful with his approach. He observed that nothing was more common than for people, "in times of heat and violence, to gratify momentary passions by letting into the government principles and precedents which afterwards prove fatal. . . . Tenderness [was] indeed due to the mistakes of those who [had] suffered too much to reason with impartiality." He acknowledged that it required a great deal of moderation on the part of the returning patriots to restrain themselves from intemperate acts of punishment against those who had held the city since 1776, but such self-restraint must be exercised.

Hamilton warned the people against the evils of "bigotry in politics," which could be as "pernicious" as bigotry in religion and which blinded the people to "the advantages of a spirit of toleration." Wreaking vengeance against their former enemies would bring no permanent benefit to the patriots, and using the processes of law for this purpose endangered the liberties of all. The loyalists had already been readmitted as citizens of the state and had been permitted to vote in the first postwar election. New legislation to penalize them was, therefore, a direct violation of their rights under the state constitution. The New York constitution was a "compact made between the society at large and each individual." Society had no more right to violate this compact than one man had to refuse to honor a contract he had made with another. Nothing could be more reckless than for a people to "make their passions, prejudices, and interests the sole measure of their own and others' rights." He commented that "honesty is still the best policy, [and] justice and moderation are the surest supports of every government." His most insistent admonition to the people was:

> Abuse not the power you possess, and you need never apprehend its diminution or loss. But if you make a wanton use of it; if you furnish another

[6] Allan Nevins, *The Evening Post: A Century of Journalism* (New York, 1922), 14 (hereafter cited as *The Evening Post*).

[7] *HWL*, IV, 230–90. The two essays total sixty-one printed pages.

example that despotism may debase the government of the many as well as the few, you, like all the others that have acted the same part, will experience that licentiousness is the forerunner to slavery.

Hamilton's opponents found it difficult to answer his charge that the antiloyalist legislation violated the state constitution. The legislature surmounted this obstacle by enacting a law providing that any American who had supported the king during the war had thereby forfeited his citizenship. Hamilton asserted that no person resident within the country could be divested of his citizenship at will. Such a principle would be "contrary to law and subversive to government," and it would be most unjust to inflict such a penalty upon any person after the event. He delved deeply into the question of the rights of the individual at the bar of justice, citing the Magna Charta, the commentaries of Coke, and other venerable sources, including the laws of ancient Rome.

Hamilton's legal evidence for his conclusions was more than sufficient, and his reasoning was reinforced by broad social and political considerations. He knew that loyalist baiting was closely related to enactments for the printing of paper money, for "stay laws" to ease the load of debtors, and for the levying of a form of taxes he considered harmful. These laws he believed illustrative of "democratic" tendencies—by which he meant mob action or irresponsible government.[8] No doubt it was as obvious to him as it was to others that the former loyalists would be inclined to support his proposals for a stronger national constitution. Many of them were wealthy, and all of them must have seen a glimmer of hope of protection in the treaty. Certainly they saw far less hope of succor in state laws or in the popular reactions then rife in New York and other states.[9]

Hamilton was almost equally interested in the diplomatic aspect of the loyalist problem, and he argued directly to that point as well. He was convinced that the New York legislature was violating certain terms of the peace treaty, and he feared Britain might reply by declaring the whole treaty void or choose to disregard whatever part of the treaty she wished. Either course would be extremely dangerous for New York, within whose borders were situated some of the frontier posts the British had agreed to evacuate but were still holding. Other Americans were aware of this danger.

[8] Hamilton to Gouverneur Morris, April 7, 1784, *ibid.*, IX, 403.

[9] Louise Irby Trenholm, *The Ratification of the Federal Constitution in North Carolina* (New York, 1932), 34–37.

Livingston, for instance, was afraid the British might hold United States territory "as pledges for the performance of the stipulations in favor of the tories."[10] Jay wrote to Hamilton from France that the loyalists were "as much pitied" in Europe as they were "execrated" in the United States and that "indiscriminate punishment" would "certainly carry the matter too far."[11]

To dishonor the treaty—the nation's solemn obligation—would, Hamilton was sure, cause Americans to become the "scorn of nations," for such action "exhibited" the nation "in the light of a people destitute of government, on whose engagements . . . no dependence [could] be placed." The United States had made a good bargain in the treaty negotiations and had received "a large tract of country to which we had even no plausible claim." Every American should be eager to preserve the gain; but even if the government had promised too much in the treaty, the objection from New York "came too late after the promise [had] been made."[12]

Hamilton rejected the contention that the new nation would be endangered by loyalists within its citizenry. He saw no likelihood that they would again take up arms against the government, for Britain would not again try to subdue the new nation. Such an attempt would be foolhardy inasmuch as the United States, even when torn by the strife between patriots and loyalists, yet "baffled all [Britain's] efforts in the zenith of her power." Good policy required that Americans forget the former strife and trust the loyalists to be faithful citizens in a land of equal opportunities.

It is impossible to measure Hamilton's influence on the public attitude on this question, but it was not great enough to stem the persecutions. Public animosity continued at a high pitch, and many more loyalists left the country, following those who had departed at the end of the war.

In 1783, Francisco Miranda, the Venezuelan apostle of Spanish American independence, came to the United States as an exile from the South American dominions of the king of Spain. He traveled widely through the Republic, moved in high social circles, became acquainted with a large number of influential persons in the land, and fixed his eyes upon Alexander Hamilton as "the one man who above all others in the United States would

[10] *RDC*, VI, 387.
[11] September 28, 1783, *ibid.*, 706.
[12] "Letters from Phocion," No. 1, 1784, *HWL*, IV, 240–43.

cooperate with him" in his ambitious project of freeing all of Spanish America from the yoke of the Bourbons in Madrid.[13]

Hamilton's friendship with Miranda was well known to the public. There were never any denials nor any embarrassments. Yet Miranda was everywhere proclaiming his revolutionary mission, and he was apparently pleased to be known by the appellation bestowed on him by President Ezra Stiles of Yale: "a flaming Son of Liberty." Miranda was undemocratic in sentiment. He was disgusted by a "turbulent popular election" he observed in the United States; he was shocked when he saw the "most ignorant people" making laws in Massachusetts; and he was offended and confused when tavern keepers expected him to eat at the same table with his servant. But his sparkling personality, his dashing ways, his interesting manner of dress, and his ebullient conversation attracted wide attention. Some Bostonians considered him a "most extraordinary and wonderfully energetic man."[14] General Henry Knox wrote of him: "He possesses an extensive knowledge of Men and things, and his opportunities have been exceeded only by his eagerness to improve them."[15]

Hamilton eagerly co-operated with the young revolutionary throughout 1784. He introduced Miranda to his friends, helped him lay plans for breaking the power of European monarchs in areas of the New World that were not yet blessed by independence, and helped the Venezuelan devise a system of government for the lands to be liberated. This phase of Hamilton's life reveals facets of his character and purpose not readily observable in other aspects of his career. It is of special importance in understanding his general attitude on foreign affairs, because it has a close bearing on his long-standing antipathy toward Spain and his initial approval of the French Revolution. Several of the Hamilton biographies, including some of the excellent productions of recent years, do not even mention Miranda's name. Studies of Miranda generally treat the relationship superficially.[16] Because of the significance of the political association of the two men, a brief summary of Miranda's career is relevant.

[13] William Spence Robertson, "Francisco de Miranda and the Revolutionizing of Spanish America," American Historical Association *Annual Report* for 1907 (1909), I, 195, 251.

[14] William Spence Robertson, *The Life of Miranda* (Chapel Hill, 1929), I, 47, 52–53, 250.

[15] Knox to Thomas Russell, April 28, 1784, Vincente Davila (ed.), *Archivo del General Miranda* (Caracas, 1925–38), V, 268.

[16] In his *Life of Miranda*, Robertson tells the story from Miranda's viewpoint. Joseph F. Thorning's *Miranda: World Citizen* (Gainesville, 1952) reveals the spirit of the "precursor of Latin American independence" but makes only brief references to his association with Hamilton (pp. 33, 36, 164, *et passim*).

Miranda was an officer in the Spanish army that took Pensacola from the British during the American Revolution. He was subsequently accused of smuggling in violation of Spanish law and of disloyalty to the king. The latter charge, at least, must have been true, for upon his arrival in the United States in 1783 he revealed that his purpose in life was to bring liberty to his own beloved Venezuela and to other millions of Americans who were not yet ruling themselves. He stated explicitly that his plans included not merely Spanish America but the entire "Continent du Nouveau Monde."[17]

Miranda considered the success of the thirteen colonies in their revolt against Great Britain an essential "preliminary of Spanish-American independence," and he expected to use that movement, and the sovereign nation it had produced, to expand the area of freedom in the Americas.[18] He visited many of the Revolutionary War battlefields and studied the tactics and the strategy of the war with many of the participants. Many believed that he came to understand the military aspects of the conflict better than most American officers who had taken part in it.

The calling cards, letters, social notes, and invitations to social events preserved in Miranda's papers suggest that he received courteous attentions from many distinguished persons in Philadelphia, Boston, and other cities he visited.[19] Hamilton's name appears frequently as Miranda's host or guest. Several of Hamilton's friends, including William Duer and General Henry Knox, came to be closely associated with Miranda.

Miranda's plans for liberating Spanish America were laid before Hamilton in July, 1784. Miranda was not planning a clearly defined movement to be undertaken at a specified time. He was engaged in a crusade to gather information, friends, and followers whom he hoped to be able to call upon at some future time for help in liberating his fellow countrymen. He held listeners spellbound with his impassioned discussions, but it is difficult to gauge how much encouragement he received from the various individuals with whom he conferred.[20] Revolutionary conspirators usually hesitate to commit all their plans to writing.

Hamilton undoubtedly gave his blessing to the Venezuelan's designs at

[17] Miranda to Hamilton, April 6, 1798, Davila, *Archivo del General Miranda*, XV, 235.

[18] Robertson, *The Life of Miranda*, I, 32.

[19] Davila, *Archivo del General Miranda*, V, 244–79; XV, 73–79. See also William Spence Robertson (ed.), *The Diary of Francisco de Miranda, Tour of the United States, 1783–1784* (New York, 1928).

[20] Robertson, *The Life of Miranda*, I, 52–53.

the time. In a letter to Miranda a few years later he expressed the hope that circumstances would soon make it possible for him "to be an instrument of so good a work,"[21] though by then he had become hesitant to become actively engaged in it.

General Knox helped Miranda work out a provisional plan by which an invading army might sometime be led from New England to the South American dominions of Spain. The army was to be made up of five thousand men, including infantry, cavalry, and artillery troops. The plan contained estimates of the expenses of the expedition, including specific amounts for salary, clothing, and rations for the troops and other supplies. This paper, now in the Miranda manuscripts, is in Knox's own hand.[22]

The young revolutionary also obtained (from Hamilton, he claimed) a list of American army officers. Beside certain names appeared a *marca de excelencia*. Apparently the mark actually indicated that the officer was deemed likely to be interested in a South American expedition, though there is no certainty of this. It could hardly have been intended to denote officers of unusual military ability; some of those so marked were not particularly able in military affairs, while others more highly regarded were not checked.

Miranda departed from American shores in December, 1784, and went to England to pursue his goal. For several years he had little success. His hopes rose during the Anglo-Spanish tensions of 1790, during the French Revolution, and again in 1798, when he believed that the United States and Great Britain would join forces to wage war on France and her ally, Spain. Those issues, however, did not bring Hamilton and Miranda together again except for a brief correspondence, which was buoyantly enthusiastic on Miranda's side but unresponsive at times and always hesitant on Hamilton's. Neither man lived to see the fulfillment of the dreams for an independent South America.

Miranda looked upon his brief sojourn in the United States as a high point in his career. It was there, he claimed, that, with the co-operation of Hamilton and Knox, he worked out a projected form of government for a liberated Spanish America. It was to resemble the British system, but provided for rule by a dictator with extensive powers in time of crisis.[23] In

[21] Hamilton to Miranda, August 22, 1798, *HWL*, X, 316.
[22] Robertson, *The Life of Miranda*, I, 54–55.
[23] *Ibid.*, I, 43, 169–229.

later years a difference in point of view arose between the two men, which may have been present to some degree from the beginning of their friendship. In writing to Hamilton, Miranda would speak of their mutual love for "unfortunate Colombia" and refer to "our dear Country America, from the North to the South,"[24] apparently meaning both continents of the New World. Such language, though calculated to win support for his cause, unquestionably arose from the heart of a sincere patriot unable to return to his homeland. Hamilton's increasing reluctance to participate in Miranda's undertaking was a logical outgrowth of his responsibilities as an official high in the national government, as well as of his intensified spirit of nationalism.

Of no less importance than Hamilton's friendship for the fiery Venezuelan were the reasons that gave rise to it. From the outset Hamilton's heart went out to the refugee. Hamilton was a singularly charitable man; his friends often expressed the fear that he would bankrupt himself by lavish giving. Another reason for Hamilton's affinity for Miranda's cause was his conviction that it was "lawful and meritorious to assist a people in a virtuous and rational struggle for liberty."[25] Finally, and most significant, was Hamilton's genuine dislike for Spain and her political system and his conviction that the Spaniards constituted an ominous threat to the future of the United States.

Hamilton's prewar expectation that Spain could be depended upon to aid America in order to disrupt the British Empire had not been fulfilled in any substantial degree. The niggardly assistance had led him to comment derisively on Spanish "indolence" and "supineness."[26] In later years he commented with some sarcasm on "the good offices of Spain in the late war."[27] As Silas Deane once wrote, Spain gave "a trifling aid in money . . . in the most secret manner, more like a bribe than a subsidy,"[28] a sentiment in which Hamilton must have concurred. Hamilton despised Spain for negotiating with the common enemy in 1781, bitterly remarking that not much could be expected from "a bigoted prince, governed by a greedy confessor."[29]

Hamilton's remark about the "greedy confessor" was no chance expres-

24 Miranda to Hamilton, November 4, 1792, Davila, *Archivo del General Miranda*, XV, 145–46.

25 Hamilton to Washington, May 2, 1793, *HWL*, IV, 402.

26 Hamilton to Robert Morris, April 30, 1781, *ibid.*, III, 358–59.

27 Hamilton to Washington, September 25, 1790, *ibid.*, IV, 319.

28 Deane to Col. Jeremiah Wadsworth, June 13, 1781, Isham, *The Deane Papers*, IV, 490.

29 Hamilton to Robert Morris, April 30, 1781, *HWL*, III, 359.

sion. During the earlier years of his career, though not during the later ones, he often cast aspersions on the practices of the Roman Catholics. In his essay "A Full Vindication" (1774) he protested indignantly against the act of Parliament establishing "Popery" in Canada; and in his "Remarks on the Quebec Bill" (1775) he called the "Popish religion" the "great engine of arbitrary power."[30] Certainly the asperity of his remarks about Spain and her rule in the Americas was sharpened by his antipathy for the religious practices of the church. Interestingly enough, his attitude toward France did not seem to be affected by religious considerations; perhaps he felt the French were less markedly influenced by their clergy.

Hamilton's writings clearly reflect Miranda's influence. In his "Letters from Phocion" Hamilton declared that the American example of freedom was attracting attention of the oppressed peoples in the "gloomy regions of despotism." The inhabitants of those lands were already experiencing a revolution in thought and attitude, he declared, and the movement seemed destined to upset the "tyrant" who dared to build his greatness on the "misery and degradation" of his subjects.[31]

Hamilton's primary object in making such statements was to contrast the institutions of his own country with those of oppressed nations; but the expression "gloomy regions of despotism" was doubtless suggested to him by Miranda's eloquent description of the blighting effects of the hand of the Spanish Bourbons in Latin America. Again, however, he did not use such language in speaking of France, which was but five years away from the revolution against despotic rule.

During the last years of the 1780's, Hamilton's antipathy toward Spain was whetted even keener by his apprehensions about the Mississippi question. He was convinced that the United States was "entitled by nature and compact" to a free use of the river, a right which was being denied by Spain.[32] The nation must have an army to meet the menace of the British on one side and the Spanish on the other, and the danger that the two countries might someday combine forces against the United States. Hamilton was also aware of the danger of hostilities from the Indians, but for obvious reasons he did not mention the ally, France, in this respect.[33]

Spain's occupation of the lower Mississippi and the desire of the United

[30] *Ibid.*, I, 37–38, 181.
[31] *Ibid.*, IV, 289.
[32] "Federalist," No. 15, *ibid.*, XI, 111.
[33] "Federalist," No. 25, December 21, 1787, *ibid.*, 195.

States for uninhibited use of the waterway planted the "seeds of enmity."[34] Spain was inclined to close the river to would-be shippers from Kentucky or Tennessee, to allow navigation only upon the payment of large fees, or to use the lower Mississippi as bait to entice the residents of the western states or counties to pull away from the United States and accept Spanish sovereignty (the last scheme came to be called the "Spanish Conspiracy"). Hamilton joined with other Americans in advocating the legal rights of all inland residents to free navigation of the river to the Gulf of Mexico. That claim had little support in international law. Perhaps the strongest argument was that those living on a thoroughfare have a natural right to the use of it; but that contention did not impress the Spaniards, who recalled that they were not allowed the full use of rivers that flowed across Portugal from Spain to the sea. In 1785 and 1786, John Jay, secretary of foreign affairs, conducted futile negotiations with Diego de Gardoqui, the Spanish envoy. Gardoqui offered America a commercial treaty, an alliance, and a pledge to help oust the British from the Northwest posts if the United States would agree to forgo the use of the lower Mississippi for a long period of time. Jay was attracted by the offer, and asked Congress to authorize him to negotiate on that basis. Congress refused, and the delegates from the southern states were so shocked by the proposal that they later took pains to make certain that the new Constitution contained a provision requiring a two-thirds vote of the Senate for the approval of a treaty.

In 1787 one of Hamilton's strongest arguments favoring a stronger national government was that only thus could the nation meet the Spanish menace in the West.[35] He continued the struggle when he was again serving as a member of the Continental Congress in 1788, during its final term. A report by a committee of which he was chairman resolved that the United States had "a clear and absolute right to the free navigation" of the Mississippi and that "the same ought in no manner whatsoever to be invalidated." On the following day the same committee called for an end to negotiations with Spain, reasserted the right of free navigation, and recommended that the whole question be "referred to the federal government, . . . to assemble in March, next."[36]

At the time these resolutions were made, the Constitution had been pre-

[34] Livingston to Adams, Franklin, and Jay, March 25, 1783, *RDC*, VI, 339.

[35] "Federalist," No. 11, November, 1787, *HWL*, XI, 84.

[36] September 15, 1788, *JCC*, XXXIV, 527; September 16, 1788, *ibid.*, 534–35. The latter was the final entry in the *Secret Journals*.

sented to the nation and ratified by eleven states, including Hamilton's own state of New York. He considered the question of the Mississippi and the Floridas of greater consequence to the nation than any other external problem, as his statements in 1790 clearly reveal; but he was also fully aware of the significance of the continuing British occupation of the posts in the Northwest and the need for a treaty of commerce with Britain. These issues also had to be turned over to the new federal government. He must have been deeply relieved by the thought that such thorny problems would be dealt with by a stronger national government.

American commerce with France failed to develop as anticipated. In 1779, Luzerne had confidently predicted that after the war ended "the commerce between the allied nations [would] shoot forth with vigor and advantage."[37] The prediction failed to come true. With the return of peace Americans began importing sizable quantities of luxury goods from France (much to the disgust of George Washington), but there was no large-scale exchange of products. The trading conditions imposed by France were relatively fair, but most Americans preferred British goods, and the British merchants extended more favorable terms of credit. Prewar channels of trade were reopened, in so far as they had been closed—a number of items of British manufacture had been available during the greater part of the war, owing to the activities of smugglers and privateers.

Postwar efforts to obtain a treaty of commerce with Britain also failed.[38] The mild cordiality of the British in 1782 passed away, and not until 1791 was a British minister sent to the United States. Treaty infractions on both sides led to bickering and ill will. Americans were importing British goods in quantity but were rigidly restricted in selling and transporting goods to Britain or the British West Indies. Under the Articles of Confederation the system of government and the recalcitrance of the states made it impossible for the United States to adopt retaliatory measures. Hamilton pointed out that under the Constitution the new government could force the English to grant more favorable terms.[39] Certainly the Confederacy had been unable to secure a treaty of commerce.

The Continental Congress expired without having resolved the controversy with Britain over the posts in the Old Northwest. That dissension

[37] Address to the Continental Congress, November 17, 1779, *RDC*, III, 409–11.
[38] *JCC*, XXIV, 321.
[39] "Federalist," No. 11, *HWL*, XI, 80.

began almost as soon as the war ended. In 1783, Congress instructed General Washington that as soon as the British withdrew he was to garrison the western posts with troops whose enlistments had not expired.[40] Then Congress began making laws for the governance of the territory and laying plans for its eventual division into states to be admitted to the Union. A proposal of 1784 called for limited self-government in the Northwest and eventual division into states; the Land Ordinance of 1785 provided for the sale of the land to the people; and the Northwest Ordinance of 1787 incorporated the two earlier proposals and added significant provisions with regard to government and a bill of rights. Despite those provisions the British continued to occupy the posts and through their friendly relations with the Indians maintained control of the territory.

The British made no claim that the Treaty of Paris awarded them the territory, but they soon began citing American violations of the treaty as justification for delaying their departure. Modern historians are aware that the day before the British government publicly proclaimed the treaty to be in effect secret orders were sent to British agents in Canada to hold the posts in spite of the treaty provisions until they received explicit orders to move out.[41]

By 1787 Hamilton had concluded that Britain intended to hold the region permanently. He had dissuaded Governor Clinton from sending the New York militia to dispossess the British in 1783, pointing out that the issue was of national concern and too large for one state to try to resolve.[42] Throughout the remainder of the decade he continued pleading with New York officials and citizenry to cease violating the treaty in order to remove Britain's pretext for holding the forts. Speaking in the legislature in 1787, he pointed out again that New York had much to gain in seeing the treaty of 1783 carried out; the western part of the state was still under British control. He did not believe that the territory would be released immediately even if the United States abided by the treaty provisions in every detail, but such a course would nevertheless weaken Britain's arguments. He assumed that the real reasons Britain held on so tenaciously were to allow her merchants to continue reaping profits from the fur trade, to induce Vermont to accept a permanent position within the empire, and to maintain a foothold from

[40] *JCC*, XXIV, 338.

[41] Bemis, *A Diplomatic History of the United States*, 71.

[42] Hamilton to Clinton, October 3, 1783, *HWL*, IX, 392.

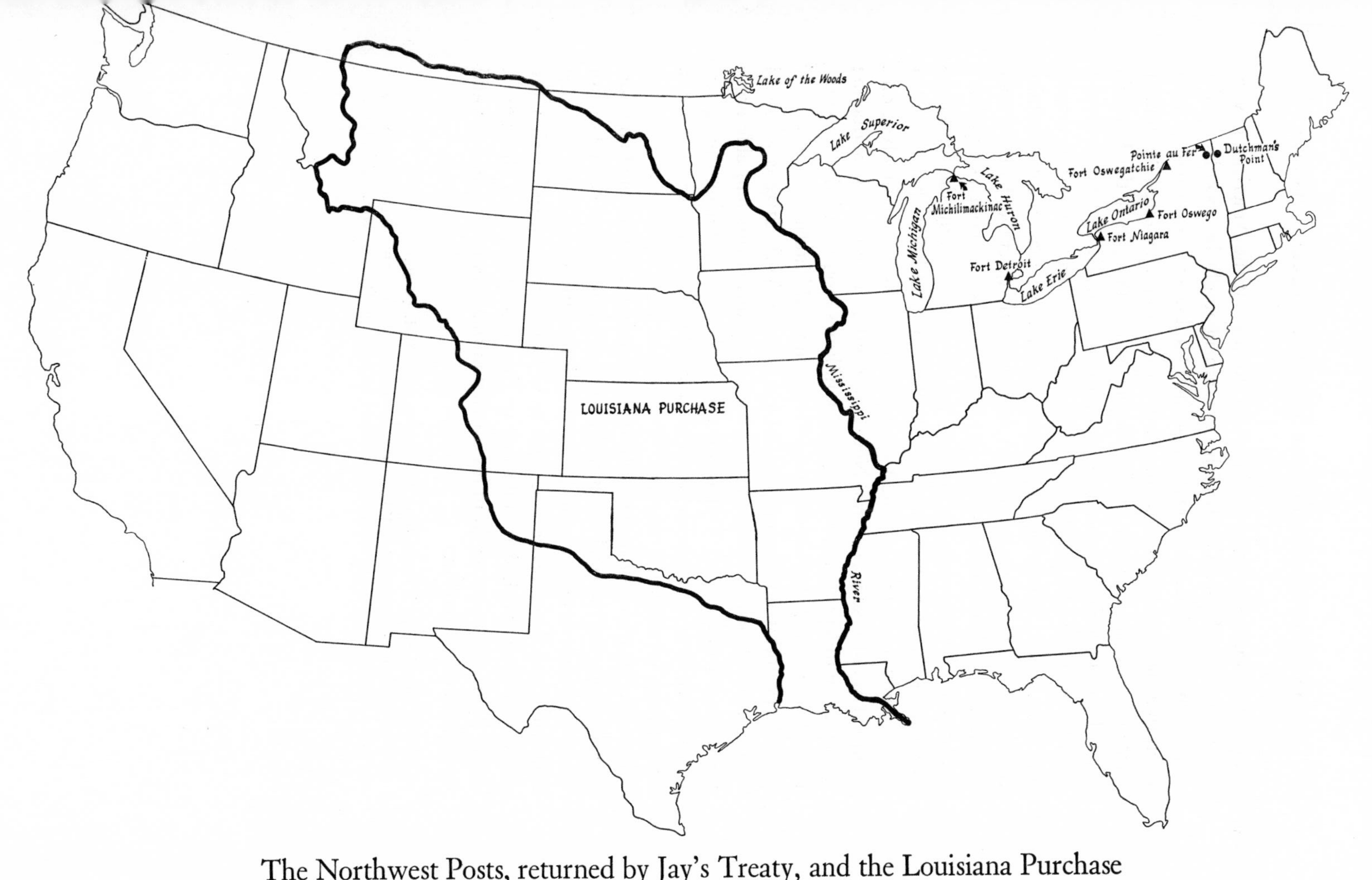

The Northwest Posts, returned by Jay's Treaty, and the Louisiana Purchase

which she could seize more territory—or all of it—if the American government should collapse. The British government might be speculating that Americans would become so weary of their "feeble and distracted" government that they would seek "a voluntary return" to the empire—"a counterpart of the restoration of Charles the Second." But even if the Republic proved able to maintain its sovereignty, it seemed likely that Great Britain and the United States would eventually go to war over the disputed territory, for, he said, "degraded as we are by our mismanagement, [Britain] can hardly entertain so mean an opinion of us as to expect we shall eventually submit to such a violation of our rights and interests without a struggle."[43]

Hamilton's speech was particularly aimed at persuading the legislators to abandon New York's claim to Vermont on condition that the latter would apply for statehood. The Vermont controversy was an involved one. Claimed by both New York and New Hampshire, Vermont was conducting herself as an independent sovereignty. Hamilton's motion failed to pass; the legislators believed that abandoning the claim would humiliate the state of New York and would mean financial loss to New York citizens who had been granted lands in Vermont. But his prodigious efforts and able arguments won wide support. One of the speeches he made during this period was printed in its entirety in the *New York Daily Advertiser* of April 5, 1787, filling "seven solid columns."[44]

It was largely because of those efforts (which in fact constituted an effort to strengthen the national government) that Hamilton was named one of New York's three delegates to the convention to meet at Philadelphia the following month to "revise" the Articles of Confederation. In his view the welfare of New York was embraced in the larger welfare of the nation. At no point did he waver from his conviction that a united republic would be secure and invincible.

[43] Speech in New York Legislature, April, 1787, *ibid.*, VIII, 55–56.

[44] An excellent brief account of this subject, based on New York and Vermont state papers, contemporary newspapers, and personal papers, may be found in Mitchell, *Alexander Hamilton*, I, 374–77.

CHAPTER VI

Beginning Again

THE NEW Constitution, which went into effect in the spring of 1789, gave the national government effective control over foreign relations. Congress was endowed with extensive authority and was backed by the Supreme Court, which could overrule actions or decisions of contrary states; and the president and his "Heads of Departments" were charged with executing the "Law of the Land," of which treaties already in effect or treaties which might be made under the powers of the president and the Senate were declared to be a part.

Hamilton was optimistic that the new system would end the "unblushing violation" of treaties, would vindicate the nation's right to navigate the "Western lakes" and the Mississippi, and would enable the country "for ages" to resist aggression from abroad.[1] Washington, referring to the Constitution as a "New Roof," anticipated that the beginning of the new government would be "an important epoch in the annals of this Country." He spoke of the establishment of the new government as a "revolution," and he believed that the accomplishment was part of God's divine purpose.[2]

Washington faced a difficult decision when it became obvious that his country intended to call him to be its chief executive. For financial reasons he needed to be at Mount Vernon, and he said frankly that life on his farm brought him great pleasure. Among the flood of letters urging him to accept the call was one from Hamilton, who told him that the entire effort to set up a better government would be "of little purpose . . . if the weightiest influence [was] not given to its firm establishment at the outset."[3] These words "stirred and alarmed Washington,"[4] who soon thereafter used this

[1] "Federalist," Nos. 8, 11, 15, *HWL*, XI, 58, 84, 111.

[2] Washington to Madison, August 3, 1788, Inaugural Address, April 30, 1789, *WW*, XXX, 33, 293.

[3] Hamilton to Washington, August 13, 1788, *HWL*, IX, 441.

[4] D. S. Freeman, *George Washington* (New York, 1948–52), V, 147.

same argument to induce supporters of the federal system to accept offices in the government or to help elect congressmen who would work to stabilize and strengthen the government. Washington's hesitation to lead that effort was sincere. Re-entering public life would be the "greatest sacrifice" of his "personal feelings and wishes" that he had ever been called upon to make. He would have to "forego repose and domestic enjoyment, for trouble; perhaps for public obloquy [in] an unexplored field, enveloped on every side with clouds and darkness."[5]

The clouds and darkness seemed to lift after a few months of reflection. In writing to his friend Lafayette, he mentioned the "embarrassments" in which America was "entangled, through lack of credit" and added that he thought he saw "a path, as clear and as direct as a ray of light," which his country should follow toward "permanent felicity." As the time approached for his departure from Mount Vernon, however, his earlier reluctance returned, and he commented that when he left he would feel like "a culprit who is going to the place of his execution."[6] He borrowed six hundred pounds, and tried unsuccessfully to borrow more, to pay debts, and on April 16, 1789, set forth on the journey to New York. The gloom of his spirit was doubtless dispelled by the ovations he received from grateful countrymen as he moved toward the seat of the government[7] and by the adulatory words in which the Senate replied to his inaugural address: "In you all parties confide; in you all interests unite."[8]

Hamilton stood near the President when he took the oath of office on April 30. Washington held the young attorney in even greater esteem than ever before. He had seen fit to praise Hamilton's "arduous and meritorious" labors in the New York ratification convention, and he had spoken in congratulatory terms of *The Federalist*. Of all the arguments he had read both for and against ratification, he said, nothing else was "so well calculated . . . to produce conviction on an unbiased Mind. . . . That Work will merit the Notice of Posterity; because in it are candidly and ably discussed the principles of freedom and the topics of government, which will always be interesting to mankind so long as they shall be connected in Civil Society."[9]

[5] Washington to Gen. Benjamin Lincoln, October 26, 1788, *WW*, XXX, 119.

[6] Washington to Lafayette, January 29, 1789, Washington to Gen. Henry Knox, April 1, 1789, *ibid.*, 186, 268. For a fuller account of Washington's correspondence and reflections on this subject, see Freeman, *George Washington*, VI, 145–59.

[7] Freeman, *George Washington*, VI, 166–84.

[8] Richardson, I, 46.

[9] Washington to John Jay, August 3, 1788, Washington to Hamilton, August 28, 1788, *WW*, XXX, 35, 66.

Organizing the new government was a slow process. Congress had been scheduled to convene on March 4, but many of the members were late in arriving. The House of Representatives finally organized on April 1, and the Senate on April 6. Even after the inauguration rules and procedures had to be formulated. The important revenue law was not enacted until July 4. Hamilton became secretary of the treasury on September 11, more than four months after Washington assumed his duties as chief of state. General Henry Knox became secretary of war on September 12. Edmund Randolph was appointed attorney general on September 26. The office of attorney general was considered a part-time job, and the salary was adjusted accordingly. Randolph was paid fifteen hundred dollars a year, compared to Knox's salary of three thousand dollars and Hamilton's of thirty-five hundred dollars, the amount the secretary of state would receive. In apology the President explained to Randolph that Congress had a "prevailing disposition to frugality" and assumed that the position of attorney general "would confer preeminence on its possessor, and procure for him a decided preference of Professional employment."[10]

Jefferson was serving as the American minister to France when the departments were set up. Upon returning to the United States early in the spring of 1790, he was greeted by an invitation to serve as secretary of state. He accepted and on March 22 entered upon his duties, which John Jay, the chief justice, had temporarily assumed.

Washington was proud of his cabinet. He wrote to Lafayette that, "by having Mr. Jefferson at the Head of the Department of State, Mr. Jay of the Judiciary, Hamilton of the Treasury and Knox of that of War, I feel myself supported by able-Coadjutors." He added that the cabinet members "harmonize extremely well together."[11] Open conflicts among them had not yet appeared. Fortunately for the student of history, Washington, Hamilton, and Jefferson carried on a long-term correspondence with Lafayette. Each wrote to the Frenchman in a manner different from that in which he communicated with any other person, and all of them confided in him information and opinions that are found nowhere else in their writings.

Washington relied heavily on Hamilton's advice. He had not hesitated to counsel with him even before the Treasury Department was set up, an easy matter to arrange since New York, the nation's capital, was also Hamilton's

[10] Washington to Edmund Randolph, September 28, 1789, *ibid.*, 419.
[11] Washington to Lafayette, June 3, 1790, *ibid.*, XXXI, 46.

home. After the young attorney entered the President's "family," as Washington sometimes referred to the cabinet, such consultations were a matter of course. The presidential cabinet developed over a period of many years, and in the early period it was not customary to draw sharp lines of distinction between one department and another. For example, when preparing his message to Congress of December, 1790, Washington asked Hamilton to "revolve in [your] mind such matters . . . as may be proper for me to lay before Congress not only in your own department, but such others of a general nature, as may happen to occur to you."[12] Because of Washington's practice of asking Hamilton's advice about a wide range of government matters, Hamilton began directing his attention to fields outside the Treasury Department, particularly diplomacy. When John Jay was appointed chief justice, his new duties made it necessary for him to devote less time to foreign affairs, and his temporary connection with the Department of State was "more nominal than real."[13] If Jefferson had been on the scene from the beginning, instead of entering the cabinet six months after Hamilton did, he would doubtless have restrained his colleague's tendency to ignore departmental boundaries—though nothing could have prevented Hamilton from speaking out. It was characteristic of him to draw to himself as much authority as came reasonably within his reach. He was convinced that "most of the important measures of every government are connected with the treasury,"[14] which, in his day, at least, was certainly true.[15] That conviction, together with his high-keyed temperament, sometimes caused him to act as if he had assumed the role of prime minister in the new government. Yet he did not deliberately claim such status; he realized that the laws conferred on him no higher rank than that of the heads of other departments.

The new government faced serious problems which the Continental Congress had been unable to solve. The most critical issues remained the territorial ones. Britain was still holding the Northwest posts. From those vantage points, and through their amiable relations with the Indians, British

[12] Washington to Hamilton, October 10, 1790, *ibid.*, XXXI, 132.

[13] Samuel Flagg Bemis, "John Jay," in Bemis (ed.), *The American Secretaries of State and Their Diplomacy* (New York, 1927), I, 280 (hereafter cited as *The American Secretaries of State*).

[14] Hamilton to Col. Edward Carrington, May 26, 1792, *HWL*, IX, 531.

[15] Leonard D. White, *The Federalists: A Study in Administrative History* (New York, 1948), 117 (hereafter cited as *The Federalists*).

agents controlled the territory south of the Great Lakes almost to the Ohio River, and they were seeking means of establishing themselves there permanently. Spain was in control of the Floridas and New Orleans, thus blocking the United States from the Gulf, and Spain's relations with the southern Indians made life hazardous for settlers in the Southwest Territory. The Indians were a serious obstacle in the new republic's path, so incompatible were the ways of life of the white man and the Indian.

The alliance with France, still in effect, was now of limited value and within a few years was to become an extremely embarrassing and finally a dangerous liability. Within a week after Washington's inauguration the States General met at Versailles, and by July the floodgates of revolution had burst, bringing to Americans a fantastic wave of hazards and opportunities. French agents, not yet fully supported by their own government, were already plotting to rob the United States of half its territory. Shortly after he became secretary of state, Jefferson learned that the formidable French minister to the United States, Éléonore François Élie Moustier, was urging his government to reacquire Louisiana and to join to it all the American territory west of the Appalachians. The French made no moves toward that end until 1795, but from 1790 Jefferson and his colleagues knew the danger was continuous.[16] The new nation was weak and almost friendless, though possessed of tremendous potential wealth, and it occupied a strategic location that stimulated the avarice of its powerful neighbors. Though now technically an independent country, its sovereignty required further vindication to assure that independence in fact.

The United States could not hope to match her opponents' strength immediately, nor did any American statesman expect her to do so. Fortunately for the security of the new republic, the nations of western Europe were jealous of each other and given to frequent combat. If the American government could successfully "exploit their mutual bickerings," all would be well.[17] That was the primary task of the new administration in the field of foreign relations.

There were also other problems with diplomatic implications. The revived American commerce was tapping new markets in the Far East but

[16] Jefferson to William Short, August 10, 1790, *JW*, VIII, 81. For an account of Moustier's plot, see E. Wilson Lyon, "Moustier's Memoir on Louisiana," *Mississippi Valley Historical Review*, Vol. XXII (September, 1935), 251–66.

[17] Henry M. Wriston, "Washington and the Foundations of American Foreign Policy," *Minnesota History*, Vol. VIII (March, 1927), 8.

struggling under handicaps in the West Indies and in Europe. A commercial treaty with Britain seemed highly desirable, as did a revised treaty with France and new ones with Spain and other European powers.

The debts to France, Spain, and the Netherlands, for money borrowed during and just after the Revolutionary War, remained unpaid. The creditors were making no peremptory demands for repayment, but the situation was embarrassing and might become urgent at an inauspicious moment. Hamilton had assured the New York legislature in 1787 that the "foreign creditors must and will be paid." They had the power to force repayment, "and sooner or later they may be expected to do it."[18] One of his arguments supporting the Union was that the country could thereby pay the foreign debt.[19]

Peace and independence did not immediately produce all the economic advantages that had been anticipated. Hamilton and most other patriots rejoiced at freedom from the burdensome Navigation Acts of pre-Revolution years. But the peace treaty that relegated those acts to the pages of history (as far as the United States was concerned), was promptly followed by new acts of Parliament that severely hampered American commerce. All nations were eager to sell their products in the United States but were determined to obstruct American exports. Great Britain adopted measures intended to keep United States vessels from the British West Indies; American lumber and wheat could be sent to the islands, only if it was transported in British ships. The West Indian market for meats and fish was reserved for shippers from Canadian and other empire ports. Raw American goods were admitted to Britain duty-free, an advantageous arrangement for the United States, but equally so for Britain and therefore no indication of favoritism on her part. In fact, Britain's liberal attitudes of 1782 and 1783, resulting in the extensive cession of territory, had given way to an attitude of cold aloofness, and through the remainder of the 1780's she refused to send a minister to the United States.

France, though an ally, gave the United States only very limited trading privileges. Article XXXII of the Franco-American treaty of 1778 had admitted American shipping to the French West Indies but reserved to France the right to "regulate" such trade.[20] An act passed in 1783 had curbed

18 *HWL*, II, 213.
19 "Federalist," No. 15, *ibid.*, XI, 111.
20 Miller, *Treaties*, II, 26–27.

American trade in the islands, but a less restrictive act in 1784 had restored many of the 1778 provisions. British and French restrictions were circumvented to some extent by smuggling, fictitious registries, and other clever ruses devised by Yankee shippers.

Britain continued to be the United States' best market and largest supplier. Favorable trade treaties negotiated with the Netherlands, Sweden, Prussia, and Morocco between 1782 and 1787 had produced no tangible results. Nor was the situation altered by the desire of Washington and others to expand Franco-American trade. Washington thought it "obvious" that "there are articles enough in France, which are wanted here; and others in turn produced here, which are wanted in France; to form the basis of a beneficial, extensive, and durable Commerce." He was not deeply interested in the West Indian trade, believing that "rum, the principle article received from thence, is . . . the bane of morals and the parent of idleness." Referring to the importation of British manufactures, he said that Americans had been "too long subject to British prejudices."[21] But the inclination toward British wares was too strong to be altered easily. In 1790, as in the days of the Confederation, nine-tenths of America's imports came from the mother country. The British manner of trading and the willingness of British merchants to extend credit also continued to prove attractive. Some improvements resulted from the law passed by Congress on July 4, 1789, placing a higher tariff on goods imported in foreign vessels and a higher tonnage fee on foreign vessels. The law brought more business to American shippers—and incidentally improved their opportunity to participate illicitly in the West Indian trade.

Before Jefferson became secretary of state, Hamilton advised Washington to try to open regular diplomatic channels with Britain with the aim of improving commercial and other relations. Gouverneur Morris was in France on private business, and it seemed particularly appropriate to entrust the mission to him. He was well acquainted with public affairs; his intellect and personality were suitable for the task; his integrity and patriotism were well known; and if the British again refused to negotiate, it would be less humiliating to the United States if the effort had been made by a private citizen. Washington instructed Morris to ask "his Britannic Majesty's ministers . . . whether there be any, and what, objections to now performing

21 Washington to the French Minister, Moustier, August 17, December 15, 1788, Washington to Lafayette, January 29, 1789, *WW*, XXX, 43–47, 163, 187.

those articles in the treaty of 1783 which remain to be performed . . . and whether they incline to a treaty of commerce with the United States, on any, and what, terms." Morris was also asked to sound out the British on an exchange of ministers and to ask them what compensation they would make for the removal of Negroes from the United States in defiance of the treaty provision. Morris was to make clear to the British ministers that, since the Constitution was in effect and the now firmly established government had a system of courts that would put an end to American treaty violations, the British were expected to evacuate the Northwest posts.[22] This candid admission by Washington that the United States had also violated the treaty was a frank challenge to Britain to reciprocate by putting a stop to her violations and fully executing the treaty.

Washington discussed this move with acting Secretary of State John Jay, who agreed with Hamilton about the need for improving relations with Britain. Madison, serving in the House of Representatives, was against the move, preferring, as he told Washington, to wait until Jefferson took charge of foreign affairs; but he was unable to give substantial reasons for his opposition, and Washington followed the advice of Hamilton and Jay.[23]

The new effort to normalize relations with Britain took full account of John Adams' failure to attain that goal in his mission of 1785 to 1788. He had been unable to negotiate a commercial treaty, though on a number of occasions the British had intimated that they would be agreeable to a commercial treaty provided the American government had enough power to require every state and every citizen to abide by its terms.[24]

Morris carried out his mission with diligence. To the Duke of Leeds, the British foreign minister, he politely affirmed his confidence in the good faith of the British government and gave assurances of American sincerity.[25] When the duke read Washington's letters, he appeared delighted and said, "I assure you it is very much my wish to cultivate a friendly and com-

[22] Washington to the Senate, February 14, 1791, giving his instructions of October 13, 1789, *ASPFR*, I, 122.

[23] *Cf.* Julian P. Boyd, *Number 7: Alexander Hamilton's Secret Attempts to Control American Foreign Policy* (Princeton, 1964), 26–27 (hereafter cited as *Number 7*). Boyd considered Washington's appointment of Morris a "surprising action" and a "puzzling fact" because he could see "no apparent urgency . . . calling for haste."

[24] Adams to Jay, February 14, 1788, *AW*, VIII, 475–76.

[25] Morris to the Duke of Leeds, April 30, 1790, PROFO 4, VIII, 483–86.

mercial intercourse," adding that "the rest of his Majesty's servants" shared the same desire.[26]

Prime Minister William Pitt was not so cordial. He, too, expressed a desire for a commercial treaty, but would make no firm commitment about negotiations. When the Northwest posts were mentioned, Morris was told they had been held because of American treaty violations and in lieu of compensation for those violations. To Morris' accusation that the British were planning to hold the forts permanently, Pitt haughtily replied, "Why, perhaps we may." Morris bristled and retorted that, while the United States did not regard it expedient to go to war immediately over the territory, "we know our rights, and will avail ourselves of them when time and circumstances may suit."[27] He strongly intimated that if Britain did not soon depart peaceably she would be forced out when next King George became engaged in hostilities with European rivals.

The British ministers seemed eager to discuss one topic only, Morris reported to Washington, and that was an alliance with the United States. Morris had neither the instructions nor the inclination to consider such an alliance, which, he said, "we shall be in no hurry to contract."[28] From 1782 to the end of the century British officials remained hopeful of reversing the verdict of Yorktown through an alliance of one form or another. In 1782, Shelburne and Oswald had followed Franklin's words eagerly when he expressed the vaguely worded hope that the future might not find Americans and Englishmen completely divided. Of course, what Franklin had had in mind was commercial intercourse, not political reunion.

While he was in London, Morris tried to soften the British mood by openly associating with Luzerne, who was then serving as French ambassador to Britain, a bold move, since France and Britain were believed to be close to hostilities. Morris reported to Washington that he kept faith with the nation's ally by informing Luzerne of Britain's refusal to remove her forces from the Northwest. Morris also took care to be seen with Charles James Fox, the leader of the minority party in Parliament. Morris probably overplayed his hand; Bemis has criticized his actions as tactless.[29] Henry

[26] Morris to Washington, April 7, 1790, *ASPFR*, I, 122.

[27] Morris to Washington, May 29, 1790, *ibid.*, 124.

[28] Morris to Washington, September 18, 1790, *ibid.*, 127.

[29] Samuel Flagg Bemis, *Jay's Treaty: A Study in Commerce and Diplomacy* (New York, 1923), 49–50 (hereafter cited as *Jay's Treaty*).

Cabot Lodge believed that the British were not particularly offended by Morris' conduct and that what complaints they made about it "were mere pretenses, put forward by the Tory Government to delay doing us justice."[30]

It would be difficult to point out any particular ill effects from Morris' brief association with Luzerne and Fox. At the time Pitt was unwilling to accede to the envoy's request anyway, and it is likely that the evidence of Franco-American intimacy led King George's ministers to understand that the United States did not stand alone.

Washington reported to the Senate that the mission had failed—that the British ministers had declared "without scruple" that they [did] not "mean to fulfill . . . the Treaty . . . 'till performance on our part, and compensation where the delay has rendered the performance now impracticable." He added, "On the subject of the Treaty of Commerce, they avoided direct answers." The British, he said, were trying to draw the United States into "a treaty of alliance offensive and defensive." Early in 1791 he instructed Morris to "discontinue his communications with them."[31] In his matter-of-fact report of the failure of the mission the President again virtually admitted that the United States had violated some of the terms of the peace treaty. It was his desire to conduct negotiations to terminate those violations or to reach agreements on compensation for mutual infringements. He was unwilling to consider an alliance "offensive and defensive" with Britain, as were Hamilton and Jefferson, though both secretaries were agreeable to surveying the possibilities of a limited alliance with the objective of seizing Spanish territory along the Gulf of Mexico (see Chapter VII).

When it was brought to Hamilton's attention that Morris had been associating with Luzerne and Fox, the secretary pointed out to Washington that Morris had had cordial relations with Luzerne when the Frenchman was minister at Philadelphia and that it would have been unnatural for him to have ignored his friend in London. Nor was it strange, said Hamilton, that Morris and Fox enjoyed one another's company. They were similar in "dispositions and character—both brilliant men, men of wit and genius, both fond of the pleasures of society." It was impossible, he felt, that there could be "anything wrong."[32]

Hamilton was, nevertheless, inwardly disturbed concerning the mission.

[30] *HWL*, IV, 343n.
[31] February 14, 1791, *WW*, XXXI, 215.
[32] Hamilton to Washington, September 30, 1790, *HWL*, IV, 343–45.

He harbored no doubts about Morris' integrity, but he felt that the mission could have been handled better. When the British asked pointedly whether Washington would send a regular minister to London if Britain would agree to send one to the United States, Morris replied that he had no direct instructions on the point but that he felt certain his country would welcome an exchange of ministers. Hamilton thought Morris was "too shy" in his reply.[33] He regretted that the response was not a simple, affirmative statement that the United States would, of course, be pleased to exchange ministers.

The report of George Beckwith, an unofficial agent sent from Canada to New York by Sir Guy Carleton (first Baron Dorchester) the governor of Quebec (see Chapter VII for details of this mission), indicates that Hamilton's criticism of Morris' conduct went further than his comments to Washington. It would be reasonable to assume that Beckwith exaggerated somewhat and that Hamilton chose his words to Washington with care. Hamilton's lack of tact can be criticized, but not his motives. Boyd referred to Hamilton's criticism of Morris as a "libel on an honorable public servant."[34] Boyd assumed that Hamilton tried to discredit Morris in Washington's eyes in order to convince the President that the cold response of the British was due to misconduct by Morris. The accusation would sound more plausible if Hamilton had not taken such pains to justify Morris' behavior to Washington and if he had not so explicitly expressed confidence in the envoy. An exchange of regular ministers, which Hamilton was trying so earnestly to arrange, according to his own testimony and Beckwith's, would certainly have removed the negotiations from Hamilton's control and placed them under Jefferson's—as actually happened in 1791, when ministers were exchanged.

Hamilton was concerned enough to try to look into the matter quietly on his own, and he proceeded to do so in a manner that revealed his inclination to play a leading role in foreign affairs. When David Humphreys was preparing to leave New York for a secret diplomatic mission to Spain and Portugal, Hamilton, "in a very confidential conversation," said that he was "not perfectly satisfied" with the manner in which Morris conducted the negotiations "with the Duke of Leeds" and asked Humphreys to talk with the

[33] Dorchester to Grenville, September 25, 1790, enclosing Beckwith's account of his conversation with Hamilton, Brymner, 149. This part of Beckwith's report, at least, rings true.

[34] Boyd, *Number 7*, 66.

"British Administration with regard to the points in agitation between the United States and Great Britain." Apparently Hamilton said nothing to Jefferson about his commission to Humphreys, perhaps only because Humphreys in turn found it impossible to accomplish anything of significance.[35]

In the meantime, Hamilton was facing pressing problems in his own department. He was well aware that one of the most urgent problems was to devise means to pay the nation's debts. Congress relied primarily on him to suggest methods for funding the debt with a view to its eventual liquidation. His astonishing success was to add immeasurably to his stature as a national leader.

In 1790 the United States owed almost $12 million to France, the Netherlands, and Spain. Americans were generally agreed that these debts should be paid in full. On the matter of the domestic debt, which was about $42 million, Americans were divided. Many believed that the government's obligations would be met satisfactorily if each creditor received 30 to 40 per cent of the face value of his holdings. The old "certificates of indebtedness," "warrants," and so on, were selling for as little as 25 per cent of their face value, and most of them were in the hands of "speculators." The secretary insisted that the nation's honor required full payment, which would also earn for the Republic the respect of other nations. His first "Report on the Public Credit" comprised sixty-four pages of convincing arguments supported by carefully arranged facts and figures.[36] The result was that Congress voted to adopt his plan for paying the national domestic debt at its full face value. The means adopted for funding both the foreign and domestic debts called for fresh loans from Dutch bankers to meet arrears owed to France and the floating of new bonds to be exchanged for the old certificates. The bonds would have a uniform value and would stimulate American financial activity. This plan was put into effect, and the results were as Hamilton anticipated.

There was heated disagreement about Hamilton's recommendation that the national government assume Revolutionary War debts incurred by the states, totaling $21.5 million. He believed that it was honorable and proper for the nation to pay the debts, and he also perceived that a unified national

[35] Humphreys to Washington, October 31, 1790, F. L. Humphreys, *The Life and Times of David Humphreys* (New York, 1917), II, 52.

[36] *HWL*, II, 227–91.

debt would augment the prestige—and support—of the national government among the citizenry. Opposition to the proposal stemmed from the fact that some states owed more than others. The Antifederalists opposed it as they did any measure that would tend to minimize the prestige of the states. The proposal was held in the House of Representatives until Hamilton and Jefferson joined forces to assure its passage. In Hamilton's over-all financial plan the need for additional revenue loomed large. The Whisky Rebellion of 1794 and the establishment of the First Bank of the United States grew out of his efforts in that direction, which lie outside the scope of this book and have been dealt with competently elsewhere.

The financial difficulties which preceded and accompanied the French Revolution gave the American debt to France particular significance. Hamilton was eager to rid the nation of the debt. He made an arrangement with the President and the secretary of state whereby official correspondence with American agents abroad, principally William Short, concerning the new loans and the funding agreements should be carried on through the Treasury Department.[37]

The financial discomforts of the French government had become so acute by 1789 that it was decided to sell the American debt to Dutch bankers for cash. While he was in Paris, Gouverneur Morris asked French officials why they were willing to discount the debt despite the fact that the United States was preparing to repay it at full face value.[38] When told that France needed the money without delay, Morris offered to take part in the transaction himself by forming a syndicate to buy part of the United States' obligations. He did not pursue the proposal, however.

When Hamilton heard of the French plans to sell the debt, he wrote to Jefferson expressing doubts whether France had the right to take such action without American consent but added that it would be poor taste to make an issue of the matter with the hard-pressed creditor.[39] He could not have failed to be aware that the United States could take advantage of the French embarrassment and redeem the debt, or part of it, at less than the amount due; but he would not have regarded that a worthy act. In his instructions to Short he expressed the hope that the French would ask for payment in provisions instead of cash. Such an arrangement would stimu-

[37] Hamilton to Short, September 1, 1790, *ibid.*, IV, 302–303.
[38] *MDFR*, I, 395–401.
[39] Hamilton to Jefferson, April 15, 1791, *HWL*, IV, 353.

late American business and commerce and would make repayment less burdensome for the United States; but he told Short not to make the proposal, for it would be discreditable to try to drive a hard bargain "at the expense of friends."[40] Hamilton did send instructions to discourage the French from selling the debt. Since the United States intended to repay it in full, he said he preferred for the French to receive it.

The projected sale did not take place, but as the French Revolution gained in fury, French authorities decided to exchange American bonds for provisions. In 1795, James Swan, an American speculator who was also serving as a purchasing agent for France, gained control of the $2 million in American bonds still held by the French. He exchanged them for United States domestic bonds that bore 0.5 per cent higher interest. These bonds he exchanged for American provisions, chiefly naval stores and salted meat, for the French navy, thereby "domesticating" the American debt and at the same time making a handsome profit for himself. Hamilton had nothing to do with this transaction. As far as France was concerned, the debt had been liquidated.

In 1792, Hamilton's opponents began charging that, despite his statements to the contrary, he did not wish to see the national debt paid but was actually trying to make it as large as possible. Jefferson commented that Hamilton planned to use the debt as a means to "corrupt and manage" Congress.[41] Hamilton's wartime statements that the debt would help to cement the Union and that national bonds would be useful in the nation's financial system were misapplied. The critics ignored or misstated Hamilton's meaning and recalled simply that the secretary believed "a national debt is a national blessing." Hamilton's correspondence with Short tells a different story. While giving Short detailed instructions for obtaining the lowest possible rate of interest on the new loan from the Dutch, he was extremely careful to see that the payments for the international exchange transactions were kept as low as possible. He cautioned Short against making agreements with the bankers that might involve large fees or initial payments that would increase the cost of the loan. He supplied Short with ample arguments to use in inducing the bankers to extend loans at favorable rates: "the economical scale of our establishments, civil and military; the comparative smallness of our debt; the reliance which may be had on the stability of our

[40] Hamilton to Short, September 1, 1790, *ibid.*, 311.

[41] Jefferson to Washington, September 9, 1792, *JW*, VIII, 401.

pecuniary arrangements; . . . the rapid progression of population and resources; . . . the hope that we shall continue in peace while other Powers are accumulating their debts by new wars." The secretary concluded, "Within due limits" these arguments should be urged "with force and assurance."[42]

In 1795, when Hamilton was preparing to resign from the cabinet, he presented to Congress another voluminous "Report on the Public Credit."[43] He spoke with scorn of persons who would support every popular demand for public expenditures and then try to win additional approval by "declaiming against a public debt" and "against every plan of taxation which is proposed to discharge old debts." He warned the nation of the dangers of excessive indebtedness, which, he said, burdens the people until it "becomes intolerable" and leads to "disorders, . . . convulsions and revolutions." There could be "no more sacred obligation" on the part of those who rule the state than to guard against such developments. The best way for those in power to demonstrate "true patriotism and genuine policy" would be by "extinguishing, with reasonable celerity, the actual debt of the country, and laying the foundation of a system . . . which, if possible, may give IMMORTALITY TO PUBLIC CREDIT."[44]

The successful funding of the debt had the results that Hamilton had predicted: it gave the United States an unequaled credit rating, it conferred on the nation an aura of respectability and stability, and it did help to cement the Union. Hamilton's measures contributed mightily toward helping the nation function effectively. Grave problems continued to beset the Republic, but at last it was now competent to deal with them.

Europe still commanded the United States' attention, for the Old World remained the center of international politics and commerce; but the New West—the lands west of the Alleghenies—also beckoned. More and more Americans heard the "horn in the West" calling them to new adventures and new homes. While the westward movement created no new diplomatic problems, it made the old ones more crucial. The complex conflicts of interests among the United States, the Indians, the British, and the Spaniards cried out for attention.

[42] September 1, 1790, *HWL*, IV, 309.
[43] January 20, 1795, *ibid.*, III, 201–301.
[44] *Ibid.*, 262–63. Hamilton's capitals.

CHAPTER VII

Western Boundaries

THE HEARTY congratulations Americans were exchanging in 1783 about the extensive western lands proved premature. The Treaty of Paris spoke of the boundaries of the Great Lakes on the north, the Mississippi on the west and the thirty-first parallel on the south; but the British remained south of the Great Lakes for thirteen years, the Indians tried to ignore the treaty, and the Spaniards remained north of the thirty-first parallel for twelve years.

Hamilton's futile recommendation to Congress in 1783 called for both land and naval forces to provide, among other things, security of "the navigation of the Mississippi."[1] Throughout the remainder of the 1780's he saw no reason to lessen his fears about Spain, and he also came to see the full import of the dangers from the British and from the Indians. "On one side of us," he wrote, "and stretching far into our rear, are . . . the dominions of Britain. . . . On the other side . . . are colonies and establishments . . . of Spain." With deep concern he described the Spanish holdings as "extending [northward] to meet the British settlements." He saw the "family compact" between Spain and France becoming constantly weaker and predicted a "future concert of views" between Spain and Britain against the United States. The "savage tribes" he "regarded as . . . natural enemies" to the United States and "natural allies" to Britain and Spain, "because they have most to fear from us, and most to hope from them." Taking a clear-eyed view of the situation, he observed that "the territories of Britain, Spain and of the Indian nations . . . encircle our Union from Maine to Georgia."[2]

Hamilton had less firsthand information about the Indians of the West than Washington and Jefferson, but he was aware of the basic American methods for handling the red men. He would not rely solely on the army

[1] *HWL*, VI, 465.
[2] "Federalist," Nos. 24, 25, *ibid.*, XI, 191–92, 195.

or the militia. He believed that, as he wrote to Governor Clinton, in dealing with the Indians "the surest as well as the most just and most humane way of removing them" was to extend American settlements "to their neighborhood." He surmised in 1783 that they might be "already willing to exchange their former possessions for others more remote."[3]

Also in 1783, Hamilton saw the possibility of selling the public lands to hasten "the extinguishment of the debts,"[4] but no such action was taken that year. Jefferson induced the Continental Congress to enact the Ordinance of 1785, providing for the rectilinear survey of the land; and during the next four years Thomas Hutchins, United States geographer, directed the survey of the Seven Ranges of townships westward from the point where the boundary lines of Pennsylvania and those of the future states of West Virginia and Ohio converged. (It was assumed that the Indians had relinquished their claims to this area in the treaties of Fort Stanwix in 1784 and Fort McIntosh in 1785.) In 1785 the government charged a minimum of a dollar an acre for the land and sold it in lots of no less than 640 acres—one section. No land office had been set up in the West, and every original purchaser in that early period had to go to New York to buy western land. Manasseh Cutler, John Cleves Symmes, and others were able to make special contracts with Congress for buying vast tracts of Ohio land, but few independent settlers could pay the $640 for a farm. Moreover, they could not tell what kind of land they were buying unless they went to Ohio to inspect it. Consequently, when Marietta was settled by the Ohio Company in 1788, it was discovered that there were squatters in the area and others downriver on lands still owned by the Indians.

In the Treaty of Sycamore Shoals signed in March, 1775, the Cherokees had "sold" most of Kentucky to the Transylvania Company, and by 1780 the white population of Kentucky had reached 74,000. Western Pennsylvania was being settled rapidly, as was the Kanawha Valley (now West Virginia). Tennessee was settled at a slower pace, but every new home established in the West added to the pressure against the British, the Indians, and the Spaniards. Land speculators were extremely ambitious and aggressive, though their profits were jeopardized by claims jumpers and squatters.

The recklessness with which the settlers moved into Indian country was

[3] Hamilton to Clinton, October 3, 1783, *ibid.*, IX, 393.

[4] *JCC*, XXIV, 256. See also William P. Cutler and Julia P. Cutler, *Life, Journals, and Correspondence of Rev. Manasseh Cutler* (Cincinnati, 1881), I, 362.

illustrated by the speed with which they began crossing the Ohio River after the Revolutionary War. They flocked in years ahead of the government surveyors, built cabins at favored spots—along the navigable rivers and near springs that would supply drinking water when the rivers were low—and claimed the land on the basis of "tomahawk rights." History can tell us little about these early "empire builders," for they left few records, but certainly their activities were concurrent with, if not prior to, legal land acquisitions.

Government officials and army officers, though aware that eager pioneers were helping strengthen the nation's hand against Britain and Spain, often looked upon them as vexatious liabilities. Many settlers were claiming land to which they had no written title, and they were impatient of the restraints of government or landlords. When the surveyors arrived in eastern Ohio to lay out the Seven Ranges, hardy squatters already settled in the region threatened their lives. The squatters claimed that they owned the land on which they were living, and they certified that "all mankind [has] an undoubted right to pass into any vacant country . . . and Congress is not impowered to forbid them [or] to make any sale of the uninhabited lands."[5] To them any unoccupied land was free, like the air they breathed, and beyond the authority of any government to sell. They harked back to colonial times, when new settlers were seldom asked to pay more than a nominal sum for unoccupied lands, the theory of the colonial governments being that the pioneers were entitled to land as a reward for helping extend the "rim of civilization." Neither Jefferson nor the Continental Congress could persuade the Ohio pioneers of the 1780's to forget the experiences of their fathers and grandfathers. The result was inevitable conflict. The squatters, and sympathetic historians of later years, charged that United States military forces looked upon them "as enemies to be punished, rather than as fellow citizens to be protected."[6]

Now and then, under orders from the Continental Congress, army troops moved up and down the north bank of the Ohio, burning the squatters' cabins; but the soldiers were few, and the cabins were soon rebuilt. The Indians slew the interlopers without mercy, but still the settlers poured in. Truly they were "the Unconquered." In all the fighting, organized and

[5] Public notice by John Emerson, March 12, 1785, in Temple Bodley, *George Rogers Clark: His Life and Public Services* (New York, 1926), 267 (hereafter cited as *George Rogers Clark*). The habits of the early settlers are described by Rufus King in *Ohio, First Fruits of the Ordinance of 1787* (Boston, 1891), 189–94.

[6] Bodley, *George Rogers Clark*, 267.

unorganized, in the Old Northwest, the Indians lost but a small fraction of the number of whites who were slain. Even in open battles far more white men than Indians were killed. General Josiah Harmar lost 200 men when he was defeated in the Maumee Valley in 1790, and the next year Major General Arthur St. Clair, the first governor of the territory, lost 630 men in the battle near Fort Wayne. In General Anthony Wayne's celebrated victory at Fallen Timbers (near present-day Toledo) in 1794, "only some fifty braves" were killed.[7]

Hamilton tried to alter the land laws and provide easier terms to encourage settlers to claim lands legally. In his "Report on Public Lands," presented on July 22, 1790, he asked Congress to establish land offices in the West, to reduce the price of public land to a minimum of thirty cents an acre, and to allow sales of tracts of as few as 100 acres to "unassociated persons."[8] He knew that the settlers were mostly young men, just married or planning to be married, and that they had little cash. Hamilton's proposed law would have enabled a man to buy a farm for $30—in contrast to the $640 required under the 1785 law. This plan was an outgrowth of Hamilton's belief that land should be held in small tracts and should be owned by the man who cultivated it. Jefferson apparently agreed; his 1785 law has been called "a temporary aberration."[9] Historians have sometimes accused Hamilton of supporting programs that would have militated against the small farmer. Morison, for instance, writes that "some . . . device for keeping the poor from the land would have been adopted in the United States if men like Hamilton, Jay, and Morris had determined the public land policy."[10] This is a good illustration of the errors that can arise when efforts are made to categorize Hamilton.

American army officers, among them Harmer, St. Clair, and John Doughty, constantly complained that British agents in Canada and in posts below the treaty border line encouraged the Indians to resist white encroachments.[11] One Indian chief told an American officer: "You invite us to stop our young men. It is impossible to do it, being constantly encouraged by the British."[12]

[7] Robert E. Riegel, *America Moves West* (New York, 1930), 62–67.

[8] *HWL*, VIII, 87–94.

[9] Riegel, *America Moves West*, 48.

[10] Samuel Eliot Morison and Henry Steele Commager, *The Growth of the American Republic*, (5th ed., New York, 1962), I, 352.

[11] William Henry Smith (ed.), *The Life and Public Services of Arthur St. Clair* (Cincinnati, 1882), I, 142, 153; II, 6–9 *et passim* (hereafter cited as *Arthur St. Clair*).

[12] *Ibid.*, I, 168.

The crushing defeat of St. Clair in 1791 convinced the Indians that they could drive the settlers back across the Ohio. United States commissioners sent to negotiate with the Indians in the summer of 1793 were told: "Brothers: We shall be persuaded that you mean to do us justice if you agree that the Ohio shall remain the boundary line between us. If you will not consent thereto, our meeting will be altogether unnecessary."[13] Not until 1794, after Wayne's slow, successful campaign, culminating at Fallen Timbers, was the Indians' resistance broken. They were unable to repel Wayne by themselves, and the British failed to give them direct aid even when Wayne's victorious forces were maneuvering outside British-held Fort Miamis, destroying crops and houses.

Spain's grasp on the territory south and west of the United States became steadily less secure. Spain's willingness to enter the Jay-Gardoqui negotiations in 1785–86 was actually a recognition of increasing pressure from frontiersmen. Unlike Jay, apparently Hamilton was never attracted by the idea of holding in abeyance American claims to navigation rights on the Mississippi in exchange for a commercial treaty with Spain. In 1787 he deplored "the disposition of Spain with regard to the Mississippi," asserting that American citizens were "entitled by nature and compact to a free participation in the navigation of the Mississippi."[14] He stressed this point again the following year when he told the Continental Congress that the navigation right "ought in no manner whatsoever to be invalidated," and as a member of Washington's cabinet he continued to seek means of upholding that right.

Jefferson was deeply interested in the West, especially in Kentucky; and his views in the 1780's coincided with Hamilton's about the importance of the western waters for shipping. "The navigation of the Mississippi," Jefferson said, "we must have." He added, significantly, "This is all we are, as yet, ready to receive."[15] In the latter view he differed from Hamilton, who had already concluded that the United States must acquire full possession of the territory all the way to the Gulf.

Madison was equally sensitive and more emotional in his attitude toward the West. In 1786, disgusted by Jay's willingness to agree not to assert navi-

[13] *Ibid.*, 182–83.
[14] "Federalist," Nos. 11, 15, *HWL*, XI, 84, 111.
[15] Jefferson to Archibald Stuart, January 25, 1786, *JW*, V, 260.

gation rights for twenty-five years, he held that in response to such neglect of their welfare western settlers would be justified in considering themselves "absolved from every federal tie" and in courting "some [foreign] protection for their betrayed rights."[16]

Washington's name has quite properly been associated with the westward expansion. His interest in the West developed early and remained unflagging, but he was less consistent than Hamilton in his attitude toward the Mississippi outlet. He was early convinced that the waters of the Potomac and the Ohio-Mississippi could be linked by a navigational canal. He thought that a careful survey of the James River might prove it to be a better waterway than the Potomac. Looking further into the future, he suggested that surveys of streams flowing into the Ohio from the north—the Muskingum and the Scioto—would probably reveal the possibility of transportation routes between the Ohio and the Great Lakes.

In 1784 Washington observed a private demonstration of "the model of Mr. [James] Rumsey's Boats constructed to work against stream." He had had "little faith" in it, he said, until he saw the demonstration, but thereafter he had "no doubt" of its future success and assumed that it would be "of the greatest usefulness in our inland navigation."[17] Washington was pledged to secrecy about the mechanical features of the craft, which was powered by a steam engine, but he was greatly impressed by the demonstration. In a letter to Dr. Hugh Williamson of North Carolina he particularly commented upon the boat's ability to move "against stream, by the aid of mechanical power and the fact that, the counteraction being proportioned to the action, [the boat] must ascend a swift current faster than a gentle stream."[18] In 1787, Rumsey gave a public demonstration of the boat on the waters of the Potomac. The "unfinished genius"[19] did not live to make his invention a practical success, but his work was a pioneer effort, and certainly it was historically significant because of its influence on Washington's thinking.

Washington's vision was a majestic one. An east-west channel penetrating the heart of the continent would bring to the interior settlers who were

[16] Brant, II, 389.

[17] Certificate to James Rumsey, September 7, 1784, *WW*, XXVII, 468.

[18] Washington to Dr. Hugh Williamson, March 15, 1785, *ibid.*, XXVIII, 107.

[19] Nathaniel W. Stephenson and Waldo H. Dunn, *George Washington* (New York, 1940), II, 206.

bound to the United States by their interest and sympathies.[20] The Spanish conspiracy to encourage defection in the West would become ludicrous. British intrusion and Indian hostility would be overcome by the power of a surging population.

Upon returning to Mount Vernon after his long western trip in the fall of 1784 Washington wrote to Governor Benjamin Harrison of Virginia, urging him to use his influence to induce the Virginia legislature—possibly in co-operation with the Maryland legislature—to order a thorough survey of the rivers preparatory to the construction of the canals.[21] Both legislatures followed his recommendations, and the Potomac Navigation Company was organized, with Washington as its president. Washington's design was not destined to become a reality—it was to be the railroads that would later help move settlers westward. The Potomac Navigation Company did render useful service, however, in constructing canals around rapids in the Potomac and removing obstructions from the river, thereby opening the way for rather extensive shipping.

It was in his letter to Governor Harrison that Washington made his famous comment that "the Western settlers . . . stand as it were upon a pivot; the touch of a feather, would turn them any way." He was alluding to the possibility of war with Spain or Great Britain over western conflicts, which he hoped would be resolved by his transportation project. He was not displeased to learn that Spanish officials were making it difficult for American frontiersmen to travel on the lower Mississippi. He did not wish to see the western settlers develop a regular course of trade to the Gulf. Experience with Great Britain had taught that when firm commercial connections were formed it was "next to impracticable to divert" them; that is, once Americans began using the Mississippi regularly it would be difficult to bring commerce to the canals and the Potomac. Washington wanted his project completed before making "any stir about the navigation of the Mississippi."[22] A month later he expressed himself more emphatically in a letter to Richard Henry Lee, president of Congress: "The navigation of the Mississippi, *at this time* ought to be no object with us: on the contrary until we have a little time allowed to open and make easy the ways between the

[20] Charles H. Ambler, *George Washington and the West* (Chapel Hill, 1936), 183–89.

[21] October 10, 1784, *WW*, XXVII, 471–80.

[22] Washington to David Humphreys, July 25, 1785, *ibid.*, XXVIII, 204–205.

Atlantic States and the Western Territory, the obstruction had better remain."[23]

The fact that Washington owned rather extensive lands in western Virginia no doubt heightened his interest in the navigation system. He could not possibly have overlooked the connection between land values and navigational facilities. Yet there are no grounds for assuming that his attitude was unduly influenced by self-seeking. His correspondence, even when he was not holding public office, always displayed more concern for public than for private affairs. He favored the rivers and canals project chiefly because he thought it would bind the Union more closely.[24]

Reports from the West made it clear that the settlers would not be denied navigation rights as they understood them. In 1787, Harmer, who was not in full sympathy with the Kentuckians, warned the secretary of war that all the inhabitants west of the Allegheny Mountains considered the free navigation of the Mississippi a vital interest. Kentucky alone, he said, could muster 5,000 fighting men, and the number was increasing rapidly. He reported that from October 10, 1786, to May 12, 1787, his "officer of the day" had counted 177 boats containing 2,689 passengers moving down the Ohio by the mouth of the Muskingum.[25] Harmar was convinced that the West could not long be denied the full use of the Mississippi.

Washington's conclusions changed when he came to understand that the Kentuckians might become "riotous and ungovernable, if the hope of traffic [was] cut off by treaty."[26] He would not ask Congress to postpone negotiations to secure rights to navigation through New Orleans if such inaction would endanger national unity. Thereafter he held essentially to the same position that Hamilton took on the Mississippi question. When he became president in 1789 he was fully alert to the dangers posed by Spanish activities in the Southwest.

In 1789 the new administration was anxious about the unwillingness of the British to abandon their hold on the territory south of the 1783 treaty boundary line. Five of the seven fortified posts were in New York: Dutchman's Point and Pointe au Fer, at the northern end of Lake Champlain;

23 Washington to Richard Henry Lee, August 22, 1785, *ibid.*, 231.
24 Ambler, *George Washington and the West*, 204.
25 May 14, 1787, Smith, *Arthur St. Clair*, II, 20.
26 Washington to Richard Henry Lee, July 26, 1786, *WW*, XXVIII, 484.

Fort Oswegatchie, on the St. Lawrence River; Oswego, on Lake Ontario; and Fort Niagara, commanding the junction between Ontario and Erie. The other two British-held posts were Detroit, strategically located between Lakes Erie and Huron, and Fort Michilimackinac, which guarded the passages connecting Lakes Huron, Michigan, and Superior. Each fort was near the border, but each was strategically located from a military point of view. The Indians living to the south depended on the post merchants to purchase their furs and to supply the goods they needed—including weapons. The British were, therefore, the Indians' friends, and the Americans, who cleared the forests and drove away the game, were their enemies. British agents constantly reminded the Indians of these factors and even went so far as to tell them that it was for their sakes, "chiefly, if not entirely," that the British continued to hold the posts.[27] British officials gave the Indians advice that made them more stubborn during treaty negotiations with the United States.

Washington always wrote resentfully when referring to the British-held forts south of the treaty border. To him they were both a national and a personal affront. He was slower than Hamilton to conclude that the British intended to stay permanently, although he did finally come to that point of view. During the 1780's he wrote to his friends from time to time expressing bitter feelings toward the British and his suspicions about the trickery to which they might resort to maintain their position. To the excuse that they needed time to arrange their departure, he retorted, "To remove their Garrisons and Stores is not the work of a week."[28] As for the suggestion that the British might release each post to American control when Congress sent a force of men to garrison it, Washington suspected that the British might give Congress notice of departure at an inconvenient time and then depart suddenly before United States forces could arrive, in which case the Indians would likely burn the forts.

Soon after taking office in 1789, Washington realized that he could not immediately find solutions to these problems or those in the West. Urgent domestic affairs coupled with an as yet somewhat disorganized manner of conducting foreign relations worked for delay in the field of diplomacy. The policies of the new government could not be formulated quickly, though the leaders were united in the conviction that they must stand firm

27 Sir John Johnson to the Indian, Brant, March, 1787, Smith, *Arthur St. Clair*, I, 153.
28 Washington to Jacob Read, November 3, 1784, *WW*, XXVII, 488.

in the assertion of the nation's rights and must be ready to take advantage of any future conflicts among the European powers.

As the year 1789 drew to a close, Washington sought advice from his cabinet about the parting thoughts he should give to the Spanish envoy, Gardoqui, who was about to return to Spain. He wanted the envoy to understand that Jay's position on the Mississippi navigation question did not represent the position of the United States government. He was convinced that "yielding the navigation," or even appearing to do so, "would occasion, certainly, the separation of the Western territory." Yet Washington's moderation and love of peace made him find it prudent to tell Gardoqui that, although America could never "lose sight of the use of that navigation," yet "by a just and liberal policy both countries might derive reciprocal advantages."[29] Gardoqui had come to the United States with explicit instructions from his government not to compromise on Spain's claim of exclusive control of the lower Mississippi. The Continental Congress had instructed Jay to make no treaty that did not concede a share in that control.[30] Though Jay and Congress wavered on this point, the American position as finally clarified by Washington's administration was firmly adhered to.

The conflict over the Mississippi exemplified the clashes of interest between the two nations. Spain clearly realized that a strong, independent republic on the North American continent might stimulate disaffection within its dominions to the south or upset the balance of power in Europe that had so far enabled the weakened kingdom to hold its extensive territories. Spanish officials in Louisiana and the Floridas developed a regular practice of giving presents to the Indians and holding banquets in their honor, and they tried to expand commercial relations to the point of making the Indians dependent allies. Southern tribes such as the Cherokees, Chickasaws, Choctaws, and Creeks inclined toward Spain just as the northern tribes leaned toward Britain, for in both regions the United States appeared to be, or was made to appear to be, the Indians' enemy.

At the beginning of 1790 the President was hopeful that the time had arrived for reaching harmonious agreements with Spain and Britain. Perhaps the new Spanish monarch, Charles IV, would not "insist upon those exclusive claims to the navigation of the Mississippi, which [had] hitherto

[29] Undated "Queries," apparently submitted to Madison or Jefferson, *ibid.*, XXX, 486–87.

[30] Bemis, "John Jay," *The American Secretaries of State*, I, 239–40.

prevented the conclusion of a treaty."[31] In his first annual message to Congress, on January 8, 1790, Washington spoke buoyantly of "the concord, peace, and plenty, with which we are blessed."[32] A month later, in a message to the Senate, he commented that, though "a difference subsists between Great Britain and the United States," he believed it "desirable that all questions between this and other nations be speedily and amicably settled."[33] He did not, however, rely entirely on the efficacy of astute diplomacy and general good will. In his January 8 message to Congress he urged the lawmakers to provide for the nation's "common defence" and observed that "to be prepared for war is one of the most effectual means of preserving peace."

Later in 1790 the web of interrelationships among the United States, Britain, and Spain assumed a new aspect following news of a British assault on Spain's boasted trade monopoly with the Indians on the northern Pacific Coast. In 1789 the crews of three British vessels, intent on fur trading, had attempted to set up a base at Nootka Sound on Vancouver Island. Spanish authorities operating from Mexico had captured the vessels and imprisoned the crews, thereby precipitating a fierce controversy between the British and Spanish governments.

William Pitt welcomed the opportunity to do battle with Britain's historic enemy. He saw a chance to expand Britain's area of trade and colonization and, at the same time, to regain the prestige lost at Yorktown. He demanded that Spain release the captives, pay reparations, and agree not to molest British traders in the area in the future. He judged, correctly, that the revolutionary tumult across the English Channel would prevent France from coming to the aid of her ally.

Spain, standing alone, had little hope of victory in a clash with Britain. Pitt was unwilling to compromise on his demands, and Spain at length capitulated. A formal agreement was reached providing for the release of the ships and crews with indemnity and conceding to the British the right to trade or make settlements on the coast at points which the Spaniards had not actually occupied. The Nootka Convention, as it came to be called, was filled with significance for the future. For Britain it opened the way into the rich Oregon country long before the United States was able to assert a

[31] Washington to Charles Pinckney, January 11, 1790, *WW*, XXX, 500–501.
[32] *Ibid.*, 491.
[33] February 9, 1790, *ibid.*, 8.

claim to it. The region was remote and little known (the British and Spaniards believed that Vancouver Island was part of the mainland). The lack of reliable information about the region is indicated by the geographical names used in a news report from Madrid, printed in the *Gazette of the United States* on September 29, 1790, referring to "the vessels detained at the port of St. Laurent, or Nootka, on the coast of California in the South Sea."[34]

When the Nootka Sound controversy erupted, Gouverneur Morris was still occupied in his futile efforts to open regular diplomatic relations with Great Britain (Chapter VI). Before he learned about the dispute, he observed a change in the attitude of the British officials with whom he was conferring. They began displaying marked satisfaction upon hearing Morris' reiterations of the United States' desire to establish cordial relations. Actually, they were disturbed by the possibility of Spanish and American co-operation in the heart of North America that might at last wrest the Northwest posts from Britain's grasp and terminate its right, provided in the Treaty of Paris, to navigate the Mississippi. It is quite possible that the British might have offered substantial concessions to win American friendship at that time if Washington had not already revealed his hand by asking Morris to try to negotiate.[35] A conflict between Britain and Spain would obviously place a premium on American friendship, and the British took important diplomatic action in the matter before learning that Spain would agree to the Nootka demands.

On May 6, 1790, Lord Grenville, then British secretary for home affairs, instructed Lord Dorchester, governor of Quebec, to prepare for a possible war with Spain. Grenville, expressing concern that the United States might join forces with Spain to force Britain out of the Northwest, ordered Dorchester to send an agent to the United States capital to observe the actions of the American government and try to win its friendship. Grenville made it clear that the emissary was to have no formal commission but was merely to establish informal contacts with American officials.[36]

The task was assigned to Major George Beckwith, who had served in the

[34] In the course of this study the Republican *National Gazette* (issues of 1791–93), and the Federalist newspapers, the weekly *Gazette of the United States* (issues of 1790–1800) and the *New York Evening Post* (issues of 1801–1804), were useful sources for determining the sentiments of the time.

[35] This view is presented by A. L. Burt in *The United States, Great Britain, and British North America, from the Revolution to the Establishment of Peace after the War of 1812* (New Haven, 1940), 109.

[36] Brymner, 131–33.

British army in the United States during the Revolution and was rather well disposed toward the new republic. Beckwith's orders reflected Grenville's instructions. He was to survey the possibility of an Anglo-American alliance against Spain, but any suggestions he made to the Americans were to be presented as though they had originated with him. He was not to make any move that could in any way obligate the British government or Beckwith's superiors in Canada.[37] Hamilton was not deceived. In an early conference at New York he had no difficulty in forcing Beckwith to reveal the true nature of his mission.

In *Number 7*, Julian P. Boyd makes a concerted attack on Hamilton for his conduct with Beckwith and for his report to Washington on their conferences. The essence of Boyd's accusation is that Beckwith did not initially propose an alliance with the United States and that Hamilton witnessed falsely to Washington when he reported that Beckwith had done so. Hamilton, Boyd asserts, "gave the false impression that the proposal of an alliance had come from the British ministry by way of Dorchester." Boyd admits that Dorchester "had indeed authorized Beckwith to say for him: 'I think the interests of the United States, in case of a war, may be more effectually served by a junction with Great Britain, than otherwise,' " but adds that "this was very far from suggesting or proposing an alliance."[38] But is there such a sharp distinction between "proposing an alliance" and urging the United States to join Britain in a war against Spain? Can one assume that Beckwith, instructed to convince the United States that it should enter the war alongside Britain against Spain, would have avoided the use of the word "alliance?"

Boyd also asserts that "nowhere" in Dorchester's letter to Beckwith can be found "a trace of a British proposal for an alliance with the United States."[39] Dorchester's letter, given in full as what Boyd calls a "supporting document," proves the opposite. In it Beckwith is instructed to "express my [Dorchester's] hope, that neither the appearance of a war with Spain, nor its actually taking place, will make any alteration in the good disposition of the United States to establish a firm friendship and Alliance with Great Britain to the Mutual advantage of both Countries; I am persuaded it can

[37] *Ibid.*, 143–44. Grenville was secretary of state for foreign affairs from 1792 to 1801 and prime minister from 1805 to 1806.

[38] Boyd, *Number 7*, 51–52.

[39] *Ibid.*, 46–47.

make none on the part of Great Britain."[40] In other words, Britain still wanted the alliance, and Dorchester hoped the United States would agree to it. Boyd tries to make the case against Hamilton more binding with censorious words and phrases, referring to Hamilton's "bold deception" and "unreliability" and terming him "as devious as he was bold." Boyd does not directly attack the wisdom of Hamilton's diplomatic goals but rather his ethics. In doing so, he relies much too heavily on the discrepancies between the respective reports of Hamilton and Beckwith on their conferences. Any student of diplomacy knows that wide variations customarily appear in reports of diplomats sitting on different sides of the conference table, with no necessary imputations of duplicity. Historians have never taken very seriously the old idea that the minister of foreign affairs expects each of his ambassadors to report every trend and every conversation with the unerring accuracy of a barometer. Relevant source materials fail to support any contention that Hamilton conducted himself in a manner that can fairly be characterized as "less than honorable."

While Beckwith was negotiating "unofficially," in London the British were drawing up plans to launch a naval attack on New Orleans. An overland campaign against Mexico from New Orleans was also being contemplated, as was a naval attack on South America, to be led by Sir Archibald Campbell.[41] Indeed, until Spain acceded to the Nootka demands, Great Britain was making ready "to seize the heart of North America for herself and erect the remainder of Spanish America into a client state."[42] Pitt believed that the Venezuelan revolutionary Miranda could induce the people of Spanish America to rise and help drive out the Spaniards. According to J. Holland Rose, Pitt's biographer, "Hopes ran high in London that Spain would be crippled by the action of her own sons in the New World, a fitting return for her assisting the revolt of the English colonists a decade earlier."[43] Apparently Miranda had no direct correspondence with Hamilton during this crisis, perhaps because the controversy was settled relatively quickly.

[40] *Ibid.*, 143.

[41] Robertson, *Life of Miranda*, I, 108.

[42] William Ray Manning, "The Nootka Sound Controversy," American Historical Association *Annual Report* for 1904 (1905), 414. This account of the controversy is the standard one. See also F. J. Turner, "English Policy Toward America in 1790–1791," *American Historical Review*, VII (July, 1902), 716.

[43] J. Holland Rose, *William Pitt and National Revival* (London, 1911), 569.

A London news dispatch of June, 1790, stated that "the question 'Are we to have a war?' had thrust 'How d'ye do?' out of place." In a British editorial written a month later it was observed that "it is more than probable, from the vigor of the Ministry, and the high and superior condition of our fleet, that an important blow may be struck before the 20th of this month."[44]

The British military plans were well under way before the Nootka Sound controversy became known in the United States. When the news, accompanied by a report that British forces in Canada were drilling intensively, reached President Washington, he concluded that the British would expect to march the Canadian troops across American territory to attack Spanish positions in Louisiana. He asked advice from each department head, the vice-president, and the chief justice about what answer to give Dorchester should he ask permission to cross United States territory.

Washington's apprehensions about a possible expedition from Canada proved groundless. Indeed, it was the one move the British had not the least intention of making. While they were mildly concerned about the possibility of a joint Spanish and American attack on the Northwest posts, they certainly did not contemplate any immediate invasion of the United States.[45]

Washington's advisers, uncertain of Britain's intentions, found the anticipated hostilities a grave issue. Washington received a number of carefully reasoned recommendations about how to contend with the immediate diplomatic situation and its ancillary issues. The advice Washington received was of a diverse nature. Secretary of State Jefferson believed that no reply at all should be given to the British if they should ask to march across American soil. He saw possibilities of driving a hard bargain with both disputants. Vice-President Adams and Chief Justice Jay would refuse to grant passage but would not favor resorting to war if the British disregarded the refusal. Secretary of War Knox and Secretary of the Treasury Hamilton did not answer the main question explicitly. They believed that the final decision should depend upon the circumstances under which permission was asked or the expedition undertaken, but essentially they were strongly inclined toward granting passage. Hamilton definitely advised granting it, provided the British would make certain concessions in return.

The positions taken by Hamilton and Jefferson during the emergency

[44] Reprinted in *Gazette of the United States,* September 4, 29, 1790.

[45] Bemis, *Jay's Treaty,* 72.

deserve detailed consideration. Hamilton believed that the crisis called for a review of all aspects of American diplomacy. His thirty-page statement to Washington is of special importance as a detailed summary of his approach to foreign policy. It is his most comprehensive discourse on the subject of America's relations with other countries.[46] Jefferson's position and the instructions he sent to the nation's representatives abroad are particularly significant, too, in that they illustrate his broad understanding of the basic ways of the European diplomats and his views on means by which American interests could be advanced during conflicts among Old World imperialists. The objectives Hamilton and Jefferson sought were similar, but there were significant differences in the procedures they recommended.[47]

Hamilton believed that the President should call a special session of Congress and make intensive preparations for war, meanwhile opening negotiations to determine what concessions could be gained in return for an agreement that the United States would not participate in the impending war, or conversely, for an agreement to support one or the other belligerent. He envisaged the possibility that the United States might go to war against either Spain or Britain, depending on military and diplomatic developments; but co-operating with Spain was far more unpalatable to him than working with Britain. He would carefully avoid any agreement with Spain unless France entered the fray, and he would make no agreement with either side until a clear understanding had been reached about the contribution the United States would make to the war effort and the territorial and other concessions that would be granted to the United States during or after the conflict.

Both Hamilton and Jefferson hoped to gain the fruits of victory without actually going to war. Both were convinced that an Anglo-Spanish conflict would present a splendid opportunity for obtaining redress of grievances from each belligerent, but both believed any such gains were to be sought primarily through negotiation. "It is certain," said Hamilton, "that there can hardly be a situation less adapted to war." The United States had "much to dread from war; much to expect from peace." He was disturbed by the possibility that the British might succeed in seizing Spanish territory on the Gulf; but even if they did, the United States would be gaining strength

[46] Hamilton to Washington, September 15, 1790, *HWL*, IV, 313–42.

[47] The most reliable collection of the opinions is found in Worthington C. Ford, *The United States and Spain in 1790* (Brooklyn, 1890).

while Britain was acquiring debts, and thereafter Britain would be cautious about provoking the new nation.

Hamilton never lost sight of the financial goals he advocated for the nation. He approached the issue with the fulfillment of those goals in mind, which called for free-flowing channels of trade within the country and with foreign nations. Washington's request for advice did not mention trade, but in his reply the young secretary pointed out the implications for United States commerce. The young nation should cultivate "commercial . . . intercourse with all the world on the broadest basis of reciprocal privilege." The nation's "true policy," therefore, was "to cultivate neutrality." Any "permanent interest" or "particular connection" with any foreign power should be avoided. Any alliance that might be made with Britain or Spain should be of short duration.

Hamilton did not reply directly to Washington's main question about how to answer a possible request for passage across American territory, but he did point out that the troops would move through uninhabited territory for the most part and that a refusal would presumably be followed by a forced passage, since Britain would not be likely to ask permission without having decided beforehand to go ahead irrespective of American wishes. He believed that the people of the United States would be inclined to consider American refusal as an attempt to protect Spain; and in such a critical situation, in which the nation was likely to become involved in war, he insisted that it was of the utmost necessity for the administration to have the support of the people. A refusal would be the wise course if it could be determined that Britain would take no for an answer, but he believed that the nation would have no feasible choice but to fight if Britain persisted in going ahead after having been told to stay out. Unlike Jefferson, he thought it would be unwise to refuse to answer the British, or even to give an evasive reply, in which case they would probably feel constrained to seize the American-held fort on the Wabash River, thereby precipitating another Anglo-American war. "It is a *sound maxim*," he declared, "that a state had better hazard any calamities than submit tamely to absolute disgrace."

For once Hamilton's clear, practical mind did not fashion a precise, detailed plan of action to be followed in the anticipated crisis. The remarkable ability he frequently displayed to come forward promptly with concrete solutions—the ability that has earned him the title "administrative architect of the new government"[48]—was not in evidence on this occasion. His hesitancy to outline particulars is obvious in the following passage:

> If even it should be taken for granted that our consent or refusal would have no influence either way, it would not even then cease to be disagreeable to concur in a thing apparently so inauspicious to our interests. And it deserves attention that our concurrency might expose us to the imputation either of want of foresight to discover a danger, or of vigor to withstand it.

The national goals, however, were perfectly clear to Hamilton, and he had no hesitation in naming them. The United States must eventually take the Northwest into its territory and must gain possession of the Mississippi Valley and the Floridas. Believing the Mississippi region of greater importance than the Northwest, he was convinced that the outlet to the Gulf of Mexico was essential for the unity of the nation.

Obviously France would not be eager to help transfer Louisiana from one ally to another, and apparently it did not occur to Hamilton to exert pressure on France toward that end. Both he and Jefferson looked with equanimity upon a course of action that would lead logically to the termination of the United States' alliance with France. In view of the long-standing rivalry for empire between Britain and Spain, Hamilton foresaw an agreement with Britain that would enrich the United States at Spain's expense. He was disposed to survey, with caution, every such possibility.

In his correspondence during this period one detects a much softer attitude toward Britain than that which was so common in his writings of the 1780's. The French Revolution had not yet reached the stage at which its repellent qualities would turn him toward Britain. Wartime passions had had time to cool, and Hamilton's admiration for the British system of government no doubt helped make the idea of a temporary alliance less repugnant.

Both Hamilton and Jefferson at length agreed that war between Spain and Britain was likely. Hamilton was the first to decide that open hostilities were inevitable. Though at the time he submitted his lengthy opinion on the crisis, he expressed doubt whether France would assist Spain. Upon receiving news from Europe the next month, however, he came to believe that war was almost certain, with France and Spain allied against Britain.[49]

[48] White, *The Federalists*, 127.

[49] Hamilton to Washington, October 17, 1790, *HWL*, IX, 472–73.

Gouverneur Morris reported from London that the general opinion there was that Spain would yield, but added his own opinion that the Spaniards would fight rather than yield the concessions Pitt demanded. "If Spain submits," Morris wrote, "she may as well give up her American dominions." Later he reported that the French National Assembly was renewing the old alliance with Spain and that the French were "arming as rapidly as their disjointed efforts would permit."[50] Jefferson believed that both Britain and Spain would pay a good price for American neutrality. Once convinced that France would participate in the conflict, Jefferson expressed the first desire of his heart—that the United States could remain neutral so that the New World might "fatten on the follies" of the Old. "If we are wise," he said, "we shall become wealthy."[51] Other Americans held a similar view. John Steele of North Carolina, among others, believed that "America must be benefited by the struggle,"[52] for they assumed that the belligerents would pay well for American products.

Jefferson gave no advice about arming the nation for possible combat. Apparently he did not think that the United States would become actively engaged[53]; but even if he had done so, his faith in the militia would have made him believe it unnecessary for the nation to undertake extensive military preparations. He hoped to utilize to the utmost the obvious diplomatic advantages the situation presented. Serious in his intentions, yet he must have smiled as he worked out his plans for extorting from the great powers of western Europe compensation for the wrongs they had inflicted upon his country.

Jefferson shared his contemporaries' suspicion of and dislike for Spain.[54] He was convinced that if Spain persisted in its autocratic behavior toward the United States, war was inevitable.[55] As Malone says, "To the Spanish Jefferson often sounded like a swashbuckler."[56] Certain that the opportunity

[50] Morris to Washington, May 29, September 18, 1790, *ASPFR*, I, 123–26.

[51] Jefferson to Edward Rutledge, July 4, 1790, Jefferson to Gilmer, July 25, 1790, *JW*, VIII, 61, 63.

[52] Steele to Joseph Winston, June 20, 1790, Henry McGilbert Wagstaff (ed.), *The Papers of John Steele* (Raleigh, 1924), I, 66.

[53] Bemis, "Thomas Jefferson," *The American Secretaries of State*, II, 42.

[54] William K. Woolery, *The Relation of Thomas Jefferson to American Foreign Policy, 1783–1793* (Baltimore, 1927), 74–75 (hereafter cited as *The Relation of Thomas Jefferson to American Foreign Policy*).

[55] Jefferson to Short, August 10, 1790, *JW*, VIII, 81; Jefferson to Carmichael, August 22, 1790, *ibid.*, XVII, 303.

[56] Malone, II, 408.

"must not be lost," Jefferson instructed William Carmichael, American chargé d'affaires at Madrid, to demand the immediate opening of the Mississippi to American navigation, along with a "port of deposit." This concession was not something to be bargained for but was to be preliminary to general negotiations.[57]

To William Short, United States representative to France, Jefferson sent instructions for dealing with the American ally. France was to understand that the United States would be hostile to Spain "if she does not yield our right to the common use of the Mississippi, and the means of *using* and *securing* it."[58] With those instructions he enclosed a communication to Lafayette, to be delivered to him in case war had already broken out, requesting the Frenchman to urge his government to impress upon the Spaniards the necessity of granting the United States' demands regarding the Mississippi. He pointed out that France should be able to impress upon Spain the wisdom of reducing the number of potential enemies. Jefferson, it is clear, was not so devoted to the Franco-American alliance that he allowed it to divert him from pursuing what he considered to be legitimate national interests.

Jefferson's approach to Great Britain was little if any more circumspect. Standing firmly on the essential feature of the "no transfer" principle (destined for a fuller expression and a long life in subsequent American diplomacy), he directed Gouverneur Morris to make it clear to the British that "we should contemplate a change of neighbors with extreme uneasiness" and that the United States was no less interested than European nations in a "due balance" on her borders. The United States would prefer to remain neutral, he assured Morris; but in a startling climax he instructed Morris to tell the British that the United States would remain neutral provided Britain would abide by the Treaty of Paris—that is, relinquish the Northwest posts—and refrain from taking over Spanish possessions north of the Gulf of Mexico. Jefferson's contempt for any government that would embark upon an unnecessary war was reflected in his comment that the British "cannot complain that the other dominions of Spain would be so narrow as not to leave them room enough for conquest."[59]

Though there was a distinctly quixotic touch to Jefferson's procedure of

[57] Jefferson to Carmichael, August 2, 1790, *JW*, VII, 71–72.

[58] Jefferson to Short, August 10, 1790, *ibid.*, VIII, 79. Italics added.

[59] August 12, 1790, *ibid.*, 85.

threatening war without recommending military preparations at home, no harm came of it. Historians have encountered greater difficulty in trying to explain his statement to Carmichael that it was "not our interest to cross the Mississippi for ages, and will never be our interest to remain united with those who do."[60] Malone believes that if Spain had been willing to cede to the United States all Spanish-held territory east of the Mississippi, Jefferson would have been "willing to guarantee all of her possessions west of that river." Jefferson was "willing to be inconsistent," says Malone, inasmuch as "the fixed point in his policy was the American interest."[61] Yet what secretary of state has not had this "fixed point"? It is a justification that can excuse discordant policies of the most inconsistent administrator who ever lived, provided only that he is patriotic.

After defending Jefferson's readiness to forgo future claims to the lands west of the Mississippi, Malone next deals Hamilton a sharp blow. Hamilton and Jay, he says, "catered to small and relatively localized economic groups," and can therefore "be more correctly described as 'sectionalists' than can Jefferson."[62] Certainly Jefferson would never have applied the word "sectionalist" to the nation's leading Federalist; on the contrary, it was Hamilton's strong nationalism that roused Jefferson's ire. No American living in 1790 was less "sectionalist" or more nationalist than Hamilton. Doubtless Jefferson knew that Hamilton was advocating the acquisition of Louisiana and the Floridas as a means of preserving the Union. There is not the slightest evidence that Hamilton ever looked upon the Mississippi as the nation's ultimate western boundary.

The answer John Adams delivered to Washington's query was clear and emphatic. If Dorchester should ask permission to take troops across American territory, "the answer . . . should be a refusal, in terms clear and decided, but guarded and dignified" and expressed in a tone that would allow the nation to refrain from going to war without humiliation if the British should march in defiance of Washington's refusal. Adams added, as did Hamilton, that the American people "would not willingly support a war" to repel or punish the British in that particular instance.[63]

Adams' note to the President had a somewhat lecturing or condescending tone. It was unfortunate, he said, that the United States did not have min-

[60] Jefferson to Carmichael, August 22, 1790, *ibid.*, XVII, 306.

[61] Malone, II, 311.

[62] *Ibid.*, 409.

[63] Adams to Washington, August 29, 1790, *AW*, VIII, 498–99.

isters "of large views, mature age, information, and judgment, and strict integrity at the courts of France, Spain, London, and the Hague. Early and authentic intelligence from those courts may be of more importance than the expense." Washington probably agreed with his vice-president on each point; but the implied criticism and the tone in which the note was written, probably explain why Adams was not thereafter regularly sought out for advice.

The Nootka Sound controversy died down when France failed to come to Spain's support. Spain's acquiescence to Britain's stern demands that her far-ranging traders be allowed to carry on their operations in the disputed area and in other territories that Spain had claimed but had not effectively occupied weakened Spanish hold on North America and indirectly enhanced the prestige of the United States vis-à-vis Spain. Anglo-American relations improved somewhat; Britain came to see that the United States could not be ignored. Yet the young nation had no reason to rejoice overmuch in Spain's losses to Great Britain, the more formidable foe, as later events proved.

Peace among the European nations was to last for a few more years. Then would come one of the most eventful decades in all of American history, commencing with the outbreak of war between France and England in 1793. During that ten-year period the American Northwest was to be secured, Spain would surrender the disputed section of West Florida to the United States and open the Mississippi to American navigation, and France would acquire and then transfer to the United States the Louisiana Territory. That series of remarkable successes would place American nationhood on a solid basis. The interesting, though finally inconclusive, year of 1790 foreshadowed the events to come. In planning how to deal with a hypothetical situation, the American leaders gained experience for coming events. It was almost as though a dress rehearsal had been staged for future drama.

CHAPTER VIII

Hamilton and the French Revolution

THE PEOPLE of the United States were elated by the news of the outbreak of the French Revolution. At the beginning this reaction was almost unanimous.[1] Americans assumed that the uprising was an afterglow of the American struggle for liberty. James Madison, a leading member in the House of Representatives from 1789 to 1797, was convinced that "the light which [was] chasing darkness and despotism from the old world [was] but an emanation from that which . . . procured . . . liberty in the new."[2] Americans had not foreseen the French Revolution, but they were generally aware of the oppressive conditions under which the French people had been living.[3] The alliance of 1778 and the resulting comradeship in arms still called forth friendly emotions from the people of the United States. They responded favorably to the watchcry of Paris: "liberty, equality, fraternity." They were delighted by the thought of "fraternal" relationships with the people of France.

Newspapers of the day, such as they were, featured the good news from France. Even the early, indecisive meetings of the States General in May, 1789, were described in glowing terms in the *Gazette of the United States* (owing to the usual delays in overseas mail, the European dispatch of May 28 was not published in the *Gazette* until August 19). The *Gazette* was jubilant in reporting that the Third Estate, presuming to act for the French nation and in defiance of the king, the nobles, and the clergy, had formed the National Constituent Assembly and that the assembly had taken the famous "tennis court oath" not to dissolve until it had written a new constitution for France and eliminated the abuses of the old regime. The *Gazette*

[1] Beveridge, *Life of John Marshall*, II, 4ff. Hamilton mentioned the American sentiment in "Americanus," No. 1, February 1, 1794, *HWL*, V, 75.

[2] Madison to Edmund Pendleton, March 4, 1790, *MW*, VI, 7.

[3] C. D. Hazen, *Contemporary American Opinions of the French Revolution* (Baltimore, 1897), 14. Hazen's work is extremely superficial and his references are unclear, yet he made some thoughtful generalizations.

declared that the people of France had "at last carried their point" and that "the calm, determined firmness of the Commons" had "overset . . . the intrigues of the Nobles."[4]

The initial American tendency to regard the radical forces in Paris as representatives of the people locked in combat with scheming nobles was of great importance in shaping American public opinion. That view persisted among a great many Americans, allowing them to condone years of anarchy and bloodshed, particularly after the Federalists, who were popularly considered to be "upper-class" Americans, began to criticize the French radicals. Four years later it was this situation that gave Genêt hope of having his way in the United States in spite of the opposition of the Federalist administration. But that was to come later. At the beginning—before the extreme radical forces formed in Paris—the Federalists were almost as exuberant as the Republicans in praising the work of the National Assembly.

Washington wrote to Michel Guillaume de Crèvecoeur in 1789, that "the American Revolution, or the peculiar light of the age seems to have opened the eyes of almost every nation in Europe." To another correspondent he expressed his joy in seeing "that the American Revolution [had] been productive of happy consequences on both sides of the Atlantic."[5] Policy, as well as emotion, helped shape Washington's attitude toward France. He treasured the alliance because he knew it could be vitally important to his country in the future, as it had been in the past. He was pleased to see that his countrymen shared his view. Soon after his inauguration as president he considered observing the anniversary of the alliance by leading the nation in a "great entertainment" every year. Such a national holiday would have kept Franco-American friendship always fresh in the people's minds. Five months later, when the revolution was expanding, he declared that it was "of so wonderful a nature that the mind [could] hardly realize the fact," and it was "of such magnitude and of so momentous a nature that we hardly yet dare to form a conjecture about it." He did not believe that the commotions in France were directed against Louis XVI, whom he still spoke of as "our great and beloved Friend and Ally."[6] Jefferson later recalled that he

[4] Dispatch dated June 29 from Paris, printed in the *Gazette of the United States* on September 12, 1789.

[5] Washington to Crèvecoeur, April 10, 1789, *WW*, XXX, 281; Washington to Catherine Macaulay Graham, January 9, 1790, *ibid.*, 497.

[6] "Queries on a Line of Conduct to Be Pursued by the President," May 10, 1789, *ibid.*, 319–20; Washington to Morris, October 13, 1789, *ibid.*, 443; Washington to Lafayette, October 14, 1789, *ibid.*, 448–49; Washington to the King of France, October 9, 1789, *ibid.*, 432.

was first to tell the President "the news of the King's flight and capture," adding, "I never saw him so dejected by any event in my life."[7]

Though from the beginning Hamilton (and other Federalists) had some reservations about the French Revolution, he was generally pleased by the news from France. To him, a nation's "struggle for liberty" was "respectable and glorious."[8] In his youth he had described the French as a people oppressed and justified in revolution. When the outbreak came, he rejoiced to see the French throw off their condition of "slavery" and claim "freedom."[9] Quick as always to determine the practical aspects of new developments, he was soon advising Jefferson that French commerce would probably expand rapidly under the new "free government" and thereby give the Franco-American commercial treaty real economic significance.[10] Other Americans, by and large, held similar views. Hamilton's Federalist friend Oliver Wolcott believed that the events in Europe were "concurring for the benefit of America."[11]

Jefferson, minister to France from 1785 to 1789, was a "privileged observer" of the outbreak. Through his advice to Lafayette and other Frenchmen he even exerted some personal influence on the movement. Unfortunately, in his letters he failed to describe the events in detail, as did Gouverneur Morris; but he made it clear that he approved the over-all purposes of the revolution, as he understood them, and his faith in the salutary effects of the uprising was enduring. France, he observed, had helped the United States win independence and had continued to be friendly to the young republic. Britain, in contrast, had tried to "exterminate" the Americans during the Revolution and had subsequently seized every opportunity to injure the new nation. In 1792, when it was called to his attention that innocent persons had met violent death in France, he compared them to innocent people who fall in battle. With "the liberty of the whole earth ... depending on the issue of the contest," he asked, "was ever such a prize won with so little innocent blood?" Indulging in his tendency toward exaggeration, he asserted that he would rather see "half the earth desolated" than to

[7] *The Anas*, *JW*, I, 301.

[8] Hamilton to Washington, April, 1793, *HWL*, IV, 386.

[9] "The Farmer Refuted," February 5, 1775, *ibid.*, I, 113; Hamilton to Washington, September 15, 1790, *ibid.*, IV, 333.

[10] Hamilton to Jefferson, January 11, 1791, *ibid.*, IV, 346.

[11] Wolcott to his father, Oliver Wolcott, Sr., May 8, 1790, Gibbs, I, 46.

see the French Revolution fail, for "were there but an Adam and an Eve left in every country, and left free, it would be better than it is now."[12]

When he assumed his duties as secretary of state in 1790, Jefferson was interested in improving trade relations with France, but he displayed less diligence than Hamilton in pursuing the matter. The French government actually did more than the American government to expand Franco-American commerce.[13] Progress was inhibited by disagreements concerning equivalents and reciprocities and by differing interpretations of terms in the existing commercial agreements and in the American tariff and tonnage laws of 1789 and 1790. Hamilton and Jefferson insisted, successfully, that these laws should apply equally to French and to other foreign ships and cargoes, even though the commercial treaty of 1778 and French legislation of 1784 seemed to imply mutually preferential treatment. Hamilton was eager for good relations with France, but he dreaded a commercial war with Britain. Jefferson thought he could attend to the disagreements with the French through direct negotiations without the necessity of making a new treaty. Both men were convinced that any new agreement or interpretation should provide full "reciprocity." Hamilton warned his colleague against making undue concessions to the French representative in the United States, a procedure that he believed might create "inconvenient precedents." The terms might not be honored by the French government, and such agreements might "beget discontents elsewhere"—that is, in Britain. Hamilton preferred that the negotiations be conducted at a high level, aimed toward a "new treaty of commerce."[14]

In *The Anas*, written several years later, Jefferson expressed his suspicion of Hamilton's motives in regard to trade treaties. He believed that the secretary of the treasury favored negotiating a commercial treaty with France as a prelude to a more binding treaty with Britain. Referring especially to Hamilton's informal discussions of November, 1791, with the French minister to the United States, Colonel Jean de Ternant, Jefferson said that his colleague's ultimate intention was to find a way to "attach" the United States to the mother country.[15] Apparently Hamilton was unaware of Jefferson's distrust, and the meager interdepartmental correspondence of

[12] Malone, II, 46, 180–237. Jefferson to Madison, August 28, 1789, *JW*, VII, 449; Jefferson to Short, January 3, 1793, *ibid.*, IX, 10.

[13] Jensen, *The New Nation*, 166–68.

[14] Hamilton to Jefferson, January 11, January 13, 1791, *HWL*, IV, 346–48.

[15] *The Anas*, JW, I, 297.

1791 indicates only mild jealousy between the two men and nowhere hints at such sharp animosity as that suggested in *The Anas*.

Discussions with French representatives, though inconclusive, were carried on in a spirit of moderation and restraint for the most part. Sometimes, however, a note of injured innocence slipped into the negotiations. Washington complained to Lafayette about the injurious "decrees of the National Assembly respecting our tobacco and oil." He added that he did not anticipate any "hasty measures" of retaliation on the part of Congress, the United States was fully aware of the "friendly disposition" of France, and he was convinced that harsh laws enacted by the assembly when it was preoccupied with other "important matters" would be corrected when a period of "calm deliberation" returned.[16] In this vein trade negotiations between the two nations continued, more or less sporadically and unmethodically, until 1793, when rising ill will toward Genêt's activities brought them to an end (see Chapter IX).[17]

Federalist approval of the revolution was, from the beginning, mixed with an element of doubt, which slowly ripened into misgivings, anxiety, and even dread. In the fall of 1789, Hamilton wrote to Lafayette confessing both "pleasure and apprehension" in the news from France. He expressed the fear that the movement might go too far and spoil through excesses the very benefits it aimed to obtain. Specifically, he feared "disagreements" among the French leaders, the "vehement character" of the French people, the "interested refractoriness" of the nobles, and "reveries" of French "philosophic politicians, who appear in the moment to have great influence, and who, being mere speculatists, may aim at more refinement than suits either with human nature or the composition of your nation." Further, he was afraid it would prove easier to "bring on" the people than to keep them "within proper bounds."[18]

Hamilton was at the point of mailing this letter when he received the startling news of the French legislation that had been passed on August 4, 1789, by which the nobility abandoned many of their ancient privileges and gave their support to the reformers. He penned a postscript to his letter

[16] Washington to Lafayette, July 28, 1791, *WW*, XXXI, 325.

[17] Alexander DeConde, "Franco-American Commerce: An Unrealized Hope," *Entangling Alliance: Politics and Diplomacy under George Washington* (Durham, 1958), Chap. V, 141–63 (hereafter cited as *Entangling Alliance*).

[18] Hamilton to Lafayette, October 6, 1789, *HWL*, IX, 460–62.

saying that the nobles' "patriotic and magnanimous policy" promised "good both to them and their country" and lessened some of his own "apprehensions." The letter foreshadowed many of his later criticisms of the revolution. He gave the uprising his fullest support as long as he believed it was promoting liberty, but he turned resolutely against it when he became convinced that it was producing too much "vehemence" and violence, moving against "human nature," and becoming too theoretical and impractical.

Americans generally failed to appreciate the magnitude of the problems facing the French people. They became uneasy and finally gravely disturbed as successive "solutions" proved ephemeral. Washington and his colleagues, though well acquainted with the history of the long-contested Civil War in England, expected the French to solve their problems promptly and in an orderly fashion. Had not the Constitution of the United States been written in a single summer and ratified without undue delay? The Federalists, particularly, tended to gloss over or ignore the fact that the French reformers were shattering centuries-old social and religious traditions, and they failed to see why so rich a nation as France could not quickly surmount its economic and financial problems. The issuance of assignats by the National Assembly appeared to illustrate the "weakness, folly and turbulence of the democratical government."[19]

Washington at length adopted this attitude, but with a keen sense of regret. He commented that solid accomplishment could be achieved only when the French leaders were imbued with "prudence," "perseverance," "disinterestedness," and "patriotism." He feared that the French were "making more haste than good speed"—a phrase he often used to criticize a skittish stagecoach driver. When the passing months failed to bring stability in France and other troubled areas of Europe, he openly deplored the "devastation," "preparations for war," "commotions," and "direful apprehensions" that seemed to be sweeping the Continent. No man was more sincere than Washington in his often expressed hopes that the condition of the people in every country would be bettered, and the happiness of mankind promoted.[20] He knew that wars in Europe might bring some advantages to the United States, but they would bring difficulties, too, on land and sea. Above all, his soul cried out against the human suffering

[19] Oliver Wolcott to his father, May 8, 1790, Gibbs, I, 46.

[20] Washington to the Marquis de la Luzerne, April 29, 1790, *WW*, XXXI, 40–41; Washington to David Humphreys, July 20, 1791, *ibid.*, 318–20.

inflicted by wars, most of which he was convinced were unnecessary. Probably no succeeding president, not even Woodrow Wilson, desired peace more ardently than did George Washington.

Gouverneur Morris was in France when the revolution began and returned there to serve as the American minister from 1792 to 1794. His correspondence of the period was characterized by cynicism about the motives of the revolutionaries and pessimism about prospects of any profitable outcome. France, he said, was "as near to anarchy as society can approach without dissolution." He regarded the failure of the Constitution of 1791, which was more than two years in formulation and survived less than a year, as "a natural accident to a thing which was all sail and no ballast." The French government, he thought, wanted to keep the peace with Great Britain, but he was afraid "the people" would not allow it. The "best picture" he could give of the French populace was that of "cattle before a thunder storm." Both Washington and Hamilton respected the quick-witted diplomat, and were doubtless influenced by his pungent criticisms.[21]

Hamilton's growing aversion to the turmoil in France was sharpened by the doom it spelled to his hopes of continued benefits from the alliance. Tones of regret permeated his references to France during the Nootka Sound controversy in 1790. He was dismayed by the possibility that the United States might have to go to war with Britain to preserve national honor and avoid further British encroachment. France was the "only weight," he said, that could be "thrown into the scale, capable of producing an equilibrium," and he did not expect to see "much order or vigor in the affairs of that country for a considerable period to come." He thought it possible that "the transition from slavery to liberty" might prove to be a "spring of great exertions" but added that "the ebullitions of enthusiasm must ever be a precarious reliance."[22]

Hamilton did not hesitate to lecture the French government whenever he felt the occasion warranted doing so. The death of Benjamin Franklin on April 17, 1790, proved to be such an occasion. The French people were deeply moved by his death, and their admiration for him brought forth a new burst of enthusiasm for things American. The French government decided to make a new effort "to cement the friendship and interests of the

[21] Morris to Washington, July 31, 1789, *MDL*, I, 143; *MDFR*, II, 572.

[22] Hamilton to Washington, September 15, 1790, *HWL*, IV, 333–34.

two nations."[23] The National Assembly conveyed to the American government a warm expression of appreciation for the great man.[24]

Hamilton drafted a reply to the National Assembly, which Washington dispatched verbatim. In the draft Hamilton elaborated upon Franklin's virtues, using those comments as a springboard into a brief discourse on the essential qualities of good government and the features of the French system that should be preserved. They complimented the French on their efforts to obtain "the blessings of liberty" and recalled in warm terms the period when "the individuals as well as . . . the government" of France helped Americans win their liberty. He expressed a "sincere, cordial, and earnest wish" that the labors of the National Assembly would produce a constitution "wisely conciliating the indispensable principles of public order with the enjoyment and exercise of the essential rights of man." He clearly related a "virtuous policy" and "the true principles of liberty" to laws and to "public order." He even tried to prop up the tottering throne of Louis XVI by calling him "the friend of the people over whom he reigns."[25]

When Hamilton received the news, in November, 1792, that Louis XVI had been deposed and that royalty had been "abolished," he adopted a sterner attitude. From his knowledge of world history—especially English history—he assumed, quite logically, that the king would eventually be restored to the throne. He saw "no ground to conclude" that the revolutionary government would "be of long duration." In the meantime, however, there was the immediate question of payments on the debt to France. For more than a year Hamilton, with Washington's approval, had been making intermittent payments to French Minister Ternant in Philadelphia, to help relieve a famine that was ravaging the French colony of Haiti.[26] Ternant had reported this assistance to his government and had praised Hamilton for the liberal manner in which he had responded to the emergency.[27]

After Louis was deposed, Hamilton, though willing to continue the payments to Ternant, advised Washington to withhold any further regular

[23] DeConde, *Entangling Alliance*, 156.

[24] Bigelow, *The Works of Benjamin Franklin*, XII, 200–201.

[25] Cabinet Paper, January 27, 1791, *HWL*, IV, 349–51. Lodge incorrectly gave the date as 1792.

[26] Hamilton to Washington, September 22, 1791, *ibid.*, 354.

[27] Ternant to Montmorin, September 28, 1791, Frederick J. Turner (ed.), *Correspondence of the French Ministers to the United States, 1791–1797*, American Historical Association *Annual Report* for 1903, (1904), II, 49 (hereafter cited as *Correspondence of the French Ministers*).

payments directly to the French government. Such payments, even though a "reimbursement, in course," might be used to bolster the strength of the revolutionaries and, in view of the probable restoration of Louis, "would doubtless be rejected" by the succeeding government.[28]

At the same time Hamilton, pointing out that Ternant had been sent to the United States by Louis, raised the question "whether the commission to Mr. Ternant was not virtually superseded." He urged the President "to avoid the explicit recognition of any regular authority in any person." Hamilton realized that he could not do business with a deposed king, but he could recommend withholding recognition and support from the upstart regime, which he clearly regarded as unprincipled and temporary.

This recommendation represented a significant shift in Hamilton's views from the previous year. Though even then he had been critical of the National Assembly, he had recognized that it had come to power in a constitutional manner and had been recognized by the king. Under those conditions he had been willing, as he had told Jefferson on April 15, 1791, to make "as large payments as . . . practicable" to France.[29] To Hamilton, the dethronement of Louis nullified the legality of the French government.

It should be pointed out that Hamilton and his colleagues lacked accurate information about the course of the French Revolution. There is but slight resemblance between contemporary French newspaper accounts reprinted in the United States during the 1790's and the accepted accounts of modern historians. Even eyewitness accounts provided Morris and Monroe were often based more on hopes or fears than on authentic information. Hamilton attributed such events as the fearful September Massacres of 1792 to explicit designs of self-seeking French politicians. This conclusion was entirely plausible, in view of the failure of the Legislative Assembly members, or of leaders like Georges Danton, of the powerful Commune of Paris, to denounce the bloody deeds; yet the modern view is that the massacres resulted as much from spontaneous outbursts of public passion as from the deliberate connivance of politicians.

According to Hamilton's later appraisal, France was the aggressor in the European wars of the 1790's, beginning with the conflict that erupted on April 20, 1792, when France declared war on Austria. In that conflict he

[28] Hamilton to Washington, November 19, 1792, *HWL*, IV, 362–66.
[29] Cabinet Paper, *ibid.*, 353.
[30] Hamilton to Washington, May 2, 1793, *ibid.*, 398–99.

knew that he lacked the "exact information" to "pronounce upon [the causes] with confidence."[30] When French armies moved successfully into the Netherlands, however, after that nation had joined a coalition to defeat the revolutionary government, he thought he perceived a predetermined plan of aggression. When it became apparent that the new French government under the National Convention keenly relished the victories its armies were winning, Hamilton grew fearful that those victories threatened the balance of power in Europe. When one nation threatened to upset the independence of neighboring countries, he said, those countries were justified in joining forces to put down the aggressor. He was exasperated by two declarations made by the French National Convention in November, 1792, offering assistance "to every people who wish to recover their liberty." He considered it "justifiable and meritorious" to assist an oppressed nation "in the act of liberating" itself, but he could not countenance "a general invitation to insurrection and revolution." By this decree, he said, France was doing what it had "most complained of"—interfering in the internal government of other nations. He was vexed still more deeply when on November 15, 1792, the convention decreed that France would "treat as enemies" any people "desirous of preserving their prince and privileged" classes. He deemed this assertion an "outrage little short of a declaration of war against every government of Europe and . . . a violent attack upon the freedom of opinion of all mankind."[31] Hamilton's friend and admirer James Kent, justice of the New York Supreme Court, also anathematized such utterances of the "French rulers," who, he said, "in 1793, adopted the intolerance of the Koran, and began to propagate their new faith by the sword."[32]

Hamilton pointed out that "France first declared and began the war against Austria, Prussia, Savoy, Holland, England, and Spain." France had violated the "laws of nations" and principles of justice by making "formal and definitive annexations" of territories over which its arms had temporarily prevailed and had explicitly violated its treaties in decreeing free navigation on the Schelde River.

The point of war guilt was very important in Hamilton's mind, and it did

[31] "Pacificus," No. 2, July 3, 1793, *ibid.*, 447–54; Hamilton to Washington, May 2, 1793, *ibid.*, 405.

[32] First published in the *Albany Centinel* following Hamilton's death in 1804; included in Coleman, *The Death of Major-General Alexander Hamilton*; reprinted, with an introduction and notes by Douglass Adair, in *The Historian*, Vol. XIX (February, 1957), 182–201. See especially p. 197.

much to influence his recommendations for action. Yet the distinctions he tried to make, and the shades of meaning he intended to convey, are not immediately obvious. In 1784, while trying to induce his fellow New Yorkers to observe the peace treaty, he had commented that, "as to the *external effects* of a war, the . . . law of nations knows no distinction between the justice or injustice of the quarrel." In the second of his "Pacificus" essays, dated July 3, 1793, he held that "when a war breaks out between two nations, all others, in regard to the *positive rights* of the parties and their *positive duties* towards them, are bound to consider it as equally just on both sides."[33]

Hamilton's point was that, in executing a treaty or in measuring the rights and duties of neutrals, a person or a government must not be influenced by the supposed guilt or aggression of one or the other party. He was firm, however, in holding that the question of war guilt should be taken into account when private or public attitudes were being formulated. Even though he had gained prominence in his own country largely through his activities in its struggle for independence—and he appeared to enjoy active field operations—yet he had a deep and lasting hatred of war. In this respect he and Jefferson were in agreement, though at times they differed widely in their beliefs about when war was necessary and what course of action should be pursued to prepare for, or prevent, one.

Hamilton's personal reactions to the most important events of the later years of the French Revolution are worthy of comment for the light they shed on his evolving theories of the United States' place in the community of nations. The mob violence that characterized the revolution evoked from Hamilton his sharpest denunciation. No other aspect of the deluge so quickly aroused his anger toward the revolutionaries. It called to mind the New York mobs attacking Tories and destroying their property in 1775. He had opposed the mobs in 1775, and the years had not tempered his antipathy for such mindless action. To him the essential element of reform was ever calm, deliberative thought and planning.[34] If fighting became necessary, it should be conducted according to a carefully prearranged plan with a definite goal in view. "Violent and unjust measures," he said, "commonly defeat their own purpose."[35] He accepted Morris' appraisal that a true picture of Paris, like that of an Indian warrior, must be painted in colors of red and black.[36]

[33] *HWL*, IV, 240–449. Italics added.
[34] "Americanus," No. 1, February 1, 1794, *ibid.*, V, 75–77.
[35] "The Warning," No. 2, February 7, 1797, *ibid.*, VI, 240.

The September Massacres of 1792 were a matter of history before news of the outrage reached the United States. The Reign of Terror, which reached its height a year later and continued its horrendous course until Robespierre died on the guillotine on July 28, 1794, drew fire from Hamilton again and again. He had no patience with Jefferson's assessment that improper trials and unjust executions were a small price to pay for the victories for freedom being won in France.[37] Hamilton did not have enough information to understand that the National Convention accepted the Reign of Terror because it seemed the only course that would assure popular support for a revolutionary government seeking to survive the onslaughts of reactionary Frenchmen at home and hostile armies abroad.[38]

Hamilton's unrelenting opposition to the revolutionaries exemplified a quality in his character that sometimes limited his vision. He was inclined to be a purist. There were but few inconsistencies in his own life, and he tended to demand comparable stability in others. Certain that his own motives were upright, he was reluctant to weigh seriously the contrary conclusions of others, especially when they appeared to involve a compromise of principles. To him the Reign of Terror violated accepted principles of law and order and the basic precepts of justice. He fiercely condemned it in the first of the "Americanus" essays, early in 1794. He lamented that the "CAUSE OF TRUE LIBERTY" had "received a deep wound in the mismanagements of it." He saw the "horrid and disgusting scenes" of the Terror as "proofs of atrocious depravity in the most influential leaders of the revolution." He called Marat and Robespierre "assassins still reeking with the blood of their fellow-citizens."[39]

Above all, Hamilton denounced the king's execution, in 1793. If the king had really committed treason, Hamilton asked, why was not the evidence of that crime published to the world? He did not dispute the right of a people to take the life of a king who was a proved traitor, but this particular act seemed to him, and others, to have been prompted only by political expediency.[40] Hamilton taunted fellow Americans who in 1792 had been

36 Morris to Hamilton, October 17, 1793, Jared Sparks (ed.), *The Life of Gouverneur Morris, with Selections from His Correspondence and Miscellaneous Papers* (Boston, 1832), II, 368.

37 Jefferson to William Short, January 3, 1793, *JW*, IX, 10.

38 For a brief but judicious appraisal of the Reign of Terror, see Paul H. Beik and Laurence LaFore, *Modern Europe: A History since 1500* (New York, 1959), 377–82.

39 *HWL*, V, 76–77. Hamilton's capitals.

40 Gouverneur Morris, who had tried to help the king escape from France, wrote ironically that Louis's chief "crime" was in "not suffering his Throat to be cut which was certainly a nefarious Plot against the People and a manifest Violation of the Bill of Rights" (*MDFR*, II, 573).

quick to denounce anybody mentioning any "bounds to our obligations to Louis" and in 1793 were so ready to believe and repeat "all the unproved and contradicted allegations" that had been brought against him.[41]

Hamilton was not moved by various French defenses based on the "brotherhood of man" or by flattering attentions paid to him. In 1792 the French government conferred French citizenship upon him because they considered him among the *amis de l'humanité et de la société* and assumed that Hamilton considered the French people *parmi vos Frères*.[42] It is likely that Hamilton's feelings were far from brotherly at the time.

At the beginning of the revolution Hamilton was convinced that the dominant interest of the revolutionaries was the welfare of France, a sentiment in which he, as a keen nationalist, heartily concurred. After only a few months of political turmoil, however, he came to believe that their concern was merely for a faction, a clique, or their own persons. He doubtless agreed with Morris' dry comment that in 1792 every individual in the French government was engaged in defending himself or attacking his neighbor.[43] In 1801, in a speech summing up the events of the previous decade, Hamilton deplored the succession by which one group of men built "their transient power . . . upon the tombs of another."[44] Taking a global view of the world, he saw it as a planet of nations, and he thought of men, not only as members of the human race, but as members of those nations. The needs of each people differed, and therefore each government "must be fitted to a nation, as much as a coat to the individual; and . . . what may be good at Philadelphia may be bad at Paris, and ridiculous at Petersburg."[45]

Until 1795, French attacks on American ships were less serious than British depredations, about which Hamilton complained vigorously. In the latter half of the 1790's—after the signing of Jay's treaty—French attacks were stepped up, an infringement of American rights which Hamilton considered unjust and which must have sharpened his antipathy toward the revolution. The abuse was made more galling when the French Directory asserted that its policy was to treat American shipping "no worse" than the

41 "Pacificus," No. 4, July 17, 1793, *HWL*, IV, 474–75.

42 Allan McLane Hamilton, *The Intimate Life of Alexander Hamilton* (New York, 1910), 300.

43 Morris to Jefferson, June 10, 1792, *ASPFR*, I, 330.

44 "Address to the Electors of the State of New York," 1801, *HWL*, VIII, 226.

45 Hamilton to Lafayette, January 6, 1799, *ibid.*, X, 337.

British treated it. Hamilton commented acidly that "France as she once was, would have blushed" at the thought of such a justification.[46]

Hamilton was among the first critics of the revolutionary government to see that it might be heading toward military dictatorship—toward becoming "the slave of some victorious Sylla, or Marius, or Caesar."[47] His discernment in this respect proved to be keener than that of Jefferson, who deplored the bloodshed but minimized the danger. Even when he received news that Napoleon had made himself first consul of France, Jefferson saw no danger of dictatorship. He predicted prompt assassination "if Bonaparte declares for Royalty" in that nation where "there must be a million of Brutuses who will devote themselves to death to destroy him."[48]

After years of alarms and disappointments Hamilton decided that civilization itself was endangered by the revolution. It came to represent to him the ultimate in evil and perversity, threatening the subversion of every good social and political institution. He repeatedly warned that the revolutionaries were "at war with the nature of man"[49] and called them supporters of infidelity and atheism.[50] A clear understanding of the final detestation with which he came to view the turmoil in France makes it easier to interpret the untiring efforts he made to thwart the designs of the Girondists, the Jacobins, and their successors upon the peace and independence of the United States.

46 "The Warning," No. 5, March 13, 1797, *ibid.*, VI, 251.
47 "Americanus," No. 1, February 1, 1794, *ibid.*, V, 77.
48 Jefferson to Henry Innis, January 23, 1800, *JW*, X, 145.
49 "Address to the Electors of the State of New York," 1801, *HWL*, VIII, 228.
50 "Fragment on the French Revolution" (undated), *ibid.*, 426.

CHAPTER IX

Genêt in America

At the beginning of 1793 the revolutionary fervor of the French National Convention was intense. The war with the Austrians was spreading, and it was obvious that Great Britain and other European powers would soon be involved. The convention, far from being dismayed by that ominous prospect, took the initiative and on February 1 declared war on Britain, Spain, and the Netherlands. The convention appealed directly to the peoples of Europe, hoping that popular uprisings would render their monarchs powerless.

It was during this militant period that the convention appointed Edmond Charles Genêt to serve as minister of the first French Republic to the United States. Genêt had established a reputation as an enthusiastic advocate of the revolution and as a rather brilliant diplomat. Those qualities, together with his youthful exuberance, seemed to mark him as the man most likely to advance the cause of the revolution with the freedom-loving Americans.

Upon his arrival in the United States, Genêt did not disembark at Philadelphia, the national capital, but instead landed at Charleston, South Carolina, explaining that the captain of his ship had been forced to veer southward to elude a British naval patrol.

The people of South Carolina greeted the young minister with cheers, and he felt so sure of American support that almost at once he began granting commissions to privateersmen to prey upon British commerce. He "conferred" upon the French consul the authority to conduct prize-court proceedings to condemn British merchant vessels captured by privateers, and he undertook preparations for irregular military operations against the Spaniards in Florida and Louisiana. He must have realized that his actions were irregular, but obviously he felt it unnecessary to wait until he was formally received by the American government. Must protocol be observed during a revolution?

Genêt took his time moving northward to Philadelphia, issuing commissions, condemning monarchy, and praising republicanism in France and America. He was acclaimed and feted everywhere he went. His warm reception increased his self-confidence. Accounts of his initial reception in Philadelphia are varied. Beveridge reflected the general view of the Republicans that Genêt was received "by the populace with a frenzy of enthusiasm almost indescribable in its intensity."[1] Hamilton, on the other hand, reported Genêt's reception as somewhat less fervid and indicated his own attitude toward the Frenchman by adding that Genêt's promoters, with few exceptions, "were the same men who [had] been uniformly the enemies and disturbers of the government of the United States."[2] The truth, no doubt, lay between the two extremes. It is clear that the minister continued to attract strong popular support until his mission ended.

Genêt's initial success in revitalizing Franco-American relations came after some years of neglect, especially on the part of the French, who had been deeply absorbed in domestic and European problems. The arrogant Moustier, minister to the United States from 1787 to 1789, had been resented by American leaders for his persistent interest in restoring Louisiana to French control, and the public had been alienated by his snobbery, illustrated by his criticism of American ways, and especially American cooking (it was reported that when he was invited to dine he sometimes took his own food with him). His successor, Louis-Guillaume Otto, the chargé d'affaires in New York, had served until August, 1791, when he was replaced by Ternant. Ternant did a creditable job but lacked the luster of Genêt.

Genêt, who arrived in the United States boasting that the sovereign people of France had done to death their "traitorous" king, had earlier been chosen to escort the deposed king and his family to the United States (where the French government had assumed Louis would be established as "an American planter").[3] Instead, Louis had been executed, and Genêt had readily adapted to the changed circumstances. When he was formally received by President Washington in Philadelphia, he pretended to be offended by Louis XVI medallions displayed on the walls of the reception room.

The British government was at least mildly alarmed by the new

[1] Beveridge, *Life of John Marshall*, II, 28.

[2] Hamilton to unnamed correspondent, May, 1793, *HWL*, X, 44.

[3] DeConde, *Entangling Alliance*, 182–83.

turn in Franco-American relations. The Foreign Office learned, presumably through its secret service, the substance of Genêt's instructions, and Grenville relayed the information to the British minister in Philadelphia, George Hammond, who passed it on to Hamilton. According to Grenville, Genêt was to send privateers against British commerce and ask the American government to supply enough provisions to discharge the balance of the debt to France. Grenville advised Hammond about how to block those schemes and supplied him with convincing arguments to persuade the Americans not to aid Genêt.[4]

Hamilton had already reassured Hammond that the 1778 treaty with France contained no "secret articles," that bogy of diplomacy. Hammond, who treasured the confidences Hamilton shared with him, transmitted Hamilton's information about the treaty to the Foreign Office, adding his own assurance that there was no reason to doubt Hamilton's sincerity in professing his desire for peace and increased commerce with Britain. In Hammond's opinion any breach in "the external tranquillity of the United States" would be fatal to the plans of the Treasury Department and to Secretary Hamilton's "present personal reputation and his future prospects of ambition."[5] On the matter of Genêt's activities Hamilton's manner toward Hammond was that of one colleague working with another in the common cause of building Anglo-American friendship. Grenville came to trust Hamilton fully, though he remained more interested in using Hamilton than in co-operating with him. Hamilton also benefited from the association; the steady stream of information supplied by Hammond undoubtedly strengthened his hand in opposing Genêt's activities.

The instructions Hammond received from his superior reveal a mature brand of diplomacy. The accurate predictions and reasonable arguments were as free of the fitful ebullience exhibited by Genêt as they were of the apprehensive spirit that colored American councils. On the day the Foreign Office received news of the French declaration of war, it sent a message to Hammond predicting that, while France would ask the United States to follow a nonneutral course of action, it would not ask the American ally to fight. Further, the British had concluded that the agreement between the United States and France was a "defensive" one which would not obligate the Americans to enter the war.

[4] Grenville to Hammond, February 8, March 12, 1793, FCA, XV.

[5] Hammond to Grenville, March 7, July 7, April 17, 1793, January 11, 1794, *ibid.*, XV, XVIII.

The state of party politics in the United States at the time would seem to render the country an easy mark for Genêt's purposes, dangerous though they were for the nation's sovereignty. Never has American public opinion been more sharply divided on foreign issues than it was in the five-year period beginning in 1793. The division had begun to appear in vague form during the ratification debates on the Constitution, and there have been attempts to trace it to an even earlier period. Party lines had hardened during the controversies over Hamilton's financial measures in 1790 and 1791, and those lines extended to diplomatic questions in 1793 and remained firmly drawn until French blunders at the time of the XYZ Affair reversed the tide of opinion.

From Genêt's point of view his mission in the United States was well timed. The American public had followed the news from Paris with heightened interest that rose to frenzy in December, 1792, when it was learned that France had declared itself a republic and that the Prussians had been turned back at the Battle of Valmy. Americans toasted the new republic, sang French songs, called one another "citizen," and displayed the tricolor. When Genêt arrived, most Americans welcomed him not only as the representative of a beneficent ally but also as a symbol of popular resistance to tyranny.[6]

The new spirit was startling to many of the Federalists, and especially to Hamilton. Even before the December crescendo of pro-French passion, he had "lamented" the "strong spirit of faction and innovation" and considered "the thing . . . alarming enough to call for the attention of every friend to government."[7] He had not forgotten French assistance in the "late revolution," and he would "always be the foremost in making . . . every suitable return"; but he saw a sharp difference between "bearing good will" toward the ally and "hating and wrangling with all those whom she hates." He believed Jefferson and Madison were too much influenced by French revolutionary thought, were too emotional in their attitude toward France—were, in short, so "unsound and dangerous" that if they were "left to pursue their own course, there would be, in less than six months, an open war between the United States and Great Britain."[8] Jefferson was unable to soften Hamilton's attitude toward the revolution. Hamilton held the up-

[6] Edward Channing, *A History of the United States* (New York, 1905–25), IV, 190; Bemis, *Jay's Treaty*, 136–37.

[7] Hamilton to C. C. Pinckney, October 10, 1792, *HWL*, X, 23.

[8] Hamilton to Col. Edward Carrington, May 26, 1792, *ibid.*, IX, 527–28.

rising "in abhorrence" and considered the public displays "a serious calamity."[9]

Jefferson, who generally stood for "reformation" rather than "revolution,"[10] understood, and probably exaggerated, the long-term benefits of the French Revolution, though he failed to grasp fully the immediate dangers it posed for his own country. He was "reluctant to believe that a beautiful dream might become a hideous, repulsive monstrosity."[11] Hamilton, for his part, failed to assess the over-all significance of the uprising but saw its dangers clearly enough to guard his nation from the day-to-day pitfalls it presented. At some points Jefferson's attitude appears naïve. In 1790, for instance, he rejoiced over the fact that "the National Convention [had] constitutionally excluded conquest from the object of their government."[12] To Joel Barlow he wrote, "God send that all the nations who join in attacking the liberties of France may end in the attainment of their own."[13] In later years Jefferson came to speak almost as derogatorily of the French violence as the Federalists did. In his autobiography he would condemn Marie Antoinette, whose "inflexible perverseness plunged the world into crimes and calamities which will forever stain the pages of modern history." Recalling, after twenty years, the animosities of 1798, he would make bitter complaints about the Federalist Charles Lee who had dared to "identify" the Republicans in the United States "with the murderous Jacobins of France."[14]

Gouverneur Morris shared Hamilton's views. He looked upon the French government of 1792 as "the worst government in Europe." He believed the "licentious [Jacobin] societies" had inspired such horror and apprehension in the minds of "the great mass of French population" that they "would consider even despotism a blessing, if accompanied by security to person and property."[15] Jefferson argued with Morris on the point, but other members of the administration took him seriously. Washington wrote Jefferson that he was appalled by Morris' "gloomy picture of the affairs of France,"

[9] *The Anas*, *JW*, I, 402, 411.

[10] Malone, II, *xvi–xvii.*

[11] Hazen, *Contemporary American Opinions of the French Revolution*, 53.

[12] Jefferson to William Short, August 10, 1790, *JW*, VIII, 81.

[13] Jefferson to Joel Barlow, June 20, 1792, *ibid.*, 383.

[14] *Ibid.*, I, 151, 281.

[15] Morris to Jefferson, June 10, 1792, *ASPFR*, I, 330.

and fearful that the reports were backed "with too much truth." Yet Washington was a patient man, and he was undoubtedly sincere when he expressed to Morris the wish that "much happiness may arise to the French nation and to mankind in general out of the severe evils which are inseparable from so important a revolution."[16]

American newspapers had opened furious fire on each other even before Genêt's arrival in the United States. The *Gazette of the United States*, a staunch supporter of Hamilton's domestic programs, was often called a Federalist organ. The *National Gazette* (which Charles Adams called the "mint of defamation"[17]), under the editorship of Philip Freneau, spoke a Jeffersonian language. Freneau, who was employed as a translating clerk in the Department of State, was often vitriolic in his attacks on Federalists and federalism and was accused of being a tool of the secretary of state. Jefferson denied the charge, insisting that Freneau wrote as he pleased. Dumas Malone has made the tongue-in-cheek suggestion that Hamilton's "unwillingness to acknowledge Freneau's independence was owing to his inability to recognize a free man when he saw one."[18] At any rate, the *National Gazette* saw the French Revolution as "one of those events, few of which occur in the rotation of many centuries." The paper presented the views of an "Old Soldier" who protested that a few days before Washington's neutrality proclamation the Pennsylvanians resembled the people of a British province, "with their panegyrics upon the measures of the British administration, and our good allies the French are branded with every felonious epithet."[19] The latter statement inadvertently appears to support Hamilton's claim that Genêt's reception at Philadelphia the following month was less enthusiastic than the Republicans claimed it was. After Genêt's arrival, Benjamin Franklin Bache's *General Advertiser* supported him even more steadfastly than did the *National Gazette*.

The strong stand taken by Hamilton and other Federalists had already had internal political repercussions. Hamilton's friend John Steele of North Carolina was slated to be elected to the United States Senate; but when the state legislature met in the autumn of 1792, it turned to William Blount

[16] Washington to Jefferson, October 20, 1792, Washington to Morris, October 20, 1792, *WW*, XXXII, 187–89.

[17] Charles Adams to J. Q. Adams, July 29, 1793, *JQAW*, I, 147.

[18] Malone, II, 462.

[19] *National Gazette*, June 19, April 20, 1793.

instead, because it had been reported that Steele had "aristocratical" views and was "the devoted . . . [*sic*] of Hamilton."[20]

The arrival of Genêt brought the United States to the sharpest diplomatic crisis it had yet faced. This time the danger was real, not hypothetical, as in 1790. Europe was aflame with war, the United States' ally was in the heart of the conflict and was sending a new minister under orders to involve the new nation in it, if only indirectly. The United States was young and weak—and divided. Washington left Mount Vernon and hastened to the nation's capital, where he arrived on April 17—a month before Genêt's arrival. On April 18, in a characteristic act, he issued to the cabinet members a list of thirteen questions asking advice about the action to be taken when Genêt arrived. Should a proclamation of neutrality be issued? Should Genêt be received, and, if so, in what manner? Were the treaties of 1778 binding under the new conditions? Did the alliance bind the nation in defensive wars only? Was the present war a defensive war on France's part? Did French warships have special privileges in American ports? If a future regent representing a French monarch should send a minister, should he also be received? Should Congress be called into session?[21]

Jefferson and some of his contemporaries, as well as later historians, recognized Hamilton's authorship of this shrewd list of questions. Jefferson later recalled that the questions were in Washington's "own hand writing," but from "their ingenious tissue and suite" he assumed that "the language was Hamilton's, and the doubts his alone."[22] If Hamilton wrote the question concerning the convening of Congress, he did so only because he knew that others would raise the point and that it could not be avoided. It may have been Washington who insisted on bringing this matter into the discussion. Hamilton thought the executive, not the legislative, branch should determine what action was called for. His handiwork is particularly evident in those questions concerning the defensive nature of the alliance and how it affected American obligations. Jefferson would not have dwelt on that point. Also, only Hamilton would have asked whether a minister from a future regent should be received. It was not really a question at all, but an argu-

20 William R. Davie to John Steele, December 16, 1792, J. G. de Roulhac Hamilton, "William Richardson Davie: A Memoir, Followed by His Letters, with Notes by Kemp P. Battle," *James Sprunt Historical Monograph*, No. VII (Chapel Hill, 1907), 26.

21 *WW*, XXXII, 419–21.

22 C. M. Thomas, *American Neutrality in 1793* (New York, 1931), 27–33; DeConde, *Entangling Alliance*, 187n.; *The Anas*, *JW*, I, 349.

ment against receiving Genêt without reservations for declaring the alliance temporarily suspended. Hamilton wrote hundreds of pages of essays, cabinet papers, and letters on those subjects during the next few months.

The President had the satisfaction of finding his cabinet members unanimous in the answers to the most crucial question. The nation, they agreed, should remain neutral in the conflict. It was in the procedures to be followed in announcing and conducting a neutral policy that differences of opinion arose.

No member of the cabinet formally advised Washington not to receive Genêt, though Hamilton might have done so had he not seen the hopelessness of such a position.[23] Gouverneur Morris had been instructed a month earlier to recognize the National Convention as the government of France. Refusing to receive the convention's accredited agent would have contradicted the American position. Jefferson's advice was to receive Genêt without reservation. Hamilton's recommendation was that when Genêt was received he should be clearly informed that the United States reserved "to future consideration and discussion the question whether the operation of the treaties . . . ought not to be deemed temporarily and provisionally suspended." Hamilton's reply to Washington on this point occupies 28 pages in his works.[24] It comprises the main body of his thought at the time on the nature of the French Revolution, the existing conditions of European diplomacy, and ways to minimize the dangers inherent in the Franco-American alliance.

Jefferson held to the unexceptionable ground that treaties are contracted by nations, not merely by governments, and he added that agreements are not nullified by a change of administration nor even by a revolution in either or both of the contracting nations. He observed that both countries had undergone revolutions since 1778. "The will of the nation" he held to be the only essential consideration. The people are the source of authority he said, and they can set up, "internally," whatever form of government they wish and change it as they will.[25]

Hamilton agreed thoroughly with Jefferson's statement as far as it went but believed that it did not go far enough. "That a nation has a right . . . to change its form of government—to abolish one, and substitute another," he said, "ought to be admitted in its fullest latitude." He added that "changes in forms of government do not of course" abrogate their treaties, that the

[23] Hamilton to John Jay, April 19, 1793, *HWL*, X, 38–39.

[24] Hamilton to Washington, *ibid.*, IV, 369–96.

[25] Jefferson to Washington, April 28, 1793, *JW*, III, 226–43; Jefferson to Morris, March 12, 1793, *ibid.*, IX, 36–40; Jefferson to Thomas Pinckney, December 30, 1792, *ibid.*, 7–8.

treaties still bind the nation making the change "and will bind the other party, unless, in due time and for just cause" the nation renounces them. In his opinion, good faith required that treaties not be renounced unless such a step seemed thoroughly justifiable. He did not recommend renouncing the alliance with France but believed it should be suspended until the military and political situation in Europe was clarified.[26] The youthful John Quincy Adams, destined to become one of America's greatest diplomats, firmly supported this view.[27]

Hamilton dipped into international law, quoting Hugo Grotius, Vattel, and Samuel von Pufendorf to the effect that an alliance might honorably be set aside if a change in the government of one party basically altered the conditions and considerations upon which the agreement was established. If, for instance, a republic entered an alliance with another republic and agreed to extend a stipulated amount of aid for their mutual defense against surrounding monarchs, after which one of the signatories underwent a sudden revolution and adopted a monarchical form of government, would the treaty still be binding? The sense of the illustration was that the new monarchy would use the aid, if delivered, to injure the republic rather than to support it.

Modern-day historians must not overlook the fact that Hamilton and most of his contemporaries believed France would eventually be defeated on the field of battle. At the time of this cabinet discussion, as in the preceding months, Jefferson showed little hope of military victory for France. In June, 1793, Jefferson wrote to Edmund Randolph that he feared summer would "prove disastrous to the French." Two months later, Washington mentioned the probability of an imminent end of the war in Europe as an argument in urging Jefferson to postpone until December his resignation from the cabinet.[28] Hamilton could not overlook the discomfort that might result from having clasped hands with a violent regime just before it was set aside by forces that could fairly claim to be acting in the name of the legal successor of Louis XVI.

The possibility that Genêt would ask the United States to join in the war against Britain—or that he would draw the nation into hostilities without a formal request—alarmed Hamilton, for he had expected France to be defeated even before Great Britain entered the lists, and he noted that the

26 Hamilton to Washington, April, 1793, May 2, 1793, *HWL*, IV, 369–96, 396–408.
27 "Menander," No. 3, *Columbia Centinel*, May 11, 1793, *JQAW*, I, 143–44.
28 *JW*, IX, 108–109; *The Anas*, *ibid.*, I, 388.

existing government in France called itself "provisional."[29] He was convinced that the brother of Louis XVI, who was calling himself Louis XVIII, had a good chance of gaining the throne; it was the avowed intention of the anti-French coalition of nations to place him there. Where, indeed, would the United States stand then, and who would be its friend?

Hamilton asked other pertinent questions. Suppose the new French monarch should send an expedition against the French West Indies, which, according to the Franco-American treaty, the United States was bound to protect. What could the United States do in such an embarrassing situation? Or suppose the Bourbons should reoccupy half of France and gain the support of half the population. Who would then be the United States' ally, the new king or the revolutionary government? Should the designated "ally" shift back and forth according to the fortunes of battle? Would it not be prudent to forestall any such disconcerting situations by telling Genêt plainly at the time of his reception that the alliance was suspended?

Such questions were not easy to set aside. Even today they are vexed questions that cannot be dismissed as "jesuitical reasoning," in Schachner's phrase.[30] At the time it appeared that Hamilton was correct in observing that France had "but one enemy, and that was all Europe." He referred to the Bourbon pretender as a "sovereign who still pursues his claim to govern, supported by the general sense and arm of Europe."[31]

Down through the years Hamilton has had a bad press in this matter, as in several others. Historians have often approached the treaty discussion by stating Jefferson's strong position—that treaties bind nations, and not merely governments—implying or claiming outright that Hamilton did not accept that principle. Some have committed the further error of claiming that Hamilton asked the President to denounce the treaties and terminate them. William E. Dodd, for instance, wrote, "Hamilton explained delightfully that since the French people had beheaded their king, all bargains with him were off."[32] Robert H. Ferrell had Hamilton arguing that "the alliance was with the monarchy and hence not valid under the republic."[33] John D. Hicks wrote, "Hamilton took the ground that the treaties were with the

[29] Hamilton to Washington, November 19, 1792, April, 1793, *HWL*, IV, 366, 384.

[30] Schachner, *Alexander Hamilton*, 318.

[31] "Pacificus," No. 4, July 17, 1793, *HWL*, IV, 478; Hamilton to Washington, April, 1793, *ibid.*, 396.

[32] William E. Dodd, "When Washington Tried Isolation," *American Mercury*, Vol. IV (March, 1925), 350.

[33] Robert H. Ferrell, *American Diplomacy: A History* (New York, 1959), 33.

King of France, and the King's government being done away with, they were no longer binding."[34] Edward Channing, one of the United States' greatest historians, said, "Hamilton argued that the treaty had been made with the king of France, and the king being dead and the monarchy destroyed, the treaty had come to an end."[35] Other historians, of course, have stated the facts correctly. Charles E. Martin, for one, treated Hamilton as practical and reasonable in urging suspension, though not termination, of the alliance.[36]

Time has proved that the secretary of the treasury and his contemporaries were mistaken in their estimates of the comparative strength of the European belligerents. But in order to evaluate his arguments, it is necessary to understand conditions as they appeared to be at the time. Viewed in that perspective, his ideas were quite plausible. To any person who has observed the diplomacy of World War II and subsequent years, there is nothing odd about the United States' granting or withholding recognition in accordance with national interest.

Hamilton was quick to point out that the alliance was stated to be a defensive one. He held that France had taken the offensive in declaring war on the powers arrayed against it. He cited authorities in international law in support of his position. For example, the eminent Swiss jurist Jean Jacques Burlamaqui had put the matter quite plainly: "The first who takes up arms, whether justly or unjustly, commences an offensive war; and he who opposes him, whether with or without reason, begins a defensive war." Jean Barbeyrac and Pufendorf, he said, held the same view.[37]

The argument did not prove convincing, and Hamilton resorted to common reasoning, using arguments roughly comparable to modern theorizing on aggression. France had violated its treaties and injured the Netherlands by declaring the Schelde and Meuse rivers free to navigation on the grounds that the old agreement was null and void because it violated "natural right." Such a position could not be held "without subverting all the foundations of positive and pactitious right among nations." He was genuinely dismayed by the French leaders' attempts to instigate revolutions in other countries—as Hamilton expressed it, "to excite disturbances in neutral and friendly

[34] John D. Hicks, *The Federal Union* (2d ed., Cambridge, 1952), 211.

[35] Channing, *A History of the United States*, IV, 128.

[36] Charles E. Martin, *The Policy of the United States as Regards Intervention: Studies in History, Economics, and Public Law* (New York, 1921), 41–46.

[37] Hamilton to Washington, May 2, 1793, *HWL*, IV, 397–98.

countries"—and emphatically asserted that nothing could be clearer to the "dictates of right reason" than that when one nation "adopts maxims of conduct tending to the disturbance of the tranquillity and established order of its neighbors, or manifesting a spirit of self-aggrandizement," those neighbors have a right to resort to arms.[38]

Hamilton was frankly fearful—John Adams and others were even more so—that the murderous orgies of Paris might spread to the United States. A more active alliance would obviously accentuate that danger. The United States' international reputation would also suffer if it clasped too fondly the bloody hands of the terrorists. Could the United States then stand forth as a nation given to "sobriety, moderation, justice, and love of order"?

It was primarily concern for the nation's honor that kept Hamilton from advising the government to abrogate the alliance. Its terms were "from the present time and forever,"[39] and it was not in Hamilton's character to treat such words lightly. "Faith and justice between nations," he reminded the public in his fourth "Pacificus" essay, "are virtues of a nature the most necessary and sacred. They cannot be too strongly inculcated, nor too highly respected." He regretted the alliance and recognized that it had become a liability, and he sometimes spoke of the possibility of future injuries by rash Jacobins that might justify abandoning it. In anticipation of that possibility he mentioned repeatedly in his essays that French assistance during the American Revolution was based on calculated national interest. France had seized the opportunity to "repress the pride and diminish the power of a dangerous rival."[40] Nations do not bestow benefits upon one another, he said, unless they expect to be repaid. He was generous enough to recall that during the American struggle for liberty French aid was not accompanied by any effort to "extort from us any humiliating or injurious concessions." Even that forbearance was "dictated by policy, yet it was a magnanimous policy, such as always constitutes a title to the approbation and esteem of mankind." He refused to concede that Americans should show "gratitude" toward the nation of France. Esteem and friendship, yes; gratitude, no. Gratitude could prove to be a shrine at which the nation's interests might be sacrificed, and he felt that those who continually harped on the theme of gratitude must base their politics on the idea "all for love, and the world well lost."[41]

[38] *Ibid.*, 399, 407.

[39] Miller, *Treaties*, II, 35–47.

[40] "Pacificus," No. 4, July 10, 1793, "Pacificus," No. 5, July 13, 1793, *HWL*, IV, 463, 467.

[41] *Ibid.*, 461–69.

George Cabot, one of the few men whose advice Hamilton greatly valued, seemed to think that a single statement from the President would lead the American people to abandon their infatuation for France. He wished the President would point out that French aid during the Revolution had been "actuated by policy, or to speak out, by ambition."[42] The remark illustrates the pompous attitude of the "High Federalist." Only a grave misunderstanding of the people could have allowed him to make the ingenuous assumption that public opinion on this emotional subject could be reversed so easily. Hamilton did not misjudge the public mind that far. He did insist that less gratitude was in order, but he used the argument as but one among many, hoping that the aggregate might alter current attitudes. The Federalists generally suffered from a blind spot in the area of sensing public will, and that was one reason for their downfall.

Jefferson's approval of the cataclysm in France caused him to warm to the alliance. Earlier, at the time of the Nootka Sound controversy in 1790, when the course of the revolution was less pronounced, his advice to Washington had indicated that he did not greatly value the French connection. He had been eager to bargain with Britain or with Spain in ways that could easily have resulted in a clash with France. By 1793 he had become more favorably inclined toward France. Only two weeks before Louis was taken from prison to the guillotine, Jefferson wrote to his son-in-law, Thomas Mann Randolph, that "news from France continues to be good." He added, significantly, that the ultimate form the American government would take would apparently depend "much more on the events of France than anybody had before imagined." News of the king's death prompted him to say that the event might lead to the founding of republics "everywhere" in Europe and that at the very least it would "soften monarchial governments" and remove that source of "insolence and oppression, the inviolability of the King's person." Even after he grew annoyed at "Genêt's machinations against our peace and friendship," he continued to believe that the French people were "constant in their friendship to us." For the United States' part, he wrote to Morris, "after independence and self-government, there is nothing we more sincerely wish than perpetual friendship with them."[43]

The cabinet members, though unanimous in the determination to try to keep the nation out of the war, were sharply divided about whether or not

[42] George Cabot to Rufus King, August 2, 1793, *KC*, I, 489–90.
[43] *JW*, IX, 13, 45, 206, 209.

to issue a proclamation of neutrality. Hamilton urged Washington to do so at once, to place the country on record before Genêt reached Philadelphia. Jefferson opposed such a proclamation, preferring to see the legislative branch of the government, rather than the executive, make such momentous decisions. As he interpreted the Constitution, only Congress had the authority to "declare" neutrality, since Congress alone was authorized to declare war. His conviction was so strong on this point that he induced Madison to enter a debate by essay with Hamilton, who, between June 29 and July 20, 1793, had published seven letters, signed "Pacificus," in the *Gazette of the United States*, supporting neutrality and the proclamation.[44] In Madison's articles, "Letters of Helvidius," which appeared in the same paper from August 24 to September 18, 1793, he maintained stoutly that Congress alone had the constitutional authority to say what treaty obligations were binding. To allow the executive branch to exercise this authority was "monarchical" and reminded him of the British system, where the conduct of foreign relations was a "royal" prerogative. Madison found the letter-writing task the "most grating one he ever experienced," and he gave it up before he had answered all of Hamilton's arguments.[45]

Though in full agreement with Madison's points, Jefferson emphasized even more strongly his desire to let the belligerents "bid" for American neutrality. He wrote Monroe that he opposed the declaration because it "would be premature, and would lose us the benefit for which it might be bartered."[46] Jefferson and Edmund Randolph differed somewhat on the matter. The former sometimes complained that cabinet decisions were two and a half versus one and a half—meaning that Hamilton and Knox were sometimes partly supported by the attorney general. On the subject Randolph, who wrote the proclamation that was finally issued, once said in a cabinet meeting that he wanted foreign nations to "understand it as . . . the President's opinion that neutrality would be our interest." Jefferson countered that he had preferred "foreign nations should understand no such thing" but should "come and bid for our neutrality."[47] Yet it must have been only the enemies of France whom he wanted to do the bidding.

[44] *HWL*, IV, 432–89.

[45] Madison to Jefferson, July 10, 1793, *MW*, VI, 138–39; "Helvidius," No. 1, August 24, 1793, *ibid.*, 144, 150. The five essays appear on pages 138–88.

[46] Jefferson to Monroe, July 14, 1793, *JW*, IX, 161; Jefferson to Madison, June 23, 1793, *ibid.*, 138.

[47] Entry dated November 18, 1793, *The Anas*, *ibid.*, I, 404.

Obviously France would not bid for American neutrality. If Washington had played the game this way, he might have gained valuable concessions from Britain in the matter of commerce or the Northwest posts, or Spain might have conceded something on the Mississippi navigation question. But such bargaining would have been perilous and might have brought the United States into the war. Jefferson's proposal illustrates his finesse in diplomacy. Yet again, as in the crisis of 1790, he saw no reason for military preparations. He objected to a proposal for the founding of a military academy on the grounds that under the Constitution Congress did not have the authority to establish one; and he advised Washington not to ask Congress to fortify American harbors.[48]

Hamilton considered the issue too dangerous to toy with. Further, the "bidding" idea was counter to his chosen means of dealing with Britain, which was to bring all issues into the open and work for an understanding on the basis of mutual interest. If the United States were then as powerful as it would be after fifteen or twenty years' growth, it might be possible to obtain "collateral advantages" before announcing neutrality, but he held that "the justice and magnanimity" of such an idea could not "be commended."[49]

The proclamation issued by the President on April 22, 1793, carefully avoided the word "neutrality." Obviously the product of strife and compromise, it briefly recognized the state of war among the European powers, affirmed the United States' intention to continue a friendly and impartial course of action toward all, and warned American citizens against committing "hostilities against any of the said powers." The proclamation indicated that violators would face rather severe punishment, but the nature of the punishment was not specified.[50]

Jefferson was eager for American citizens to observe in good faith the principles of neutrality—as he understood those principles—though he assumed that it would not preclude a limited amount of friendly co-operation with the French. Before learning that the British had entered the war, he wrote to a friend in Europe that the United States had no desire "to meddle with the internal affairs of any country, nor with the general affairs of Europe." Two days before the proclamation was issued, he assured

[48] Cabinet Meeting, November 23, 1793, *The Anas*, *JW*, I, 409.
[49] "Pacificus," No. 7, July 20, 1793, *HWL*, IV, 484.
[50] *ASPFR*, I, 140.

Thomas Pinckney, minister to Great Britain, that the United States intended "to preserve a fair neutrality in the present war." Before Genêt's arrival he told Minister Ternant that if any American citizens committed "hostilities at sea" against any belligerent the government would make every effort to bring the offender "to condign punishment."[51]

Washington and his "coadjutors" had made their decision: Congress would not be called into immediate session, the treaty of alliance and the treaty of amity and commerce with France would not be suspended, the United States would try to remain neutral, and Genêt's formal reception by the President would be as cool as possible without actually offending the young diplomat. He was so received by President Washington on May 17, 1793. Genêt's prior information and instructions had led him to prepare himself for a cool official reception. His hopes lay in appealing directly to the American people, and what Girondist could doubt that the public will must prevail?

The government leaders in Philadelphia must have been greatly relieved when Genêt made it known that France did not intend to request all-out American assistance against Britain or Britain's cobelligerents. Determined to gain every possible psychological advantage from the situation, however, Genêt described the French decision as an act of rare magnanimity by a self-sacrificing elder sister. He grandiloquently pointed to his country as standing "single, against innumerable hordes of tyrants and slaves, who menace her rising liberty."[52]

If the sole intention of Genêt in America had been to antagonize the secretary of the treasury, he could hardly have chosen a better course than the one he followed. As noted earlier, appealing to the "passions" of the people was to Hamilton a peculiarly subversive and objectionable practice. Issuing privateering commissions to Americans within their own country ran counter to his concept of sovereignty. Organizing naval expeditions inside American ports to attack a third power seemed to him a violation of the country's neutral status, an affront to the government, and a rude assault upon the basic concept of justice among nations. Conferring casually with the people of South Carolina and the back country during his month-

[51] Jefferson to C. F. W. Dumas, March 24, 1793, Jefferson to Pinckney, April 20, 1793, Jefferson to Ternant, May 15, 1793, *JW*, IX, 46, 67, 94.

[52] Genêt to Jefferson, May 23, 1793, Turner, *Correspondence of the French Ministers*, II, 147. Genêt's instructions are given on pages 202–11.

long trip from Charleston to Philadelphia stirred Hamilton to the highest pitch of indignation.

The war between republican France and her monarchist enemies was far more bitter than the earlier succession of "dynastic" wars. The French, asserting that the cause of human liberty rode under their banner, maintained that not all the usual rules of warfare and diplomacy should be binding upon them. Their enemies held that the revolutionaries were determined to destroy the foundations of decent society, that France had become a "nation in arms," and that it would be as imprudent as it would be unjust for neutrals to demand the observance of the customary rules of naval warfare.

Troubles came fast. Britain insisted on seizing enemy property on neutral vessels, and neutral ships as well, if they were engaged in commerce between the French colonies, such as the West Indies and France. American ships carrying food products to France were forced to put in at British ports, though the cargoes were usually paid for. Such practices, considered violations of international law, made it extremely difficult for Washington to avoid war with Britain. Boisterous pro-French factions exploited every possible means of arousing American ire about British depredations, including demands for a declaration of war against Britain. Washington and Hamilton began looking for ways to prepare the nation for a war it might not be able to avoid. Though King George's government did not want another conflict with the United States, it was willing to try American forbearance to the utmost.

British interference with American shipping gave Genêt a theme that never failed to produce a hearty response from American audiences at mass meetings he was soon addressing. A few days after he reached Philadelphia he helped found a pro-French society called the "Democratic Club."[53] Similar clubs sprang up in other parts of the country, to the chagrin of the President, who came to associate them with the Republican party and often applied the epithet "French faction" indiscriminately to Republicans and to the Democratic clubs.

Genêt had scarcely had time to settle down in Philadelphia when he broached the subject of a new "commercial treaty"—a "true family compact" —with the United States. He assured Jefferson that such an arrangement would bring great advantages to each signatory.[54] His proposals, which

[53] DeConde, *Entangling Alliance*, 252–53.

also referred to closer political connections, convinced Jefferson that the time was highly inauspicious for any formal discussions. Not wishing to offend the minister or his government, Jefferson delayed the issue by pointing out that treaties required Senate action and that Congress would not convene for several months.

Hamilton fought with all his strength against the idea of a new treaty—even a commercial one—at this particular time. He insisted that it was but a device of the French to aid themselves during the war. He warned the people to be wary of any tempting offers from the French, for only terms of "permanent, mutual interest" would be of any value. Nothing could be gained from a wartime treaty that might quickly be repudiated when peace was restored.[55] In this instance, Jefferson's tactics proved sound: while Hamilton was railing against the proposal, Jefferson quietly killed it.

Genêt's privateering activities against British commerce, sometimes carried out in American territorial waters, constituted such a grave offense that it was feared Britain would declare war on the United States if it was not stopped.[56] From the beginning the cabinet was united in opposing such activities, and eventually they were stopped, though Genêt resisted the American government with every possible means. Scarcely six weeks after the issuance of the neutrality proclamation, one Gideon Henfield was arrested for privateering. An interesting legal battle followed. Attorney General Randolph prosecuted, and the government tried hard for a conviction.[57] Genêt unsuccessfully demanded the "releasement" of the defendant and then undertook to finance a strong defense. The jury found that Henfield's action violated the peace treaty with Great Britain and that the treaty was, according to the Constitution, the supreme law of the land; but it refused to convict Henfield because of his good record as a patriotic citizen, his professions of loyalty to his country, his plea that he did not know privateering for France was a violation of American law, and his expression of regret for his activities. Immediately after his acquittal, Genêt and his friends held a rousing "victory feast," during which Henfield reenlisted as a privateersman.[58]

[54] Genêt to Jefferson, May 22, 1793, *ASPFR*, I, 142.

[55] "Pacificus," No. 7, July 20, 1793, *HWL*, IV, 485.

[56] See Hamilton's essay "Camillus," No. 16, 1795, *ibid.*, V, 385.

[57] M. D. Conway, *Omitted Chapters of History Disclosed in the Life and Papers of Edmund Randolph* (New York, 1888), 162–86 (hereafter cited as *Edmund Randolph*).

[58] The Henfield case has attracted the attention of several competent historians. See Thomas,

The rude behavior and interference in governmental matters by the French minister, whose chief interest was supposed to be the improvement of relations between his country and the United States, evoked from the usually tolerant secretary of state the bitter remark that Genêt's conduct "is indefensible by the most furious Jacobin." After the Henfield trial Genêt continued his newspaper advertisements inviting Americans to enlist in the service of France. This defiance brought from Jefferson the acid comment that, "when the government forbids their citizens to arm and engage in the war [Genêt] undertakes to arm and engage them. When they forbid vessels to be fitted in their ports for cruising on nations with whom they are at peace, he commissions them to fit and cruise."[59] Yet Jefferson tried hard to save Genêt. He assured Genêt many times of Americans' friendly disposition toward France. He did his best to "moderate the impetuosity of [Genêt's] movements" and convince him of the folly of appealing to the people against the will of the President.[60] He also tried to cultivate public favor for Genêt, as far as possible, assuring the people that "nothing could be more affectionate or [more] magnanimous" than Genêt's basic purposes. When the young man's rashness became insupportable, Jefferson tried to persuade the people not to blame the French government and nation for his behavior. Madison was willing to consider Genêt's conduct the result of the failure of Congress "in the outset . . . to favor the commerce of France more than that of Great Britain."[61]

In one notable violation of American sovereignty, the French privateer *L'Embuscade* captured the British merchant vessel *Grange* in Delaware Bay. George Hammond promptly and successfully demanded the return of the vessel to its owners. He informed Grenville that he was convinced of the sincerity of American intentions to observe a fair neutrality, and Grenville agreed.[62] Jefferson dealt with both Ternant and Genêt on this occasion, and soon thereafter informed Genêt, firmly but civilly, that he was convinced by the minister's professions of friendship that he would not give "further umbrage."[63] Further umbrage was forthcoming, nevertheless. A French

American Neutrality in 1793, 170–74; Conway, *Edmund Randolph*, 182–86; Francis Wharton, *State Trials of the United States* (Philadelphia, 1849), 49–89.

[59] Jefferson to Monroe, July 14, 1793, Jefferson to Morris, August 16, 1793, *JW*, IX, 164, 201.

[60] Jefferson to Monroe, June 28, 1793, *ibid.*, 146.

[61] Jefferson to Madison, May 19, 1793, *ibid.*, 97; Madison to Jefferson, *MW*, VI, 195.

[62] Hammond to Grenville, May 7, 1793, October 12, 1793, Grenville to Hammond, January 1, 1794, FCA, XV, XVIII.

[63] Jefferson to Ternant, May 3, 1793, Jefferson to Genêt, June 5, 1793, *JW*, IX, 74, 111.

privateer brought in another British ship, the *Little Sarah*. It was renamed *La Petite Democrate*, and preparations were made to arm it for privateering activities. Hamilton and Knox wanted to set up a battery to prevent the crew from putting out to sea, but Jefferson feared that such action might lead to war with France, since French warships that were expected to arrive soon might join in the fray. He could not bear the thought of "the only two republics on earth destroying each other" and prayed that it not be "from our hands that the hopes of man receive their last stab."[64] He urgently requested Genêt to promise that the vessel would not go to sea until Washington, who had left the capital, could return. Genêt replied that the ship was not yet fit to go to sea, anyway. Jefferson evidently believed Genêt's response sufficient; but by a ruse the vessel managed to leave port and escape to sea. It was a crude blunder on Genêt's part, for it cost him Jefferson's friendship. Governor Mifflin of Pennsylvania sent A. J. Dallas, his secretary of state, to try to induce Genêt to stop the vessel. Mifflin reported that the Frenchman spoke lightly of Washington and threatened to appeal directly to the people. These comments hastened Genêt's political downfall.[65]

Holding the American people to the promise of maintaining neutrality proved a difficult task. An act of Congress seemed to be the only way to stop impetuous Americans from committing acts of "hostility." One of Genêt's strongest arguments in support of Americans who accepted his privateering commissions was that there was "no law against it." Hamilton, Jefferson, and Randolph agreed, as the President's proclamation indicated, that international law was a part of the law of the land, and they held that the treaty of 1783 with Britain could not be infringed by Americans without penalty. The pro-French Americans of 1793 and 1794 required a lot of convincing.[66] The President therefore asked Congress to enact a law stating explicitly that it was illegal for any American to commit an unneutral act. Congress was slow to act. Washington had first mentioned such a law late in 1792 when he became aware of the dangers of siding with one or another of the belligerents. In their reply the legislators had evaded the issue. When the regular session opened in December, 1793, the presidential message gave

[64] *The Anas*, *ibid.*, I, 368.

[65] Washington to Jefferson, July 11, 1793, *WW*, XXXIII, 4; Hamilton to King, August 13, 1793, *HWL*, X, 50–53.

[66] "Pacificus," No. 1, June 29, 1793, *HWL*, IV, 444; Jefferson to Genêt, June 5, 1793, *ASPFR*, I, 152; Conway, *Edmund Randolph*, 183.

greater emphasis to the necessity for specific legislation.[67] This time Congress promised to act, though nearly six months passed before it did so. The resulting neutrality law, approved on June 5, 1794, was intended to remove all doubt about the nation's ability and determination to prevent American citizens from committing acts of hostility like those Genêt had been promoting.[68] This law—hammered out on the anvil of grim necessity—was to be copied by other countries of the Western world.[69]

Another scheme of Genêt's was to recruit armies and generals in the United States for an assault on Spain's possessions on the Gulf of Mexico. Here again Jefferson tried to give the young man friendly counsel—to no avail. Genêt may actually have misunderstood Jefferson when the secretary of state told Genêt that he "did not care what insurrections should be excited in Louisiana" but that in enticing Kentuckians to fight Spain, a nation with which the United States was at peace, Genêt was "putting a halter about their necks."[70] Genêt may have thought the demurral was merely for the record.

Hamilton was more emphatic in his objection to Genêt's recruiting. He again quoted Vattel, who had written: "To enlist soldiers in a foreign country without the permission of its sovereign . . . is . . . kidnapping. . . . Foreign recruiters are hanged without mercy, and justly so." The recruiter could not plead, in defense, that he was acting under orders from his own sovereign, for no ruler has the right to "command things contrary to the natural law."[71] According to Hamilton, commissioning privateers was an even more serious violation of the nation's sovereignty. The trend of Hamilton's thought is clear enough, but he was too sensible to propose seriously that the objectionable Girondist be hanged.

Jefferson seems to have been in virtual agreement with his colleague in this matter. In his instructions to the American minister at Paris he protested in strong language: "No foreign power or person can levy men within [another nation's territory] without its consent; and he who does,

67 *ASPFR*, I, 19, 22.

68 *The Statutes at Large of the United States of America* (Boston, 1845–73; Washington, 1875–77), I, 381–84.

69 Charles S. Hyneman, "Neutrality During the European Wars of 1792–1815," *American Journal of International Law*, Vol. XXIV (April, 1930), 285.

70 *The Anas*, *JW*, I, 361–62.

71 Emmerich de Vattel, *The Law of Nations* (tr. by Charles G. Fenwick), (Washington, 1916), 240. Hamilton to Washington, May 15, 1793, *HWL*, IV, 410–12.

may be rightfully and severely punished."[72] He had every intention of preserving American neutrality, and how could it be preserved when men were being recruited within United States borders for the purpose of attacking an ally of Britain?

Jefferson was well aware of Genêt's scheme of conquest. Upon his return from Paris Colonel W. S. Smith had reported it to Jefferson, three months before Genêt's arrival. The plan, worked out in collaboration with Miranda, called for a determined movement to capture Louisiana, the Floridas, and the West Indies, as well as Mexico and all of South America, if possible. These plans, which were laid before Great Britain entered the war, called for "forty-five ships of the line" from France. The United States was expected to supply "provisions" and thereby discharge the balance of the debt to France. In return there would be "no objection" if the United States annexed the Floridas.[73] In this form the idea was quite attractive to Jefferson; he "snapped at the bait."[74] He relayed information about the plan to Carmichael and Short, the American representatives in Madrid, and told them that the United States must remain "free to act . . . according to circumstances" and that they must avoid giving any guarantee of the Spanish colonies "against their own independence, nor indeed against any other nation." He added that his earlier suggestion to guarantee to Spain all Spanish-held territory west of the Mississippi in exchange for the Floridas had been made at a time when it was feared that Louisiana might be "seized by Great Britain."[75]

After Britain entered the war, Genêt held to the plan to seize Spanish territories; but to carry out the conquest while Britain and France were at war made it necessary to recruit forces in the United States. The warfare in Europe, and particularly the military reverses of the French army under General Charles Dumouriez in the Netherlands in March, 1793, had changed the picture—and also changed Jefferson's attitude.[76] In spite of his earlier predictions Britain and Spain had become allies. American assistance in a projected invasion of Louisiana might lead to war with Great Britain, which Jefferson most emphatically did not want, especially in view of the

[72] Jefferson to Morris, August 16, 1793, *JW*, IX, 185.

[73] *The Anas, ibid.*, I, 334–35.

[74] DeConde, *Entangling Alliance*, 199; Frederick J. Turner, "The Policy of France Toward the Mississippi Valley in the Period of Washington and Adams," *American Historical Review*, Vol. X (January, 1905), 259–60.

[75] Jefferson to Carmichael and Short, March 23, 1793, *JW*, IX, 55–56.

[76] E. Wilson Lyon, *Louisiana in French Diplomacy, 1759–1804* (Norman, 1934), 71.

likelihood, as he told Carmichael and Short, that Spain's colonies would break away "soon enough," without the need for the United States to risk a war for them.

Genêt tried to make Jefferson an unequal partner in the projected attack on Spanish territories. Jefferson was given only limited information about the scheme. Genêt took a patronizing attitude toward the long-suffering secretary of state, despite which Jefferson gave Genêt a letter of introduction for Genêt's agent, Andre Michaux, to Governor Shelby of Kentucky. Jefferson, aware that the agent was to gather an army of Kentuckians,[77] apparently hoped that the Kentuckians would leave United States territory before actually enlisting.

In spite of its dangers, the scheme evidently interested the members of Washington's cabinet. By this time they were incensed at Spain for repeatedly delaying negotiations about disputed rights and territory at the mouth of the Mississippi and for arming the Indians and encouraging them to violate their treaties with the United States and to attack American frontiersmen. Jefferson was convinced that Spain was "picking a quarrel" with the United States and that war had become "inevitable."[78]

Military expeditions cost money, and Genêt had a scheme for raising it. Some would come from the sale in the United States of captured British merchant ships. The rest he hoped to obtain by persuading the United States to make advance payments on the debt to France. The payments, he told Jefferson, could be made in provisions, some of which would be used to outfit the troops.[79] The rest he evidently expected to sell on the American market. One must give Genêt credit for inventiveness, not to mention self-confidence. At a time when the British navy had virtually cut him off from his homeland, he had undertaken to conquer an empire for France.

Debt payments were the province of the Department of the Treasury, and there Genêt met one of his most formidable obstacles. Hammond had forewarned Hamilton that Genêt would make the request. Undoubtedly it would have been easier for the American government to repay the debt in provisions, for that procedure would have removed the problems involved in international monetary exchange and would have placed upon France the responsibility of delivering the goods to their destinations. But Hamilton

[77] *The Anas*, *JW*, I, 337.
[78] Jefferson to Monroe, June 28, 1793, *ibid.*, IX, 144.
[79] Genêt to Jefferson, May 22, 1793, *ASPFR*, I, 142.

was no longer interested in paying the debt this way. By 1793 he was determined that the Treasury Department would do nothing to help finance the revolution.

Now that the United States had full diplomatic relations with France, Hamilton agreed that regularly scheduled debt payments must be made to whatever regime "acquires *possession*" of the nation's "political power" and "becomes master of its *goods*."[80] But he was sharp and clear in his opposition to granting requests for additional money or provisions. Again he reminded the President that, upon the restoration of the monarchy, the king might disavow such payments and might, moreover, resent the fact that the United States had abetted the revolutionaries.[81] Later he argued against prepayment on the grounds that it might then become impossible to meet payments to Dutch creditors on time.[82]

Hamilton's position was considerably eased by further occasions for making advance payments to relieve the famine in Haiti. Hamilton had two reasons for helping the Haitians: he was sincerely compassionate, and he believed that payments made for that purpose would win further good will in France, as they had two years earlier.[83] He tried to make certain that the relief funds were not by some means diverted to France or to Genêt. When creditor agents spoke of payments of $400,000 at a time, Hamilton informed the President that, while there was "little doubt" that it was "in the power of the Treasury to furnish the sum," he preferred to remit the funds monthly and to take "precise measures" to see that they were spent solely to relieve the distressed colony.[84] Nor did he think that Genêt was entitled to any reason for the refusal of prepayments. None but "true ones" could be given, he observed, and they would only irritate the Frenchman.[85]

Jefferson disagreed with Hamilton on the last points. Reasons would have to be given, he said, if Genêt's request was refused. In June, 1793, Jefferson suggested that the government should at that time pay Genêt all the money due for the remainder of that year.[86] Hamilton refused to do so.

Genêt did succeed in diverting a small amount of relief funds to his

[80] Hamilton to Washington, April, 1793, *HWL*, IV, 395.

[81] Hamilton to Washington, November 19, 1792, *ibid.*, 363.

[82] Hamilton to Washington, November 23, 1793, *ibid.*, V, 62–63.

[83] Ternant to Montmorin, September 28, 1791, Turner, *Correspondence of the French Ministers*, 49.

[84] Hamilton to Washington, November 19, 1792, *HWL*, IV, 363–65.

[85] Hamilton to Washington, June 5, 1793, *ibid.*, 418–20.

[86] Jefferson to Washington, June 6, 1793, *JW*, IX, 114–17.

scheme, but not enough to meet his needs. Hamilton's financial strictures were the major reason for the failure of the scheme,[87] for it was only lack of funds that prevented him from bringing Louisiana under French control, at least temporarily. The men of Kentucky and Tennessee were eager to march, and George Rogers Clark was eager to lead them, as "Major-General in the Armies of France, and Commander-in-Chief of the Revolutionary Legions on the Mississippi."[88] Clark thought the expedition would prove highly beneficial to his country, and Governor Shelby evidently agreed, because he refused to intervene. The Spanish governor at New Orleans, Barón Francisco Carondelet, saw no hope of withstanding the impending attack. If the Kentuckians marched, he said, Louisiana would "fall into their hands with the greatest rapidity and facility."[89]

Genêt's downfall was gradual and somewhat anticlimactic. His appeals to the American people—never direct or formal, but nonetheless quite open—failed, partly because of the ravages of a yellow-fever epidemic in Philadelphia, in which many of his followers perished, but primarily because of the popularity of George Washington, the belated but powerful opposition of Jefferson and some of his high-level friends, and the writings and influence of Hamilton and other Federalists. Finally, the correct behavior of the national government convinced many Americans that the choice before them was not between France and Britain but between France and American independence—if not, indeed, between Genêt and Washington. Lack of funds deprived the scheme of its motive force, but in the end it was the steady opposition of the national government that spelled its death.

Genêt did not give up easily. He was not yet convinced that he had failed. He remembered the welcome he had received in the South, and he believed he had a reservoir of influence there that could help him overcome the opposition of the government. James Monroe, who was not in close touch with national affairs at the time, also believed that the people of Virginia at least would support Genêt. Jefferson wrote to Monroe in Albemarle, Virginia, that Genêt was probably injuring his own country by his imprudent actions. Monroe replied that he was "well assured" that the residents of his state would consider Genêt's "errors" the result of "the intemperate zeal of an

87 Ford, *Alexander Hamilton*, 288; Richard K. Murdoch, "Citizen Mangourit and the Projected Attack on East Florida in 1794," *Journal of Southern History*, Vol. XIV (November, 1948), 531.

88 Smith, *Arthur St. Clair*, I, 201.

89 Bodley, *George Rogers Clark*, 345–48.

honest heart active in the support of the best of causes, whilst they would deem those of his antagonists as the effect of unsound hearts and wicked heads planning the ruin of that cause."[90] This view, extremely pro-French and anti-administration in tone, was to cause Monroe great embarrassment in years to come.

Genêt and his agent in Charleston, Michel-Ange-Bernard de Mangourit, believed that Governor William Moultrie, one of the "brave republicans of South Carolina," was on their side. But the governor proved to be unwilling to resist the authority of the government and the president. In December, 1793, the South Carolina legislature investigated the Florida invasion plans, and the governor followed the investigation with a proclamation designed to quell them.[91] A "second proclamation of neutrality" issued by Washington on March 24, 1794, was designed to dampen the Kentuckians' enthusiasm for the venture.[92] The movement did not finally die away, however, until Genêt's successor, Joseph Fauchet, formally renounced it.

Official American complaints to the French government about Genêt's activities were couched in terms of friendship and trust, but the detailed instructions sent by the secretary of state to Gouverneur Morris in Paris on August 6, 1793, reviewing and condemning Genêt's practices, and the use Morris made of those instructions must have given the French authorities a fairly clear impression that their minister had blundered.[93] By that time Washington's cabinet had agreed unanimously to ask the French government to recall Genêt. When the question arose about the tone to be taken in the communication, Jefferson commented that he favored "great delicacy." He hoped to avoid offending the French and at the same time to avoid shocking the American people out of their enthusiasm for the revolutionaries. Other cabinet members favored "peremptory terms." Jefferson became exasperated with Hamilton, who said that Genêt's recall should be demanded "even if it should lead to war."[94]

French attacks on American commerce during the summer of 1793—which were not really as serious as they were reported to be—produced more war talk.[95] It seems clear that if the French government had seen fit

[90] Monroe to Jefferson, August 21, 1793, *JMW*, I, 271.

[91] Genêt to Jefferson, December 25, 1793, *ASPFR*, I, 311; John Harold Wolfe, *Jeffersonian Democracy in South Carolina* (Chapel Hill, 1940), 73–74.

[92] *WW*, XXXIII, 304–305.

[93] *JW*, IX, 180–209.

[94] *The Anas*, *ibid.*, I, 379, 406.

[95] Cabinet Opinion draft by Hamilton, August 31, 1793, *HWL*, V, 60.

to support Genêt the United States could not long have remained at peace. The decision at Paris was thus of momentous significance. George Hammond, apparently prompted by Hamilton, asked the British government to try to find out whether the National Convention would stand behind Genêt.[96] Apparently neither Hammond nor Hamilton learned anything conclusive at that time.

As mentioned earlier, it came to be widely believed in the United States that Genêt's ultimate intent was to bring the United States into the war. Hamilton reached that conclusion early and also accused some of Genêt's Republican friends of desiring war.[97] His cabinet opinion of July 8, 1793, referred to Genêt's actions in connection with the *Little Sarah* as part of "a regular plan to force the United States into the war."[98] After several months Jefferson, angry with Genêt for throwing down "the gauntlet to the President," concluded that "his object was evidently, contrary to his professions, to force us into the war."[99] Actually this was not Genêt's aim; his government much preferred to encourage the United States to remain neutral but benevolent.

No American dreaded war with Britain more than Hamilton did. He dwelt at length on the possibility in his correspondence and in his two "Americanus" essays of February, 1794. It would be difficult to finance such a war, he said, unless the nation was rendered desperate by outright invasions. The United States had no army or navy to come to France's aid in Europe. The powerful British navy would make it difficult for the United States to attack Canada and Florida. The nation might be invaded by both British and Spanish forces, which would almost certainly be aided by the Indians. Yet Hamilton's faith in his country did not allow him to countenance the possibility of defeat. The United States would maintain its independence. If Britain should try to take that away, "she would run . . . greater risks of bankruptcy and revolution than we of subjugation."[100]

Hamilton firmly disagreed with the opinion frequently expressed in the Republican press that if the European monarchies managed to defeat the French they would turn on the United States and make it the "next victim,"

[96] Hammond to Grenville, August 10, 1793, FCA, XV.

[97] Hamilton to unnamed correspondent, May, 1793, *HWL*, X, 44.

[98] *Ibid.*, V, 6.

[99] Jefferson to Madison, June 9, 1793, *JW*, XI, 121; Jefferson to Morris, June 9, 1793, *ibid.*, 184; Jefferson to Madison, August 25, 1793, *ibid.*, 211.

[100] *HWL*, V, 93. The two essays appear on pages 74–96.

in order to restore monarchical rule on both continents. Hamilton argued that the American struggle for independence bore no resemblance to the French Revolution and that European monarchs would not make the mistake of equating them. The American uprising had been orderly and in accordance with the laws of nations. It had been free of attacks on the principles of private property and personal security or upon the morals and religion of the people. The people of Europe would not permit such an attack, Hamilton predicted, and, moreover, they would be preoccupied with considerations of the balance of power and other controversies nearer home. Moreover, he was convinced that once the monarchy was restored in France the French people would, upon "sober reflection," agree that the United States had given them no just cause for resentment.[101]

As the war progressed, Hamilton was quick to point out French violations of the treaties between the two countries. On August 31, 1793, he drafted a paper, which was signed by all the cabinet members, asserting that the French government had violated the law of nations and the treaties by ordering the seizure of neutral vessels carrying provisions to British ports.[102] Before the end of the year such violations had become so flagrant that Washington mentioned them in a message to Congress. France, he said, had violated treaty agreements by decreeing that enemy goods were "lawful prize in the vessel of a friend."[103]

Even after the administration requested Genêt's recall, his following in the United States continued to be a threat to the nation's independence. The Democratic clubs were ugly and unpredictable. According to numerous reports, they would toast Genêt at their dinners but often refuse to toast the President. Members would surround Washington's residence in Philadelphia and shout offensive remarks. As late as May 1, 1794, they held a mass rally to celebrate "the success of the French Republic," and they gave threatening toasts "aimed directly at Washington and his administration."[104] Twenty years later John Adams recalled the frightening scenes of 1793 when "ten thousand people in the streets of Philadelphia, day after day, threatened to drag Washington out of his house, and effect a revolution in the government, or compel it to declare war . . . against England." Adams

[101] Hamilton to Washington, April, 1793, *ibid.*, IV, 389–90.

[102] *Ibid.*, V, 60.

[103] *ASPFR*, I, 141.

[104] Harry Marlin Tinkcom, *The Republicans and Federalists in Pennsylvania, 1790–1801* (Harrisburg, 1950), 80–87.

accurately predicted that it would be difficult for "posterity" to believe such events could have occurred. He was convinced that only the yellow-fever epidemic, which dispatched some of the mob's leaders and drove others from the capital, "saved the United States from a fatal revolution."[105]

Relations between Jefferson and Genêt were strained while the administration waited for a reply from Paris to the request for his recall. Genêt remained convinced that the people and Congress would rally to his support, and Jefferson did not find it easy to persuade him otherwise.[106] A cabinet meeting was held on November 18 to consider dismissing him outright. Jefferson opposed the action on the grounds that France was "the only nation on earth sincerely our friend."[107]

In the end Genêt turned against Jefferson—an act of monumental ingratitude toward the man who had supported him and given him wise counsel. Genêt appeared to develop an even greater dislike for Jefferson than for Hamilton, who had been openly and consistently opposed to him. Some of the Federalists viewed with glee Genêt's frustration and Jefferson's embarrassment. Robert Troup, one of Hamilton's closest friends, commented: "What a pleasant thing it is to see Jefferson, Randolph and Genêt by the ears! All has ended well."[108]

The aftermath of Genêt's adventure is well known. He was denounced by his own government, and through the good graces of the administration he had affronted he was allowed to take up residence in the United States as a political exile. In time he became an American citizen.

But Troup had rejoiced too soon. All had not "ended well." The wars in Europe still raged, American commerce was unsafe at sea, Americans were divided, and the nation was on the verge of war with Great Britain.

[105] Adams to Jefferson, June 30, 1813, *AW*, X, 47.

[106] Genêt to the Minister of Foreign Affairs, August 15, 1793, Turner, *Correspondence of the French Ministers*, 240–41.

[107] *The Anas*, *JW*, I, 405.

[108] Robert Troup to Rufus King, January 1, 1794, *KC*, I, 540.

CHAPTER X

Commerce and the Borderlands

By the early 1790's Hamilton's views on foreign policy had reached maturity. Thenceforth he would display no such indecisiveness as that characterizing his opinion to Washington during the Nootka Sound dispute. His direction had become clear. He was firm in his concept of the proper goals toward which he believed his country should steer.

Harmonious relations with Great Britain were at the heart of Hamilton's purpose. English law and system of government appealed to him. He was repelled by the institutions of France and Spain. He viewed with favor the economic practices of the British. He disliked Spanish restrictions on business and distrusted French instability.[1] He saw no reason for future conflict with the mother country, assuming that she would eventually honor her obligations under the Treaty of Paris. Along with Jefferson and most other Americans of that generation, he believed that hostilities with Spain were almost inevitable. The United States needed British goods and British capital, and Britain could not prosper without continued access to the products of American farms and forests. Mutual interests, both material and ideological, called for Anglo-American co-operation; and Hamilton undertook the enormous task of bringing both nations to an awareness of their interdependency.

He was aware of the ill will that clouded the vision of leaders and ordinary citizens on both sides of the Atlantic, and he realized that it constituted a formidable obstacle. He took comfort, however, from the fact that few people of either nation any longer wanted open hostilities, and he was convinced that time, patience, and an eventual recognition of mutual interests would drive away lingering resentments. Hamilton was supremely confident of his ability to guide the actions of the American government, and he intended to play a leading role in bringing the British to his point of

[1] Outline of speech, January, 1794, *HWL*, IV, 213ff.

view. Believing that men's actions are based largely on self-interest, he looked forward to renewed cordiality between the English-speaking countries.

As far as relations with Britain were concerned, Hamilton was the chief author of United States foreign policies from 1791 to 1798—from the end of the Nootka Sound conflict through the ratification of Jay's Treaty, the British evacuation of the Northwest, and the subsequent controversy with France.[2] The diplomatic settlements of those years made the United States' independence secure and provided the indispensable conditions for future national development. From the informal negotiations and discussions between Hamilton and British representatives in New York and Philadelphia came the materials from which the final structure of agreement was formed. This chapter presents an account of the proceedings up to the spring of 1793, when Washington's administration received the news that war had broken out between Great Britain and France.

Hamilton was aware that the task of reconciliation would not be easy. Indeed, he shared in some of his fellow Americans' animosities toward the British. He resented, though less bitterly than others did, Britain's continued occupation of the Northwest, and he stated publicly and repeatedly that the British must eventually withdraw or the United States would have to resort to the "arbitrament of the sword."[3] Yet he did not really think that war would be necessary. He believed that the British soldiers would be withdrawn peaceably as a logical step in Anglo-American rapprochement. He also believed that the United States was still too weak to bring Britain to terms by military means, by retaliatory methods such as those Madison came to advocate, or by cleverly shaped arguments such as those Jefferson began to produce. Hamilton would dispense with the suave discourses of the practiced diplomats and patiently lead both sides to recognize the advantages of concord.

Hamilton was less excited than Washington, Jefferson, and Madison

[2] This period of American history has long been the object of serious study. Bemis' *Jay's Treaty* is the pre-eminent work on the Jay-Grenville negotiations. Burt, *The United States, Great Britain, and British North America,* is also a major contribution, and there are many other works of note. Unfortunately, Hamilton's biographers have given less attention to the diplomatic scene than did Dumas Malone and Irving Brant in their works on Jefferson and Madison. Consequently, Hamilton's motives and achievements in foreign relations have been overlooked or misinterpreted.

[3] Hamilton's speech, "The Independence of Vermont," in the New York Assembly, April, 1787, *HWL*, VIII, 56.

about British occupation of the Northwest posts because he regarded that area of the continent as far less important to his country's future development than the Floridas and Louisiana. His West Indies background may have influenced his convictions about the importance of the Gulf region.

It has been pointed out earlier that most of the disagreements between Britain and the United States had arisen from violations by both nations of the peace treaty and from Britain's unwillingness to begin negotiations for a treaty of commerce. By 1791 many Americans had come to believe that only through such a treaty could friendly relations be restored. It is not surprising that the terms of the treaty were often violated. The treaty was a compromise, and powerful groups in both countries were convinced that their negotiators had sold them out. British delays in withdrawing troops were viewed by the Republicans, who were increasing in numbers, as perfidious behavior. The British continued to encourage the Indians in warfare along the frontier and refused to pay for the slaves that had been taken away by departing British forces at the end of the Revolution. The indefinite boundary line between Maine and New Brunswick stirred further contention. The British, in turn, complained that Americans were not paying debts they owed to British merchants and were continuing to harass the loyalists.

The Nootka Sound controversy revitalized Anglo-American relations. The British government did not immediately reverse its surly attitude, but there was a new awareness of the importance of British interests in North America and commerce with the United States, and a determination to maintain a close watch on the new republic, to warn the American government about the dangers of legislating against British commerce, and to obtain, if possible, concessions that would soften the terms of the peace treaty. It was for those purposes that Major Beckwith was sent to the United States in 1789 (he was promoted to the rank of lieutenant colonel that year). He was to observe, to hold informal talks, to report attitudes and developments in the United States, and to do what he could to influence the American government to remain neutral or pro-British if Britain should go to war with Spain.

Such an emissary could not of course be received as an official representative from the British government. Nevertheless, after discussing the matter with Hamilton and Jay, Washington decided that Hamilton should hold talks with Beckwith in New York and learn what he could about Britain's intentions.[4] Jefferson did not reach New York until about five months after Colonel Beckwith had arrived. In the meantime, the secretary of state opened his own channel of communication to the envoy through James Madison, who lodged in the same house with him. After Hamilton began conferring regularly with Beckwith, Jefferson customarily spoke of the procedure in terms of disgust. He believed that Hamilton was overplaying—and misplaying—his hand. Moreover, it did not escape Jefferson that Hamilton was crossing departmental lines.

Beckwith's letter of credentials from Lord Dorchester did not reveal that his mission had been ordered by the government in London. Hamilton played upon the colonel's pride to learn how much authority Beckwith had and the degree to which he could express the official British view. He called Beckwith's attention to the irregularity of his mission—a point which the colonel had apparently failed to grasp—and to the limitations it placed upon what the envoy could say. Upon reading the letter from Dorchester, Hamilton remarked that it seemed "to speak only the sentiments of his lordship."

Hamilton's strategy was successful. Beckwith immediately revealed the true authors of his mission: "His lordship knew too well the consequences of such a step, to have taken it without a previous knowledge of the intentions of the British cabinet."[5] As their friendship warmed, Beckwith doubtless told Hamilton about the frequent conversations he had had the previous year with high British officials, including Lord Grenville. He relayed Grenville's grave concern about the news of a movement in the United States to place severe restrictions on British trade.

It was obvious to Hamilton that Beckwith's mission was also the result of apprehensions that if war should erupt between Britain and Spain the United States might try to drive a hard bargain in return for remaining neutral. After the Nootka Sound crisis subsided at the end of 1790, Hamilton was pleased to hear that Britain was now eager to improve relations with the United States. Beckwith frequently brought up the subject of an "alliance" between Britain and America. Hamilton replied that he would not "raise or repress expectation" along that line, but added that the American government had "a sincere disposition to concur in obviating with candor and fairness all grounds of misunderstanding" about the execution

[4] Entry dated July 4, 1790, John C. Fitzpatrick (ed.), *Diaries of George Washington, 1748–1799*, (New York, 1925), IV, 143.

[5] Hamilton to Washington, July, 1790, *HWL*, IV, 298.

of the treaty and "in laying the foundation of future good understanding, by establishing liberal terms of commercial intercourse."[6]

Beckwith was an appropriate instrument for Hamilton's purpose of persuading Britons and Americans alike of the benefits that would result from harmonious relations. In a few weeks it became clear that Beckwith was indeed a ready channel to the British government. The Foreign Office maintained regular exchanges with him, and he reported to Grenville in detail about his experiences, conferences, and proposals. Along with his regular dispatches he enclosed notes penned by Hamilton and sometimes by Washington, Jay, and others. These dispatches and enclosures furnish information about the issues of the day that is not obtainable from any other source.

Hamilton, for his part, reported to Washington, and sometimes to the cabinet members, about his discussions with Beckwith. The President relayed some of the information to Congress. This procedure was precisely what Hamilton wanted, for he was as intent on influencing Americans as he was on swaying the British. Formal notes from a recognized minister would necessarily have gone to the secretary of state, and perhaps to the President, in their entirety, whereas in these informal circumstances Hamilton could be selective in the items he transmitted. He took great pains with the wording of his reports. His handwritten draft of a letter to Washington about an early conference with Beckwith shows exhaustive editing, with many interlinear corrections, deletions, and changes in wording. It bears evidence of more reworking than any other Hamilton paper observed in the course of this study.[7]

Spanish policies and possessions in North America brought about a complex diplomatic triangle. Britain's primary aim was to destroy Spain's trade monopoly in the Spanish American colonies, but in crisis after crisis during the 1790's the two countries found themselves in temporary alliances that made it impossible for Britain to seize Spanish territory. It was characteristic of French policy that when Britain and Spain were allied, as they were in 1793, France would immediately begin laying plans to take over Spain's American dominions.[8]

Hamilton's interest in Spanish Florida, dating from prerevolutionary

[6] Hamilton to Washington, July 22, 1790, *ibid.*, 300–301.
[7] *Ibid.*, 299–302. The original draft of the letter is in HPLC, VIII.
[8] Lyon, *Louisiana in French Diplomacy, 1759–1804*, 68.

days, had become even more intense. His determination that the United States must have navigation rights on the lower Mississippi, with a port of deposit, had broadened to a conviction that only by securing the Gulf regions could the United States maintain its territorial unity.

The British government was eager to draw the United States into controversies with Spain. Grenville was sure that the Americans would be interested in obtaining a share of the trade in the Spanish colonies, and he hoped that the Washington administration would agree that the navigation of the Mississippi was of primary importance to the United States. Moreover, he believed that it would be easier for the United States to secure Mississippi navigation rights through British aid than to gain control of the Northwest posts through Spanish aid.[9] Accordingly, Beckwith employed that approach with Hamilton. To soften American resentment, he assured Hamilton that Dorchester had always tried to encourage a friendly attitude toward the United States among the northwestern Indians, while Spain had pursued the opposite course (Hamilton was not convinced that Dorchester had played any such kindly role). Beckwith again mentioned his government's desire for alliance with the United States and asked if there were any binding agreements between the United States and Spain. Hamilton, with Jefferson's approval, assured Beckwith that there were none, hoping thereby to place the United States in the best possible bargaining position with both sides in case they should come to the point of open warfare.[10]

Despite his favorable attitude toward Britain, Hamilton did not want that country to take over Spain's colonial territories. In his view it would be "safer . . . to have two powerful but *rival* nations bordering upon our two extremities than to have one powerful nation pressing us on both sides, and in capacity, hereafter, by posts and settlements, to envelop our whole interior frontier."[11]

By December, 1791, Jefferson was convinced that Spain was ready to negotiate a treaty granting the United States free navigation of the Mississippi. It was at that time that Washington nominated William Carmichael and William Short as envoys to Spain.[12] This move annoyed Grenville, who promptly instructed the new minister to the United States, George Hammond, to keep him fully informed about the progress of negotiations and to

[9] Grenville to Dorchester, May 6, 1790, Brymner, 133.

[10] Hamilton to Washington, July, 1790, July 22, 1790, *HWL*, IV, 296–99, 299–302.

[11] Hamilton to Washington, September 15, 1790, *ibid.*, 319.

tell the American leaders that he hoped they would make "no engagements with the Court of Madrid . . . prejudicial to the interests of Great Britain."[13] Hammond was particularly concerned about Britain's navigation rights on the Mississippi—"rights" Britain and the United States had "granted" each other in the Treaty of Paris.

Hamilton reassured Hammond that the negotiations in Madrid would not lead to any infringements on British rights on the Mississippi. Hamilton expressed his government's pleasure in Britain's interest in shipping on the river; presumably Britain might someday help the United States vindicate its own rights if Spain proved unwilling to concede them. A few months later Hamilton informed the British minister that Spain was balking on the matter of allowing American shippers to establish a port of deposit near the mouth of the Mississippi and predicted that if Spain did not eventually alter its position armed conflict was bound to result. Everything that the Americans proposed in Madrid, he added, was "clogged by some strange absurd impediment or other."[14]

Despite the impediments the treaty negotiations continued. In formulating the proposals pertaining to commerce, Jefferson relied heavily on Hamilton's advice. He believed that Carmichael and Short might be "out of their depth in the details of commerce." Jefferson asked Hamilton specifically what proposals should be made to Spain "on the subject of our fish, grain, and flour" and what should be proposed "as an equivalent." Hamilton gave a carefully prepared reply containing a number of suggestions for alterations and additions. He advised the secretary of state to accept a commercial treaty like the one contemplated, even though the United States failed to gain broad concessions, provided the treaty was "coupled with a satisfactory adjustment of the *boundary* and *navigation*." He was far more interested in those adjustments than in any trade concession Spain was likely to grant. He made no direct comment on Jefferson's concern about inabilities of the American negotiators, but he did suggest that the treaty proposals should be transmitted to the United States for "the participation of the Senate."[15] No doubt Hamilton wanted to observe the trend of the negotiations at first hand, to be sure that no harmful concessions were granted and that no opportunity was overlooked for acquiring the Mississippi outlet.

[12] Washington to the Senate, January 11, 1791, *WW*, XXXI, 456–57.

[13] Grenville to Hammond, January 5, 1792, PROFO, 4, XIV.

[14] Hammond to Grenville, April 5 and July 3, 1792, *ibid.*, XIV, XVI.

[15] Jefferson to Hamilton, March 5, 1792, Hamilton to Jefferson, March, 1792, *HWL*, IV, 358–62.

Actual commerce between the United States and Spain was relatively insignificant in 1792, too minor an issue to carry the burden of the concessions the United States wanted. Jefferson overargued the American case for boundaries and navigation, discussing at length the web of treaties that had been negotiated among the United States, Britain, Spain, and France in efforts to settle the disputed claims to the New Orleans area. He held that by the treaty of 1783 the United States had acquired legal right to navigate the full length of the Mississippi. Though Spain had wrested the Floridas from Britain during the American Revolution, it had not conquered the "waters," which still belonged to Britain in 1782 when the peace treaty was drawn up. Hamilton tried to save Jefferson from this blunder by including in his comments the question, "Is not the conquest of a water an incident to that of territory?" Bemis has characterized Jefferson's arguments on this point as "casuistry."[16] Even Malone described the secretary of state as "legally and philosophically . . . on shaky ground."[17]

The Spanish officials were alarmed by the American secretary's claim to lands which seemed to them unquestionably Spanish. They resorted to dilatory tactics in Madrid and undertook renewed anti-American activity in their Gulf possessions. The Indians in the Southwest Territory were encouraged to intensify their attacks on white settlers.[18] Spanish forts and garrisons along the Mississippi were reinforced to some extent.[19] When the alliance was formed between Britain and Spain the following year, Jefferson perceived a "lowering disposition" on the part of both nations. Spain continued to avoid arriving at a treaty settlement and, Jefferson reported, "sent 1,500 men to New Orleans, and greatly strengthened her upper posts on the Mississippi."[20] At the same time Spain stepped up efforts to bring about disaffection among settlers along the Mississippi and Ohio rivers. Disposition of the real issues would not be made until three years later, when Spain found itself isolated in Europe and hard pressed by frontiersmen in the American territories.[21]

16 Bemis, "Thomas Jefferson," *The American Secretaries of State*, II, 46–57.

17 Malone, II, 409.

18 Hammond to Grenville, December 4, 1792, PROFO, 4, XVI; Jefferson to Carmichael and Short, May 31, 1793, *JW*, IX, 101.

19 Governor St. Clair to Hamilton, August 9, 1793, Smith, *Arthur St. Clair*, II, 318.

20 Jefferson to Madison, June 2, 1793, *JW*, IX, 106.

21 T. M. Green, *The Spanish Conspiracy; a Review of Early Spanish Movements in the Southwest* (Cincinnati, 1891); A. P. Whitaker, *Spanish-American Frontier, 1783–1795* (New York, 1927).

Washington's administration was keenly disappointed by the turn of events. Jefferson, whose resentment of both nations led him to expect the worst of them, spoke gloomily of a possible common stand by Britain and Spain against the United States, even while they remained enemies in Europe.[22] He adopted an attitude of waiting and glaring. Hamilton was not content to take a passive role toward Spain, though he was to display remarkable patience in times of severe crisis, such as that of 1794 with Britain and that of 1796–98 with France. Like Jefferson, he distrusted Spain; but, unlike his colleague, he looked toward Britain in hopes of joining that nation in bringing pressure on the Spaniards. For the time, however, the issues remained unsettled.

One of the foremost problems that continued to face Washington's administration was the control of the nation's foreign commerce, three-fourths of which was carried on with Great Britain. Trade regulations had remained unstable since the end of the Revolutionary War. At one stage in the peace negotiations in 1782 the Americans had convinced Richard Oswald, a British negotiator, that the peace treaty should provide for Anglo-American trade to "go on precisely as if the separation had not taken place."[23] This stipulation had not been included in the treaty, but Prime Minister Shelburne had been determined to be generous with the United States, not only in ceding territory westward to the Mississippi but also in granting liberal terms for commercial intercourse. Before the Revolution the United States had been Britain's best customer. British merchants, recalling that brisk prewar trade, had been "loud and insistent in their demands" for the free flow of commerce advocated by Adam Smith.[24] Merchants in the British West Indies preferred to import food and lumber directly from the United States to avoid the higher costs of the triangular Britain-Canada-West Indies exchanges.[25]

Those liberal attitudes did not prevail. Shelburne found, as Hamilton would later, that most of his fellow countrymen were not ready for any such "advanced doctrine." Canadians fiercely protested the territorial conces-

[22] Jefferson to Washington, September 9, 1792, *HWH*, IV, 294.

[23] Report on conversation with John Jay, Beckwith to Grenville, August 31, 1791, PROFO, 4, XII.

[24] Jensen, *The New Nation*, 157. See pages 154–66 for a clear exposition of Britain's treatment of American commerce following the Revolution.

[25] Bemis, *Jay's Treaty*, 31.

sions, and they, together with like-minded Englishmen, were able to rally enough votes in the House of Commons to censure the treaty and force Shelburne's resignation. Canadians, including new arrivals who had been loyalists in the American Revolution, demanded the right to supply the West Indies with lumber and fish. Conservative members of Parliament still cherished the Navigation Acts as a bulwark of the nation's economy and a nursery for seamen and demanded caution in taking any measures that might enable the United States to develop a mighty merchant marine or set up its own factories.[26]

The Navigation Acts remained in force, but through a series of modifying statutes and regulations Parliament and the Privy Council provided means of accommodating trade between the United States and the British Isles. Trade with the West Indies was placed on a much more restricted basis, an act that was to remain a source of irritation for more than a generation.

On April 8, 1789, James Madison introduced a bill in the House of Representatives designed to levy a low tariff on imports and low tonnage dues on ships. He tried to make the bill noncontroversial, pointing out the immediate need for revenue and the fact that though the Continental Congress and the state legislatures had agreed to a tariff, they had been unable to put it into effect nationally because of the "state of imbecility" of the national government under the Articles of Confederation.[27]

Prompt enactment of his bill was necessary, said Madison, if revenue was to be collected on the "spring importations." Congress delayed action to await the arrival of representatives from Georgia and the Carolinas and to discuss the respective advantages of ad valorem and specific duties. The real point of controversy was the last part of Madison's bill, dealing with tonnage rates for vessels of foreign countries; ships and goods from nations having commercial treaties with the United States were to be charged less than those from countries that had not yet made such treaties.

Madison apparently did not expect the protracted debate that the bill engendered, but he defended it vigorously and fought passionately for the discrimination clause. He demanded to know why foreign nations would bother to make favorable trade treaties with the United States if it did not show favor to those who did. When France and Great Britain were brought into the discussion, he frankly admitted he was partly moved by a senti-

[26] *AW*, VIII, 291.
[27] *Annals*, I, 102–103.

mental desire to favor the ally. He also saw a direct national interest involved in bringing the nation's commerce into a more "natural channel." To illustrate the point, he reported that Britain was annually importing "eighty or ninety thousand hogsheads" of American tobacco, consuming "scarcely 15,000," of it and exporting the remainder, of which 20,000 hogsheads went to France. Obviously the British middlemen were taking a profit. Proper discrimination against British ships, he held, would result in the shipment of tobacco from the United States directly to France, presumably with higher profits for the American producers.[28]

Hamilton had no direct part in this debate, of course, but his position was reflected in the speeches of New York Representatives Egbert Benson and John Laurance.[29] Benson saw no good reason why "Dutch and French ships should be preferred to English" ships, unless preferential treatment was stipulated in the United States' treaties with those nations. Laurance believed that the nation's trade with Britain, Spain, and Portugal was "as lucrative and useful" as that with nations that had made commercial treaties with the United States—France, the Netherlands, Sweden, and Prussia. In his judgment a treaty with Britain was "more likely to be brought about by moderation than by a war of commercial regulations." In such a contest the United States would suffer more than Britain, which was firmly established and had enough capital "to bear the loss of a suspension of trade."[30]

Madison and others tried to refute the contention that Britain would have an advantage in a commercial contest. Thomas Fitzsimmons of Pennsylvania was convinced that the British West Indies would be ruined if trade with the United States was closed off. Roger Sherman of Connecticut held that Britain imported from the United States only those goods which "she cannot get anywhere else." Madison fully agreed with these statements and later summarized the position neatly by saying, "We can do better without Great Britain than she can do without us; articles of luxury can be retrenched with advantage."[31]

The British government, concerned by the debates in Congress, instructed its minister to the United States to threaten retaliation by Parliament. It did not, however, take any action against the mild measures that were

[28] May 4, 1789, *ibid.*, 236–40.

[29] Occasionally spelled Lawrence in the *Annals*.

[30] April 21, May 4, 1792, *Annals*, I, 176–81, 234–36.

[31] April 21, 25, 1789, May 13, 1790, *ibid.*, 188, 206, II, 1624.

finally enacted by Congress in 1789. The House of Representatives voted for the discriminatory tonnage rates against Britain but acquiesced in the Senate's proposal to charge instead a rate of fifty cents a ton on all foreign ships. Madison's proposal of six cents a ton for American ships proved acceptable to both houses of Congress, and a tariff averaging 8½ per cent was enacted. A drawback of 10 per cent of the tariff was to be allowed on goods imported in American-built or owned ships. Mild as these measures were, and in spite of the pressing need for revenue, they were not sent to President Washington for his approval until July. At first some merchants feared that the duties would prove injurious to "shipbuilding, fishery, and carrying trade"; but this fear soon vanished amid the rising prosperity of the period.[32]

Political alignments began to reveal themselves in the arguments for and against the discrimination clause. Though Madison tried to serve the interests of the nation—not merely those of his own state or class—he emerged as the leader of the southern agrarians who would form the nucleus of the Republican party. Opponents of discrimination, predominantly of the northern and central parts of the country, were more inclined to speak for financial and commercial interests. Many of the latter joined the Federalists. There was more than a sprinkling of opposition to Madison from Federalists of the South.[33] Party lines were drawn more sharply during the 1790's by Hamilton's financial measures, the impact of the French Revolution, Jay's Treaty, and other features of the Federalist program. The Federalists, now the spokesmen for commercial interests, came to favor closer relations with Britain, while the Republicans advocated coercive legislation that would force Britain to open the West Indies to American shipping. On the surface, therefore, it appeared that despite the Federalists' apparent representation of commercial interests it was the southerners who were actually most concerned with expanding commerce (and later the most determined to halt British impressment of American seamen). The explanation of this seeming paradox is related to the party complex that developed in regard to diplomatic relations with Britain and France. The men of commerce had more to lose at the outset from a break with Britain, for they were enjoying profitable trade in spite of British restrictions and annoyance. The people of the

[32] Christopher Gore of Massachusetts to Rufus King, April 25, 1789, *KC*, I, 360.

[33] William Barry Grove, Federalist representative from North Carolina, to James Hogg, a merchant at Wilmington, North Carolina, January 23, 1794, K. P. Battle (ed.), "Letters of Nathaniel Macon, John Steele, and William Barry Grove," *James Sprunt Historical Monograph*, No. III, (Chapel Hill, 1902), 99–100.

South, on the other hand, could see no economic dangers in their restrictive proposals. Apparently only a few southern leaders realized that commercial restrictions might bring acute distress to their region, when agricultural products might "rot in warehouses."[34] The people of the South, especially those of Virginia and North Carolina, were haunted by fears of a possible movement to restore to British owners landed estates confiscated during the Revolution. Finally, the South had suffered grievously from marauding redcoats and Tories during the Revolution. It was not strange that bitter anti-British feeling lingered in the region.

Madison was by far the most prominent congressman in the first House of Representatives. He took the floor 124 times during the five-month session, more than twice as many times as his nearest contenders, Congressmen Elbridge Gerry and Thomas Fitzsimmons.[35] The members finally tired of him, however, as the months passed and he displayed such dogged determination to force enactment of some form of discriminatory legislation. When the Senate struck the discriminatory article from the original tonnage bill and the House agreed to the amendment, Madison rose to complain that his fellow congressmen were "afraid of losing all in endeavoring to attain all." He vowed to continue to support the original clause, adding that if the Senate refused to "adopt what is for the common good" they would "be answerable for the consequences."[36] He voted with the minority and refused to give up the fight.

Jefferson was never as determined as Madison upon retaliation against the British, but the young congressman found some encouragement in the attitude of his older friend. Before resigning from his post as minister to France, Jefferson had written to Madison that he remembered Britain as the nation that had tried to annihilate his country and, having failed in that effort, was continuing to inflict every possible injury. In disparaging anti-Madison forces in the congressional debate in 1790, he wrote, "The fear is that it would irritate Great Britain were we to feel any irritation ourselves."[37] Such thoughts were expressed again and again by Madison in House de-

[34] Thomas Tucker of South Carolina, April 9, 1789, and James Jackson of Georgia, May 5, 1789, *Annals*, I, 107–108, 252.

[35] Brant, III, 246.

[36] July 1, 1789, *Annals*, I, 615–19.

[37] Jefferson to Madison, August 28, 1789, *JW*, VII, 449; Jefferson to Edward Rutledge, July 4, 1790, *ibid.*, VIII, 60.

bates on discrimination that continued intermittently until the ratification of Jay's Treaty in 1795.

The House toiled diligently, especially during the month of May, 1790, over a bill to charge all foreign ships a "tonnage of one dollar." The petition was put in the form of a bill and brought up for discussion. Inasmuch as the tonnage would be charged against French vessels as well as British ones, Madison opposed the bill. When it was amended to apply only to "bottoms belonging to nations not in commercial treaty with the United States," it received a favorable vote of thirty-two to nineteen. During the debate before the vote was taken, Madison commented that "there are cases in which it is better to do nothing than not to do a great deal" and suggested that "it might be good policy to interdict the vessels of all nations from carrying our produce." On the following day, May 14, 1790, Madison moved to amend the resolution with a statement that "no such vessel be permitted to export from the United States any unmanufactured article being the growth or produce thereof."[38]

In this extreme form the proposal produced exasperated opposition. Theodore Sedgwick of Massachusetts called it a "measure of passion" and of "very great impropriety." Hamilton's friend William L. Smith of South Carolina called it "highly impolitic" and saw no reason to condemn Britain "for following her usual policy in her navigation laws," which had been "originally aimed at the Dutch." He called for time to negotiate a treaty and pointed out that Britain's "stable and permanent administration . . . might cripple our commerce exceedingly from one Congress to another." He added that some products from the United States were admitted to Britain duty-free, though the British charged a duty on similar articles from other countries.

Madison countered by drawing attention to British discrimination against American trade with the West Indies—which trade he claimed was about one-fourth the amount of commerce between the United States and all of Europe—and by demanding discrimination in turn as the only way to "teach" other countries the value of "a treaty with us" and to strengthen the hand of the President in negotiating trade treaties. In time Britain would succumb to such pressure, for it could not "bear to see between five and six hundred vessels rotting in port [and] seven or eight thousand seamen thus turned out of employment." A break in Anglo-American trade, he added,

[38] May 13, 1790, *Annals*, II, 1624–26.

would also bring unemployment in British industries while stimulating American industrial development and would "increase the spirit of emigration, already so much dreaded" by Britain. The bill was passed by the House of Representatives, but was rejected by the Senate, where Hamilton exerted greater influence.[39]

Though other pressing matters were requiring the attention of the legislators, on June 30 Madison again renewed the controversy by introducing a long, carefully worded resolution that in effect would have prohibited United States–British West Indies trade as long as British restrictions remained in effect. According to the *Annals of Congress*, four members spoke briefly in favor of the motion; then James Jackson, the "militant Georgia republican,"[40] brought forth a blast of opposition that killed the measure for that year. He maintained that the proposed resolution would be disastrous to Georgia—and to North Carolina, too, he believed, in spite of the contrary view of some members from that state. It was "extraordinary indeed," he commented, that "the gentleman from Virginia should come forward with one exceptional proposition after another . . . so tenacious is he of his object."[41] (The records of the early *Annals* are incomplete and inexact, and it is probable that Jackson used far stronger words than "extraordinary" and "exceptional." According to reports, his speeches were delivered so lustily that when he spoke in the House the senators sometimes had to close the windows of their chamber to deaden the noise.)

Britain and France followed the debates in Congress with keen interest. Sir John Temple, the British consul at New York, was instructed to report on the new port charges and duties enacted by Congress and the differences in charges imposed in various other countries.[42] The French chargé d'affaires, Louis-Guillaume Otto, reminding Jefferson of the "principles of friendship and attachment" with which France had regarded the United States, declared that the new tonnage law, which did not exempt the French vessels, was "directly contrary to the spirit and to the object of the treaty of commerce" between the two countries.[43] Jefferson was able to show that no treaty violation had taken place, since each ally was pledged only to grant

[39] May 14, 1790, *ibid.*, 1628–35. The Senate debates were not published at the time.

[40] Brant, III, 245.

[41] *Annals*, II, 1712–14.

[42] See Jay's report to the President, entry dated October 7, 1789, Fitzpatrick, *Diaries of Washington, 1748–1799*, IV, 15.

[43] Otto to Jefferson, December 3, 1790, January 8, 1791, Jefferson to Washington, January 18, 1791, *Annals*, II, 2173–80.

to the other terms as favorable as those applying to the "most favored nation." Jefferson did recommend, however, that the United States make some special concession to France. French decrees of 1787 and 1788 had granted Americans a monopoly on the shipment of whale oil to France. Also, as he said, nearly two-thirds of the produce of American cod fisheries found a free market in French colonies. Jefferson feared that this highly profitable commerce might be curtailed by French retaliation.

In this instance Hamilton joined in the debate. He differed with the secretary of state, though amicably, to judge from his correspondence. Before Jefferson sent his report on the matter to President Washington, Hamilton first read it "with attention."[44] He agreed with Jefferson's interpretation of the Franco-American treaty but did not approve of making unilateral concessions to France. Otto was asking for concessions that would permit French vessels to be admitted to American ports duty-free while offering in return merely a continuation of most-favored-nation treatment of American ships in French ports, which meant that American ships would pay the same duty as "the mass of foreign vessels." Hamilton did not minimize the importance of commerce with France; on the contrary, he looked for a "probable increase" in it; but he advocated negotiating a "new treaty of commerce with France" that would set forth in explicit terms mutually acceptable concessions. Such a treaty would benefit the United States and, unlike direct concessions, probably would not antagonize Britain. He warned of the "inconvenience and injury" of "commercial warfare," which might lead to a "worse kind of warfare." For the next two years—until the difficulties with Genêt arose—Hamilton showed more interest than Jefferson did in negotiating a new treaty with France.

Hamilton tried to use French interest in American trade to expedite similar treaty discussions with the British. He told Beckwith that, shortly before Ternant had become minister to the United States, the French National Assembly had authorized the formation of a new treaty with the United States. Of course, the British were already aware of the fact, but Hamilton cleverly added that France had become alarmed and jealous because Britain was beginning to devote more attention to the new nation.[45] It was a ploy reminiscent of Franklin's procedures in Paris in 1782, and it had similar results. Beckwith immediately began urging Grenville to em-

[44] Hamilton to Jefferson, January 11, 13, 1791, *HWL*, IV, 345–48.
[45] Beckwith to Grenville, August 31, 1791, PROFO, 4, XII.

bark on treaty discussions as a means of undermining French influence in the United States.

After relations between Hamilton and Jefferson grew strained, Jefferson came to believe that Hamilton was pressing for a new treaty with France only to obtain a treaty with Britain—one so binding as to limit American sovereignty.[46] Jefferson's suspicions were unfounded. There are no grounds for doubting Hamilton's own statement, made several years later, that he never desired a treaty with Britain "giving to her any privilege or advantage which was not to be imparted to other nations."[47]

Britain, which had less justification than France for protesting the American tonnage laws, tried to forestall further restrictive legislation. Beckwith reported to Grenville about his warnings to American leaders that Britain could, if necessary, do without American trade and that retaliation would be met by retaliation.[48] When Gouverneur Morris conferred with Prime Minister Pitt in 1790, Pitt insisted that American commerce was so favorably treated in England that American laws should in turn favor British commerce.[49]

Beckwith was jolted when Washington reported to the Senate that Morris' dispatches had convinced him of Britain's disinterest in a treaty of commerce except as part of a "treaty of alliance offensive and defensive, or unless in the event of a rupture with Spain."[50] In a dispatch to Grenville, Beckwith enclosed a copy of the President's message, along with a note from Hamilton assuring him that Washington was not prejudiced against Britain because of the treatment that had been accorded Morris in London. Hamilton added significantly that "such views," however, had probably influenced the thinking of "certain persons"—meaning, no doubt, Madison and Jefferson.[51]

Beckwith's mission in America was not lacking in results. Like Hamilton he worked hard to improve Anglo-American relations. Their common cause was largely the reason for the cordiality and close association that developed between them. Beckwith was soon advocating to his government precisely those courses of action that Hamilton wanted the British to adopt.

[46] *The Anas, JW*, I, 297.
[47] Hamilton's letter attacking John Adams in 1800, *HWL*, VII, 358.
[48] Beckwith to Grenville, March 3, 1791, PROFO, 4, XII.
[49] Morris to Washington, May 29, 1790, *ASPFR*, I, 125.
[50] Washington to the Senate, February 14, 1791, *ASPFR*, I, 121.
[51] Beckwith to Grenville, March 3, 1791, PROFO, 4, XII.

Beckwith also reported to Grenville that most "sensible" Americans were eager to reach fair adjustments of the controversies between the two nations. He was convinced that a commercial treaty would serve Britain's interests, for the United States, facing a glorious future, was beginning to "feel its own importance." Beckwith commented that he had come to look upon the birth of every child from "New Hampshire to the river Mississippi" as a potential consumer of British goods. Everywhere in the new nation he saw "a spirit of order, industry, and improvement."[52]

Beckwith came to have absolute confidence in Hamilton. Again and again he praised Hamilton's veracity and integrity. He considered Hamilton a source of confidential information about American affairs and urged Grenville to avoid making any statement that might reveal to the United States Senate how close the relationship between the two men had become. Following Hamilton's own line, Beckwith relayed his conviction that though the secretary of the treasury was motivated by a desire to promote American interests, his program would also advance the welfare of Great Britain.

Beckwith fell so completely under Hamilton's influence that he even imitated the latter's literary style. Toward the end of his sojourn in the United States his dispatches took on an unmistakable Hamiltonian idiom.

Hamilton was embarrassed and disquieted by Madison's seemingly endless proposals for retaliatory measures. In principle Hamilton was opposed to trade restrictions, especially tariffs, except for military purposes, for temporary protection of infant industries, or as a defense against the tariffs of other countries.[53] Once, in exasperation, Hamilton protested that the Republicans were determined to upset their "competitors" even if they had to destroy the national government in the process. He pleaded, unavailingly, for a "neutral and pacific policy"[54] and exerted his influence in the Senate against the discriminatory resolutions. Early in 1791, to prevent the British from becoming aroused and to gain time to allow his own policies to develop, he told Beckwith that nothing would "take place during the present session to the injury of your trade." But determined to make the most of the situation, Hamilton added that Congress would probably enact a law copied after the British Navigation Acts to prohibit the importation of non-British goods in British vessels. Though he predicted that such a law would have

[52] *Ibid.*; Beckwith to Grenville, June 14, 1791, *ibid.*

[53] Louis M. Hacker, "The Report on Manufactures," *The Historian*, Vol. XIX (February, 1957), 144–67.

[54] Hamilton to Col. Edward Carrington, May 26, 1792, *HWL*, IX, 530.

no profound effect, he must have known how deeply such a course would be resented, for again he urged the negotiation of an Anglo-American trade treaty. He added profound assurances that a great many Americans longed for improved relations with the mother country and that their numbers would rapidly increase if British authorities would give them some grounds for encouragement.[55]

Beckwith did not seem eager to prolong his visit to the United States. From time to time he suggested to his superiors that the British government should send a regular minister to Philadelphia. In the spring of 1791 he predicted flatly that if his government remained inactive British commerce would "not remain on its present footing beyond the month of November next."[56]

By the time Beckwith's dispatch reached London, the British government had already decided to send a minister, George Hammond, to the United States. Though avoiding unseemly haste in the matter, Grenville wanted the decision to be relayed to Philadelphia as soon as possible to preclude further untoward legislation. He chose to convey the tidings through Colonel William S. Smith, Vice-President Adams' son-in-law and secretary of the American legation at London. Hamilton learned of the new development unofficially at the end of June, 1791. He expressed gratification and restrained optimism, observing that "if some liberal arrangement with Great Britain should ensue, it [would] have a prodigious effect upon the conduct of some other parts of Europe."[57] Madison was less sanguine. In a letter to his father he commented that if the British minister brought "powers and dispositions" to make a reasonable treaty they would represent "an interesting change in the councils of that nation."[58]

George Hammond was, at twenty-eight, rather youthful to be representing Britain in the United States. His efforts in Philadelphia bore little evidence of the diplomatic ability he was to display in later life. He was sincere in his desire to improve Anglo-American relations, but he lacked Beckwith's sympathy for the Americans, and of course his actions as an official representative from Britain were more closely circumscribed by the Foreign Office. The American leaders' expectations of progress were soon replaced

[55] Beckwith to Grenville, January 20, 1791, PROFO, 4, XII.

[56] Beckwith to Grenville, March 3, 1791, *ibid.*

[57] Hamilton to Benjamin Goodhue, representative from Massachusetts, June 30, 1791, *HWL*, IX, 484.

[58] July 2, 1791, *MW*, VI, 54.

by general disappointment when they learned that Hammond could only discuss the issues; he was not empowered to make binding agreements.[59] His primary mission was to study carefully and report on American attitudes and intentions and to prevent, through his presence and "a procrastinated negotiation," any serious anti-British moves by the American government.[60] Americans were not interested in his suggestions for an alliance, and his proposal for settling the western disputes by ceding the land to the Indians shocked Federalists and Republicans alike.

Hamilton established with the new minister the same kind of relationship he had maintained with Beckwith. Like Beckwith, Hammond became thoroughly convinced of Hamilton's good faith and desire for a just settlement. Hammond closely guarded his confidential conversations with Hamilton; in some of his "secret and confidential" dispatches he gave Hamilton's name in cipher—a secret within a secret. In praising Hamilton's character he commented that all the secretary's "interests, political and personal, are so implicated in the preservation of peace as to leave me no doubt of his sincerity."[61] When Hamilton inadvertently gave him some incorrect information about Carmichael's and Short's mission to Spain, Hammond attributed the episode to "an alteration of system in the Spanish court rather than to any deception on the part of Mr. Hamilton." In all his communications with Hamilton, he said, he had "never yet at any time had reason to suspect him of artifice or imposition."[62] Both Beckwith and Hammond were right in trusting Hamilton's sincerity, as they were right in believing that he was genuinely striving to advance American interests. The ultimate failure of governments to accept Hamilton's point of view was a serious misfortune.

Hamilton took up with Hammond the same points he had raised with Beckwith, in even greater detail. Acknowledging the fact that the loudest complaints of Madison and others were directed toward the restrictions on American exports to the West Indies, Hamilton urged "with much force and emphasis" the need for some moderation, even though exporters remained limited in the "size and tonnage of the vessels employed in the trade." He had no objection to measures that would prevent the traders

[59] For Hammond's instructions, see Mayo, 2–13.

[60] Bemis, *Jay's Treaty*, 94.

[61] Hammond to Grenville, April 2, 1793, FCA, XV.

[62] Hammond to Grenville, July 3, 1792, PROFO, 4, XVI.

from assuming a share of transporting West Indies exports to Britain.[63] Hammond listened attentively but noncommittally in accordance with his instructions, as well as his awareness of Britain's adherence to the Navigation Laws. Yet Hamilton's persuasiveness soon convinced him that trade relations should be improved; and there were rays of hope, as when Grenville instructed him to open negotiations for a commercial treaty based on reciprocal advantages and most-favored-nation treatment.[64] But such negotiations were peripheral to Hammond's primary tasks. From the British point of view there was no reason for haste. Britain had a near monopoly on the delivery of foreign goods to the American market; and Americans were generally eager to sell their products to Britain with or without a treaty.

After a reminder from Jefferson about the removal of the slaves in 1783, Hammond took up the subject with Hamilton. The British held that the action was not actually a violation of the treaty because the slaves had become free men upon entering British camps. Hamilton did not press the matter, which in his view was of secondary importance. Hammond reported that in the same conversation St. Croix River—the unsettled northeastern boundary of the United States—was discussed and that Hamilton again failed to express great interest. Later he learned that both Hamilton and Jefferson thought the boundary could readily "be adjusted by commissions."[65]

The crucial issue was, of course, the western territories. Some members of Congress gave their support to Madison's discrimination proposals mainly because of their keen resentment of Britain's retention of the military posts.[66] Correspondence among Canadians following the treaty of 1783 had been "alive with chagrin at the boundary which the United States had secured."[67] They were convinced that transferring the Northwest to the United States would put an end to the trade with the Indians. Britain encouraged disaffection among Americans in Vermont and in the Mississippi Valley to try to hold the west and warned the Indians that the encroaching settlers would destroy them.[68] Two-thirds of Hammond's original instructions dealt with

[63] Hammond to Grenville, January 9, 1792, *ibid.*

[64] Grenville to Hammond, September 1, 1791, Mayo, 17–19.

[65] Hammond to Grenville, January 9, October 3, 1792, PROFO, 4, XIV, XVI.

[66] *Annals*, II, 1628, 1633.

[67] Bemis, *Jay's Treaty*, 9.

[68] Col. Josiah Harmar to Henry Knox, June 1, 1785, Capt. John Doughty to Henry Knox, October 21, 1785; Smith, *Arthur St. Clair*, II, 9–10; Washington to Jefferson, April 4, 1791, *WW*, XXXI, 267.

the posts, and they were the primary subject of Grenville's later instructions, as well as of Hammond's dispatches. Hammond was cautioned about the "great importance" of the posts "both in a commercial and political view." He was directed to transmit everything Washington or the cabinet members said about the posts, as well as anything else he could learn on the subject "from any quarter." According to his instructions it was "to be wished" that the posts "should remain in His Majesty's possession, if the conduct of the United States should continue to justify this measure." Hammond was to state that Britain would have "restored these posts and forts immediately after the ratification of the treaty, if the said States had complied with the fourth and fifth articles of the said treaty [those having to do with repayment of debts] in favor of British creditors."[69]

It is difficult to see what the "said States" could have done at that point to persuade the British to give up the posts, in view of Grenville's instruction to Hammond two months later not to accept any offer that the Americans might make to repay the debts in return for the posts. Hammond was to point out that losses to British creditors were in many cases irrecoverable owing to the disappearance of records and the deaths of witnesses during the intervening years. Hammond was also to insist that American settlers must not be permitted to enter the Northwest Territory; the dispute should be handled by negotiations between the two governments, not by "individual action."[70] Individual action was taking place, nevertheless. Settlers continued to pour across the Ohio River to establish settlements[71] and thereby make the situation even more tense.

In point of fact, it was not American violations of the treaty that had influenced the British to hold the posts. During the first months after the treaty went into effect, they made no issue about American violations. The real reason the British refused to leave was the fur trade. Even before the treaty was proclaimed, fur-trading interests were insisting that the posts must not be abandoned. Each year the Indians were selling furs worth £200,000 to Canadian dealers, and half the furs were thought to be coming from regions south of the treaty boundary. This commerce "furnished huge profits to the Montreal traders, valuable freight for English navigators, rich tariffs to the English exchequer, [and] a lucrative turnover to the London

[69] Instructions drafted by Lord Hawkesbury (president of the Board of Trade), July 4, 1791, Mayo, 7–9.

[70] Grenville to Hammond, September 2, 1791, Mayo, 13–14.

[71] Gen. Arthur St. Clair to Hamilton, May 25, 1791, Smith, *Arthur St. Clair*, II, 209–11.

importers."[72] Great pressure was brought to bear on the British government not to make any move that would endanger that trade.

Governor Clinton of New York continued to be acutely disturbed by British occupation of the Northwest. Washington, who realized that military action was out of the question, urged upon the governor "a conduct of circumspection, moderation and forbearance."[73] It was a course that Washington himself must have found difficult to maintain. Perhaps no American resented more deeply than he British presence within United States borders. For that reason he had not shown much eagerness about the talks between Hamilton and Beckwith about a commercial treaty. To Washington, the first step was for the British to "fulfill what they already stand engaged to perform."[74]

Negotiations between Hammond and Jefferson opened with recriminations. After months of diplomatic sparring, Hammond addressed to the secretary of state a long, detailed note accusing the United States of violating the treaty on many occasions.[75] Jefferson's devastating rejoinder is perhaps the best illustration of his competence and shrewdness in the field of diplomatic repartee.[76] Hammond had listed several instances in which, he claimed, American courts had refused to require Americans to pay what they owed to British creditors. Jefferson submitted proof that in some of the cases full payment had been made and that in others there were no such persons as Hammond had listed. Jefferson used his evidence in such a manner as to make it appear to nullify all of Hammond's accusations. He then proceeded to cite glaring British infractions of the treaty. The impression one receives from his notes is that of an unoffending United States victimized by the outrages of an arrogant bully.

The exchange brings into focus the difference between Hamilton's diplomatic methods and Jefferson's. The latter pursued the ancient crafts of diplomacy by marshaling his arguments into their most powerful form and using them to bludgeon those of his opponent. The question was, Would the secretary's adroitness succeed in redeeming American soil from the clutches of the British? In this instance Jefferson again relied too heavily on the force of words. He despised Hamilton's approach of amiability and

[72] Bemis, *Jay's Treaty*, 3–11.
[73] Washington to Clinton, September 14, 1791, *WW*, XXXI, 369.
[74] Entry dated July 8, 1790, Fitzpatrick, *Diaries of George Washington, 1748–1799*, IV, 139.
[75] Hammond to Jefferson, March 5, 1792, *ASPFR*, I, 191–200.
[76] Jefferson to Hammond, May 29, 1792, *ibid.*, 201–37.

patience; yet he also opposed strengthening American military might. In 1792 he did not join Washington and Hamilton in requesting Congress to augment the armed forces. Instead, he told the President that he regretted the failure of the Constitution to guarantee to the people "freedom from standing armies."[77] He continued to believe that the nation could safely rely on the militia, the position he had taken in 1791, when British authorities were trying to force American settlers out of the Northwest. At that time Jefferson had suggested (and Washington had agreed) that the settlers should seek protection from the militia in the area.[78]

Hamilton read a draft of Jefferson's reply to Hammond's charges and induced him to omit certain features, such as those which made basic assumptions about the right and wrong of the dispute. To Hamilton, the "rule in construing treaties" should be "to suppose both parties in the right, for want of a common judge."[79] Then and later, Hamilton protested publicly and privately about American treaty violations. Official denials of violations which were common knowledge offended his sense of honor. As he pointed out to Hammond, he believed that the weakness of the Continental Congress had been the primary reason for the nation's failure to abide by the treaty terms.[80]

Jefferson rejected some of his colleague's recommendations to moderate the reply. He insisted on justifying American action rather than explaining the extenuating circumstances and then trying to work for mutual understanding. Hamilton was so disturbed by this procedure that he never forgot it. Ten years later he was to write that Jefferson's handling of negotiations with the British in 1792 had seemed designed "to widen, not to heal, the breach between the two countries."[81] "To heal the breach," not to win a contest of words, was the essence of Hamilton's policy toward the British (as it would later be toward the French).

These exchanges and attitudes illustrate the bearing both statesmen's political philosophies had on their concepts of sound diplomacy. Hamilton seized upon the occasion to point out the weaknesses of the Confederation and of the attendant states' rights doctrine. Jefferson was just as eager to utilize the opportunity to make an indirect attack on federalism.

[77] Jefferson to Washington, September 9, 1792, *JW*, VIII, 400.

[78] Washington to Jefferson, April 1, 1791, *WW*, XXXI, 260.

[79] Hamilton to Jefferson, March, 1792, *HWL*, IV, 357.

[80] Hammond to Grenville, January 9, 1792, PROFO, 4, XIV.

[81] "Examination of Jefferson's Message to Congress of December 7, 1801," Essay No. 18, April 8, 1802, *HWL*, VIII, 368.

Unfortunately, Washington's hands were not at the controls as the ship of state passed through these stormy waters. The topics covered in Jefferson's reply had been discussed in cabinet meetings, but not the final draft. Washington was in Virginia while Hamilton and Jefferson were exchanging comments about the draft. He returned just in time for a consultation with Jefferson before the note was handed to the British minister. Hamilton thought that the note was delivered prematurely—before he had had a chance to explain his point of view to Washington.

No doubt it was Washington's resentment of British intransigence that allowed him to sanction the caustic terms in which the reply was couched. Hamilton was probably right in his assumption that, if he had had the opportunity, he could have induced the President to overrule Jefferson. Like Hamilton, Washington had admitted and deplored American treaty violations both publicly and in private correspondence,[82] and three years earlier he had instructed Morris to inform the British that under the Constitution the government would be able to enforce compliance with the treaty. There seems little doubt that Hamilton could have convinced him of the futility of denying actions that were common knowledge. But even if such a conference had been held and Washington had supported Jefferson, the outcome would have been far better for the nation than to allow the matter to rest, as Hamilton believed it did, on divided counsel.

As it was, Hammond, smarting from Jefferson's reply, promptly appealed to Hamilton for balm, placing the secretary of the treasury in an uncomfortable situation. He could not have failed to be somewhat diverted by the minister's discomfort; Hamilton had long been convinced that the very existence of the United States was dependent upon British accession to the territorial provisions of the treaty. Yet he remained convinced that his own course of patient conciliation was the only path to a peaceable settlement, and Jefferson's reply seemed to clutter the path with obstacles.

If Hamilton's situation was uncomfortable, Hammond's was acutely so. He doubtless feared that his blunder in making accusations without first checking their accuracy would blight his career. In his desperate efforts to clear himself, he tried to lay the blame on Phineas Bond, the British consul at Philadelphia, for supplying him with inaccurate information,[83] meanwhile contradictorily assuring Grenville that he could demonstrate the truth

[82] As, for instance, to William Grayson, July 26, 1786, *WW*, XXVIII, 487.

[83] Hammond to Grenville, June 8, 1792, PROFO, 4, XIV.

of nearly all the points on which Jefferson had said he was in error. He further reported that Hamilton had deprecated Jefferson's "intemperate violence" and had assured him that the reply did not represent the position of the administration. There is no reliable record of what Hamilton actually said to Hammond, and the latter statement was almost certainly exaggerated. Hammond was well aware that little else would have served to turn away the probable wrath of his superiors than just such a compromising statement by Hamilton.

American historians have criticized Hamilton's conduct in this affair, too readily accepting Hammond's statement. Schachner, for instance, called Hamilton's behavior "intervention with a vengeance!"[84] Malone's condemnation went even further: "There would have been a memorable scene if either Washington or Jefferson had known" what Hamilton had said to the minister.[85] The available records are entirely too meager to justify speculation about the kind of "scene" that might have ensued had Washington known all the facts.

After this jarring encounter Hammond appeared more reluctant than ever to talk with Jefferson. The secretary of state succeeded in inveigling the minister into enumerating the points of controversy between the two countries as seen from the British side: mistreatment of loyalists, nonpayment of debts, the disposition of private property of British nationals living in the Northwest posts, and the location of the national boundaries at the upper Mississippi and the St. Croix rivers. But when Jefferson expressed willingness to negotiate on every point, Hammond again backed away.

Hammond did, however, continue his discussions with Hamilton. In 1792 and 1793 the two men discussed nearly every point that was later to be embodied in Jay's Treaty. Indeed, that treaty was based largely on those informal conversations. The two men went even further to a brief consideration of limiting the fortifications along the United States–Canadian border.[86] Hammond was pleasantly surprised by Hamilton's suggestion that British fur traders might be allowed to continue their operations south of the border after all the forts were evacuated. The Indians could carry the furs

84 Schachner, *Alexander Hamilton*, 298.

85 Malone, II, 419.

86 Samuel Flagg Bemis, "Alexander Hamilton and the Limitation of Armaments," *The Pacific Review*, Vol. II (March, 1922), 587–602.

87 Hammond to Grenville, July 3, 1792, PROFO, 4, XVI.

over the border unmolested and sell them in Canada, provided a reciprocal agreement was made that United States citizens could trade with Indians living in Canada.[87]

Hamilton's reassurance given in January, 1792, that American courts would uphold the treaty and compel American debtors to pay British creditors failed to satisfy Hammond and his superiors. They continued to demand immediate payment and displayed contempt and impatience when British violations were put forth as justification for delaying payments.[88] As the year 1792 wore on, they became more and more reluctant even to talk about withdrawing from the posts, meanwhile sharply insisting that Americans should not be allowed to settle in the disputed regions.[89] In a conversation with Hammond on June 3, Jefferson finally came to understand that Britain intended to keep the posts.[90]

Canadian officials and businessmen, especially fur traders and their associates (usually referred to as the "Montreal Merchants"), sent increasingly urgent petitions to London begging the government to hold the Northwest Territory permanently. Grenville's instructions to Hammond reflected the merchants' sentiments and also some of their specific proposals. The immediacy of the problem stimulated their powers of imagination, and they produced a variety of suggestions for relieving the British Empire of the obligations of 1783.[91]

An oft-repeated recommendation was for "mediation" by British authorities to restore peace between the United States and the Indians who inhabited portions of the disputed territories. Such a peace, which would acknowledge the Indians' ownership of the territory, would effectively bar Americans from the region. This recommendation was vigorously pressed immediately after the American forces under St. Clair were defeated by the Indians in November, 1791. Wrote William Dundas, representing both military and merchant factions in Canada, "This is the important moment in which the unfortunate terms of that peace [of 1783] may be altered."[92] He gleefully transmitted details about St. Clair's defeat—the large amount of flour and other staples seized by the Indians, the failure of repeated

88 Hammond to Grenville, January 9, 1792; Dorchester to Dundas, March 23, 1792, *ibid.*, XIV.

89 Grenville to Hammond, September 2, 1792, Mayo, 15.

90 Notes on his conversation with Hammond, *JW*, XVII, 328.

91 Montreal Merchants to Governor Simcoe, April 23, 1792, PROFO, 4, XVI.

92 Hammond to Grenville, December 19, 1792, enclosure dated November 24, 1791, *ibid.*, XI.

American bayonet charges, the final disordered retreat, and the small, scantily supplied American garrisons.

The governor of Canada seemed confident that the Americans would ultimately be required to pay the debts stipulated in the treaty, and he also expected that the fur trade, as well as the Northwest Territory would remain in British control. He reported that in parleys with various tribes he had found them willing to claim all the land along the southern edge of the Great Lakes. He had not yet succeeded in finding a tribe willing to claim the area at the northern end of Lake Champlain, but, he said, he was still looking and hoping. He suggested that if no such claims could be advanced Britain should hold the Champlain area simply on the ground that the United States had no need for it—unless it expected to use the region as a base for smuggling operations or for an invasion of Canada.

The Montreal Merchants also spoke of setting up a neutral territory, a no man's land forbidden to British and American armed forces alike; an arrangement for reciprocal trade across the border; and an agreement for territorial changes that would give substance to the treaty stipulation about mutual navigation rights on the Mississippi.

Grenville was heartily in favor of the mediation plan and returned to it again and again. Beckwith mentioned it to Hamilton before Hammond's arrival. Hamilton, apparently considering it merely an illustration of Beckwith's naïveté, patiently explained why the United States could not consider the idea. At the beginning of Hammond's mission Grenville told him that "nothing would be more satisfactory to His Majesty" than to be able to arrange such a peace.[93] When Hammond first brought up the proposal, Hamilton, who was, of course, firmly opposed to it from first to last, again calmly explained why it was utterly unacceptable to the United States. He told Hammond that if the British really wanted to be helpful they should advise the Indians to ask the United States government for peace terms.

Undaunted, Hammond continued to work on the project. In the spring of 1792, Hammond again outlined the plan for Hamilton, this time point by point: the tribes were to be recognized as sovereign, Britain and the United States were to withdraw all their armed forces from the territory and relinquish all claims to it, and the subjects of both nations were to be enjoined

[93] Grenville to Hammond, September 2, 1791, Mayo, 16.

[94] Hammond to Grenville, December 19, 1791, March 7, 1792, June 8, 1792, PROFO, 4, XI, XIV, XV.

from acquiring land or establishing settlements in the region. At that point Hamilton realized that the project was officially sanctioned by the British government. Thereupon he told the minister, "briefly and coldly," according to Hammond, that he wished him "to understand that any plan, which comprehended anything like a cession of territory or right or allowance of any other power to interfere in the dispute with the Indians would be considered by [his] government as absolutely impracticable and inadmissible."[94]

Hammond was convinced that this stiff rejection was final and feared that any further mention of it would antagonize the secretary; but the persistent Grenville ordered him to renew the offer repeatedly, continuing to push the proposal even after he had negotiated the treaty with Jay in 1794.[95]

Finally the harried minister even laid the subject before the secretary of state.[96] Jefferson was as adamant as Hamilton had been, and for good measure tried to argue Hammond out of his government's claim that the treaty of 1783 had granted to each signatory free navigation of the Mississippi. Jefferson astutely held that the joint-navigation article was placed in the treaty at a time when it was assumed that Britain would retain the Floridas—which then extended westward to the Mississippi—and that the article had no possible reference to navigation of the river north of Florida. Britain's subsequent cession of the Floridas to Spain, he added, had removed all occasion for the British to use the river and all claims that she might have had earlier.[97] Jefferson's sensitive and suspicious mind grasped the enormous dangers inherent in the British scheme. It reinforced and amplified his attitude toward that country and made him more apprehensive than ever of Hamilton's policy of seeking to conciliate Britain. He even went so far as to suspect Hamilton of being in sympathy with the proposal,[98] a misjudgment that is difficult to excuse.

In spite of the brevity and coldness with which Hamilton dismissed the mediation proposal, he tirelessly pressed upon Hammond his own design for a peaceful solution to Anglo-American disagreements. When from time to time Hammond broached the subject of Britain's Mississippi navigation rights, Hamilton, far from arguing against them, commented that the

[95] Bemis, "Alexander Hamilton and the Limitation of Armaments," *The Pacific Review*, Vol. II (March, 1922), 601; Grenville to Hammond, November 20, 1794, Mayo, 71–73.

[96] Hammond to Grenville, July 3, 1792, PROFO, 4, XVI.

[97] "Notes on a Conversation with George Hammond, June 3, 1792," *JW*, XVII, 326–27.

[98] *The Anas*, *ibid.*, I, 298–99; Woolery, *The Relation of Thomas Jefferson to American Foreign Policy*, 94.

administration considered "the participation of Great Britain in the navigation of that river as an object of benefit rather than disadvantage, inasmuch as it involves the two countries in one common connection of interest against any attempt of the Court of Spain to exclude both or either of them from the navigation of that river."[99] Clearly Hamilton and Jefferson, who by now were not working closely together, held opposite views on the matter. Not long after Jefferson tried to refute British Mississippi claims, Hammond returned to the subject in a conversation with Hamilton, proposing that the boundary west of the Great Lakes be dropped southward far enough to "afford to His Majesty's subjects an effectual communication" with the river. Hamilton commented that it "would well deserve the attention of the United States to consent to as liberal a measure of accommodation in that respect as would not be detrimental to [American] interests."[100]

Hamilton's goal was to take advantage of the long-standing enmity between England and Spain to resolve his country's most crucial diplomatic problems in one bold stroke. Though Jefferson was mistaken in assuming that Hamilton was willing to cede any part of the territory south of the Great Lakes, Hamilton would have the United States cede Britain a region in the Far Northwest, from Lake of the Woods to the present site of Minneapolis and St. Paul, in exchange for equivalent concessions. He would tie together Britain's supposed desire for access to the Mississippi and his own desire for the United States to gain Spanish territory north of the Gulf of Mexico.[101] Accordingly, at a cabinet meeting a few months later Hamilton recommended that an agreement be sought with Britain to give substance to that nation's "right" of navigation of the Mississippi by moving the Canadian boundary south to a navigable point on that river and then to join forces with the British to seize and divide the territories of Spain on the Gulf. Jefferson and Randolph opposed the idea, and Secretary of War Knox, who usually stood with Hamilton, apparently gave him no support. Washington would have none of it, commenting, according to Jefferson's statement, that the remedy was worse than the disease.[102]

99 Hammond to Grenville, April 5, 1792, PROFO, 4, XIV.

100 Hammond to Grenville, July 3, 1792, *ibid.*

101 Hamilton's position on this point is adversely criticized by J. Fred Rippy and Angie Debo in "The Historical Background of the American Policy of Isolation," *Smith College Studies in History*, Vol. IX (1924), 155. The writers appeared to accept Jefferson's erroneous view that Hamilton was willing for the United States to cede territory south of the Great Lakes.

102 Entry dated October 31, 1792, *The Anas*, *JW*, I, 322–23; Conway, *Edmund Randolph*, 199.

It would be impossible to say what the long-term results of such an undertaking might have been—whether harmful or beneficial to the United States. Nor can it be said that Britain would have been willing to co-operate. The British leaders north of the Canadian border and across the Atlantic were focusing their attention on the northern basin of the Ohio River. They might have rejected the plan as coldly as Washington did.

There was an element of melancholy in the episode. Under adverse circumstances Hamilton was trying to induce both nations to leave off their petty bickering, their resentments, their recriminations, and their jealous rivalries. He was seeking to point out a path of friendship and amicable commerce that he was certain would lead to a bright future for coming generations of both nations. There is no positive measure by which the wisdom of any governmental policy, past or present, can be objectively assessed. The century of sputtering compromises that followed the War of 1812 would finally lead to the adoption of Hamilton's live-and-let-live attitude, a fact which argues strongly for the basic soundness of his proposal.

A small but powerful circle of Federalist friends agreed with him, but they were in a minority. Beckwith and Hammond were convinced, but their superiors had eyes on other goals. Grenville persisted in his effort to use Hamilton's magnanimity as a wedge to split off the Northwest, to promote a project which he called "mediation between the United States and the Indians" and "peace" but which Hamilton knew would maim if not destroy the new republic. Truly, it was no easy task that faced the young peacemaker.

CHAPTER XI

Party Politics and Diplomacy

BRITAIN did not want war with the United States, but neither did it display any eagerness to settle the unresolved disputes between the two countries. In 1793, Britain's position in the Northwest was secure. British forces held the territory south of the Great Lakes, and British merchants were thriving on the fur trade. The Navigation Acts continued to prevail; impressment of American seamen and other affronts to American commerce brought strongly worded but ineffectual protests from the American government. Jefferson in particular was sharp in his complaints, but they were made less effective by rumors that he would soon resign. For the moment Hamilton's policy of conciliation made it easier for Hammond to postpone negotiations. Moreover, the French armies were hard pressed from their setbacks of March, 1793. Peace in Europe, should it come, would remove the excuse for wartime obstruction of American shipping, but it would leave Britain in a powerful position on all the other issues in dispute.

Hamilton tried hard to get negotiations under way. He expressed to Hammond deep concern that there had been no understanding reached on "matters that still remained undecided between the two countries." Hammond replied that "the pressure of temporary business alone had hitherto prevented His Majesty's Ministers from attending to this object."[1] Such a weak apology did not satisfy Hamilton, and it was galling to Jefferson, who had even less success than his colleague in drawing Hammond into meaningful discussions. Jefferson expressed his frustration to Thomas Pinckney, who had been named United States minister to Great Britain in 1791. Jefferson wrote him that negotiation with Hammond was "exactly in the state in which it was when you left America." He complained that Hammond "waits for instructions, which he pretends to expect from packet to packet. But sometimes the [British] ministers are all in the country, some-

[1] Hammond to Grenville, March 7, 1793, FCA, XV.

times they are absorbed in negotiations nearer home, sometimes it is the hurry of impending war, or attention to other objects, the stock of which is inexhaustible."[2]

Written communications brought no better results than personal interviews. In a stern note to Hammond in June, 1793, Jefferson reminded him that British presence in the Northwest was costing the United States daily in "blood and treasure"—a reference, of course, to clashes with the Indians. The state of affairs could not but produce "anxiety," he said, and he asked when he could "expect the honor of a reply" to his letter of the previous year. In December, two weeks before he resigned from the Department of State, he made a final attempt, but again to no avail.[3] His efforts were not totally wasted, however. He kept the record straight, and he numbered the heavy losses his country was suffering. A gifted lawyer, he knew that the written protest could prove invaluable at some future date, when, under different circumstances, Britain might be forced to an accounting.

In spite of persistent French avowals of friendship for the United States, the National Convention tried to match British measures to restrict neutral commerce. A decree issued by the convention on May 9, 1793, provided for seizure of neutral-owned foodstuffs for pre-emptive purchase. Enemy-owned provisions were to be taken as prize, even from neutral vessels. Though American vessels were specifically exempt from the latter provision, in fact they were preyed upon relentlessly. Washington informed Congress that such acts constituted a violation of the treaty of 1778 with France but indicated that it would not be hard to induce the French to stop the depredations.[4]

Hammond's situation was eased by the problems the Americans were having with the French government—and with Genêt. Hammond's protests about seizures of British ships by American privateersmen or by French warships operating inside American territorial waters were promptly attended to by Jefferson. Hammond, convinced that the United States intended to maintain a fair neutrality, did not try to turn such incidents into grievances against the United States. His attitude helped lessen tensions in Anglo-American relations and diminish the threat of war—but also probably made the British less hesitant to raid American shipping. Since 1776 the

[2] Jefferson to Pinckney, April 20, 1793, *JW*, IX, 66.

[3] Jefferson to Hammond, June 19, December 15, 1793, *ibid.*, 138, 271–72.

[4] December 5, 1793, Richardson, I, 138.

United States had been trying to promote the rule "free ships, free goods," which in its extreme form would have given American shippers the right to transport noncontraband French cargoes. Britain, loath to accept the rule, since it would limit the effectiveness of the British navy, extended the list of contraband goods, and took measures to prevent American vessels from carrying on commerce with the French West Indies.

An order in council of June, 1793, played havoc with the American position on contraband goods. Holding that food products bound for a "nation in arms" were contraband, the order provided that all neutral vessels carrying corn, flour, or meal to France were to be brought into British ports. The blow was lightened when Britain announced that it would purchase the cargoes. The following November another order was issued to interrupt neutral shipping to or from the French West Indies. Within four months a torrent of complaints had poured into Philadelphia about the seizure of some three hundred American vessels in the Caribbean. The United States could not now look to an "armed neutrality" in Europe like the one of 1780 to restrain Britain's maritime practices, for some of the nations that had stood for restraints in 1780 were now joined in an active coalition with Britain against France. Moreover, the French, though restrained by the British navy, found other methods of molesting neutral trade with its enemies. It sent out privateers and frigates and penalized neutral vessels in French harbors that were suspected of trading with enemies.

Many of the American shipping losses were not directly related to the laws enacted by Parliament or the National Convention, or to interpretations of international law. Not long after he succeeded Jefferson as secretary of state, Edmund Randolph made a long report to the President on the "vexations and spoliations on our commerce since the commencement of the European war." The allegations of American shippers were that (1) vessels were held so long in British ports that the owners were ruined financially even though the ships were eventually released by the prize courts; (2) British courts condemned vessels before the American owners had time to prepare legal defense against their captors; (3) British captors practiced "barefaced bribery" to induce "unwary boys" and others to give false testimony about the ships' cargoes or destinations to ensure condemnation by the prize courts; (4) American captains and crews were subjected to "insults and outrages"; (5) Britain had arranged a peace settlement between Portugal and the Algerians that had permitted the latters' ships to emerge from the Mediterranean and attack American ships in the Atlantic; (6) in many instances vessels were condemned because the courts connived in the "suppression of papers, registers, etc"; and (7) the British Admiralty was "impeachable for an excess of rigor and a departure from strict judicial purity."

After this painstaking enumeration of complaints against Britain there followed a much briefer statement that French "privateers harass our trade no less than those of the British," that French "Courts of Admiralty are guilty of equal oppression," and "that a very detrimental embargo has been laid upon large numbers of American vessels in the French ports." Most significant of all, perhaps, was the allegation that France had violated the treaty of 1778 "by subjecting to seizure and condemnation our vessels trading with their enemies in merchandise which that treaty declares not to be contraband."[5]

It became obvious that an ardent desire for neutrality had not prevented the United States from becoming deeply involved in the war. Washington's administration was grimly determined to negotiate for a redress of grievances, and some high-level officials were determined that the nation should look to its military and naval defenses. The Republicans, under the leadership of Madison, renewed their efforts to enact retaliatory legislation against British commerce. The debate on this subject opened even before the attacks on neutral commerce reached their height, and for some months it was conducted along lines similar to those of 1789–91.

On December 16, 1793, at the request of the House of Representatives, Jefferson prepared a long report on the "Privileges and Restrictions on the Commerce of the United States in Foreign Countries."[6] Omitting "minute details," he prepared a clear, statistical summary of conditions in the summer of 1792, "when things were in their settled order." The report showed that of the United States' chief exports—which were, in the order of their value, breadstuff, tobacco, rice, wood, and salted fish—Britain received almost half, valued at $9,363,416. "France and its dominions" received goods worth $4,698,735, while Spain and the Netherlands each bought about half as much as France. Britain and its dominions imported to the United States goods valued at more than $15,000,000—more than 70 per cent of all imported goods. Only slightly more than 10 per cent of United States imports came from France and its colonies.

[5] March 5, 1794, *Annals*, IV, 1303–1306.
[6] *Ibid.*, 1288–99.

Jefferson's report also catalogued the restrictions and tariffs imposed by various countries on American exports and shipping. The statements, which were brief and clear, had the effect of emphasizing British restrictions and underplaying those imposed by France. Additional comments inclined in the same direction; for example, the report stated that "before the war" four-fifths of American tobacco and rice imported by Britain was "re-exported to other countries, under the useless charges of an intermediate deposite [*sic*], and double voyage." That claim supported Madison's contention that, dollar for dollar, exports to France were more profitable than those to England, since the French consumed their imports and presumably remitted to American shippers a larger share of the selling price. Jefferson also gave explicit support to Madison's main argument for retaliation against Britain. He asked how Britain's restrictions and those imposed by other nations might "best be removed, modified, or counteracted" and answered his own question by suggesting either "friendly arrangements" or acts of Congress "for countervailing their efforts." Since Britain had refused to enter into agreements to ease trade conditions, he urged retaliatory legislation, since "free commerce and navigation are not to be given in exchange for restrictions and vexations; nor are they likely to produce a relaxation of them."

Yet in spite of these assertions, Jefferson did not wholeheartedly support retaliation. Though it might be the only way to obtain fair treatment from other nations, and tariff protection might prove an "encouragement to domestic manufacturers" and an attraction to potential immigrants, he remained convinced that free trade was ultimately in the best interests of his country. "Would even a single nation begin with the United States this system of free commerce," he thought it "advisable to begin it with that nation."[7]

The case against Britain, as outlined in Jefferson's report, was, briefly, that the British West Indies was virtually closed to American commerce; importation to England of salted fish and other salted foods was prohibited; American bacon and whale oils were subject to prohibitory import duties; American grain was not admitted to Britain except when scarcities forced up the price of English wheat; no American manufactured goods were admitted; serious restrictions were imposed on American-built ships sold abroad; and those American imports that were allowed to enter Britain

[7] See Koch, *Jefferson and Madison*, 147.

could do so only under a law by which permission was granted from year to year, whereas the exports of other nations to Britain were secured by "standing laws."

Washington sent Jefferson's report to Congress when it convened in December, 1793, and the debate opened immediately. Madison offered a new resolution, far less extreme than those he had proposed in earlier sessions. Now he would merely place higher tariff rates and tonnage duties on goods or ships from countries "having no commercial treaty with the United States." His initial argument took into account the reasons for earlier opposition; he said that he would not recommend rates high enough to "wound public credit"—a point certain to be raised again by Hamilton's allies.[8]

The most thoroughly prepared statement of opposition came from the South Carolina Federalist, Congressman William Loughton Smith, who, according to his biographer, "just missed the top rung" in a ranking of the brilliant Charleston lawyers of the period.[9] Smith's speech, based on an "outline" drafted by Hamilton,[10] was polished and detailed—about twice as long as Jefferson's report, to which Smith was ostensibly replying.[11] Smith argued that British commercial regulations were more favorable to the United States than were French regulations. Though acknowledging the fact that a much greater volume of American exports went to Britain, he pointed out that "six of our most valuable staples" were admitted to Britain at a lower rate of tariff than that nation charged on the same goods from any other country, while France gave American shippers favorable rates on nothing but "fish oil." He did not dwell on the exclusion of United States ships from the British West Indies but held that "several of our productions" were being admitted here, though similar articles from other countries were prohibited. The British ban on American wheat except when the price rose to a certain point was imposed equally on wheat from all foreign nations, not merely the United States.

Smith pointed out some errors and omissions in Jefferson's report. The tariff on American tobacco in Britain was less than half the rate imposed on tobacco from all other sources. The East India Company was required to

[8] January 3, 1794, *Annals*, IV, 152–58.

[9] George C. Rogers, Jr., *Evolution of a Federalist: William Loughton Smith of Charleston (1758–1812)*, (Columbia, S.C., 1962), 123 (hereafter cited as *William Loughton Smith*).

[10] *HWL*, IV, 205–24.

[11] *Annals*, IV, 174–209.

pay a higher rate on rice than was charged to American shippers. In England and the British West Indies, American timber exports fared better than like products from other countries—a fact, Smith asserted, which enabled Americans to sell those products in competition with the countries of northern Europe. He pictured both France and Britain as nations looking to their own commercial advantages, not to a deliberate effort either to aid or injure the United States. Retaliation such as Madison proposed might stimulate other nations to export some of the goods currently being imported from Britain, but the prices would be higher, and American consumers would suffer. Improvements in trade relationships should rather be sought through "temperate negotiation and reasonable equivalent." He restated earlier arguments against retaliation: Britain could be expected to return like for like, and the older country, with more capital to sustain her economy, could better withstand commercial warfare, which would involve but "one-sixth of her trade . . . and more than one-half of ours." Even worse, such strife could lead to war.

Madison, unable to refute Smith's points about comparative rates, fell back on his earlier arguments that Britain had had abundant time to agree to a commercial treaty if she had been so inclined and that the only recourse was an increase in American rates. He resorted to a touch of humor, rare for Madison, commenting that a West Indian planter might aptly say to the United States, "We will agree to buy your provisions rather than starve, and let you have our rum, which we can sell nowhere else; but we reserve out of this indulgence a monopoly of the carriage to British vessels."[12]

The debate, as such, was never resolved. Before definitive action could be taken on tariff rates, other retaliatory proposals were made. Jonathan Dayton, representative from New Jersey, moved to sequester "all the debts due from the citizens of the United States to the subjects of the King of Great Britain"—to indemnify Americans who had suffered financial losses through British acts violating international law.[13] His proposal was quite modest, Dayton claimed, in view of the fact that American property had so frequently been "plundered on the high seas" by the British. Indeed, outright confiscation of the debts would be justifiable. Dayton's motion was countered by alternative proposals. Young John Quincy Adams took a particularly grave view of the proposal. Sequestration of British debts would

[12] January 14, 1794, *ibid.*, 217–18.
[13] March 27, 1794, *ibid.*, 535.

undoubtedly constitute "a direct act of hostility." It seemed to him that Dayton was saying, in effect, "We cannot fight [the British] and therefore we should cheat them."[14]

Congressman Abraham Clark, also from New Jersey, exasperated by Britain's behavior, introduced a motion to exclude all imports from that country. Madison offered an amendment to the motion stating that "from the —— day of —— next, our commercial intercourse with that nation be suspended" (leaving the date open, Madison said, might persuade Britain to make concessions). Congress could then decide whether or not the terms offered by the British were acceptable.[15] In this form the bill passed the House by a vote of fifty-eight to thirty-eight. The bill was defeated in the Senate.

Hamilton and leaders of like convictions seized the occasion to promote building a navy and forming an army. The Republicans, the most anti-British spokesmen in the nation, remained firmly opposed to any measures to strengthen naval or military defenses. Washington's fifth annual message to Congress, presented on December 3, 1793, strongly recommended "placing ourselves in a condition of complete defense." He added the now-famous words, "If we desire to secure peace, . . . it must be known that we are at all times ready for war."[16] Attacks by Algerian pirates gave some impetus to the defense movement. Congressmen Madison and William B. Giles, also of Virginia, suggested hiring Portuguese ships of war to fight the pirates, and William Lyman suggested encouraging "private individuals . . . to fit out vessels for attacking the Algerines." Other congressmen thought it would be futile to oppose the pirates; John Smilie of Pennsylvania was sure that "Britain would assist the Algerines underhandedly," just as it was encouraging the Indians in the Northwest. When it was reported that Britain's aim in arranging the truce between Portugal and Algeria was to draw the former into the anti-French coalition, Giles took the position that all members of the coalition would then support the "corsairs" against American attacks. He agreed with those who had suggested that "a peace may be effected by money"—in effect, bribery of the Algerians to spare American shipping, after the practice of several European countries.[17] Madison predicted that Britain would intercept any American squadron

[14] John Quincy Adams to John Adams, April 22, 1794, *JQAW*, I, 187–88.

[15] April 18, 1794, *Annals*, IV, 600–602.

[16] *WW*, XXXIII, 165–66.

[17] *Annals*, IV, 436, 438, 439, 445, 488–90.

that might try to enter the Mediterranean to strike Algeria. Monroe said that he "would not be surprised" if the British government tried to draw the United States into war "by every species of insult and outrage which a proud, selfish, and vindictive nation can impose."[18]

When Sedgwick, a Federalist from Massachusetts, urged the formation of an army of fifteen thousand troops as a defense against possible invasion, Monroe charged that Sedgwick's purpose was to use such an army to remodel the government "and form it by the English standard."[19] Jefferson, who still resisted defensive measures, wrote to Madison that it was "not that the monocrats and paper men want war; but they want armies and debts."[20]

Partisan considerations seemed to have unseated reason, at least for the time. The Republicans would enter a commercial war with Britain, and some would even appropriate British property, but they rejected all measures for national defense. The Federalists generally held to a moderate defensive attitude. Hamilton tried to get Washington to speak out once again for a "respectable military posture" for the nation, "because war may come upon us, whether we choose it or not."[21] Congressman Fisher Ames supported measures of defense, but urged caution: "America is rising with a giant's strength, [but] its bones are yet but cartilages."[22] But Federalists could also speak in extreme terms, as when the Reverend Timothy Dwight wrote to Oliver Wolcott: "A war with Great Britain, we, at least, in New England will not enter into. Sooner would ninety-nine out of a hundred of our inhabitants separate from the Union."[23]

On February 21, 1794, after several weeks of unmethodical consideration, the House voted forty-three to forty-one to build four warships carrying forty-four guns each and two ships carrying twenty guns each. The cost was to be met by slight increases in tariff rates. It took time to work out details of the tariff increases, especially since the opposition (predominantly though not exclusively made up of Republicans) deliberately sought delays. The following month the Republicans nearly mustered enough votes to kill the measure by recommitting it. The navy bill finally was enacted late in March, but only after it had been amended to provide that construction on

[18] Monroe to Jefferson, May 28, 1793, *JMW*, I, 258.
[19] Monroe to Jefferson, March 16, 1794, *ibid.*, 285–87.
[20] April 3, 1794, *JW*, IX, 282.
[21] Hamilton to Washington, March 8, 1794, *HWL*, X, 63–64.
[22] January 27, 1794, *Annals*, IV, 349.
[23] Dwight to Wolcott, 1793, Gibbs, I, 107.

the ships would stop when and if the Algerians stopped their attacks on American vessels. For his efforts Madison received praise and congratulations from many sources. Because he had spoken out against Britain and for France, the Republican society of Charleston, South Carolina, heaped adulation upon him, addressing him as "Citizen Representative James Madison," and they hanged and burned in effigy William Smith, Fisher Ames, Benedict Arnold, General Dumouriez (who had been defeated in Europe and had defected to the British), and the devil.[24]

In the meantime, Britain and the United States seemed to be moving ever closer to war. A new order in council, dated November 6, 1793, softened somewhat by a revised version issued on January 8, 1794, brought added tribulation to American shippers. In an attempt to establish Britain's Rule of 1756, providing that colonial commerce closed in peacetime cannot be opened in wartime, the new orders clamped down even more tightly on French West Indies trade and heralded further restrictions on trade with continental French ports. News of the orders and the resultant seizure of hundreds of American ships reached Philadelphia at the same time the government learned of a highly provocative speech Lord Dorchester had addressed to the Northwest Indians. In the speech Dorchester had told the Indians that the land was theirs, that efforts on Britain's part to persuade the Americans to acknowledge the fact had failed, and that the war that would erupt between Britain and the United States within a year would drive out the white settlers and place the Indians in firm possession.

The prospect of war now appeared undeniable. Even so stalwart a Federalist as Rufus King became convinced that Britain had decided to attack.[25] Madison now considered his resolutions, which were still before the House, too tame to meet the crisis. In the heat of the excitement, he could probably have obtained a favorable vote on them; but, in keeping with the Republican tendency to "bend the bow too far" diplomatically, he did not push for enactment, hoping to get much more. The Republicans did call for more drastic measures, for which they drew some support from the Federalist camp. The proposal to sequester debts owed to British subjects was resubmitted by Jonathan Dayton. It was hotly debated and failed to pass. Congress settled for placing a one-month embargo on exportation of American goods, which was later extended to a second month. The embargo

[24] Madison to Jefferson, March 26, 1794, Brant, III, 396.
[25] King's memo, April 7, 1794, *KC*, I, 524.

was justified on the basis of the 1778 treaty with France, in which the United States had promised to help check British efforts to conquer the French West Indies.

Some Federalist-inspired measures were also adopted. Laws were enacted to raise a force of eighty thousand militia and to provide for other measures of defense; but Congress remained unwilling to go as far in military preparedness as Hamilton had recommended to Washington.[26]

The House of Representatives asked for Hamilton's assistance in devising means of financing the threatening war with Britain. The moderate tax that had earlier been proposed to finance construction of the six warships had met strong opposition in Congress. Paying for a war against the Mistress of the Seas would be far more difficult. Less than two months earlier the secretary of the treasury had stated that nine-tenths of the national revenue was "derived from commercial duties."[27] Obviously a war with Britain would reduce this income drastically, though it would not wipe it out—some trade and privateering activities would continue, as they had throughout the Revolution.

Hamilton met with a committee of fifteen representatives, including Madison, to discuss new sources of revenue. On that occasion Madison gave the floor to Hamilton and listened rather than talked. Another committee member reported that Hamilton "appeared cursedly mortifyed" at the thought of raising enough revenue to fight Britain but that he assured the committee the money could be obtained.[28] No precise record was kept of Hamilton's recommendations, but it is likely that they were the same ones he had made two months earlier in his two "Americanus" essays. There he had warned that it might prove impossible to finance a war that was not clearly defensive—"an external war . . . for a foreign and speculative purpose." He had expressed his conviction, as he always did, earlier and later, that the United States could sustain a war that was supported by an aroused and unified people. "To subvert by force republican liberty in this country," he had written, "nothing short of entire conquest would suffice," and that venture "would be absolutely ruinous to the undertakers." He rejected outright the proposal to issue paper money as a means of financing a war at

[26] Hamilton to Washington, March 8, 1794, *HWL*, X, 63–65.

[27] "Americanus," No. 2, February 8, 1794, *ibid.*, V, 87.

[28] William Barry Grove of North Carolina to John Steele, April 2, 1794, Battle, "Letters of Nathaniel Macon, John Steele, and William Barry Grove," *James Sprunt Historical Monograph*, No. III, 109.

that time. Foreign loans would be "out of the question," since "the principal lending powers would be our enemies." Domestic loans would be but a slender resource "in a community where capitals are so moderate as in ours." Therefore, "pecuniary taxes, taxes on specific articles, [and] military impress" would be "the resources upon which we should have chiefly to rely."[29]

Madison found his tongue readily enough, and his pen as well, when Congress took up the discussion of specific items to be taxed. An unseemly contest arose between North and South, between representatives of stockholders and of landowners, between those who wished to tax carriages and snuff and those who would tax public securities and bank stocks.[30] Hamilton won a victory when Congress placed a tax on auction sales, carriages, snuff, and sugar; but the revenue from the tax was not enough, and the quarrel grew louder. Moreover, the Republicans rallied to choke off further military preparations. When the Senate tried to raise an army of ten thousand men, Madison reported that the measure "was strangled more easily in the House of Representatives than I had expected."[31]

The nation was aroused, true enough, but it was far from united. It was clearly in no position to embark on a major war, nor would it be unless it was pressed to the final extremity.

In the "Americanus" essays Hamilton had made a forceful attempt to calm the talk of war. Revolutionary France could not be trusted as an ally, he warned; she had deeply wounded the "cause of true liberty," was showing "marks of an unexampled dissolution of all the social and moral ties," and might "find herself at length the slave of some victorious Sylla, or Marius, or Caesar." He pointed to the domestic "state of prosperity," which would be disrupted by war. War might become necessary, he agreed; but he urged that, before putting "so vast a stake upon the chance of the die, we ought at least to be certain that the object for which we hazard is genuine, is substantial, is real."[32]

Jefferson, commenting on the crisis from Monticello, expressed the hope that war would be avoided but also the belief that the passionate hatred the people felt toward Great Britain made them willing to undergo the rigors of conflict.[33] Jefferson spoke for a large segment of the South; he did not appear fully aware of the determination of the North to avoid hostilities.

[29] *HWL*, V, 74–96.
[30] Brant, III, 398–400.
[31] *Ibid.*, 399.
[32] *HWL*, V, 74–96.
[33] Jefferson to Madison, April 3, 1794, *JW*, IX, 282.

About the middle of March rumors began circulating that the administration was planning to send a special envoy to London. To many, Hamilton appeared to be the likely choice for the mission.[34] Congressman William Barry Grove, the lukewarm Federalist from North Carolina, expressed alarm at the prospect of war but was comforted by the assumption that Hamilton would be the commander-in-chief on the field of battle.[35]

In April, Secretary of State Randolph, acutely aware of the heavy responsibilities of his office in the crisis, wrote to Washington recommending a direct approach to negotiations with Britain. Though he was considered a Republican, his reasoning was much like Hamilton's on the merits of direct negotiations.[36] According to Senator Rufus King, however, Randolph made "every effort" to prevent the President from sending Hamilton to London.[37]

Washington found it very difficult to decide on the course to follow. He did not want to alienate the French. He saw less to criticize in the French Revolution than Hamilton did, and he still valued the alliance, despite Madison's accusation of the previous year that "the unpopular course of Anglomany [was] openly laying claim" on the President.[38]

While Washington was pondering the next move, Monroe also undertook to oppose Hamilton's appointment as envoy to Britain. He wrote a rather imperious letter to the President asking for an interview and declaring that Hamilton's nomination would be "injurious to the public interest" and damaging to Washington personally.[39] The latter comment was apparently a reference to a charge the Republicans were bandying about that Hamilton was using the Chief Executive to promote Federalist party issues. Monroe may have felt himself called upon as a fellow Virginian to warn the President about the accusation.

Monroe's letter raised the constitutional question of how much influence a senator could exert concerning a nomination that had not yet been formally submitted to the Senate. Washington sought Randolph's counsel on the question, and was advised that Monroe's position justified granting the

[34] Conway (*Edmund Randolph,* 214) refers to this rumor and cites an unpublished letter from Monroe to Jefferson, March 16, 1794.

[35] Grove to Steele, April 2, 1794, Battle, "Letters of Nathaniel Macon, John Steele and William Barry Grove," *James Sprunt Historical Monograph,* No. III, 106–107.

[36] April 6, 1794, Conway, *Edmund Randolph,* 214–15.

[37] *KC*, I, 519.

[38] Madison to Jefferson, June 10, 1793, *MW*, VI, 127.

[39] April 8, 1794, *JMW*, I, 291–92.

interview.[40] Washington thought otherwise and sent a caustic reply to Monroe to the effect that he had not yet decided whom he would appoint, if anyone, and that if Monroe had information that would "disqualify Colo. Hamilton for the mission" he should submit it "in writing." The President added, "I *alone* am responsible for a proper nomination."[41]

Monroe was not the only Republican from whom Washington received unsolicited advice. Congressman John Nicholas of Virginia is said to have written a vitriolic letter expressing astonishment at the rumor of the impending nomination of Hamilton, whose power, he said, frightened Americans more than the possibility of a British attack. Nicholas is supposed to have called Hamilton "the avowed friend of Great Britain" and to have suggested that Britain's "present hostility" was probably "intended to aid [Hamilton's] well known attachment to it."[42] If such a letter was sent to Washington, it merited no reply, and none is recorded.

George Hammond, though sincerely interested in maintaining peace, found that there was not much he could do to soften American antipathies. He tried to convince Hamilton that the new British restrictions were necessary and legal; but Hamilton dismissed his explanations and insisted that Britain must compensate American citizens for their losses.[43] Hammond told Senator Rufus King that Dorchester's speech to the Indians had not been authorized by London, that Grenville was making strenuous efforts to see that American merchants would be justly treated in the future, and that the animosity of Americans would lessen once they learned that their merchants had been resorting to "unworthy" practices in misusing the American flag to cover French property. King rejected the explanation, stressing the gravity of the crisis and insisting, as Hamilton did, that Britain "would be bound to give . . . compensation."[44]

Washington considered the crisis the gravest one he had faced since taking office. His deepest concern was not the power of Great Britain but the divided sentiments of his own countrymen. Despite his urging Congress had failed to strengthen the nation's defenses. He asked the governors to call out the state militias, if necessary, to enforce the embargo on exports to Britain; but his Revolutionary War experiences had left him with far less

[40] *Ibid.*, 292n.
[41] April 9, 1794, *WW*, XXXIII, 320–21.
[42] *JMW*, VI, 292–93n.
[43] Hammond to Grenville, April 17, 1794, FCA, XV.
[44] King's personal memorandum, April 7, 1793 [1794], *KC*, I, 523–25.

confidence in the militia than Jefferson frequently expressed. He believed that Dorchester's speech indicated a design on the part of the "British Cabinet" to seize the Northwest; but he had hopes that the military and diplomatic "disappointments" of "the combined powers in Europe" had caused Britain to hesitate. Meanwhile, he urgently requested Governor Clinton to survey and report to him the "state of things in upper and lower Canada."[45]

Washington's thoughts on many significant details of this critical situation remain a mystery. The historian is frustrated by inadequate records, and by Washington's taciturn manner. Certainly he wrote and spoke sparingly on the danger of war. It seems clear that in his general attitude toward Britain he stood about midway between Hamilton and Jefferson. He did not go as far as Jefferson in his sympathy for the French, nor as far as Hamilton in the desire for establishing a close relationship with Britain. Apparently he would gladly have sent—or led—an army into the Northwest to seize the territory from the British if he could have been sure that the nation would unite behind him. He must have asked himself repeatedly what reactions such a move might bring from the agrarians of the South and from the merchants of the North, and what these diverse groups would do if the British should force him into war. He hesitated; and he did not seek advice from all sides, as he had four years earlier during the Nootka Sound crisis. He was lonely. A marked coolness had entered relations between him and Republican leaders. There was even a breach between him and Hamilton. He continued to respect Hamilton's judgment, but at the moment he did not feel for him the warm affection of earlier years. Apparently the breach had come early in the year, when the Republicans, criticizing financial measures of 1791, had forced Hamilton to turn over to a House committee a letter from Washington that had deeply embarrassed the President.[46]

Though we have few indications of Washington's thoughts during the

[45] Message to the Senate and House of Representatives, March 28, 1794, Washington to Clinton, March 31, 1794, *WW*, XXXIII, 306–307, 310–11.

[46] Hamilton's opponents in the House, having probed the books of the Treasury Department, charged Hamilton with using money borrowed in the Netherlands at the beginning of the decade to support the Bank of the United States in a manner not authorized by Congress. After repeated efforts to refute the charge had failed, Hamilton felt compelled to submit to the House a letter written by the President in 1791 authorizing the act. Washington was annoyed and embarrassed, as Hamilton knew he would be, for the President had forgotten that he wrote the letter, and by 1794 the issue had taken on a highly partisan tone. The President's coolness toward his secretary of the treasury was not of long duration, but it must have contributed to his silence in this period. See Brant, III, 396–97.

critical spring months, his actions bear out his retrospective comment four years later when, in answer to Monroe's peevish complaints against Washington's French policy, he asked the rhetorical question: "Did the then situation of our affairs admit of any other alternative than Negotiation or War?"[47]

Others might hesitate, but the leaders of the Federalist party could not. On March 10, Senators Rufus King, Oliver Ellsworth, George Cabot, and Caleb Strong met, surveyed their country's critical position, and decided to induce Washington to send Hamilton to London, meanwhile seeing that vigorous measures were undertaken at home to place the nation in a defensive posture—"to save the national honor, and to procure indemnification for the wrongs that our merchants had already suffered." When Ellsworth laid before him the views of the Federalist leaders, Washington was "at first reserved"; when he did warm to the general proposals, he told them frankly that Hamilton failed to "possess the general confidence of the country," a factor which would probably disqualify him for the mission.[48] The practical-minded President would not be one to overlook such a point.

Robert Morris also tried to persuade Washington to send Hamilton, but without success. Washington even told Morris that he had considered sending Jefferson, a statement that is revealing of Washington's hostile attitude toward Britain at the time. He must have known that his former secretary of state would be certain to approach Britain coldly and make extreme demands.

Rufus King and his co-Federalists came to see that they must forgo Hamilton's nomination; but they decided to play him as their top card to win Washington's approval of the over-all project. This strategy proved to be a winning one.

Hamilton co-operated eagerly and with a sense of deep urgency. He realized that his pen might be the only tool standing in the way of the sword. He composed a long, powerful letter to Washington presenting arguments that in the end induced Washington to choose the course of direct, extraordinary negotiation.[49] It was truly "one of the most important letters ever penned by Hamilton."[50]

Acknowledging the "perilous crisis" and the "violent resentment for recent and unprovoked injuries," Hamilton presented his recommendations

[47] *WW*, XXXVI, 195.

[48] Intimate details of this episode are given in Rufus King's memorandum, *KC*, I, 517–23.

[49] April 14, *HWL*, V, 97–115.

[50] *Ibid.*, 115n.

early in the letter: (1) "take effectual measures of military preparation"; (2) seek new sources of revenue; (3) obtain, somehow, special powers for the President during the emergency; (4) make "another effort of negotiation, confided to hands able to manage it, and friendly to the object," to "obtain reparation for the wrongs" Britain had done to the United States and to lay out a line of conduct for the future; (5) avoid retaliatory measures against Britain during the course of the negotiations; and (6) if the negotiations should fail, "then and not till then . . . resort to reprisals and war."

Hamilton was convinced that most Americans did not want war and would be "impatient under the measures which war would render unavoidable." If the government should resort to war without a final effort at the conference table, northerners, especially, would be convinced that the conflict came about through "the design of some and the rashness of others" (he could have added that some New Englanders were proclaiming that they would secede before they would go to war with Britain).[51] Those persons "whose measures [had] a war aspect [were] under the influence of some of the strongest passions that can actuate human conduct"—passions arising from "an implacable hatred to Great Britain and a warm attachment to France." His abhorrence of the French Revolution was illustrated by his comments that war with Britain would strengthen the pro-French faction in the United States, that the French Republic could not give the Americans any aid, and that the newly founded, barbarous institutions of France might infect American domestic life and lead to "disorganization and anarchy."

He accused the Republicans not of wanting war with Britain, but of accentuating the danger by indulging in ill will toward that country. They hoped, said Hamilton, to "hector and vapor with success," thus "perpetuating animosity between the two countries without involving war." Such proposals as those of Madison, Dayton, and Clark to cut off—or at least threaten to cut off—Anglo-American commerce and to sequester British debts, would "change negotiation into peremptory demand" and might actually convince Britain that the United States had deliberately chosen the path of war because of France's recent improved military position. Though Madison and his colleagues spoke of retaliation as a means of forcing the British to "do us justice," such measures would create a situation where that nation could not accede to American demands without "the disgrace or disrepute of having receded through intimidation [and] without renounc-

[51] Timothy Dwight to Oliver Wolcott, 1793, Gibbs, I, 107.

ing her pride and her dignity [and] losing her consequence and weight in the scale of nations." He was "morally certain" that Britain would not risk such a humiliating course under any terms. Those who opposed negotiation that was "conducted with ability and moderation" were actually afraid that such an effort might be successful and restore amity between the two nations, thereby dashing the hopes of certain Republican leaders for "permanent alienation from Great Britain." He found evidence of "a common sentiment between the advocates and opposers" of moderate negotiations that the moment was "peculiarly favorable to such an attempt."

Further, Hamilton warned that sequestration of British debts might immediately lead that government to seize "our vessels wherever they are found, on the ground of keeping them as hostages for the debts." Any American move to interrupt commerce with Britain was particularly unwise at the moment; the possibility of war made it necessary to continue importing items as long as possible to strengthen American defenses.

Throughout this period Hamilton never underestimated the danger that British obstinacy and American antipathy might make war unavoidable despite anything the executive branch could do. Yet nothing Hamilton said justifies the position sometimes taken by historians that he believed a rupture with Britain would bring "the collapse of the new nationality of 1787." There are also misleading implications in the statement that "*even* Hamilton advocated raising a federal army and fortifying the principal ports."[52] At the hint of danger Hamilton always thought first of military preparedness. In this highly-charged letter he underscored the sentence including the core of his recommendations for military and naval preparations.

Other portions of the letter illustrate Hamilton's long-range foreign policy. He made it clear that national affairs must be conducted in a manner that would leave no doubts of the country's sincere desire for peace. Coercive acts and threats were especially to be avoided. Rather, an appeal should be made to Britain's sense of justice and magnanimity, and to her self-interest in establishing a firm peace with the rich and growing young nation.

Near the close of the letter, Hamilton switched to the customary intimate tone with which he addressed the President. He said that he was aware that Washington had considered him, among others, for the post of special envoy to London. He would not have written the letter, he said, had he not firmly resolved to recommend "another character" for the mission. "Mr. Jay" was

[52] Bemis, *A Diplomatic History of the United States*, 100–101. Italics added.

"the only man in whose qualifications for success there would be thorough confidence." He closed with the prophecy that if the President succeeded in "rescuing the country from the dangers and calamities of war" there would be no part of his life that would produce "more real satisfaction or true glory."

Washington was convinced. Hamilton had won. The President now moved swiftly. He let it be known that he would follow the course laid out by the High Federalists. On April 16—just two days after Hamilton wrote his letter—Washington placed Jay's name before the Senate. His message clearly reflected Hamilton's sentiments: "Peace ought to be pursued with unremitted zeal" before recourse to war, and Jay's mission would "announce to the world a solicitude for a friendly adjustment of our complaints and a reluctance to hostility."[53]

Jay was evidently eager for the appointment.[54] Indeed, on the day of his nomination he told Senator Ellsworth that he was determined to accept it.[55] The intense political partisanships had forced the President's hand. He chose the right path, but it was unfortunate that he was thereby precluded from placing a different name before the Senate. Hamilton had a better mind than Jay had, a stronger will, and an intimate knowledge of every point in dispute. Moreover, he was highly regarded by Grenville and other high-ranking British officials. If the temper of the country had made it possible for Washington to send Hamilton to London, the negotiations would have been in stronger hands. Though desirous of reconciliation, Hamilton had always held, to Washington, and, through his essays in the press, to the people, that there was no hope for permanent peace unless Britain abandoned the disputed Ohio-Great Lakes area and made compensation for damages inflicted on American commerce. He would not have conceded either demand to the British. He would have understood full well that any treaty would have to be acceptable to the United States, at many points, or the Senate would not ratify it. There seems every reason to believe that he would have brought back treaty terms broader in scope and far more effective than Jay was able to achieve. Most important of all for the course of history the mission would have given him an unparalleled opportunity to reconcile the two nations.

But Jay, not Hamilton, was to be United States envoy to Britain. The

[53] Richardson, I, 145–46.
[54] *KC*, I, 520.
[55] Ellsworth to Oliver Wolcott, Sr., April 16, 1794, Gibbs, I, 135.

Senate confirmed his appointment on April 19 by a vote of eighteen to eight. At that time, Senate debates were not published, and little is known about what opposition, if any, there was to the appointment. From the information that can be gleaned from the writings of the men who were present, it appears that the nomination was "rammed through."[56] Madison wrote to Jefferson that on a preliminary ballot there were ten votes against Jay and that the appointment passed the Senate only because of "some adventitious causes,"[57] about which he did not elaborate. There was some opposition on the grounds that Jay was known to be pro-British, that when negotiating with Gardoqui he had shown a willingness to relinquish the nation's navigation rights on the Mississippi, and that it was improper to send the nation's chief justice on a diplomatic mission. No doubt some objections were raised simply because the project was Federalist-inspired.

In spite of Jay's nomination, the House of Representatives refused to halt the debate on Congressman Clark's motion to bar British imports. House records show that one or more unnamed members suggested terminating or postponing the discussion, since if the motion passed it would be not only a hindrance to Jay but also an infringement on the power of the executive branch to carry on negotiations and an "indelicacy" to the President. These considerations eventually closed the debate, but at the time "it was answered," as the *Annals of Congress* recorded, "that the Legislature have solely a right to regulate commerce" and that any indelicacy in the matter was committed by the executive, since the debate "had been several days pending in the House before the nomination."[58]

Such comments, and others indicating downright disapproval of Jay's mission, did not bode well for its success. Hamilton was right in saying that the nation was not united for war. It was also clearly not united for peace.

[56] DeConde, *Entangling Alliance*, 103.
[57] April 28, 1794, *MW*, VI, 212.
[58] *Annals*, IV, 600.

CHAPTER XII

Jay's Treaty

SECRETARY of State Randolph had advised Washington to open special negotiations with Great Britain, but he did not favor Jay's nomination as the envoy to Britain. He seems to have been indecisive when the time came to write Jay's instructions. Randolph, who was well aware that the mission was being guided by persons with the ear of the President, was torn by conflicting pressures because he had chosen the path of moderation in an era of ardent partisanship. He was not Republican enough to remain securely in the good graces of the Jeffersonians, and certainly he was not Federalist enough to be trusted by Hamilton and his allies. Indeed, Hamilton looked upon him as one of those "characters, not numerous," constantly fluctuating "between reason and passion."[1]

Because of Randolph's hesitancy, Hamilton stepped in to help draft the instructions Jay took with him to London. At a meeting held on April 21, 1794, at which Hamilton, Ellsworth, Cabot, King, and Jay were discussing the mission, one member of the group reported that in a recent conversation Randolph had indicated a desire to leave the negotiations largely to Jay's discretion—usually a difficult position for a diplomat, who, facing a task of such gravity, prefers to proceed under instructions. Those attending the meeting were convinced that the President had the constitutional authority to "give the instructions without consulting the Senate," and, fearing the turmoil and delay which a Senate discussion would involve, they believed it "most advisable so to conduct the business," although the treaty would be signed "subject to the approbation of the Senate." They agreed that Britain must be required to observe the Treaty of Paris: "Strenuous efforts should be made to obtain satisfaction for the spoliations on commerce, and to establish rules" for the future. If these points were gained, they believed, it would be reasonable for the United States to pay half a million pounds to

[1] Hamilton to Washington, April 14, 1794, *HWL*, V, 99.

discharge the pre-Revolutionary War private debts to British subjects. Other points discussed at the meeting were a commercial treaty, the Northwest posts, Indian trade, navigation of the Great Lakes, "the West Indies, etc., etc."[2]

Soon thereafter both Hamilton and Senator King took a much stronger stand on the subject of compensation for British molestation of American commerce. The next step toward preparing instructions was the writing of a cabinet paper by Hamilton, at Washington's request.[3] In the paper Hamilton suggested that the treaty should include a definite rule for settling claims against the British for "depredations upon our commerce." The term "contraband" should be applied only to articles that could reasonably be called "instruments of war." Only such articles should be liable to confiscation, and they should not be deemed to "infect other parts of a cargo, nor even a vessel carrying them, where there are no appearances of a design to conceal."

If these terms proved unobtainable, the British should agree to pre-emptive purchase of all provisions seized when the ship was bound for an enemy port that was not actually blockaded. Hamilton appears to have been willing to acquiesce in the British seizure of French West Indies goods in American bottoms going to France—thus abandoning the "free ships, free goods" rule. Paper blockades should be proscribed. Each nation should agree to refrain from selling to the American Indians more than the usual amount of supplies when the other signatory was at war with the Indians, and each nation might allow free trade with Indians living within the other's boundaries.

In fulfillment of the treaty of 1783 the British should pay for the slaves removed from American soil and surrender the Northwest posts, and the United States should agree to pay a specified sum to settle the claims of British creditors in those cases where there were legal obstructions in the United States. An effort should be made to reach agreement on the mutual disarmament of the land-and-water boundary between the United States and Canada.

Hamilton still favored a commercial treaty, but he did not see how it could greatly alter conditions at the moment, except that Britain should be asked to open the West Indies trade to American vessels of sixty to eighty tons' burden and to allow American manufactured goods into Great Britain

[2] *KC*, I, 523.
[3] April 23, 1794, *HWL*, V, 115–19.

and Ireland on a most-favored-nation basis. In return the United States might agree to admit on the same basis manufactured goods from Britain, to remove the extra tonnage and duties on British ships and on goods imported in British ships, and not to levy a duty of more than 10 per cent on British goods. If it proved impossible to obtain a treaty containing these terms, even one with less favorable provisions might be advisable "for preserving peace between the two countries."

Randolph amplified Hamilton's suggestions and worked them into a formal set of instructions.[4] In addition, he gave Jay permission to confer with the Baltic powers concerning a new "armed neutrality" to curb Britain and stated emphatically that no terms could be agreed to that would violate the United States' arrangements with France, nor was any commercial treaty to be negotiated if Britain did not agree to open the West Indies to American commerce. Randolph's instructions on provisions to be included in any treaty of commerce were far more favorable to the United States than the terms listed by Hamilton—including, for example, the principle of "free ships, free goods"—but to points that were "purely the ideas of Randolph, Jay paid little serious attention."[5]

Obviously the High Federalists were willing to agree, by treaty, that the United States would not enact anti-British laws like those proposed by Madison and other Republicans. It is highly significant, as Randolph's biographer has pointed out, that the Federalists did not reveal their proposals for a commercial treaty until after the Senate had confirmed Jay's appointment.[6] Certainly Washington, in his brief Senate communication nominating Jay, did not make the slightest reference to a commercial treaty. The violent resentment later shown by the Republicans was based in part on this procedure, which seemed to them highly partisan and, even worse, unconstitutional. Madison had often advocated a treaty that would open the West Indies and regulate trade with Britain, and he mentioned the absence of such a treaty as justification for levying higher duties on British imports from that country; but he would never have trusted the Federalists to negotiate the treaty. If Washington had mentioned the subject when nominating Jay, he would have aroused furious opposition.

The Federalists were disturbed by continuing Republican efforts, es-

[4] *ASPFR*, I, 472–74.
[5] Bemis, *Jay's Treaty*, 210.
[6] Conway, *Edmund Randolph*, 220.

pecially in the House, to penalize British commerce after the executive branch had decided to make the move toward conciliation. Senator King observed with regret that, "as the prospects of peace brighten, the efforts of these Sons of Faction are redoubled."[7] In great indignation, George Cabot wrote to Senator Ralph Izard, a wealthy South Carolina planter, that "the combination of Fools with Knaves must eventually be too powerful for the friends of genuine liberty."[8] Monroe referred to Jay's nomination as a "submissive measure . . . to court [Britain's] favor and degrade [the United States'] character." He believed that a measure to ban the importation of British goods would have passed the House had it not been for the "executive maneuver" by which Jay's nomination had been announced during the course of the discussion, a nomination which had been called a "measure of conciliation" that should not be obstructed by acts of retaliation. Monroe also recalled that Jay had previously "well nigh bartered away the Mississippi."[9] This was an unjustified exaggeration, as were those of anti-Federalist historians of later years, one of whom jibed, "Washington sent the best American Englishman he could find, Chief Justice Jay, to London."[10]

The Senate, of pronounced Federalist complexion, sought to play a steadying role by voting down, fourteen to eleven, an anti-British bill that had passed the House.[11] Hamilton tried to lessen Randolph's asperity toward Hammond by advising him against "too much tartness" in his communications. "We are still in the path of negotiation," he reminded the secretary of state; "let us not plant it with thorns."[12]

Federalists and Republicans alike realized that Anglo-American conciliation would be repugnant to France. The French Republic could hardly be expected to take a moderate view on negotiations between its ally and its most persistent enemy. By 1794, Washington had come to detest the policies of the French revolutionaries, but he was still determined to preserve the alliance if possible.

It was time to send a new minister to France—not for extraordinary negotiations, but to replace Gouverneur Morris, who had become the "toast

[7] King to unnamed correspondent, April 16, 1794, *KC*, I, 562.

[8] Cabot to Izard, August 19, 1794, "South Carolina Federalist Correspondence, 1789–1797," *American Historical Review*, Vol. XIV (July, 1909), 780.

[9] Monroe to Jefferson, May 4, 24, 1794, *JMW*, I, 293–94.

[10] Dodd, "When Washington Tried Isolation," *American Mercury*, Vol. IV (March, 1925), 351.

[11] April 28, 1794, *Annals*, V, 89.

[12] Hamilton to Randolph, April 27, 1794, *HWL*, V, 121.

of French aristocrats" and thus *persona non grata* to the revolutionaries.[13] A Republican thoroughly acceptable to the Jacobins seemed called for. Senator Monroe relished the administration's embarrassment. Two weeks after Jay's nomination he wrote to Jefferson that the executive was "reduced to the dilemma of selecting from among its enemies" to nominate "a person who would be acceptable" to the French. He had heard, he wrote, that Robert R. Livingston, chancellor of New York State, had been offered the appointment, and he believed that Livingston would accept. He understood that Senator Aaron Burr of New York had also been mentioned.[14]

Apparently Monroe had no idea that he himself might be appointed to the post. His criticisms of the government had been extremely caustic. He had supported Genêt long after Jefferson had lost confidence in the French minister. During the previous year Madison had shown Monroe a letter from Jefferson sharply criticizing Genêt for appealing directly to the people and meddling in government affairs. Monroe had then written to Jefferson, trying to justify Genêt's actions by laying the blame on Jay and King and on the Federalists generally, charging that "the object of this party is to separate us from France and ultimately unite us with England is what I am well assured of."[15] Two years before, Monroe had protested the appointment of Morris as minister to France and, incidentally, the commissioning of General Anthony Wayne to fight the Indians, claiming both appointments to be "generally reprobated" and adding, "It is said that it would have been difficult to have found more unfit persons for those stations, even if some industry had been used to select them out."[16]

Monroe's speeches in the Senate were not, of course, published, owing to that body's policy of secret debate, and Washington may have been unaware of Monroe's extreme position. He also may not have known that Monroe considered the appointment of Jay plus the administration's coolness toward France as proof that an alliance with Britain was "the real object of the Executive."[17] It is understandable that Monroe was surprised when he received the call to represent the United States in France. He accepted the appointment, on the advice of Madison and other friends, because of "the

[13] Gilbert Chinard, *Thomas Jefferson, the Apostle of Americanism* (Boston, 1929), 323.

[14] Monroe to Jefferson, May 4, 1794, *JMW*, I, 295–96.

[15] Monroe to Jefferson, September 3, 1793, *ibid.*, 274.

[16] Monroe to Jefferson, June 17, 1792, *ibid.*, 232.

[17] Monroe to Jefferson, May 4, 1794, *ibid.*, 295.

necessity of cultivating France; and the uncertainty of the person upon whom it might otherwise fall."[18]

Monroe's instructions, less specific than Jay's, were general ones for strengthening friendship with France.[19] Lord Grenville was disturbed by the enthusiasm and fraternal embraces with which Monroe was received in France,[20] but apparently his concern did not soften his attitude toward Jay.[21] Washington later had cause to regret having sent Monroe to France (see Chapters XIII and XVI), and the assignment brought bitterness to Monroe as well. There is some justification for Monroe's subsequent conclusion that Washington had sent him to France to placate the allies while Jay negotiated a treaty which the French considered loathsome.

Hammond was pleased by Jay's appointment. He discussed with Hamilton the objectives the American government hoped to reach and then relayed to Grenville the substance of Jay's instructions.[22] Hammond objected when Hamilton told him that, "as an indispensable basis of friendly adjustment," Jay would insist on compensation for American vessels that had been seized without conclusive proof that the cargoes were French or without recourse to appeal. In a second conference the following day, Hammond returned to the subject and asked casually whether he had understood Hamilton correctly that Jay would unequivocally demand compensation in such cases. Hammond reported that Hamilton replied in the affirmative, without qualification, but added that the demand would be made in a reasonable manner and assured him that the American government was sincere in trying to establish a durable peace with Britain.

The purpose of Hamilton's strong statement was to strengthen Jay's bargaining position in London, as he explained in a candid letter to Jay a few days before the latter's departure. The "indispensability" of the demand, he said, should apply only when "the affair of indemnification [was] standing alone." If Britain was willing to carry out its obligations under the treaty of 1783—the primary one being abandonment of the Northwest posts—and would agree to "a truly beneficial treaty of commerce, embracing

[18] Monroe to Jefferson, May 27, 1794, *ibid.*, 299–301.

[19] June 10, 1794, *ASPFR*, I, 668–69.

[20] Bemis, *Jay's Treaty*, 243, *passim*.

[21] Monroe's reception is described by Louis-Guillaume Otto, the French charge d'affaires in the United States from 1790 to 1791, in *Considérations sur la conduite du gouvernement américain envers la France, depuis le commencement de la révolution jusqu'en 1797* (intro. by Gilbert Chinard), (Princeton, 1945), 17–18.

[22] Hammond to Grenville, April 17, 28, 1794, FCA, XVIII.

privileges in the West India Islands," it might be reasonable for the United States to compensate "its own citizens who [had] suffered." He agreed that British depredations on shipping were "atrocious" and that they had greatly angered the American people. He was convinced that no arrangement should be made on the "*mere appearance* of indemnification." No agreement should be reached that would not "stand the test of the severest scrutiny." If Britain would not contract to make substantial payments, it would be better to leave the subject unadjusted so that the United States would be free "to act afterwards as they deem proper."[23]

In this significant communication Hamilton reiterated eloquently his conviction that solid agreement between the two nations would contribute richly to the welfare of both. He pointed out again that the United States was Britain's best customer and that American purchases would rapidly increase along with the population. Britain needed American trade in times of war and of peace and would be wise indeed to conclude a firm treaty to regularize trade relationships—to place them above the hazards of "interruption and derangement" (no doubt a reference in part to Madison's retaliation proposals). He added that the treaty terms might also include "a renunciation of all pretensions of right to sequester or confiscate debts."

Jay, aware of the affinity of Washington's and Hamilton's views, correctly considered this letter highly significant. He showed parts of it to Grenville—apparently with good results.[24]

Hamilton's spirits were high; the long-festering sore of Anglo-American antagonism was at last to undergo treatment, and he grew more hopeful about his nation's future than he had been for several years. He wrote to his wife, "Tell your father that our affairs continue to mend, and that there is every prospect that we shall not put on the French yoke."[25]

When Jay sailed for England, in May, 1794, the British government was not aware of the precariousness of relations with the United States. His Majesty's government, preoccupied with the war with France, had probably placed too much reliance on Hamilton's ability to counteract anti-British sentiment in the United States. Soon after Jay's arrival in London, on June 12, Grenville received disturbing dispatches from Hammond "telling of the increasing popular bitterness, the various proposals of inimical

[23] Hamilton to Jay, May 6, 1794, *HWL*, V, 123–28.

[24] Hamilton to Jay, August 19, 1800, Jay to Hamilton, September 28, 1800. Transcripts of these letters, from the Jay Papers, were supplied by Frank Monaghan.

[25] Hamilton to Mrs. Hamilton, June 8, 1794, HPSCLC, Box 2.

legislation—passed through everything but the final stage of enactment—the *sine qua non* as expressed by Hamilton, the certainty that if the coming negotiation should fail the legislation would pass the next session of Congress, [and] the imminent danger of war itself."[26] Moreover, a new threat was in the offing. Sweden and Denmark were trying to organize a new "armed neutrality" like that of 1780 which had embarrassed Britain and had somewhat limited maritime hostilities during the final phase of the American Revolution.

If Jay had been able to negotiate a treaty promptly, during that somewhat threatening period, he would probably have been able to secure more favorable terms than those embodied in the treaty that was eventually worked out. But the British procrastinated, and procrastination worked in their favor. Soon British naval victories and news of triumphs in the West Indies offset French successes in land warfare and gave the English people fresh hope. In such circumstances troubles with the United States seemed relatively minor.

No formal instructions were issued to Grenville, and neither he nor Jay kept complete records of their conferences. One of the few documents dealing with the negotiations is a memorandum, apparently prepared by Grenville for his own guidance before the meetings began.[27] It outlined the terms he considered "desirable" though not necessarily mandatory. It included most of the points that comprised the final treaty, except for a provision calling for closing the Northwest boundary gap south of Lake of the Woods, on a line from Lake Superior to a navigable point on the Mississippi.

By September 19 the negotiators had reached agreement on several important points, including evacuation of the posts, but these points were essentially the ones both sides had been willing to accept from the beginning. The British had come to see that they must give up the posts in order to avoid war with the United States. Jay had won no victories, and there remained unsettled the crucial problems of contraband and the position Britain would take toward American shipping in the future.[28]

On September 30 Jay made a vigorous effort to obtain a favorable settlement by presenting a complete draft of a proposed treaty. It included the United States' small-navy principles—essentially "free ships, free goods"

[26] Bemis, *Jay's Treaty*, 202.
[27] *Ibid.*, Appendix II, 278–85.
[28] For a summary of the points agreed upon by September 19, see *ibid.*, 237–38.

and liberal definitions of contraband—that had been incorporated in American commercial treaties of 1778 with France and later with the Netherlands, Prussia, and Sweden. Jay probably injured his cause by making such demands, which Grenville had never shown the slightest inclination to accept. Britain could not place France under a real blockade—that is, deploy its warships in such a manner that they could intercept neutral vessels seeking to enter or leave French ports—without dangerously dividing the war fleet and making it vulnerable to the French navy. Britain's right to seize contraband goods aboard neutral vessels on their way to France was incontestable under international law, and such action did not reduce the effectiveness of the navy. Thus the point at issue was the definition of contraband. Britain's choice of definition would allow that nation an easy, inexpensive way to choke off the flow of neutral goods to the enemy. A liberal definition such as that most small-navy powers preferred would strike from British hands one of their most effective weapons. Jay was demanding the right of vessels from neutral United States to carry large quantities of goods (though not implements of war) to French purchasers. Nothing could induce Britain to concede this right but a threat of force far beyond the capacity of the United States to carry out, or the threat of a strangling embargo which the United States could not put into effect. The two month-long embargoes Congress had imposed had proved ineffective. Americans were too divided to make a general embargo successful, as Grenville was well aware. He also knew that Britain's command of the seas and its many alliances kept open to it most of the markets of the world except those in western Europe. He hoped to keep open the American market as well, but he was unwilling to pay the price Jay was asking.

Historians have often speculated whether the United States could have brought more pressure on Britain by joining with other neutral nations who were eager to establish a liberal definition of contraband, a rejection of any blockade not actually maintained close by an enemy port, and less rigid prize-court procedures. Though Jay's instructions had authorized him to sound the ministers of Russia, Denmark, and Sweden "upon the probability of an alliance" if the British government offered no satisfaction,[29] he was not given permission to make a treaty with those powers, nor was he instructed about specific terms that he might propose to them.

When Randolph indicated a willingness to allow Jay more leeway in the

[29] *ASPFR*, I, 473.

matter, Hamilton called him sharply to account. In a brief letter dated July 8, Hamilton reminded the secretary that the instructions did not authorize Jay "to establish *by treaty* a concert with Sweden and Denmark." In any such treaty, he added, the United States' "peculiar advantages . . . would . . . be thrown into common stock without an equivalent." Those nations were "too weak and too remote to render a co-operation useful; and the entanglements of a treaty with them might be found very inconvenient" (a comment foreshadowing the Farewell Address). His conclusions, he said, were "the final result of full reflection."[30]

Several weeks later Hammond broached the subject to Hamilton and was given essentially the same arguments. Even if there should come "an open contest with Great Britain," the United States would enter no such alliance with the Baltic powers, said Hamilton, for it might later "involve [the United States] in disputes wherein it might have no possible interest, and commit it to a common cause with allies from whom, in the moment of danger, it could derive no succor."[31]

Hammond's report on this interview reached Grenville about September 20. Some six weeks earlier, Russia, now Britain's ally, had informed Sweden and Denmark that it would station a fleet in the Baltic to check all neutral vessels bound for France.[32] Grenville must have known that this action rendered the would-be "armed neutrality" nugatory—or "abortive," as it is commonly described.[33] Russia, the primary force of the armed neutrality of 1780, had not been a major obstacle to Britain. Moreover, the Baltic neutrals were no more interested in forming an alliance with the United States than Hamilton was in forming an American alliance with them. A Swedish representative made a tentative move toward Jay, but after Danish admonitions he quickly drew back.

One can criticize as improper Hamilton's assurances to Hammond that the United States would enter no Baltic "alliance." In fact, it has been called "the betrayal of a state secret."[34] Hamilton has also been described as "standing behind Jay . . . holding a mirror, however unconsciously, which reflected the American negotiator's cards to the enlightenment of the suave and

[30] Hamilton to Randolph, *HWL*, V, 135–36.

[31] Hammond to Grenville, August 3, 1794, FCA, XIX.

[32] Bemis, *Jay's Treaty*, 251.

[33] The conclusion of Burt (*The United States, Great Britain, and British North America*, 155n.), based on a thorough study of British sources.

[34] Arthur Burr Darling, *Our Rising Empire, 1763–1803* (New Haven, 1940), 184.

smiling Grenville."[35] It seems only just to point out that Hammond's report arrived in London too late to have any influence on the discussions. But there is no doubt that Hamilton made a serious mistake. If conditions in Europe had been different, his revelation to Hammond might have injured the American cause.

Yet there is something to be said in Hamilton's defense. His candor must have added weight to his earlier statement that an agreement to make compensation for the molestation of American commerce was a *sine qua non*. Hamilton never retreated an inch from his demands for the evacuation of the posts. This concession, together with the continuation of peace, was to be the United States' real gain in the treaty.

Jay's methods and convictions made it impossible for him to use the Baltic states as a threat against Grenville.[36] He never thought well of the idea. If he had been possessed of the diplomatic cleverness of a Benjamin Franklin, at the outset of negotiations he could have jolted Grenville by affecting an interest in building a new armed neutrality, about which the British foreign secretary was somewhat apprehensive.[37] But he could not have carried out the threat; the Russian move and Danish irresolution rendered it a hollow one, and Grenville then could have voided earlier concessions granted because of the threat and could have made new demands for equivalents.

The British knew full well that the real threats were the disruption of commerce and the possibility of war with the United States. Those dangers were the true source of Jay's strength. Hostilities might well lead to the dissolution of British power in North America. Wartime blockades and embargoes would have presented Britain with real difficulty in finding other sources for materials it was receiving from the United States. During the Revolutionary War American privateers had made heavy inroads on British shipping. Could they not do the same thing again, and worse?

During the summer of 1794 the precarious peace was almost broken. As mentioned earlier, Dorchester had decided that war was inevitable, and John Graves Simcoe, lieutenant governor of Upper Canada, agreed with him. They believed that Wayne's campaign, ostensibly against the Indians north of the Ohio, was really directed against the British fort at Detroit. In

35 Claude G. Bowers, *Jefferson and Hamilton: The Struggle for Democracy in America* (Boston, 1925), 270 (hereafter cited as *Jefferson and Hamilton*).

36 See John C. Fitzpatrick's review of *John Jay, Defender of Liberty*, by Frank Monaghan, in *American Historical Review*, Vol. XLI (April, 1936), 552.

37 Grenville to Hammond, May 10, 1794, Mayo, 54–55.

January authorities in London, still hoping to persuade the United States to agree to a neutral barrier state inhabited by Indians, had instructed Dorchester to try to keep the frontier quiet.[38] Dorchester's famous speech to the Indians (discussed in Chapter XI) had been delivered before he received those instructions, but he had been persuaded by Simcoe that overt action was, nevertheless, called for. After Jay's departure for London news had reached Philadelphia that Simcoe had completed and garrisoned a fort at Miamis, sixty miles south of Detroit. Washington was angered and humiliated by the act, and seriously considered military measures against the fort. On May 30, Theodore Sedgwick stated in the House of Representatives that war was not a "distant prospect" and claimed that Washington had declared he would drive Simcoe out.[39] On May 25, Fauchet, the French envoy, reported to his government that Britain and the United States were moving into war.[40]

Sedgwick's statement was made in a speech in support of a new bill, just received by the House from the Senate, to increase American military forces. Madison had opposed the new measure in the House, claiming that he feared the President would use the force "for the sake of the influence to be acquired by the command" and that the bill was unconstitutional because it granted too much power to the President.[41] Monroe, who had not yet been appointed minister to France, wrote to Jefferson in an oddly different tone. He referred to Simcoe's action as "an actual invasion" and said he assumed that it would be treated as such by the President, "whose powers are competent by the existing law to its repulsion." Passage of the bill in the Senate was easy, Monroe said, "for the Republican party [was] entirely broken in that branch."[42]

In August the administration learned that Simcoe had protested a new settlement at Sodus Bay on Lake Ontario, established by Americans with a land title granted by the state of New York.[43] Washington was outraged by the protest. Britain had ceded the region to the United States in 1783 and had never since laid claim to land south of Lake Ontario. In angry tones Washington wrote to Jay describing the protest and predicting that war

38 Bemis, *Jay's Treaty*, 184n.
39 *Annals*, IV, 738.
40 Turner, *Correspondence of the French Ministers*, 351.
41 *Annals*, IV, 738.
42 Monroe to Jefferson, May 26, 1794, *JMW*, I, 296–97.
43 Bemis, *Jay's Treaty*, 179.

would be "inevitable" unless the Northwest posts were soon evacuated. He blamed British agents for Indian hostilities against American frontiersmen and observed bitterly that those agents had not been punished by their own government.[44] His letter, though informal in style, actually constituted the strongest instructions Jay received on the subject of the Northwest. Though Hamilton's views on the subject generally coincided with those of his chief, of all the hundreds of extant Hamilton letters, public and private, not one blazes with the incandescent anger of this one from Washington's hand.

On November 19, 1794, after five months of give-and-take, Jay and Grenville met to sign the treaty.[45] It opened with a statement affirming a "firm inviolable and universal peace, and a true and sincere friendship" between the two nations. It provided that the British posts were to be evacuated by June 1, 1796, after which Indians living on either side of the border were to be free to cross it to carry on normal trade without payment of fees or duties. Citizens of Canada and the United States would have access to inland waterways of both countries. The Mississippi would be "entirely open to both parties."

Under the terms of the treaty the United States agreed to pay for British vessels seized by Genêt's privateersmen, and in the future captured privateersmen who had been commissioned by a third power and had operated against the ships of either signatory would be tried and punished as pirates. Citizens of one signatory would not be allowed to perform regular military service in the forces of an enemy of the other signatory (in other words, American citizens would not join the French army or navy). The United States would pay private debts of Americans to British subjects in cases where payment had been prevented by legal obstructions. Britain was to pay for American ships seized "under color," and commissions were to be set up to determine the amounts of those obligations. Commissioners were also to be appointed to survey and establish the boundary line between Maine and New Brunswick and to survey the upper Mississippi and Lake of the Woods area in preparation for future negotiations on the Northwest boundary gap. Citizens of each nation currently holding lands in the territories of the other would "continue to hold them according to the nature and tenure of their respective estates and titles therein." This provision gave rise to fears, probably unforeseen by Jay, that it would reinstate British or

44 Washington to Jay, August 30, 1794, *WW*, XXXIII, 483–85.

45 The text of the treaty, with useful supplementary material is given in Miller, *Treaties*, II, 245–74.

Gouverneur Morris (1779)

From a drawing by Pierre Eugène du Simitière

COURTESY OF EMMET COLLECTION, MANUSCRIPT DIVISION,
NEW YORK PUBLIC LIBRARY, ASTOR, LENOX, AND TILDEN FOUNDATIONS

Nothing can be more ridiculous than the idea of expelling a few from this city and neighbourhood, while there are numbers in different parts of this and other ſtates, who muſt neceſſarily partake in our governments, and who can never expect to be the objects of animadverſion or excluſion. It is confirming *many* in their enmity and prejudices againſt the ſtate, to indulge our enmity and prejudices againſt a few.

The idea of ſuffering the Tories to live among us under diſqualifications, is equally miſchievous and abſurd. It is neceſſitating a large body of citizens in the ſtate to continue enemies to the government, ready, at all times, in a moment of commotion, to throw their weight into that ſcale which meditates a change whether favourable or unfavourable to public liberty.

Viewing the ſubject in every poſſible light, there is not a ſingle intereſt of the community but dictates moderation rather than violence. That honeſty is ſtill the beſt policy; that juſtice and moderation are the ſureſt ſupports of every government, are maxims, which however they may be called trite, are at all times true, though too ſeldom regarded, but rarely neglected with impunity.

Were the people of America with one voice, to aſk, What ſhall we do to perpetuate our liberties and ſecure our happineſs? The anſwer would be, GOVERN WELL, *and you have nothing to fear either from internal diſaffection or external hoſtility. Abuſe not the power you poſſeſs, and you need never apprehend its diminution or loſs. But if you make a wanton uſe of it, if you furniſh another example, that deſpotiſm may debaſe the government of the many as well as the few, you like all others that have acted the ſame part, will experience that licentiouſneſs is the fore-runner to ſlavery.*

How wiſe was that policy of Auguſtus, who after conquering his enemies, when the papers of Brutus were brought to him, which would have diſcloſed all his ſecret aſſociates, immediately ordered them to be burnt. He would not even know his enemies, that they might ceaſe to hate when they had nothing to fear.

How laudable was the example of Elizabeth, who when ſhe was transferred from the priſon to the throne, fell upon her knees and thanking Heaven, for the deliverance it had granted her, from her bloody perſecutors; diſmiſſed her reſentment. "This act of pious gratitude, ſays the hiſtorian, ſeems to have been the laſt circumſtance in which ſhe remembered any paſt injuries and hardſhips. With a prudence and magnanimity truly laudable, ſhe buried all offences in oblivion, and received with affability even thoſe, who had acted with the greateſt virulence againſt her." She did more — ſhe retained many of the oppoſite party in her councils.

The reigns of theſe two ſovereigns, are among the moſt illuſtrious in hiſtory. Their moderation gave a ſtability to their government, which nothing elſe could have effected. This was the ſecret of uniting all parties.

Theſe ſentiments are delivered to you in the frankneſs of conſci-

ous

LIBRARY OF CONGRESS

Excerpt from "Letter from Phocion"

Pamphlet published by Hamilton in New York, 1784

COURTESY OF THE GRANGER COLLECTION

Mrs. Alexander Hamilton (1787)

From a portrait by Ralph Earle

COURTESY OF COLLECTION, UNIVERSITY ART MUSEUM, UNIVERSITY OF CALIFORNIA, BERKELEY, GIFT OF MRS. MARK HOPKINS

Washington at the Battle of Monmouth

On June 28, 1778, Washington rode to the scene of threatening disaster, rallied the troops and avoided defeat. Washington is facing General Charles Lee, who had ordered the retreat. Just behind Washington are Hamilton (left) and Lafayette (right).

COURTESY OF THE GRANGER COLLECTION

Revolt of Wayne's Brigade (1781)

From a steel engraving by Robert Thew (1863)

COURTESY OF INDEPENDENCE NATIONAL
HISTORICAL PARK COLLECTION, PHILADELPHIA

James Madison

From a painting by Catherine Drinker, 1875, after Gilbert Stuart

COURTESY OF METROPOLITAN MUSEUM OF ART, NEW YORK, GIFT OF FREDERIC W. STEVENS, 1908

Albert Gallatin (ca. 1803)

From a portrait by Gilbert Stuart

WIDE WORLD PHOTOS

John Jay

From a steel engraving, artist unknown

COURTESY OF THE GRANGER COLLECTION

Edmond Charles Genêt

Nineteenth-century wood engraving from a French aquatint engraving of 1793

COURTESY OF INDEPENDENCE NATIONAL
HISTORICAL PARK, PHILADELPHIA
NATIONAL PARK SERVICE PHOTO

General James Wilkinson

From a portrait by Charles Willson Peale

WIDE WORLD PHOTOS

General George Rogers Clark

Clark shared Hamilton's views about the vital importance of the West in America's future development.

COURTESY OF THE METROPOLITAN MUSEUM OF ART, NEW YORK, BEQUEST OF WILLIAM NELSON, 1905

Washington and Lafayette at Mount Vernon

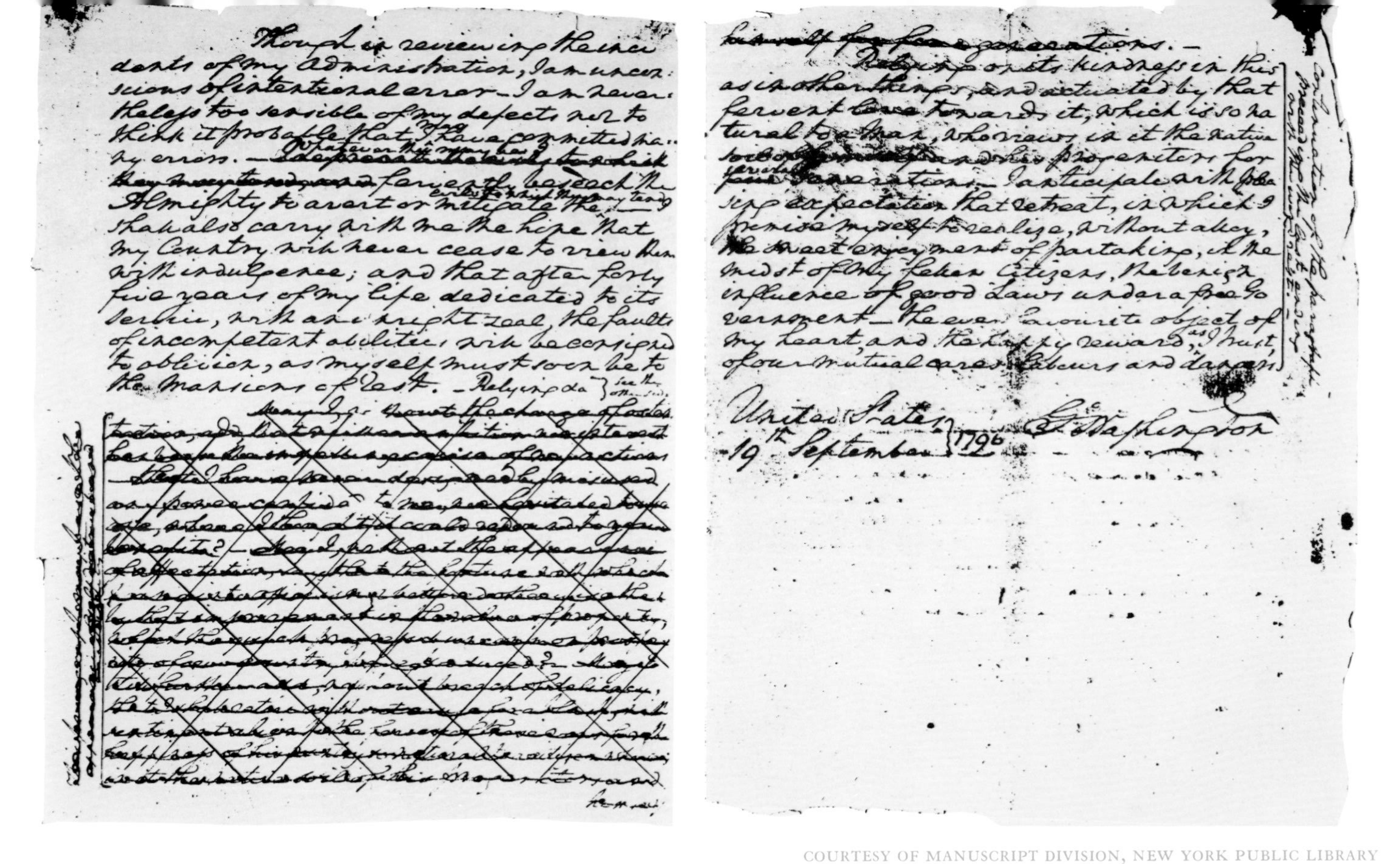

Though in reviewing the incidents of my Administration, I am unconscious of intentional error — I am nevertheless too sensible of my defects not to think it probable that I have committed many errors. — Whatever they may be I fervently beseech the Almighty to avert or mitigate the evils to which they may tend — I shall also carry with me the hope that my Country will never cease to view them with indulgence; and that after forty five years of my life dedicated to its Service, with an upright zeal, the faults of incompetent abilities will be consigned to oblivion, as myself must soon be to the Mansions of rest. — Relying &c. } see the other side.

Continuation of the paragraph preceding the last ending with the word rest. —

Relying on its kindness in this as in other things, and actuated by that fervent love towards it, which is so natural to a Man, who views in it the native soil of himself and his progenitors for several generations — I anticipate with pleasing expectation that retreat, in which I promise myself to realize, without alloy, the sweet enjoyment of partaking, in the midst of my fellow Citizens, the benign influence of good Laws under a free Government — the ever favourite object of my heart, and the happy reward, as I trust, of our mutual cares, labours and dangers.

United States } 1796
19th September }

G° Washington

COURTESY OF MANUSCRIPT DIVISION, NEW YORK PUBLIC LIBRARY
ASTOR, LENOX, AND TILDEN FOUNDATIONS

Washington's Farewell Address (1796)

From the original draft of the closing paragraphs. For the complete text of the address, see the Appendix of this book.

COURTESY OF THE BOSTON ATHENAEUM

John Adams (1788)

From a portrait by Mather Brown

COURTESY OF NEW-YORK HISTORICAL SOCIETY

Thomas Jefferson (1803)

From a portrait by Rembrandt Peale

COURTESY OF HOUGHTON MIFFLIN COMPANY

The *Constellation* Vanquishes *L'Insurgente* (1799)

From a painting by E. Savage Maya

loyalists' titles to lands such as the vast Granville and McCulloch estates in North Carolina that had been confiscated during the Revolution.

In spite of the earlier Republican motion in the House of Representatives to confiscate British debts, the treaty contained the provision that private debts would not be confiscated, even in the event of war. In a statement that would give further affront to Republican sentiments, the treaty declared it "unjust and impolitic" that such debts be "destroyed or impaired . . . on account of national differences and discontents."

The commercial articles of the treaty were to be binding for twelve years from the date of ratification. East Indies trade was opened to Americans, though since trade with that area was slight, the article was of little consequence. The West Indies were to be opened to American vessels of not more than seventy tons' burden; but to make doubly sure the Americans would not take over the carrying trade between the islands and Britain, an encumbrance was added prohibiting the exportation in American vessels of "molasses, sugar, coffee, cocoa, or cotton," even from the United States, the assumption being that these items would have originated in the West Indies. This restriction (the despised Article XII), was rejected by the Senate before ratification.

As if to place further curbs on the Republicans in the House, the treaty included guaranties against future tariff and tonnage discrimination. It specifically provided that Britain might levy additional duties against American ships and cargoes entering British ports to offset charges provided by American discriminatory laws enacted since 1789.

The treaty included a long list of contraband items, from obvious ones such as "cannon, muskets, bombs," to naval stores and materials such as "timber for shipbuilding, . . . sails, hemp, and cordage." These products were declared liable to confiscation if seized en route to an enemy of either signatory. Food and other provisions were omitted from the list, and it was provided that if such products were seized they would not be confiscated but would be "speedily" paid for by "the captors, or, in their default, [by] the Government." Pre-emptive purchase of such provisions had already become the regular practice of the British government; the treaty sought to regularize the procedure and to protect the rights of neutral shippers by providing that the amount to be paid must include "the full value of all such articles, with a reasonable mercantile profit thereon, together with the freight, and also the demurrage incident to such detention."

This guaranty of profit was one of the reasons New Englanders found the treaty less odious than did southerners and Republicans, who considered it a national disgrace to agree in writing to let the Mistress of the Seas intercept goods sorely needed by France.

To the disappointment of many Americans, the treaty failed to deal with some serious problems, among them the impressment of American seamen by the British navy. That omission was all the more vexing because a provision was included that officers of "ships of war" of either nation visiting in the other country were to be "treated with that respect which is due to the commissions which they bear." If those visitors were insulted, the offenders were to be punished for disturbing "the peace and amity between the two countries." Yet it must have been difficult for Americans to show respect to British officers suspected of impressing American seamen.

Another omission was the question of compensation for the Negroes carried away by the British in violation of the Treaty of Paris. Jay, like Hamilton and many others, found the subject of slavery embarrassing. There was little interest in the United States in the return of the Negroes, but slaveowners who had suffered financial losses were sorely disappointed to learn that their losses appeared to be permanent.

Jay had tried to induce Grenville to accept Hamilton's proposal to disarm the Canadian-American border. Grenville rejected the proposal because it interfered with his own project to erect a "neutral" barrier Indian state south of the boundary. He continued to cherish this idea even after he had agreed to evacuate the posts. The day after the treaty was signed, he instructed Hammond to discuss the subject again with Hamilton, and preferably not with Randolph, whom he considered too pro-French.[46] Inasmuch as both Beckwith and Hammond had utterly failed to interest Hamilton or any other prominent American in the barrier-state idea, it appears incredible that Grenville still hoped to see it fulfilled. The only explanation can be his extremely inadequate grasp of American public opinion.

It is one of the misfortunes of history that Hamilton did not live to see the border disarmed. It had been a cherished goal almost throughout his career of public service.[47] As a member of the Continental Congress he had urged that it be included in the peace treaty,[48] and he did not abandon the

[46] Grenville to Hammond, November 20, 1794, FCA, XIX.

[47] Bemis, "Alexander Hamilton and the Limitation of Armaments," *The Pacific Review*, Vol. II (March, 1922), 587–602.

[48] Mitchell, *Alexander Hamilton*, I, 314.

goal even when Jay failed in his effort with Grenville. An unguarded border was a vital element in Hamilton's design for Anglo-American harmony, and was consistent with his conviction about the mutuality of interests of the two nations. It was evidence of his foresight and statesmanship in an era when few could foretell the course of American history.

The first copy of Jay's Treaty reached Philadelphia on March 7, 1795. The Senate was not in session, but Washington had already issued the call, and the upper house convened on June 8. The treaty was promptly laid before it with special injunctions of secrecy. After two weeks of unrecorded, but reputedly heated, discussion, the Senate ratified it (except for Article XII) by a vote of twenty to ten, exactly the required two-thirds majority. Despite the injunctions of secrecy, the contents of the treaty were immediately divulged to the country by Senator Pierce Butler of South Carolina, and by others, and the nation responded with an outcry of protest. The move that had secured "peace abroad" had kindled "war at home."[49]

In the initial wave of protest the people generally overlooked or failed to appreciate the concessions gained by the treaty. Complaints were centered on the provisions allowing Britain to seize French goods aboard American ships, classifying naval stores as contraband, and agreeing to pay pre-Revolutionary War debts. The last provision drew particularly heated opposition from planters in Virginia and South Carolina who were not to be compensated for losses of slaves.[50] When, in 1784, Virginia had opened its courts to British nationals to sue to collect such debts, it had made the action conditional upon compensation for the slaves. Even the agreement to evacuate the posts met opposition because it was to be delayed for two years. The boundary commissions were denounced as devices to facilitate British trickery.

The spirit of opposition was contagious, and Federalists were not immune. Even the "merchants and steady men" of Boston felt the "prevailing fever," though they later came to support the treaty.[51] At a public meeting held in Faneuil Hall in Boston to discuss the treaty, not a single voice was raised in its favor.[52] In Charleston, South Carolina, the people reacted "in much the same manner as they had greeted the news of the Stamp Act." South Carolina Federalist John Rutledge thundered against the treaty, and General Charles Cotesworth Pinckney refused even to read it or to attend public

[49] Fisher Ames to Thomas Dwight, February 3, 1795, Ames, *Works of Fisher Ames*, I, 166.

[50] Rogers, *William Loughton Smith*, 279.

[51] Fisher Ames to Oliver Wolcott, July 9, 1795, Gibbs, I, 210.

[52] Morison, *The Life and Letters of Harrison Gray Otis*, I, 55.

meetings where it was to be discussed. Later, upon sober reflection, Rutledge moved quietly to the other side of the argument and let it be known that he regretted having spoken intemperately against it.[53]

Soon "Sir John Jay," as he was called, became "the most hated man in America."[54] At mass meetings in several cities resolutions were passed and toasts offered to convince Washington that he must reject the treaty. Many Fourth-of-July celebrations were transformed into anti-treaty demonstrations. On July 10 the *Philadelphia Aurora* reported the toast: "May the cage constructed to coop up the American eagle prove a trap for none but Jays and King-birds."[55] A visitor to Philadelphia reported that all the people of the city who did not ride in "elegant carriages" were protesting the treaty.[56]

Timothy Pickering, the uncompromising Federalist, told President Washington that the complaints were coming from the lowest class of society in America, very few of whom "would be fit to serve on a jury."[57] Despite Pickering's assessment, however, men in high places also opposed the treaty. Jefferson denounced it and its supporters. He repaid the Federalists who had characterized the Republicans as a "party" or a "faction"—with their imputations of sedition—in kind. This treaty, he wrote, he regarded as the boldest "party stroke ever struck" and called it an effort to "undermine the government."[58] It was "a treaty of alliance between England and the Anglomen of this country against the legislature and people of the United States."[59] "A rogue of a pilot" had run the ship of state "into an enemy's port."[60] He allowed Washington the dubious credit of being "the only honest man who has assented to" the treaty.[61] But after the President had signed it, Jefferson would write the famous letter to Phillip Mazzei in which he lamented, "Men who were Samsons in the field and Solomons in the council . . . have had their heads shorn by the harlot England."[62]

Earnest effort has been made to support Jefferson's "explanation," offered

[53] Rogers, *William Loughton Smith*, 276–81.

[54] DeConde, *Entangling Alliance*, 114.

[55] Bowers, *Jefferson and Hamilton*, 276.

[56] Dodd, *The Life of Nathaniel Macon*, 351.

[57] Ford, "Timothy Pickering," in Bemis, *The American Secretaries of State*, II, 173–74.

[58] Jefferson to Madison, September 21, 1795, *JW*, IX, 310.

[59] Jefferson to Edward Rutledge, November 30, 1795 (Rutledge Papers, Dreer Collection, Historical Society of Pennsylvania, Philadelphia), quoted in Rogers, *William Loughton Smith*, 280.

[60] Jefferson to Mann Page, August 30, 1795, *JW*, IX, 307.

[61] Jefferson to Madison, March 27, 1796, *ibid.*, 331.

[62] Jefferson to Phillip Mazzei, April 24, 1796, *ibid.*, 336.

only after Washington's death, that he was not really referring to the President in the Samson allusion. But Jefferson's intimate friends, among them Monroe, certainly thought that he was speaking of the President,[63] and apparently everyone else also thought so at the time. The contention that he was not alluding to Washington leads one inevitably to ask why, in that case, Jefferson did not explain his allusion immediately. It is difficult to support the contention that Jefferson did not attack the character of his political opponents when he differed with their principles.[64] He clearly implied that all others who "assented" to the treaty were not "honest" and made the explicit accusation that through intrigue "a faction" had "entered into a conspiracy with the enemies of their country to chain down the Legislature at the feet of both."[65]

Madison shared Jefferson's opposition to the treaty, though he couched it in milder terms. He thought that the treaty granted "everything to Great Britain for nothing in return" and would make it impossible thereafter to get a good commercial treaty with "any other nation." It irked him to see that persons who were actually engaged in the carrying trade generally took the other side of the argument, though "the whole treaty" appeared to him "to assassinate the interest of that part of the Union."[66] For his part, Senator William Maclay of Pennsylvania, wished that Washington were dead so that he would not be "brought forward as the constant cover to every unconstitutional and irrepublican act."[67] This sentiment was a far cry, indeed, from the attitude of the nation toward Washington expressed by the Senate just a few years earlier: "In you all parties confide; in you all interests unite."[68]

Jefferson's characterization of the treaty as an "alliance" against the legislature and people reflected his particular resentment of the articles proscribing the sequestration of debts and the enactment of retaliatory commercial legislation, like that which had been near passage in the spring of 1794. Admittedly, it was a rather highhanded act on Hamilton's part to forestall the Republican representatives through this maneuver—and his draft of instructions to Jay, as well as his later correspondence with the

[63] Monroe to Jefferson, July 12, 1797, *JMW*, III, 88.

[64] Malone, III, 302–22.

[65] Jefferson to Madison, March 27, 1796, *JW*, IX, 330–31.

[66] Madison to unnamed correspondent, August 23, 1795, *MW*, VI, 242–43.

[67] Tinkcom, *The Republicans and Federalists in Pennsylvania, 1790–1801*, 30.

[68] "Address of the Senate to George Washington," May 7, 1789, Richardson, I, 46.

envoy, referred to above, shows clearly that that was his deliberate design. Moreover, in a communication to the President, Hamilton had recommended that Jay be instructed to "insert a formal *stipulation*" in the treaty agreeing to pay the British for vessels seized by American privateersmen commissioned by Genêt. If the matter was handled that way, he observed, "the Senate only will have to concur. If provision is to be made by law, *both Houses* must concur. The difference is easily seen."[69] Hamilton's usual rule in such a serious game was to play his hand for all it was worth, as long as it was in the nation's interest and did not violate the Constitution as he interpreted it.

By the time public opposition to the treaty began to be felt, Hamilton was no longer in the cabinet. His salary as secretary of the treasury was, he felt, insufficient to meet the needs of his growing family. He had delayed his resignation because of the British negotiations, but on January 31, 1795, he had stepped out, and was soon making almost three times as much money in his New York law practice as he had received in public office. The President had written him a generous letter of appreciation. "In every relation which you have had to me," he had assured the departing secretary, "I have found that my confidence in your talents, exertions, and integrity, has been well placed." He had added, "I speak from opportunities of information which cannot deceive me."[70] Washington continued to depend on Hamilton for advice, relying on him particularly heavily since he no longer felt free to call on Jefferson or Madison now that his fellow Virginians had become alienated from him politically.

Washington knew that Jay's Treaty left much to be desired, but he was struck by the widespread opposition to it. People looked upon it as though it were a mad dog, he observed, and nearly everybody seemed "engaged in running it down."[71] He sent Hamilton a copy of the treaty and requested his opinion on each article and his evaluation of the entire instrument.[72]

Hamilton replied voluminously, as usual.[73] Most of what he wrote no doubt simply reinforced the President's own position, and much of it had been said before. The evacuation of the British posts was, he said, of "signal

[69] Hamilton to Washington, June 22, 1794, *HWL*, V, 133–34.
[70] Washington to Hamilton, February 2, 1795, *WW*, XXXIV, 109–10.
[71] Washington to Hamilton, July 29, 1795, *ibid.*, 262.
[72] Washington to Hamilton, July 3, 1795, *ibid.*, 226–28.
[73] Hamilton to Washington, July 9, 1795, *HWL*, V, 138–81. In print the letter is forty-three pages long.

importance." The delay until June, 1796, was regrettable but should give no reason for suspecting British intentions to comply with the agreement. They needed time to avoid upsetting their relations with the Indians and to avoid appearing to have been forced into a sudden withdrawal. The private debts should have been paid even "had their been no article," for confiscation was bad policy, and the legal impediments in some of the states were unjustifiable. He supported the surveys and arbitrations provided for in the treaty as the best means of seeking accommodation. Concerning the relationship between the treaty-making power and the prerogatives of legislating bodies, he observed that the authority to make treaties did not extend far enough to allow a violation of the Constitution but that it would be "difficult to assign any other bounds to the power." He noted the objections to Article X, by which the United States agreed not to pass laws to sequester foreign debts, but dismissed them with the comment that the unlikely enactment of such a law would be a "disgrace" to the country.

Hamilton approved the Senate's rejection of Article XII. The small increase the provision would have brought in West Indian trade would not have justified prohibiting the United States from exporting the specified items. Moreover, the article might have given France a "reasonable cause of dissatisfaction," for some of the "molasses, sugar, coffee, cocoa, or cotton" to be exported from the United States might have originated in the French-owned islands. The article had grown from Hamilton's own proposals, and it must have been somewhat embarrassing to him to denounce it. Such reversals were rare in his life.

In his opinion, the provisions on commerce and on the pre-emptive purchase of contraband goods were generally satisfactory. They were an improvement over previous conditions, and there were stipulations against abuses to American shipping. He was aware of the complaints that those points would give "umbrage to France," but he considered that likelihood "improbable," for there was "no cause given," and France had shown no indication of willingness to "make a better bargain." On the whole, he considered the treaty beneficial to the United States, and, provided Article XII was removed, he recommended ratification.

Hamilton soon became known as the treaty's chief American sponsor, a reputation which earned him considerable abuse. When he tried to speak for it at a mass meeting in New York in July, 1795, he was stoned[74] (an

[74] Frank Monaghan, *John Jay, Defender of Liberty* (New York, 1935), 393.

episode which gave rise to the Federalist gibe that the Republicans had tried to reduce him to their own level by knocking out his brains[75]).

He next reached for the pen, always his mightiest weapon. In the "Camillus" essays,[76] published in the *New York Argus* during the remainder of 1795 and into the following year, he displayed his deep understanding of the diplomatic needs of his nation and of international relations generally. He also demonstrated his power to influence the public mind. The "Camillus" essays are a tour de force in the literature of American diplomacy.

In the essays Hamilton asked the people to reflect upon the dangers and uncertainties of war, the nation's need for time for peaceful development, the ordinary prudence of compromise in quarrels between men or nations, and the degree of prosperity and happiness the nation was enjoying in peacetime. Thrusting barbs into the leaders of the opposition, he said that only a "rage for objections" would have inspired them to complain about Article I, for example, which was nothing more than the customary declaration of peace between the two contracting powers. Those who demanded that American retaliation should precede negotiations were, in his estimation, desirous of war. Critics who spoke out against Jay's conciliatory attitude must have expected him to address the British authorities in the tones of "an imperious Bashaw to his trembling slave."

The article providing for British evacuation of the posts was highly advantageous to the United States, he said; yet it was condemned as severely as if the posts had been ceded outright to the British. He presented elaborate proofs that the treaty conferred real benefits on the nation: payment for British depredations, cession of the Northwest, and some improvement in trade privileges. The article reiterating the rights of both the United States and Britain to free navigation on the Mississippi would help keep Spain from blocking American shipping in that region.

America's honor was not besmirched by the treaty, Hamilton insisted. "True honor is a rational thing" and "cannot be wounded by consulting moderation.... The ravings of anger and pride" must not be "mistaken for the suggestions of honor.... How afflicting, that imposture and fraud should be so often able to assume with success the garb of patriotism, and that this

[75] George Cabot to Rufus King, July 27, 1795, Henry Cabot Lodge, *Life and Letters of George Cabot* (Boston, 1877), 82.

[76] *HWL*, V, 189–491, VI, 3–197.

sublime virtue should be so frequently discredited by the usurpation and abuse of its name!" "The true patriot" is one "who never fears to sacrifice popularity to what he believes to be the cause of public good." Americans should "aspire to the glory of the greatest triumph which a people can gain, a triumph over prejudice!"

"For God's sake," wrote Jefferson to Madison, "take up your pen and give a fundamental reply to ... Camillus." "Hamilton is a colossus.... Without numbers, he is an host within himself."[77]

Madison declined the task but predicted that the essayist would be "betrayed by his anglomany into arguments as vicious and as vulnerable as the treaty itself."[78] He hoped—vainly, it proved—that Hamilton in defending the treaty would become as unpopular as Jay had become for negotiating it.

Hamilton's friends recognized his ability to influence public opinion, but thought the attempt was beneath his dignity. Fisher Ames compared him to "Jove," who "holds his bolts in his talons, and hurls them not at the Titans, but at sparrows and mice."[79]

Washington, though "not favorable to" the treaty because it lacked many hoped-for concessions by Britain, came to believe it "better to ratify it ... than to suffer matters to remain" as they were.[80] He abruptly changed his mind upon learning that the British were again seizing provisions as contraband aboard American ships. These acts shocked the nation, which interpreted them as new violations of international law—as indeed they were later declared to be by the arbitral commission formed in accordance with the provisions of the treaty. The new seizures were carried out under a special order in council designed to intercept the shipment of a large purchase of food supplies by the French government.[81] The order was soon rescinded, but the United States did not receive the news until after final ratification of the treaty.

Hamilton was exasperated by the renewed attacks on American shipping and strongly advised against exchanging ratifications until the order was

[77] Jefferson to Madison, September 21, 1795, *JW*, IX, 309–11.

[78] Madison to [Jefferson], August 23, 1795, *MW*, VI, 239. Hunt does not give Jefferson's name as the addressee, for it did not appear on the draft he used; but this letter is undoubtedly a reply to Jefferson's request.

[79] Ames to Dwight Foster, January 4, 1796, Ames, *Works of Fisher Ames*, I, 183.

[80] Washington to Randolph, July 22, 1795, *WW*, XXXIV, 244.

[81] Josiah T. Newcomb, "New Light on Jay's Treaty," *American Journal of International Law*, Vol. XXVIII (October, 1934), 685–92.

set aside. He urged the government to make a "remonstrance . . . well considered and well digested." To complete the treaty in the face of a new unrequited injury would offend France, allow misinterpretation of the treaty, and destroy confidence in the American government. "It would scarcely be reputable to a nation to conduct a treaty with a Power to heal past controversies, at the very moment of a new and existing violation of its rights."[82]

Washington was so provoked by these "high-handed measures" that it seemed to him it had become "next to impossible to keep peace between the United States and Great Britain."[83] Randolph, who was opposed to signing the treaty under the circumstances, came to believe that the President would not sign it until the order was withdrawn.[84] But after the furor over the British seizures calmed, a domestic crisis arose in high government circles that changed Washington's mind. British authorities turned over to Oliver Wolcott, who had succeeded Hamilton as secretary of the treasury, some intercepted dispatches from the French minister Fauchet to his government, one of which indicated that Randolph was working at cross-purposes to the administration.[85] Wolcott gave the dispatches to Secretary of War Timothy Pickering, who dramatically informed the President that Randolph was a traitor. The revelation convinced Washington that he must sign the treaty. Randolph's intimacy with Fauchet had destroyed the weight of his counsel.

Having made the decision to sign the treaty, Washington confronted his secretary of state with the French dispatch and asked for an explanation. Randolph was overwhelmed by the accusation. After a brief attempt to explain that the message had been misinterpreted, he suddenly resigned. The evidence against him was not conclusive,[86] and treason was apparently too strong a word for describing his actions and intentions; but he was clearly not working in harmony with the administration. Timothy Pickering was appointed to succeed him as secretary of state, and sent the youthful

[82] Hamilton to Oliver Wolcott, August 10, 1795, *HWL*, X, 113–14.

[83] Washington to Hamilton, August 31, 1795, *WW*, XXXIV, 295.

[84] Conway, *Edmund Randolph*, 269.

[85] Turner, *Correspondence of the French Ministers*, II, 444–45, reprints Fauchet's famous dispatch No. 10, which contains the damaging references to Randolph.

[86] Irving Brant, "Edmund Randolph, Not Guilty!" *William and Mary Quarterly*, 3d Ser., Vol. VII (April, 1950), 179–98. A firsthand account hostile to Randolph may be found in Wolcott's letter to John Marshall, June 9, 1806, Gibbs, I, 241–46. For a much fuller treatment and extensive correspondence, see Gibbs, I, 232–80. An account favorable to Randolph is given by D. Robins Anderson, "Edmund Randolph," in Bemis, *The American Secretaries of State*, II, 149–59.

and rising John Quincy Adams to London with instructions to exchange ratifications of the treaty. There was no question about Adams' support of it; he had held from the first that it was "better than war."[87] He was to inquire whether the objectionable order in council had been withdrawn. If not, he was to try to persuade the British to rescind it, but was to exchange ratifications in any case, which he did on October 28, 1795. The treaty was proclaimed in Philadelphia on February 29, 1796.

Now the scene shifted to the House of Representatives. On March 1, Washington sent to the Senate and the House a simple, one-sentence message to the effect that the treaty had been concluded, ratified, exchanged, and promulgated and that he was therewith transmitting "a copy thereof for the information of Congress."[88] Information appeared to be just what the House was looking for. On March 2, Edward Livingston of New York presented a resolution requesting the President to "lay before [the] House a copy of the instructions to the Minister of the United States, who negotiated this treaty . . . together with the correspondence and other documents relative" thereto,[89] thereby launching a long, fierce argument about the constitutional authority of the House in treaty making.[90]

Washington was embarrassed by the move, the report of which he read in the March 3 issue of "Bache's Paper," the *Philadelphia Aurora*. He had no desire, in most cases, to conceal information from the nation's lawmakers, and he had great respect for the House. There is no evidence that he ever regretted having made the fight in the Constitutional Convention of 1787 for a broadly representative lower chamber. Yet he dreaded the spectacle of a public argument on prerogatives, and he knew that the House Republicans were trying to vitiate the treaty, which he had already proclaimed to be in effect. He had laid the instructions and correspondence in question before the Senate, and he must have realized that the senators who had prematurely revealed the treaty's contents had also given a full account of the accompanying papers. The ensuing debate in the House made it clear that the members already knew the contents of the papers they had requested.

Once more the President turned to Hamilton. The latter had recently arrived in Philadelphia, and Washington asked Wolcott to see the former

87 Upham, *Life of Timothy Pickering*, III, 243; J. Q. Adams to John Adams, October 23, 1794, *JQAW*, I, 203.

88 Richardson, I, 184.

89 *Annals*, V, 426.

90 The *Annals* give the debate consecutively, *ibid.*, 426–783.

secretary, "if he has not left the city," and learn about his views on the House request.[91] The message was delayed in reaching Hamilton, and so Washington wrote directly to him,[92] but this letter also failed to reach Hamilton promptly. Meanwhile, on March 24, Livingston's resolution had passed by a vote of sixty-two to thirty-seven, after an amendment had been added "excepting such of said papers as any existing negotiation may render improper to be disclosed." On the following day a House committee had presented the resolution to Washington. The members reported to their fellow legislators: "The President answered that he would take the resolution into consideration."[93]

A long delay at this point by the executive would have played into the hands of the treaty's opponents, for it would have appeared difficult to find arguments to support a refusal. Washington wrote to the secretaries of state, treasury, and war and to the attorney general, asking them to submit their opinions "in writing" and also to consult with him personally on the matter.[94]

When Washington's letter finally reached Hamilton on March 22, he hastily dashed off a brief reply and soon followed it with a fuller statement, after having discussed it with Jay.[95] He also submitted a complete draft of a message in a form to be presented to the House.[96] It was well polished and phrased in noncontroversial language, but filled with cogent arguments. Hamilton pointed to the harm that might befall the nation if it should become known that the details of its negotiations with foreign powers were to be laid open to public gaze. Furthermore, each nation had a right to assume that it could make binding agreements with duly constituted authorities of the other—in the case of the United States, the President and the Senate, under the provisions of the Constitution—and any government would be reluctant to enter into agreements with the United States if some other organ of its government could, at its own discretion, nullify a treaty.

[91] Washington to Wolcott, March 3, 1796, *WW*, XXXIV, 482.

[92] Washington to Hamilton, March 22, 1796. This letter is not in *WW* and apparently is no longer extant but is referred to, by date, in Hamilton's reply.

[93] *Annals*, V, 759–60.

[94] Washington to members of the cabinet, March 25, 1796, *WW*, XXXIV, 505.

[95] Hamilton to Jay, March 24, 1796, Hamilton to Washington, March 28, 1796, *HWL*, X, 151–55.

[96] March 20 [?], 1796, *HWL*, VIII, 161–81. This letter is misdated; either it was sent about a week after March 20, or it was prepared following the receipt of a communication from Wolcott or Senator King conveying the President's request, before Hamilton received Washington's letter of March 22.

Finally, the Constitution, which all public officials were solemnly sworn to uphold, placed the treaty-making authority in the hands of the President and the Senate, and any other arrangement would be a usurpation of power. The President, therefore, had no legal right to comply with the House request.

Hamilton observed privately to Washington that there were "things in the *instructions* to Mr. Jay—which good policy, considering the matter *externally* as well as *internally*, would render it inexpedient to communicate." The section in Jay's instructions on which Article IX, relating to land titles, was based spoke of acceding "to the entire *abolition of alienism*." This wording he knew would intensify opposition to that article. Jay had also been instructed to make an agreement "against the employment of privateers in war." The critics might think that this agreement would be harmful to the interests of the United States, for in war "it is chiefly by privateers that we could annoy the trade of Great Britain." Hamilton aimed a blow at Randolph, saying that he, "who was in the habit of saying much and saying little," had drawn up the instructions so poorly that they might be "censured as altogether deficient in firmness and spirit."[97]

Washington, with the aid of his cabinet, had already drafted a message to the House when Hamilton's powerful statement arrived. Since it would take considerable time to copy Hamilton's paper, and in view of the "anxious solicitude" for the executive's reply and the possibility of "a fresh demand with strictures," Washington decided to send the prepared message. But he was unusually profuse in expressions of appreciation for Hamilton's efforts and assured him "over and over of the warmth of my friendship and of my affectionate regard."[98]

The President's reply to the House, delivered on March 30, 1796, contains essentially the same points that Hamilton had made. It is couched in clear, emphatic language, but in style it compares to Hamilton's draft as ore compares to gold. It lacks the refinement and the tone of gracious amiability that pervades Hamilton's draft. It must have acted as an abrasive on the sensibilities of the representatives who had voted for Livingston's resolution.

Asserting his continuing desire to work in harmony with all branches of the government, Washington observed that, nevertheless, "foreign negotiations [require] caution, and their success must often depend on secrecy." That was why the Constitution placed the treaty-making power in the hands

[97] *Ibid.*

[98] Washington to Hamilton, March 31, 1796, *WW*, XXXV, 6–8.

of the President and the Senate, the latter being made up of "a small number of members." Bearing in mind, no doubt, that Madison had played a large role in writing the Constitution, Washington recalled that he, himself, had been a member of the Constitutional Convention. He cited precedent by reminding the representatives that "in this construction of the constitution every House of Representatives has hitherto acquiesced" and that the House had heretofore "made all the requisite provisions for carrying [treaties] into effect." He added that according to the journals of the Constitutional Convention, which he had "deposited in the office of the Department of State," when a motion was made "that no treaty should be binding . . . which was not ratified by a law" the motion had been "explicitly rejected." He could not see that the documents called for could serve any constitutional purpose of the House, "except that of an impeachment, which the resolution has not expressed." He closed the message with the abrupt statement that his duty under the Constitution "forbids a compliance with your request."[99]

The House responded with renewed hostility. Some efforts were made to center attention on the question of the constitutional authority of the lower house. Thomas Blount of North Carolina moved that the House had the right to ask the President for papers without stating the purpose for which they were desired,[100] an allusion to Washington's point that the only legitimate purpose would be for impeachment proceedings. Representative Andrew Moore of Virginia insisted that the executive and Senate were, through the treaty, violating the constitutional prerogatives of the House. Articles of the treaty binding the nation not to enact certain types of retaliatory commercial legislation placed "an eternal veto . . . against our ever carrying . . . measures" like those that had been under consideration in the spring of 1794. Thus "the Executive claims not only the constitutional right of forcing this House to pass what laws they please [to implement the treaty], but also by treaty, to declare what they shall not do."[101]

The debate then turned to the merits and flaws of the treaty. Madison moved that "with such information as the House possesses, it is not expedient at this time to concur in passing the laws necessary for carrying the said treaty into effect."[102] House action would be necessary to appropriate money for payments by the United States of the delinquent private debts

[99] Richardson, I, 186–88.
[100] April 6, 1796, *Annals*, V, 771–72.
[101] April 21, 1796, *ibid.*, 1122.
[102] April 14, 1796, *ibid.*, 971.

and for the expenses of boundary surveys and commissions called for by the treaty. Madison's effort was destined to fail, but if that motion had been passed and had been adhered to, it would have forced the President to submit the requested documents; alternatively, it would probably have nullified the treaty.

Jefferson, believing that a grave constitutional question was at hand and considering the treaty an act of sedition by the Federalists, gave strong moral support to the House dissidents. He credited Randolph with hitting upon "the true theory of our constitution; that when a treaty is made involving matters confided by the constitution to the three branches of the Legislature conjointly, the Representatives are as free as the President and the Senate were to consider whether the national interest requires or forbids their giving the forms and force of law to the articles over which they have a power."[103]

It was widely believed by members of both factions that the controversy threatened the survival of the government. Hamilton did not see how any man who valued his "reputation for discernment or sincerity" could maintain that the treaty was unconstitutional and warned that blocking it would "prostrate the government."[104]

"Since the 4th of July, 1776, the councils of America have not been agitated by so momentous a question," Representative John Wilkes Kittera of Pennsylvania declared, and all but accused the supporters of Madison's motion of desiring the downfall of the government.[105] Fisher Ames also believed that the controversy brought the Union into grave danger,[106] and in "The Anas" Jefferson reported having been told that Senators King and Strong had threatened that if the House broke the treaty they would stall the Senate and consider the government no longer in existence.[107] Nathaniel Macon said that if Article IX was interpreted to mean reinstatement of titles to former Granville lands in North Carolina, which comprised half of the state, it would be "of greater importance to the state . . . than the Declaration of Independence." In the next to last recorded comment on the treaty before the final vote, Representative James Holland added that any such claim on behalf of the Granville estate "would certainly be resisted by force."[108]

103 Jefferson to William B. Giles, December 31, 1795, *JW*, IX, 315.

104 "Camillus," No. 36, 1796, *HWL*, VI, 160–62.

105 April 21, 1796, *Annals*, V, 1124.

106 Ames to Thomas Dwight, March 9, 1796, Ames, *Works of Fisher Ames*, I, 188.

107 *The Anas*, *JW*, I, 422.

108 April 29, 30, 1796, *Annals*, V, 1281, 1291.

When the long debate drew to a close on April 30, 1796, the House was evenly divided, forty-eight to forty-eight, on a motion to declare the treaty "highly objectionable." Speaker Jonathan Dayton of New Jersey "decided in the negative." There was another equal division, forty-nine to forty-nine, on declaring the treaty "objectionable." Again the speaker "decided in the negative." Meanwhile, public opinion in favor of the treaty had begun to be felt. Washington noted what he called a "torrent of Petitions, and remonstrances" from the eastern and middle states, as well as some from Virginia, calling on the representatives to enact "the necessary provisions for carrying the treaty into effect." Washington probably exaggerated the magnitude of the "torrent," but he was doubtless correct in believing that it was those expressions of public will that finally moved the House to allow the treaty to take effect.[109] Even so, the final vote was an embarrassing fifty-one to forty-eight.[110]

It was a momentous victory, nonetheless. Washington might have found ways to implement some parts of the treaty without the approval of the House, but those who feared that adverse action would have endangered the national government were correct in their fears. Even if the government had managed to survive, those seeking a détente with Britain would have been overwhelmed by the pro-French elements to the point that war might have followed. The transfer of the posts would have been delayed indefinitely, for British officials in North America had been instructed by their home government not to give up the Northwest holdings if the House of Representatives prevented the treaty from going into effect.[111]

The British government had difficulty understanding American opposition to Jay's Treaty. They considered it so favorable to the United States that it must quickly lay to rest anti-British sentiment and prove a foundation for "permanent harmony and good understanding," thereby permanently silencing the pro-French faction.[112] The French were fearful of just such an outcome. Though they could not point to any particular article in the treaty

[109] Washington to Thomas Pinckney, May 22, 1796, *WW*, XXXV, 62. See also Beveridge, *Life of John Marshall*, II, 146–56.

[110] *Annals*, V, 1291.

[111] Grenville to Phineas Bond, January 18, 1796, Mayo, 106–10.

[112] Grenville to Hammond, November 20, December 10, 1794, August 31, 1795, *ibid.*, 69, 76, 92.

[113] Alphonse Bertrand, "Les États-Unis et la révolution française," *Revue deux mondes*, 5th Ser., Vol. XXXIII (1906), 427.

that explicitly violated the treaty of alliance of 1778, the spirit of the alliance seemed to be destroyed.[113] A crisis in Franco-American relations loomed.

Jay's Treaty resulted in many long-term advantages for the United States. The disappointing features proved to be transitory and not crippling in their immediate effects, whereas the advantages were permanent. For the first time the young nation had undisputed possession of all its territories. Perhaps even more important, peace had been assured, and time for the nation to develop. The margin by which the treaty was ratified by the Senate, the House, and the nation was so narrow that without the enormous efforts Hamilton made in its behalf it would almost unquestionably have failed. As Bemis has commented, it might be more aptly called Hamilton's Treaty.[114]

The rancorous controversies over the treaty brought to Washington a temporary but nonetheless damaging loss of prestige, late in his second term. A cloud of bitterness and pain had moved across his path,[115] which would persist until the end of his term in office and would be intensified by antagonisms with the French, which would create for him a new complex of disconcerting problems.

[114] Bemis, *Jay's Treaty*, 271.
[115] Washington to Jay, May 8, 1796, *WW*, XXXV, 36–37.

CHAPTER XIII

A Dying Alliance

ONE immediate effect of Jay's Treaty was to alter the source of tensions under which Americans had been living. Relations with Britain became bearable—though only bearable, for the war in Europe and in the Atlantic continued unabated. Nothing but peace in Europe could end the molestation of American commerce by both the British and the French. But the treaty widened the breach between the United States and France. The French government assumed that the Americans had broken the alliance of 1778 and had moved into the British sphere. The ferocity of the war, supposedly waged in the cause of human freedom to which both allies were committed, made the French incapable of weighing the dangers faced by the Americans or of recognizing the injuries which French naval action had inflicted on their commerce-minded allies. France felt deserted and betrayed by the nation it had so recently befriended.

America's relations with Spain, on the other hand, took a sharp turn for the better. Spain, like France, had feared that Jay's negotiations would lead to an Anglo-American alliance. Spain was not overjoyed by the fact that its new ally, England, was whittling down the French navy—Spain's erstwhile defense for its own empire. After all, the assailants of the Bastille were not the only enemies Spain might face in a world of violence and uncertainty. Who could say that its ancient foe, England, might not soon renew the contest in empire building? And what more likely area for such a contest could be found than Spain's lush dominions in the Western Hemisphere? It is not strange that when the young Spanish prime minister Manuel de Godoy worked out the Treaty of Basel with France in 1795 he was awarded the august title "Prince of the Peace."[1]

[1] For an excellent account of this phase of America's diplomacy, based on multiarchival research, see Samuel Flagg Bemis, *Pinckney's Treaty, America's Advantage from Europe's Distress, 1783–1800* (rev. ed., New Haven, 1960).

Anticipating the renewal of Spanish and British rivalries, Godoy approached Carmichael and Short, the American commissioners in Madrid, with a proposal for an alliance of Spain, France, and the United States against Britain. Though the idea was not acceptable to the United States at the time, when the special envoy, Thomas Pinckney (brother of Charles Cotesworth Pinckney), reached Madrid in July, 1795, he found conditions ripe for a favorable settlement of differences with Spain. Fortunately, he was able to proceed on the basis of negotiations carried on by Monroe in Paris and by Short in Madrid.[2]

In exchange for promises of peace between the two nations, Spain recognized the United States' claim to the territory on the east bank of the Mississippi from 32°20′ latitude southward to 31° (organized as Mississippi Territory in 1798) and to grant Americans freedom of navigation on the river with a port of deposit at New Orleans. Thus, by conceding nothing that the United States wished to withhold, Pinckney obtained everything his country claimed in the region.[3]

Americans looked upon the Treaty of San Lorenzo el Real, often called Pinckney's Treaty, as the one bright event during a period of gloom. By that time Washington had long since abandoned his position that the issue of navigation on the Mississippi could be delayed until after a canal was built to connect the Potomac and the Ohio. In 1790 he had written to Lafayette that the United States must have "free navigation of the Mississippi" and "as certainly shall have [it] as we remain a nation." He had expressed the belief that success would eventually result from a "just steady and prudent national policy . . . whether the powers of the old world may be in peace or war, but more especially in the latter case."[4] Hamilton, too, had long considered the navigation rights essential to the United States and had said that the continued denial of those rights would result "infallibly in a war with Spain, or separation of the western country."[5] In the short run he feared that "a general Indian war [might be] excited by the united influence of Britain and Spain, [which] would not fail to spread desolation throughout our frontier."[6] He realized that Jay's Treaty had reduced the likelihood of "a community of views between Great Britain and Spain";

[2] Monroe to Pickering, November 20, 1794, *JMW*, II, 117–21.

[3] For the text of the treaty see Miller, *Treaties*, II, 318–38.

[4] Washington to Lafayette, August 11, 1790, *WW*, XXXI, 88.

[5] Hamilton to Washington, September 15, 1790, *HWL*, IV, 324, 336.

[6] "Americanus," No. 2, February 8, 1794, *ibid.*, V, 87.

but until he learned of Pinckney's success, he wrote often of the likelihood of war with Spain.[7]

That was the general view in the United States during those difficult years, among Federalists and Republicans alike. In 1793 Jefferson had written to Madison that "there is no one of us who doubts" the probability of war.[8] As late as October, 1795, in the absence of any good news from Madrid, Washington complained that Spain was encroaching on American territory, meanwhile conducting negotiations that were "procrastinating, trifling, undignified, . . . and insulting." By then he was almost convinced that he would have to lay the matter "fully before Congress."[9]

The 1794 dispatches of Sir Robert Liston, the new British minister at Philadelphia, made frequent reference to American talk of war, as well as to rumors that Britain was planning to attack the weak "Spanish American Settlements."[10] Liston's home government was indeed considering such an attack and asked its representatives in the United States to sound out the reactions of the American people. Later, when the Madrid negotiations opened, Grenville asked the British consul at Philadelphia, Phineas Bond, to find out whether Pinckney had instructions to negotiate an alliance with Spain, which in his understandably one-sided view could not be as advantageous to the United States as a concert of interests with Britain.[11]

Bond asked Wolcott and Pickering about Pinckney's instructions and was given a frank account of their contents. Wolcott reiterated the intention of the United States to avoid any additional alliances, and Bond reported to Grenville that he was impressed by the "sincerity of the assurances."[12]

Pinckney's Treaty lightened the nation's mood, at least temporarily. Washington's seventh annual address to Congress, presented on December 8, 1795, was glowing with warmth and happiness—peace with Britain, peace with the Indians (following Wayne's victory in the Northwest), peace with Morocco, and now peace with Spain.[13] Hamilton declared that the provisions of the treaty were "equal to our most sanguine wishes." Yet he

[7] "Camillus," No. 7, 1795, *ibid.*, 254.

[8] Jefferson to Madison, *JW*, IX, 139.

[9] Washington to Hamilton, October 29, 1795, *WW*, XXXIV, 351.

[10] Liston to Grenville, May 10, 1794; FCA, XVIII.

[11] Grenville to Phineas Bond, October 10, 1795, *ibid.*, XXV.

[12] Bond to Grenville, January 2, 1796; *ibid.*, XXVIII.

[13] Richardson, I, 174–76.

was not without some apprehension; he expressed the hope that "no future embarrassment" would arise.[14]

The French government was in no position to protest the Spanish-American rapprochement openly. By the stipulations of the treaties of Basel and San Lorenzo the three nations were ostensibly on friendly terms. But the French did not relish Americans coming into possession or use of territories which they coveted for themselves. By 1795 the Directory had quietly adopted Moustier's scheme for reacquiring the Mississippi Valley,[15] which made it more difficult to adjust the issues intensified by Jay's negotiations in London and by the vehement debates within the United States over the ratification and execution of the treaty with Britain.

Hamilton foresaw this reaction and hoped to minimize the harmful effect it would have on Franco-American relations. It will be recalled that one reason he gave for eliminating Article XII from Jay's Treaty was that France might reasonably consider it a cause of "dissatisfaction."[16] Throughout the period of negotiation the French were "bristling with distrust."[17] Monroe tried earnestly to pacify them, but he was handicapped by his own serious reservations about what was transpiring in London. In accordance with his instructions, he assured the French ministers that Jay would agree to nothing that would impinge upon the terms of the alliance with France. Unconvinced, they had pressed Monroe for information about the agreements being reached. To Monroe's embarrassment, Jay proved uncommunicative, and Monroe promised to report the terms of the treaty as soon as he learned about them.

Finally, after several unsatisfactory exchanges of letters between the two American ministers, Jay sent the artist John Trumbull, who was serving as his secretary, to Paris with instructions to give Monroe a copy of the treaty, provided the latter agreed not to reveal the contents.[18] This arrangement would only have further complicated Monroe's position, and he refused to accept the treaty on those terms. The incident heightened his antipathy toward Jay, the Federalists, and the treaty; and it intensified French suspicions.

14 "The Warning," No. 4, February 27, 1797, *HWL*, VI, 247; Hamilton to King, May 4, 1796, *ibid.*, X, 163.

15 Turner, "The Policy of France Toward the Mississippi Valley in the Period of Washington and Adams," *American Historical Review*, Vol. X (January, 1905), 242–49.

16 Hamilton to Washington, July 9, 1795, *HWL*, V, 163.

17 W. P. Cresson, *James Monroe* (Chapel Hill, 1946), 137.

18 Monroe to Randolph, March 17, 1795, *JMW*, II, 229–34. The letter gives Monroe's objections to Jay's decision.

Franco-American friendship, which had survived the Genêt episode, foundered on Jay's Treaty. It has been called "the blow from which the alliance never recovered."[19] It had corroding effects on the French attitude toward the United States.[20] William Branch Giles, the firebrand Republican of Virginia, declared in 1796 that French bitterness "certainly may be ascribed to that instrument."[21]

The bitterness was not all one-sided. Resentments were building in the United States over French "machinations" against American independence, which Hamilton repeatedly denounced, and deep-lying conflicts between the two countries over territory on the Gulf of Mexico.[22] The French were able to convince Monroe that they were not interested in obtaining Louisiana, except, possibly, to keep England from acquiring it—in which case, they assured him, they would keep the United States fully informed of developments.[23] John Quincy Adams, at The Hague, had what proved to be a more nearly correct impression of French intentions. As early as August, 1796, he was writing to his father that the Directory was trying to wrest Louisiana from Spain, and early the following year he wrote of French designs to build a "Western Republic." Jay's Treaty, he said, was being used by the Directory as a "stalking horse."[24] The British-American contest for territory had been sharply reduced by Jay's efforts. The British people had acquiesced to American independence, and, with the relinquishment to the United States of the territory south of the Great Lakes, Americans were reasonably willing for the British flag to fly over Canada. Such evidence of accord was extremely unpalatable to the French.

From the outset Monroe's mission to Paris was ill-starred. Washington did not really want to send him, a member of the "opposition," and for the same reason Monroe did not relish the assignment. It was a choice made necessary by French dislike of the Federalist convictions of Gouverneur Morris and of his astringent criticism of the French Revolution. It was hoped that Monroe could lessen tensions that were bound to rise over the treaty negotiations. Monroe's reluctance was offset by the hope that he could "cultivate" good relations between the two nations, which another Wash-

[19] Alexander DeConde, "Washington's Farewell, the French Alliance, and the Election of 1796," *Mississippi Valley Historical Review*, Vol. XLIII (March, 1957), 641–58.

[20] Bertrand, "Les États-Unis et la révolution française," *Revue deux mondes*, 5th Ser., Vol. XXXIII (1906), 427.

[21] December 14, 1796, *Annals*, VI, 1631.

[22] See Hamilton's "Horatius" essay, May, 1795, *HWL*, V, 183.

[23] Monroe to Pickering, September 10, 1796, *JMW*, III, 62.

ington appointee might fail to achieve.[25] In his letter of acceptance he avoided any words of praise for the President, and to his friend Jefferson he acknowledged that, in appointing any Republican, Washington had to surmount "some objections of a personal nature."[26]

The French foreign minister delayed his formal reception of Monroe, but the new envoy was determined to carry out his mission. He appealed to the Directory, and then was received by the National Convention. His reception by the latter was so warm that it produced no little consternation in the United States and in London.[27] He had some success in persuading the leaders to moderate French depredations on American ships and seamen, but his failure to calm the furor over Jay's Treaty placed all the issues on a new level. Washington and his cabinet failed to appreciate the difficulty of Monroe's position, as well as the seriousness of French objections to the treaty. Not long before he resigned from his post as secretary of state, Randolph wrote to Monroe explaining that the treaty embraced a broader range of subjects than the French had been given to understand but that they would share in all the commercial provisions and that there was nothing in the treaty injurious to them.[28] One of Pickering's first acts as secretary of state was to send Monroe a set of arguments to convince the French that the treaty was in no way violative of the alliance or likely to injure French interests.[29] When he received the letter, Monroe decided that was not the time to pursue the points and decided to wait for a more propitious moment.[30] Upon learning of the delay, the administration was convinced that Monroe had let a golden opportunity slip by and concluded that he was using his office to advance the cause of the Republican party in the United States, as well as to block Jay's Treaty.

When the provisions of the treaty became known, the Directory seriously considered declaring war against the United States, but soon realized that such a course would drive the United States still closer to Britain and cut off American imports. After repeated requests from Monroe, the French at

24 John Quincy Adams to John Adams, August 13, 1796, April 3, 1797, May 20, 1797, *JQAW*, II, 20, 155–57, 169.

25 Monroe to Jefferson, May 27, 1794, *JMW*, I, 300.

26 Monroe to Washington, May 26, 1794, *ibid.*, 298.

27 Cresson, *James Monroe*, 133; Bemis, *Jay's Treaty*, 242.

28 February 15, March 8, 1795, *ASPFR*, I, 696, 699.

29 *Ibid.*, 596–98.

30 Cresson, *James Monroe*, 143.

last presented a detailed statement of their objections.[31] They were especially bitter about the provisions allowing Britain to cut off American provisions and shipbuilding supplies. In reply, Monroe made no claim that Jay had negotiated a good treaty—the French knew that Monroe detested it—but, like the able attorney he was, he presented a strong case in an effort to prove that there was no infringement of the alliance and that Jay's commercial concessions did not violate any generally recognized principles of international law. He admitted that the treaty had abandoned the free ships, free goods principle which was a part of the Franco-American treaty; but the British had never fully observed that principle, and the United States did not have the power to force them to do so. Moreover, it could not be shown that free ships, free goods had been a general rule among nations, and its inclusion in the treaty between the United States and France did not make it binding as international law applicable to other nations.[32]

This reasoning was not convincing to the French, who held to their position that the alliance had been broken. They informed Monroe of their intention to send a special envoy to Philadelphia to declare the alliance terminated and diplomatic relations severed.[33] Monroe claimed credit for delaying this ominous move for several months by pointing out that it would but bring joy to those opposed to the alliance and horror to friends.[34] The comprising nature of his position can be seen in a letter he wrote to Madison, "I have detained them seven months from doing what they ought to have done at once."[35]

John Quincy Adams, deeply suspicious of both Britain and France, believed that France was trying to use the United States as it was using the Dutch provinces and that it would rejoice in a war between the United States and Britain, which would destroy Anglo-American commerce. He did not believe that France would agree to make "common cause" with its ally against Britain, though the Directory "would give us as many fair words as we could wish." Later he accused that "malevolent" body of circulating the ugly rumor, picked up from Monroe, that Jay had been bribed

[31] March 9, 1796, *ASPFR*, I, 732–33.

[32] Monroe to the French Minister of Foreign Affairs, March 15, 1796, *JMW*, II, 467–82; Monroe to same, July 14, 1796, *ibid.*, III, 27–34.

[33] Monroe to Pickering, February 16, 1796, *ibid.*, II, 455.

[34] Monroe to Pickering, February 20, 1796, *ibid.*, 457ff.

[35] Monroe to Madison, September 1, 1796, *ibid.*, III, 52–53.

in London and that members of the House of Representatives had been bribed to accept the treaty.[36]

Thomas Paine, now a French citizen, resided with Monroe in France for several months, and the association apparently sharpened Monroe's pro-French leanings. Now that Paine had transferred his loyalties to France, he was particularly lavish in his praise of the Republican party, which he called "the sincere ally of France."[37] Along with other Republicans, Monroe blamed Hamilton rather than Washington for the "evil" treaty with Britain. In a letter to Madison he complained that Pickering wrote to him in the tone of an "overseer on the farm to one of his gang," but added that Pickering's style "corresponds so much" with Hamilton's "Camillus" essays that he suspected both "were written by the same hand" (a surmise that was not far wide of the mark). Monroe ended the letter: "Poor Washington. Into what hands has he fallen!"[38]

Washington was incensed by a rumor circulated in the spring of 1796 that France was preparing to declare war on the United States and launch an invasion if the government did not renounce Jay's Treaty. The President wrote to Hamilton that "were it not for the unhappy differences among ourselves" his "answer would be short and decisive, to this effect. We are an independent nation and act for ourselves. . . . We will not be dictated to by . . . any nation under heaven." If any nation could tell the United States what to do and what not to do, beyond treaty agreements, "we have independence yet to seek, and have contended hitherto for very little."[39]

Hamilton's reply urged moderation and conciliation. He would have Monroe remind the French government that it had concurred in United States neutrality, which alone could assure that American goods would reach France. That assistance was far more useful to France than any belligerence would have been. Moreover, Monroe should observe that the United States had been faithful to the Franco-American Treaty, though France had not; that war would have placed the "infant state" in grave jeopardy; that the treaty with Britain "involved no ingredient of political connection"; and that for the United States to refuse to observe the commercial agreements so recently made with Britain would be "an act of

[36] John Quincy Adams to John Adams, May 22, September 12, 1795, January 14, 1797, *JQAW*, I, 356–58, 412–13; II, 85.

[37] Beveridge, *John Marshall*, II, 222–23.

[38] Monroe to Madison, September 1, 1796, *JMW*, III, 53–54.

[39] Washington to Hamilton, May 8, 1796, *WW*, XXXV, 40.

perfidy which would destroy the value of our friendship to any nation."[40]

In the meantime, suspicions were growing that Monroe's convictions were doing harm to the American cause. Hamilton was prominent among those who began demanding his recall. First he wrote to Secretary of War James McHenry, suggesting that Monroe "be superseded with a kind letter to him." He commented that "we must not quarrel with France for *pins* and *needles*." He added that he had not yet suggested recalling Monroe to the President or to the secretary of state but that he believed McHenry should bring it to their attention, "even at the expense of being a little officious."[41] Two weeks later he made the same suggestion to Wolcott, who stood higher in Washington's esteem than McHenry did. To Wolcott, Hamilton expressed the opinion that the best man to succeed Monroe was probably McHenry himself, who was "not yet obnoxious to the French."[42] Wolcott replied that he had "for some time been inclined to think that Mr. Monroe ought to be recalled" as one means of stopping "the channels by which foreign poison is introduced into the country."[43] Finally Hamilton approached the President directly on the matter, saying that it seemed "more and more urgent that the United States should have some faithful organ near the French government to explain their real views and to ascertain those of the French."[44]

No doubt the idea had already occurred to the President, for he was greatly displeased with Monroe's efforts, partly because of his failure to grasp the difficulties Monroe was facing. He did understand, however, that Monroe's Republican attitudes and his antipathy for Jay's Treaty made it impossible for him to serve a Federalist administration effectively. Realizing that an outright recall would further intensify party strife in America, he toyed with the idea of leaving Monroe in the position and in effect superseding him with the appointment of an envoy extraordinary to France. In a carefully reasoned letter written from Mount Vernon, he asked Hamilton to confer with Jay in New York and give him their views on four points: whether he had the constitutional authority to send an envoy extraordinary when the Senate was not in session; whether the Directory might raise the question of the constitutionality of the appointment as a pretext to refuse

40 Hamilton to Washington, May 20, 1796, *HWL*, X, 165–70.

41 Hamilton to James McHenry, June 1, 1796, *ibid.*, 171.

42 Hamilton to Wolcott, June 15, 1796, *ibid.*, 174–75.

43 Wolcott to Hamilton, June 17, 1796, Gibbs, I, 361.

44 Hamilton to Washington, June, 1796, *HWL*, X, 179.

to recognize such an envoy; whether the Senate should be called into special session; and how the problem of dealing with Monroe should be handled.[45]

Hamilton and Jay quickly conferred, and Hamilton's reply was prompt. It was their conclusion, he wrote, that it did not appear to be within the President's constitutional authority to send a special representative without Senate approval and that relations with France did not seem critical enough to justify calling the Senate into special session. To the question of how to deal with Monroe, Hamilton and Jay suggested a direct solution. They would simply remove Monroe from the office and thereby create a vacancy that could be filled by a new appointment at the ministerial level and in that way avoid any question of constitutionality. It would be an immense problem, they felt, to find a man suitable for the position. He would have to be both "a friend to the government"—that is, a Federalist—and at the same time "understood to be not unfriendly to the French Revolution." General Charles Cotesworth Pinckney was the only man they could think of "who fully satisfies the idea," and they were afraid that he would refuse to serve. In any event, proper means would have to be taken to answer the French complaints. To fail to do so would "bring serious censure upon the Executive. It will be said that it did not display as much zeal to avoid misunderstanding with France as with Great Britain, [and] that discontents were left to rankle."[46] It was sound advice.

In the meantime, an urgent message from Philadelphia convinced Washington that he must act before the Hamilton-Jay letter reached him (no doubt he had already learned of Hamilton's views from McHenry and Wolcott). Before leaving for a stay at Mount Vernon, he had asked the cabinet to meet in Philadelphia in his absence to consider a new envoy. Now they reported to the President that there was a new, impressive reason for dismissing Monroe—a private letter from him which had fallen into their hands after the President had departed. The letter was addressed to Dr. George Logan, a strong advocate of peace with France.[47] Pickering became even more virulent than usual. On July 21, 1796, he wrote to Washington that he had received confirmation of "the suspicions some months since entertained that the ominous letters of Mr. Monroe composed a part of a

45 Washington to Hamilton, June 26, 1796, *WW*, XXXV, 101–103.

46 Hamilton to Washington, July 5, 1796, *HWL*, X, 180–81.

47 Cresson, *James Monroe*, 152; Washington to Pickering, July 27, 1796, *WW*, XXXV, 156–57.

solemn farce to answer certain party purposes."[48] Rufus King, the new minister to Great Britain, circulated the same charge,[49] and John Quincy Adams wrote from The Hague that the French people's anger over Jay's Treaty did not "proceed from themselves" but was "inspired by Americans at Paris," including Monroe. "The greatest enemies of America in France," he said, "are Americans themselves."[50]

The cabinet was convinced that "a minister who has thus made the notorious enemies [that is, the Republicans] of the whole system of government his confidential correspondents in matters which affect that Government, cannot be relied on to do his duty to the latter."[51] Monroe's letter to Logan, together with earlier ones, reinforced the Federalists' suspicions that Monroe was using his office and information to give the game away in France and augment Republican strength at home.

The President conferred with Attorney General Charles Lee, who was in Alexandria, Virginia, at the time. It was Lee's opinion, too, that the President did not have the authority to send an envoy extraordinary without the prior approval of the Senate but that Monroe, who was filling an office already approved by the Senate, could be removed and replaced. On July 8, Washington announced to Pickering his decision to recall Monroe, and on the same day he wrote General Pinckney a persuasive letter urging him to assume the office of minister to France. The President had first asked John Marshall to accept the position but had not pressed him seriously, assuming correctly that he would refuse.

In Washington's letter to Pinckney the President gave his views of the situation with France and the gravity of dissensions at home and abroad. He described the purpose of the mission in words almost identical to those Hamilton had used in his earlier letter. The person to replace Monroe must be "well attached" to the American government and "not obnoxious" to the French. The greatest embarrassment of the government was the "counteraction of people among ourselves, who are more disposed to promote the views of another [country] than to establish a national character of their own." "Virtuous and independent men" must come forward; if they did not, it would not be "difficult to predict the consequences." Able men in the

[48] *JMW*, II, 482n.

[49] King to Wolcott, August 14, 1796, Gibbs, I, 376.

[50] John Quincy Adams to John Adams, April 4, *JQAW*, I, 481–82; John Quincy Adams to John Adams, June 7, 1796, *ibid.*, II, 177.

[51] Pickering, Wolcott, and McHenry to Washington, July 2, 1796, Gibbs, I, 366–67.

executive and legislative branches had been "so decisive in their politics, and, possibly, so frank and public in their declarations, as to render it very difficult to choose from among them one, in whom the confidence of this country could be placed, and the prejudices of the other not excited." No other man, he concluded, could fill the need as well as Pinckney.[52]

The appeal was successful—it would have been difficult for any patriot to refuse it. In September, 1796, Pinckney left for France with instructions to listen to complaints and explain his country's actions and intentions.[53] Little could be said that Monroe had not already been instructed to say, but now there was a greater sense of urgency.

The French were in no mood for explanations. For three years they had been violating the treaty of alliance, though their behavior had briefly improved after Monroe arrived.[54] From the time the negotiations began in London, France had tried to keep its ally in line with a combination of threats, promises, and abuse. Monroe's assurances that the treaty would include nothing objectionable to France and, later, that it would be rejected in Philadelphia served as a deterrent until news reached Paris that the treaty had been ratified. On July 2, 1796, the Directory issued a decree that the French would treat neutral vessels "as they suffer the English to treat them."[55] To John Quincy Adams it appeared that the French were saying, " 'We will insult and injure you, because we see you are too weak to resent the insults and injuries to others.' "[56] They had already been doing what they now threatened to do, but after the July 2 decree was issued, ship seizures were carried out on flimsier pretexts, and treatment of American seamen was even more abusive. Rufus King, the new American minister in London, reported having met an American captain who had been tortured with thumbscrews by his French captors until he agreed to make a false statement to justify confiscation of his vessel.[57]

The French decree was communicated to the Department of State by the French minister, P. A. Adet, on October 27, 1796. Adet's note contained a list of complaints, most of which were based on provisions of Jay's Treaty.

52 Washington to Pinckney, *WW*, XXXV, 127–31.

53 Gibbs, I, 368–69.

54 Washington's special message to Congress, December 5, 1793, Richardson, I, 138. See also Hamilton's "No Jacobin," No. 3, 1793, *HWL*, V, 39.

55 *ASPFR*, I, 745.

56 John Quincy Adams to Joseph Pitcairn, in Paris, October 2, 1796, *JQAW*, II, 32.

57 King to Pickering, April 19, 1797, *KC*, II, 172–73.

Adet claimed that earlier protests, of specified dates, had gone unanswered.[58] A copy of the protest, written in a churlish, self-righteous tone, was released to the press, and Adet appeared to relish the whole affair. His attitude from the outset had been one of aversion toward the United States, unlike that of his predecessor, Fauchet, who had some sympathy for his host country. Soon after his arrival in Philadelphia, Adet had informed his government that it was a mistake to assume that the United States was friendly toward France.[59] Unlike Monroe, he made no effort to improve relations.

Washington was provoked by Adet's conduct and especially by the publication of the note before the government had had a chance to reply to it.

Once again he wrote to Hamilton for advice. In his letter he sought to justify his actions. Some of Adet's previous "remonstrances" had not been answered because they "were accompanied by as indecent charges, and as offensive expressions as the letters of Genêt." Some of Adet's complaints "had been replied to (as the Secretary of State informs me) over and over again." Washington recoiled from the indignity of "a newspaper dispute with the Minister of a foreign nation," yet he knew that a failure to reply promptly would feed the fires of factionalism. He closed the letter by asking advice about how he should receive Adet if the minister attended a presidential levee to be held in a few days.[60]

Hamilton replied that Adet should be received "with a *dignified reserve*, holding an *exact medium* between an *offensive coldness* and *cordiality*." He added, "The point is a nice one to be hit, but no one will know better how to do it than the President." (One wonders whether Hamilton detected the humorous elements in his advice. He was not endowed with a lively sense of humor.) A further word of caution was added: Hamilton was "afraid of Mr. Pickering's *warmth*."[61]

The next day Hamilton wrote to the President again, referring to the prompt and cutting reply that Pickering had already made to Adet's charges.[62] Hamilton did not take issue with Pickering's position, which was essentially the same as that contained in Hamilton's own earlier letters to the secretary—that it was the French rather than the Americans who had violated the treaty. But Hamilton was appalled by the caustic tone of the

[58] October 27, 1796, *ASPFR*, I, 576–77.
[59] Turner, *Correspondence of the French Ministers*, 735.
[60] Washington to Hamilton, November 2, 1796, *WW*, XXXV, 251–55.
[61] Hamilton to Washington, November 4, 1796, *HWL*, X, 198–200.
[62] *ASPFR*, I, 578.

note; he found it "epigrammatical and *sharp*," whereas "the card now to be played is perhaps the most delicate that has occurred in our administration, [and] nations, like individuals, sometimes get into squabbles from the manner more than the matter that passes between them." He considered it "all-important . . . if possible, to avoid rupture with France, and if that cannot be, to evince to the people that there has been an unequivocal disposition to avoid it." Discussions should be "*calm*" and "*smooth*," in the "language of moderation, and, as long as it can be done, of friendship . . . Mr. Pickering, who is a very worthy man, has nevertheless something warm and angular in his temper, and will require much a vigilant, moderating eye."[63]

Receiving no immediate reply to this letter, and aware of Washington's own tendency to strong statements in international relations, Hamilton turned again, unbidden, to the subject. He wrote that his mind "kept dwelling" on Pickering's reply to Adet, and the more he considered it the less he liked it. He believed that Pickering had mishandled one complaint, that regarding British impressments of American seamen. France had a right to raise the issue, since the impressments had increased Britain's strength. The secretary of state should have explained explicitly, and in a calm tone, why the government was unable to prevent such acts. The "possibility of connivance" gave France a "right to inquire" and placed upon the United States "an obligation to enter into friendly explanation." Pickering's manner of expression was "untenable." Hamilton closed the letter with the hope that the President would not consider his observations "officious."[64] In replying to the letters, Washington wrote rather coolly that he would "be mindful of their contents" and that "due consideration" would be given to them.[65]

In Paris, Monroe could no longer forestall the Directory's determination to sever diplomatic relations. In September the Directory had informed Monroe that the decision had been made to instruct Adet to protest and withdraw.[66] Even before the decision could be acted upon, a "foolish report" began circulating to that effect.[67] It seemed incredible that such a thing could happen. Pickering thought the rumor a "farce,"[68] and Wash-

[63] Hamilton to Washington, November 5, 1796, *HWL*, X, 200–201.
[64] Hamilton to Washington, November 11, 1796, *ibid.*, 206–208.
[65] Washington to Hamilton, November 12, 1796, *WW*, XXXV, 271–73.
[66] Monroe to Madison, September 1, 1796, *JMW*, III, 52–53.
[67] William Vans Murray to McHenry, November 9, 1796, Steiner, 201.
[68] Pickering to Washington, July 21, 1796, *JMW*, II, 482n.

ington was "unable to account" for what he thought was a pretended preoccupation with Jay's Treaty. He was convinced that the French were using it as an excuse to carry out "other ulterior measures."[69]

The blow fell on November 15, 1796. In a long note addressed to Secretary of State Pickering and to the American people, Adet declared that the leaders of the American government had forsaken the glorious ideals for which Americans and Frenchmen had laid down their lives during the American Revolution. The American government, he continued, had even betrayed its pledged word and violated the alliance of 1778 through which American independence had been won. Under those conditions his government had instructed him to suspend diplomatic relations with the United States. He hoped, however, that the American government might soon adopt a different course, so that the friendship could be renewed. He made a careful distinction between the American government and the American people (the latter being addressed as "O ye Americans") and maintained that the French still had the warmest feelings of friendship for the people.[70]

Federalists were aghast at the move. "Nothing can be more insolent than Adet's appeal to the people of the United States against their government," declared Samuel Johnston, the North Carolina Federalist.[71] "Outrageous beyond conception," protested Washington.[72] "An insult that marked the utmost insolence of spirit," fumed Fisher Ames.[73] Adet had written in "the most approbrious and contumelious language," scolded John Adams.[74] At any rate, Adet had written plainly, a fact George Cabot thought one good aspect of the crisis, observing, "If the devil is in company it is always best to see his cloven foot."[75]

Though as shocked as the Federalists by the move, the Republicans were not all displeased. Monroe had worked hard to forestall it, but he was in no mood to regret that the Directory had decided on it.[76] The Republicans, for so long critical of the administration's British policy, were not particularly offended by French animadversions on that policy. Speaking in favor of

[69] Washington to Pickering, October 17, 1796, *WW*, XXXV, 244.

[70] *ASPFR*, I, 279–583.

[71] Johnston to Judge James Iredell, December 25, 1796, G. J. McRee (ed.), *Life and Correspondence of James Iredell* (New York, 1857–58), II, 438.

[72] Washington to Hamilton, January 22, 1797, *WW*, XXXV, 372.

[73] December 15, 1796, *Annals*, VI, 1650.

[74] Adams to Elbridge Gerry, February 13, 1797, *AW*, VIII, 523.

[75] Cabot to Wolcott, November 30, 1796, Gibbs, I, 404.

[76] September 1, 1796, *JMW*, III, 53.

restoring good relations between the United States and France, Congressman Josiah Parker of Virginia reminded his fellow representatives that the two countries "have fought for freedom" and added, "I wish to see Republican liberty spread itself over the world."[77]

It was obvious, as the French intended it to be, that Adet's pronouncement was designed to influence the forthcoming presidential election. The aim was to bring the Republicans to power. At first, Washington was their target. They reportedly hoped that if they could not "turn the balance of election" they could "induce [his] retirement or resignation from the disgust of ill treatment."[78] The Farewell Address was published before Adet's shot could be fired, however, whereupon the sights were turned on Adams. French agents openly electioneered for Jefferson,[79] and the Republicans utilized their assistance to the fullest, claiming that a vote for Adams was a vote for war.[80] William Smith, a South Carolina Federalist, had suspected some such maneuver when he read Adet's note of October 27. He had prophesied that it would have "an effect directly the reverse of that which [was] so palpably intended."[81] No doubt some Republicans were affected in this manner, but not as many as Smith had hoped. Adams was elected to the presidency, but Jefferson, in second place, became vice-president. The citizens of Philadelphia voted overwhelmingly for Jefferson. Many of them were Federalists who turned to the other party, believing that "the election of Mr. Jefferson was necessary to prevent a rupture with France."[82]

It is possible that the Directory based the idea of influencing the election on casual remarks by Monroe. Once, while trying to persuade them not to break off relations, he said, "Left to ourselves, everything will, I think, be satisfactorily arranged and *perhaps in the course of the present year*." That year was election year. To Monroe's credit, it must be recorded that he said further that it would be better "to make such arrangements ourselves than to be pressed to it."[83]

[77] December 15, 1796, *Annals*, VI, 1640.

[78] John Quincy Adams to John Adams, April 4, 1796, *JQAW*, I, 486.

[79] DeConde, "Washington's Farewell, the French Alliance, and the Election of 1796," *Mississippi Valley Historical Review*, Vol. XLIII (March, 1957), 652.

[80] Nathan Schachner, *Founding Fathers* (New York, 1954), 408.

[81] William Smith to Senator Ralph Izard, November 3, 1796, "South Carolina Federalist Correspondence, 1789–1797," *American Historical Review*, Vol. XIV (July, 1909), 781.

[82] Oliver Wolcott, Jr., to Oliver Wolcott, Sr., November 27, 1796, Gibbs, I, 401.

[83] Samuel Flagg Bemis, "Washington's Farewell Address: A Foreign Policy of Independence," *American Historical Review*, Vol. XXXIX (January, 1934), 258. Bemis' italics.

Washington wrote to Hamilton that his "sentiments in this interesting crisis will always be thankfully received."[84] The sentiments were rather more promptly forthcoming than Washington expected. Hamilton had not waited for an invitation but had already written to him. Their letters crossed in the mails. Hamilton's expressed "the greatest anxiety" and then turned to the matter of the President's reply to Adet, which had not yet been delivered. The response, he emphasized, "should be managed with the utmost possible prudence and skill," expressing "a dignified seriousness—reluctant to quarrel, but resolved not to be humbled."[85] Hamilton's letter was brief and contained no extensive arguments. He had decided to bring his influence to bear on the administration primarily through Secretary of the Treasury Wolcott, with whom he maintained a close, sympathetic relationship. Since Washington had treated his communications of November 5 and 11 with something less than warmth (and also because several months earlier the President had expressed to Hamilton his heartfelt desire to speak to the French in a "short and decisive" manner), Hamilton feared that the President might approve a reply by Pickering that was inadequately reasoned or unduly offensive. A letter of admonition to Pickering might be disregarded or buried in the files of the Department of State. There was no ill will between Hamilton and Pickering, but the latter was more impatient, was inclined to speak more sharply to France, and had less dread of war with that country. Hamilton knew that the momentous diplomatic move called for would be made only after extended discussions in the cabinet, where Wolcott would have a voice. Accordingly, he wrote to Wolcott. His carefully presented statement represents one of the major efforts of his career.

Hamilton opened by entreating the administration to exert "all its prudence, all its wisdom, all its moderation, all its firmness." The communication should be sent through Pinckney, at Paris, rather than to Adet, since he had broken off relations. It "should be *calm, reasoning*, and *serious*, . . . having force in the idea rather than in the expression." Then he outlined his ideas, point by point, showing how each of Adet's complaints should be met. It should appeal to the "justice and magnanimity of France" and ask for a retraction of statements reflecting on the honor and integrity of the American government. The note should declare readiness "for meeting [France] freely in the complete restoration of a friendly intercourse." If

[84] Washington to Hamilton, November 21, 1796, *WW*, XXXV, 289.
[85] Hamilton to Washington, November 19, 1796, *HWL*, X, 209.

France proved willing to do so amiably, the two nations should discontinue the old alliance.[86]

Washington was soon convinced that caution was necessary. He instructed Pickering to make sure that the statement was "without asperity." To that end he asked for it to be "revised over, and over again."[87] Instructions were sent to Pinckney along the lines Hamilton had suggested.[88] They were "outlined by Hamilton and ably penned by Secretary of State Pickering."[89] They comprised a massive document, going over with meticulous attention all the French complaints. Pickering sent a copy to Hamilton, who "read it with great pleasure" and commented that it would "do good in this country; . . . as to France, . . . events will govern there."[90] But France was not yet ready to listen to calm reasoning.

In the meantime, relations with Britain continued to improve, a logical result of the disharmony between the United States and France and of Britain's continuing reliance on wartime imports from America. The British were pleased with the new American minister, Rufus King. At the time of his appointment Liston informed Grenville that King, "a gentleman high in character," had contributed to the ratification of Jay's Treaty.[91] Grenville also was well disposed toward him and instructed Liston to relay to the secretary of state "the favorable impressions which [were] entertained respecting Mr. King's conduct."[92]

Though the British had long overridden American rights, they expressed moral indignation at French movements "exciting internal discontents" in America and French threats to attack the United States merely because the latter had tried to establish "good understanding" with Britain. Liston was "distinctly authorized by His Majesty" to assure the Americans that the king was ready to "make common cause" with them.[93] Even if open hostilities did not develop between America and France, the British demonstrated willingness to extend naval protection to American commerce, indirectly through the continuing belligerent actions of the British navy against France, and directly by allowing American vessels to move in British con-

[86] Hamilton to Wolcott, November 22, 1796, *ibid.*, 209–13.

[87] Washington to Pickering, January 4, 1797, *WW*, XXXV, 352.

[88] January 16, 1797, *ASPFR*, I, 559–76.

[89] Bemis, *A Diplomatic History of the United States*, 113.

[90] Hamilton to Pickering, February 6, 1797, *HWL*, X, 236.

[91] Liston to Grenville, May 28, 1796, FCA, XXIX.

[92] Grenville to Liston, January 27, 1797, *ibid.*, XXXIII.

[93] Grenville to Liston, March 18, 1797, *ibid.*, XXIX.

voys. King at first refused to sanction British convoys of American vessels and asked for instructions on the point.[94] Pickering told him not to request such protection but, on the other hand, not to refuse it.[95]

Hamilton was pleased by this new evidence that Britain was acting more peaceably. Such actions would strengthen "the hands of the friends of order and peace."[96] Actually he had anticipated the latest move; he had written to Wolcott a few months earlier that if the English were "wise they would neither have harassed our trade themselves, nor suffered their trade with us to be harassed. . . . A frigate or two to serve as convoys would not be amiss. . . . A *hint* might not perhaps do harm."[97]

Any approach toward harmony with Britain was good news to the Federalists. King cheerfully observed that the people of England held George Washington in higher esteem than any other man on earth except their own monarch.[98] George Cabot believed that American tranquillity ultimately depended on "the fate of England" in its conflict with France,[99] and Noah Webster trusted that "the British Ministry could be convinced of the utility of conciliating the attachment of the Americans."[100] All these observations were to prove too optimistic.

To counter the menacing gestures of the French, Hamilton took up his pen and produced a series of essays designed to hearten the American people. He wrote: "In the eyes of France the unpardonable sin" of Jay's Treaty was that "it roots up for the present those germs of discord" with Britain.[101] France had addressed America "*in the tone of reproach, instead of the language of friendship*." One by one he reviewed articles of the treaty to demonstrate that the United States was nowhere in default.[102] The French aim, he wrote, was "to seduce the [American] people from their government, and, by dividing, to conquer and oppress." Some Americans were "depraved enough" to help play the French game, though it meant stooping "to the ignominious level of vassals." The French were treating American commerce worse than the British ever had; and if they persisted,

[94] King to Pickering, March 12, 1797, *KC*, II, 152–53.
[95] King to Pickering, May 9, 1797, *ibid.*, 178–79.
[96] Hamilton to King, December 16, 1796, *HWL*, X, 217.
[97] Hamilton to Wolcott, June 15, 1796, *ibid.*, 176.
[98] King to Hamilton, February 6, 1797, *KC*, II, 142.
[99] Cabot to King, May 9, 1797, *ibid.*, 181.
[100] Webster to King, May 30, 1797, *ibid.*, 182.
[101] "France," 1796, *HWL*, VI, 206–14.
[102] "The Answer," December 6, 1796, *ibid.*, 215.

"open war" would have to be the American reply. Yet there was still hope that the nation would not be driven to that "disagreeable extremity," and the "true policy" for the United States was "to remain at peace if we can, to negotiate our subjects of complaint as long as they shall be at all negotiable, to defer and to wait."[103]

In the meantime, Hamilton urged, military and naval preparations must not be delayed. From the time of his failure to induce the Continental Congress to provide for a "Military Peace Establishment"[104] in 1783, he never gave up the effort. He became more insistent during periods of national crisis—especially in 1794, when war with England threatened, and again when France was threatening American independence.

In the summer of 1796, to counter the rigorous opposition to a preparedness program, he suggested a rather odd expedient to provide for the construction of three frigates to resist French privateers. Since Congress had not appropriated money for the construction of the ships, he suggested that "the merchants, by secret movements," should be asked to make a loan to the government to cover the expense. The ships could be built ostensibly to fight the Algerians, but the real purpose could be allowed to "circulate in whispers."[105] In his letter to Washington suggesting material for the President's eighth annual address to Congress, to be delivered December 7, 1796, he also recommended the construction of a military academy and of publicly owned factories to provide military and naval equipment and "the *gradual* and *successive* creation of a navy."[106] The President agreed, particularly on the last recommendation, and emphasized it in his address: "A naval force is indispensable. . . . It is in our own experience that the most sincere neutrality is not a sufficient guard against the depredations of nations at war."[107]

The Senate, reflecting a Federalist majority, replied to the President, "We perfectly coincide with you in opinion that the importance of our commerce demands a naval force," and promised to try "to attain that object." The House of Representatives, less inclined to agree, stated merely, "The various subjects of your communication will respectively meet with the attention that is due to their importance."[108]

103 "The Warning" essays, six in number, January 27–March 27, 1797, *ibid.*, 229–59.
104 *Ibid.*, 463–83.
105 Hamilton to Wolcott, June 16, 1796, *ibid.*, X, 176–77.
106 Hamilton to Washington, November 10, 1796, *ibid.*, 204–205.
107 Richardson, I, 193.
108 *Ibid.*, 196–201.

While discussing the President's message, the House members fell into a wrangle over the French question. It was clear that defense measures faced fierce opposition. Those measures called for appropriations, and the Republicans had far more power in Congress than in the executive branch. Moreover, many Republicans adhered to Jefferson's conviction that democracy would be endangered if the federal government had any considerable number of armed men under its command. In 1793, as secretary of state, Jefferson had opposed fortifying the harbors and had rejected a proposal to build a military academy, arguing that Congress did not have constitutional authority to do so.[109] In 1797 he and his party were opposed to building up armaments that might be used against France. When Congress did appropriate money to build three frigates, it was over Republican opposition. Representative John Nicholas of Virginia protested that the law had been "an unfortunate business. [It] had been passed by surprise, . . . and was carried by a small majority."[110] Nathaniel Macon of North Carolina persuaded the House to pass a resolution providing that none of the frigates could operate outside American waters. The bill failed to pass in the Senate.[111]

"A war with France," wrote Madison to Jefferson, "and an alliance with G. B. enter both into print and conversation."[112] He was alarmed by both prospects. Representative Thomas Claiborne of Virginia thought a defense program would interfere with proper negotiations with France. He told the House, "We ought not to pretend to negotiate with a sword in our hand."[113]

Taxes frightened the Republicans and even wilted some of the Federalists. Hamilton asserted positively that adequate revenues could be raised, if Congress would but put out its hand and take them. He wrote to Wolcott, Sedgwick, and Smith, urging the imposition of taxes on buildings, horses, and salt and the passage of a stamp tax; but many congressmen were determined to avoid new levies on their regions or constituents. "Overdriven theory," moaned Hamilton, "everywhere palsies the operations of our government."[114]

By this time the French plan for seizing the Mississippi Valley was reaching maturity. The scheme, if successful, would extend French control all

109 Cabinet meeting, November 23, 1793, *The Anas*, *JW*, I, 409.
110 February 10, 1797, *Annals*, VI, 2116.
111 Dodd, *The Life of Nathaniel Macon*, 100–101.
112 Madison to Jefferson, January 29, 1797, *MW*, VI, 307.
113 December 15, 1796, *Annals*, VI, 1663.
114 Hamilton to William Smith, 1797, *HWL*, X, 224–26.

the way to the Allegheny Mountains. Disgust with eastern apologists for the French made the administration doubly aware of this additional menace. In May, 1796, the War Department informed General St. Clair, governor of the Northwest Territory, that French agents named Powers, DeCollot, and Warren would soon be circulating through the territory to promote secession. The general was ordered to seize the agents' papers and send them to the President and to arrest them if he could obtain sufficient proof of seditious activities.[115]

Talleyrand, now back in France after a two-year exile in the United States, had become a leading advocate of the plan. During his exile he had been the object of much kindness, and had become acquainted with many American leaders, including Hamilton. He had criticized the offensive behavior of French ministers in the United States. He had written to Hamilton that he was telling everyone he did not believe the Americans would become estranged from France but that if they should it would be a natural result of the bold and unfriendly policies of the French ministers.[116] Yet soon after his return to France in 1796 he was reported to have assured French leaders that "America is not of greater consequence to them, nor ought to be treated with greater respect, than Geneva or Genoa."[117] Hamilton saw the aptness of the comparison, though his conclusions were different. In his essays he later described the drastic terms the French had just imposed on the "little republic" of Genoa, and he observed that its neutrality had not saved it from the wrath of France.[118]

From Paris, Monroe reported having been told that a treaty was "in great forwardness" between France and Spain "whereby the latter cedes to the former Louisiana, and, perhaps the Floridas."[119] Wolcott thought the cession had actually been made.[120] Since the summer of 1796, American newspapers had been expressing alarm at the prospect of losing the West.[121] The English co-operated by informing the Americans about French and Spanish conspiracies.[122] Washington instructed Pickering to "let Mr. Pinck-

[115] Smith, *Arthur St. Clair*, II, 395–96.

[116] Talleyrand to Hamilton, November 12, 1796, HPSCLC, Box 2.

[117] Charles Cotesworth Pinckney to Pickering, December 20, 1796, *ASPFR*, II, 8.

[118] "The Warning," No. 3, February 21, 1797, *HWL*, VI, 240–41.

[119] Monroe to Pickering, August 4, 1796, *JMW*, III, 50.

[120] Oliver Wolcott, Jr., to Oliver Wolcott, Sr., November 1, 1796, Gibbs, I, 390. See also *ibid.*, 351–55 for a memorandum and extracts from letters on the subject.

[121] DeConde, *Entangling Alliance*, 450.

[122] Liston to Grenville, November 18, 1796, January 25, 1797, FCA, XXIX, XXXIII.

ney know how unpleasant to this country it would be that the French should be possessed of Louisiana and the Floridas."[123] The secretary of state also informed King in London of the threatening danger, though he confessed he did "not know what opportunity" might occur to King "for throwing obstacles in the way."[124] John Trumbull, now a commissioner overseeing Article VII of Jay's Treaty, wrote from London that the question "ought to be terminated by the immediate seizure of Florida and New Orleans" by the United States.[125]

Some of the Federalists who had lost patience with France began questioning Hamilton's policy of moderation. His reply to them was straightforward: "It is much to our interest to preserve peace, if we can with honor, and if we cannot, it will be very important to prove that no endeavor to do it has been omitted."[126] He remained constantly aware of the power of public opinion during peacetime and of its vital importance in war.

Hamilton did not try to outguess the intentions of the French. He assumed that they had not chosen a definite course but were constantly trimming sail to take advantage of varying winds. Though he resented Adet's insolent behavior, he assumed that it was designed to "leave France at liberty to slide easily either into a renewal of cordiality or an actual or virtual war with the United States."[127] In his view the French would, of course, follow the course of self-interest. He was convinced that if the United States acted promptly—before the Directory made a decision for war—it should be possible to convince the French that their interests called for peace with America. In 1796, Americans had shipped to France goods valued at $11,623,314, half the value of goods shipped to Britain.[128] It seemed obvious that if France resorted to open hostilities "the consequence may be to turn [American commerce] more entirely into the channels of Great Britain."[129] He would not use threats, but in a nonmenacing manner he would have the French reminded of the "consequences" of war.[130] He thought it worthwhile to "appeal to the justice and interest of France."[131] Republican Con-

123 Washington to Pickering, February 14, 1797, *WW*, XXXV, 388.

124 *KC*, II, 147.

125 Trumbull to Wolcott, January 15, 1797, Gibbs, I, 474.

126 Hamilton to Theodore Sedgwick, February 26, 1797, *HWL*, X, 239.

127 Hamilton to King, December 6, 1796, *ibid.*, 215.

128 *Annals*, VI, 2109.

129 Hamilton to King, December 16, 1796, *HWL*, X, 215.

130 Hamilton to Wolcott, November 22, 1796, *ibid.*, 211.

131 Hamilton to Washington, January 19, 1797, *ibid.*, 230.

gressman Giles, on the other hand, argued that French interests would be promoted by a war with the United States, which would quickly ruin American commerce with England.[132]

To Hamilton, the time for negotiation seemed to be running out. French attacks on American commerce were too severe to be endured for long. He was especially concerned by the "picaroon privateers hovering on our coast."[133] If the nation submitted to such continued assaults, the outcome would be "absolute degradation from the rank of sovereign and independent states." "If France, after being properly called upon to renounce [her hostile actions] shall persevere, . . . there cannot be a question but that open war will be preferable to such a state."[134] There should be a "final effort to accommodate, and then resort to measures of defense."[135]

When Adet had announced the severance of Franco-American relations, he had placed those relations on a new plane. Pinckney had left for Paris some two months earlier, and following Adet's protest the Department of State had sent him additional elaborate instructions; but Hamilton knew that Pinckney was authorized only to tell the French what they had earlier dismissed or refused to hear. He began to feel that more could be done to avert hostilities. A new note appeared in his correspondence—a suggestion that a "final appeal" be made. Affairs with France were at "the same point" as they "were with Great Britain when Mr. Jay was sent there."[136] Writing to Congressman Theodore Sedgwick the following day, he expressed the same thought and added, "We ought to make a final effort to accommodate."[137] Then he spelled out his proposal to Washington: an "extraordinary mission" of three men should be sent to France. One of the envoys should be a Republican, to minimize political repercussions at home if the mission should fail and to soothe the "pride" of France and provide a "bridge over which she may more easily retreat." The three envoys should be Pinckney, who was already in Europe, Madison, well known as a Republican, and George Cabot, a strong Federalist with a wide knowledge of commercial matters. They should be empowered to work for a settlement at a much higher level than had yet been attempted. They should try to agree on

132 December 14, 1796, *Annals*, VI, 1631–32.
133 Hamilton to Wolcott, June 16, 1796, *HWL*, X, 176.
134 "The Warning," Nos. 1, 3, January 27, February 21, 1797, *ibid.*, VI, 230, 243.
135 Hamilton to Sedgwick, January 20, 1797, *ibid.*, X, 232.
136 Hamilton to William Smith, January 19, 1797, *ibid.*, 231.
137 Hamilton to Sedgwick, January 20, 1797, *ibid.*, 232.

"mutual compensations" for past injuries, modify the commercial treaties, and terminate or alter the terms of the alliance.[138]

The Republicans were demanding a similar move, though apparently they had in mind a one-man mission.[139] Washington had heard of the suggestion, and on the same day Hamilton wrote to him, he wrote to Hamilton requesting his opinion. He, too, was thinking of the mission in terms of one man only, but he saw difficulties in the way. Had not Pinckney recently been sent to France "for the express purpose of explaining matters, and removing inquietudes? With what more could another be charged?" And what would Pinckney think of "having a person treading on his heels by the time he had arrived in Paris"? (As it turned out, Pinckney proved to have a more magnanimous spirit than the President thought. He asked John Quincy Adams, at The Hague, to inform the administration that his only object was to serve the country and that he would not resent it in the least if another envoy was sent to Paris.[140]) The President appeared perplexed and undecided; he closed the letter by saying, "The sooner you can give me your sentiments on these queries the more pleasing will they be."[141]

Again, Hamilton's suggestions arrived sooner than expected. His letter was already in the mail, and probably reached Washington by January 24. The minds of these two statesmen were so closely attuned that all the President's questions were answered, and apparently there was no further communication between them on the subject. Hamilton had even anticipated the possible embarrassment to Pinckney. "Cogent motives of public utility," he wrote, "must prevail over personal considerations. Mr. Pinckney may be told, in a private letter from you, that this is an unavoidable concession to the pressure of public exigency and the state of *internal parties*."[142]

Hamilton was so determined on further negotiations with France that he decided to plant the idea in Congress as well. To that end he wrote to Sedgwick reiterating the advice he had given to Washington, with some further elaboration. One of the three commissioners should be "a man as influential with the French as Mr. Madison," but Madison could not be sent alone, "lest his Gallicism should work amiss"; and it might "wound Mr. Pinckney" to be superseded by one man. Pinckney, therefore, should be one

138 Hamilton to Washington, January 22, 1797, *ibid.*, 233–35.

139 Ames to Hamilton, January 26, 1797, *HWH*, VI, 198–99.

140 John Quincy Adams to John Adams, May 11, 1797, *JQAW*, II, 166.

141 Washington to Hamilton, January 22, 1797, *WW*, XXXV, 373.

142 Hamilton to Washington, *HWL*, X, 235.

of the three. George Cabot, as the third, "would mix very useful ingredients in the cup." The envoys should aim for cancellation of the treaty of alliance "by mutual consent," for "a definite duration" for the treaty, or for a provision specifying that the assistance to be rendered should be "so many men, so many ships, or so much money," and that only in "a clearly defensive war." The Senate should be kept in session so that it could give its approval to the mission, which, as Hamilton had previously observed, was required by the Constitution. Sedgwick was to use the letter however he saw fit (such letters were customarily written to be shown around).[143]

The end of Washington's administration was clouded by unresolved diplomatic controversies abroad and by factionalism at home. He pointed unhappily to Jefferson and Madison as the leaders of the "opposition."[144] He was aware that "the Republican movement" was growing into a "Republican party."[145] "Parties" and "factions" were much the same to him, and such groups, in his view, verged on treason. It evidently never occurred to him that the Federalists also constituted a party. Both he and Hamilton looked upon the Federalists simply as those Americans who were supporting good government.

Washington's aversion to parties stemmed from the days of the Whisky Rebellion, when the participants had received moral support from the Republicans. He believed that the inevitable differences of opinion should be resolved by the people's representatives at the nation's capital. Stirring up agitation throughout the country was, to him, sheer demagoguery, placing the nation in peril. Moreover, the faction that had supported the Whisky Rebellion was now giving friendly countenance to France even after that country had hurled insults, a tenth part of which would cause the average American of a later generation to turn purple with rage. The French had seized American vessels and imprisoned seamen on trivial and even false pretexts and were unwilling even to discuss the matter with the American government. The French were striving to divide the people of the United States and stir some areas to rise against the legally constituted government, meantime preparing to seize territories in the West. It seemed to Washington that through this siege of injury and conspiracy the Republicans were

[143] Hamilton to Sedgwick, February 26, 1797, *ibid.*, 239–41.
[144] Washington to Hamilton, May 15, 1796, *WW*, XXXV, 49.
[145] William Nisbet Chambers, *Political Parties in a New Nation: The American Experience, 1776–1809* (New York, 1963), 80.

serving as eager coadjutors of the adversary. Though angered and dismayed, he performed ably until the end of his administration. He was ready to lay down his burdens—but not until he had given his fellow countrymen some thoughtful words of advice for the future.

CHAPTER XIV

The Farewell Address

THE enduring fame of a statesman often depends as much on what he writes as on what he does. Among American statesmen this observation particularly applies to Jefferson and to a lesser extent to Lincoln and Wilson, and to Hamilton. Washington's immortality is assured for his deeds, but his Farewell Address has brought him to the attention of succeeding generations of Americans who might otherwise have had but a superficial knowledge of his achievements. In the address the man of action emerges as a man of thought as well, one who foresaw clearly the path his country could safely follow to fulfill its destiny.

The Farewell Address, which has been called the Second Declaration of Independence,[1] is one of the great American state papers, and continues to merit careful study. Some of Washington's premises no longer apply to modern-day government. World political conditions make foreign alliances necessary, and political parties have long since come to play an essential role in government. But the greater part of Washington's counsel is for man and the ages, and is as sound today as when it was written. The complete text of the address is given at the end of this book.

The influence of the address is incalculable. It encompassed the essence of the wisdom of the Revolutionary generation. The political attitudes of the people—and therefore their actions—during the nineteenth and twentieth centuries have been profoundly affected by it.

Hamilton contributed notably to the composition of the Farewell Address. He is responsible not only for its beautiful style but also for many of its best-known principles. His role in its creation, though second to that of Washington, is one of his greatest legacies to his nation.

Washington had intended to retire from the presidency at the end of his

[1] Bemis, "Washington's Farewell Address: A Foreign Policy of Independence," *American Historical Review*, Vol. XXXIX (January, 1934), 250–68.

first term and in 1792 had asked Madison's assistance in preparing a parting message to the people.[2] In earlier years Washington and Madison had been very close. Madison had been an honored guest "for a week's stopover" at Mount Vernon, in December, 1788, and the President had been impressed by his judgment and had thereafter regularly conferred with him, especially concerning appointments to federal offices and congressional matters.[3]

Madison had reluctantly agreed to help prepare a farewell message in 1792 but had appeared infinitely more interested in persuading the President not to retire. The likely successor, he had reportedly told Washington, would be one of three men, Jefferson, Adams, or Jay. Jefferson, he thought, might be unwilling to leave his "farm and his philosophy" to take up such a burden and would face powerful opposition from the northern states because of their "local prejudices" and from Pennsylvania because of his efforts in plans to move the Capital from Philadelphia. Adams would be looked upon with suspicion because of his unconcealed "monarchical principles." Jay, having "the same obnoxious principle," and being "less open," would be "more successful in propagating them." Moreover, the "Western people" considered Jay "their most dangerous enemy" because of his "negotiations for ceding the Mississippi to Spain."

Madison, believing that Washington's gravest apprehensions stemmed from the growth of political parties in the country,[4] pointed out that the best means conceivable for holding them in check was for the President to remain in office. No doubt this point had far more weight with the President than the aspersions Madison cast on Adams and Jay, both of whom Washington trusted. The President was not yet convinced, however, and seeing that for the moment he was unable to alter Washington's determination to retire, Madison prepared and submitted a brief farewell message.[5] Madison's thought is evident in the final form of the address presented in 1796, but the Virginia congressman's most important contribution was his suggestion that the message be delivered, not to Congress, but directly to the people through the press. He observed that "the people" were the President's "only constituents,"[6] and apparently Washington never wavered, then or later, from his determination to follow that advice.

[2] Madison's memorandum, May 5, 1792, *MW*, VI, 106–10, describes the conversation in detail.

[3] Brant, III, 281–88.

[4] Memorandum, May 5, 1792, *MW*, VI, 108.

[5] *Ibid.*, 113–16.

[6] Madison to Washington, June 21, 1792, *ibid.*, 112.

Washington later expressed deep regret that he allowed the counsel of Madison and others to persuade him to continue in office for another four-year term.[7] During that period his broad-minded tolerance of his fellow Virginians Jefferson and Madison gave way, and he came to view them as party-minded men. He must have been offended by Madison's "Helvidius" essays, published in the *Gazette of the United States* in August and September, 1793. There Madison had made a show of affection and respect for the President, meanwhile attacking Hamilton's efforts, in the "Pacificus" essays, to justify the Neutrality Proclamation of 1793.[8] Washington had never disclaimed responsibility for the proclamation. He was aware that Jefferson believed the executive had no more authority to declare neutrality than to declare war, and he must have winced at the words "tyranny," "monarchical," and "royal prerogatives" which Madison employed to condemn Hamilton's thesis.[9] Nevertheless, not long after the "Helvidius" essays appeared, Washington wrote to Madison and others, asking them whether they considered it within his constitutional authority to convene Congress to meet at some place other than Philadelphia, where the fever was raging.[10] In this matter he could hardly overlook Madison, who rated so highly in Congress and who had helped write the Constitution; but, as Madison's editor observed, "This was the last opinion given by Madison to Washington. Their relations were no longer cordial."[11]

In the early summer of 1796, while the address was being prepared, Washington wrote to Hamilton that the contents of the 1792 message were known to Jefferson and Madison, who were "strongest and foremost in the opposition to the Government" and antagonistic toward him because he was conducting the government in ways "contrary to their views."[12] It is distressing to read of the acrimony and distrust that had developed between these patriots, which Washington blamed on the developing party lines. His apprehensions about the danger of parties are clearly reflected in the anti-party statements in the address, and they are one reason why he drew so close to Hamilton in the closing months of his presidency.

The association of Washington and Hamilton from 1777 to 1799—from

[7] According to a conversation of August 2, 1793, reported by Jefferson in *The Anas*, *JW*, I, 382.

[8] *MW*, VI, 138–88.

[9] "Helvidius," No. 1, August 24, 1793, *ibid.*, 144–50.

[10] Washington to Madison, October 14, 1793, *WW*, XXXIII, 122–25.

[11] *MW*, VI, 199n.

[12] Washington to Hamilton, May 15, 1796, *WW*, XXXV, 49.

the day Hamilton became the General's aide-de-camp to the end of Washington's life—reached its apex in their work on the Farewell Address. Because of its importance to this climactic political work, a brief review of that relationship seems in order. In the early years of their association Washington had a paternal attitude toward the younger man, writing congratulatory lines about his devotion to duty and his "probity and sterling virtue."[13] Washington's esteem survived Hamilton's abrupt resignation from the general's staff in 1781, and was undoubtedly strengthened by the young colonel's valor at Yorktown. When he was a member of the Continental Congress from 1782 to 1783, Hamilton displayed warm friendliness toward Washington and showed him marked courtesy and kindness.[14] He saw Washington's star rising, and he was too much of a realist to ignore the advantages of being associated with him. Yet Hamilton made no compromise with integrity; he remained independent of thought and action. A mutual "reverence for law and constituted authority" drew the two men together.[15] Hamilton helped persuade Washington to attend the Constitutional Convention at Philadelphia in 1787, and in those arduous days their mutual respect increased. Washington heaped praise on the authors of the "Federalist" papers,[16] knowing that they were mostly the product of Hamilton's pen.[17]

Washington's regular custom as president of seeking advice on a wide range of matters led to the accusation that he had fallen under the influence of Hamilton, with his alert mind and ready answers.[18] Certainly this charge was an exaggeration. Randolph's biographer stated that after Hamilton's view was accepted by Washington in the controversy regarding the founding of the Bank of the United States in 1791, Jefferson and Randolph won fourteen successive victories on the issues.[19] In 1796, angered by newspaper reports that Jefferson accused Hamilton of having led the administration into grievous errors, the President reminded Jefferson—in wording revealing that his emotions were barely under control—that if he would search his

13 Washington to Hamilton, November 15, 1777, *ibid.*, X, 67; Washington to John Sullivan, February 4, 1781, *ibid.*, XXI, 181.

14 *JCC*, XXIV, 142 *et passim.*

15 Monaghan, *John Jay*, 342.

16 Washington to Hamilton, July 10, 1787, *WW*, XXIX, 246.

17 Washington to Hamilton, August 28, 1788, *ibid.*, XXX, 66.

18 This was a common Republican accusation. See especially E. S. Maclay (ed.), *The Journal of William Maclay, United States Senator from Pennsylvania, 1789–1791* (New York, 1927), 319.

19 Conway, *Edmund Randolph*, 199–200.

memory of the period when he was secretary of state he could not fail to recall that "there were as many instances" when the President had "decided *against* as in *favor of* the opinions" of Hamilton.[20] Yet it was Hamilton's doctrines that came to set the tone of the administration—especially after 1793, when Jefferson was no longer in the cabinet. It is impossible to evaluate Jefferson's belief that by that time the President's mind had lost some of its keenness.

Washington's reliance on Hamilton was not interrupted by the latter's return to his law practice in 1795. Hamilton continued to give unstintingly of his time in service to the President—sometimes to the President's embarrassment, as when Hamilton wrote a small-sized book evaluating Jay's Treaty when Washington had merely asked for his opinion. After expressing his deep appreciation of the effort, the President added, "I am really ashamed when I behold the trouble it has given you."[21] He continued to ask Hamilton's advice on important appointments and on many of the issues of the day. He especially depended on Hamilton for help in refuting or avoiding criticism. A Hamilton biographer has presented the following capsule of questions and requests which Washington addressed to Hamilton in New York:

> What am I to do for a Secretary of State? . . . You have seen the long promised vindication, or rather accusation. What do you think of it; and what notice shall be taken of it? . . . What measures might be taken with the Senate with reference to the treaty with Great Britain? . . . What do you think ought to be said in case G——— M———'s information should prove true *in all its parts*? . . . . Do you suppose that the Executive, in the recess of the Senate, has power . . . to send a special character to Paris as Envoy Extraordinary? . . . And what shall be done with Mr. M——— in that case? That the letter which he has now given to the public will be answered, and (to the candid mind) I hope satisfactorily, is certain; but ought it to be published *immediately*, or not?[22]

Frequently Hamilton appeared to be reminding the President of his duty, though always in terms of deepest respect. In 1788, when urging him to accept the presidency, Hamilton asserted, "It would be inglorious in such a situation not to hazard the glory, however great," which Washington had "previously acquired."[23] Similarly, in 1792 he wrote that Washington must

20 Washington to Jefferson, July 6, 1796, *WW*, XXXV, 119.

21 Washington to Hamilton, July 13, 1795, *ibid.*, XXXIV, 237–40.

22 Johan J. Smertenko, *Alexander Hamilton* (New York, 1932), 217.

23 Hamilton to Washington, September, 1788, *HWL*, IX, 445.

accept a second term as President because duty required it and his reputation would be endangered if he declined.[24] In 1794, in his letter recommending Jay's appointment as envoy to England, he declared it "the duty of every man, according to situation, to contribute all in his power towards preventing evil and producing good."[25] In 1798, when war with France seemed likely, he wrote regretfully that he knew Washington would be sacrificing well-deserved comforts at Mount Vernon if he came forth to command the American armies, but, he added, "you will be compelled to make the sacrifice."[26]

One cannot help but wonder why the elder statesman did not sometimes lose patience and rebuke his adviser with some such comment as, "Young man, I am competent to decide for myself what duty demands of me!" On the contrary, he regularly expressed appreciation for advice[27] and only rarely reacted coolly.

Washington's literary style was profoundly influenced by Hamilton. From the time Hamilton joined the general's "military family," as Washington called it, he was the aide chosen to write the most important letters and reports "to Congress, to governors, and state legislatures."[28] Hamilton was so honored because of "his quickness to grasp and execute the plans of his chief, [and] his clear style as a writer of good English."[29] In fact, "Few men in any age have so well advanced their fortunes by tongue and pen as he."[30] Timothy Pickering, who became the President's closest associate in the cabinet after Hamilton's departure, pointed out that Washington's grammar and spelling, defective during the early years of the Revolution, improved through his association with Hamilton.[31] Thus, in many areas, Washington was "perhaps Hamilton's greatest admirer and certainly his chief disciple."[32]

It was to be expected, therefore, that in the summer of 1796 the President

[24] Hamilton to Washington, July 30, 1792, *ibid.*, X, 7–8.

[25] Hamilton to Washington, *ibid.*, V, 97.

[26] Hamilton to Washington, May 19, 1798, *ibid.*, X, 286.

[27] Notably, Washington to Hamilton, March 4, 1783, *WW*, XXVI, 185; Washington to Hamilton, October 3, 1788, *ibid.*, XXX, 110.

[28] *Ibid.*, Introduction, I, *xliv*.

[29] Humphreys, *The Life and Times of David Humphreys*, I, 167.

[30] Bower Aly, *The Rhetoric of Alexander Hamilton* (New York, 1941), 3.

[31] Pickering to Richard Peters, January 5, 1811; Upham, *Life of Timothy Pickering*, II, 96.

[32] Richard B. Morris (ed.), *Alexander Hamilton and the Founding of the Nation, vii.* See especially his eight-page introductory essay, "Alexander Hamilton after Two Centuries," a good appraisal of Hamilton's mind and statesmanship.

would turn to Hamilton for assistance in preparing his last official message to his countrymen. It has been truly said that "two men were never better fitted for just such a joint work," for no man knew better than Hamilton "what Washington felt and thought,"[33] and no man knew as well as Hamilton the foreign problems and dangers that faced the young nation. It could be debated whether Hamilton could have analyzed the nation's domestic problems as well as Jefferson or Madison, but the survival of his principles in American government and the gradual abandonment of many of the concepts of Jefferson and Madison is a strong argument in favor of Hamilton's pre-eminence in this realm as well. Hamilton remained "a colossal pillar" of the administration, and his "wise and disciplined mind" had much to offer.[34]

Washington first asked Hamilton's help in writing the message, which he usually referred to as his "valedictory address."[35] Apparently the President was to write a first draft and send it to Hamilton, who was eager to get on with the work, though he urged the President to keep his mind open a few months longer on the subject of stepping down from office. The foreign situation might suddenly become more critical. "If a storm gathers," he anxiously inquired, "How can you retreat?"[36] Yet he made no determined effort to prevent the retirement—apparently assuming that no conceivable arguments except a new "storm" would alter the President's decision. It is barely possible that Hamilton may also have been harboring an ambition to become the nation's second president, as some writers have assumed,[37] though there appears to be no written evidence to support such an assumption. There may be some significance in Jefferson's later conclusion that the only way to prevent Hamilton from becoming the third president was to work out a friendly agreement with Adams.[38]

When Washington's draft of the address failed to reach Hamilton in New York as promptly as he expected, he wrote to the President warning against delay. It was necessary that the work "be done with great care, and much

[33] Horace Binney, *An Inquiry into the Formation of Washington's Farewell Address* (Philadelphia, 1859), 85 (hereafter cited as *An Inquiry*).

[34] Jared Sparks (ed.), *The Writings of George Washington* (Boston, 1834–37), XII, 391. Though this compilation has been superseded by the Fitzpatrick edition, Sparks's own observations are useful.

[35] Washington to Hamilton, May 15, 1796, *WW*, XXXV, 50.

[36] Hamilton to Washington, July 5, 1796, *HWL*, X, 181.

[37] John C. Miller, *Alexander Hamilton: Portrait in Paradox* (New York, 1959), 445 (hereafter cited as *Alexander Hamilton*).

[38] Jefferson to Madison, January 1, 1797, *JW*, IX, 359.

leisure, touched and re-touched."[39] Washington then sent him a copy of Madison's draft of 1792, along with additional points he wished to include.[40]

Washington intended to open the message by quoting all of the document prepared by Madison, to prove that he had not desired a second term, and then to make additional points. Hamilton realized that this format would weaken the impact of the speech, yet he seemed embarrassed in recommending the deletion of Madison's contribution. He may have feared that the President would think he was moved by petty considerations growing out of the rupture between him and Madison. In trying to prepare a paper "digesting" Washington's recent points with Madison's work, he found "a certain awkwardness in the thing" which would seem to imply, he said, that the President's avowal that he had planned to retire in 1792 would not be believed unless the "evidence" was given. The more he "considered the matter, the less eligible" the 1792 statement appeared to be.[41]

Washington agreed, and Madison's paragraphs were deleted, though some of his thoughts and better phrases were retained in the final document. This decision was the correct one. Madison's reasoning was sound, but his style was generally poor. He had not put forth much initiative to polish it, observing that he had had "little more to do as to the matter than to follow the very just and comprehensive outline which [Washington] had sketched." Madison's statement was at times harsh and almost grating, and in places wordy and tendentious. In his first sentence, for example, he wrote, "It may be requisite to a more distinct expression of the public voice that I should apprize . . . ." Deeper in the body of his draft is a sentence containing 212 words.[42]

Hamilton decided to write an address that could be read aloud with ease and pleasure. The measure of his success is the continuing response it has drawn in succeeding years. Perhaps no other state paper of its length is so appealing to the ear. In her later years Mrs. Hamilton described how her husband had her "sit with him, that he might read to me as he wrote,"

[39] May 10, 1796, *HWL*, X, 165.

[40] All the drafts exchanged by the two principals, as well as pertinent communications by other persons, are collected in Victor Hugo Paltsits' useful publication *Washington's Farewell Address, in Facsimile, with Transliterations of All the Drafts of Washington, Madison, and Hamilton, Together with Their Correspondence and Other Supporting Documents* (New York, 1935) (hereafter cited as *Washington's Farewell Address*). Paltsits analyzes the documents and, to some extent, evaluates the relative contributions of those involved.

[41] Hamilton to Washington, July 30, 1796, *HWL*, X, 186.

[42] Madison to Washington, June 21, 1792, *MW*, VI, 113–15.

remarking, " 'My dear Eliza, you must be to me what Molière's old nurse was to him.' " Practically all of the paper was read to her "as he wrote it."[43]

It was rare for Hamilton to devote so much time to a single effort. Most of his papers were prepared in haste, under pressing deadlines, and many of the literary gems to be found in his letters and essays are so closely tied in with the problems of the day that they are scarcely quotable in any length. He was one of the most overworked statesmen who ever lived. If he had had more time to elaborate his themes, he might hold a higher rank as a political philosopher.

In Washington's first draft were four paragraphs describing his good intentions and honesty during his years in office and recalling the injustice of the attacks that had been made upon him. Hamilton modified the tone of this section and reduced it to one short paragraph.[44] The President was reluctant to accept those changes. He had suffered in silence for a long time. The attacks, he said, related to "facts which are but little known to the Community," and his address was directed primarily to "the Yeomanry of this Country."[45]

Hamilton was better able to take a long-range view of the matter. He correctly assumed that the criticisms would soon be forgotten, and, in order to make the paper "importantly and lastingly useful," he wanted it to "embrace such reflections and sentiments as will wear well, progress in approbation with time, and redound to future reputation."[46]

Historians have long theorized about the manner in which the Farewell Address was produced. One view was that "the germinal thought is Washington's, the germination is Hamilton's."[47] Another was that "the arrangement and the language . . . were very largely the work of Alexander Hamilton, but the ideas were Washington's own."[48] Jared Sparks, who must have seen all the relevant papers, went so far as to say that Hamilton "suggested some of the topics and amplified others."[49] None of these theories go far enough. Only by textual comparison can it be determined which ideas were added to the Address through Hamilton's drafts.

[43] This interesting memorandum, dated August 7, 1840, is in HPLC, Library of Congress.

[44] Paltsits, *Washington's Farewell Address*, 171–73.

[45] Washington to Hamilton, May 15, and August 25, 1796, *WW*, XXXV, 50, 190–91.

[46] Hamilton to Washington, July 30, 1796, *HWL*, X, 186.

[47] Binney, *An Inquiry*, 109.

[48] Elbert J. Benton, "The Spirit of Washington's Foreign Policy," *The Review*, Vol. I (October 11, 1919), 471.

[49] Sparks, *The Writings of George Washington*, XII, 397.

The foreign-policy sections of the document, aimed at keeping the nation out of the war in Europe, resisting the French effort to subvert the nation's independence, and guiding the future course of the Republic, may be summarized as follows:

1. The need for unity in facing foreign nations
2. The need for military preparedness
3. The danger of permanent alliances
4. The possible need for temporary alliances
5. The value of recent treaties in protecting the interests of all sections of the country
6. The danger that the "spirit of party" may lead to foreign domination
7. The dangers of foreign influence
8. The need to avoid "inveterate antipathies" and "passionate attachments" for other nations
9. The wisdom of practicing good faith and justice toward all nations
10. The need for cultivating foreign trade
11. The need for establishing foreign commercial relations with as little political connection as possible
12. The need for an impartial commercial policy toward all nations
13. The need for awareness that Europe's "primary interests" are those with which the United States has little concern
14. The folly of expecting disinterested favors from another nation[50]

Three of the fourteen points above, 4, 5, and 12, were not mentioned in any of Washington's drafts. Each of the three is highly significant. The nation would have been grievously handicapped in its foreign relations had it forsworn all resort to alliances (point 4). Jefferson had been more determined than any other American in holding to the possibilities of future alliances, as he had emphasized during the Nootka Sound affair in 1790; but Washington and Hamilton had also seen that the United States would probably face crises in the future which would make it necessary to resort

[50] Paltsits credits Hamilton also with the remarkable passage beginning, "Of all the dispositions and habits which lead to political prosperity, religion and morality are indispensable supports." It is one of the most widely quoted paragraphs in the address. It is not the purpose of this chapter to search out Hamilton's contributions other than those in the area of foreign policy. The tone of the passage and its import are characteristic of both Washington and Hamilton.

to co-operation with certain European powers as a defense against others. Important as this point was, it was suggested, not by the President, but by Hamilton.

Both Hamilton and Washington were well aware that the people of the West had been deeply dissatisfied with the national government, had been vulnerable to the wiles of Genêt, and had considered secession. Westerners' apprehensions had not been allayed by Jay's Treaty, though Pinckney's Treaty, which had opened the Mississippi to commerce, had greatly lessened their suspicions that eastern interests were willing to barter away their rights. Hamilton was thus presented with a capital opportunity (point 5) to link the eastern-favored Jay's Treaty and the Mississippi-oriented Pinckney's Treaty as illustrations of the prudence of adhering closely to "the Union by which they were procured." Hamilton had enough prudence and judgment to restrain himself from pointing out that Jay's Treaty, which had been denounced in the West, had by this time led to withdrawal of British troops from the Northwest.

Washington offered no objection to referring to the two treaties to bolster his effort to promote greater devotion to the Union. It was one of the major goals of the address and has remained an effective plea for unity long after the provisions of the treaties were forgotten.

Point 12 in the list above was in part Hamilton's answer to efforts to discriminate against British commerce. No doubt Washington realized that; at any rate he was willing to support the principle in his parting message. He was well aware, as judicious historians have realized in later years, that Hamilton never wanted or recommended special, uncompensated advantages to British commerce. How could the United States adhere steadily to a policy of neutrality in wartime if its peacetime commercial policy was not impartial?

Other intimates of the President had some influence on the contents of the address. Hamilton conferred with Jay while he was working on it, but apparently he did not reveal the magnitude of the work, and Jay later exaggerated his own contribution.[51] John Quincy Adams also helped stimulate Washington's thinking. It has been suggested that the President may have had one of Adams' essays on the desk before him as he worked on his

[51] See the exchange of letters between Jay and Judge Richard Peters, February 14, March 29, 1811, and editorial comments, Paltsits, *Washington's Farewell Address*, 263–71. See also Binney, *An Inquiry*, 154–59.

first draft.[52] Certainly it was the product of "recent and painful experiences."[53] It remains significant that some of the basic premises of the address were placed there by Hamilton, and not by Washington. It is not enough to say, therefore, that "the trunk and branches" were Washington's and the "foliage" was Hamilton's.[54] The message contained Hamilton's own "structure of thought" and some salient points that were distinctly his contributions.[55]

Washington, of course, made the final decisions about the content. He struck out a sentence in Hamilton's final draft: "In my opinion, the real danger in our system is, that the general government, organized as at present, will prove too weak rather than too powerful."[56] Here Hamilton's genius had erred and, as sometimes in earlier years, was corrected by "the steadiness of Washington."[57] The sentence and Washington's reaction to it provides an interesting contrast in the outlooks of the two men. It was not unusual for Hamilton to give way, from time to time, to pessimism of this kind. Washington was always more hopeful, and certainly he would not agree that the Constitution he had helped write and the government over which he had presided for more than seven years might "prove too weak."

It is not likely that Washington deleted the sentence because of its partisan flavor. In so far as the message was aimed at influencing public opinion at the time, it was an attack on Republican concepts. It has also been pointed out that in persuading Washington not to complain about unfair criticism Hamilton saved the address "from the appearance of a defensive maneuver against Republican critics" and thereby succeeded in making it "an offensive weapon against them."[58] One historian has called the address "a campaign document" and "a piece of partisan politics directed specifically against Republican and Francophiles who had made Washington's last years miserable."[59] That is probably too caustic a statement, but it has the germ of

[52] Bemis, "John Quincy Adams and George Washington, "*Proceedings of the Massachusetts Historical Society*, Vol. LXVII (October, 1941–May, 1944), 381.

[53] Bemis, "Washington's Farewell Address: A Foreign Policy of Independence," *American Historical Review*, Vol. XXXIX (January, 1934), 261.

[54] *Ibid.*, 262.

[55] Felix Gilbert, *To the Farewell Address: Ideas on Early American Foreign Policy* (Princeton, 1961), 132, 168 (hereafter cited as *To the Farewell Address*).

[56] *HWL*, VIII, 201.

[57] White, *The Federalists*, 6.

[58] Brant, III, 441.

[59] DeConde, *Entangling Alliance*, 465; DeConde, "Washington's Farewell, the French Alliance, and the Election of 1796," *Mississippi Valley Historical Review*, Vol. XLIII (March, 1957), 648.

truth. The interesting suggestion has been offered that Washington may have hoped to employ both Hamilton and Madison in the composition of the address to illustrate how Americans of different political views could work together if they would try.[60] That approach would have been consistent with the President's outlook in 1792, but by 1796 he had grown too hostile toward Republican leaders to have considered any such means of appeasing them.

Bitter strife later arose among the Federalists concerning Hamilton's part in the writing of the address. The only two persons who could have clarified the issue died within a decade after its publication. "Whisperings arose, grew to murmurings, and then became vocal in a controversy that parted friends of years."[61] Hamilton's friends claimed that they could produce a draft of the address in Hamilton's own hand. They were referring, of course, to Hamilton's final draft; but it alone would not have proved Hamilton's authorship. The President's nephew, Bushrod Washington, wrote that neither he nor Chief Justice Marshall had ever "met with any letter or copy of a letter ... which could warrant the conclusion" that Hamilton wrote the address.[62] Mrs. Hamilton resorted to court action to try to recover possession of some Hamilton papers from Rufus King. She was frustrated at nearly every turn and must have felt that there was a conspiracy to deny her dead husband his rightful place on history's page.[63] Her own statements of August 7, 1840, quoted above, directed to her children and to posterity, represented a dedicated effort to set the record straight. She erred in a few minor details because she was not fully aware of Washington's contributions. [Despite her efforts the dispute was not resolved during her lifetime.]

The copy Hamilton sent to the President disappeared from the Washington papers, under what Lodge called "suspicious" circumstances.[64] Fortunately Hamilton kept a copy for himself (and was unjustifiably criticized for not destroying communications with Washington "in a case of so confidential a nature"[65]). Today, of course, "all the papers, whether drafts

60 Gilbert, *To the Farewell Address*, 124.

61 Paltsits, *Washington's Farewell Address*, 75.

62 Bushrod Washington to Charles King, October 6, 1825, *KC*, VI, 618.

63 Several papers relating to the Hamilton family's dispute with King are in HPSCLC, Box 2. See also Paltsits, *Washington's Farewell Address*, 75–94, 263–304, for an account of the controversy and the more important correspondence relating to it.

64 *HWL*, VIII, 188n.

65 Sparks, *The Writings of George Washington*, XII, 396.

or correspondence, that can be conceived to have been written in connection with the formation of the Farewell Address, are extant,"[66] and the contributions of both men are a matter of record.

As the address neared completion, Washington became increasingly eager to present it to the public. As Madison had suggested in 1792 Hamilton thought that the month of October was the proper time to release it, though by June, 1796, Washington was wishing that it had already been published.[67] After a last few days spent in final polishing it was published on September 19 in David C. Claypoole's *American Daily Advertiser*. It was soon being read and acclaimed throughout the United States, and came to the attention of the chancellories of Europe.[68] None but a few of the most inflexible Republicans dared attack it openly.

The manner in which Washington and Hamilton complemented each other is well illustrated in the address. Washington's mind was deliberate and stable; Hamilton's was quick and penetrating. Both were firm in holding to basic principles, but the younger man more readily perceived the specific applications and results of given policies. Both men were remarkably consistent in adhering to a chosen course—an uncommon characteristic in statesmen. Their political ideologies were similar, and their views on diplomacy were almost identical. "Washington's foreign policy . . . was Hamilton's foreign policy."[69] "The story of the one is almost the story of the other."[70] Timothy Pickering, who knew both men better than any other contemporary, wrote: "Washington's acts . . . are so blended with the efficiency of Hamilton that I fear it will be difficult to find a biographer bold enough to do justice to the latter." He was writing in 1822, when the memory of Washington was universally cherished but Hamilton's claim to greatness was not yet recognized. Pickering was convinced that any writer would lose stature if he tried to give Hamilton his just due, and thus seem to diminish Washington's greatness.[71]

It seems reasonable to conclude that if Hamilton had written a farewell

66 Paltsits, *Washington's Farewell Address*, 75.

67 Washington to Hamilton, June 26, 1796, *WW*, XXXV, 101–104.

68 John Quincy Adams to Abigail Adams, February 8, 1797, *JQAW*, II, 109.

69 DeConde, *Entangling Alliance*, 508.

70 Broadus Mitchell, "Alexander Hamilton, His Friends and Foes," *The Historian*, Vol. XIX (February, 1957), 135.

71 Pickering to Nicholas Fish, July 30, 1822, Pickering Papers, Massachusetts Historical Society, Boston, XV, 279*a*. Pickering himself gathered material for a biography of Hamilton but never completed the task.

message entirely his own it would have differed in but few points from the joint production. It is unquestionably Washington's Farewell Address; but it is Hamilton's as well. It is the clearest statement ever made of Hamilton's mature political, diplomatic, social, and economic philosophy. "The memory of Hamilton shall live forever in the work."[72]

[72] Binney, *An Inquiry*, 115.

CHAPTER XV

The Adams Administration and the Quest for Peace

THE PRESIDENTIAL election of 1796, though dominated by the French question, brought no particular change in the nation's diplomatic perplexities. As vice-president, Adams had not greatly influenced foreign policy, for Washington had not often sought his advice. Upon assuming the presidency, Adams presented no new or startling proposals, and it was generally expected that he would continue along the path laid out by Washington and Hamilton. His son, still serving as minister at The Hague, wrote to him of the "delicate situation" in Europe and called attention to the need for preserving "the firmness, the spirit, and the dignity" of the government, while at the same time avoiding "a rupture with France."[1]

The election returned Thomas Jefferson to an active role in the national government. The possibility that he might be elected to the presidency had caused a wave of alarm throughout New England, as Madison had predicted. While the outcome of the election was still in doubt, Oliver Wolcott, Sr., claimed that all the Connecticut electors looked upon the election of Jefferson as "the worst of evils" and even expressed the hope that "the northern states would separate from the southern the moment that event shall take effect."[2] Jefferson was concerned about the northerners' hostile attitudes toward him. In an effort to counter them, he tried to cultivate Adams' friendship. He recognized Adams' talents and felt no jealousy at his success in the election; in fact, he appears actually to have preferred that Adams be elected. When it appeared that the electoral vote might result in a tie, he urged Madison to use his influence in the House of Representatives to assure Adams' election.[3] "I am his junior in life," wrote Jefferson, "was his junior in Congress, his junior in the diplomatic line, [and] his junior

[1] John Quincy Adams to John Adams, December 30, 1796, *JQAW*, II, 69.
[2] Oliver Wolcott, Sr., to Oliver Wolcott, Jr., December 12, 1796, Gibbs, I, 408–409.
[3] Jefferson to Madison, December 17, 1796, *JW*, IX, 351.

lately in the civil government." He suggested to Madison that the Republicans should work out an understanding with Adams if his policies proved satisfactory.[4]

When it became clear that Adams was the winner, Jefferson wrote a letter of congratulation, assuring Adams that he had never desired a different outcome and expressing the hope that the President would "be able to shun for us this war."[5] The letter was sent to Madison, who was then in Philadelphia, to be delivered or not, according to his judgment. Madison decided not to forward it, not because he disagreed with the purpose, but because he knew that Jefferson's modesty during the election had already made Adams kindly disposed toward Jefferson, and the letter might have the opposite effect.[6] Adams also showed a willingness to narrow the breach between the parties. He called on Jefferson at Philadelphia the day before the inauguration and entered into a "free conversation" concerning "the situation of our affairs with France."[7]

Any genuine rapprochement failed to be attained, however. Jefferson recorded that in the first cabinet meeting, held on March 6, 1797, Adams abandoned his impartial stance "and returned to his former party views."[8] Less than a month after the "free conversation" Adams wrote to Henry Knox that he was shocked by the thought that "such a character as Jefferson" might be elected president.[9] It soon became clear to Jefferson that Adams had indeed chosen to follow the Washington-Hamilton course in dealing with France. Later the Alien and Sedition Acts would accentuate party animosities. But Adams himself never moved as far from Jefferson as Hamilton or Washington had, nor did he later express the malignant feelings for Jefferson that he did for Hamilton. George Gibbs, who edited the Wolcott papers and spoke for the Hamilton Federalists, had as little use for the Adams wing of that party as he did for the Republicans. He accused Jefferson of deranging Adams' principles and setting him against Hamilton.[10]

The Adams administration "was born to trouble,"[11] and the discord with France, which was not of Adams' making, continued to harass the govern-

4 Jefferson to Madison, January 1, 1797, *ibid.*, 358.
5 Jefferson to Adams, December 28, 1796, *ibid.*, 357.
6 Madison to Jefferson, January 15, 1797, *MW*, VI, 303.
7 *JW*, I, 413–14.
8 *Ibid.*, 415.
9 March 30, 1797, *AW*, VIII, 535.
10 Gibbs, I, 457–59.
11 Stephen G. Kurtz, *The Presidency of John Adams* (New York, 1957), 239.

ment. Adams retained Pickering, Wolcott, and McHenry in his cabinet. Their loyalties were with Hamilton, who was cool toward Adams and was soon to become his enemy. Elbridge Gerry, archflatterer of Adams, intimated to the President that Pickering might not be entirely faithful to him.[12] Adams replied that "Pickering and all his colleagues are as much attached to me as I desire."[13] Time would prove him wrong.

Adams' inaugural address, presented on March 4, 1797, was characterized by statesmanship, scholarship, style, and solemnity appropriate to the occasion. Free of fulminations or bluster, it professed "esteem for the French nation" and a desire to preserve the Franco-American friendship through "amicable negotiations." Yet it also warned of "the pestilence of foreign influence." The nation's hard-won freedom to govern itself could be destroyed if the vote of but one presidential elector was "obtained by foreign nations by flattery or menaces, by fraud or violence, by terror, intrigue, or venality." If patient and reasonable negotiations should prove insufficient to vindicate the nation's rights and obtain "a reparation for the injuries that have been committed on our commerce, . . . by whatever nation," the facts would be laid before the members of Congress "that they may consider what further measures" should be taken.[14]

Hamilton thought that the change of administrations, "however undesirable in other respects," might work to the nation's advantage in resolving the controversy with France. Adams had not roused French "passion," and the change might "furnish a bridge [for France] to retreat over."[15]

It was a mistaken hope. The French were not yet ready to retreat and were not interested in any kind of bridge that Adams might be willing to provide. They were sorely disappointed to see one Federalist president replaced by another.

There was no friendship between Adams and Hamilton, though it is not clear when their coldness first arose. There is evidence that Adams resented being excluded from Washington's councils after 1790, when Hamilton was constantly being called upon for advice. Hamilton no doubt sensed Adams' attitude toward him, though there would be no open antagonism between them until 1798, when Adams would try to avoid giving Hamilton an army command. Their ill will cannot be attributed solely to their personality

[12] February 3, 1797, *AW*, VIII, 521.

[13] Adams to Gerry, February 13, 1797, *ibid.*, 523.

[14] Richardson, I, 218–22.

[15] Hamilton to Theodore Sedgwick, February 26, 1797, *HWL*, X, 239.

differences, great though they were, for in this respect Hamilton was farther from Washington than from Adams.

The new President received advice from many quarters—chiefly from those who respected him as a seasoned diplomat and a mature statesman. Henry Knox urged him to send Jefferson on a special mission to France. The latter would be warmly received by the French, Knox believed, because of his well-known views and his high position in the government; and the people at home would be likely to accept a treaty negotiated by the vice-president. The crisis was so great that Pinckney could hardly object.[16] The idea had already occurred to Adams; he had offered Jefferson such an appointment, but it had been politely declined.[17] Adams told Knox about the offer but added that upon further reflection he had concluded that it was improper to send so high-ranking an official on a diplomatic mission. Sending Jay to London in 1794, he said, had lowered the United States in the eyes of Europeans. Moreover, he was convinced that the French had no real respect for Jefferson, nor for any other American. He was convinced that the recent effort of the Directory to help Jefferson gain the presidency had been part of a larger plan. A Frenchman, he observed, "thinks that France ought to govern all nations, and that he ought to govern France."[18]

Hamilton did not feel close enough to the President to advise him directly, but he found indirect means to do so. In the interval between the election and the inauguration he showered letters upon important political leaders urging the appointment of two envoys to join Pinckney in Paris.[19] The day before the inauguration he sent Fisher Ames to the President to press upon him the necessity of such a commission. Adams was too busy at the time to consider the proposal thoroughly, but he did not reject it. He replied that the idea had occurred to him but that he wanted more time for thought and consultations and would "determine nothing suddenly." Unlike Washington and others, Adams was not in the least deterred by any thought of offending Pinckney by sending another envoy, but he had considered sending Madison and Hamilton "to join Mr. Pinckney, in a new commission."[20]

Adams sometimes failed to take his cabinet fully into his confidence—with unfortunate results. While he was considering the possibility of send-

[16] Knox to Adams, March 19, 1795, *AW*, VIII, 534.
[17] *JW*, I, 413–14.
[18] Adams to Knox, March 30, 1797, *AW*, VIII, 535–36.
[19] *HWL*, X, 200–41.
[20] Letter No. XII to the *Boston Patriot*, 1809, *AW*, IX, 282–84 and n.

ing Hamilton and Madison to France, he asked Wolcott merely what he would think of sending Madison. Wolcott, assuming the responsibility of speaking for the cabinet, amazed Adams by saying, "Mr. President, we are willing to resign." Adams rejected the offer, of course, and, assuming that he would have to forgo sending Madison also, abandoned the thought of sending Hamilton, though apparently Hamilton's name had never entered the discussion. Later he wrote that he had known the French would resent the appointment of Hamilton but would welcome that of Madison and that he had hoped they would "tolerate one for the sake of the other."[21] There for the moment Adams let the matter rest. He had yet not learned of Pinckney's reception in Paris and assumed that negotiations of some kind were under way.

Wolcott's shocked reaction to Adams' proposal to send Madison to Paris was understandable. He considered Madison to be Adet's choice for the appointment.[22] Madison had condemned Washington's French policy and had been the loudest Republican of them all in denouncing Jay's Treaty. From the floors of Congress he had continued demanding revisions in the treaty even after it had been ratified and proclaimed and offering "proofs" that Britain would not in consequence declare war on the United States.[23] Wolcott could have expected nothing less than that Madison, as the lone envoy, would have found a way to reopen the controversy, irritating the British and reinvigorating the pro-French party in the United States,[24] and in the process casting away the gains of the 1796 election, in which the people had demonstrated enough independence to place in office the man whom Adet had tried so hard to defeat. The cabinet would have been equally appalled if Adams had suggested sending Jefferson to Paris. That was one reason why the idea was so quickly abandoned.

In the third week after the inauguration the government was jolted by the news that the Directory members had refused to receive Pinckney and had driven him from the country under threat of arrest.[25] The rebuff was made more pointed by the affectionate farewells simultaneously bestowed on Monroe. "Depart with our regret," they told the latter. "In you we give up [an American representative] whose personal qualities did honor to that

[21] *Ibid.*, 286.
[22] Wolcott to Hamilton, March 31, 1797, Gibbs, I, 487.
[23] April 15, 1796, *Annals*, VI, 987.
[24] Oliver Wolcott, Jr., to Oliver Wolcott, Sr., March 20, 1797, Gibbs, I, 475–76.
[25] *ASPFR*, II, 6–10.

title." In keeping with the French strategy of separating the American people from the American government, the president of the Directory asked Monroe to "assure the good American people . . . that like them we adore liberty, . . . and they will find in the French people republican generosity."[26]

In response to this newest affront Adams called Congress into special session on May 15.[27] He told the members that the occasion was "extraordinary," but he did not become heated. The members of the Directory had assumed that Adet had broken off relations; they had nothing more to say and supposed that Pinckney could say nothing that would interest them. The Federalists considered the insult another step along a path of ill will, injury, and perverseness. "We must have war with them," declared Congressman Uriah Tracy, of Connecticut, "unless there is an alteration, either of men or measures."[28] Congressman Jeremiah Wadsworth, also of Connecticut, reported the "general opinion" in his state to be that "France intends war" and commented that, to him, war was better than a continuation of "our present state."[29] Hamilton complained that the French action had caused "the bitter cup of our sufferings to overflow."[30] Fisher Ames observed that, though war was a dreadful thing, so was "preference of peace to honor and real independence." He added bitterly, "France is feared as if her cut-throats could fraternize us, and loved by the multitude as if they were not cut-throats."[31]

George Washington, now a private citizen but still deeply concerned about foreign affairs, saw the nation facing a test that would determine whether it would "stand upon independent ground, or be directed in its political concerns by any other nation." It would soon be revealed "who are true Americans."[32]

In this critical period Hamilton let pass an opportunity to serve any personal political ambitions he may have had. If he had chosen, he could have raised a battle cry that, coming from him, would have carried the ring of consistency. For years he had anathematized the French revolutionaries. Though he had pressed for negotiations with them, at the news of Pinckney's rebuff he could have taken the logical position that further discussions

[26] Communicated by President Adams to Congress, May 16, 1797, *ibid.*, 12.
[27] March 25, 1797, Richardson, I, 222–23.
[28] Tracy to Oliver Wolcott, Sr., March 26, 1797, Gibbs, I, 478.
[29] Wadsworth to Oliver Wolcott, Jr., March 26, 1797, *ibid.*, 478–79.
[30] "The Warning," No. VI, March 27, 1797, *HWL*, VI, 257.
[31] Ames to Wolcott, March 24, 1797, Gibbs, I, 477.
[32] Washington to Thomas Pinckney, May 28, 1797, *WW*, XXXV, 452–53.

would be futile and dishonorable. As a persistent champion of resistance to French menaces he would have drawn a large following—although in a divided nation. A man of fewer principles or narrower vision might well have assumed that such a course would lead him to higher levels of power and fame; and even if it failed, the attempt would likely have been charged to zealous patriotism. Yet Hamilton was never an opportunist. To judge by his acts and his writings, he was not in the slightest degree tempted to such a course. The Federalists had a narrow majority in Congress, but with so many Americans still opposed to war with France, Hamilton's good sense told him that it would be folly to "rush the country into war."[33] Instead of calling for war, he held to his stated principles, which had proved successful during the crisis with Britain in 1794, and set out to prepare for the country a program of action. The underlying premise remained peaceful negotiation.

For their part, the Republicans maintained that Jay's Treaty was the source of the trouble. Upon hearing of the failure of Pinckney's mission, Madison said that French "resentment is the fruit of the British Treaty, which many of its zealous advocates begin now to acknowledge was an unwise and unfortunate measure."[34] In truth the French were venting their anger on the wrong man. Pinckney was no enemy of the French. Neither he nor his views were well known, even in the United States, and Adet, who evidently considered all Federalists inimical to the revolutionary cause, had misinformed the Directory.[35] Actually, Pinckney was a lukewarm Federalist at best and had often spoken in support of the French Revolution. He had the confidence of "the Jacobins of most of the southern states."[36] Hamilton described him as a "middle character" who had "too much French leaning to consider him, in conjunction with Jefferson or Madison, as perfectly safe." Therefore it seemed clear to Hamilton that at least one member of the proposed commission must be a strong Federalist.[37]

When it became generally known that Adams was planning further efforts to reopen discussions with France, the Republicans unanimously favored the move, but strong opposition rose among the Federalists. Hamilton was soon caught up in the controversy and found himself in the curious

[33] Morison, *The Life and Letters of Harrison Gray Otis*, I, 72.

[34] Madison to his father, March 12, 1797, *MW*, VI, 309.

[35] E. Wilson Lyon, "The Directory and the United States," *American Historical Review*, Vol. XLIII (April, 1938), 516–17.

[36] Rogers, *William Loughton Smith*, 299.

[37] Hamilton to Pickering, May 11, 1797, *HWL*, X, 262.

position of agreeing, at least on one point, with the Republicans. Though more insistent than ever before about the absolute necessity of defense measures, he continued to advocate negotiation. He deplored the "indignity" of the Directory's treatment of Pinckney, but "at this delicate crisis" he was concerned that "a course of conduct exactly proper . . . be adopted." He offered the secretary of state detailed recommendations: there should be a day of "humiliation and prayer," for Americans might be called on to defend their "firesides and . . . altars"; Congress should be convened at the earliest possible moment; the special commission should be approved by the Senate and sent to Paris without delay; new taxes should be levied to provide for national defense, including a navy and an army of 25,000 men; commerce should be convoyed or embargoed.[38]

Pickering's reaction to Hamilton's suggestions was not favorable. He replied that the decision to convene Congress had already been made and that the President himself had conceived the idea of proclaiming a national day of humiliation and prayer. The secretary could not see the "propriety" of initiating further discussions with France. The Directory had stated that it would not receive another emissary from the United States until the "grievances" had been redressed, and "all the important acts of the government must therefore be reversed before a minister can be admitted." Moreover, Pickering said, "this new mission is what the enemies of our government wish for." Careful not to offend Hamilton, Pickering "presumed" that Hamilton did not know the French had been "so peremptory" and urged him "to continue to communicate on public affairs, especially at the present interesting period."[39]

Pickering need not have worried on that score. Hamilton continued to plead for negotiations, to meet the French "on their own ground and disarm them of the argument that all has not been done which might have been done towards preserving peace." It seemed impossible to him that "the Directory can mean to say that they will shut the door to all explanations, even as to the *nature* and *measures* of redress of grievances which they require." Even if he were sure that the Directory would refuse all new representations, he would send the commission anyway for the effect it would have on the American people. It would be sound policy, "if such a

[38] Hamilton to Pickering, March 22, 1797, *ibid.*, 243–46.

[39] Pickering to Hamilton, March 26, 1797, Pickering Papers, Massachusetts Historical Society, Boston, VI, 249.

temper exists [in the Directory], to accumulate the proofs of it with a view to union at home." He had "not only a strong wish, but an extreme anxiety, that the measure in question . . . be adopted." The "interest" of the United States in peace was "a very powerful reason for attempting everything."[40]

Thus Hamilton's reasoning in 1797 was the same as that in 1794: peace was in the nation's interest. In his most personal correspondence with close friends in positions of power there is not the slightest indication that he ever desired war with France at any time, then or in the future—or that he was playing a well-calculated game to checkmate the Republicans. Yet in view of the great personal popularity gained from his peace efforts of 1797, his conduct has been characterized as merely "a good political move."[41]

Hamilton was well aware that his position was not a popular one among his fellow Federalists. Many of them had reached a "grim determination to have war with France."[42] Pickering was increasingly looked upon as a leader of this group. At first Hamilton was tactful in his efforts to influence the secretary. He employed political subtleties in reporting to Pickering that there was "an opinion industriously inculcated (which nobody better than myself knows to be false), that the *actual* administration are endeavoring to provoke a war." He added, "It is all important by the last possible sacrifice to confound this charge."[43]

The following day Hamilton wrote to Wolcott covering the same ground and then pointing out that France might ultimately win the war in Europe and that the United States might then have to stand alone. It was even possible that France might seek to "get rid of troublesome spirits" at home by sending them in an army to attack the United States. "Will it be wise," he asked, "to omit any thing to parry, if possible, these great risks?" In closing, he stated his position succinctly: "As in the case of England, so now, my opinion is, to exhaust the expedients of negotiation; and, at the same time, to prepare *vigorously* for the worst."[44]

The Federalists' prowar sentiments were growing steadily, however. George Cabot, the Federalist whom Hamilton wanted to serve on the commission, thought a "new embassy . . . would be disgraceful," would embroil

[40] Hamilton to Pickering, March 29, 1797, *HWL*, X, 246–47.

[41] Dumas Malone and Basil Rauch, *Empire for Liberty* (New York, 1960), I, 314.

[42] Bowers, *Jefferson and Hamilton*, 345. It would be impossible to substantiate Bowers' further conclusion that the New England Federalists were "in high glee over the prospects," unless he was referring solely to the prospects of discomfiting the Republicans.

[43] Hamilton to Pickering, March 29, 1797, *HWL*, X, 246–47.

[44] Hamilton to Wolcott, March 30, 1797, *HWL*, X, 248–49.

America in new controversies with Britain, and would strengthen "the French party within our country." The Republican on the commission would be sure to bring about these dire results by making senseless pro-French "propositions."[45] Caleb Strong, a High Federalist of Massachusetts, saw no hope for reaching any reasonable understanding with France, for the Directory members had indicated that they would not negotiate further unless the United States first performed "the penance they have prescribed." Without such abject submission the "new messengers" would be "kicked from the door."[46]

Wolcott believed that the time for negotiations had passed. As he wrote Hamilton, he too believed that any Republican serving on the commission could be expected to agree to damaging concessions to France. The result would be no new agreement—or at best an unpopular one—and the Republican emissary would find ways to cast all the blame on the Federalists and Jay's Treaty. The political repercussions at home "would deliver the country, bound hand and foot, to French influence." The administration must sail the ship of state with the force of the "steady gale" then blowing against France "or be assailed with a tornado which will throw everything into confusion."[47]

Hamilton thought that Wolcott was too pessimistic. "If Madison is well coupled," he wrote, "I do not think his intrigues can operate as you imagine." Referring again to the nation's interest in peace, Hamilton called attention to young Napoleon's recent victory over the Austrians and correctly predicted the dissolution of the European coalition against France. Moreover, the envoys to France could be given strict "instructions from which they may not deviate." Hamilton's earlier comradeship with Madison was reflected in his closing sentence: "Besides that, it is possible too much may be taken for granted with regard to Mr. Madison."[48]

From London, Rufus King had been supplying Hamilton with disheartening news and gloomy predictions. He had pointed out that the Directory had rebuffed Pinckney just after it had received news of Napoleon's victory in Italy. Austria was doggedly trying to continue the war, but could not do so without financial aid from Britain, and every bank in England, to the "dismay" of all, had stopped specie payment and could

[45] Cabot to Jeremiah Smith, April 17, 1797, Gibbs, I, 495.
[46] Caleb Strong to Wolcott, April 17, 1797, *ibid.*, 493.
[47] Wolcott to Hamilton, March 31, 1797, *ibid.*, 487.
[48] Hamilton to Wolcott, April 5, 1797, *HWL*, X, 251–52.

extend little aid to the Austrian emperor. France, he predicted, would continue to "harass and waste our commerce, regardless of justice," using Jay's Treaty as a pretext to cover the real design to subvert American independence. "Had we made no treaty her conduct would have been the same," he believed. France had demanded that Hamburg and Bremen cut off all commerce with Britain but had not, in return, treated them any better.[49]

In reply Hamilton agreed that if France continued to be successful on the field of battle it would "be too violent and imperious to meet us on any admissible ground." Yet he reaffirmed his policy of trying to renew diplomatic discussions while making preparations for war. He added that, on the brighter side, the misconduct of France was proving to be a "very powerful medicine for the political disease of our country" and that the President was following a course of prudence and firmness.[50] Those comments were echoed by George Cabot, who wrote to King that "opposition to the tyranny of France is every day growing more popular."[51]

Congressman William Smith of South Carolina, who had long fought Hamilton's battles in the House, now turned from him. Smith saw grave dangers in sending a new diplomatic mission to France. He seemed actually to fear the effects in the United States of an improvement in French conduct. If France saw that it could not overthrow the American government or force the abrogation of Jay's Treaty, it might "suddenly wheel about and generously forgive us." And "such a change favorable to us" would, he thought, "drive the great mass of knaves and fools [in the United States] back into her arms."[52]

Hamilton did his best to calm these fears. It was "unpleasant" to know, he wrote, that he "had for some time differed materially" from many of his friends on how to deal with the French menace, a difference resulting from his abhorrence of the prospect of war "with a political monster, which seems destined soon to have no competitor but England." The Federalists must not "feel and reason as the *Jacobins* [that is, the Republicans] did when Great Britain insulted and injured us." He would rather perish, with his family, he said, "than see the country disgraced"; nevertheless, the United States must "combine energy with moderation." "God grant that the public

[49] King to Hamilton, March 8, 1797, *KC*, II, 154.

[50] Hamilton to King, April 8, 1797, *HWL*, X, 255.

[51] Cabot to King, *KC*, II, 170.

[52] Smith to King, April 3, 1797, *ibid.*, 165–66.

interest may not be sacrificed at the shrine of irritation and mistaken pride."[53]

Smith was not convinced. Any further discussions, he thought, should be conducted through Pinckney alone, who could be sent new instructions and augmented powers to negotiate. Dispatching additional envoys might offend Pinckney and thereby alienate many of the administration's friends in the south.[54]

The cabinet "rebellion" against Hamilton was not of long duration. Nor was the disagreement an acrimonious one. Relations between the cabinet members and Hamilton remained cordial—evidence of his continuing influence upon them. Moreover, Pickering and Wolcott had little chance of carrying the day, since Hamilton's position largely coincided with Adams'.

In the course of preparing his message to Congress, the President wrote to the members of his cabinet requesting their opinions about whether another envoy should be sent to Paris and what proposals or demands should be made.[55] His questions revealed his clear comprehension of the issues and of the procedures that would have to be followed.

The heads of departments in turn wrote to Hamilton requesting his views. McHenry relayed Hamilton's reply to him directly to the President.[56] Thus it was that some of Hamilton's proposals—even to exact wording—found their way into the President's message.

The nation remained divided, and not altogether along party lines. Thoughts turned toward the next session of Congress. Pickering thought that it would be a good idea to publish the official reports about the treatment Pinckney had been subjected to in Paris. Hamilton advised against immediate publication, which, he said, might add to the current "calumny" that the government was courting trouble with France; instead, he would present the reports to Congress (and thus the nation) during the forthcoming session of the legislature. This procedure would not appear to be an

[53] Hamilton to Smith, April 5, 10, 1797, *HWL*, X, 253–54, 256.

[54] Smith to Hamilton, May 1, 1797, HPLC; cited by Rogers, *William Loughton Smith*, 299. This exchange between two friends and allies of many years is interesting for the light it sheds on their relationship. Jefferson spoke of Smith as a mere tool of Hamilton, and some historians have accepted that appraisal. On the contrary, Rogers establishes beyond question that Smith was a man of superior ability, fully capable of independent thought. These qualities are evident in the *Annals*. In Congress, Smith delivered carefully prepared speeches, which seem to reflect Hamilton's influence, but he also carried arguments through long debates, speaking repeatedly on the issues at hand and displaying excellent powers of reasoning.

[55] April 14, 1797, *AW*, VIII, 540–41.

[56] Hamilton to McHenry, March, 1797, *HWL*, X, 241–43.

artful maneuver and would probably be more damaging to the Republican position.[57]

Adams completed his message to Congress. Though he complained to Henry Knox of the "multiplicity of business" his duties entailed in that critical period, he indicated his determination to do everything reasonable to settle the disputes with France. He would not see his nation's honor violated, however. "America is not scared," he wrote to his son, and added, "I have great confidence in my saddle."[58] In this spirit he went before Congress on May 16, 1797.

The President's message, though firm, was conciliatory toward France. In reviewing America's actions, he said, he had found nothing that should have given offense to France. The Directory's refusal to receive a minister from the United States "until we have acceded to their demands with discussion . . . is to treat us neither as allies nor as friends, nor as a sovereign state." Yet, he said, he had decided to "institute a fresh attempt at negotiation," and he was ready to "redress" any injuries the Directory could prove had been perpetrated by the American government. In the meantime he recommended that Congress find new sources of revenue and attend to the nation's defense.[59]

The message evoked praise from the Federalists and condemnation from the Republicans. According to the accepted rules of courtesy of the time, each house of Congress went to work preparing an address to the President setting forth its own position on major points mentioned in the President's message. Since the Federalists were in the majority, the drafting committees of both houses produced statements supporting Adams' position. The result was weeks of acrimonious debate in both houses, which gradually encompassed the whole field of Franco-American relations. The incomplete reports of the debates in the House of Representatives reveal a conflict that few, if any, wanted though for many days none could check.[60] The more moderate legislators tried again and again to halt the debate and settle for a polite and noncontroversial response to the President; but emotions were too strong, and too many men wanted the last word. The Republicans would not agree with the President that American policy had been fair and just

[57] Hamilton to Pickering, April 1, 1797, *ibid.*, 250.

[58] Adams to Henry Knox, March 30, 1797, Adams to John Quincy Adams, March 31, 1797, *AW*, VIII, 535–37.

[59] Richardson, I, 223–29.

[60] *Annals*, VII, 67–232.

toward France and that France had broken off diplomatic relations for no adequate reason. The proposals for defense measures raised the controversy to its highest pitch throughout the government; and in the heat of the argument words were exchanged that make strange reading for twentieth-century Americans.

Jefferson condemned the "threatening posture" of Adams' speech, which he feared would "provoke hostilities."[61] To him Jay's Treaty was still the root of the trouble. "Common error, common censure, and common efforts of defense had formed the treaty majority into a common band," and they had "feared to separate even on other subjects." Early in the year their ties had begun to loosen, and their phalanx separate a little, but this favorable development he saw "blasted . . . by the nature of the appeal which the President made to the nation, the occasion for which had confessedly sprung from the fatal British treaty."[62]

The Federalists held that the increasing French depredations on American commerce, coupled with their refusal to negotiate, had resulted from their victories over their enemies on the Continent and their determination to defeat Britain by cutting off British commerce by any means, fair or foul. The French would have proceeded on that course, they believed, treaty or no treaty.[63] The Federalists professed to be shocked by Republican intemperance. William Smith wrote, "Giles, Gallatin, Nickolas, Livingston, Swanwick, and Sam Smith have disgraced the country by their speeches; Giles and Livingston were hours in apologizing for France and abusing the government of this country and the British treaty; but Sam S[mith], who spoke yesterday, surpassed them all."[64]

The Republicans chose to cast the blame, not on the President directly, but, as in Washington's administration, upon his advisers. The Republican newspaper, the *Philadelphia Aurora,* which had been heartened by the earlier prospect of winning Adams over to Jefferson's views, tried to explain the President's sternness in his May 16 address: "His men Timothy and Oliver have fed him upon pepperpot these three weeks past in order to bring his nerves to a proper anti-gallican tone."[65]

[61] Jefferson to Colonel Bell, May 18, 1797, *JW*, IX, 386.

[62] Jefferson to Burr, June 17, 1797, *ibid.*, 400–401.

[63] William Smith, House of Representatives, May 22, 1797, *Annals*, VII, 57.

[64] Smith to Ralph Izard, May 23, 1797, "South Carolina Federalist Correspondence, 1789–1797," *American Historical Review*, Vol. XIV (July, 1909), 787.

[65] Cited by Kurtz, *The Presidency of John Adams*, 232.

In 1797 party loyalty had not yet become a primary force in American politics. Each side reached out for adherents, not to gain offices and patronage, but with the larger purpose of advancing policies it considered essential for the nation's welfare. Opponents were therefore looked upon not merely as political adversaries but, more important, as enemies of the country. Hamilton and others of the Federalist persuasion believed the country's independence to be jeopardized by the Republicans, who had established a working arrangement with the French revolutionaries, now arrogant from European successes. Jefferson and his Republican followers were convinced that the Federalists had already undermined the nation's independence by accepting Jay's Treaty and that they were now trying to plunge the nation into war with France, the world's champion of human liberty.

Republicans and Federalists were in agreement about the need for national unity, and each group strove to rally the nation around its own standards. Jefferson deplored the "higher style of political difference" in the country. "Political dissension" he considered "a less evil than the lethargy of despotism, but still . . . a great evil, and it would be worthy the efforts of the patriot as of the philosopher to exclude its influence . . . from social life."[66]

Gouverneur Morris had long held that "the French Directory would not risk high language to us, if they had not received previous assurances that the [American] people would force our government to sacrifice the national interest."[67] Washington was sure that the French would not have gone so far if they had not been "encouraged to do so by a party among ourselves." That party, he feared, was "determined to advocate French measures under *all* circumstances."[68] The same view was often expressed in Hamilton's writings.

At length the special session of Congress did enact defense measures, but by narrow margins, and with the Republicans fighting the bills step by step. They preferred to leave the harbors unfortified, believing that the administration would not then dare adopt a "haughty" attitude toward France; and they did not want American warships to put to sea lest they "provoke" the French to combat. Until 1798 few Republicans were convinced by Federalist arguments that preparedness makes for peace or that during a period of naval warfare prudence called for defensive measures or even that armed

[66] Jefferson to Thomas Pinckney, May 29, 1797, *JW*, IX, 388–89.

[67] Morris to Hamilton, March 4, 1796, *HWH*, VI, 90.

[68] Washington to Pickering, August 29, 1797, *WW*, XXXVI, 19; Washington to King, June 25, 1797, *ibid.*, XXXV, 475.

vessels were needed to repel French privateers. While the three frigates authorized earlier by Congress were under construction, Joshua Coit of Connecticut expressed the hope that "the most distant idea of manning them would not enter gentlemen's minds."[69] Albert Gallatin told the House of Representatives that he was voting against an appropriation to complete them for fear they would go to sea.[70] While the Senate was debating the naval bill, designed to protect "the citizens of the United States and the seacoasts of the United States," a motion was offered to amend it to read "*within* the harbors and *on* the seacoast." The motion was narrowly defeated by a vote of 15 to 13.[71] Hoping to prevent the use of warships as escorts for American merchant vessels, Giles moved to restrict the armed ships to action "within the jurisdiction of the United States." Rutledge objected that this restriction would prevent an American ship of war from pursuing a pirate vessel "across the line." Even so, Giles refused to alter his stand. His lack of understanding of naval warfare and hostile landing operations was shown in his opposition to fortifying harbors on the grounds that the nation had an "extensive seacoast, and it was not to be expected that an enemy would choose to come to precisely the place where a fortification stands."[72]

A House amendment to the military appropriation bill called for an additional $16,085 to provide for "the purchase of horses and the equipment of the cavalry." The amendment passed, over the protest of Joseph B. Varnum of Massachusetts, who "could not see why a body of cavalry should be kept up in a time of peace."[73]

Jefferson watched with dismay as the Senate voted out naval and military bills, modest though their provisions were. He hoped that "the Representatives will concur in none of these measures, though their divisions hitherto have been so equal as to leave us under doubt and apprehension." Learning of a rumor that the Directory had proposed to declare war against the United States and had only been restrained by the Council of Ancients (the upper chamber of the French legislature), he observed dolefully, "Thus we see two nations who love one another affectionately, brought by the ill temper of their executive administrations, to the very brink of a necessity to

69 House of Representatives, February 18, 1797, *Annals*, VI, 2201.
70 March 2, 1797, *ibid.*, 2341.
71 March 2, 1797, *ibid.*, 2337. Italics added.
72 June 5, 10, 1797, *ibid.*, VII, 240, 294.
73 March 2, 1797, *ibid.*, VI, 2337.

imbrue their hands in the blood of each other." By now he saw "little hope of peace" and anticipated "the burning of our seaports, [and] havoc of our frontiers." He could barely restrain himself, he said, "from joining in the wish of Silas Deane, that there were an ocean of fire between us and the old world."[74]

Problems multiplied. How could the nation finance an effective defense program, much less a war with France? Wolcott foresaw that "finances will be hereafter difficult to manage." Hamilton was more hopeful. He perceived many untapped sources of revenue—"nor is the field narrow," he observed. He believed that two million dollars could be collected annually through a tax on buildings, at so much a room, stamp taxes, and taxes on saddle horses and salt. He would not recommend a federal tax on land unless war broke out.[75]

In the midst of these critical decisions, the old conflict with Spain over Mississippi River rights flared up again, a conflict that had presumably been settled by Pinckney's Treaty of 1795. Prime Minister Godoy had thought that the treaty barred Britain from the Mississippi. When in 1796 the United States and Britain had proclaimed as still binding the provisions of Jay's Treaty and the Treaty of Paris, recognizing mutual navigation rights on the river, Godoy had suspended execution of Pinckney's Treaty and refused to remove the remaining Spanish troops from the region north of the thirty-first parallel. He had hoped thereby to so agitate the Americans in the West that they would either force their government to revoke Jay's Treaty or rebel. When the westerners failed to react as he hoped, Godoy began searching for some profitable means of getting rid of Spanish-held territory on the lower Mississippi.[76] The French tried to use the Anglo-American "entente" to persuade Spain to cede Louisiana to France on the grounds that the territory would then serve as a buffer to prevent further encroachments by the United States into Spanish possessions. But Godoy was looking for a better bargain than that.[77]

While in Paris, Monroe had foreseen the possibility of some such transaction but had placed his faith in French good will. As late as the fall of

[74] Jefferson to French Strother, June 8, 1797, Jefferson to Aaron Burr, June 17, 1797, Jefferson to Thomas Pinckney, May 29, 1797, Jefferson to Elbridge Gerry, May 13, 1797, *JW*, IX, 396–97, 404, 389, 385.

[75] Wolcott to Hamilton, March 31, 1797, Hamilton to Wolcott, June 6, 1797, Gibbs, I, 488, 544–45.

[76] A. P. Whitaker, "The Retrocession of Louisiana in Spanish Policy," *American Historical Review*, Vol. XXXIX (April, 1934), 460–62.

[77] Lyon, *Louisiana in French Diplomacy*, 83.

1796 he had fancied that the French might induce Spain to cede the region to the United States.[78] It was clear to United States officials at home, however, that France was the only logical European "purchaser" of the territory. Andrew Ellicot, the American surveyor commissioned to work with the Spaniards in laying out the boundary line called for in Pinckney's Treaty, was sent to Natchez to look for conspiracies. He found a "tropical profusion" of them, but none that was yet ripe for action.[79]

Some Federalists, having little understanding of the attitudes of the western settlers, assumed that they were ready to defect. Early in 1797, Fisher Ames commented that "the western country scarcely calls itself dependent on the Union" and added that "France is ready to hold Louisiana."[80] Wolcott recommended to President Adams that if negotiations with France reached the point that a revision of the alliance seemed feasible, the United States should insist on stipulations that would prevent France from acquiring Canada or Louisiana.[81] Adams, deeply disturbed by the developments, informed Congress on June 12, 1797, that Spain had refused to complete the demarcation of the treaty boundary line.[82] Pickering sent the same information to King in London. He was afraid that France was trying to acquire Louisiana in order to gain control of the United States, "a plan so dangerous to our union and peace."[83] Similar apprehensions were felt in the South. Congressman William Barry Grove of North Carolina thought that it was "pretty well understood that French influence" was controlling Spanish action. The prospect of French acquisition of Louisiana and Canada was an alarming one; the French were so powerful and ambitious that they would "become troublesome neighbors."[84] Later in the year Grove heard a "flying report" that French garrisons were already taking over some of the posts on the Mississippi.[85]

Adams moved steadily ahead with his announced plan of sending new envoys to France. He decided that Pinckney, who was awaiting instructions at Amsterdam, should be one of the three nominees. He also wanted to send

78 Monroe to William Short, May 30, 1795, Monroe to Pickering, September 10, 1796, *JMW*, II, 289–90.

79 A. P. Whitaker, *The Mississippi Question, 1795–1803* (New York, 1934), 102–103.

80 Ames to Hamilton, January 26, 1797, *HWH*, VI, 200.

81 Wolcott to Adams, April 25, 1797, Gibbs, I, 513.

82 Richardson, I, 236.

83 Pickering to King, June 20, 1797, *KC*, II, 192.

84 Grove to James Hogg, June 24, 1797, Henry Gilbert Wagstaff (ed.), "Letters of William Barry Grove," *James Sprunt Historical Publications*, Vol. IX, No. 2, 62.

85 Grove to Hogg, December 18, 1797, *ibid.*, 65.

John Marshall of Virginia. These men would represent the Federalists. For the third envoy, a Republican, the choice seemed to lie between Francis Dana and Elbridge Gerry, both of Massachusetts. Adams conferred with his cabinet and congressional leaders. He found that "they all preferred Mr. Dana." When Dana declined the appointment, Adams again proposed Gerry's name to the cabinet. The members "unanimously were against him." Adams later wrote of the incident: "Such inveterate prejudice shocked me. I said nothing, but was determined I would not be the slave of it. [Gerry] was nominated and approved."[86] The President emphatically warned Gerry not to engage in strife with his Federalist colleagues. "You have known enough of the unpleasant effects of disunion among ministers," he wrote, "to convince you of the necessity of avoiding it, like a rock or quicksand."[87] Gerry's nomination was a plausible one, and Adams was not precipitate in his decision. But the criticism of the appointment, plus Gerry's behavior in Paris, was to call for years of explaining on Adams' part.

Gerry and Marshall were on their way by midsummer, and on October 4, 1797, the three men were in Paris, eager to begin their mission. A significant step had been taken. By sending the emissaries to France the American government had again demonstrated its preference for settling disputes at the conference table, even in the face of continuing provocation. The world paid little attention, but the American people were impressed, though not entirely favorably.

Jefferson expressed "infinite joy" at Gerry's appointment[88] but was unhappy about the two Federalist appointments. "If strong and earnest negotiations had been meant," he wrote to Burr, all envoys chosen for the task would have been "persons strongly and earnestly attached to the alliance of 1778." He deplored the "secrecy and mystery" of Adams' actions, which he compared to that of Washington's administration.[89]

A segment of Federalists were equally unreconciled to the inclusion of a Republican in the mission; Theodore Sedgwick, for example, thought that no appointment could have been "more injudicious" than Gerry's. But most Senate Federalists apparently voted for the appointment; otherwise it could not have been approved.[90]

86 Letter No. XIII to the *Boston Patriot*, 1809, *AW*, IX, 287.
87 Adams to Gerry, *ibid.*, VIII, 547–48.
88 James T. Austin, *The Life of Elbridge Gerry* (Boston, 1827–29), II, 154.
89 June 17, 1797, *JW*, 402–403.
90 Sedgwick to King, June 24, 1797, *KC*, II, 193.

Once the mission was under way, there was some lessening of tension—and of pro-French enthusiasm. Supreme Court Justice James Iredell, North Carolina Federalist, reported, "The French fever is abating in the country, but is still much higher than I could wish."[91] In June, 1797, Hamilton sensed that the temper of the country was mending daily and that the subversive French influence was waning.[92] The administration had adopted his recommendations for dealing with the crisis, and he was hopeful, though not so sanguine that he would be totally unprepared for the new storm that was soon to sweep the nation.

[91] Iredell to Wolcott, June 5, 1797, Gibbs, I, 542–43.

[92] Hamilton to King, June 6, 1797, Hamilton to Washington, August 28, 1797, *HWL*, X, 267, 273.

CHAPTER XVI

Hamilton and the XYZ Affair

THE DEPARTURE of Marshall, Pinckney, and Gerry for Paris was not the personal victory for Hamilton that Jay's mission to London had been. Unlike Washington, Adams did not have to be convinced of the need for negotiation. Yet, for all that, it was a triumph worth noting. The Federalists in the Senate would probably have defeated the move if Hamilton had remained quiet, and they would certainly have blocked it if Hamilton had added his influence to that of the Federalist cabinet members and senators who opposed it. In that case Adams, whose messages to Congress had already offended the Republicans, would quickly have found himself a man without a party.

Now Americans could but wait—some with hope, some with apprehensions—while their emissaries made yet another effort at conciliation. Perhaps the United States showed too much forbearance. France had violated the treaties of 1778 from the opening of the war with Britain in 1793. There is merit in the observation that Washington should have declared the "treaties with France ended" in 1793. It may be true that both Washington and Adams were "too patient."[1] But there were many factors to be considered. The war in Europe might soon end, and the French alliance could prove a valuable counter to subsequent British and Spanish moves. Moreover, terminating the alliance might lead to war with France—a possibility not to be dismissed lightly, in view of the nation's divided and defenseless condition. Therefore, most Americans supported their government's determination to avoid hasty action and to try once more to reach an amicable agreement.

While Adams waited for news from Paris, Monroe enlivened the scene at Philadelphia. After his departure from Paris he had spent some time touring Europe and awaiting a propitious season to cross the Atlantic.[2] Upon returning to Philadelphia in the summer of 1797, he was honored at a public dinner by a number of Republican notables, who dined with the flag of France flying over their heads. General Victor Collot, who had been spying out the Mississippi area to facilitate the Directory's scheme to seize it, also attended the celebration. The Federalists were scandalized. As Hamilton's son later described the occasion, Jefferson gave a toast to the "success and prosperity" of France, at a time, as the younger Hamilton pointed out, that that country was engaged in "open hostilities" against the United States. "After an American envoy had been menaced with imprisonment and driven ignominiously from Paris to a land not permitted to be neutral," Hamilton wrote, "the second officer of this Republic is seen, amid loud applauses, pouring out libations to the prosperity of a nation then plundering her commerce—to the success of the enemy of his country."[3]

Monroe, deeply resentful about his recall, seized the occasion to demand that Secretary of State Pickering give the reasons for his dismissal so that he could defend himself from imputations of incompetence or poor judgment. He acknowledged the authority of the executive to "censure and remove a public minister," but that authority, he said, should "be exercised according to the rules of justice." He demanded a "statement as a matter of right."[4] He wrote again the following day, a Saturday, demanding a reply by "Thursday next."[5] Failing to receive one, he became even more pointed in his demands: "I put too high a value upon the blessings of an honest fame, and have too long enjoyed that blessing, in the estimation of my countrymen, to suffer myself to be robbed of it by any description of persons, and under any pretense whatever." He asked whether the President had constitutional authority to censure or remove an officer without sufficient cause. Was not the President accountable, both to the public and to the injured party? He asked for an enumeration of the charges against him and the names of the "informers."[6]

These demands placed Pickering in an embarrassing situation. He could scarcely refuse to answer questions from so notable a public servant as Monroe; yet he knew that any frank explanation of the reasons for the recall would be fuel for the fires of the opposition. Consequently, he sought safety

[1] Bemis, *A Diplomatic History of the United States*, 112–13.

[2] Cresson, *James Monroe*, 154.

[3] John Church Hamilton, *History of the Republic of the United States, as Traced in the Writings of Alexander Hamilton and His Contemporaries* (New York, 1857–64), VII, 74.

[4] Monroe to Pickering, *JMW*, III, 67.

[5] Monroe to Pickering, *ibid.*, 68.

[6] Monroe to Pickering, July 19, 1797, *ibid.*, 70–73.

in generalities. In reply he referred to the Constitution, noting that all appointive officers except judges "hold their offices during the pleasure of the President of the United States." Compliance with the former envoy's request for particulars might "form an improper, inconvenient, and unwise precedent." He could not, "for the sake of indulging [Monroe's] sensibility, sacrifice a great national principle" and in the future "expose the Executive to perpetual altercations and controversies with officers removed." After this disclaimer Pickering proceeded to answer Monroe, though he wrote in general terms. Although a minister's "official communications" might have "a fair appearance," he said, that minister might deserve dismissal if he had held "intimate and improper correspondence on political subjects with men known to be hostile to the government he represents and whose actions tend to its subversion. He may even from mistaken views of the interests of his own country countenance and invite a conduct in another, derogatory from its dignity and injurious to those interests."[7]

Monroe was outraged. In reply he paraphrased Pickering's letter, making it sound much more offensive than the original. Surely, said he, if a minister allowed himself to become a "tool" or "partisan" of another government and worked for the "disorganization" of his own country, he "should be dismissed and punished.... But do you mean to apply any of those imputations to me?" he asked baldly. "If so, why not avow it and present your proof?" He probably stung the secretary most severely with his added comment that the Washington administration had been fully aware of the sentiments he had expressed in the Senate (presumably concerning the controversies with Britain and France) before asking him to take on ministerial functions.[8] He thus implied, as he had earlier to Madison, that Washington sent him to Paris to keep the ally pacified while Jay was in London negotiating away the interests of both France and the United States. John Quincy Adams later observed that Monroe seemed to think that "the tenure of the President's pleasure . . . meant the pleasure of Mr. Monroe."[9]

There followed an exchange of private, unofficial letters between Monroe and Pickering in which the latter offered to give Monroe the information he wanted "as an individual citizen." McHenry and Attorney General Charles Lee, he said, were willing to do the same thing.[10] Monroe refused to deal

[7] Pickering to Monroe, July 24, 1797, *ibid.*, 75–76n.

[8] Monroe to Pickering, July 31, 1797, *ibid.*, 79–81.

[9] John Quincy Adams to William Vans Murray, October 26, 1797, *JQAW*, II, 217.

[10] Pickering to Monroe, July 25, 1797, *JMW*, III, 84n.

with the situation on any but an official basis and wrote Pickering another official letter condemning the secretary in abusive terms. He had not really expected "a candid answer," he said, but one "dealing in hints and innuendos," disguising the facts "by every possible artifice which interest and ingenuity could suggest, because I knew the real motive could not be avowed."[11]

Pickering sought to calm his nerves by writing to Washington about the exchange. He told his former superior that Monroe's refusal to keep the information confidential proved the correctness of his original supposition that the demand had been made "*in order to be denied*."[12] It is obvious that Monroe was not really trying to learn the reasons for his dismissal; his correspondence with friends reveals that he felt certain that he already knew them. And there is no doubt that it would have gratified him to have an official acknowledgment from the Department of State that he had been recalled for opposing Jay's Treaty, for expressing friendship for France, and for carrying on "subversive" correspondence with pro-French Americans. Such an admission would have been a choice weapon for Republican propagandists.

Washington refused to take the matter seriously. He was convinced that Monroe had spent more time in Paris promoting the interests of the Republican party than he had spent advancing the interests of the United States. It was Pickering's intention to send Washington copies of the Monroe correspondence; but before he could do so, Monroe released it to the newspapers. The former President then observed laconically, "I perceive Mr. Monroe has opened a battery," and predicted, "His artillery will recoil upon himself."[13] The attitude of the Sage of Mount Vernon would have been no surprise to Monroe, for their distrust was mutual.

During his correspondence with Pickering, Monroe urged Jefferson to "acknowledge" his authorship of the famous letter to Philip Mazzei and justify the letter on the basis that "the principles of our Revolution and of Republican government have been substantially swerved from of late in many respects." In this way, Monroe said, the question could be brought before the public and lift "the spirits of the honest part of the community."[14]

[11] Monroe to Pickering, July 31, 1797, *ibid.*, II, 75, 84–85.

[12] Pickering to Washington, August 9, 1794, *ibid.*, 384 n.

[13] Washington to McHenry, August 4, 1797, *WW*, XXXVI, 8.

[14] Monroe to Jefferson, July 12, 1797, *JMW*, III, 69–70. In the letter to Mazzei, written on April 24, 1796, and later published in the United States, Jefferson indirectly criticized both Washington and Hamilton as "Samsons in the field & Solomons in the councils, but who have had their heads shorn by the harlot England."

The advice was of no avail; Jefferson was too discreet to attack Washington in the open.

Monroe, feeling certain that the people were "ready to back those who go most forward,"[15] decided to place the issue before the public himself. In his final letter to Pickering he maintained that since their fellow citizens were interested in the problem and could properly "estimate yours and my conduct," it was his intention "to carry the subject before that enlightened and impartial tribunal, with all the lights" he possessed.[16] He then took up the task of writing an exhaustive account of his ministry to Paris. It was a laborious undertaking, as revealed by his correspondence with Jefferson and Madison. He was careful with details, gave the dates of relevant documents, and cited many illustrations of the French resentments growing out of Jay's Treaty and other acts and slights of the administration. He employed all his skills to produce a lengthy, polished, persuasive treatise. He sometimes referred to it as his "book."[17] He entitled the work "A View of the Conduct of the Executive . . . ," thus making it clear that his chief purpose was not to defend his own conduct but to impeach the President, Secretary of State, and the Federalists generally.

In the work he described the circumstances of his appointment as minister to France in 1794, noting his surprise at the appointment and the administration's assurance that the central purpose of the mission was to work for an improvement in relations with France. He had been officially informed, he said, that he was being asked to replace Morris because of his sympathy for France. Monroe did not explicitly accuse Washington of sending him to deceive the French while Jay was negotiating an anti-French treaty at London, but he presented the facts in such a light and in such a sequence as to convince any Republican, at least, that that was the President's real motive. He first reported that the Department of State had informed him that Jay was instructed "to obtain immediate compensation for our plundered property and restitution of the posts." Later he described these two subjects as the "only" business Jay was authorized to discuss. Several pages later he described his annoyance at learning that Jay might be negotiating for a commercial treaty beyond the area "to which his [Jay's] powers were restricted," and still later he emphasized his shock at the news of a "commercial treaty actually concluded."

[15] Monroe to Jefferson, November, 1797, *ibid.*, 88.

[16] Monroe to Pickering, July 31, 1797, *ibid.*, 84.

[17] *Ibid.*, Appendix, 383–457.

Monroe also described his great embarrassment when the French officials became convinced that he had been sent to Paris only to "amuse and deceive" them. He had wanted to leave France, he wrote, as soon as he learned that Jay had agreed that British cruisers could intercept American foodstuffs en route to famine-ridden France—an agreement he described as indicating an American preference for "the system of kings [over] starving France." He remained in France only because he realized that his departure would simply confirm French suspicions of him and deepen their resentment against the United States. The French grew cold toward him, nevertheless, until they learned that he had been repudiated and recalled by the authorities at Philadelphia.

The most telling blow that Monroe struck against Washington and Pickering was his insistence that the French government and people had America's best interests at heart, that they had responded cordially to his message of good will and had checked their attacks on American commerce, and that, until the signing of Jay's Treaty, they had had every intention of continuing as a faithful ally of the United States. In short Monroe himself, like Adet and other French leaders, looked upon that treaty as a willful abandonment of republicanism at home and abroad.

Monroe's work gave renewed hope to his fellow Republicans, and both they and the Federalists hurried to obtain copies. The first printing was not large enough to meet the demand, and the report soon went through three editions. The Federalists hoped that it would provide evidence of the faithlessness of Republicans and Frenchmen and of Monroe's supposed betrayal of Washington. Republicans hoped for a view of the inner workings of the Federalist administration and of European diplomacy, as well as for further proofs of the "monarchical" trends of the Federalists and the evil results of Jay's Treaty. It is so well written that it remains an absorbing document today; to Monroe's contemporaries, whose lives were intimately involved in the events, it was enthralling.

Reactions were immediately forthcoming. Apparently the adherents of each party found exactly what they were looking for. There followed a series of pamphlets and letters to the newspapers in which "Federalists and Republicans damaged each other's reputations as much as they could."[18] Monroe's editor presented an interesting collection of comments on the work from undated correspondence of leading Republicans and Federalists. Jeffer-

[18] Daniel C. Gilman, *James Monroe* (Boston, 1883), 71.

son had heard "unqualified eulogies both on the matter and manner by all who are not hostile to it from principle." Madison wrote to Jefferson that if the account did not "open the eyes of the people, their blindness must be incurable." John Taylor of Carolina read it with "warmest approbation," though he found its contents "not at all surprising."

On the Federalist side, Robert Goodloe Harper found the work a "complete justification . . . for Monroe's recall." Wolcott predicted that it would make "no impression beyond the circle of Tom Paine's admirers." Pickering saw it as Monroe's "death warrant" (presumably because of its attack on Washington).[19] John Quincy Adams wrote that "Monroe's greatest enemy is himself, and his own book."[20] Washington pored over Monroe's "View" and wrote profuse comments in the margin of his copy that make clear his final position on Monroe and the unfortunate mission.[21] In fact, it would be impossible to gain a clear understanding of Washington's attitude toward the Jay negotiations and the controversy with France without this remarkable set of comments.[22]

Washington had too much self-assurance to react to Monroe's work with bitterness. In a few places he even responded with some mild flashes of humor, and he made numerous points in rebuttal, elaborating the positions he had taken earlier. He reaffirmed his belief in the necessity for the Jay negotiations and in his conviction that they were properly conducted. He denied having dealt with Monroe or with the French deceitfully, and he continued to hold Monroe guilty of having bungled his task at Paris by disseminating Republican propaganda. He supported the accusations of Pickering and John Quincy Adams that French "disgust" at Jay's Treaty was an outgrowth of Monroe's own objections to it. "Who were the contrivers of this disgust?" asked Washington. "Let the French Party in the United States and the British debtors therein answer the question." That comment was a reflection of John Quincy Adams' charge that Americans in England were "almost universally" in debt to British merchants and would therefore welcome an Anglo-American war in hopes that it "would serve as a sponge for their debts." The young Adams even accused Monroe of

[19] *JMW*, III, 385n.

[20] John Quincy Adams to William Vans Murray, December 8, 1798, *JQAW*, II, 379.

[21] *WW*, XXXVI, 194–237.

[22] Gilman, *James Monroe*, 70. When writing his biography of Monroe in the 1880's, Gilman was unable to find the copy of the "View" in which Washington had written his comments and therefore used Sparks's transcription of the notes. The copy with Washington's original notes is now in the Harvard College Library.

deliberately encouraging the Directory to rebuff Pinckney upon his arrival at Paris.[23] Washington was deeply influenced by Adams' correspondence.

Washington's notes were written for posterity. It would have been beneath his dignity to strike back publicly at Monroe, whom he considered a man of small caliber. He was willing to leave the subject before "the tribunal [of public opinion] to which [Monroe] himself [had] appealed."[24] Had he published a crushing rebuttal, Monroe's subsequent political career might well have suffered severe damage.

During the course of the controversies produced by Monroe's reports, Americans were besieged by reports of continuous French attacks at sea. The fate of the peace mission in France was not yet known, and Republican ardor for the French began to die away. Hamilton was relieved to observe that "the public mind [was] adopting more and more sentiments truly American, and free from foreign tincture."[25]

Washington too sensed an improvement in the public mind. He continued to believe that the "mass of our citizens" would act correctly when they came to understand a question. If the mission to France should fail, it would "open the eyes of all . . . who are not wilfully blind and resolved to remain so." He scorned political leaders who were so ready to believe that the executive branch was willing to violate the Constitution and, at the same time, so eager to explain away the Directory's overthrow of the French constitution on September 4, 1797. Americans who expressed such views were, he believed, "governed more by party passion and party views than by the dictates of justice, temperance and sound policy."[26] But he did not lose hope, though he was deeply disappointed in the attitudes of many of his fellow Americans. A religious man, he was sustained and comforted by his belief in the kind providence of God.

Jefferson also noted a lessening of "the republican majority in Congress," but he explained it in quite a different light. He had hoped that conditions would improve when Washington retired, but he had found that Washington's "ungrateful predilections in favor of Great Britain," which had "alienated" France, had in turn created a reaction "on the minds of our

[23] John Quincy Adams to John Adams, June 24, 1796, April 30, 1797, *JQAW*, I, 506, II, 160–61.

[24] Washington to John Nicholas, March 8, 1798, *WW*, XXXVI, 183.

[25] Hamilton to Washington, August 28, 1797, *HWL*, X, 273.

[26] Washington to John Marshall, December 4, 1797, *WW*, XXXVI, 93–94.

citizens [producing] an effect which supplies that of the Washington popularity."[27]

On September 25, 1797, appeared the mysterious "Langhorne letter," which all but destroyed what good feeling Washington may have had for Jefferson. Some of the facts surrounding the incident still elude the historian. It appears that Jefferson's nephew Peter Carr wrote the letter to Washington, without Jefferson's knowledge, trying to trap the former President into a compromising statement. The name Langhorne was evidently fictitious. John Nicholas called Washington's attention to part, but not all, of the facts, and the former President concluded that Jefferson was the writer. Washington made no public accusation, but he lost all confidence in Jefferson, and he used the occasion to observe that the attempts of the Republicans "to explain away the Constitution, and weaken the Government are now become so open; and the desire of placing the Affairs of this Country under the influence and controul [*sic*] of a foreign Nation is so apparent and strong, it is hardly to be expected that a resort to covert means to effect these objects, will be longer regarded." Such men were "blinded by Party views," he added, "and determined at all hazards to catch at any thing that, in their opinion, will promote them."[28]

By this time there was much apprehension about whether the Directory had received the three Americans. There had been no indication that they would do so. They had earlier rejected the Federalist Pinckney. Why would they welcome three commissioners, two of whom were Federalists? It had seemed so obvious to John Quincy Adams that they would not that he had not thought the government would even appoint a successor to Pinckney.[29] Underlying the Federalists' reiteration of their wish for the success of the envoys lurked the conviction that failure at Paris would bring one blessing at least—it would upset the Republican party at home. Similarly, one senses in Republican correspondence an undertone of conviction that a diplomatic success with the French would dull the edge of the criticism of Jay's Treaty and thereby neutralize one of the Republicans' best weapons for belaboring the Federalists.

[27] Jefferson to Burr, June 17, 1797, *JW*, IX, 402–403.

[28] Washington to John Nicholas, March 8, 1798, *WW*, XXXVI, 183–84. See Manning J. Dauer, "The Two John Nicholases: Their Relationship to Washington and Jefferson," *American Historical Review*, Vol. XLV (January, 1940), 338–48. Dauer found some evidence that Jefferson did not instigate the writing of the Langhorne letter.

[29] Adams to Joseph Pitcairn, January 13, 1797, *JQAW*, II, 76.

Wolcott expected that "the Ministers, after being treated with insult and indignity," would eventually be received, for he thought that the Directory would have better judgment than to make a move that would "rouse and unite the country."[30] Washington, eager to look on the bright side, was delighted by reports that French public opinion was turning from the Directory and toward the United States.[31] Yet rumors persisted that the French were about to declare war on the United States. President Adams thought that "a continued appearance of umbrage, and continued depredations on a weak, defenseless commerce, will be much more convenient for their views."[32] Hamilton, though as always confident that a war could be financed if necessary, was less confident about the friends of the government; he feared that they lacked "sufficient capaciousness of views for the greatness of the occasion."[33] From Jefferson's correspondence through this period it is clear that he dreaded both the political effects of armaments and the economic burden of higher taxes. Adams genuinely feared that taxing the people beyond a certain point would lead to revolt.[34]

Washington could not believe that France would declare war on the United States "without a *semblance of justice*." But if war should come, he wrote, he was convinced that the mass of Americans would prove true to their country. Yet he may have had lingering doubts, for he added, "I pray devoutly that the Directory will not bring the matter to trial."[35] Of course, in expressing that hope he may only have been reiterating his ceaseless hatred for war.

From London, Rufus King warned the government to prepare for war, saying, "You will deceive yourselves if you rely too confidently on peace; it is too problematical to be considered probable." On the same day he wrote to Hamilton giving an alarming picture of the seemingly irresistible power of French arms in Europe and the blighting results of French conquests. Hamilton, himself, never expressed a more pessimistic view of the French system than King did when he made the ominous prediction that "we seem to be doomed to witness, if not to suffer, in the dissolution of the present

[30] Oliver Wolcott to his brother Frederick Wolcott, February 27, 1798, Gibbs, II, 13.

[31] Washington to Pickering, July 31, 1797, *WW*, XXXV, 514.

[32] Adams to Pickering, October 31, 1797, *AW*, VIII, 560.

[33] Hamilton to Wolcott, 1797, *HWL*, X, 274.

[34] Manning J. Dauer, *The Adams Federalists* (Baltimore, 1953), 65–66.

[35] Washington to Pickering, August 29, 1797, Washington to Pinckney, December 4, 1797, *WW*, XXXVI, 19, 90.

social organization."[36] Wolcott relayed the grim warning to Adams, whose reply illustrates his frustration and uncertainty. He could not, for example, understand Talleyrand's hostility in light of the "cordial hospitality" he had received in the United States; yet "the French Directory," it appeared, "must have war. War, open or understood, is their eternal doom."[37]

Jefferson, on the other hand, was alarmed only by Federalists, whom he accused repeatedly of coveting the profits and the power that would come from a war with France. Along with other Republicans he was apprehensive about what the Federalist administration might do with a navy, and as long as it was possible to do so he continued to oppose even as modest a defense measure as fortifying the harbors of the United States.[38] Jefferson continued to maintain that the Directory was eager for peace and would be willing at any time to negotiate reasonably with acceptable envoys. He believed that the outcome would be favorable and that, "if there were danger of war, we should have heard from the envoys."[39]

Hamilton, who never believed in doing things by halves, continued his industrious correspondence with members of the cabinet and Congress, urging them to arm the nation. At a strategic moment, at the opening of the special session of Congress in May, 1797, he sent Senator Tracy of Connecticut a number of suggestions for increasing armaments and taxes and for enacting other laws to prepare the nation for a possible "trial of strength." Tracy took the letter directly to President Adams, who was shocked by the magnitude of the program, which called not only for a navy but also for an army of fifty thousand men (including ten thousand cavalry), increased taxes, and other measures. Recalling the incident twelve years later, Adams declared with some indignation that the letter "contained a whole system of instructions for the conduct of the President, the Senate, and the House of Representatives" and that it had had a great deal of influence on "both houses of Congress," though none on himself. He was as yet unaware that his cabinet looked chiefly to Hamilton for guidance.[40] His conservative instincts told him, nevertheless, that the times called for an improvement in the nation's warmaking potential. In his message to the special session he

[36] King to Wolcott, August 6, 1797, Gibbs, I, 570; King to Hamilton, August 6, 1797, *KC*, II, 211.

[37] Adams to Wolcott, *AW*, VIII, 558–59.

[38] John C. Miller, *Crisis in Freedom: The Alien and Sedition Acts* (Boston, 1951), 36 (hereafter cited as *Crisis in Freedom*).

[39] Jefferson to Peregrine Fitzhugh, February 23, 1798, *JW*, X, 2.

[40] Letter No. XIII to the *Boston Patriot*, 1809, *AW*, IX, 289.

committed the task to Congress. As "effectual measures of defense," he spoke of "the naval establishment," "an addition to the regular artillery and cavalry," "arrangements for forming a provisional army," and "laws for organizing, arming, and disciplining the militia."[41] His message was couched in grave terms, but at no point did he appear to command Congress. He conveyed the assurance that the lawmakers would enact necessary measures in the manner they saw fit.

Detailed resolutions were duly introduced providing for the fortification of harbors; the construction and purchase of warships; the arming of merchant vessels; artillerists, engineers, and cavalry; and increased taxes and authorizing the President to borrow money.[42] Enacting these proposals into law proved to be quite another matter. Taxes were the main stumbling block. Representatives of various sections and interests introduced tax bills that would weigh most heavily on other sections and interests. There was also argument over priorities—whether first attention should be given to the provisional army, the militia, or the navy. There was still a widespread belief that actual resistance to France would eventually prove to be unnecessary, and the leading Republicans felt that the whole defense program would play right into the hands of the Federalists—that every increased expenditure would strengthen that party at home and encourage it to launch an unnecessary war at sea. Action was consequently slow-paced.

The tenor of the two parties had reversed itself from that of two years earlier. Then it had been the Republicans who were disposed to call their opponents "traitors" and "allies of Britain." By 1797 the Federalists were hurling at the Republicans such epithets as "traitors" and "adherents to France." In condemning Jay's Treaty in 1795, Jefferson had said that he hoped the government would learn "the eternal truth that acquiescence under insult is not the way to escape war."[43] The same attitude was adopted by the Federalists when France became the primary aggressor.

It proved impossible for the Federalists to get their defense program under way as long as there was no word from Marshall, Pinckney, and Gerry.[44] Though the President might declare, "Old as I am, war is, even to me, less dreadful than iniquity or deserved disgrace," Congress was rendered

[41] Adams to Congress, May 16, 1797, Richardson, I, 226–28.

[42] *Annals*, VII, 239.

[43] Jefferson to Henry Tazewell, September 13, 1795, *JW*, IX, 308.

[44] Morison, *The Life and Letters of Harrison Gray Otis*, I, 76–77.

almost powerless by a stream of petitions against war measures and war taxes.[45]

By January, 1798, Adams had become sufficiently concerned to ask for his secretaries' opinions about what action should be taken if France refused to negotiate with the envoys. Should war be declared? Should an embargo be placed on American shipping? What advances should be made toward Spain, Holland, and England?[46] McHenry promptly wrote to Hamilton for counsel, saying, "I am sure I cannot do justice to the subject as you can."[47] Hamilton, as usual, responded freely, recommending a "truly vigorous defensive plan" and "mitigated hostility" that would still leave "a door open to negotiate." He saw "nothing to be gained" by a formal war with France. In their respective communications both Adams and Hamilton expressed opposition to a formal alliance with Britain even if France and the United States went to war. In that event arrangements should be made to co-operate with Britain, but Hamilton assumed that "mutual interest will command as much from her as a treaty," and Adams asked his secretaries, "What aids or benefits can we expect from England by any stipulations with her, which her interest will not impel her to extend to us without any?" Joining with Britain "on the brink of the dangerous precipice," he said, might cause both nations to fall together. Moreover, there might be a revolution in England, followed by a "wild democracy" like that which had overtaken France, and such an eventuality would create "the danger of reviving and extending that delirium in America." Hamilton also thought that "the overthrow of England [was] very possible" and might be followed by a French invasion of the United States.

Gifted with longer vision than Adams, Hamilton looked into the future and tried to foresee means of Anglo-American co-operation. Britain, he decided, should be asked to send a naval force to America, under the command of the British minister to the United States, to be employed in seizing "the Floridas, Louisiana, and South American possessions of Spain, if rupture, as is probable, will extend to her."[48] This action would help forestall a French invasion up the Mississippi or through the Floridas and would perhaps make such a war ultimately profitable to the United States. Adams evidently entertained no such ambitious plans, but the two men

[45] Adams to Knox, March 30, 1797, *AW*, VIII, 535; Beveridge, *Life of John Marshall*, II, 337.

[46] Adams to the cabinet, January 24, 1798, *AW*, VIII, 561–62.

[47] McHenry to Hamilton, January 26, 1798, Steiner, 291.

[48] Hamilton to McHenry, n.d., Steiner, 291–95.

held similar views on the immediate measures to be taken, though they had no direct communication with each other and were barely on speaking terms.

Vice-President Jefferson, though unable to exert much direct influence on foreign policy, did not remain silent. Like Hamilton, he had spokesmen in each branch of Congress, and his correspondence was weighted with questions of diplomacy and world affairs. He agreed that France would probably overcome Britain and thereby revolutionize the British government. The prospect did not disturb him. He did not wish "to see any nation have a form of government forced upon them; but if it is to be done, I should rejoice at its being a free one."[49]

King continued to send warnings from London that it would be "weakness instead of prudence" to delay defense measures.[50] King had been well received in England, and the British were pleased with Adams' election as president.[51] British officials no longer refused to confer with the American minister. Indeed, King thought that they were rather candid with him. At that time Britain was dickering with Miranda, the Venezuelan revolutionary, who had been disappointed in the response to his schemes in France and was now placing his hopes on an Anglo-American attack on Spanish America. King embraced the idea with enthusiasm and tried to keep Pickering and Hamilton informed about British attitudes toward it. In early 1798 he reported to Pickering that the current British position was (1) not to interfere in Spanish America if Spain remained "independent" but (2) to request American co-operation in carrying out Miranda's project if France should take over Spain. King, aware that the success of such an undertaking would bring valuable new territories to the United States, was equally interested in helping free the Spanish colonies and building a basis for future good relations between those peoples and the United States. He reported that he understood Liston, the British minister at Philadelphia, would approach Pickering with the proposal and expressed his hopes that President Adams would agree to co-operate with Britain and "by great and generous Deeds to lay deep and firm the foundations of lasting accord between [America's] rising Empires."[52]

The French government issued a decree that brought the two nations still closer to war. Henceforth it would be French policy "to make prize and

[49] Jefferson to Peregrine Fitzhugh, February 23, 1798, *JW*, X, 4.
[50] King to Pickering, February 7, 1798, *KC*, II, 280.
[51] Liston to Grenville, February 13, 1797, FCA, XXXIII.
[52] February 26, 1798, *KC*, II, 283–84.

confiscate every vessel and cargo infected by a single parcel of goods of British produce."[53] As the British quickly pointed out, this decree was more belligerent than any preceding one and if it was enforced it would ruin all neutral commerce. To Grenville it was a sure sign that the Directory had decided on "the dismissal of the American Ministers in France" and on open war against the United States.[54]

The Atlantic was a serious obstacle to communication in the eighteenth century. Americans were prepared for an extended period of silence from their diplomats in Europe, but apparently no one had anticipated that Marshall and his colleagues would be so long detained in Paris. The urgency of the situation clearly called for prompt action, but months passed without any direct reports of progress. Rumors and indirect reports were mostly adverse. Soon after his arrival in Europe, John Marshall wrote rather gloomily to Washington that constitutional liberty was "dead or dying" in France.[55] John Quincy Adams wrote that France had forced its "ally" the Netherlands to break off diplomatic relations with Portugal for no other reason than to compel Portugal to come to terms with France. He gloomily predicted that France would try to force the United States to break with Britain as a prelude to any Franco-American settlement.[56] Such predictions convinced the President that the nation was probably close "to another trial of . . . spirits."[57] Mistrust between the two parties deepened. Monroe, "anxious to hear the results of our mission to France," suspected that reports might be "purposely kept back by the administration."[58]

At long last, on March 4, 1798, the fateful dispatches from France arrived in Philadelphia. They revealed an account of insult and threat unparalleled in the history of the United States. The envoys had never been officially received; bribes had been not merely asked for but demanded; and the United States had been threatened with "the fate of Venice" if the recent policies of neutrality were not repudiated. The episode had one good result: it cleared the air and made the administration fully aware of where it stood with France.[59]

[53] John Quincy Adams to William Vans Murray, January 27, 1798, *JQAW*, II, 240.

[54] Grenville to Liston, January 15, 1798, Mayo, 148–49.

[55] September 15, 1797, Beveridge, *Life of John Marshall*, II, 242.

[56] November 14, 1797, *JQAW*, II, 227.

[57] Adams to James Wilkinson, February 4, 1798, *AW*, VIII, 564.

[58] Monroe to Jefferson, January 27, 1798, *JMW*, III, 98.

[59] Beveridge, *Life of John Marshall*, II, 200–373. The episode is vividly related in Beveridge's biography.

Part of the difficulty lay in the fact that the American commissioners arrived in Europe at a time when France was shaken by a new convulsion. The Directory, under the leadership of Talleyrand, who had been appointed minister of foreign affairs, had taken over the control of both domestic and foreign matters. Napoleon, though not yet in the center of the stage, was moving into a leading role. The streets of Paris were "resounding to the shouts of French victories."[60] The Americans were not driven from Paris as Pinckney had been, because Talleyrand was convinced that he could compel them to do his bidding. They were approached by three of Talleyrand's agents, Jean Conrad Hottinguer, a Swiss; a Mr. Bellamy, an American banker in Hamburg; and Lucien Hauteval, also a Swiss—later referred to as X, Y, and Z (see Chapter XVII). The agents demanded a bribe of fifty thousand pounds for Talleyrand and his friends and a large loan to the French government before negotiations opened. Talleyrand himself talked with the envoys a few times, but he refused to open any serious negotiations unless the bribe was paid. Young Adams accused Monroe of having given the French the idea of demanding money from the United States, and one of Monroe's biographers has concluded that the demand grew out of Monroe's effusive cordiality.[61]

The Americans presented their country's position in a powerfully worded statement, but it left the French unmoved.[62] They demanded that the commissioners withdraw all American complaints about French mistreatment. Adams' resolute message to the special session of Congress on May 16, 1797, also came under heavy attack.[63]

As Pickering and other Federalists had predicted, Gerry broke away from his colleagues and tried to persuade them to agree to at least a part of Talleyrand's financial demands.[64] Marshall and Pinckney stood firm and for months tried by every proper means to open normal negotiations, but in vain.

Talleyrand probably had an exaggerated estimate of the size of the pro-French party in the United States, though he could not have overlooked the fact that the Republicans had failed to capture the presidency in 1796. He continued to believe that his demands, coupled with the power of the

[60] *Ibid.*, 215.

[61] John Quincy Adams to William Vans Murray, January 27, 1798, *JQAW*, II, 246; Cresson, *James Monroe*, 136.

[62] *ASPFR*, II, 170–82.

[63] *Ibid.*, 159 *et passim*.

[64] Beveridge, *Life of John Marshall*, II, 314–17.

Republicans, could break the resistance of the Federalists, and he frankly said so to Marshall and Pinckney. Gerry's attitude also encouraged him. Marshall and Pinckney labored to alter Talleyrand's appraisal of American attitudes, and they succeeded, at least in part. When they continued to meet his demands with firm resistance, he began threatening to destroy American independence. It was no empty threat; mighty France had succeeded in crushing Venice, Genoa, Geneva, and the Netherlands. As the weeks passed, Talleyrand's stance grew even more threatening. After the news of Napoleon's victory over Austria in 1797, Hottinguer, one of Talleyrand's agents, told Marshall that the Directory had determined "that all nations must aid [the French] or be considered and treated as enemies."[65] Another member of the XYZ trio alluded to the ruins of Venice and asked the Americans to consider well before courting a similar fate.[66]

Gerry was convinced. When Pinckney and Marshall, convinced that the mission was hopeless, prepared to leave France, Gerry refused to join them. He lamely observed that under the Constitution not even the president had the authority to make war, much less he, who was only a minister.[67] When his colleagues accused him of dishonoring his country by remaining behind, he replied that "the honor of a country . . . could never be consulted by adopting a measure which hazarded its existence."[68] Marshall had already exhausted his influence with Gerry through discord, but Pinckney tried hard to persuade him to leave with his colleagues.[69] John Quincy Adams was scandalized by the break in the commission and wrote to Gerry that "there is a point beyond which every sacrifice to preserve peace only serves to defeat its own purpose, and . . . perfidy or dishonor are too high a price to pay."[70] But in the face of Talleyrand's threat of war Gerry was impervious to his countrymen's pleas.

While Marshall and Pinckney were preparing to depart, Talleyrand played his final card. His agents reminded the envoys of the large pro-French party in the United States and promised to contrive ways to cast on Marshall and Pinckney all the blame for the failure of the mission. The envoys would return home in disgrace, and the American people would repudiate the

[65] *Ibid.*, 293; *ASPFR*, II, 161–62.
[66] Beveridge, *Life of John Marshall*, II, 278.
[67] Gerry to Pickering, October 1, 1798, *ASPFR*, II, 204–208.
[68] Austin, *The Life of Elbridge Gerry*, II, 216.
[69] Beveridge, *Life of John Marshall*, II, 333.
[70] John Quincy Adams to Gerry, February 20, 1798, *JQAW*, II, 260.

Federalist administration.[71] Diplomats of less resolution might have been deterred by this threat, which must have evoked memories of the rioters who had greeted John Jay upon his return three years earlier. But these men would risk personal disgrace rather than betray their country.

And so the mission ended. Pinckney was detained in southern France by his daughter's illness, and Marshall returned alone to the United States—and to a hero's welcome.[72] The political climate had undergone a rapid change. On March 3, 1798, even before all the dispatches about the mission were decoded, President Adams had warned Congress that the nation was facing an emergency. Two weeks later, after all the facts were disclosed, he told Congress that all efforts at negotiation had failed, that no terms short of a surrender of American sovereignty appeared acceptable to France, and that the United States must look to its defenses. He reminded the legislators of his earlier recommendations but did not chide them for having done so little in the intervening ten months. He confined himself to a new entreaty for "replenishing our arsenals, establishing foundries and military manufactures, and [providing] such efficient revenue as will be necessary." He no longer avoided the language of urgency, however. He "exhorted" the lawmakers to act "with promptitude, decision, and unanimity."[73] The nation was confronted with an emergency that would allow no further delay.

[71] Beveridge, *Life of John Marshall*, II, 279; *ASPFR*, II, 164.
[72] Beveridge, *Life of John Marshall*, II, 344–45.
[73] Richardson, I, 255.

CHAPTER XVII

Hamilton Versus Talleyrand

By the summer of 1798, Hamilton's turn had come to reap the harvest of his labors. He had always advocated maintaining basic military and naval strength in peacetime. He had shown that it would not be an unbearable financial burden and that it would facilitate rapid and effective expansion of defensive forces to meet emergencies. Peaceful negotiations as long as practicable had always been his preference over the use of force; yet his call for military preparations against Britain in 1794 was as firm and insistent as his recommendations for negotiations. His call for resistance to French aggression was always coupled with pleas for negotiation, until Marshall returned from Paris empty-handed. After the failure of Pinckney's mission Hamilton had used all his powers of persuasion to prevail on the administration to invite France once again to the peace table, and all who knew him well were convinced of his sincerity in those efforts. With the failure of the negotiations, Hamilton stood out as a man of moderation and foresight who could lead the resistance to a nation that no longer seemed to understand any language but that of the cannon.

As soon as Hamilton learned that the American envoys to France had been rebuffed, and even before the final official dispatches had been received and made public, he began a series of seven essays, "The Stand," in the *New York Commercial Advertiser*, summing up the American side of the long controversy with France and setting forth a comprehensive plan of action.[1] At the same time he maintained his correspondence with his friends in power, outlining the same policies. The purpose of the essays was to make the public aware of the grave dangers the nation faced and of the need for national unity and prompt action.

In "The Stand," Hamilton first reviewed French aggressions against American commerce, painting them in somber colors. He referred to the

[1] *HWL*, VI, 259–318.

repeated attempts of the American government to draw France into a reasonable discussion of grievances and the "insupportable outrage" of the Directory's rejection of every endeavor to "appease and conciliate." He also described French aggressions against European neutrals, Belgium, Genoa, Venice, the Swiss cantons, and others, which, he was convinced, illustrated a design to establish a "universal empire." France had in effect declared war against all states "not in league" with her and did not recognize the right of any nation to choose the path of neutrality.

He next reopened his attack on French revolutionary excesses. The Directory was composed of five "implacable tyrants" who would not "endure a murmur at the blows they inflict." In sum, the Directory was a "horrid monster." The French Revolution had, in his view, proved to be "a prodigy of human wickedness and folly," "a volcano of atheism, depravity, and absurdity," "an instrument of cruelty and bloodshed," "an engine of despotism and slavery," and "a drama of iniquity . . . exceeding in turpitude" all earlier appraisals of it.

Hamilton did not minimize the power of France. Britain, he said, had so far been an obstacle to the "grasping ambition of France," but Britain might yet be defeated by France, after which "there would be no insuperable obstacle to the transportation" of a French invading force across the Atlantic. It would be foolhardy to discount the probability of such an attempt, and the United States could not safely rely on the militia alone to repel an invasion. A navy should be established, seaports should be fortified, foundries and arsenals should be established, and the "utmost diligence" should be applied to raising "a considerable army." The United States was now much stronger than it had been when it stood up to the power of Britain in 1775. "With respectable revenues and a flourishing credit," and "with many of the principal sources of taxation yet untouched," it could face France in battle. The nation's commerce would suffer from a war, but "independence and liberty are of more consequence than . . . trade." Peace, though precious, was "a bauble compared with national independence." French action had "filled up the measure of national insult and humiliation." Further unresisted encroachments would blot the United States from the list of independent nations. There was "no choice left but between resistance and infamy."

Hamilton dwelt at length on the need for national unity. He scorned those Americans who still tried to excuse French action. Alluding to Talleyrand's behavior and threats, he saw "strong symptoms that men in power in France understand better than ourselves the true character of their faction in this country." He accused the leaders of the faction of a desire "to prepare the way for implicit subjection" to the will of France. He believed that those faithless leaders, "unmasked in all their intrinsic deformity," would presently be deserted by their erstwhile followers and would "shrink from the scene appalled and confounded."

Hamilton was careful to point out that the occasion did not call for a declaration of war by the United States, or for open hostility beyond sinking or capturing "assailants" and bringing in "privateers found hovering within twenty leagues of our coast." Such acts might imply "a state of war," but if so, it would be a limited state of war, to grow into a general war or not at the election of France. He believed that "want of success" might bring "the despots to reason" and that a new revolution might place better men in charge of the French government "and lead to honorable accommodation."

The essays were widely read and raised Hamilton higher than ever in public esteem. He had long been a leader of the leaders; in the early part of 1798 he came closer than at any other time in his life to being a leader of the people. Before the public he maintained an air of moderation, and he never adopted an "I told you so" attitude. Yet it was obvious to the people and their leaders alike that he was placing the capstone on his structure of logical and prudent policy. The letters of his contemporaries and speeches in Congress vibrated with phrases from "The Stand." Talleyrand's attempt to seize control of American minds had failed. Hamilton had won.

To Pickering, Hamilton gave detailed suggestions for arming the nation and mobilizing public opinion, as well as suggestions about what the President should say to Congress. His recommendations on military affairs were similar to those he had given Pickering the year before. Yet he continued to warn against "proceeding to final rupture."[2] To make certain that his views were understood in Congress, he wrote to Theodore Sedgwick, summarizing his recommendations for defensive measures and closing with advice that "especial care" should be taken to see that "merely defensive views" were expressed.[3] He was as eager to avoid full-scale war as he was to move forward with defensive measures. He feared the "warlike ardor" of President Adams and "the militant Federalists."[4]

[2] Hamilton to Pickering, March 17, 1798, *HWL*, X, 275–78.

[3] Hamilton to Sedgwick, March, 1798, *HWL*, X, 278–79.

[4] Miller, *Alexander Hamilton*, 468–69.

Hamilton's influence over the national government was never more powerful. The cabinet had much greater respect for his opinions than they had for those of the President. Adams' control was further weakened by his frequent absences for long periods from the Capitol. Hamilton did not gain everything he wanted from Congress, but his views dominated the Senate and more often than not won out in the House.[5] As Morison wrote, "Back of Congress and the Executive stood Alexander Hamilton, ruling the Federal party, and through it the nation, from his law office in New York."[6] Thus, as Dauer pointed out, he was able to "integrate the operations of the legislative and executive branches."[7]

Congress plunged into a prolonged debate. Some Federalists were prepared to make a declaration of war. Among them was William Smith of South Carolina, who had previously adhered closely to Hamilton's views.[8] So insistent were they that the British government was also convinced a war was certain.[9] But in Congress the advocates of war were a few votes short of those needed to carry through a declaration.[10] Jefferson remained hopeful that war could be forestalled. "If we could but gain this season," he wrote, "the affairs of Europe would of themselves" make war unnecessary.[11] He was assuming that peace was near in Europe. Unlike Hamilton, he was not alarmed by the thought of a final French victory, for, as he saw it, peace in Europe would mean peace on the Atlantic and an end to the molestation of American commerce. He did not take seriously the postwar designs France had on the United States. For several months he had been predicting that the current French military campaign would be the last one and that the United States would be safe if it could just "rub through" for a little longer.

Since the Federalists could not summon enough votes for an open declaration of war, the House Republicans proposed a resolution to the effect that it was not expedient to enter full-scale hostilities with France.[12] Robert G. Harper, the Federalist leader in the House, at first indicated that there would be no Federalist opposition to the resolution, but the Federalists had

[5] Darling, *Our Rising Empire, 1763–1803*, 307–10; Smertenko, *Alexander Hamilton*, 217–22.

[6] Morison, *The Life and Letters of Harrison Gray Otis*, I, 99.

[7] Dauer, *The Adams Federalists*, 122.

[8] Rogers, *William Loughton Smith*, 319.

[9] Grenville to Liston, June 8, 1798, Mayo, 155.

[10] Whitaker (*The Mississippi Question, 1795–1803*, 116) incorrectly concluded that Hamilton wanted a declaration of war at this time.

[11] Jefferson to Madison, March 21, 29, 1798, *JW*, X, 11, 17.

[12] March 27, 1798, *Annals*, VIII, 1319.

second thoughts and voted it down lest it put a damper on public support of defensive measures.

To most Americans in the spring of 1798, French military strength seemed almost invincible. Britain appeared exhausted and beaten. The Bank of England had suspended specie payments; Ireland was poised to revolt; there were reports of mutinies in the British navy; and the French "Army of England" was forming on the Channel, ostensibly for an invasion of England. If the protective force of the British navy was lost, Federalist Harrison Gray Otis predicted, "it will be time for us to prepare to be good and dutiful subjects of the French."[13] In like vein Republican William B. Giles, whose pro-French sentiments were weakening, told the House that Britain was at the verge of national bankruptcy and "must fall" even if there was no invasion. He could not see how the young nation could resist the power of victorious France, a nation of thirty million people with a well-equipped army led by skillful generals and flushed with victory.[14] The name Bonaparte began to appear with increasing frequency in American correspondence and congressional debates.

The House debates soon turned to the larger questions of national defense. Republicans began demanding that the President release detailed information about the abortive negotiations. The bombastic Giles accused Adams of trying to place Congress in "a degraded state" by requesting the enactment of hostile measures against France and the levying of new taxes, meanwhile "keeping back all information from Congress."[15] Congressman John Allen, Federalist from Connecticut, tried to forestall the Republicans by moving to ask the President to "communicate to this House the dispatches" mentioned in his message of March 19, "or such parts thereof as considerations of public safety and interest, in his opinion, may permit." Giles objected to the latter part of the motion. The President should not be allowed to exercise his judgment about which papers should be submitted to Congress. According to the genteel language of the *Annals of Congress*, Giles "was not himself satisfied as to the sincerity of the proceedings of the Executive."[16]

Vice-President Jefferson and other Republicans strongly supported the

[13] Otis to his wife, March 14, 1798, Morison, *The Life and Letters of Harrison Gray Otis*, I, 69.

[14] March 29, 1798, *Annals*, VIII, 1352.

[15] *Ibid.*, 1349.

[16] *Ibid.*, 1358.

call for the dispatches and were backed by the Republican *Aurora*.[17] At first there was a noticeable spirit of impudence in the demand. The Republicans remembered how they had mortified Washington in 1796 by clamoring for papers dealing with Jay's negotiations, and they hoped to score a point if the Chief Executive refused for a second time to take the representatives into his confidence. But upon reflection the Republicans grew disturbed at the possibility of unforeseen results. Washington would have been seriously embarrassed by a comparison of Jay's instructions with his accomplishments; but this time the situation might be reversed. Adams might reveal the intrigues of Talleyrand. The Federalists in the House made it more difficult for the Republicans by supporting Allen's motion, and they did not fight hard for the stipulation that would have allowed the President to decide which papers he would submit. To avoid appearing to contradict the Federalist position of two years earlier, Harper pointed out that the papers were needed as information to help guide the House in taking action on matters within its constitutional authority—implying that in 1796 the papers were called for as a move to block the implementation of Jay's Treaty, which had already been ratified.[18]

The resolution passed the House by a vote of sixty-five to twenty-seven, and on the following day, April 3, 1798, President Adams sent them copies of the envoys' letters of credence, instructions, and dispatches.[19] In these documents the letters X, Y, and Z were used in place of the names of Talleyrand's agents, thereby giving the notorious diplomatic episode the name XYZ Affair. The Federalists in the Senate pushed through a motion to print ten thousand copies of the papers for nationwide distribution. The Jeffersonians were hard pressed for arguments to block the measure; they had long contended that the people should be kept informed about national and international affairs. The best they could do was to assert that the papers did not tell the whole story and were so voluminous that they would confuse the people. "In endeavoring to give so much information," said Nathaniel Macon of North Carolina, "they would give none."[20]

The papers were duly distributed, nonetheless, and the nation was presented with the ugly picture of Talleyrand and his agents rejecting America's effort at conciliation, soliciting bribes, and making threats. "The

[17] Beveridge, *Life of John Marshall*, II, 336–39.
[18] April 2, 1798, *Annals*, VIII, 1369.
[19] *ASPFR*, II, 152–68.
[20] April 6, 1798, *Annals*, VIII, 1379.

system of France," Wolcott said, was "the most insolent, presumptuous, and profligate which the annals of mankind have disclosed."[21] Washington thought the affair should "open the eyes of the blindest" but predicted that it would produce no change in the "leaders of the opposition, unless there should appear a manifest desertion of their followers."[22]

Federalists throughout the country saw to it that the XYZ papers were distributed in a manner that would make the people fully aware of the danger and the need for united resistance. The papers were also put to political use. In North Carolina, for example, the Federalist William R. Davie asked Pickering to send him North Carolina's quota of papers before Congress adjourned so that he could circulate them in his state before Republican congressmen could come home to mislead the people.[23] The papers were delayed in reaching him, and Davie accused unnamed Republicans of intercepting them. When they finally arrived, they were "sent off by mail as fast as they could be carried."[24] Colonel William Polk assisted Davie in placing copies of the documents in the hands of "federal men" in various counties for distribution. Polk informed Davie that the dispatches had been "distributed amongst the Citizens who appear eager to read them and to give them all that just credit they so well deserve."[25] The people of North Carolina responded. Late in the same year Davie was elected governor, and North Carolina sent almost a full slate of Federalists to Congress. Similarly, of the six representatives elected in South Carolina, five were Federalists.[26]

The outburst of public wrath throughout the nation at first appeared to forecast the doom of the Republican party. On his return to Philadelphia, Marshall was feted and acclaimed. No other American save Washington had ever been accorded such honor.[27] In New England public demonstrations were held to demand a declaration of war. If that declaration had been made, one historian has observed, "the Republican party would have dis-

[21] Wolcott to Washington, March 9, 1798, Gibbs, II, 13.

[22] Washington to Pickering, April 16, 1798, *WW*, XXXVI, 249.

[23] Davie to Pickering, August, 1798, Papers of William R. Davie, North Carolina Department of Archives and History, Raleigh, 15; Delbert Harold Gilpatrick, *Jeffersonian Democracy in North Carolina* (New York, 1931), 94.

[24] Davie to Pickering, August 24, 1798, Papers of William R. Davie, North Carolina Department of Archives and History, Raleigh, 38.

[25] Polk to Davie, October 27, November 30, 1798, *ibid.*, 33–34.

[26] Dodd, *The Life of Nathaniel Macon*, 129. Henry McGilbert Wagstaff, *Federalism in North Carolina* (Chapel Hill, 1910), 30–31.

[27] Beveridge, *Life of John Marshall*, II, 344.

appeared in the political chasm."[28] Robert Troup, a close friend of Hamilton's, noted a "growing unanimity throughout the whole extent of our territory," and Fisher Ames concluded that "folly had nearly burnt out its fuel."[29] Such comments as, "Alas! How silly I have been," came from the pens of leaders who had trusted in the good will of France.[30] Hamilton sensed "an extraordinary union among the people in the support of their own government" and consequently saw "nothing to be feared for our future security."[31] In Boston it was reported that Federalists were carrying elections by majorities of fourteen to one, and all but a few people of diminishing influence were firmly in support of Adams' policy toward France.[32] As a nineteenth-century historian rather extravagantly described it, the Republican party, "having come forward as advocates of submission, . . . withered and wasted under the meridian blaze of an excited patriotism."[33]

Eager to extract from the situation the last ounce of benefit, Hamilton advised Washington to make a tour of the southern states, where the Republicans still had considerable strength. Washington might explain the tour, Hamilton suggested, by saying that he was traveling for his health. He would be honored along the way, and in toasts and speeches he could express his thoughts on national and international affairs and thereby improve the morale of the people[34]—and incidentally win more southerners to the Federalist position. Washington rejected the idea, stating that his health "never was better" and that the "enemies" of strong government, "always more active and industrious than friends," might "turn it to their own advantage, by malicious insinuations."[35]

The Republicans were not wholly defeated, however. They retained their strength in some parts of the country, put up a strong battle in Congress,

[28] John Austin Stevens, *Albert Gallatin* (Boston, 1899), 167.

[29] Troup to King, June 10, 1798, *KC*, II, 344; Ames to Otis, April 23, 1798, Ames, *Works of Fisher Ames*, I, 225.

[30] Representative W. B. Grove of North Carolina to Hogg, March 23, 1798, Henry McGilbert Wagstaff (ed.), "Letters of William Barry Grove," *James Sprunt Historical Publications*, Vol. IX, No. 2, 74.

[31] Hamilton to Count Latour Dupin Gouvernet, October 3, 1798, *HWL*, X, 324.

[32] Pickering to John Quincy Adams, April 10, 1798, Pickering Papers, Massachusetts Historical Society, VIII, 323.

[33] Richard Hildreth, *The History of the United States of America* (New York, 1856–60), V, 325.

[34] Hamilton to Washington, May 19, 1798, *HWL*, X, 285–86.

[35] Washington to Hamilton, May 27, 1798, *WW*, XXXVI, 271.

and soon rallied. Joseph Hopkinson (the composer of "Hail Columbia") was "mortified" to find that the "tri-coloured cockade" was "by no means an infrequent sight" in New York City and that "the federal spirit" there was "not worth a farthing."[36] Federalist Congressman Uriah Tracy of Connecticut, reflecting on the congressional scene, lamented, "Our best men are so timid, and our worst so active and profligate, that nothing is done but with excessive fatigue and industry."[37] It was not a hopeful description of the body that would have to bear so much responsibility. For now it was up to Congress to decide the nation's course of action. The wheels of diplomacy had stopped turning. The President had spoken, calling for congressional action. The public was aroused and confused by conflicting arguments. There was little that could be done until Congress gave the signal.

Madison was no longer in the House of Representatives, and Albert Gallatin led the debate for the Republicans, assisted by John Nicholas of Virginia and Nathaniel Macon of North Carolina. Robert G. Harper of South Carolina led the Federalists, with powerful assistance from Harrison Gray Otis of Massachusetts and Jonathan Dayton of New Jersey. Though Dayton was speaker of the House, he did not allow his position to deter him from taking the floor for frequent verbal encounters.

The Republicans were on the defensive during most of the session—an uncommon and unhappy role for them. They were kept busy explaining their motives and defending themselves from "calumnies" and "slanders." The Federalists had become newly aggressive and passionate. They showed no reluctance to impugn the motives of their opponents and to expose inconsistencies in Republican arguments. Gallatin, resourceful and well informed and adept at debate, nevertheless made the Federalists work hard for every point they gained. He scrutinized their every word, often demonstrating weaknesses in their positions or presentations. Many a Federalist, under Gallatin's pommeling, had to withdraw and start over again. There were repeated calls to order as members became too candid about one another's motives and personalities. It was a lively, if grave, debate.

Working steadily through the summer of 1798, Congress gradually fashioned laws establishing a small army and navy, severing trade relations with France and suspending the alliance, and authorizing merchant ships to

[36] Hopkinson to Wolcott, May 17, 1798, Gibbs, II, 49.
[37] Tracy to Hamilton, May 17, 1798, *HWH*, VI, 287.

arm and to defend themselves when attacked. The naturalization period for immigrants was increased from five to fourteen years. It was declared illegal to write or speak against the government in a manner that might bring it into disrepute. The Republicans opposed each measure, but they realized that until the national mood changed it was futile to try to regain the ground they had lost. Provision was made for increasing the regular army to thirteen thousand men, though that total was not reached because action was delayed at so many points. At Federalist insistence a provisional army of fifty thousand men was authorized, to be called into being at the President's discretion. Even those most strongly favoring the measure realized that it would not pass in any stronger form, and the President's opposition to a large standing army meant that a force that size was unlikely to be called up. The President was also authorized to call up eighty thousand militia if circumstances warranted.

The House continued to exercise a restraining force. Senate bills calling for more troops and ships were regularly pared down in the House. There was some alarm in the nation, especially in the South, at rumors that the French were preparing an invasion from Haiti with an army of Negroes. The cry, "Take your daughters to the mountains!" became common.[38] But a strong core of Jeffersonians in Congress proved immune to such rumors. Again and again they reiterated that France had no intention of attacking the United States and that the seizure of ships was but a logical consequence of Federalist foreign policy—especially of the "odious" treaty with Britain. Jefferson, calling the Federalists "war hawks" to contrast them with the "peace party," his term for the Republicans, insisted that in spite of Jay's Treaty and other injustices France would make a reasonable peace, provided the "insult" of Adams' message to Congress of March 19 was first "wiped away."[39] Such statements illustrate why Jefferson proved unable to carry through his professed desire of March, 1797, to work harmoniously with Adams.

No part of the defense program had Jefferson's support. As each provision was adopted, he rallied support to try to block the next step. When passage of defense measures appeared certain, he vowed that the Republicans would "oppose all external preparations." As always, he considered the

[38] Miller, *Crisis in Freedom*, 6.
[39] Jefferson to Madison, April 6, 26, 1798, *JW*, X, 25, 33.

militia the most appropriate defensive force. Noting that naval bills were passing the House, he commented that the army bill "would surely be rejected if all our members were here."[40]

The Federalists advocated a navy as necessary to provide minimal defense for the nation. Furthermore, they believed that the French had pushed the nation to the ultimate point at which independence could be preserved. The United States did not have a choice between "peace or war," warned Speaker Harper. The only choice was "to resist or submit."[41] The House was well aware of this fact, he asserted, thus by implication—and sometimes in direct language—accusing the Republicans of advocating abandonment of America's sovereignty and submission to France. Harper reminded the congressmen of the French army, five thousand men strong, under the French administrator Victor Hugues in the West Indies, "ready to make a blow upon the Southern country whenever the word of command shall be given." He also reminded his listeners of the French practice of invading a nation at a time of "domestic insurrection." He feared not only that the invaders would arm the slaves but also that some white Americans might support them. When pressed by his opponents, he refused to qualify the statement.[42]

Other southern congressmen shared his fears. Representative Grove of North Carolina protested that none of the defense money was being allocated to fortify his state's four-hundred-mile coastline, where the enemy might land unmolested and "put arms into the hands of at least five thousand men, who might be ready to receive them" (presumably he was referring to slaves).[43] Sewall and others pointed to the danger that a French army might be invited into "the Mississippi" by the Spaniards at New Orleans and come ashore in Tennessee.[44]

When the Republicans spoke disparagingly of these fears, the Federalists reminded them that Talleyrand's agents had specifically threatened to "ravage our coasts" if "bribes and tribute" were not paid. Harper thought that "the army on the coast of France, which, in gasconading style, they call the Army of England, may be the *Army of America*; and the transports

[40] Jefferson to Peter Carr, April 12, 1798, Jefferson to Madison, April 26, 1798, *ibid.*, 30, 31. For a good, brief description of Jefferson's attitude on defense measures see Morison, *The Life and Letters of Harrison Gray Otis*, I, 75.

[41] March 28, 1798, *Annals*, VIII, 1341.

[42] April 24, 1798, *ibid.*, 1530–31.

[43] April 11, 1798, *ibid.*, 1397.

[44] April 24, 1798, *ibid.*, 1528.

collecting at Bordeaux and Brest, instead of being intended to go against London, may be sent to Florida, or against Rhode Island."[45] His opponents made light of such forebodings and continued to condemn the navy bills as unnecessary, unjust, immoral, and suicidal.

It became obvious that a large segment of the "peace party," somewhat more attached to the agrarian way of life than the Federalists were, simply considered commerce not worth fighting for. Nicholas of Virginia touched on this point several times. The merchant class, he said, had no right to ask for protection that was unduly expensive and dangerous to the rest of the nation. Jefferson wearily observed that it was "better for us to continue to bear from France through the present summer, what we have been bearing from both her and England these four years."[46] Advocates of resistance stubbornly refused to concede that French aggressions of 1797 and 1798 were no worse than British acts of 1794. Unlike the French, the British had not seized vessels merely because their papers were not in order or on other trivial grounds.

In addition, said Congressman John Allen, Britain did not "avow the wrongs she had committed on us, nor did she threaten to continue them and ravage our coasts."[47] The one point above all others that gave the Republicans difficulty—one they were never able to counter satisfactorily—was the continued French refusal to meet with Americans in open, honorable negotiation.

Naval appropriations passed Congress more easily than army appropriations, for it was at sea that injuries were being felt. Adams, too, showed much more interest in the navy than in the army. Yet even naval bills met heavy resistance. Even after the XYZ Affair became common knowledge, motions were made to restrict the navy's activities to American harbors and coastal waters.[48] Such a motion had been narrowly defeated in 1797 by a vote of thirteen to fifteen. The motion was offered again on April 20, 1798, but failed by a vote of thirty-two to fifty.[49]

In the late eighteenth century, war was considered a formal undertaking, hedged about by rules of legality. Secretary of War James McHenry asked Hamilton the extent of the President's authority to order warships into action. In spite of his well-known "loose construction" theories, Hamilton

[45] May 11, 1798, *ibid.*, 1691.
[46] Jefferson to Samuel Smith, August 22, 1798, *JW*, X, 57.
[47] April 20, 1798, *Annals*, VIII, 1479.
[48] June 9, 1797, *ibid.*, VII, 19.
[49] *Ibid.*, VIII, 1520–21.

replied that Congress alone could constitutionally make war—that without legislative authorization the President could only "employ the ships as convoys, with authority to *repel* force by *force* (but not to capture), and to repress hostilities within our waters, including a marine league from our coasts." To overcome these restrictions, he suggested that the President should go before Congress and ask for authority to give American commerce "a more extensive protection." The request would place the responsibility plainly upon Congress "in a shape which cannot be eluded" and would gain for the President "credit for frankness and an unwillingness to chicane the Constitution."[50]

True to his threat, Talleyrand did make an effort to throw upon Marshall and Pinckney all the blame for the failure of the negotiations. John Quincy Adams reported a story circulating in Europe that Talleyrand was saying the American commissioners had kept themselves "studiously distant" while in Paris and was denying that he had requested a loan. Talleyrand's version of events fell flat when word reached Europe of the publication of the XYZ papers, which raised America's standing in the eyes of Europeans.[51] Even so, the story gave Republicans in Congress a fresh defense. Macon asked the rhetorical question whether there was "a man in the country . . . not blinded by party spirit who [could] believe that the French Government knew anything of the unauthorized conversations held with our Commissioners in Paris."[52] Joseph McDowell of North Carolina described the statements of X, Y, and Z as "unofficial information" from private persons and suggested that the United States would find itself always in trouble "if the opinions of individuals in any country were to be taken and acted upon as the opinions of the nation."[53]

Anti-Federalist Congressman Joseph Bradley Varnum of Massachusetts deplored the behavior of the agents but "could not believe" that they represented Talleyrand and assumed that the Directory would "punish these persons for their conduct."[54] Republican Gallatin conceded that the demands for money were evidence of corruption in the French government, but he could not see that they were grounds for war. He taunted the Federalists by saying that the publication of the XYZ papers made it more

[50] May 17, 1798, *HWL*, X, 281–82.

[51] John Quincy Adams to William Vans Murray, June 19, 1798, John Quincy Adams to Abigail Adams, June 22, September 14, 1798, *JQAW*, II, 309, 311, 360.

[52] May 11, 1798, *Annals*, VIII, 1699.

[53] May 8, 1798, *ibid.*, 1645.

[54] May 7, 1798, *ibid.*, 1628.

difficult to maintain peace.[55] Jefferson shared Gallatin's views; the French desire for American money did not "offer one motive the more for our going to war."[56] The XYZ picture was so ugly and alarming, however, that such arguments were unconvincing to the people. Allen quoted a paragraph in which Y threatened to make it appear that Marshall and Pinckney were to blame for the failure of the negotiations and then asserted, "Were France herself to speak through an American mouth, I cannot conceive" what more could be said "than what we have heard from certain gentlemen to effect her purposes."[57] When he was asked what member he was accusing of having made such utterances, he replied that he referred to Gallatin. Such exchanges were all too common in and out of Congress.

Fears of a French invasion grew apace. Republican spokesmen pronounced the idea fatuous. To Gallatin it was a mere "bugbear."[58] W. C. Claiborne of Tennessee reasoned that an invasion would be pointless because the nation had nothing "to court [French] avarice."[59] Adams, with heavy humor, observed that there was "no more prospect of seeing [a French] army here than . . . in heaven."[60] Washington, on the other hand, was moving slowly toward Hamilton's view that a truce in Europe or a French victory over Britain might leave France free to send an army across the Atlantic. He had previously thought such a thing impossible, but now, he said, he was living in the "Age of Wonders," when it was "reserved for intoxicated and lawless France . . . to slaughter its own Citizens and to disturb the repose of all the World besides." It would be "dangerous and improper" not to prepare to meet an invasion. If one came, he predicted, it would be in the South, for that section was "weakest," the French would expect to find more friends there, and they could count on arming the slaves. Too, the South was close to bases he thought the French might soon be establishing in Louisiana or Florida.[61]

Taxes remained the most unpopular element in Hamilton's program. Few Americans shared his view that there were abundant tax sources that could be tapped without injuring the nation's economy. Large sums of

[55] April 19, 20, 1798, *ibid.*, 1512–13, 1475.

[56] Jefferson to Madison, April 6, 1798, *JW*, X, 26.

[57] *Annals*, VIII, 1482.

[58] House of Representatives, May 8, 1798, *ibid.*, 1633.

[59] May 10, 1798, *ibid.*, 1652.

[60] John Adams to McHenry, October 22, 1798, *AW*, VIII, 613.

[61] Washington to Adams, July 4, 1798, Washington to Pickering, October 18, 1798, Washington to McHenry, July 11, 1798, *WW*, XXXVI, 313, 497, 324.

money were raised by private subscriptions in Boston, New York, Philadelphia, Baltimore, and Charleston to build warships "to be loaned to the Government";[62] yet every tax bill called forth groans and exclamations. Representative William Findley of Pennsylvania, arguing against the land tax, requested at least a postponement on the grounds that France could not invade the United States before the next session of Congress.[63] He was not moved by arguments that it might be too late to begin taxing the citizens once the enemy was on the doorstep.

Jefferson was repelled by the prospect of "great expenses [being] incurred" but gained some comfort from the thought that "it [would] be left to those whose measures render them necessary, to provide to meet them."[64] Adams, calling regiments "costly articles," predicted that "if this nation sees a great army to maintain, without an enemy to fight, there may arise an enthusiasm that seems to be little foreseen."[65] As though to fulfill Adams' prophecy, "Fries's Rebellion" erupted in western Pennsylvania, a revolt against land and house taxes. Once again Hamilton erred, as he had during the Whisky Rebellion in 1794, by calling for a large army to move against the rebellious farmers, on the grounds that there was a danger of "magnifying a riot into an insurrection by employing, in the first instance, an inadequate force." "Whenever the government appears in arms," he wrote, "it ought to appear like a Hercules, and inspire respect by the display of strength."[66] The administration followed the advice and sent in a force of regular army troops and militia. No resistance was encountered. Arrests were made, fines imposed, and John Fries and two others were sentenced to death for treason. Adams belatedly made amends for the unduly rigorous action by issuing pardons for the three men. Republican politicians and journals laid the blame mostly on Hamilton and grossly exaggerated the "excesses" of the troops. Hamilton's popularity of early 1798 waned.[67] In retrospect, ten years later, Adams held that the tax laws sponsored by Hamilton caused the downfall of the Federalist party.[68]

[62] William Barry Grove to James Hogg, July 8, 1798, Wagstaff, "Letters of William Barry Grove," *James Sprunt Historical Publications*, Vol. IX, No. 2, 62, Wolfe, *Jeffersonian Democracy in South Carolina*, 121.

[63] May 7, 1798, *Annals*, VIII, 1623.

[64] Jefferson to Madison, April 12, 1798, *JW*, X, 28.

[65] John Adams to McHenry, October 22, 1798, *AW*, VIII, 613.

[66] Hamilton to McHenry, March 18, 1799, *HWL*, X, 349.

[67] Miller, *Alexander Hamilton*, 505–507.

[68] Letter No. XIII to the *Boston Patriot*, 1809, *AW*, IX, 290.

While Congress was struggling with problems of army, navy, and taxes, President Adams turned his thoughts toward appointing officers to build and command the army. Conscious of his lack of military experience, he wrote an exploratory letter to Washington, regretting the impossibility of bringing the Virginian back to the presidency and requesting advice whether "to call out all the old Generals, or to appoint a young set."[69]

In reply, Washington expressed reluctance to offer his services in a military capacity but wrote that in case of a formidable invasion he would not "intrench" himself "under the cover of Age and retirement" if his assistance was necessary. It would not be easy "to find among the old set of Generals, men of sufficient activity, energy and health, and of sound politics" to do the strenuous work required; therefore, he recommended reliance, for the most part, on "the well known, most experienced, best proved, and intelligent Officers of the late Army; without respect to Grade."[70] Washington was sixty-six years old at the time but in excellent health. Hamilton had tried to prepare Washington for emerging from the retirement he had so recently entered and which he loved so well. Hamilton "deplored" the necessity of drawing Washington from his well-deserved rest, but reported that "it is the opinion of all those with whom I converse, that you will be compelled to make the sacrifice."[71]

Washington's reply to Hamilton expressed extreme reluctance to leave his "present peaceful abode." He believed that there were other men "more in [their] prime" who could command the armies better than he, and he would not accept command unless the public demand was "unequivocally known." Further, he wanted to know who would be his "coadjutors" and whether Hamilton "would be disposed to take an active part."[72] The younger man immediately gave his assurance that the nation's desire for Washington's leadership would be "ardent and universal" and that he himself was ready to re-enter army life if he was offered a post high enough to enable him to render services "proportionate to the sacrifice" he would be making. He would like to be appointed to the second-highest post, "Inspector-General, with a command in the line."[73]

Washington's choice for second-in-command was Charles Cotesworth

[69] Adams to Washington, June 22, 1798, *ibid.*, VIII, 573.
[70] Washington to Adams, July 4, 1798, *WW*, XXXVI, 313–14.
[71] Hamilton to Washington, May 19, 1798, *HWL*, X, 285–86.
[72] Washington to Hamilton, May 27, 1798, *WW*, XXXVI, 272–73.
[73] Hamilton to Washington, June 2, 1798, *HWL*, X, 287.

Pinckney, who had been breveted brigadier general during the Revolution. Washington trusted Pinckney; moreover, he thought it good policy to appoint a southern general inasmuch as the campaign, if any, would probably take place in the South. Hamilton summoned all his influence and that of his friends in high places to secure the post for himself. It would be a position of great importance, for Washington was understood not to plan to leave Mount Vernon unless it became necessary to lead the army into battle. Pickering had suggested Hamilton for commander-in-chief before he learned that Washington would serve.[74] Now he and McHenry and other Federalists went to work to assure Hamilton's appointment as second-in-command.

Intrigue was no part of Hamilton's makeup. His life had been so open to public view and he had always been so candid in expressing his opinions that he had frequently incurred ill will for supporting propositions he thought were right even though unpopular. Adams later accused Hamilton of intrigue in his efforts to influence the cabinet during this period. Yet, as has been repeatedly illustrated, Hamilton had always given his advice freely. He had tried to counsel Adams directly but had been rebuffed, and most of the advice he gave to the cabinet had already appeared in his essays. On the few occasions when Hamilton did resort to surreptitious methods—as later in the election of 1800—he blundered precisely because he was not experienced in intrigue. In 1798 he succeeded because of the assistance of his friends and because the position called for a man with his energy and astuteness.

Adams disliked Hamilton and considered him a climber, but he had intended to offer Hamilton a high commission. He stoutly resisted the idea of placing him in so important a post, however, preferring Horatio Gates, Benjamin Lincoln, Daniel Morgan, or Henry Knox, and at first rejected outright the cabinet's recommendation of Hamilton.[75] Adams asked the Senate to approve his appointment of Washington for command. It promptly did so, and McHenry delivered Washington's commission in person, seizing the opportunity to advance Hamilton as second-in-command. Washington was offended at Adams for placing his name before the Senate without his explicit consent, though the President had some grounds for

[74] Pickering to Hamilton, August 21, 1798, *HWH*, VI, 343–46; Pickering to King, August 29, 1798, *KC*, II, 404.

[75] Miller, *Alexander Hamilton*, 475.

assuming that Washington had given his assent in his letter of July 4, 1798, in which he wrote, "You may command me without reserve."[76] McHenry and Hamilton made special efforts to soothe the general's ruffled feelings. "Convinced of the goodness of the motives" of Adams, Hamilton wrote that "it would be useless to scan the propriety of the step."[77] Washington's principles would not have allowed him to refuse the commission in any event, but Adams' precipitous manner probably made Washington more amenable to the idea of making Hamilton second-in-command. Washington was told by the High Federalists that public opinion in the East and Northeast was calling insistently for Hamilton and would give less support to the war if a southerner was appointed to the second post.

When Washington gave Pickering his reasons for suggesting Pinckney, he strongly implied that he actually preferred Hamilton.[78] He wrote candidly to Hamilton, "My wish to put you first, and my fear of losing him [Pinckney] are not a little embarrassing."[79] Hamilton took his own cause in hand and replied, also candidly, that service during the Revolution had given him better training for generalship than Pinckney had received, that he would have risen to a higher rank if he had been placed in command of one of the "regiments of artillery" in 1777 instead of becoming Washington's aide-de-camp, and that he did not believe Pinckney would object to being appointed to third place. He was emphatic in declaring that he would not allow personal "ambition or interest" to stand "in the way of the public good"—so emphatic, in fact, that it would have been virtually impossible for him to refuse third place for himself. Before the final decision was reached, he wrote to Washington again, saying, "I shall cheerfully place myself in your disposal, and facilitate any arrangement you may think for the general good."[80] A refusal to serve would have denied him a role in the drama, and would have shaken Washington's confidence in him, which Hamilton would have viewed as a personal catastrophe.[81]

At last Washington gave in. He wrote to McHenry that he had always insisted on being allowed to choose such officers "as will be agreeable."[82]

[76] Washington to Adams, July 4, 1798, *WW*, XXXVI, 312.

[77] Hamilton to Washington, July 8, 1798, *HWL*, X, 295.

[78] Washington to Pickering, July 11, 1798, *WW*, XXXVI, 323–25.

[79] Washington to Hamilton, July 14, 1798, *ibid.*, 332.

[80] Hamilton to Washington, July 29, August 20, 1798, *HWL*, X, 299–303, 311.

[81] Cf. Miller, *Alexander Hamilton*, 476, who implies that Hamilton might have refused to serve if denied the post he wanted.

[82] Washington to McHenry, July 5, 1798, *WW*, XXXVI, 318.

When Washington learned that Adams wished to appoint his fellow New Englander Henry Knox to the second post, he expressed himself plainly to the President, in one of the longest letters he ever wrote, saying that he had accepted his commission with the understanding that he would determine the rank of the generals. He all but threatened to resign unless Adams agreed to appoint Hamilton. He tried hard to avoid a tone of arrogance and to avoid offending the President, illustrating at some length why Hamilton was qualified for the command, mentioning the nature of his duties during the Revolution and his superb energy and abilities. "By some," he wrote, Hamilton "is considered an ambitious man, and therefore a dangerous one. That he is ambitious I shall readily grant, but it is of that laudable kind which prompts a man to excel in whatever he takes in hand. He is enterprising, quick in his perceptions, and his judgment intuitively great—qualities essential to a Military character."[83]

Adams knew that he was beaten. With as much dignity as possible, he replied that he had always intended to defer to Washington in disputes over rank. He added, however, that he had the authority to allow Washington to make such decisions, for under "the present Constitution of the United States, the President has authority to determine the rank of officers."[84] Thus he conceded the point while holding intact the constitutional powers of his office.

This was Hamilton's most triumphant hour. As inspector general he would be responsible for building an army, and he was eager for the task. He had promoted every stratagem to maintain the peace, but if war must come he wanted to be in the thick of it, as in his youthful days during the Revolution. He had used his energy and his talents in counseling statesmen and the people in the ways of peace. Now that he thought peace was impossible, he would promote the nation's interests by direct action.

He was soon to find that his course was crowded with obstacles. His colleagues did not share his energy, nor the nation his enthusiasm.

[83] Washington to Adams, September 25, 1798, *ibid.*, 453–62.
[84] Adams to Washington, October 9, 1798, *AW*, VIII, 601.

CHAPTER XVIII

Major General Hamilton

MANY FORCES combined to delay the organization of the army. It was a difficult task, involving much more than calling out the militia, as had been the case in 1794, and "the art of administration" had not yet been developed in the new nation.[1] What army existed was a mere shadow army, and there was no recruiting system. Washington pointed out that the President could not create an army of ten thousand men merely by blowing a trumpet, and the generals were soon exasperated by the tardiness of the administration.

It was left to Hamilton, now major general, to do much of the work that should have been carried out by the War Department, and Hamilton himself was delayed by several attacks of illness. For some time he had no secretarial help except what his nephew Philip Church, his only aide, could give him. Yet it fell to Hamilton to formulate programs for recruitment, mobilization, and discipline, and even to fashion uniforms for the various branches of service.[2] Large numbers of Republicans in and out of Congress resorted to every conceivable tactic for delay. "Why call out an army," they asked, "with no enemy in sight?" The passage of the Alien and Sedition Acts brought the accusation that the Federalists were chiefly interested in creating an army to move against their democratic opponents at home.

Secretary of War McHenry became the target of Hamilton's sharpest criticism. Hamilton was vexed by the "want of energy" in the government, though he expected that a favorable "progress of opinion" would "shortly overcome this obstacle."[3] The force of public opinion proved less effective than he had hoped, and so he sought to prod McHenry directly, though tactfully. He informed the secretary that General Washington would like

1 White, *The Federalists*, 8.
2 Mitchell, *Alexander Hamilton*, II, 438–42.
3 Hamilton to King, June 6, 1798, *HWL*, X, 291.

"frequent communications" concerning "public supplies, . . . the quantities on hand and the measures in execution to procure others."[4] He had already prepared the way by advising Washington to request the information from McHenry.[5] Washington had promptly complied, but to little effect. "I hear nothing of nominations," Hamilton complained. "What malignant influence hangs upon our military affairs?"[6] Continued delays led him to write to Congressman Otis, urging him to "interrogate the Minister."[7] Though aware that Washington was on intimate terms with McHenry, Hamilton commented to his chief that "my friend McHenry is wholly insufficient for his place, with the additional misfortune of not having himself the least suspicion of the fact."[8] Washington replied that he had known since he appointed McHenry in 1796 that the secretary had small abilities—that he was "a Hobson's choice"—but he asked, "What is to be done?"[9]

Adams remained lukewarm about the expansion of the army, though he supported the navy energetically. Seeing no real prospect of a French invasion, he remained opposed to the taxes that would be required to equip and support an army. Many years later he retrospectively concluded that his defeat at the polls in 1800 was the result of the high taxes imposed for military expenses during his last year in office.[10]

Republican congressmen objected, though unsuccessfully, to the procedure of authorizing the President to raise an army. Nicholas held that Congress alone should make the decision about the need for an army, and he believed it to be so utterly unnecessary at that time that he tried to prevent the discussion of any proposal for it. Gallatin, in his precise, methodical manner, showed that the Constitution plainly stated that the power to raise armies was given to Congress, not to the president. A successful Federalist effort to reverse this authority, he maintained, would reduce the Constitution to "a piece of blank paper."[11] The Federalists met this objection much as twentieth-century Americans would meet it, but the discussions worked for delay.

Hamilton, who served as major general for several months before he

[4] Hamilton to McHenry, August 25, 1798, *ibid.*, 317–18.
[5] Hamilton to Washington, August 1, 1798, *ibid.*, 304.
[6] Hamilton to McHenry, December 26, 1798, *ibid.*, VII, 48.
[7] Hamilton to Otis, December 27, 1798, *ibid.*, X, 326.
[8] Hamilton to Washington, July 29, 1798, *ibid.*, 302.
[9] Washington to Hamilton, August 9, 1798, *WW*, XXXVI, 394.
[10] Letter No. 13 to the *Boston Patriot*, 1809, *AW*, IX, 289.
[11] *Annals*, VIII, 1525–26.

began receiving a salary, grew hard-pressed financially. Adams had asked the generals to serve without pay until they were called into active service. Hamilton was too proud to reject the condition, but an exception should have been made in his case. Unlike other officers, he was soon spending nearly all his time at his new military duties, and he was unable to support his family without a salary. He threw himself so freely into his military tasks that his law practice dwindled. In October, 1798, he went to Philadelphia, attired in an expensive uniform, and spent six weeks conferring with Washington and Pinckney. By January his resources were so nearly exhausted that he felt constrained to swallow his pride and write to McHenry for relief.[12] Adams promptly gave instructions to commence the young general's salary—$268.35 a month—retroactive to the previous November 1.[13]

The process of choosing officers for commissions was drawn out over an incredibly long period. First it must be decided how many officers should be recruited in each state. Then the generals in the various states apportioned the commissions to counties or groups of counties. For example, Secretary McHenry asked General William R. Davie of North Carolina to select ten or twelve captains, twenty-four lieutenants, and twenty-four ensigns. McHenry stipulated that these officers should be selected from among men "whose attachment to the Government is unequivocal" and who had never shown "a decided inclination toward France, or French principles."[14] The generals duly wrote to political friends soliciting nominations, usually relaying the admonition about political principles. The Federalist captains were supposed to choose the men in their localities to fill up their companies. The politicians were unconscionably slow in making their nominations. Delay was the order of the day. After they were finally commissioned, several officers resigned in disgust, after waiting for months to be called into action.[15]

Only when the political tensions of 1798 are recalled is it possible to understand why responsible national leaders would set up such a partisan system. Washington commanded in this respect, as in others. For years he had stoutly opposed political parties, and certainly he had no personal political aspirations during these closing years of his life. Yet his antagonism toward the "French faction" continued unabated. When it was reported to

[12] December 16, 1798, *HWL*, VII, 43.

[13] Mitchell, *Alexander Hamilton*, II, 439.

[14] McHenry to Davie, September 12, 1798, Papers of William R. Davie, North Carolina Department of Archives and History, Raleigh.

[15] Washington to Hamilton, April 10, 1799, *WW*, XXXVII, 182.

him that some Americans who had formerly spoken out in support of revolutionary France were professing to have altered their views and were seeking commissions in the army, he was gravely disturbed. He warned the secretary of war that "you could as soon scrub the blackamore white, as to change the principles of a profest Democrat." He believed that such persons would "leave nothing unattempted to overturn the Government" and that in case of an invasion they would promptly join the enemy.[16] He wrote to General Davie that at the officer level "all violent opposers of the Government, and French Partisans should be avoided; or they will disseminate the poison of their principles in the Army, and split, what ought to be a band of brothers, into parties."[17]

Davie needed no such warning. When requesting nominees, he informed key Federalists in the state that it was "indispensable that the Gentlemen should be warm and attached friends to their country and untainted in every manner by French politics or principles."[18] Such language would not likely be misunderstood. The recommendations that came back to the general seldom failed to mention that the nominees had "ardent attachment to the Government of the United States" or were "strongly attached to the Government" or had "federal or governmental principles."[19] Might not such men gain in political stature as a result of their prospective military careers? Might they not become centers of Federalist influence during later years and help keep the state from wandering again after the enticements of Republicanism?

Hamilton, having no interest in political parties as such, was less insistent than Washington, McHenry, and Davie on federalism in the army. First and foremost he wanted an effective army. He found it regrettable "that the objection against anti-federalism has been carried—so far." He agreed that it was important to appoint "friends of the government" generally, but he would "relax the rule in favor of particular merit in a few instances."[20] Thus he favored the appointment of Aaron Burr,[21] and he was disappointed when

[16] Washington to McHenry, September 30, 1798, *ibid.*, XXXVI, 474.

[17] Washington to Davie, October 24, 1798, *ibid.*, 516.

[18] Davie to Major General Smith et al., September 27, 1798, Papers of William R. Davie, North Carolina Department of Archives and History, Raleigh.

[19] John Stanley to Davie, December 27, 1798, Wallace Alexander and John Moore to Davie, January 3, 1799, Wallace Alexander to Davie, January 27, 1799, John Davis to Davie, February 14, 1799, Governor's Papers, State Series, North Carolina Department of Archives and History, Raleigh, XXII, 12, 16, 32, 49.

[20] Hamilton to McHenry, February 6, 1799, *HWL*, VII, 63.

[21] Miller, *Alexander Hamilton*, 481.

Caleb Gibbs was refused a commission. He might have prevailed over Washington in any given case, but the Federalists in the Senate were adamant.

Speculation continued about the probability that France would declare war. The British remained convinced that war was at hand.[22] John Quincy Adams, on the other hand, still thought that the United States could avoid war and at the same time protect its commerce by joining with the neutral nations of Europe in a system comparable to the Armed Neutrality of 1780.[23] Rufus King, United States minister to Great Britain, was as uncertain as any of his Federalist friends. In June, 1798, he predicted, "France will not declare war against us." Yet by the following month he had altered his opinion and believed that Americans' unwillingness to submit would impel the Directory "to declare war against us." In August he felt confident that the United States was in a favorable position because of "the spirit of our people" but warned that relaxation would ruin everything. In September, observing the flow of events in Europe, he was convinced that there would be no outright war, but he continued to warn against French designs to take over the United States by internal division.[24]

William Vans Murray, the new United States representative at The Hague, appears to have analyzed Talleyrand's intentions more accurately. The French were "alarmed," he wrote, "by American preparation, . . . spirit and will." He believed that Talleyrand did not want a "rupture" but that the French would continue to "plunder as much [as ever] and whine more."[25] Pickering also thought it "probable that France will continue her actual hostilities against the commerce of the United States without a formal declaration of war." Yet he authorized King to employ a fast sailing vessel to rush the news to the United States in case of such a declaration. Pickering recalled that it was Talleyrand who had stated "that the United States merited no more consideration than Genoa or Geneva," which had fallen into the clutches of France.[26] In the summer of 1798, Pickering probably knew that Talleyrand had written confidentially to Jefferson that he "would not be tricked into a war with America," but it would have been difficult for

[22] Liston to Grenville, May 2, 1798, FCA, XXII.

[23] *JQAW*, II, 263.

[24] King to Hamilton, June 6, July 14, September 23, 1798, King to Pickering, August 5, 1798, *KC*, II, 338, 365, 382, 424.

[25] Murray to John Quincy Adams, July 3, 1798, American Historical Association *Annual Report* for 1912 (1914), 426–27.

[26] Pickering to King, May 3, November 7, 1798, *KC*, II, 320, 459.

any American, especially a Federalist, to take comfort from that declaration, coming from one who had attained such a reputation for mendacity.[27]

Jefferson wrote as though he had abandoned all hope for peace, but it is not clear whether he was speaking out of conviction or merely using his pen to attack the Federalists. In protesting against Adams' "thrasonic" answers to anti-French "addresses" from various towns, Jefferson stated that "whatever chance for peace might have been left us after the publication of [the XYZ dispatches], is completely lost by these answers." A little later (presumably before he received the communication from Talleyrand), he saw the nation "proceeding further and further in war measures. I consider that event as almost inevitable."[28]

Hamilton, also growing slowly and reluctantly convinced that war was inevitable, did not overlook what he always regarded as the greater threat—internal enemies working on behalf of France. He wrote to Washington about the "great probability that we may have to enter into a very serious struggle with France; and it is more and more evident that the powerful faction which has for years opposed the government, is determined to go every length with France. I am sincere in declaring my full conviction, as the result of a long course of observation, that they are ready to *new-model* our Constitution under the *influence* or *coercion* of France, to form with her a perpetual alliance, *offensive* and *defensive*, and to give her a monopoly of our trade by *peculiar* and *exclusive* privileges. This would be in substance, whatever it might be in name, to make this country a province of France."[29] Washington subscribed fully to this view and to the further view that relaxation would be ruinous.[30]

A careful scrutiny of Hamilton's works fails to reveal at what date he first came to see outright war as a near certainty. In March, 1798, he spoke of Americans' choice "between a tame surrender of our rights, or a state of mitigated hostility."[31] Evidently he was not then envisioning an unlimited war. During the summer of 1798 his expectation of all-out hostilities increased, and by October he was relatively sure that they could not be avoided, for then he referred to a recent period when "it became unequivocal that

[27] Lyon, "The Directory and the United States," *American Historical Review*, Vol. XLIII (April, 1938), 525.

[28] Jefferson to Madison, May 2, 1798, Jefferson to General Thaddeus Kosciusko, June 1, 1798, *JW*, X, 33–34, 49.

[29] Hamilton to Washington, May 19, 1798, *HWL*, X, 284–85.

[30] Washington to McHenry, December 13, 1798, *WW*, XXXVII, 35.

[31] Hamilton to Pickering, March 17, 1798, *HWL*, X, 277.

we must have a decisive rupture with France."[32] Upon becoming major general he had perforce to turn his thoughts to war, and no doubt his military concerns influenced his opinions and reinforced the severe disappointments he had witnessed in the field of diplomacy. Once war seemed to him unavoidable, for reasons of morale he hoped that France would make the declaration. When 1798 had passed without such a break, he came to wish that Congress would declare war. He suggested to Congress a dramatic plan for doing so in a manner that would enhance American morale and at the same time advance his own strategy for conducting the war. Before Congress adjourned, he would have it enact a law "empowering the President, at his discretion, . . . to declare that a state of war exists," if "a negotiation between the United States and France should not be on foot by the first of August next, or being on foot should terminate without an adjustment of differences." He suggested that the law also authorize the use of the nation's land and naval forces to frustrate the "hostile designs of France, either directly or *indirectly through any of her allies*."[33] The latter provision would facilitate action against the Spaniards in Louisiana and Florida.

The Federalists in Congress made their own survey of the possibilities of declaring war, being aware, as Ames put it, "of the danger and folly of keeping multitudes long in suspense."[34] When Hamilton failed to support them, preferring to wait for France to make the break or to authorize the President to declare war "on the first of August next," they tried to draw Adams into the plan. He refused, even though he had recently "given the impression that he could not wait to be off to the wars."[35] Realizing that they did not have enough votes to pass the measure, they decided not to bring the subject up for debate.

Adams later pointed to Hamilton as the instigator of the move for the immediate declaration of war.[36] Adams' biographer, his grandson Charles Francis Adams, tried to prove the point. He even cited Gibbs, who was emotionally pro-Hamilton, in support of the accusation.[37] But Gibbs offered no evidence that would bear out the contention. According to him, of the two anti-Adams factions of Federalists, one wanted to continue the nation's

[32] Hamilton to King, October 2, 1798, *ibid.*, 321.
[33] Hamilton to Otis, January 26, 1799, *ibid.*, 338.
[34] Ames, *Works of Fisher Ames*, I, 228.
[35] Miller, *Alexander Hamilton*, 471.
[36] See his letter No. 18 to the *Boston Patriot*, 1809, *AW*, IX, 305.
[37] Charles Francis Adams, *Life of John Adams*, *ibid.*, I, 538–39.

preparations and await a French declaration, while the other preferred to see the United States take more precipitate action. He did not state or imply that Hamilton supported the latter group, though he offered several reasons of his own for believing that the United States should have declared war in 1798.[38]

The difficulties facing the nation were further complicated by the fact that the British continued their irritating attacks on American shipping. Hamilton was upset by news of the operations of the particularly bold Captain Cochran, who commanded the *Thetis* in the West Indies and off the southern coast of the United States. Hamilton was convinced that such attacks must not be allowed to continue. They were injurious to the country and might revive the strength of the Republicans and dampen American resistance to France. He advised the secretary of state that the country should "act with spirit and energy as well toward Great Britain as France. I would mete the same measure to both of them, though it should even furnish the extraordinary spectacle of a nation at war with two nations at war with each other. One of them will quickly court us." He would send one of the new American frigates to Charleston to protect American commerce and, "if necessary, control the *Thetis*. This conduct will unite and animate."[39]

The proposal was perfectly consistent with the attitude Hamilton held toward Britain throughout his life and is reminiscent of his firm avowals to Hammond during the dark days of the Jay negotiations that the United States would make no peaceful settlement with Britain if she did not evacuate the Northwest Territory. It is in interesting contrast to the attitude of Jefferson, who also resented the injuries of both belligerents but thought that war must be avoided with both.[40] Each man was interested primarily in the domestic scene—Hamilton believing that resistance was essential to the maintenance of national independence and the avoidance of mob rule, and Jefferson believing that American freedom would be endangered by a strong government and by the high taxes military defense would require.

It was through such opposing views that each man, from positions of patriotism, came to consider the other the nation's deadliest enemy. In Jefferson's view, it was "the irresistible influence and popularity of General

[38] Gibbs, II, 216–17.

[39] Hamilton to Pickering, June 7, 8, 1798, *HWL*, X, 293–94.

[40] Jefferson to Gerry, January 20, 1799, Jefferson to Edmund Pendleton, February 14, 1799, *JW*, X, 79, 107–108.

Washington played off by the cunning of Hamilton, which turned the government over to anti-republican hands, or turned the republicans chosen by the people into anti-republicans."[41] Jefferson failed to see that French ambitions, unchecked, would have destroyed the United States, and he was mistaken in assuming that Hamilton's political principles endangered liberty. Very little actual expenditures for the army or the navy would have been necessary if the Republicans had not been so long-winded in apologizing for France. "The difficulties with France would have been of short duration," wrote Morison, "had not the blind infatuation of Jefferson's party for France encouraged the rulers of that country to use them as instruments to keep the United States in tutelage."[42]

Jefferson wanted Congress to adjourn early in the summer of 1798 so that the administration could no longer use that body as a sounding board to alarm the nation about France. The Federalists were determined, he said, that Congress should "stay together to keep up the inflammation of the public mind." To separate Congress now," he wrote, would "be withdrawing the fire from under a boiling pot."[43] If the members would go home and mingle with their constituents, he was confident that they would find more resistance against the high taxes recently levied and the Alien and Sedition Acts than against the French privateers.[44]

Some of the Republicans in Congress were proclaiming that the United States could not afford war measures even if a more passive policy meant the loss of the nation's foreign commerce. When the Federalists decried "counting the cost" when the nation's defense was at stake, John Williams of New York replied that if the "rights" being violated concerned subjects outside the national territory "it was perfectly right to sit down and calculate the expense."[45]

Representative Livingston, assuming that Elbridge Gerry was still lingering in France (though Pickering had ordered him unequivocally to return to the United States),[46] offered a resolution calling on the President to instruct Gerry to proceed alone to negotiate a treaty with France according to previous instructions. The move was apparently aimed at covering up

[41] Jefferson to John Taylor, June 1, 1798, *ibid.*, 44.
[42] Morison, *The Life and Letters of Harrison Gray Otis*, I, 70.
[43] Jefferson to Madison, June 21, 1798, *JW*, X, 51–52.
[44] Jefferson to Edmund Pendleton, February 14, 1799, *ibid.*, 105.
[45] House of Representatives, May 5, 1798, *Annals*, VIII, 1595 ff.
[46] Pickering to Gerry, June 25, 1798, *ASPFR*, II, 204.

Gerry's questionable behavior and was not a serious proposal. Federalist Representative John Wilkes Kittera of Pennsylvania derisively offered an amendment: "... and in case the said Envoy shall have been ordered out of the French Republic, or taken into custody, then with such other person or persons as the French Directory may select." Congressman George Thacher of Maine seconded the amendment, but Otis expressed the hope that the amendment would be withdrawn because it cast too slight a censure on the motion.[47] The amendment was withdrawn, and the motion failed.

Philadelphia was caught up in a new sensation in November, 1798, when the Quaker Dr. George Logan returned from his private peace venture to Paris convinced that the Directory was eager for further negotiations to put an end to the long-standing controversy.[48] The Federalists reacted furiously, recalling that this was the man who had "treasonously" published in a Philadelphia newspaper Monroe's letters from Paris but had withheld the author's name. Logan's reputation as a man of high moral principles was not enough to protect him, especially when it became known that he had carried a letter of recommendation from Jefferson and was looked upon in Europe as Jefferson's agent. Jefferson told his friends that the purpose of the letter was merely to protect Logan in "turbulent and suspicious" Europe, that he had given Logan no instructions, and that he had been led to believe the journey had to do with Logan's "private affairs." "The part [the Federalists] ascribed to me," he declared, "was entirely a calumny." Jefferson reacted in much the same way the Republicans in Congress did when they were on the defensive. He complained that he had been "a constant butt for every shaft of calumny which malice and falsehood could form and the presses, public speakers, or private letters disseminate."[49]

With the assistance of a mutual friend, Logan gained access to Washington's home, but the general treated him and his message with contempt and recorded for posterity a memorandum of the encounter that is the best surviving illustration of his considerable ability at biting rejoinder.[50] Logan received a more favorable reception by the public at large, however, and he did not consider his mission a failure.

The Federalists responded by pushing through the famous Logan Act,

[47] *Annals*, July 2–3, 1798, VIII, 2083–86.

[48] Moore, *A Digest of International Law*, IV, 448–49.

[49] Jefferson to Gerry, January 26, 1799, Jefferson to Pendleton, January 29, 1799, *JW*, X, 75–76, 88–89.

[50] "Memorandum of an Interview," November 13, 1798, *WW*, XXXVII, 18–20.

making it illegal for a private citizen to undertake diplomatic negotiations with a foreign government on any subject other than redress for injuries he had personally sustained from that government. But the Federalists gained no strength from the Logan controversy. The word of an honored citizen that high French officials had expressed a desire for peace was not lost on a public that had already grown irritable at high taxes and oppressive wartime laws enacted without a declaration of war. The Republican *Aurora* heaped praise on Logan and asserted that if war with France was avoided it would be attributable to his heroic action.[51]

The tide began to turn in Congress, as the Republicans took new courage. Gallatin asked what harm Logan had done and added that if it was a crime for a private American citizen to correspond with a foreign government it should also be illegal for American officials to negotiate with foreign citizens—as Marshall and Pinckney had done with Talleyrand's agents.[52] Representative Nicholas agreed that a person should be punished for trying to involve his country in war, but he did not understand the objection to trying to obtain peace. He pointedly asked the Federalists if they were afraid the country would be "forced into a peace which they did not want." He pointed out that Logan had simply informed the French that their actions were building up hatred in the United States and strengthening the Federalists. "Even a child," he said, "could have illuminated France on this subject."[53] That was too obvious to be denied; and Harper, the most outspoken Federalist in the House, came to the point where he merely characterized Logan's effort as "a very silly affair." The Federalists' strong point was that no nation could afford to allow its citizens to carry on unauthorized negotiations with other governments, and it was on this principle that they wrote the Logan Act.

The Republicans drew comfort from the President's annual address to Congress on December 8, 1798. Again Adams condemned the hostility of the French and their refusal to enter negotiations, but he expressed gratitude to the "Supreme Being [for] our well-being and safety." He praised the successes of the American navy in checking the attacks on American commerce and said, "Perhaps no country ever experienced more sudden and remarkable advantages from any measure of policy than we have derived

[51] *Aurora*, November 29, 1798.

[52] House of Representatives, December 27, 28, 1798, *Annals*, IX, 2496–97, 2538.

[53] December 27, 1798, *ibid.*, 2495, 2518.

from the arming for our maritime protection and defense." He recommended a continuous program of naval building and said that the causes for delay in building the army had been removed and that "it is expected that the raising and organizing of the troops will proceed without obstacle and with effect." All of this surprised nobody; it simply called for a continuation of previous policies. But the nation noted more particularly his statements about further negotiations with France. The French government, he said, appeared "solicitous to impress the opinion that it is averse to a rupture with this country" and had "in a qualified manner" indicated a willingness to "receive a minister from the United States." To send another minister under existing circumstances would be "an act of humiliation to which the United States ought not to submit," but he would "respect the sacred rights of embassy," a statement which seemed to be an invitation to France to send an envoy to Philadelphia.[54]

Generals Washington, Hamilton, and Pinckney sat at the right of the President during his address to lend a military air to the occasion, but Hamilton felt that something was amiss. He continued with military preparations, but a new element of doubt crept into his correspondence. A few days later, when drafting for Washington a long report to the secretary of war on military matters, he stated, "Nothing has been communicated respecting our foreign relations, to induce the opinion that there has been any change . . . as to external danger." "Late occurrences," he agreed, might have rendered a French invasion of the United States less likely, but the "rapid vicissitudes . . . of political and military events" and the "extraordinary fluctuations" in the European contest were such that the only prudent course for the United States was full attention to preparations for war.[55] Two weeks later he wrote that he could not "conceive why nothing has yet gone to Congress" to facilitate the military build-up.[56]

Nicholas was on a sounder course than usual when he remarked in the House of Representatives that he sensed a "general impression" that relations with France "were mending." He thought that his opponents had altered their tone. In the previous session they had been loud "in their cry for war," but now he heard "nothing of that kind."[57] As was often pointed out, it

[54] Richardson, I, 261–65.

[55] December 13, 1798, *HWL*, VII, 9–10.

[56] Hamilton to Otis, December 27, 1798, *ibid.*, X, 326.

[57] December 27, 1798, *Annals*, IX, 2493–94.

appeared that the French had reduced the severity of their attacks on American commerce.[58]

The Federalists remained firm on the point that any improvement had resulted from the American show of force and that a relaxation would lead rapidly to worse conditions. Defense measures and appropriations continued, and the army began to take shape, but now it was the Federalists who often found themselves on the defensive. They began to show keen irritation at repeated avowals by Republicans that if war should come they would fight as hard as anyone else in defense of their country. Jefferson had continually made this point clear in correspondence with his friends. If war should "actually take place," he had declared, "no matter by whom brought on, we must defend ourselves. If our house be on fire, without inquiring whether it was fired from within or without, we must try to extinguish it. In that, I have no doubt, we shall act as one man."[59]

Such statements were frequently made in Congress, where the Federalists ridiculed them and characterized them as hypocritical statements from men tinged with treason. They kept asking why the Republicans did not demonstrate their patriotism by supporting naval defenses against recurring attacks on Americans at sea and why they did not, while there was still time, support measures to prepare an army to meet the land invasion that had been explicitly threatened by Talleyrand's agents. Congressman James A. Bayard of Delaware finally blazed out with the accusation that what the Republicans were really saying to France was: "Capture our vessels; destroy our commerce; . . . imprison our seamen; insult and trample upon [our] rights; but don't bring an army among us, because then we can no longer hoodwink the people; . . . our party will be ruined. . . . We shall be deserted and annihilated; we must fall never to rise again."[60]

There was no question that American naval action greatly diminished the attacks on American commerce. The publication of the XYZ papers proved to Talleyrand that he could not overcome the Americans by threats of force or subvert the United States through the Republican party. Thus he became an "apostle of peace" with the United States.[61] But his earlier duplicity made

[58] Morison, *The Life and Letters of Harrison Gray Otis*, I, 155.

[59] Jefferson to James Lewis, Jr., May 9, 1798, *JW*, X, 37.

[60] January 17, 1799, *Annals*, IX, 2714–15.

[61] Lyon, "The Directory and the United States," *American Historical Review*, Vol. XLIII (April, 1938), 524; E. Wilson Lyon, "The Franco-American Convention of 1800," *Journal of Modern History*, Vol. XII (September, 1940), 305.

it difficult for him to convince Adams that he wished to change diplomatic course. Moreover, it was not a "peace among equals" that he wanted, but new negotiations to terminate commercial grievances and give him time to concoct new schemes to further French designs on the United States. He came to feel a greater urgency to carry through his project to seize control of the Mississippi Valley. If he could carry out this plan, he believed, he could still prevail. Fortunately, there were a great many Americans who had followed the game so well that they knew what to expect and what moves to make to block his play.

As early as 1790, Jefferson had been aware of Moustier's scheme to detach the Mississippi area from the United States. As secretary of state, Jefferson had instructed William Short to try to convince the French government that it would be of no advantage to the French to reacquire the territory since they could carry on commerce there under American sovereignty as well as under their own.[62] Jefferson had also been fully aware of Genêt's earlier plans to seize Louisiana with the help of American frontiersmen, though he had not appeared disturbed by the idea.[63]

In 1798 Hamilton called the nation's attention to the French menace on the Gulf. Spain, he said, was "enjoying the fruits of her weakness." The French demand for Louisiana, long pressed, had "at length become categoric. The alternative was to comply or offend." Hamilton described the French goal as the acquisition of all Spain's dominions in the Western Hemisphere and the "dismembering" of the United States.[64]

Moustier's memoir of January, 1789, had probably been "the first serious suggestion by a responsible official that France recover her former colony."[65] In March, 1796, Adet had sent General Victor Collot, former governor of Guadeloupe, to make a ten-month survey of the Ohio and Mississippi country. Adet had urged his government to acquire the Mississippi basin, east and west, all the way to the Alleghenies and to fortify the Allegheny passes against the United States.[66] Talleyrand at length adopted this plan as a national goal for France. Americans were not fully aware of the details

[62] Jefferson to Short, August 10, 1790, *JW*, VIII, 81.

[63] Genêt to Jefferson, December 25, 1793, *ASPFR*, I, 311.

[64] "The Stand," No. 4, April 12, 1798, *HWL*, VI, 284.

[65] Lyon, "Moustier's Memoir on Louisiana," *Mississippi Valley Historical Review*, Vol. XXII (September, 1935), 252.

[66] Turner, "The Policy of France Toward the Mississippi Valley in the Period of Washington and Adams," *American Historical Review*, Vol. X (January, 1905), 249, 272.

of the scheme, but the Federalists frequently expressed alarm about it, and their suspicions proved to be correct.[67]

The fertile lands of the Mississippi Valley and the lush hammocks of Florida had never attracted the Spaniards into establishing settlements on any important scale. They were interested in gold and silver and in settled Indian nations that were numerous enough and rich enough to support a ruling class. They had such colonies in Mexico and South America. They considered Louisiana and the Floridas a fence to exclude the United States from the Gulf of Mexico and thus from aggressive incursions into their more greatly prized possessions. By 1795, Spain had become reconciled to losing Louisiana, but preferably to France, not to the United States. As mentioned earlier, Godoy had refused to cede the territory to France in the Treaty of Basle, for he wished to use navigational rights on the Mississippi as bait to obtain a friendly treaty with the United States.[68] After that he had planned to cede the territory to France for the best bargain he could get.[69] Pinckney's Treaty, which followed, was always considered highly beneficial to the United States, but under the circumstances it represented no loss to Spain.

American diplomats at home and abroad had followed Godoy's moves. In December, 1795, the British representative in Philadelphia had reported that the Americans understood Spain would cede Louisiana to France at the end of the war.[70] Spain had been so displeased by the Anglo-American "explanatory article" to Jay's Treaty, indicating the United States' willingness to share with Britain the navigation of the Mississippi, that it had rashly sacrificed its new-won friendship with the United States by refusing to carry out promptly all the provisions of Pinckney's Treaty, withdrawing the right of deposit at New Orleans, refusing to hand over Natchez and the territory north of the thirty-first parallel, and again stirring up the Indians against the Americans.[71]

[67] Bemis, *John Quincy Adams and the Foundations of American Foreign Policy*, 100.

[68] A. P. Whitaker, "Louisiana in the Treaty of Basle," *Journal of Modern History*, Vol. VIII, (March, 1936), 23–24.

[69] Whitaker, "The Retrocession of Louisiana in Spanish Policy," *American Historical Review*, Vol. XXXIX, (April, 1934), 459.

[70] Bond to Grenville, December 20, 1795, FCA, X.

[71] Whitaker, "The Retrocession of Louisiana in Spanish Policy," *American Historical Review*, Vol. XXXIX, (April, 1934), 426. James Wilkinson, *Memoirs of My Own Times*, (Philadelphia, 1816), I, 434 (hereafter cited as *Memoirs*); Steiner, 258–74. Catharine Van Cortlandt Mathews, *Andrew Ellicott: His Life and Letters* (New York, 1908), 129–57 (hereafter cited as *Andrew Ellicott*).

The Indian menace, nourished by Spanish intrigue, brought consternation to Americans of all shades of thought. When Jefferson was secretary of state he mentioned it frequently.[72] By the time of the XYZ Affair the Federalists, at least, had come to look upon the French, the Spaniards, and the Indians as equal partners in conspiracy. It was assumed that the Indians, unsupported, would not prove formidable, and it was known that Spain was militarily weak; but the prospect of France coming into the scene created an alarming picture. The Americans were convinced that Spain could not resist French encroachment and that French occupation of Louisiana and the Floridas was but a matter of time.[73] "Poor Spain," King wrote to Hamilton, "is completely under the influence of the Directory."[74] France had come to look upon Louisiana as one of its own dominions. In 1797 it had offered to cede the territory to Great Britain if the latter would cede to France territorial gains in Europe.[75]

American frontiersmen were not without plots of their own. The surveyor-statesman Andrew Ellicott, looking over the situation in 1797, found some settlers mulling over plans to drive out the Spaniards by force as a prelude to joining the United States or Britain, and others even contemplating securing navigation rights by joining with Spain.[76]

When Senator William Blount of Tennessee came under fire as a result of his scheme to draw the frontiersmen and Indians together and join the British in an attack on Spanish Florida and Louisiana, Pickering found the plot incredible, so accustomed had he been to considering it "a fixed point that the French were to obtain possession of Louisiana" and then stir up disaffection against the United States.[77] The British minister Liston had given some support to Blount's scheme, and was embarrassed when Pickering offered him the opportunity to make a written statement, to be presented Congress, denying Britain's part in the affair. Liston evidently assumed that the territory in question would go to the United States, despite Britain's help in driving out the Spaniards. He had to resort to evasive

[72] *JW*, VIII–IX.

[73] Wolcott to Hamilton, July 10, 1795, *HWH*, VI, 15.

[74] King to Hamilton, December 19, 1798, *KC*, II, 495. For a fuller story of Spain's Mississippi policy during this period, see Franklin L. Riley, "Spanish Policy in Mississippi after the Treaty of San Lorenzo," American Historical Association *Annual Report* for 1897 (1898), 177–92.

[75] Whitaker, "The Retrocession of Louisiana in Spanish Policy," *American Historical Review*, Vol. XXXIX (April, 1934), 464; Lyon, "The Directory and the United States," *American Historical Review*, Vol. XLIII (April, 1938), 526.

[76] Whitaker, *The Mississippi Question, 1795–1803*, 103.

[77] Liston to Grenville, June 24, 1797, FCA, XVIII.

language to avoid denying his approval of an undertaking which he believed would have been acceptable to the American government "if it could have been effected with a rapid success."[78] Blount's scheme and others like it were all the more alarming to the Federalists because they had slight confidence in the frontiersmen, whom they feared might become dangerous tools in the hands of Talleyrand.

In the spring of 1798 the air was full of rumors that the French had arrived at Gulf posts. Pickering received "advice from Charleston" that "the French flag was flying at Pensacola," which he interpreted as a "prelude to its appearance in Louisiana."[79] The same report appeared in English newspapers, with the comment that Spain had already "ceded to France eastern Louisiana."[80]

The Republicans continued to discount both French and Spanish dangers in the Mississippi region, taking comfort from the fact that the frontiersmen were by no means unified in their attitudes. The citizens of Natchez were so angered by the Spaniards' delay in withdrawing from the fort that in the spring of 1797 they offered to raise one hundred volunteers, to serve under the command of General James Wilkinson or Major Andrew Ellicott, and force them out.[81] Nothing came of the proposal, but it was evidence of strong anti-Spanish feeling. On the other hand, in Frankfort, Kentucky, there was a strong movement for peace.[82] Jefferson spoke lightly of the "acrimonious altercations" between the Spanish minister and Pickering and added that if hostilities failed to take place in Natchez it was not "for want of endeavors to bring them on by our agents."[83] In Congress the observation was made that war with France would close navigation on the Mississippi, to which Gallatin replied that there was no reason why the river should be closed, since war with France should not lead to one with Spain.[84]

The Federalists deplored the light dismissal of the tensions in the Mississippi region. To them, French occupation of the territory constituted a grave danger. In the summer of 1799, Washington expressed the fear that danger might not be understood "until it is felt; and yet no problem in

[78] Liston to Grenville, March 16, July 8, 1797, *ibid.*

[79] Pickering to General George Matthews, April 1, 1798, Pickering Papers, Massachusetts Historical Society, Boston, VIII, 286.

[80] King to Miranda, May 15, 1798, Davila, *Archivo del General Miranda*, XV, 261.

[81] Mathews, *Andrew Ellicott*, 153.

[82] Whitaker, *The Mississippi Question, 1795–1803*, 127.

[83] Jefferson to Madison, January 25, 1798, *JW*, IX, 436.

[84] June 13, 1798, *Annals*, VIII, 1918.

Euclid is more evident." A little later he wrote that if the French "possess themselves of Louisiana and the Floridas, either by exchange or otherwise, I venture to predict, without the gift of second sight that there will be 'no peace in Israel.' "[85]

What could be done to avert or mitigate this danger? Hamilton was repeatedly asked this question by men in high places. When Pickering wrote confidentially to Hamilton about the failure of Gerry, Marshall, and Pinckney in Paris, he put the question directly: "What ought we to do in respect to Louisiana?" He added a significant comment: "The Spanish force in all Louisiana is small; probably not rising to a thousand men."[86] Washington put the question in the most formal manner possible, in a communication as commander-in-chief to "Major Generals Hamilton and Pinckney." "What measures," he asked, "will be best to counteract [the French]?"[87]

Hamilton had a plan that he was certain would meet the threat; but he would have many obstacles to overcome in seeking to put his plan into effect.

85 Washington to John Trumbull, June 25, 1799, Washington to Governor Jonathan Trumbull, August 30, 1799, *WW*, XXXVII, 250, 348.

86 Pickering to Hamilton, March 25, 1798, *HWH*, VI, 276–77.

87 Washington to Hamilton and Pinckney, November 10, 1798, *WW*, XXXVII, 14.

CHAPTER XIX

Hamilton Looks Toward Louisiana

From late 1798, Hamilton based his program on the conclusion he had finally reached that war with France could not be avoided. His first goal was to build up the military forces to the point where they could forestall any invasion attempt by France. His second concern was to resolve the Indian problem, which also gave anxiety to other American leaders. The third and most colorful feature of his program was to lead an army down the Mississippi and seize Louisiana and the Floridas, territories he had long considered "essential to the unity of the empire" and "the permanancy of the Union."[1]

His primary efforts were devoted to preparations to repel a French invasion of the type threatened by Talleyrand's agents. He was less inclined than formerly to predict the course France would take, but he believed it possible that England and its allies might withdraw from the European struggle, through defeat or weariness. He was convinced that a united America need not quail before the prospect of facing France alone. Comparing the nation in 1798 with its condition in 1775, he found it stronger and wealthier. He looked upon the Republican leaders as the "Tories" of 1798 but thought that they would attract a smaller following than had the insurgents of the 1770's.

Hamilton continued his efforts as inspector general of the army. His prodigious achievements in the face of mounting difficulties have amazed military men of later years. At no time in his life did he display greater ability, enterprise, and persistence.[2]

Hamilton's biographers have devoted relatively little attention to his

[1] Hamilton to Washington, September 1, 1790, *HWL*, IV, 334; Hamilton to Otis, January 26, 1799, *ibid.*, X, 339.

[2] For details of his military achievements see Miller, *Alexander Hamilton*; and Mitchell, *Alexander Hamilton*. Schachner (*Alexander Hamilton*) dwelt on some of the human-interest aspects of this period in Hamilton's life.

interest in the Indian question. As inspector general he spoke of that concern almost as often as he did the French issue. Unlike Washington, Jefferson, and Wilkinson, he did not have much firsthand information about the frontier; but no man saw more clearly than he the dangers of collaboration between the Indians and America's potential enemies, the likelihood of Indian attacks on frontier settlements at a time when the army might be preoccupied with a European foe, and the possibilities of Indian obstruction of army movements in the West.

The Indians occupied an important position in the concerns of the nation's leaders during the early years of the Republic. The Battle of Fallen Timbers had taken place less than four years before Hamilton was called to his role in national defense. The Indians of the Northwest had been defeated, but, like the Indians in the Southwest Territory, the possibility that they might join forces with enemies of the United States was a continuing one. In Hamilton's communications with Brigadier General Wilkinson and other officers in the West, he never failed to take the Indians into account. Wilkinson shared his concern and frequently reported to Hamilton that the Indians were being encouraged by the Spaniards, who were, in turn, being urged on by the French.[3] The Indians, the Spaniards, and the French in the Gulf territories posed a constant threat to the United States.[4]

Though many historians and biographers have mentioned Hamilton's Louisiana policy, none have treated it fully or described it in its proper setting. It has often been confused with Miranda's schemes to liberate Spanish America. Hamilton was well aware of those schemes and gave them some consideration, but his interests were concentrated on Louisiana.

In 1790, when Britain and Spain had been thought to be near war, Hamilton had toyed with the thought of seizing Spain's Gulf territories adjacent to the United States.[5] He had told Washington that "when we are able to make good our pretensions, we ought not to leave in the possession of any foreign power the territories at the mouth of the Mississippi."[6] He continued steadily in that conviction. It will be recalled that when Spain's grasp on the region was imperiled by Genêt's schemes in 1793, Hamilton blocked

[3] Wilkinson to Hamilton, April 15, 1799, HPLC, XXXIX.

[4] Hamilton's most thorough statement on the Indian problem is his letter to Colonel Strong, May 22, 1799, *ibid.*, XLII.

[5] Beckwith to Grenville, November 3, 1790, PROFO, 4, XII.

[6] Hamilton to Washington, September 15, 1790, *HWL*, IV, 337.

the Frenchman by rigidly controlling his money supply. Even Jefferson's support proved unavailing.[7]

The first step in Hamilton's Louisiana program was to build up the forces in the West. Working through Washington, he managed to prevent the withdrawal of forces from that region to reinforce the "Atlantic frontier." He obtained the command over Wilkinson's western army, most of which was stationed on the Ohio and the Mississippi, though other regions of Kentucky and Tennessee were under the command of General Pinckney. Washington agreed that "frequently the most effectual way to defend is to attack."[8] It seemed logical that when France went to war Spain would do so as well. Even if Spain chose to assume a neutral posture, Hamilton believed that the French would use Spanish harbors, and that, together with other unneutral acts, would cause Adams and Congress to consider Spain a belligerent in the conflict.[9] Surely France would demand no less of Spain than Genêt had requested of the United States five years earlier. Thus, with an army in readiness, Hamilton could descend the Mississippi and occupy Spain's weakly protected territories.

Hamilton hoped to make the gifted intriguer Brigadier General Wilkinson his right-hand man, for Wilkinson was acquainted with the West and supposedly had the region well in control. Hamilton gave no credence to widespread stories that Wilkinson had treasonable associations with Spain. Nor did Adams, who learned about the rumors from his son-in-law, Colonel William S. Smith. Adams replied to Smith's charges that he was "too precipitate" and that Smith's own conduct had been criticized just as severely as Wilkinson's. He also rebuked Smith soundly for having gone to Detroit to engage in questionable land speculations while pretending to be on a mission for the President.[10]

Adams nevertheless wrote to Wilkinson reporting that nearly every traveler from the Mississippi claimed that the general "held a commission and received pay as a Colonel in the Spanish service." Then he assured Wilkinson that he did not believe the reports. He reminded the general of the gathering war clouds and expressed full confidence in his loyalty.[11]

[7] Darling, *Our Rising Empire, 1763–1803*, 152–56.

[8] Washington to McHenry, December 13, and 16, 1798, January 24, 1799, *WW*, XXXVII, 37–38, 61.

[9] Liston to Grenville, September 27, 1798, FCA, XXII.

[10] Adams to Smith, February 16, 1798, *AW*, VIII, 566–67.

[11] Adams to Wilkinson, February 4, 1798, *ibid.*, 536–64.

In recommending Wilkinson's promotion to the rank of major general, Hamilton reported to Adams that he "had heard hard things said of the General" but that he had "never seen the shadow of proof" and had himself been "too much the victim of obloquy, to listen to detraction, unsupported by facts." Furthermore, he said, he held "nothing so unwise in public affairs, as half confidence." He believed that Wilkinson would give his faithful assistance in making the country great if he was assured a chance to share in that greatness.[12] For good reason Washington was doubtful about Wilkinson's reliability (the general had taken part in the cabal against Washington in the 1780's), but he supported Hamilton's recommendation on the grounds that it would "feed [Wilkinson's] ambition, soothe his vanity, and by arresting discontent, produce the good effect you contemplate."[13] McHenry pleaded with Hamilton not to rely on Wilkinson, but Hamilton persisted, and the promotion was granted.[14]

It was a risk, for Wilkinson was indeed engaged in private dealings with the Spaniards, as well as in speculations in land and army contracts. He had a long-established reputation for intrigue. But apparently Hamilton's faith in him proved justified. There is no evidence of active disloyalty on the part of the "Tarnished Warrior" during this period, and according to his biographer the general told a Spanish agent that his "honor and position would not allow him to continue his former connection."[15]

Hamilton knew, through Wilkinson and other sources, that Spain's military position at New Orleans was precarious. Since 1793, Spain had "trusted to God to protect its border provinces and assisted Him as best it could through the foreign office."[16] As Hamilton's plans matured, Spanish officials in America began requesting military reinforcements, without which, they said, the Americans could seize the Mississippi and move westward unimpeded into Mexico. Godoy replied that he could not send reinforcements and observed that "you can't lock up an empty field."[17] The prize awaited; if he was permitted to do so, Hamilton could reach out and take it.

For all his courage, however, Hamilton was not one to take unnecessary risks. He would be no diminutive conqueror; as he once said in a different

[12] Hamilton to Adams, September 7, 1799, Wilkinson, *Memoirs*, II, 158. The letter is in the Adams Papers, Massachusetts Historical Society, Boston.

[13] Washington to Hamilton, June 25, 1799, *WW*, XXXVII, 246.

[14] McHenry to Hamilton (private and confidential), June 27, 1799, *HWH*, V, 283.

[15] James Ripley Jacobs, *Tarnished Warrior* (New York, 1938), 166.

[16] Whitaker, *The Mississippi Question, 1795–1803*, 179–80.

[17] *Ibid.*

connection, he would have the "government in arms" appear "like a Hercules, and inspire respect by the display of strength."[18] He prepared his Mississippi expedition with care. While men were being recruited and trained in the West, he worked out with Wilkinson a project to build seventy-five boats on the Ohio, each capable of transporting forty men with "baggage and stores," at a proposed cost of two hundred dollars a boat. By this means he could move an army of three thousand men against St. Louis and New Orleans.[19]

It was characteristic of Hamilton that, having exerted every possible effort to prevent the war, once it appeared certain, he tried to extract from it every benefit he could. Soon after a long planning session with Washington and Pinckney, in October, 1798, he informed a Federalist senator that the army would need a goodly provision of heavy artillery. "This," he said, "looks to offensive operations. . . . Our game will be to attack wherever we can. France is not to be considered as separated from her ally. Tempting objects will be within our grasp."[20] Washington, looking toward "offensive operations," also did all he could to build up the army.[21]

Again Hamilton urged the establishment of "an academy for military and naval instruction" and recommended the establishment of a secret-service fund of half a million dollars.[22] He probably hoped to use some of those funds to promote military operations in the West without prematurely revealing to potential enemies the plan he and Washington were working out.

Washington, Hamilton, and Pinckney decided that it was necessary to summon Wilkinson to Philadelphia to make concerted plans for western operations. Hamilton issued the summons, observing that "much may be examined in a personal interview, which, at so great a distance, cannot be effected by writing." It is not clear how much Hamilton had already told Wilkinson about the plans for operations down the Mississippi. It is significant that he admonished the general to leave a prudent officer in command while he was in Philadelphia—an officer charged only with duties "indispensable for defensive security." That officer should not be entrusted

18 Hamilton to McHenry, March 28, 1799, *HWL*, X, 349.
19 Hamilton to McHenry, October 29, 1799, HPLC, LVIII.
20 Hamilton to General James Gunn, December 22, 1798, *HWL*, VII, 46.
21 Washington to John Trumbull, June 25, 1799, *WW*, XXXVII, 250.
22 Undated document, apparently written early in 1799, for circulation among Hamilton's friends in high places, *HWL*, X, 48–49.

with all the "discretionary powers" that had been conferred upon Wilkinson, lest he "commit prematurely the peace of the United States." The key sentence in the communication, as given in Wilkinson's memoirs, reads, "Care must be taken that the nation *be not embroiled,* but in consequence of a *deliberate policy in the government.*"[23] In his edition of Hamilton's works, Lodge has the passage, "Care must be taken that the nation be not embroiled, in consequence of a *liberal* policy in the government."[24] The copy of the letter in the Hamilton Papers in the Library of Congress is not clear, but it definitely includes the word "but," and the key word looks much more like "deliberate" than "liberal." Moreover, Lodge's rendition does not fit the context. Lodge apparently wanted to play down Hamilton's plan for attacking New Orleans. He did not print Hamilton's letter to McHenry prescribing the number of boats and men to be used in the Louisiana campaign.[25]

Before Wilkinson left for Philadelphia Hamilton wrote to him again concerning the "objects" which he should be prepared to discuss in the Capitol. Those topics included the "disposition" of "our Western inhabitants" and of the Indians and the Spaniards, and the strength of the latter "in number and fortification." Hamilton also wanted to know "the best mode (in the event of a *rupture with Spain*) of attacking the two Floridas."[26] In his correspondence Hamilton often referred to such a "rupture" as a prerequisite for attacking that country's territories in America, but his letters to friends and associates such as Washington, King, McHenry, and Otis reveal that he fully intended that war with France should be tantamount to a rupture with France's ally as well.

There is no indication that Washington differed with Hamilton on this point. Both men assumed that France might try to invade the United States through Louisiana (just as Andrew Jackson, sixteen years later, looked for the appearance of a British army at Pensacola), and they considered themselves justified in action anticipating such an invasion. It was "the penalty"

23 Hamilton to Wilkinson, February 12, 1799, Wilkinson, *Memoirs*, I, 436. Apparently Wilkinson underscored the phrases shown here in italics (a common practice of his), without indicating that they were not underscored in the original.

24 *HWL*, VII, 66. Italics added.

25 In his edition of Hamilton's works Lodge claimed to have presented every letter of historical importance and personal interest, but throughout the edition disconcerting inaccuracies and unaccountable omissions can be detected.

26 Hamilton to Wilkinson, April 15, 1799, *HWL*, VII, 75–76.

Spain would have to pay for her "subserviency to the Jacobins."[27] At this time Hamilton wrote an essay (apparently not published) sharply protesting that the French armies invading Germany were treating as "rebels and criminals" all German peasants who had joined the armies resisting them. To Hamilton this behavior was additional proof that, like the "ancient Romans," the French "considered themselves as having a right to be the masters of the world, and to treat the rest of mankind as their vassals."[28] The French conquerors, he said, were casting aside international law and precedent.

Before he conferred with Hamilton in 1799, Wilkinson advocated a direct assault on Spanish strongholds. He recommended fortifying Loftus Heights, on the Mississippi, as a point from which "to carry a coup-de-main against the capital below" and thereby a "direct route into the Mexican provinces of Texhas (*sic*), St. Afee (*sic*), and St. Andrea."[29]

Any such military movement required a high degree of secrecy, of course; thus the written records of these plans are rather scanty. Edward Everett Hale, in his delightful work, *Memories of a Hundred Years*, reported seeing in 1876 a trunkful of Wilkinson's papers at Louisville, Kentucky, containing the Hamilton-Wilkinson correspondence about the projected attack on New Orleans.[30] Hale's vague reference to the dates and contents of the papers gives the historian little to go on, but other evidence makes it almost a certainty that Hamilton brought Wilkinson into the plan at an early stage and found Wilkinson an eager ally.[31] Wilkinson reported that, though the residents of Louisiana were mostly French, they had "changed masters" so often that they had no "permanent attachment" to any government.[32] He spoke of the "imbecility of the Spanish government on the Mississippi" and expressed a belief that "a single individual of hardy enterprise" with a proper commission from the government at Philadelphia hoisting the American flag at New Orleans "might depose the Spanish administration in one hour, and have the population of the country at his disposal for any

27 Whitaker, *The Mississippi Question, 1795–1803*, 118. Cf. Jacobs (*Tarnished Warrior*, 191), who believes that after consideration Washington rejected Hamilton's plan for attacking New Orleans.

28 "The War in Europe," 1799, *HWL*, VI, 331–32.

29 Wilkinson to Hamilton, April 15, 1799, HPLC, XXXIX, 39.

30 (New York, 1904), 57, 65. When the owner of the correspondence was unable to sell the papers at what he thought a justifiable price, he burned them in disappointment.

31 Wilkinson to Hamilton, December 6, 1798, HPLC, LXXXIII.

32 Wilkinson to Hamilton, April 15, 1799, *ibid.*, XXXIX.

chivalrous enterprise." The Mississippi and its tributaries, Wilkinson added, "bathe the most extensive tract of luxuriant soil in the universe." He thought the "capture of New Orleans" the best way to provide for "the safety, the subordination, and prosperity of our western possessions."[33] Hamilton replied optimistically and said that Wilkinson's report would be submitted to General Washington.[34] Wilkinson also spoke of attacking New Orleans in case of a "rupture with Spain," though in September, 1799, he referred to such an attack as "unwarrantable" at that time. No doubt he would have considered a full-scale war with France as a suitable excuse for the attack, since "the Spaniards [were] subordinate to the French."[35]

In those years Congress was reluctant to make military appropriations without itemized statements showing how they were to be used. Hamilton tried to get his western program under way by asking in a general way for money to construct a "schooner, galleys, etc." to be built at Pittsburgh and Detroit. The House asked for details. Representative Harper, chairman of the Ways and Means Committee and a friend and supporter of Hamilton, admitted that he knew of no law "for erecting the schooner and galleys on the Ohio and Mississippi" but assumed that the War Department had requested them "for sufficient reason." At length he decided to omit the item, to be restored to the bill later if necessary.[36] Hamilton had much better support in the Senate, where the bill was amended to increase the total appropriation and strike out the words "which sums shall be solely applied to the objects for which they are respectively appropriated." The lower house accepted the amendment.[37] In light of the emergency Hamilton's requests were not unreasonable. In fact, he sometimes found it advisable to restrain his friends in the Senate, who were willing to make larger appropriations than he thought prudent.[38]

Hamilton well understood the importance of propaganda in wartime. He seized every opportunity to strengthen the nation's resolution and condition men's minds for fighting. In the summer of 1799, upon learning that the French fleet had put to sea, he immediately recommended posting fast ships outside America's main harbors to assure advance notice of any attempted

[33] Wilkinson to Hamilton, September 4, 1799, Wilkinson, *Memoirs*, I, 447–49.

[34] *Ibid.*, 458.

[35] Wilkinson to Hamilton, April 15, 1799, HPLC, XXXIX.

[36] April 15, 1798, *Annals*, VIII, 1543–44.

[37] June 7, 1798, *ibid.*, 1874.

[38] Hamilton to Gunn, December 22, 1798, *HWL*, VII, 45.

invasion. The recent French invasion of Egypt had led him to believe that a similar movement against the United States should not be considered "impracticable." Despite the French naval defeat at Abukir Bay, France was still strong enough at sea to launch a naval attack on the United States, provided the British withdrew from the war. The government should inform the people of its vigilant actions so that they would see it did "not deem an invasion impossible."[39]

Some of Hamilton's friends were soon calling his attention to a project far more extensive than the seizure of Louisiana. They would have the United States join forces with Britain and drive the Spanish forces from both the Americas. According to this scheme, the United States would take Louisiana and the Floridas, while Britain took Santo Domingo, which though promised to France in 1795 was still held by Spain out of fear of the British. The remaining Spanish colonies would be helped to set up independent governments. Thus the Anglo-American project was put forward as a movement for defense and liberation—not one of conquest.

Rufus King, minister to Great Britain, was the foremost advocate of the scheme. Miranda also wholeheartedly supported it. John Jay and other Americans were in favor of it.[40] Britain was eager to go forward with it. Hamilton, though hesitant, hoped that conditions would make it possible. The Republicans thought the idea was self-defeating and dishonorable, and Washington and Adams were also firmly opposed to it.

King opened his correspondence on the subject in February, 1798, when he informed Pickering that he believed the British government was holding consultations with Miranda about ways and means to effect the "complete independence of South America."[41] Britain made it clear that it would not act unless Spain entered the European war or fell under more direct French influence. If that should happen, King said, he was convinced that Britain would be eager to liberate Spanish America and would request the cooperation of the United States in doing so. King hoped that his government would respond favorably and "by great and generous deeds lay deep and firm the foundations of lasting accord between [the] rising Empires" of the "New World."[42] Pickering's reaction was favorable. He was well disposed

[39] Hamilton to McHenry, June 16, 1799, *ibid.*, 94.

[40] Jay to Adams, January 3, 1799, *AW*, VIII, 620.

[41] February 7, 1798, *KC*, II, 281.

[42] King to Pickering, February 26, 1798, *ibid.*, 283–84.

toward Britain during this period, grateful that the British were accepting American vessels in their convoys to protect them from the French.[43]

In his dispatches King mentioned the connection between the South American venture and the French threat in Louisiana. He quoted a prominent Frenchman as having said that "France wants only a footing upon the continent to regulate the destinies of the citizens of the United States." King was particularly alarmed by the prospect that France would institute its own brand of revolution in the New World, a real possibility, he felt, without the intervention of the United States.[44] King wanted his nation to play a grand role in world affairs and to save itself and the rest of the hemisphere from the fate of the Continent. "Europe cannot be saved," he concluded, "but this is no reason why America should perish likewise." France was the only European nation that "projects enterprises"; the other nations were "puzzled in a perpetual effort to find out and defeat the plans of France." Americans should "do more than merely defend" themselves; they should take the initiative and co-operate with Britain in liberating South America. He warned against making a permanent alliance with Britain, however, being "averse to indissoluble engagements with any one."[45]

When Hamilton and Pickering failed to reply promptly, King became even more insistent. "For God's sake, attend," he begged. "Providence seems to have prepared the way, and to have pointed out the instruments of its will. Our children will reproach us if we neglect our duty."[46] He made but brief reference to Louisiana, a region that, in his view, was incidental to the grand venture in South America.

Hamilton replied that he was eager for the "enterprise in question" to be carried out. The United States was not quite ready for it, he said, "but we ripen fast." He was willing to join forces with Great Britain, but "the principal agency [should] be in the United States—they to furnish the whole land force if necessary." He would, "very naturally," command the expedition. The new nations to be established should have "moderate government," and Britain and the United States should have "equal privileges in commerce" with them.[47] It is noteworthy that in this letter Hamilton did not mention Louisiana or the Floridas.

43 Pickering to King, April 2, 1798, *ibid.*, 296–97.
44 King to Pickering, April 6, 1798, *ibid.*, 305.
45 King to Hamilton, July 14, 1798, *ibid.*, 656.
46 King to Hamilton, January 1, 1799, *ibid.*, 519.
47 Hamilton to King, August 22, 1798, *HWL*, X, 314–15.

This project has often been referred to as Hamilton's "vision of empire," which some historians have called "chimerical," expressing wonderment that Hamilton seriously considered it.[48] In this context Channing warned that "it is easy to make assertions which no amount of research can prove to be false"[49]—sound advice to any student of history. Yet the evidence does seem conclusive that Hamilton seriously contemplated the South American enterprise in case of "a decisive rupture with France"[50] and that he would have embarked upon it with enthusiasm if he had received adequate support at home and an official arrangement had been worked out with the British government. He expressed this view in several letters to King, to McHenry, and to others.[51] Moreover, it would be difficult to find any grounds for impeaching the accuracy of his son's statement that "Hamilton felt all the importance of this great reformation" and "believed in its easy accomplishment" with the use of "ten thousand men . . . aided by an adequate marine." It seems quite reasonable to assume that he hoped "his name would descend to a grateful posterity, as the Liberator of Southern America."[52] Hamilton made it quite clear, however, that he would have nothing to do with Miranda's scheme unless it was "patronized" by the American government.[53] As Darling pointed out, it was that stipulation which distinguished Hamilton's "plot" from the schemings of John Chisholm, William Blount and others.[54]

Miranda, the persistent revolutionary, used every inducement to enlist British aid. To the same end, he conferred with King, wrote to Adams, and renewed his contacts with Hamilton.[55] It is clear that Miranda and Hamilton had different views about the part Hamilton was to play. Miranda, who fancied himself an able general, still looked upon Hamilton as a genius in the science of government, as he had in 1784, and he would have the American draw up constitutions for the new countries to be established.[56] Hamilton would not have refused that task, but he assumed that his first duty

[48] Whitaker, *The Mississippi Question, 1794–1803*, 117.

[49] Channing, *A History of the United States*, IV, 197.

[50] Hamilton to King, October 2, 1798, *HWL*, X, 321.

[51] Hamilton to McHenry, June 27, 1799, *ibid.*, VII, 97.

[52] John C. Hamilton, *History of the Republic of the United States as Traced in the Writings of Alexander Hamilton and His Contemporaries* (New York, 1857–64), VII, 218.

[53] Hamilton to Miranda, August 22, 1798, *HWL*, X, 316.

[54] Darling, *Our Rising Empire, 1763–1803*, 322.

[55] Robertson, *The Life of Miranda*, I, 170; Miranda to Adams, March 24, 1798, *AW*, VIII, 569–72; Miranda to Hamilton, *Archivo del General Miranda*, XV, 234–36.

[56] Miller, *Alexander Hamilton*, 497.

would be to direct military operations. He thought that it would be "extremely essential" for Miranda to come to the United States if the project was undertaken. No doubt he expected to utilize Miranda's military and political abilities.[57]

Apparently the British did not place much reliance on Miranda, nor did they make a serious effort to learn the "temper, disposition, or plans" of the peoples in the Spanish colonies.[58] They were primarily interested in cutting off Spanish American commerce with France and in obtaining free access to that commerce themselves. Moreover, Britain took a more pragmatic view of Spanish neutrality than Hamilton ever did. As long as Spain refrained from putting forces into the European conflict, kept French armies out of Spain, and refused to allow the French to march across Spain to attack Portugal, Britain would respect Spain's colonies.

Apprehensive that Spain might prove unwilling or unable to maintain so neutral a posture, Grenville made an effort to draw the United States into an agreement to carry out the plans advocated by King and Miranda if they became feasible. Grenville's approach had little of the altruism expressed by King. The British minister saw the undertaking as one by which Britain and the United States could satisfy their respective interests in a material sense and improve their relative positions in the world power structure.

Dispatches received from Liston in Philadelphia probably kept Grenville better informed than King was about the trends in American public opinion and Hamilton's views. In January, 1798, Grenville instructed Liston to make a special effort to convince the Americans they should "look to Great Britain as their most natural friend and support."[59] Subsequently for several months Liston's reports were optimistic: Americans were expecting to go to war with France; war fever had for the first time made President Adams a popular figure; Americans expected to take Louisiana and the Floridas, but would be happy for Britain to take Santo Domingo and would, if necessary, send an army to defend Canada for Britain. Indeed, Grenville was sure, Talleyrand's chief grievance against the United States was its growing friendship for Britain.[60]

Warming to the subject, Grenville told Liston to assure Adams that

[57] Hamilton to Miranda, August 22, 1798, *HWL*, X, 316.

[58] Robertson, *The Life of Miranda*, I, 168–69; King to Pickering, August 17, 1798, *KC*, II, 393.

[59] Mayo, 149.

[60] May 2, June 25, 1798, FCA, XXII.

Britain would consider it "a matter of satisfaction" for the United States to take Louisiana and Florida, and asked him to point out to the President that American interests would be well served by Britain's acquisition of Santo Domingo. By way of a mild threat Liston was to mention the possibility that, without such a prior understanding, if Britain and France came to a peaceful agreement, the United States would find itself in an uncomfortable position.[61] Grenville's immediate purpose was to seize Santo Domingo before France could take possession of it and to gain the United States' full commitment in the war against France. Though he was interested in South America, he had no intention to move into that region if Spain remained neutral. He made no proposal to Adams about Miranda's scheme. Unlike Hamilton, he hoped that Spain would not enter the war.

Liston industriously promoted the Louisiana–Santo Domingo project. He discussed it frequently with Pickering, and sometimes also with Adams. When Pickering told him that the United States was opposed to entering another alliance, Liston assured him that Britain would not insist on it, wishing only to carry out a project that would be of great benefit to both nations. Sensing the Americans' hesitation, Grenville instructed Liston to work for an agreement at Philadelphia even if each participant retained the right to make a separate peace—providing the peace terms did not harm the interests of the other nation.[62] Grenville's plan called for the use of British vessels, to be manned partly by American recruits, and an American army. He preferred to make the final arrangements himself with Rufus King in London, but he did not hold that essential. He was so eager to take New Orleans and Santo Domingo from Spain and to get the United States into the war that he would agree to "any other Principles that may be equally beneficial to both Countries."[63]

Liston went to Adams' home, at Braintree, Massachusetts, to talk with him. He found the President favorably disposed toward the undertaking but inclined to await a more positive expression of the people's will. Liston thought that this was a prudent attitude. He was convinced that all reasonable men were in favor of the plan and that the nation as a whole was rapidly moving to support it.[64] Actually the President's hesitation was based partly on renewed hopes for peace with France. The following month

[61] June 8, 1798, Mayo, 157.

[62] Grenville to Liston, June 8, 1798, Mayo, 155–58.

[63] Grenville to Liston, December 8, 1798, *ibid.*, 165.

[64] Liston to Grenville, September 27, 1798, FCA, XXII.

Liston reported to his home government that both Adams and Pickering agreed to the proposal of using American seamen on British vessels as a fair and reasonable one but were afraid that Congress would not agree. Adams looked forward eagerly to the time when the public would "be prepared for that important measure," Liston reported, but added that the President had disclaimed the authority to force Americans to serve aboard foreign vessels. When Liston suggested that British officers be permitted to recruit in American ports and to reclaim British deserters, Adams reportedly made no comment. Undoubtedly he was appalled by the thought of British press gangs operating in American cities, but he refrained from saying so. With war so near, it would be "the height of folly for a people . . . not to secure the assistance and defense that may be derived from another nation engaged in the same common cause."[65]

As time passed and the likelihood of a French declaration of war diminished, Liston noted a change in Adams' attitude. He thought it best not to be the first to return to the subject of joint naval action, and he came to believe that Adams had been mistaken in anticipating the support of the American people. On the contrary, Liston believed that they were moving in the opposite direction. He had learned that a few Americans suspected Britain of a "secret desire" to overthrow American independence, that others feared misunderstandings would arise in co-operative action, and that a few boastful young Americans were claiming that the United States alone was more than a match for any nation in Europe.[66] Liston viewed these attitudes with misgivings and regret. He sincerely wanted to see the United States prosper. He was sure that it would benefit by expanding its boundaries to the Gulf of Mexico, a goal that Grenville's offer of assistance seemed to guarantee.

It is clear that at that time Hamilton and other Federalist leaders were opposed to an alliance with Britain; Pickering emphatically denied the Republican charge that either he or Adams was seeking one.[67] Liston understood that fact, and when he proposed co-operation he was meticulously careful to make it clear that he was not seeking an alliance. Jonathan Trumbull, who was second only to John Quincy Adams in his suspicions

[65] Liston to Pickering, November 7, 1798, *ibid.*

[66] Liston to Grenville, January 29, 1799, *ibid.*, XXV.

[67] Pickering to Col. James Hendricks, September 28, 1798, Upham, *Life of Timothy Pickering*, III, 392.

of the British, wrote from London warning against making any alliance with them, observing that they would go to any length to get the United States into the war with France, looking forward to "the happy day when the two sister vipers [the United States and France] shall sting each other to death."[68] King, though eager for joint action, was also opposed to a formal alliance.[69]

Many reputable historians have misunderstood this point and have repeated the charge of the Jeffersonians that the Federalists were working for an alliance with England. DeConde, for instance, says, "Since the Hamiltonians were anti-French, in their view the French alliance was entangling. Ironically, they saw no evil in close connections with Great Britain."[70] Actually, while from 1793 to the end of the eighteenth century the Federalists spoke often of plans to use the British to promote America's interests, they opposed all kinds of "connections," even temporary ones. Hamilton was so strongly opposed to an alliance that he wanted to carry out his Louisiana project without a written agreement of any kind. He wanted to be sure the country did not become "entangled." Britain's self-interest, he said, was a sufficient guarantee of its co-operation, and a treaty might embarrass the nation if France should suddenly make "satisfactory" offers for peace. He expressed the hope that, without a treaty, the British government would send a fleet to American waters and confer upon Liston "powers commensurate with such arrangements as exigencies may require."[71] Obviously Hamilton hoped that such a procedure would enable him to direct the entire operation—and it probably would have, for the movement of American forces down the Mississippi would almost certainly have been co-ordinated with a naval attack on New Orleans.

In spite of the weakness of the Spanish position at New Orleans, such naval assistance would have provided a comforting reassurance of success to both Hamilton and Wilkinson. In discussing land and river action, Wilkinson cautioned Hamilton: "We dare not move out of the Ohio until we have built a river navy of decided superiority; for it may be received as a truth, that an expedition after four day's sail down the Mississippi, must succeed, surrender, or perish; as we can find no retreat for an army through

68 Trumbull to Wolcott, June 8, 1798, Gibbs, II, 52–53.

69 *KC*, II, 339.

70 DeConde, *Entangling Alliance*, 505.

71 Hamilton to Pickering, March 27, 1798, *HWL*, X, 280.

deep, difficult, extensive, and trackless wilds; for . . . [it] must fall a prey to hostile savages or starve."[72]

Hamilton showed no fear of such alternatives. He proceeded with his plans on all fronts, hoping soon to have in Tennessee and Kentucky "two regiments of infantry; a battalion of riflemen, and a regiment of dragoons . . . for defensive or offensive measures as future exigencies may dictate."[73] He regularly urged Wilkinson to avoid any rash act that might put the Spaniards on notice of the impending invasion. When he learned that Wilkinson was making extensive preparations at Natchez, he decided that the concentration of forces should be much farther upstream.[74] Washington emphatically agreed, observing that activities could be carried out on the Ohio, "exciting no alarm"; from that point, when the time came, the army could "descend the stream like lightning."[75] Those words must have heartened Hamilton, for a rapid descent of the Mississippi was the core of his strategy.

But Hamilton's project was not to be fulfilled—or at least not by him, and not in the manner he had planned. The long-anticipated French declaration of war failed to materialize, and Adams, Congress, and even the formerly submissive McHenry grew cool toward extensive military operations. For lack of funds and support, Hamilton and Wilkinson had to bring their western operations to a halt. Regretfully, Hamilton ordered Wilkinson to suspend the plan to build boats for the expedition and to erect no more "permanent fortifications without [further] instructions."[76]

Some of the Republicans began accusing "the Executive" of planning to use the army to set up a military dictatorship in the United States,[77] an accusation directed as much against Adams as against Hamilton. In the course of time it became clear that the charge against Adams had no basis, for he had starved the army; but he, in turn, made the same accusation against Hamilton. Charles Francis Adams and later historians have repeated the charge that Hamilton sought to become a military dictator.[78]

[72] Wilkinson, *Memoirs*, I, 448.

[73] Hamilton to Wilkinson, October 31, 1799, *HWL*, VII, 162.

[74] Hamilton to Washington, September 9, 1799, *ibid.*, 124.

[75] Washington to Hamilton, September 15, 1799, *WW*, XXXVII, 364.

[76] Hamilton to Wilkinson, October 31, 1799, *HWL*, VII, 168; Hamilton to Wilkinson, November 15, 1799, HPLC, LXI.

[77] Gallatin, in the House of Representatives, December 27, 1797, *Annals*, IX, 2514. See also Jefferson to S. T. Mason, October 11, 1798, *JW*, X, 62.

[78] John Adams' Letter No. XIII to the *Boston Patriot*, 1809, *AW*, IX, 290; Charles Francis

Bowers also made the accusation. "We may be sure," he said, that it was true, "albeit the public, and even John Adams, was ignorant of it."[79] Morison struck hard at the fabrication and should have laid it to rest;[80] yet Dauer and other later writers have appeared willing to give it credence.[81]

Hamilton's life is an open book to any person who cares to read it. Every page clearly disproves any such plot. True, he desired to strengthen the national government; but, as illustrated earlier, succeeding generations have strengthened it far beyond what he advocated. When the Kentucky and Virginia Resolutions were passed in opposition to the Alien and Sedition Acts, at the time he was planning the Louisiana invasion, he showed no desire to send the army against those states except in the event of outright treason.[82] That any competent historian could credit the accusation is beyond comprehension.

Miranda, failing to obtain a definite commitment from Grenville or from Hamilton, decided to present his plan for liberating South America directly to Adams. The President was suspicious of Miranda's "full powers" and of his claim that he had strong support in South America; moreover, he apparently had no idea that Hamilton favored the scheme.[83] The President evidently reacted strongly to Miranda's letter, for he later wrote about it at some length. He had long since become convinced that Latin Americans were "not capable of a free government," and according to his own statement he "laughed heartily" at the idea that South America could be revolutionized as easily as Miranda thought. He considered the project "visionary, though far less innocent than that of his countryman González, of an excursion to the moon, in a car drawn by geese trained and disciplined for the purpose."[84] He did not reply to Miranda directly. He sent Pickering a copy of Miranda's letter, adding his own disparaging comments and asking, "If we were enemies [of Spain] would the project be useful to us?"[85] Pickering did not contest Adams' views on the matter.

Adams, *Life of John Adams*, *ibid.*, I, 526, 531, 540, 541. In a modified form the accusation was repeated by Henry Adams in his *Life of Albert Gallatin* (Philadelphia, 1897), 170.

79 Bowers, *Jefferson and Hamilton*, 426.

80 Morison, *The Life and Letters of Harrison Gray Otis*, I, 102–103.

81 Dauer, *The Adams Federalists*, 47.

82 Hamilton to Jonathan Dayton, 1799, *HWL*, X, 335; Hamilton to Sedgwick, February 2, 1799, *HWL*, X, 340–42.

83 Adams to James Lloyd, March 26, 1815, *AW*, X, 142–43; Charles Francis Adams, *Life of John Adams*, *ibid.*, I, 532.

84 Adams to James Lloyd, March 26, 27, 1815, *ibid.*, X, 141, 146.

85 Adams to Pickering, October 3, 1798, *ibid.*, VIII, 600.

Washington also reacted with sharp disapproval when Jonathan Trumbull presented Miranda's project to him. He was firmly opposed to it unless it had the unanimous support of the people, an unlikely prospect at that time, when the country was deeply divided over projects at home, with one strong party "hanging upon the Wheels of Government, opposing measures calculated solely for Internal defense."[86]

As president, Adams was a careful man and a conservative diplomat. In earlier years he had risked everything for American independence. But his gambling days were over. In 1799 he gave a new turn to the course of American history by deciding to seek negotiations with France once more.

[86] Washington to Trumbull, August 30, 1799, *WW*, XXXVII, 348.

CHAPTER XX

The Adams Treaty

BY EARLY 1799 there was growing feeling in the United States that the limited conflict with France was wearing out. French decrees against American commerce had been mitigated. The American navy was proving effective in repelling French attacks at sea. In February, 1798, one of the three new frigates, the *Constellation*, had vanquished *L'Insurgente*. French privateers had been driven from American shores and were being hunted through the West Indies and beyond. These successes tended to lessen American anger, and as tempers cooled toward France, the antipathy toward high taxes rose. The nation began to listen again to Republican contentions that France had no desire to make war on America.

France, a nation long inured to battle, would not have been dispirited by the naval setback they had received at American hands. But now it became clear that it was not Talleyrand's intention to subdue the United States by force of arms. What Talleyrand had sought was control of the will of the American people. In that contest Hamilton had won, for no man had done more than he to strengthen Americans' spirit of defiance. Talleyrand knew perfectly well that Hamilton was his adversary, an awareness that did not diminish his respect for the man, whom twenty years later he characterized as one of the world's greatest statesmen.[1]

Talleyrand had not given up his determination to acquire Louisiana, however, and he hoped that that accomplishment would achieve what threats and naval action had failed to gain. (Hamilton had the answer to that menace also, but his opponents blocked it.) The insolent manner in which Adet broke off relations with the United States in 1796 and the subsequent refusal of Talleyrand to confer with Marshall and Pinckney made it difficult for Americans to believe that the Directory was willing to enter

[1] Charles Maurice de Talleyrand-Périgord, *Memoirs* (tr. and ed. by Raphael Ledas de Beaufort), (New York, 1891–92), I, 182.

serious negotiations. Yet it was true. The firm stand taken by the United States convinced the French that negotiations were necessary.[2] The French government was not interested in justice—only in keeping the United States quiescent until Spain could be inveigled into relinquishing its hold on Louisiana. The French realized that they had reacted too vigorously to the pro-British terms of Jay's Treaty. Belatedly they saw that it would be poor policy indeed to drive the United States into Britain's orbit. Joel Barlow, the radical expatriate, revealed his understanding of Talleyrand, if not of Adams, when he wrote from Paris on April 12, 1799, that the Directory knew that Adams was "mad for war, and that his object is to provoke them to declare it, but they are determined to disappoint" him.[3]

Lafayette, who despite his country's abusiveness was still held in high esteem by both Federalists and Republicans, considered assuming a diplomatic role to try to bring the two countries together. Hamilton advised him against such a move. Lafayette, he said, would be more likely to compromise himself with all parties than to please any.[4] Liston was relieved that Lafayette did not go on with the idea—probably fearing that he might have been successful.[5] Lafayette did what he could in an unofficial capacity, however. He wrote to Washington, assuring him that the Directory wanted peace with the United States. Washington's reply was, "Let them evidence it by actions."[6]

Secretary Pickering had reprimanded Gerry for succumbing for so long to Talleyrand's enticements in Paris, but when at last Gerry returned to the United States, Adams gave him a sympathetic hearing and was almost convinced that the officials of the Directory wished "to retrace their steps."[7] He grew even more willing to await developments and less so to continue the expense of building up a large army. He instructed Pickering to draw up "a treaty and a consular convention" that might be acceptable to the United States "if proposed by France."[8] The secretary was told to seek advice from

[2] Lyon, "The Directory and the United States," *American Historical Review*, Vol. XLIII (April, 1938), 518.

[3] Barlow to Dr. Hopkins, Pickering Papers, XXV, Massachusetts Historical Society, Boston.

[4] Hamilton to Lafayette, January 6, 1799, *HWL*, X, 337.

[5] Liston to Grenville, June 17, 1799, FCA, XXV.

[6] Washington to Lafayette, December 25, 1798, *WW*, XXXVII, 68.

[7] Charles Francis Adams, *Life of John Adams*, *AW*, I, 533.

[8] Adams to Pickering, January 15, 1799, *ibid.*, VIII, 621.

all other members of the cabinet and was asked to keep the matter secret. Apparently Pickering ignored the request.[9]

By now both the Spanish and the French governments were aware that the United States had designs on Louisiana. Pickering had so persistently questioned Carlos M. de Irujo, the Spanish minister to the United States, about rumors that Spain was about to cede the territory to France that the minister grew suspicious and warned his home government that if such a cession was contemplated it must be kept a secret until France was ready "to take possession of Louisiana with a large force," for the United States would fight to prevent it.[10] The secret would be difficult to keep in view of the protracted negotiations with France that would be necessary.

Talleyrand, trying to move gradually into renewing diplomatic relations with the United States, sent Victor du Pont, former French consul for the Carolinas and Georgia, to serve again as consul. Adams refused to issue him an exequatur or to enter into discussions with him, but Jefferson seized the opportunity to see that the French knew exactly what was happening in the United States. He told Du Pont that French behavior was driving the United States toward an alliance with Britain and was a source of strength to the Federalist party. If Americans could be persuaded that France had peaceful intentions, he believed, the Republicans would win the presidential election of 1800. Gerry and Logan had already implied the same thing to Talleyrand, but Jefferson reinforced his comments with further startling information. He revealed the United States' military plans to Du Pont. Hamilton and Washington had tried hard to keep the western military operations secret, even from Congress. They could not keep them from the Vice-President, however, and Jefferson told all. Upon receiving the information, Talleyrand, according to the Spanish ambassador in Paris, said that he would do everything in his power to avert Hamilton's projected seizure of New Orleans.[11] He had no military means to oppose Hamilton as long as Britain controlled the Atlantic, and so he resorted to the only deterrent available to him: more determined diplomatic action.

[9] Charles Francis Adams, *Life of John Adams*, *ibid.*, I, 540.

[10] Whitaker, *The Mississippi Question, 1795–1803*, 122.

[11] Whitaker, "The Retrocession of Louisiana in Spanish Policy," *American Historical Review*, Vol. XXXIX (April, 1934), 467; Lyon, "The Directory and the United States," *American Historical Review*, Vol. XLIII (April, 1938), 529; J. A. James, "Louisiana as a Factor in American Diplomacy, 1795–1800," *Mississippi Valley Historical Review*, Vol. I (June, 1914), 54.

Had the Federalists known of Jefferson's revelation, they would of course have denounced him as a traitor—though Washington, at least, would not have been surprised. It is probably the only time in American history when so high an official of the government gave away so many of the nation's military secrets. Jefferson acted out of patriotic motives, but it was a potentially dangerous move and under different circumstances might have impelled France to gain firm control of New Orleans. The outcome, however, was to hasten the end of the Franco-American controversy, just as Jefferson hoped.

When discussing Hamilton's intimate conversations with Hammond in 1792, Malone commented that "one would have to search far in American history to find a more flagrant example of interference by one high officer of the government with the policy of another which was clearly official policy, and to attempt to defeat it by secret intrigue with the representative of another country."[12] The search need not go beyond Jefferson's revelations to Victor du Pont.

As Bemis has written, "Abruptly the Directory changed front."[13] Because of Adet's blustering attitude of 1796 it was almost impossible for Talleyrand to send an envoy to Philadelphia, though Gerry had begged him to do just that;[14] but it was no longer sufficient to wait "expectantly for overtures from the United States."[15] Talleyrand sent a letter to the French chargé d'affaires in the Netherlands, L. A. Pichon, which was to be shown to the American minister, William Vans Murray and which promised that if the United States would send another envoy to France he would "be received with the respect due to the representative of a free, independent, and powerful, nation." This was the condition that Adams had insisted upon. The rather circuitous means of communication was made necessary by the fact that neither the United States nor France had a representative residing in the other nation's capital. The information, dutifully relayed to the President, was reinforced by a "flood of private letters" from other Americans in Europe (as Adams recalled ten years later), urging renewal of negotiations.

The correspondence had a powerful cumulative effect on the President. It gave him a more commanding view of the situation than either Washing-

[12] Malone, II, 419.

[13] Bemis, *A Diplomatic History of the United States*, 123.

[14] Gerry to Talleyrand, July 1, 1798, *Annals*, IX, 3497.

[15] Lyon, "The Directory and the United States," *American Historical Review*, Vol. XLIII (April, 1938), 518.

ton or Hamilton had. Yet it was not the sole reason for Adams' decision to test Talleyrand's sincerity. Another was his preference for neutrality and his opposition to any kind of alliance with Britain. If the United States must choose a partner in Europe, he looked upon France as the "natural ally."[16] He was also worried about the apparent willingness of some Americans to support Miranda's schemes in South America. Finally, one must not overlook Adams' personal dislike for Hamilton and his reluctance to do anything that would augment the latter's prestige.[17]

In Adams' reminiscences there are many contradictions about his reasons for renewing negotiations. At one point he mentioned the Pichon letter as the determining factor.[18] Later he referred to Gerry as the man who "saved the peace of the nation," since "he alone brought home the direct, formal, and official assurances upon which the subsequent commission proceeded, and peace was made."[19] Adams must also have been influenced by his son's letters from Europe (though the senior Adams' later writings do not mention that correspondence). Shortly after Gerry left France, the younger Adams wrote to his mother that Talleyrand was at last eager to negotiate with the United States. To his father, a few days later, he made the point even stronger, showing why peace was becoming a necessity for France because of deepening military involvement in Europe.[20]

On February 18, 1799, Adams sent to the Senate his nomination of William Vans Murray, minister to the Netherlands, to undertake a peace mission to Paris.[21] Predictably, Republicans were pleased and Federalists protested vehemently. Adams had not consulted the cabinet, knowing that their answers would have been "flat negatives." "If I had asked their reasons," Adams later recalled, there would be "such arguments as Hamilton has recorded."[22]

Pickering informed Hamilton of the President's step, which, he said, was "wholly *his own act*."[23] Theodore Sedgwick, now a senator, expostulated to Hamilton, "Had the foulest heart and the ablest head in the world been permitted to select the most embarrassing and ruinous measure, perhaps it

16 Adams to James Lloyd, March 29, 1815, *AW*, X, 147.
17 Morison, *The Life and Letters of Harrison Gray Otis*, I, 163.
18 Letter No. II to the *Boston Patriot*, 1809, AW, IX, 244.
19 Letter No. XIII to the *Boston Patriot*, 1809, *ibid.*, 287.
20 *JQAW*, II, 362, 367–69.
21 *ASPFR*, II, 239.
22 Letter No. X to the *Boston Patriot*, 1809, *AW*, IX, 271. See also Steiner, 370.
23 Pickering to Hamilton, February 25, 1799, *HWH*, VI, 398.

would have been precisely the one which has been adopted." He realized that the state of domestic politics would make it ruinous to reject the nomination; yet he believed it would be extremely hazardous to the nation's peace and safety to agree to it. In his dilemma he asked for Hamilton's advice,[24] as he had on so many earlier occasions.

The reply was quickly forthcoming: the nomination "would astonish, if anything from that quarter could astonish." Hamilton agreed that the nomination should not be disapproved by the Senate but added that Murray was "certainly not strong enough for so immensely important a mission." Rather, there should be "a commission of three."[25]

The Senate referred the nomination to a committee of five, with Sedgwick the chairman. The committee called on Adams, questioned him about his purposes, and gave their reasons for advocating delay. The President, though angered by what he chose to consider an attempt by the legislative branch to overrule the executive, agreed to confer with them. Since their objections seemed to be primarily directed against Murray, he agreed to nominate two additional envoys. Acting quickly, before the Senate could vote against Murray, he nominated Oliver Ellsworth, chief justice of the Supreme Court, and Patrick Henry, who had become a determined Federalist. He promised that Ellsworth and Henry would not depart until further assurances were forthcoming that they would be properly received in Paris.[26]

Henry's health was so poor that he was unable to undertake the mission (he died the following June). In his place William R. Davie, Federalist governor of North Carolina, was offered the nomination and accepted. He had appeared to be a firm Hamilton man, and he was a major general in the new army, but his apathetic recruiting in North Carolina suggested a lessening of his earlier enthusiasm for military action against France. At the beginning of the year he had taken the trouble to write Adams a letter commending the President's handling of the French question.[27] It was rumored that both Davie and Ellsworth were planning to use their diplomatic achievements as a springboard to the presidency.[28]

Washington, filled with good intentions and free from personal ambition,

[24] Sedgwick to Hamilton, February 19, 1799, *ibid.*, 396.

[25] February 21, 1799, *HWL*, X, 345–46.

[26] *ASPFR*, II, 240. See Charles Francis Adams, *Life of John Adams*, *AW*, I, 546–47.

[27] Davie to Adams, January 3, 1799, William R. Davie Letter Book, 1799, North Carolina Department of Archives and History, Raleigh, 7.

[28] *The Anas*, *JW*, I, 430–31.

was perplexed about the stand he should take on the new negotiations. He had recently received a letter from Joel Barlow assuring him that the Directory was eager to renew talks with the American government. Washington forwarded the letter to Adams, with an offer to reply to it if Adams thought that it might lead to a restoration of peace "upon just, honorable, and dignified terms."[29] Upon being informed by Pickering and another, unnamed, person that France had made no "*direct* overture," Washington concluded that "Talleyrand was playing the same loose, and round-about game he had attempted the year before with our Envoys." He would have replied to Talleyrand "through the channel of his communication" and apparently would have stipulated that a French envoy be sent to the United States for the negotiations.[30] When Adams wrote to tell him of Murray's nomination, Washington's reply merely acknowledged receipt of the letter. He made no comment about the appointment, thus implying disapproval of the move, though he again expressed hopes that peace would be achieved "in an honorable and dignified manner." He mentioned the Barlow letter but appeared to regret having forwarded it.[31] In spite of the cold tone of Washington's letter, Adams, defending his peace move, tried to use it in later years to prove that Washington had approved the nomination.[32]

Liston was as displeased as the Federalists were by Adams' action. He reported to his government that some Americans attributed it to Adams' "old age" and "dotage," adding, "of this, however, I can discover no marks." Others had pointed out to Liston that "precipitation and inconsistency have always been conspicuous features in [Adams'] character." He reported that Adams no longer appeared to accept advice from anyone but Mrs. Adams, who was quite ill. He thought it possible that the idea might have originated with John Quincy Adams, who had reported from Berlin that "Europe was so depraved in spirit as soon to fall completely to the French and leave the United States to face her arms and arts alone." Liston concluded that it was likely the President was acting only to meet "French protestations of friendship" but had little real hope that the mission would succeed.[33] His conclusions were close to the truth. Adams did have little expectation of success.

Peacemaking proved to be a slow process, accompanied by partisan

[29] Washington to Adams, February 1, 1799, *WW*, XXXVII, 120.
[30] Washington to Pickering, March 3, 1799, *ibid.*, 142.
[31] *Ibid.*, 143–44.
[32] Letter No. I to the *Boston Patriot*, 1809, *AW*, IX, 241–42.
[33] Liston to Grenville, March 4, 1799, FCA, XXV.

rancor and personal invective. The followers of Hamilton and Pickering worked desperately for delay, while Jefferson's hopes were "entirely dashed" by the decision to send two additional negotiators—and by the stipulation that they were not to leave until assured a welcome in France.[34] The High Federalists saw clearly the danger the nominations portended for the 1800 elections. As Dodd wrote, they knew that they were not doing very well with Adams, "but that he would destroy at one blow all their schemes by sending another representative to Paris was a bolder step than they thought his love of office would allow him to take."[35]

Adams was not swayed by the pleas of the Federalists. At last he had come to realize that the cabinet and Congress were largely under Hamilton's influence.[36] He returned to this point again and again in his writings of later years, protesting that Hamilton had had "a spy in the cabinet" and that "I was as President a mere cipher."[37] Some historians have sympathized with Adams. The cabinet, said Bowers, disregarded the President's wishes, "conspired against him," and took orders "from a private citizen who was his political rival and personal foe." "Ali Baba among his Forty Thieves," Bowers added, "is no more deserving of sympathy than John Adams shut up within the seclusion of his Cabinet room with his official family of secret enemies."[38]

The fact is that during this period Adams was not often in his "Cabinet room." He stayed at home for a surprisingly large part of the time and made little effort to work with the cabinet in the day-to-day details of government. He was in no position to cultivate Congress, and he offered little by way of guidance to a nation torn by divisions at home and assailed by enemies abroad. It is not surprising that Hamilton stepped into the breach.

The summer of 1799 would probably have been the best time to drive a good bargain with France. The anti-French coalition was victorious in Italy, and Bonaparte was stranded in Egypt.[39] Murray, acting alone, could have gone to Paris at that time, but the mission was delayed while Adams awaited

[34] Jefferson to Bishop James Maidon, February 27, 1799, *JW*, X, 122.

[35] Dodd, *The Life of Nathaniel Macon*, 141.

[36] Morison, *The Life and Letters of Harrison Gray Otis*, I, 161–63. Schachner, *Alexander Hamilton*, 387.

[37] Letter No. XVIII to the *Boston Patriot*, 1809, *AW*, IX, 305. Morison, *The Life and Letters of Harrison Gray Otis*, I, 158.

[38] Bowers, *Jefferson and Hamilton*, 315.

[39] Lyon, "The Directory and the United States," *American Historical Review*, Vol. XLIII (April, 1938), 532.

Talleyrand's specific assurance that the two additional commissioners would be received. Pickering tried to make the most of the delay. He informed King in London that "we shall recover from the shock of Murray's nomination; no preparation for war is lessened."[40] George Cabot expressed the hope that "the new nominations of Ellsworth and Henry" constituted "a real relinquishment of the original measure" to send only Murray, but added, "It is still pernicious."[41]

In reply to Pickering, King commented that the subject of the nominations was too painful to discuss. France, he said, was in an even worse military situation than it had been in 1793, and "prudence seems to require that we should not be in haste" to negotiate.[42] He was hopeful of an imminent defeat of the French forces.

Pickering tried to persuade Washington to support a delay in the negotiations. He was only partly successful. Washington would only comment that the commissioners should not be sent until the French government stated "*officially and unequivocally*" that it would treat with them seriously and that "the embarrassments occasioned by the late appointment of envoys, begin now to show themselves."[43] But Adams would not wait for a French defeat in Europe. He was evidently uncertain about how or when Talleyrand would reply to his stipulation. When Davie's commission was sent to him on June 1, 1799, it was accompanied by a statement that inasmuch as it was "uncertain whether any negotiations [would] take place" he need not accept the appointment immediately but merely indicate whether, if necessary, he would accept.[44] (Upon receipt of Murray's dispatch late in July enclosing Talleyrand's eager and favorable response, Davie was requested to lay "aside all other employments" and "make immediate preparations for embarking."[45])

The cabinet continued to oppose the President and seized on every possible pretext for calling off the negotiations. Pickering complained that Talleyrand, in his reply, had criticized Adams for delaying discussions; but Adams dismissed this objection lightly. He considered it "far below the dignity of the President of the United States to take any notice of Talley-

40 Pickering to King, March 6, 1799, *KC*, II, 549.

41 Cabot to King, March 10, 1799, *ibid.*, 552.

42 June 5, 1799, *ibid.*, III, 31.

43 Washington to Pickering, August 4, 11, 1799, *WW*, XXXVII, 323, 329.

44 Pickering to Davie, Davie Collection, Private Collection 78, p. 50, North Carolina Department of Archives and History, Raleigh.

45 Pickering to Davie, August 12, 1799, *ibid.*, 53.

rand's impertinent regrets, and insinuations of superfluities." "Although I have little confidence in the issue of this business," he added, "I wish to delay nothing, to omit nothing." He made it clear that he expected "the co-operation of the heads of departments," and he complained about Pickering's tardiness in sending him the final draft of the envoys' instructions—instructions which had already been agreed upon by the President and the cabinet. He insisted that all military and naval operations should proceed, "animated with fresh energy";[46] nevertheless, he continued to delay further increases in the army.

A recurrence of yellow fever in Philadelphia made it necessary for the cabinet to shift its headquarters to Trenton. Adams went home to Massachusetts. Secretary of the Navy Benjamin Stoddert, an Adams supporter, urged the President to come to Trenton before the envoys departed so that he would be able to change the instructions or postpone the mission in the event of new developments in Europe.[47] Unwilling to leave home at the time, Adams replied that he was "well aware" that conditions might make it necessary to suspend the mission, in which case, or in the event of disagreements "between the heads of department," he would go to Trenton later.[48]

Upon receiving news of the imminent overthrow of the Directory and the revival of the Jacobin clubs, Pickering once more asked Adams to give "serious consideration [to] suspending the mission."[49] The news brought "great anxiety" to Adams, and he replied that he could not make a decision immediately. He did observe, though with apology, that the United States had always been more successful in negotiating with French terrorists than with royalists or aristocrats.[50] Looking back on this correspondence ten years later, Adams wrote that he was "astonished at this unexpected, this obstinate and persevering opposition."[51] That reaction was not evident in his reply to Pickering, however. At any rate he lost no time in hastening to Trenton to take the affair into his own hands. He found Davie and Ellsworth willing to leave for Europe immediately, though Ellsworth had earlier covertly helped Pickering seek a postponement.

[46] Adams to Pickering, August 6, 1799, *AW*, IX, 10–11.
[47] Stoddert to Adams, August 29, 1799, *ibid.*, 18–19.
[48] Adams to Stoddert, September 4, 1799, *ibid.*, 19–20.
[49] Pickering to Adams, September 11, 1799, *ibid.*, 23–25.
[50] Adams to Pickering, September 19, 1799, *ibid.*, 32–33.
[51] Letter No. V to the *Boston Patriot*, 1809, *ibid.*, 252.

By coincidence Hamilton was also in Trenton at the time. He called on Adams and argued vehemently for delaying the mission until more could be learned about developments in France. Adams listened politely but would not be swayed. With the cabinet he reviewed instructions to the envoys and sent them on their way. They sailed from Newport, Rhode Island, on November 3, 1799.

The instructions were explicit. The diplomats were told that the differences between the United States and France were so well understood that a "speedy decision" should be reached and that they should be ready to leave France by the first of April of the following year. If they were not properly and honorably received, they were to leave France immediately. If they should "resolve to terminate the mission," they were not to resume it, "whatever fresh overtures or assurances may be tendered . . . by the French government." They were to demand from France "full compensation" for all "irregular or illegal captures" of American vessels. A new commercial treaty should be negotiated, but there should be no alliance, and "no aid or loan [should] be promised in any form whatever."[52]

Rarely has an American president taken such heavy responsibility upon himself as Adams did when he sent the delegation to France. Most of his cabinet members were utterly opposed to the move, and he did little to change their views. Most of the leaders of his party were also opposed, but his only compromise was to appoint two additional envoys—and that only to prevent Senate rejection of the first one. The fact that the Republicans were pleased also had little influence on him; he held them in such contempt that he made no effort to win their support. Nor did he seek public support for his policy. Too late he recognized his mistake. Ten years later he said that if he had published the information he had at the time he could have prevented "the mischief . . . and innumerable prejudices and errors propagated all over the nation."[53]

Hamilton's hopes were dashed by the renewal of negotiations. It effectively put a stop to his enterprise in the West at a time when victory was already in sight. From the moment they learned of Murray's nomination, most people apparently anticipated an imminent peace. As shown in Washington's, Hamilton's, McHenry's, and Davie's correspondence, qualified candidates began refusing commissions in the army and officers began

[52] Pickering to Davie, Ellsworth and Murray, October 22, 1799, *ASPFR*, II, 301–306.
[53] Letter No. VII to the *Boston Patriot*, 1809, *AW*, IX, 261.

resigning. As Whitaker expressed it, "Hamilton's game was up."[54] In July, 1800, Hamilton turned in his accounts as inspector general and, though he did not resign his commission, returned to his law practice.

Once the mission was on its way, Washington revealed his true opinion of it. Less than a month before his death he wrote to McHenry that he had been "stricken dumb" by Adams' action. He had "for sometime past, viewed the political concerns of the United States with an anxious, and painful eye."[55] He had earlier written to Hamilton that he had been "exceedingly" surprised by the measure and "much more so at the manner of it"—alluding to Adams' refusal to heed the advice of cabinet and Senate. It was "incomprehensible" to him why the President did not use the "door" that was opened by the news of the fall of the Directory to "retreat" from "the first faux peaux [*sic*]."[56]

In confidence McHenry gave Hamilton the details of the wrangle between Adams and the cabinet, emphasizing Adams' unwillingness to be swayed by the counsel.[57] George Cabot expressed the basic fear of the Federalists: "the triumph of Jacobinism in the United States."[58]

The British also resented the move for peace. They could hardly react otherwise; they had been at war with France for nearly seven years. They appeared certain that the peace effort would be successful[59] and showed their resentment by blocking efforts to settle the claims provided under Jay's Treaty. They became so obstructive that Adams felt there was "no business before the government . . . more important than this."[60] Hamilton shared Cabot's fear that a new treaty with France might result in bringing the United States into the war as an ally of France against England.[61] Anything might happen, he said, to a nation under the leadership of a man with Adams' "perverseness and capriciousness." He saw the President's action as "too much the effect of momentary impulse. Vanity and jealousy exclude all counsel. Passion wrests the helm from reason."[62] Pickering poured out his fears to Murray and emphasized the opposition of Hamilton, Cabot,

[54] Whitaker, *The Mississippi Question*, 129.

[55] Washington to McHenry, November 17, 1799, *WW*, XXXVII, 428.

[56] Washington to Hamilton, October 27, 1799, *ibid.*, 409.

[57] McHenry to Hamilton, November 10, 1799, HPLC, LX.

[58] Cabot to Pickering, October 21, 1799, Pickering Papers, Massachusetts Historical Society, Boston, XXV, 261.

[59] Grenville to Liston, May 9, 1800, Mayo, 186.

[60] Adams to Pickering, December 7, 1799, *AW*, IX, 42.

[61] Hamilton to Washington, October 21, 1799, *HWL*, X, 356.

[62] Hamilton to King, January 5, 1800, *ibid.*, 358.

Ames, and others to the negotiations.[63] It is difficult to see what he expected to gain from his tirade; he did not imply that Murray should sabotage the negotiations.

In France the scene had shifted dramatically. The Directory had fallen, and Napoleon had taken over the reins of government. Fortunately, he was well disposed toward the United States, though when the Americans reached Paris in March, 1800, he was away on military action. Moreover, his first concern in America was to pry Louisiana from Spain, believing that it would provide him the area for empire building that had been denied him in Egypt.[64] These factors worked for delay, but Davie, Ellsworth, and Murray were courteously received, and there was no talk of bribes or threats.[65] While seven months were to elapse before a treaty was executed, the newspapers of Paris became "much less insolent" toward the United States, and all the French "plundering and barbarous decrees against neutral navigation [were] rescinded."[66]

Again, as during the XYZ period, the Americans had to endure a long period of waiting and speculating on the course of events. Hamilton recalled that in 1794 he had written a letter to Jay to be shown to Grenville, stating that "unless an arrangement on solid terms" could be made with Britain it would "be better to do nothing." He asked and received verification of that communication from Jay.[67] Dismayed by the move for French negotiations, by the consequent renewal of British depredations at sea, and by the "jealousy," "envy," and "miserliness" of many Americans, Hamilton morosely observed that his country could but "creep" toward greatness. Yet he consoled himself that "slow and sure is no bad maxim. Snails are a wise generation." And ultimately the country was "too young and vigorous to be quacked out of its political health."[68]

[63] Pickering to Murray, October 25, 1799, American Historical Association *Annual Report* for 1912 (1914), 610–11.

[64] Albert Sorel, *L'Europe et la Révolution Française* (Paris, 1885–1904), VI, 75.

[65] Albert du Casse, *Histoires des Négociations diplomatiques relatives aux traités de Mortefontaine, de Lunéville et d'Amiens* (Paris, 1855), I (hereafter cited as *Histoire des Négociations*). Presents from the French point of view Franco-American relations through the signing of the treaty of 1800.

[66] John Quincy Adams to Murray, May 18, 1799, John Quincy Adams to Abigail Adams, June 12, 1800, *JQAW*, II, 421, 462.

[67] Hamilton to Jay, August 19, 1800, Jay to Hamilton, September 22, 1800, Jay Papers; obtained through the courtesy of Frank Monaghan.

[68] Hamilton to Sedgwick, February 27, 1800, Hamilton to Henry Lee, March 7, 1800, *HWL*, X, 362–63.

During this period of uncertainty Adams had slight expectation of success. He had never been sanguine about the chances of the mission. He had confessed to Pickering that he believed the envoys would return without a treaty and that he would then have no choice but to ask Congress to declare war, "having exhausted the last means of reconciliation."[69] Adams' often-expressed doubts in 1799 and 1800 conflict sharply with his arguments a decade later in which he maintained that his action was logical and inescapable. From the vantage point of hindsight he ridiculed Hamilton, point by point, for the latter's doubts and opposition.[70]

In May, 1800, Adams abruptly dismissed Pickering and McHenry from their posts—heedless of the political repercussions that were bound to follow. He retained Wolcott, he said, to avoid "derangements in the affairs of the Treasury."[71] He may also have decided to keep him partly because of his friendship for Wolcott's father and because Wolcott had ingratiated himself with the President. Charles Francis Adams wrote, "To the day of his death" Adams never suspected that Wolcott supplied Hamilton with confidential information for use against him.[72] Yet Adams could hardly have failed to realize that Wolcott was also working closely with Hamilton.

Adams at length grew impatient at "the long delay of our envoys." In the summer of 1800 he wrote to John Marshall, the newly appointed secretary of state, that "it will be our destiny, for what I know, republican as we are, to fight the French republic alone."[73] Marshall also expected the mission to be unfruitful. He asked the President what measures should be taken in that likely eventuality—quite a contrast in procedure from Pickering's bold self-assurance.[74] Adams replied that he had not yet reached a decision and that the matter should be considered by the cabinet "in all its lights." He repeated that he would not be surprised if the negotiations came to naught and confided that he was considering recommending to Congress in December an "immediate and general declaration of war against the French republic." Though a limited state of war already in fact existed, "the public mind cannot be held in a state of suspense," and he was seriously considering

[69] Pickering to Ames, November 20, 1799, Pickering Papers, Massachusetts Historical Society, Boston, XII.

[70] The central theme of Adams' letters to the *Boston Patriot*, 1809, *AW*, IX, 241–311.

[71] McHenry to John McHenry, May 20, 1800, Gibbs, II, 348.

[72] *AW*, I, 590.

[73] Adams to Marshall, August 30, 1800, *ibid.*, IX, 80.

[74] Marshall to Adams, August 25, 1800, *ibid.*, IX, 81 n.

taking off "all the restrictions and limitations."[75] He wrote a little later, "These Federalists may yet have their fill at fighting." But, he asked, "What has been lost? Certainly nothing, unless it be the influence of some of the Federalists."[76]

The Federalists he was referring to were, of course, Pickering and McHenry, whose loss of influence Adams had abetted by ejecting them from the cabinet. He was also referring to Hamilton, who upon Washington's death had become the highest-ranking officer in the army. It appears unlikely that Adams would have dismissed Hamilton if war had been declared, though more than likely he would have appointed another officer to take Washington's place. But Adams himself would lose if he failed to be re-elected, which appeared likely.

Meanwhile, though negotiations proceeded slowly in Paris, Davie, Ellsworth, and Murray did not have the frustrations and disappointments the earlier mission had encountered. Napoleon showed every inclination to re-establish cordial relations with the United States, as did the French people. The envoys' hearts were warmed by the many expressions of grief relayed to them when news of Washington's death reached Paris.[77] The Americans could only mark time and wait for Napoleon to conclude his military affairs and complete secret negotiations with Spain concerning Louisiana. When discussions did at last get under way, the chief point of disagreement was the Americans' demand for compensation for illegal molestation of American commerce. John Quincy Adams and others had foreseen that that demand would be the main obstacle to negotiations.[78] In the younger Adams' view, if France defeated the European coalition it would be unwilling to pay, and if France lost the war it would be unable to pay.[79]

The treaty (officially called the Convention of Mortefontaine), signed on October 2, 1800, left the question of indemnities for future negotiations—which never came about. But there were some achievements. The treaty, and the diplomatic exchanges the following year, nullified the treaties of 1778, halted French attacks on American commerce, put an end to hostilities between the two countries, and renewed commercial relations on a

[75] Adams to Marshall, September 4, 1800, *ibid.*, 80–81.

[76] Adams to John Trumbull, September 10, 1800, *ibid.*, 83.

[77] Du Casse, *Histoire des Négociations*, I, 185–86.

[78] John Quincy Adams to Murray, May 24, 1799, *JQAW*, II, 415.

[79] John Quincy Adams to King, May 25, 1799, *ibid.*, 422.

most-favored-nation basis. Napoleon was astute enough to include the "small naval power" principle of free ships, free goods, except for war contraband, as well as liberal principles for regulating neutral trade.[80] By this means he hoped to draw the United States into the Armed Neutrality then being re-formed by the nations of northern Europe.

When the treaty reached the United States in December, 1800, most of Hamilton's followers attacked it for its failure to bind France to pay indemnities. Sedgwick reported to Hamilton in confidence about the provisions of the treaty and the adverse comments about them.[81] Senator James Gunn called the treaty "detestable" and declared that "the independence of our country is humbled to the dust."[82] Gouverneur Morris sardonically observed that the negotiations had been "very well conducted on the part of France" and that the treaty, if ratified, could well lead the United States into "war against France or England."[83]

Hamilton understood Napoleon's purpose in imposing the neutrality provisions, observing that they would render the United States a "makeweight in the wrong scale";[84] yet he believed that the treaty should be ratified. In the national election Adams and Pinckney, the vice-presidential candidate, had lost; either Jefferson or Burr would be the next president, and Hamilton thought it better to accept the treaty, taking the good with the bad, "than to leave it to a Jacobin to do much worse." "Indemnification for spoliations . . . was rather to be wished than expected, while France [was] laying the world under contribution." "A definitive rupture with France" should not "be hazarded on this ground."[85] When it began to appear that Burr might become president, Hamilton, who deeply distrusted Burr, redoubled his efforts to assure ratification of the treaty.[86] Indeed, ratification, which came only after much wrangling, was largely the result of his labors.

The agreement should properly be called the Adams Treaty. Certainly Adams had more to do with its consummation than any other single person. For technical and political reasons it was called a "convention," a term Jefferson properly criticized, saying, "It is a real treaty."[87] Napoleon in his

[80] *ASPFR*, II, 295, 345.
[81] Sedgwick to Hamilton, December 17, 1800, *HWH*, VI, 492.
[82] Gunn to Hamilton, December 18, 1800, *ibid.*, 492.
[83] Morris to Hamilton, December 15, 1800, *ibid.*, 493.
[84] Hamilton to Sedgwick, December 22, 1800, *HWL*, X, 397–98.
[85] Hamilton to Morris, December 24, 1800, *ibid.*, 400.
[86] Robert Trout to King, February 12, 1801, *KC*, III, 391.
[87] Jefferson to Madison, December 19, 1800, *JW*, X, 185.

memoirs, as well as the French historian Du Casse, also usually referred to it as a treaty.

Viewing the situation as a whole, Hamilton found reasons for optimism. He had not won the Mississippi outlet for his nation, but he had helped save American independence. He had restrained Federalist impetuosity in 1796 and 1797 and had successfully promoted further negotiations. The XYZ fiasco had brought about unity that rendered the nation immune to Talleyrand's designs. Hamilton's pen had proved mightier than his sword, but the United States had weathered formidable dangers.

It is a deplorable fact that Hamilton's contributions during this period have often been overlooked. It has been said that after New York ratified the Constitution "his life's work was done," with the later comment that "certainly there was little in these years [1795–1804] to magnify his reputation."[88] Another historian has commented that Hamilton's "great work was over" when he left Washington's cabinet in January, 1795.[89] These appraisals not only overlook Hamilton's contributions to the Farewell Address but also ignore his brilliant service in saving the nation from the machinations of Talleyrand.

The ratification of Adams' Treaty signalized the end of Federalist leadership of the national government. The Federalists had no formal party organization and very little sense of party affiliation.[90] When they referred to themselves as a party, they were speaking of individuals who shared one another's political ideas and attitudes. They would doubtless have been shocked by the party systems of modern times, embracing every precinct in the country and organized through hierarchies of committees into nationwide power structures. For that matter, the Republicans of 1800 also saw little usefulness in an organized national political party in the conduct of day-to-day operations of government, though they were willing to use whatever organization and propaganda was available to unseat the Federalists.

The decline of the Federalists was no sudden phenomenon. The Alien and Sedition Acts, passed in the heat of nationalistic fervor and anti-French feeling, demonstrated the Federalists' loss of touch with the people. The

[88] Tugwell and Dorfman, "Alexander Hamilton: Nation-Maker" Part I, *Columbia University Quarterly*, Vol. XXIX (December, 1937), 226; Part II, *ibid.*; Vol. XXX (March, 1938), 66.

[89] Padover, *The Mind of Alexander Hamilton*, 18.

[90] William Nisbet Chambers, *Political Parties in a New Nation: The American Experience, 1776–1809* (New York, 1963), 153.

absence of a firm, consistent attitude toward France also hurt them. Adams' unwillingness to support Hamilton in the capture of Louisiana and the Floridas was probably the glaring failure of the administration. The renewal of negotiations with France apparently cost Adams the 1800 election. Though McHenry and others charged that the move was made specifically to help him win,[91] Adams' assertion that it was one of the most "disinterested and meritorious" acts of his life has the ring of sincerity, particularly in view of his comment that he was delighted to be relieved of the burden of office.[92] On the other hand, Adams' own emphasis on the general unpopularity of the military measures and the opposition to high taxes that almost produced civil war[93] lends some credibility to McHenry's accusation.

Adams' dismissal of Pickering and McHenry no doubt also cost him votes. Washington had appointed both men, and there was strong feeling that officials who had been satisfactory to Washington should have been equally so to Adams. Hamilton, angered by the dismissals, was even more deeply offended when Adams referred to him in conversations as a member of a "British faction" and, when Hamilton protested, refused to avow, disown, or explain the accusation.[94] Despite such affronts Hamilton had at first urged the Federalists of New York and New England to support Adams and Pinckney, to save the country from the fangs of Jefferson, though he had hoped that Pinckney would draw enough support in the South to gain him the presidency.[95] Later, in bitterness and frustration he had made the grave error of attacking Adams in a long pamphlet setting forth in exaggerated form all his foibles and weaknesses.[96] Hamilton had intended the pamphlet to be circulated only among his friends, but Aaron Burr obtained a copy and published part of it. Hamilton was then impelled to publish the entire work, further lessening Adams' chances in the election and permanently damaging his own reputation, though some of his friends remained personally and politically loyal. As Nevins says, "No other leader [in 1800]

[91] McHenry to John McHenry, May 20, 1800, Gibbs, II, 347.

[92] Adams to James Lloyd, January, 1815; Letter No. XII to the *Boston Patriot*, 1809, *AW*, X, 113, IX, 281.

[93] Adams to James Lloyd, February 6, 1815, *ibid.*, X, 115.

[94] Hamilton to Adams, August 1, October 1, 1800, *HWL*, X, 382, 390–91.

[95] Hamilton to Sedgwick, May 4, 1800, *ibid.*, 371.

[96] "The Public Conduct and Character of John Adams, Esq., President of the United States," *ibid.*, VII, 309–64.

approached him in brilliance, but his genius was not unmixed with an erratic quality."[97]

Hamilton had been a supremely important influence in national affairs since 1782, when he took his seat in the Continental Congress. Now the days of his mighty deeds were ended. Twilight was falling upon him.

[97] Nevins, *The Evening Post*, 10.

CHAPTER XXI

Closing Accounts

THE YEAR 1800 had been one of multiple disappointments for Hamilton. His military efforts had failed. Pickering and McHenry had been forced out of the cabinet, the Republicans had won the presidential election, and, for the first time since revolutionary days, Hamilton had had to carry on without the support of George Washington. Washington's death was a severe personal loss to Hamilton. It is doubtful that he ever fully appreciated Washington's true greatness, but he certainly understood how helpful Washington had been in supporting his proposals and often in serving as the agent through whom his projects were put into effect. Earlier in his career Hamilton had been assisted by various influential persons, but now he had grown so tall himself that there was no man who could replace Washington.

Hamilton was acutely aware of his loss. He wrote that he had "been much indebted to the kindness of the General," who "was an *Aegis very essential*" to him.[1] Looking into the future, he wrote to Mrs. Washington, "I cannot say in how many ways the continuance of that confidence and friendship was necessary to me in future relations."[2] These were sincere expressions; yet even if Washington had lived, it is doubtful that he could have done his friend any political service, for Hamilton was resolved that "nothing short of a general convulsion" could bring him back again into public life.[3]

The election of 1800 terminated Hamilton's political career. His support of Jefferson over Burr could not possibly have gained Jefferson's favor, nor did Hamilton expect that it would. Though he spoke better of Jefferson than he had for several years, commenting that there was "no fair reason to suppose him capable of being corrupted," it was generally believed that he looked upon Jefferson merely as the lesser of two evils.[4] He expected Jeffer-

[1] Hamilton to Tobias Lear, January 2, 1800, *HWL*, X, 357.

[2] Hamilton to Mrs. Martha Washington, January 12, 1799, *ibid.*, 361.

[3] Robert Troup to King, August 8, 1801, *KC*, III, 496.

[4] Hamilton to James A. Bayard, January 16, 1801, *HWL*, X, 413–14.

son to be a weak and indecisive president, but not otherwise dangerous. He was not acutely disturbed by Jefferson's earlier expressions regarding "strict construction"; he observed that when Jefferson was in Washington's cabinet he had never hesitated to depart from that theory in order to support any measure he deemed useful. Burr he considered a traitor at heart who would "certainly attempt to reform the government *à la Bonaparte*." He considered Burr "unprincipled and dangerous, . . . as true a Catiline as ever met in midnight conclave."[5] He thought Burr would lead the nation into the European war to promote his own personal power.[6] He saw a great difference between the two men, unlike Senator Gunn, who observed that in the final choice in the House of Representatives the Federalists would have "to choose among rotten apples."[7]

When the movement arose to amend the Constitution to provide that electors would vote separately for president and vice-president, to avoid another tie by candidates of the same party, Hamilton gave it his support. "It is in itself right," as he saw it, "that the people should know whom they are choosing"; and he was eager to help strengthen "the connection between the Federal [government] and the people." Moreover, he wished to narrow the "scope to intrigue," for "in everything which gives opportunity for juggling arts, our adversaries will nine times out of ten excel us." The proposed amendment would also diminish "the means of party combination, in which also, the burning zeal of our opponents will be generally an over-match for our temperate flame."[8]

Hamilton's loss of influence among the Federalists following his slashing attack on Adams was of less consequence, in his view, than the loss of the presidency to the Republicans. Moreover, he expected to regain ground on both fronts. "I shall not despair of the public weal," he wrote, "as long as the federal party pursue their high ground of integrity and principle."[9]

In the spring of 1801, Hamilton and several of his friends in New York founded the *Evening Post*, a newspaper designed to promote their brand of federalism and establish Hamilton as the recognized leader of the party.[10] Federalists in other parts of the country soon followed suit. In 1802, Davie

[5] Hamilton to Bayard, August 6, 1800, *ibid.*, 387.
[6] Hamilton to Gouverneur Morris, January 10, 1801, *ibid.*, 411.
[7] Gunn to Hamilton, December 18, 1800, *HWH*, VI, 492.
[8] Hamilton to Gouverneur Morris, March 4, 1802, *HWL*, X, 427.
[9] Hamilton to John Rutledge, December, 1800, *ibid.*, 404–405.
[10] Nevins, *The Evening Post*, 9.

and other North Carolina Federalists founded the *Raleigh Minerva* to strengthen the cause in that area;[11] and in 1803 the *Charleston Courier*, a "vigorous party newspaper," was established by the South Carolina Federalists.[12] The various leaders exchanged correspondence, but there was no concerted effort to establish a national organization.

Newspapers of that period were more given to editorializing than to news reporting, and therefore it was expected that they would reflect partisan inclinations. William Coleman, the editor of the *Evening Post*, was strongly pro-Hamilton in his views and personal feelings. He regularly visited Hamilton's home to listen and take notes while Hamilton discussed leading issues of the day. The *Post* editorials were basically Hamilton's views, expressed in Coleman's words. Hostile journalists and critics called Coleman "Hamilton's editor" and "Hamilton's typographer." Hamilton did not deny the association,[13] though Coleman sometimes embarrassed him by expressing views in a cocksure and exaggerated fashion. Occasionally Hamilton himself wrote editorials for the *Post*, particularly on significant issues about which he was determined to make his weight felt. His style was more elegant than Coleman's, and his writings were much more convincing.

Hamilton often dwelt on the subject of Louisiana. He could not reconcile himself to the thought of leaving the territory in foreign hands. Though he supported ratification of the Adams Treaty, he knew it would not bring about "perpetual peace."[14] He anticipated a day when war would bring the territory into his country's possession. Jefferson was frequently taken to task for his complacent attitude toward the Mississippi question. As Nevins has pointed out, the opinions expressed in the *Post* "upon the diplomatic aspects of the Louisiana treaty . . . and the navigation of the Mississippi certainly represented Hamilton's views."[15]

Hamilton remained convinced that steady adherence to upright principles would return the Federalists to power.[16] He tried to comfort himself and his Federalist friends with the hope that, now that the Republicans were in control of the government, the people would more readily perceive the

[11] Wagstaff, *Federalism in North Carolina*, 38.

[12] Wolfe, *Jeffersonian Democracy in South Carolina*, 182.

[13] Nevins, *The Evening Post*, 21, 29.

[14] Hamilton to Gouverneur Morris, January 10, 1801, *HWL*, X, 410; *New York Evening Post*, December 7, 1801.

[15] Nevins, *The Evening Post*, 27–28.

[16] Hamilton to John Rutledge, December, 1800, Hamilton to King, June 3, 1802, *HWL*, X, 404, 441.

fallacies and dangers of the Republican system and would soon be ready to throw it off.[17] Beginning in late 1801 he wrote a series of eighteen essays undertaking an "Examination of Jefferson's Message to Congress of December 7, 1801."[18] He criticized the President for announcing that, even though Tripoli had declared war on the United States and was in fact committing acts of war, he could not make a stand until Congress acted. In attacking Jefferson's move to eliminate some forms of internal revenue, he tossed back at the President the old accusation of the Republicans that, as secretary of the treasury, Hamilton had called the public debt a "public blessing." His position was that the taxes should be used to pay the national debt, enlarge the navy, and provide for other public needs.[19]

The public did not respond to Hamilton's attack on Jefferson's procedures, and Republican writers took up the cause. The controversial James Thomson Callender, who had not yet deserted his patron Jefferson, tried to shame Hamilton for opposing Jefferson's measures for peace, which Callender was sure would continue to thrive "in despite of all the Macbeth witchcraft of the fallen angels."[20]

The failure of the people, and especially of the Federalists, to respond to his criticisms plunged Hamilton into gloom. Early in 1802 he expressed the fear that the people had not come to the point where they were willing "to make an effort to *recover* the Constitution." Those who were so inclined were so few that they "must wait a while."[21]

Hamilton still believed that Republican leaders appealed to men's baser passions rather than to their legitimate interests or their sense of justice.[22] But in 1802 he revealed a plan for a "Christian Constitutional Society" which would also lay more emphasis on emotion than on clear thinking. He envisioned the society as a nationwide movement to act in co-operation with the churches. His friends did not think well of the idea, and it was soon abandoned. But it should be noted that even in this rather ill-considered venture Hamilton insisted that every act must be in accordance with the Constitution and the laws of the land and that any proposed change

[17] Address to the Electors of the State of New York, 1801, *HWL*, VIII, 224–25.

[18] December 17, 1801–April 8, 1802, *ibid.*, 246–373.

[19] *Ibid.*, 224–57.

[20] Letter No. III in a pamphlet printed in New York in 1802 by Richard Reynolds.

[21] Hamilton to Gouverneur Morris, February 27, 1802, *HWL*, X, 426.

[22] "Camillus," No. 1, July 22, 1795, *ibid.*, V, 191; Hamilton to Gouverneur Morris, April 6, 1802, *ibid.*, X, 430.

in government must be effected through procedures provided by the Constitution.[23]

From some points of view those years should have been happy ones for Hamilton. He was freed of the heavy public responsibilities he had carried through almost all his adult life. He enjoyed his family and his friends. He was head of the New York bar and had a successful and remunerative practice. Yet his gloom persisted. Had he been asked the source of his unhappiness, in deepest sincerity he would have attributed it to his conviction that the American society could not long maintain peace and harmony unless it provided for a stronger government than Jefferson's.[24]

Hamilton's interest in diplomacy revived in 1802 with news that Spain had formally ceded Louisiana to France. He was further agitated when news arrived that American commerce was again being harassed by Spanish authorities at the mouth of the Mississippi. He reminded Pinckney that he had "always held that the *unity of our empire* and the best interests of our nation require that we shall annex to the United States all the territory east of the Mississippi, New Orleans included." Surely, he wrote, Jefferson must be planning to go to war to gain possession of the region, and he reflected that the President must now be regretting Republican financial measures, for "the pretty scheme of substituting economy to taxation will not do here."[25]

Through the *Evening Post* the Federalists took up the cry for positive action. When Jefferson failed to respond as they expected, they tried to win the western settlers to their cause, accusing Jefferson of ignoring the welfare of the West. The frontiersmen were suspicious of the Federalists' proposals, however, and decided to give Jefferson time to work out the problem.

By now Jefferson was no less interested in New Orleans than Hamilton was. He was less concerned about Florida, and neither man had shown any great interest in western Louisiana. As secretary of state, Jefferson had told Carmichael, the American representative to Spain, to assure the Spaniards that it was not "our interest to cross the Mississippi for ages" and would "never be our interest to remain united with those who do."[26] At no time would Hamilton have considered making any such concession.

[23] Hamilton to Bayard, April, 1802, *ibid.*, X, 432–37.

[24] *MDL*, II, 454.

[25] Hamilton to Pinckney, December 29, 1802, *HWL*, X, 445–46.

[26] "Heads of Consideration on the Navigation of the Mississippi, for Mr. Carmichael," August 22, 1790, *JW*, XVII, 306.

Jefferson was deeply aware of the grave responsibilities of the office he held. There is a distinct echo of the Hamilton of 1799 in Jefferson's instructions of April 18, 1802, to Robert R. Livingston, minister to France. He wrote that New Orleans was the "one single spot, the possessor of which is our natural and habitual enemy." On that occasion it was Jefferson who commented, "The day that France takes possession of New Orleans, . . . we must marry ourselves to the British fleet and nation."[27] Converts to a faith are sometimes more devout than lifelong adherents. Since the early 1790's, Hamilton had worked for harmonious relations with Britain, but he had utterly rejected the idea of an alliance with that country in 1799, when full-scale war with France had appeared certain. Now again Hamilton was recommending a military expedition to seize New Orleans, and he was hopeful of British co-operation; but, true to his previous stand, he remained opposed to a treaty with Britain. As in 1799, he would rely upon British self-interest and would merely ask Britain to "hold herself in readiness" to co-operate.[28] In power or out, Hamilton remained true to his principles.[29]

Understandably, Republican officials did not supply Hamilton with confidential information about the currents of diplomacy, and thus his recommendations were not as precise or well suited to the circumstances as they had been in the past. He was unduly impatient with Jefferson's leisurely procedure. Through editorials in the *Evening Post* and in other writings, Hamilton repeatedly called for military measures. He ridiculed the to him fatuous proposal to purchase the Floridas and New Orleans, assuming that it had not the remotest chance of success.[30] Jefferson, who of course took the correct step in offering to buy the territory, did not really think that the move would succeed either. "I did not expect [Napoleon] would yield," he wrote later, "till a war took place between France and England, and my hope was to palliate and endure . . . until that event."[31] Hamilton feared that further delay would give the French time to fortify New Orleans. News that Monroe had been sent to France to join Livingston in the negotiations prompted the *Evening Post* to gibe that "Patriot Monroe is gone with two millions of money in his hand, to buy some partial privilege, with which

[27] Jefferson to Livingston, *ibid.*, X, 312–13.

[28] "Pericles," 1803, *HWL*, VI, 336.

[29] Cf. Whitaker (*Mississippi Question*, 213–14), who believes that Hamilton's statements at this point were for partisan purposes.

[30] "Pericles," *HWL*, VI, 334.

[31] Jefferson to Dr. Joseph Priestley, January 29, 1804, *JW*, X, 446–47.

money the *Emperor of the Gauls* will build a fort at New Orleans."[32] Such comments demonstrated the extent to which Hamilton had lost touch with the currents of European diplomacy.

Hamilton was thus as much surprised as Jefferson by the success of the negotiations. Yet when the treaty, amazingly providing for the purchase of the entire Louisiana Territory, reached the United States, he rose again to greatness and supported it with every ounce of his energy. Other Federalists balked—some out of jealousy of Republican successes and others out of fear that their commercial interests would be permanently jeopardized by the addition of the vast new territory, whose inhabitants' chief interests would be agricultural. "The purchase of an immense territory which we did not want," lamented Pickering, "and at such a price."[33] Hamilton was far above such considerations. The purchase was a happy solution to the Louisiana problem, and he rejoiced in it. Again, as on many earlier occasions, he did not hesitate to differ with his friends when he thought the nation's welfare demanded it.

Now it was Jefferson's turn to be embarrassed. He could find no constitutional authority for the next step. "The Constitution has made no provision for our holding foreign territory," he pointed out, and "still less for incorporating foreign nations into our Union."[34] He thought that it would be just as unconstitutional to acquire Louisiana as to "receive England, Ireland, Holland, etc."[35] At first he thought it would be a relatively simple matter to amend the Constitution to make the cession legal. He considered the amendment: "Louisiana, as ceded by France to the United States, is made a part of the United States"; and "Florida also, whensoever it may be rightfully obtained, shall become a part of the United States." Upon further contemplation, he decided that "the less that is said about any constitutional difficulty, the better; . . . it will be desirable for Congress to do what is necessary, *in silence*."[36] The strength of northern opposition to the purchase was so great that it appeared such an amendment might not be ratified. On October 17, 1803, Jefferson laid the treaty before the Senate for its advice and consent.[37]

32 March 21, 1803.

33 Pickering to Governor Strong, November 22, 1803, Pickering Papers, Massachusetts Historical Society, Boston, XIV.

34 Jefferson to John Breckenridge, August 12, 1803, *JW*, X, 411.

35 Jefferson to W. C. Nicholas, September 7, 1803, *ibid.*, 418.

36 Jefferson to Levi Lincoln, August 30, 1803, *ibid.*, 416–17.

37 Richardson, I, 350.

One historian has sought to explain the contradiction between Jefferson's approval of the treaty and his doctrine of strict construction by saying that "Jefferson knew himself and his Cabinet to be free of dictatorial ambitions" and that "he had the welfare of the nation . . . closely in view."[38] These comments are correct, of course, but the main point is that when the theory of strict construction was confronted by this momentous test Jefferson saw that it would not serve and was open-minded enough to discard it. It should be added that he was no freer from "dictatorial ambitions," nor more interested in the "welfare of the nation," than Hamilton had always been.

Senate action was so prompt and so favorable that four days after the President submitted the treaty he could inform the House of Representatives that the treaty had "been ratified and my ratification exchanged for that of the First Consul of France in due form." He did not specifically ask for an appropriation of funds to pay for the territory, though the request was implied. His immediate concern was for House action providing for "the occupation and government of the country."[39] Exchanging ratifications without awaiting action by the representatives was also a shift from his earlier position on Jay's Treaty; in 1795 he had held that if a treaty contained provisions requiring House action—that is, appropriations to implement the treaty—the instrument could not legally go into effect until approved by the lower house.

Though Hamilton praised the treaty in the columns of the *Evening Post*, his praise did not go as far as to include any gracious expressions for the negotiators, or for their chief in the White House. "The acquisition has been solely owing to a fortuitous concurrence of unforeseen and unexpected circumstances, and not to any wise or vigorous measures on the part of the American government." As for Monroe, he deserved no credit whatever, according to the *Post*, for he arrived on the scene after the French had already decided to sell the territory.[40]

In a sense the Louisiana Purchase was a victory not only for Jefferson but for Hamilton as well. Before the American Revolution, as a mere youth, he had expressed an interest in the Gulf region.[41] In his first term in the Continental Congress, while the peace treaty with Britain was being worked out, he reaffirmed the importance of the region to the United States,[42] and

[38] Koch, *Jefferson and Madison*, 242 n.

[39] Richardson, I, 350–51.

[40] *New York Evening Post*, July 5, 1803.

[41] "A Full Vindication," December 15, 1774, *HWL*, I, 29.

[42] *JCC*, XXIV, 194.

in his second term in Congress he went on record as emphatically favoring the removal of obstacles to commerce on the Mississippi.[43] He dwelt at length on the subject in the "Federalist" essays.[44] As secretary of the treasury and later as Washington's adviser, in his counsel to Adams' cabinet, in his personal correspondence, and in his communications with the public, he kept the subject alive. He recognized the vital economic importance of access to the Gulf. He knew that the nations of Europe were envious of the United States' potential wealth and greatness and would continue to obstruct American commerce and encourage disaffection among the westerners to hamper the nation's growth. Again and again he emphasized that the unity of the nation depended on the acquisition of Louisiana and the Floridas.

In short, Hamilton did more than any other American to convince the people about the vital importance of the area. If he had not thwarted Talleyrand's schemes, French control might have been firmly established at New Orleans and even farther north before Napoleon appeared on the scene. Under such circumstances the West might have found a new loyalty and might even have evolved into a separate country. Now the nation had secured its future. Neither the objections of his dissident friends nor his understandable jealousy of the success of his political foes could dull his elation when Louisiana Territory was joined to his nation.

It is one of the ironies of American history and one of the misfortunes of life that he who had laid the groundwork, and who had come so close to winning the territory in 1800, was forced to step aside and watch his greatest rival gain enduring fame for the achievement.

In New England Federalist resentment of the Louisiana Purchase continued so intense that by 1804 a dangerous secessionist plot had developed. Apparently Hamilton did not realize how far the plot had gone until he heard that Aaron Burr, that gifted schemer, was also supporting it.[45] Hamilton was, of course, shocked by the idea of disunion, which he opposed "with every fiber of his being."[46] He took up his pen to prove to the subversives that secession would be "a clear sacrifice of great positive advantages without any counterbalancing good."[47]

[43] *Ibid.*, 534–35.

[44] "Federalist," No. 11, November, 1797, *HWL*, XI, 84.

[45] Harvey Putnam Prentiss, *Timothy Pickering as the Leader of New England Federalism, 1800–1815*, (Salem, 1934), 30.

[46] Schachner, *Alexander Hamilton*, 420.

[47] Hamilton to Sedgwick, July 10, 1804, *HWL*, X, 458.

No doubt he would have traveled through New England in person to speak against the plot, but a black cloud had descended upon his life. Hamilton made some remarks casting doubt on Burr's loyalty to the United States. In answer Burr challenged Hamilton to a duel.[48] Hamilton could not deny that his statements had been tantamount to calling Burr a traitor. He decided, though reluctantly, to go through with the encounter and sent Rufus King to New England in his place to bear his message opposing secession.[49] Arguments proved unnecessary, however, for when the news spread that Hamilton had died at the hands of the man thought to be a leader in the plot, the movement collapsed.[50] As in life, so in death, Hamilton served his country well.

48 Burr to Hamilton, June 18, 1804, *ibid.*, 460.
49 Hamilton to Sedgwick, July 10, 1804, *ibid.*, 458.
50 Mitchell, *Alexander Hamilton*, II, 518–23.

Washington's Farewell Address

FAREWELL ADDRESS.[1]

UNITED STATES, *September 17, 1796*.

Friends and Fellow-Citizens:

The period for a new election of a citizen to administer the Executive Government of the United States being not far distant, and the time actually arrived when your thoughts must be employed in designating the person who is to be clothed with that important trust, it appears to me proper, especially as it may conduce to a more distinct expression of the public voice, that I should now apprise you of the resolution I have formed to decline being considered among the number of those out of whom a choice is to be made.

I beg you at the same time to do me the justice to be assured that this resolution has not been taken without a strict regard to all the considerations appertaining to the relation which binds a dutiful citizen to his country; and that in withdrawing the tender of service, which silence in my situation might imply, I am influenced by no diminution of zeal for your future interest, no deficiency of grateful respect for your past kindness, but am supported by a full conviction that the step is compatible with both.

The acceptance of and continuance hitherto in the office to which your suffrages have twice called me have been a uniform sacrifice of inclination to the opinion of duty and to a deference for what appeared to be your desire. I constantly hoped that it would have been much earlier in my power, consistently with motives which I was not at liberty to disregard, to return to that retirement from which I had been reluctantly drawn. The strength of my inclination to do this

[1] Reprinted from James D. Richardson (ed.), *A Compilation of the Messages and Papers of the Presidents, 1789–1897 (Published by Authority of Congress)* (Washington, 1896), I, 213–24.

previous to the last election had even led to the preparation of an address to declare it to you; but mature reflection on the then perplexed and critical posture of our affairs with foreign nations and the unanimous advice of persons entitled to my confidence impelled me to abandon the idea. I rejoice that the state of your concerns, external as well as internal, no longer renders the pursuit of inclination incompatible with the sentiment of duty or propriety, and am persuaded, whatever partiality may be retained for my services, that in the present circumstances of our country you will not disapprove my determination to retire.

The impressions with which I first undertook the arduous trust were explained on the proper occasion. In the discharge of this trust I will only say that I have, with good intentions, contributed toward the organization and administration of the Government the best exertions of which a very fallible judgment was capable. Not unconscious in the outset of the inferiority of my qualifications, experience in my own eyes, perhaps still more in the eyes of others, has strengthened the motives to diffidence of myself; and every day the increasing weight of years admonishes me more and more that the shade of retirement is as necessary to me as it will be welcome. Satisfied that if any circumstances have given peculiar value to my services they were temporary, I have the consolation to believe that, while choice and prudence invite me to quit the political scene, patriotism does not forbid it.

In looking forward to the moment which is intended to terminate the career of my political life my feelings do not permit me to suspend the deep acknowledgment of that debt of gratitude which I owe to my beloved country for the many honors it has conferred upon me; still more for the steadfast confidence with which it has supported me, and for the opportunities I have thence enjoyed of manifesting my inviolable attachment by services faithful and persevering, though in usefulness unequal to my zeal. If benefits have resulted to our country from these services, let it always be remembered to your praise and as an instructive example in our annals that under circumstances in which the passions, agitated in every direction, were liable to mislead; amidst appearances sometimes dubious; vicissitudes of fortune often discouraging; in situations in which not unfrequently want of success has countenanced the spirit of criticism, the constancy of your support was the essential prop of the efforts and a guaranty of the plans by which they were effected. Profoundly penetrated with this idea, I shall carry it with me to my grave as a strong incitement to unceasing vows that Heaven may continue to you the choicest tokens of its beneficence; that your union and brotherly affection may be perpetual; that the free Constitution which is the work of your hands may be sacredly maintained; that its administration in every department may be stamped with wisdom and virtue; that, in fine, the happiness of the people of these States, under the auspices of liberty, may be made complete by so careful a preservation and so prudent a use of this blessing as will acquire to them the glory of recommending it to the applause, the affection, and adoption of every nation which is yet a stranger to it.

Here, perhaps, I ought to stop. But a solicitude for your welfare which can not end but with my life, and the apprehension of danger natural to that solicitude, urge me on an occasion like the present to offer to your solemn contemplation and to recommend to your frequent review some sentiments which are the result of much reflection, of no inconsiderable observation, and which appear to me all important to the permanency of your felicity as a people. These will be offered to you with the more freedom as you can only see in them the disinterested warnings of a parting friend, who can possibly have no personal motive to bias his counsel. Nor can I forget as an encouragement to it your indulgent reception of my sentiments on a former and not dissimilar occasion.

Interwoven as is the love of liberty with every ligament of your hearts, no recommendation of mine is necessary to fortify or confirm the attachment.

The unity of government which constitutes you one people is also now dear to you. It is justly so, for it is a main pillar in the edifice of your real independence, the support of your tranquillity at home, your peace abroad, of your safety, of your prosperity, of that very liberty which you so highly prize. But as it is easy to foresee that from different causes and from different quarters much pains will be taken, many artifices employed, to weaken in your minds the conviction of this truth, as this is the point in your political fortress against which the batteries of internal and external enemies will be most constantly and actively (though often covertly and insidiously) directed, it is of infinite moment that you should properly estimate the immense value of your national union to your collective and individual happiness; that you should cherish a cordial, habitual, and immovable attachment to it; accustoming yourselves to think and speak of it as of the palladium of your political safety and prosperity; watching for its preservation with jealous anxiety; discountenancing whatever may suggest even a suspicion that it can in any event be abandoned, and indignantly frowning upon the first dawning of every attempt to alienate any portion of our country from the rest or to enfeeble the sacred ties which now link together the various parts.

For this you have every inducement of sympathy and interest. Citizens by birth or choice of a common country, that country has a right to concentrate your affections. The name of American, which belongs to you in your national capacity, must always exalt the just pride of patriotism more than any appellation derived from local discriminations. With slight shades of difference, you have the same religion, manners, habits, and political principles. You have in common cause fought and triumphed together. The independence and liberty you possess are the work of joint councils and joint efforts, of common dangers, sufferings, and successes.

But these considerations, however powerfully they address themselves to your sensibility, are greatly outweighed by those which apply more immediately to your interest. Here every portion of our country finds the most commanding motives for carefully guarding and preserving the union of the whole.

The *North*, in an unrestrained intercourse with the *South*, protected by the equal laws of a common government, finds in the productions of the latter great additional resources of maritime and commercial enterprise and precious materials of manufacturing industry. The *South*, in the same intercourse, benefiting by the same agency of the *North*, sees its agriculture grow and its commerce expand. Turning partly into its own channels the seamen of the *North*, it finds its particular navigation invigorated; and while it contributes in different ways to nourish and increase the general mass of the national navigation, it looks forward to the protection of a maritime strength to which itself is unequally adapted. The *East*, in a like intercourse with the *West*, already finds, and in the progressive improvement of interior communications by land and water will more and more find, a valuable vent for the commodities which it brings from abroad or manufactures at home. The *West* derives from the *East* supplies requisite to its growth and comfort, and what is perhaps of still greater consequence, it must of necessity owe the *secure* enjoyment of indispensable *outlets* for its own productions to the weight, influence, and the future maritime strength of the Atlantic side of the Union, directed by an indissoluble community of interest as *one nation*. Any other tenure by which the *West* can hold this essential advantage, whether derived from its own separate strength or from an apostate and unnatural connection with any foreign power, must be intrinsically precarious.

While, then, every part of our country thus feels an immediate and particular interest in union, all the parts combined can not fail to find in the united mass of means and efforts greater strength, greater resource, proportionably greater security from external danger, a less frequent interruption of their peace by foreign nations, and what is of inestimable value, they must derive from union an exemption from those broils and wars between themselves which so frequently afflict neighboring countries not tied together by the same governments, which their own rivalships alone would be sufficient to produce, but which opposite foreign alliances, attachments, and intrigues would stimulate and imbitter. Hence, likewise, they will avoid the necessity of those overgrown military establishments which, under any form of government, are inauspicious to liberty, and which are to be regarded as particularly hostile to republican liberty. In this sense it is that your union ought to be considered as a main prop of your liberty, and that the love of the one ought to endear to you the preservation of the other.

These considerations speak a persuasive language to every reflecting and virtuous mind, and exhibit the continuance of the union as a primary object of patriotic desire. Is there a doubt whether a common government can embrace so large a sphere? Let experience solve it. To listen to mere speculation in such a case were criminal. We are authorized to hope that a proper organization of the whole, with the auxiliary agency of governments for the respective subdivisions, will afford a happy issue to the experiment. It is well worth a fair and full experiment. With such powerful and obvious motives to union affecting all parts of our country, while experience shall not have demonstrated its impracticability, there will always be reason to distrust the patriotism of those who in any quarter may endeavor to weaken its bands.

In contemplating the causes which may disturb our union it occurs as matter of serious concern that any ground should have been furnished for characterizing parties by *geographical* discriminations—*Northern* and *Southern*, *Atlantic* and *Western*—whence designing men may endeavor to excite a belief that there is a real difference of local interests and views. One of the expedients of party to acquire influence within particular districts is to misrepresent the opinions and aims of other districts. You can not shield yourselves too much against the jealousies and heartburnings which spring from these misrepresentations; they tend to render alien to each other those who ought to be bound together by fraternal affection. The inhabitants of our Western country have lately had a useful lesson on this head. They have seen in the negotiation by the Executive and in the unanimous ratification by the Senate of the treaty with Spain, and in the universal satisfaction at that event throughout the United States, a decisive proof how unfounded were the suspicions propagated among them of a policy in the General Government and in the Atlantic States unfriendly to their interests in regard to the Mississippi. They have been witnesses to the formation of two treaties—that with Great Britain and that with Spain—which secure to them everything they could desire in respect to our foreign relations toward confirming their prosperity. Will it not be their wisdom to rely for the preservation of these advantages on the union by which they were procured? Will they not henceforth be deaf to those advisers, if such there are, who would sever them from their brethren and connect them with aliens?

To the efficacy and permanency of your union a government for the whole is indispensable. No alliances, however strict, between the parts can be an adequate substitute. They must inevitably experience the infractions and interruptions which all alliances in all times have experienced. Sensible of this momentous truth, you have improved upon your first essay by the adoption of a Constitution of Government better calculated than your former for an intimate union and for the efficacious management of your common concerns. This Government, the offspring of our own choice, uninfluenced and unawed, adopted upon full investigation and mature deliberation, completely free in its principles, in the distribution of its powers, uniting security with energy, and containing within itself a provision for its own amendment, has a just claim to your confidence and your support. Respect for its authority, compliance with its laws, acquiescence in its measures, are duties enjoined by the fundamental maxims of true liberty. The basis of our political systems is the right of the people to make and to alter their constitutions of government. But the constitution which at any time exists till changed by an explicit and authentic act of the whole people is sacredly obligatory upon all. The very idea of the power and the right of the people to establish government presupposes the duty of every individual to obey the established government.

All obstructions to the execution of the laws, all combinations and associations, under whatever plausible character, with the real design to direct, control, counteract, or awe the regular deliberation and action of the constituted authorities, are destructive of this fundamental principle and of fatal tendency. They serve to organize faction; to give it an artificial and extraordinary force; to put in the place of the delegated will of the nation the will of a party, often a small but artful and enterprising minority of the community, and, according to the alternate triumphs of different parties, to make the public administration the mirror of the ill-concerted and incongruous projects of faction rather than the organ of consistent and wholesome plans, digested by common counsels and modified by mutual interests.

However combinations or associations of the above description may now and then answer popular ends, they are likely in the course of time and things to become potent engines by which cunning, ambitious, and unprincipled men will be enabled to subvert the power of the people, and to usurp for themselves the reins of government, destroying afterwards the very engines which have lifted them to unjust dominion.

Toward the preservation of your Government and the permanency of your present happy state, it is requisite not only that you steadily discountenance irregular oppositions to its acknowledged authority, but also that you resist with care the spirit of innovation upon its principles, however specious the pretexts. One method of assault may be to effect in the forms of the Constitution alterations which will impair the energy of the system, and thus to undermine what can not be directly overthrown. In all the changes to which you may be invited remember that time and habit are at least as necessary to fix the true character of governments as of other human institutions; that experience is the surest standard by which to test the real tendency of the existing constitution of a country; that facility in changes upon the credit of mere hypothesis and opinion exposes to perpetual change, from the endless variety of hypothesis and opinion; and remember especially that for the efficient management of your common interests in a country so extensive as ours a government of as much vigor as is consistent with the perfect security of liberty is indispensable. Liberty itself will find in such a government, with powers properly distributed and adjusted, its surest guardian. It is, indeed, little else than a name where the government is too feeble to withstand the enterprises of faction, to confine each member of the society within the limits prescribed by the laws, and to maintain all in the secure and tranquil enjoyment of the rights of person and property.

I have already intimated to you the danger of parties in the State, with particular reference to the founding of them on geographical discriminations. Let me now take a more comprehensive view, and warn you in the most solemn manner against the baneful effects of the spirit of party generally.

This spirit, unfortunately, is inseparable from our nature, having its root in the strongest passions of the human mind. It exists under different shapes in all government, more or less stifled, controlled, or repressed; but in those of the popular form it is seen in its greatest rankness and is truly their worst enemy.

The alternate domination of one faction over another, sharpened by the spirit of revenge natural to party dissension, which in different ages and countries has perpetrated the most horrid enormities, is itself a frightful despotism. But this leads at length to a more formal and permanent despotism. The disorders and miseries which result gradually incline the minds of men to seek security and repose in the absolute power of an individual, and sooner or later the chief of some prevailing faction, more able or more fortunate than his competitors, turns this disposition to the purposes of his own elevation on the ruins of public liberty.

Without looking forward to an extremity of this kind (which nevertheless ought not to be entirely out of sight), the common and continual mischiefs of the spirit of party are sufficient to make it the interest and duty of a wise people to discourage and restrain it.

It serves always to distract the public councils and enfeeble the public administration. It agitates the community with ill-founded jealousies and false alarms; kindles the animosity of one part against another; foments occasionally riot and insurrection. It opens the door to foreign influence and corruption, which find a facilitated access to the government itself through the channels of party passion. Thus the policy and the will of one country are subjected to the policy and will of another.

There is an opinion that parties in free countries are useful checks upon the administration of the government, and serve to keep alive the spirit of liberty.

This within certain limits is probably true; and in governments of a monarchical cast patriotism may look with indulgence, if not with favor, upon the spirit of party. But in those of the popular character, in governments purely elective, it is a spirit not to be encouraged. From their natural tendency it is certain there will always be enough of that spirit for every salutary purpose; and there being constant danger of excess, the effort ought to be by force of public opinion to mitigate and assuage it. A fire not to be quenched, it demands a uniform vigilance to prevent its bursting into a flame, lest, instead of warming, it should consume.

It is important, likewise, that the habits of thinking in a free country should inspire caution in those intrusted with its administration to confine themselves within their respective constitutional spheres, avoiding in the exercise of the powers of one department to encroach upon another. The spirit of encroachment tends to consolidate the powers of all the departments in one, and thus to create, whatever the form of government, a real despotism. A just estimate of that love of power and proneness to abuse it which predominates in the human heart is sufficient to satisfy us of the truth of this position. The necessity of reciprocal checks in the exercise of political power, by dividing and distributing it into different depositories, and constituting each the guardian of the public weal against invasions by the others, has been evinced by experiments ancient and modern, some of them in our country and under our own eyes. To preserve them must be as necessary as to institute them. If in the opinion of the people the distribution or modification of the constitutional powers be in any particular wrong, let it be corrected by an amendment in the way which the Constitution designates. But let there be no change by usurpation; for though this in one instance may be the instrument of good, it is the customary weapon by which free governments are destroyed. The precedent must always greatly overbalance in permanent evil any partial or transient benefit which the use can at any time yield.

Of all the dispositions and habits which lead to political prosperity, religion and morality are indispensable supports. In vain would that man claim the tribute of patriotism who should labor to subvert these great pillars of human happiness—these firmest props of the duties of men and citizens. The mere politician, equally with the pious man, ought to respect and to cherish them. A volume could not trace all their connections with private and public felicity. Let it simply be asked, Where is the security for property, for reputation, for life, if the sense of religious obligation *desert* the oaths which are the instruments of investigation in courts of justice? And let us with caution indulge the supposition that morality can be maintained without religion. Whatever may be conceded to the influence of refined education on minds of peculiar structure, reason and experience both forbid us to expect that national morality can prevail in exclusion of religious principle.

It is substantially true that virtue or morality is a necessary spring of popular government. The rule indeed extends with more or less force to every species of free government. Who that is a sincere friend to it can look with indifference upon attempts to shake the foundation of the fabric? Promote, then, as an object of primary importance, institutions for the general diffusion of knowledge. In proportion as the structure of a government gives force to public opinion, it is essential that public opinion should be enlightened.

As a very important source of strength and security, cherish public credit. One method of preserving it is to use it as sparingly as possible, avoiding occasions of expense by cultivating peace, but remembering also that timely disbursements to prepare for danger frequently prevent much greater disbursements to repel it; avoiding likewise the accumulation of debt, not only by shunning occasions of expense, but by vigorous exertions in time of peace to discharge the debts which unavoidable wars have occasioned, not ungenerously throwing upon posterity the burthen which we ourselves ought to bear. The execution of these maxims belongs to your representatives, but it is necessary that public opinion should cooperate. To facilitate to them the performance of their duty it is essential that you should practically bear in mind that toward the payment of debts there must be revenue; that to have revenue there must be taxes, that no taxes can be devised which are not more or less inconvenient and unpleasant; that the intrinsic embarrassment inseparable from the selection of the proper objects (which is always a choice of difficulties), ought to be a decisive motive for a candid construction of the conduct of the Government in making it, and for a spirit of acquiescence in the measures for obtaining revenue which the public exigencies may at any time dictate.

Observe good faith and justice toward all nations. Cultivate peace and harmony with all. Religion and morality enjoin this conduct. And can it be that good policy does not equally enjoin it? It will be worthy of a free, enlightened, and at no distant period a great nation to give to mankind the magnanimous and too novel example of a people always guided by an exalted justice and benevolence. Who can doubt that in the course of time and things the fruits of such a plan would richly repay any temporary advantages which might be lost by a steady adherence to it? Can it be that Providence has not connected the permanent felicity of a nation with its virtue? The experiment, at least, is recommended by every sentiment which ennobles human nature. Alas! is it rendered impossible by its vices?

In the execution of such a plan nothing is more essential than that permanent, inveterate antipathies against particular nations and passionate attachments for others should be excluded, and that in place of them just and amicable feelings toward all should be cultivated. The nation which indulges toward another an habitual hatred or an habitual fondness is in some degree a slave. It is a slave to its animosity or to its affection, either of which is sufficient to lead it astray from its duty and its interest. Antipathy in one nation against another disposes each more readily to offer insult and injury, to lay hold of slight causes of umbrage, and to be haughty and intractable when accidental or trifling occasions of dispute occur.

Hence frequent collisions, obstinate, envenomed, and bloody contests. The nation prompted by ill will and resentment sometimes impels to war the government contrary to the best calculations of policy. The government sometimes participates in the national propensity, and adopts through passion what reason would reject. At other times it makes the animosity of the nation subservient to projects of hostility, instigated by pride, ambition, and other sinister and pernicious motives. The peace often, sometimes perhaps the liberty, of nations has been the victim.

So, likewise, a passionate attachment of one nation for another produces a variety of evils. Sympathy for the favorite nation, facilitating the illusion of an imaginary common interest in cases where no real common interest exists, and infusing into one the enmities of the other, betrays the former into a participation in the quarrels and wars of the latter without adequate inducement or justification. It leads also to concessions to the favorite nation of privileges denied to others, which is apt doubly to injure the nation making the concessions by unnecessarily parting with what ought to have been retained, and by exciting jealousy, ill will, and a disposition to retaliate in the parties from whom equal privileges are withheld; and it gives to ambitious, corrupted, or deluded citizens (who devote themselves to the favorite nation) facility to betray or sacrifice the interests of their own country without odium, sometimes even with popularity, gilding with the appearances of a virtuous sense of obligation, a commendable deference for public opinion, or a laudable zeal for public good the base or foolish compliances of ambition, corruption, or infatuation.

As avenues to foreign influence in innumerable ways, such attachments are particularly alarming to the truly enlightened and independent patriot. How many opportunities do they afford to tamper with domestic factions, to practice the arts of seduction, to mislead public opinion, to influence or awe the public councils! Such an attachment of a small or weak toward a great and powerful nation dooms the former to be the satellite of the latter. Against the insidious wiles of foreign influence (I conjure you to believe me, fellow-citizens) the jealousy of a free people ought to be *constantly* awake, since history and experience prove that foreign influence is one of the most baneful foes of republican government. But that jealousy, to be useful, must be impartial, else it becomes the instrument of the very influence to be avoided, instead of a defense against it. Excessive partiality for one foreign nation and excessive dislike of another cause those whom they actuate to see danger only on one side, and serve to veil and even second the arts of influence on the other. Real patriots who may resist the intrigues of the favorite are liable to become suspected and odious, while its tools and dupes usurp the applause and confidence of the people to surrender their interests.

The great rule of conduct for us in regard to foreign nations is, in extending our commercial relations to have with them as little *political* connection as possible. So far as we have already formed engagements let them be fulfilled with perfect good faith. Here let us stop.

Europe has a set of primary interests which to us have none or a very remote relation. Hence she must be engaged in frequent controversies, the causes of which are essentially foreign to our concerns. Hence, therefore, it must be unwise in us to implicate ourselves by artificial ties in the ordinary vicissitudes of her politics or the ordinary combinations and collisions of her friendships or enmities.

Our detached and distant situation invites and enables us to pursue a different course. If we remain one people, under an efficient government, the period is not far off when we may defy material injury from external annoyance; when we may take such an attitude as will cause the neutrality we may at any time resolve upon to be scrupulously respected; when belligerent nations, under the impossibility of making acquisitions upon us, will not lightly hazard the giving us provocation; when we may choose peace or war, as our interest, guided by justice, shall counsel.

Why forego the advantages of so peculiar a situation? Why quit our own to stand upon foreign ground? Why, by interweaving our destiny with that of any part of Europe, entangle our peace and prosperity in the toils of European ambition, rivalship, interest, humor, or caprice?

It is our true policy to steer clear of permanent alliances with any portion of the foreign world, so far, I mean, as we are now at liberty to do it; for let me not be understood as capable of patronizing infidelity to existing engagements. I hold the maxim no less applicable to public than to private affairs that honesty is always the best policy. I repeat, therefore, let those engagements be observed in their genuine sense. But in my opinion it is unnecessary and would be unwise to extend them.

Taking care always to keep ourselves by suitable establishments on a respectable defensive posture, we may safely trust to temporary alliances for extraordinary emergencies.

Harmony, liberal intercourse with all nations are recommended by policy, humanity, and interest. But even our commercial policy should hold an equal and impartial hand, neither seeking nor granting exclusive favors or preferences; consulting the natural course of things; diffusing and diversifying by gentle means the streams of commerce, but forcing nothing; establishing with powers so disposed, in order to give trade a stable course, to define the rights of our merchants, and to enable the Government to support them, conventional rules of intercourse, the best that present circumstances and mutual opinion will permit, but temporary and liable to be from time to time abandoned or varied as experience and circumstances shall dictate; constantly keeping in view that it is folly in one nation to look for disinterested favors from another; that it must pay with a portion of its independence for whatever it may accept under that character; that by such acceptance it may place itself in the condition of having given equivalents for nominal favors, and yet of being reproached with ingratitude for not giving more. There can be no greater error than to expect or calculate upon real favors from nation to nation. It is an illusion which experience must cure, which a just pride ought to discard.

In offering to you, my countrymen, these counsels of an old and affectionate friend I dare not hope they will make the strong and lasting impression I could wish—that they will control the usual current of the passions or prevent our nation from running the course which has hitherto marked the destiny of nations. But if I may even flatter myself that they may be productive of some partial benefit, some occasional good—that they may now and then recur to moderate the fury of party spirit, to warn against the mischiefs of foreign intrigue, to guard against the impostures of pretended patriotism—this hope will be a full recompense for the solicitude for your welfare by which they have been dictated.

How far in the discharge of my official duties I have been guided by the principles which have been delineated the public records and other evidences of my conduct must witness to you and to the world. To myself, the assurance of my own conscience is that I have at least believed myself to be guided by them.

In relation to the still subsisting war in Europe my proclamation of the 22d of April, 1793, is the index to my plan. Sanctioned by your approving voice and by that of your representatives in both Houses of Congress, the spirit of that measure has continually governed me, uninfluenced by any attempts to deter or divert me from it.

After deliberate examination, with the aid of the best lights I could obtain, I was well satisfied that our country, under all the circumstances of the case, had a right to take, and was bound in duty and interest to take, a neutral position. Having taken it, I determined as far as should depend upon me to maintain it with moderation, perseverance, and firmness.

The considerations which respect the right to hold this conduct it is not necessary on this occasion to detail. I will only observe that, according to my understanding of the matter, that right, so far from being denied by any of the belligerent powers, has been virtually admitted by all.

The duty of holding a neutral conduct may be inferred, without anything more, from the obligation which justice and humanity impose on every nation, in cases in which it is free to act, to maintain inviolate the relations of peace and amity toward other nations.

The inducements of interest for observing that conduct will best be referred to your own reflections and experience. With me a predominant motive has been to endeavor to gain time to our country to settle and mature its yet recent institutions, and to progress without interruption to that degree of strength and consistency which is necessary to give it, humanly speaking, the command of its own fortunes.

Though in reviewing the incidents of my Administration I am unconscious of intentional error, I am nevertheless too sensible of my defects not to think it probable that I may have committed many errors. Whatever they may be, I fervently beseech the Almighty to avert or mitigate the evils to which they may tend. I shall also carry with me the hope that my country will never cease to view them with indulgence, and that, after forty-five years of my life dedicated to its service with an upright zeal, the faults of incompetent abilities will be consigned to oblivion, as myself must soon be to the mansions of rest.

Relying on its kindness in this as in other things, and actuated by that fervent love toward it which is so natural to a man who views in it the native soil of himself and his progenitors for several generations, I anticipate with pleasing expectation that retreat in which I promise myself to realize without alloy the sweet enjoyment of partaking in the midst of my fellow-citizens the benign influence of good laws under a free government—the ever-favorite object of my heart, and the happy reward, as I trust, of our mutual cares, labors, and dangers.

G°. WASHINGTON.

Bibliographical Essay

Among the varied works and sources used in this study the following deserve special mention.

Bibliographies and Guides

The most useful bibliographical aids for this study were Samuel F. Bemis and Grace Gardner Griffin, *Guide to the Diplomatic History of the United States, 1775–1921* (Washington, 1953); and Paul Leicester Ford, *Bibliotheca Hamiltoniana* (New York, 1886). Ford corrects Sabin concerning authorship of many pamphlets published by Hamilton's contemporaries. Other works consulted were Charles Evans, *American Bibliography* (12 vols., Chicago, 1903–34); Paul Leicester Ford, *Bibliography and Reference List of the History and Literature Relating to the Adoption of the Constitution of the United States, 1787–1788* (Brooklyn, 1888); E. B. Greene and R. B. Morris, *Guide to the Sources for Early American History (1600 to 1800) in the City of New York* (New York, 1929); A. P. C. Griffin, *List of Works Relating to the French Alliance in the American Revolution* (Washington, 1907); Grace Gardner Griffin, *Writings on American History, 1906* (New York, New Haven, and Washington, 1908–, continued subsequently by various editors and at irregular dates. Oscar Handlin *et al.*, *Harvard Guide to American History* (Cambridge, 1954), proved indispensable. Allan Nevins, "Alexander Hamilton," *Dictionary of American Biography* (New York, 1932), VIII, 171–79, is a good critical analysis of Hamilton biographies. Also useful were Joseph Sabin, *A Dictionary of Books Relating to America* (24 vols., New York, 1868–1934); and A. C. Wilgus, *The Histories of Hispanic America* (Washington, 1932). Good use can be made of the selective bibliographies given by Nathan Schachner, *Alexander Hamilton* (New York, 1946), 373–81; John C. Miller, *Alexander Hamilton: Portrait in Paradox* (New York, 1959), 623–39; Broadus Mitchell, *Alexander Hamilton: Youth to Maturity* (New York, 1957), 647–66; and Broadus Mitchell, *Alexander Hamilton: The National Adventure* (New York, 1962), 775–92; but the present work was laid out before these biographies were published.

Newspaper and archival guides consulted were C. S. Brigham, *History and Bibliography of American Newspapers, 1690–1820* (2 vols., Worcester, 1947); A. G. Slauson, *A Check List of American Newspapers in the Library of Congress* (Washington, 1901); Yale University, *A List of Newspapers in the Yale University Library* (New Haven, 1916); R. A. Billington, "Guides to American History Manuscript Collections in Libraries of the United States," *Mississippi Valley Historical Review*, XXXVIII (June, 1951), 467–96; J. C. Fitzpatrick, *Manuscripts in Public and Private Collections in the United States* (Washington, 1924); Curtis Wiswell Garrison, *List of Manuscript Collections in the Library of Congress to July, 1931* (Washington, 1932); *Guide to the Material in the National Archives* (Washington, 1940).

MANUSCRIPTS

The Library of Congress has a large collection of Hamilton papers—first series, 85 volumes; second series, 24 volumes—mostly concerned with his legal practice in New York. These papers include many important documents that have never been printed. A special collection of four boxes, containing 479 papers, never before open to the public, was made available for the present study through the kindness of Alexander Hamilton of New York. These documents add appreciably to an understanding of Hamilton's life and work, but they do not hold the answers to any of the unresolved problems concerning Hamilton.

The Library of Congress also has a useful collection of the instructions and dispatches between the British Foreign Office and its representatives in the United States, 1783 to 1792 (Foreign Office, Series 4, Vols. 1–12 and 14–16), as well as the Henry Adams Transcripts, continuing this correspondence from 1793 to 1801 (Vols. 15–37 in the old classification, Foreign Office, Series 5, modern system).

Important Hamilton material may be found almost throughout the 60 volumes of Pickering Papers, in the Massachusetts Historical Society, Boston. In life the two men were closely associated, and after Hamilton's death Pickering gathered material for a Hamilton biography, which he never wrote. Oliver Wolcott succeeded Hamilton as secretary of the treasury and continued in that office until 1800. Collaboration between the two men was close and constant for several years. The Connecticut Historical Society has 50 volumes and 24 boxes of Wolcott Papers, which include many unpublished Hamilton letters. Most of them pertain to other matters than foreign policy and will be essential for any complete biography of Hamilton.

The North Carolina Department of Archives and History, Raleigh, has a collection of the papers of William R. Davie, who, as major general and as governor of North Carolina, worked closely with Hamilton in 1799 in efforts to build an army. These papers are mostly in Private Collections 78 and 176. Several others are in the Governor's Letter Book No. 13, and Governor's Papers, State Series, Vol. XXII.

Newspapers

The Federalist *Gazette of the United States*, 1790 to 1800, and the Republican *National Gazette*, 1791 to 1795, give a clear picture of the contentious spirit of the times. The course of Hamilton's thought after the inauguration of Jefferson as president can be followed in the *New York Evening Post*, 1801 to 1804. The editor, William Coleman, was an enthusiastic disciple of Hamilton and incorporated into his editorials Hamilton's views on foreign affairs.

Printed Sources

Nearly all the collected works of Hamilton's contemporaries and many of the standard government publications contain material relating to his foreign policy.

Official Documents:

Douglas Brymner (ed.), "Relations with the United States after the Peace of 1783," *Report on Canadian Archives, 1890* (Ottawa, 1891), covers the Beckwith mission. F. J. Turner, ed., *Correspondence of the French Ministers to the United States, 1791–1797*, American Historical Association *Annual Report* for 1903, II (1904), contains indispensable documents dealing with French foreign policy. Bernard Mayo (ed.), *Instructions to the British Ministers to the United States, 1791–1812* (Washington, 1941), supplements Library of Congress transcripts and photostatic copies of British manuscripts of this period and is very useful.

Francis Wharton (ed.), *Revolutionary Diplomatic Correspondence of the United States* (6 vols., Washington, 1889), gives special attention to Hamilton's contribution. W. C. Ford (ed.), *Journals of the Continental Congress, 1774–1789* (34 vols., Washington, 1904–37), provides important data on the period. Max Farrand (ed.), *Records of the Federal Convention of 1787* (4 vols., New Haven, 1927–37), gives Hamilton's notes and his contribution to the work of the Constitutional Convention. Other documentary sources are Charles C. Tansil (ed.), *Documents Illustrative of the Formation of the Union of the United States* (Washington, 1927); *Annals of Congress* (42 vols., Washington, 1834–46), I–XIV; and Hunter Miller (ed.), *Treaties and other International Acts of the United States of America, 1776–1883* (8 vols., Washington, 1931–48). John Bassett Moore, *A Digest of International Law* (8 vols., Washington, 1906), provided background information on interpretation of international law of the period. Walter Lourie *et al.* (eds.), *American State Papers*, Class I, *Foreign Relations* (6 vols., Washington, 1832–56).

Published Works:

Charles Francis Adams (ed.), *The Works of John Adams* (10 vols., 1850–56). W. C. Ford (ed.), *The Writings of John Quincy Adams* (7 vols., New York, 1913–17). Seth Ames (ed.), *Works of Fisher Ames* (2 vols., Boston, 1854). Henry Cabot Lodge (ed.), *Life and Letters of George Cabot* (Boston, 1877). William P. Cutler and Julia P. Cutler (eds.), *Life, Journals, and Correspondence of Rev. Manasseh Cutler* (2 vols., Cincinnati, 1881). John Bigelow (ed.), *The Works of Benjamin Franklin* (12 vols., New York, 1904). John C. Hamilton (son of Alexander Hamilton), *The Works of Alexander Hamilton* (7 vols., New York, 1850–51). Henry Cabot Lodge (ed.), *The Works of Alexander Hamilton* (12 vols., New York, 1904). Harold C. Syrett (ed.), *The Papers of Alexander Hamilton* (7 vols., in process, 1961–). G. J. McRee (ed.), *Life and Correspondence of James Iredell* (2 vols., New York, 1857–58). Henry P. Johnston (ed.), *The Correspondence and Public Papers of John Jay* (4 vols., New York, 1893–94). Julian P. Boyd *et al.* (eds.), *Papers of Thomas Jefferson* (60 vols., in process, Princeton 1950–). A. A. Liscomb and A. E. Bergh (eds.), *The Writings of Thomas Jefferson* (20 vols., Washington, 1903–1904). Charles R. King (ed.), *The Life and Correspondence of Rufus King* (6 vols., New York, 1894–1900). E. S. Maclay (ed.), *Journal of William Maclay, United States Senator from Pennsylvania, 1789–1791* (New York, 1890). Bernard C. Steiner (ed.), *Life and Correspondence of James McHenry* (Cleveland, 1907). Gaillard Hunt (ed.), *The Writings of James Madison* (9 vols., 1900–10). Vincente Davila (ed.), *Archivo del General Miranda* (15 vols., Caracas, 1929–38). Stanislaus Murray Hamilton (ed.), *The Writings of James Monroe* (7 vols., New York, 1898–1903). Jared Sparks (ed.), *The Life of Gouverneur Morris, with Selections from His Correspondence and Miscellaneous Papers* (3 vols., Boston, 1832). Samuel Eliot Morison (ed.), *The Life and Letters of Harrison Gray Otis* (2 vols., Boston, 1913). Octavius Pickering and C. W. Upham (eds.), *Life of Timothy Pickering* (4 vols., Boston, 1867–73). M. D. Conway (ed.), *Omitted Chapters of History Disclosed in the Life and Papers of Edmund Randolph* (New York, 1888). William Henry Smith (ed.), *The Life and Public Services of Arthur St. Clair* (2 vols., Cincinnati, 1882). Henry McGilbert Wagstaff (ed.), *The Papers of John Steele* (2 vols., Raleigh, 1924). Charles Maurice de Talleyrand-Périgord, *Memoirs* (tr. and ed. by Raphael Ledas de Beaufort), (5 vols., New York, 1891–92). John C. Fitzpatrick (ed.), *The Writings of George Washington* (39 vols., Washington, 1931–44). John C. Fitzpatrick (ed.), *Diaries of George Washington, 1748–1799* (4 vols., New York, 1925). W. Davis (ed.), James Wilkinson, *Memoirs of My Own Times* (3 vols., Philadelphia, 1816).

SECONDARY WORKS

General Histories:

Henry Adams, *History of the United States During the Administration of Jefferson and Madison*, (New York, 1889), I–II, describes Hamilton's influence in the Federalist party during the early part of Jefferson's term as president. Rafael María Baralty Ramón Díaz, *Resumen de la Historia de Venezuela desde el Año de 1797 hasta el de 1830* (2 vols., Paris, 1939) has interesting conclusions about Hamilton's relations with Miranda. Samuel Flagg Bemis, (ed.), *The American Secretaries of State and Their Diplomacy*, I–II, is especially useful for the studies of Jay, Randolph, and Pickering. Samuel Flagg Bemis, *A Diplomatic History of the United States* (4th ed., New York, 1955), gives a basic treatment of this period, but places too much emphasis on Hamilton's supposed dependence on revenue collected from Anglo-American commerce. Edward Channing, *A History of the United States* (New York, 1917–18), III–IV, makes interesting observations regarding Hamilton's foreign policy but does not enter deeply into the subject. Richard Hildreth, *The History of the United States of America* (6 vols., New York, 1856–60), clearly describes the partisan feelings of the Hamilton-Jefferson period. J. B. McMaster, *A History of the People of the United States*, (New York, 1883), I, presents a clear picture of the political and social conditions in which Hamilton worked. W. A. Ward and G. P. Gooch, *Cambridge History of British Foreign Policy* (Cambridge, 1922), I, is useful for giving the British side of diplomacy in which Hamilton was involved.

Biographies:

Until recent years nothing approaching a complete biography of Hamilton had been published. For many years the reading public was subjected to a stream of biased biographies of Hamilton and Jefferson that exaggerated the acrimony between them. Most of these works did little more than proclaim the political convictions and historical predilections of their authors. Only a few made more than incidental references to Hamilton's foreign policy.

All the Hamilton biographies were consulted in the course of this study, and several of them were helpful. Charles F. Dunbar, "Some Precedents Followed by Alexander Hamilton," *Quarterly Journal of Economics*, III (October, 1888), 32–59, shows that Hamilton leaned heavily on English precedent and was not inclined toward experimentation. Henry Jones Ford, *Alexander Hamilton* (New York, 1920), a balanced account of Hamilton's influence in the creation of the new government, corrects a number of errors of previous writers. James A. Hamilton (Hamilton's son), *Reminiscences* (New York, 1869), has much firsthand information concerning Hamilton's personal feelings and aspirations. John C. Hamilton (Hamilton's son), *History of the Republic of the United States as Traced in the Writings of Alexander Hamilton and his Contemporaries* (7 vols., New York, 1857–64), must be classified as controversial and used with care. The chief value of the work arises from the fact that the author drew much of his information directly from his memories of his father and from family traditions. Allan McLane Hamilton (Hamilton's grandson), *The Intimate Life of Alexander Hamilton* (New York, 1910), is another personal work. Henry Cabot Lodge, *Alexander Hamilton* (Boston, 1882), though definitely pro-Hamilton, displays a deep understanding of the Federalists. It gives the best account of the rise of the animosity between Adams and Hamilton. William Graham Sumner, *Alexander Hamilton* (New York, 1890), contains interesting sociological interpretations based on limited knowledge of the facts. Roland J. Mulford, *The Political Theories of Alexander Hamilton* (Baltimore, 1903), is a detailed study by a political scientist. John T. Morse, Jr., *Life of Alexander Hamilton* (2 vols., Boston, 1876), reflects the spirit of the period in which it was published and sees Hamilton's enemies as predominantly southerners. Allan Nevins, "Alexander Hamilton," *Dictionary of American Biography*, (New York, 1932), VIII, 171–79, states some pertinent facts of Hamilton's life, and discusses rather fully some weaknesses of his character. Nathan Schachner, *Alexander Hamilton* (New York, 1946) represents the most thorough study of Hamilton published to that date. It is objective in most points, and brings to light a number of new facts, though Schachner does not go as far in interpreting Hamilton and the issues of his times as some readers might desire. Rexford G. Tugwell and Joseph Dorfman, "Alexander Hamilton: Nation-Maker," *Columbia University Quarterly*, Vol. XXIV (December, 1937), Vol. XXX (March, 1938) treats both Hamilton and Jefferson harshly and minimizes their importance. The authors' view is that only in the earlier years were Hamilton's services beneficial to the country.

The approach of the Hamilton bicentennial in the mid-1950's brought renewed interest in Hamilton, and the best biographies yet produced. Louis M. Hacker, *Alexander Hamilton in the American Tradition* (New York, 1957), describes Hamilton's role in establishing a centralized government but holds that he would not approve of the present "big government" designed to extend direct aid to many individuals. John C. Miller, *Alexander Hamilton: Portrait in Paradox* (New York, 1959), is a fine interpretation of Hamilton and the political currents of his time, based on extensive research; yet it sometimes criticizes too sharply Hamilton's motives or behavior without adequate analysis. Broadus Mitchell, *Alexander Hamilton* (2 vols., New York, 1957, 1962), is the most thorough and objective study ever made of Hamilton and presents clearly Hamilton's contributions in building the nation.

There are some excellent biographies of other statesmen and some that, though not particularly thorough, are, nevertheless, useful. Charles Francis Adams, *Life of John Adams*, Vol. I of *Works of John Adams* (Boston, 1850); Zoltan Haraszti, *John Adams and the Prophets of Progress* (Cambridge, 1952); Gilbert Chinard, *Honest John Adams* (Boston, 1933); Samuel F. Bemis, *John Quincy Adams and the Foundations of American Foreign Policy* (New York, 1949); and Samuel F. Bemis, "John Quincy Adams and George Washington," Massachusetts Historical Society *Proceedings*, 1941–44, Vol. LXVII (1945), 365–84, generally represent thorough research and brilliant scholarship, but claim for Adams certain influence over Washington that I believe should be attributed to Hamilton instead. George Adams Boyd, *Elias Boudinot: Patriot and Statesman, 1740–1821* (Princeton, 1952), considers Hamilton a protégé of Boudinot. Charles J. Stillé, *The Life and Times of John Dickinson, 1732–1808* (Philadelphia, 1891), and Catharine Van Cortlandt Mathews, *Andrew Ellicott: His Life and Letters* (New York, 1908), reflect the attitudes of their subjects. Henry Adams, *Life of Albert Gallatin* (Philadelphia, 1879), reflects John Adams' suspicions about Hamilton's attitude toward the republican form of government. Frank Monaghan, *John Jay, Defender of Liberty* (New York, 1935), is a clear presentation of Jay's approach. Claude G. Bowers, *Jefferson and Hamilton* (Boston, 1952), though strongly pro-Jefferson, pictures Hamilton as a man of broad vision working among contemporaries who were devoted to sectional interests. Gilbert Chinard, *Thomas Jefferson, the Apostle of Americanism* (Boston, 1929), gives a reliable account of the Hamilton-Jefferson disputes in the cabinet. Dumas Malone, *Jefferson and His Time* (3 vols., Boston, 1948–62), is objective and scholarly in dealing with Jefferson but in speculations subtly cuts Hamilton to pieces. William K. Woolery, *The Relation of Thomas Jefferson to American Foreign Policy, 1783–1793* (Baltimore, 1927), gives most of his attention to the period before 1790. Adrienne Koch, *Jefferson and Madison* (New York, 1950); and Irving Brant, *James Madison* (6 vols., Indianapolis, 1941–61), present excellent discussion of the relations between Hamilton and Madison, especially during the period when both men were members of the Continental Congress. Albert J. Beveridge, *Life of John Marshall* (2 vols., Boston, 1916–19), II, shows how profoundly America was affected by the French Revolution. William Spence Robertson, *The Life of Miranda* (2 vols., Chapel Hill, 1929), describes Hamilton's influence on Miranda's thinking. Daniel C. Gilman, *James Monroe* (Boston, 1883), is a valuable biography. Theodore Roosevelt, *Gouverneur Morris* (Boston, 1888), a broad interpretation of the men and policies of the post–Revolutionary War period. Harvey Putnam Prentiss, *Timothy Pickering as the*

Leader of New England Federalism, 1800–1815 (Salem, 1934), gives Hamilton credit for halting the New England secession movement. George C. Rogers, Jr., *Evolution of a Federalist: William Loughton Smith of Charleston (1758–1812)* (Columbia, S.C., 1962), is instructive concerning Hamilton's relations with Congress. James Ripley Jacobs, *Tarnished Warrior* (New York, 1938), is an illuminating study of James Wilkinson's military life, with some attention to his relations with Hamilton. John Marshall, *The Life of George Washington* (5 vols., London, 1804–1807), reveals much firsthand knowledge and understanding. Nathaniel W. Stephenson and Waldo H. Dunn, *George Washington* (2 vols., New York, 1940), is weak on foreign affairs and fails to bring Hamilton prominently into the discussion of Washington's foreign policy. D. S. Freeman, *George Washington* (6 vols., New York, 1948–52), is the most thorough study of Washington to date. J. D. Fitzpatrick, *George Washington Himself* (Indianapolis, 1933), is also useful.

Hamilton's British Policy:

Samuel Flagg Bemis, "Alexander Hamilton and the Limitation of Armaments," *Pacific Review*, Vol. II (March, 1922), 587–602, describes Hamilton's plan for disarming the border between Canada and the United States. Samuel Flagg Bemis, *Jay's Treaty: A Study in Commerce and Diplomacy* (New York, 1923), concludes that Jay's Treaty was based on Hamilton's negotiations with Hammond and that the discussions in 1794 weakened Jay's position in the negotiations at London. A. L. Burt, *The United States, Great Britain, and British North America* (New Haven, 1940), after thorough research, attributes Britain's retention of the Northwest posts after 1783 to the Indian problem rather than to the fur trade, as Hamilton supposed. It minimizes the damage done by Hamilton's interference in the Jay negotiations in 1794. F. J. Turner, "English Policy Toward America in 1790–1791," *American Historical Review*, Vol. VII (July, 1902), 706–35; Vol. VIII (October, 1902), 78–86, presents a brief discussion of the Nootka Sound affair and the Pitt-Miranda plans of 1790 to attack New Orleans and Mexico.

Hamilton's French Policy:

A. Aulard, "La dette américaine envers la France sous Louis XVI et sous la révolution," *Revue Paris*, Vol. XXXII (1925), 319–38, 534–50; and further discussion by the same author in *Révolution française*, New Series, No. 26 (1925), 111–24, gives the French side of this subject. Alphonse Bertrand, "Les États-Unis et la Révolution française," *Revue des Deux Mondes*, 5th Series (1906), 392–430, reviews the diplomacy and sentiments, 1788–1796. E. S. Corwin, *French Policy and the American Alliance of 1778* (Princeton, 1916), gives an interpretation of the influence of the alliance, but is not based on extensive study of documents. Manning J. Dauer, "The Two John Nicholases: Their Relation to Washington and Jefferson," *American Historical Review*, Vol. XLV (January, 1940), 338–48, discusses the "Langhorne letter." Albert du Casse, *Histoire des négociations diplomatiques relatives aux traités de Mortefontaine, de Lunéville et d'Amiens* (3 vols., Paris, 1855), is weak on American history but points out French mistakes. C. A. Duniway, "French Influence on the Adoption of the Federal Constitution," *American Historical Review*, Vol. IX (January, 1904), 304–309, shows that Hamilton was mistaken in his belief that French agents tried to obstruct the ratification of the Constitution. C. D. Hazen, *Contemporary American Opinion of the French Revolution* (Baltimore, 1897), is drawn mostly from Jefferson's writings. James Alton James, "French Diplomacy and American Politics, 1794–1795," American Historical Association *Annual Report* for 1911 (1913), I, 151–63; and James Alton James, "French Opinion as a Factor in Preventing War Between France and the United States, 1795–1800," *American Historical Review*, Vol. XXX (October, 1924), 44–55, are partly superseded by later researches but give a clear description of French fears that the United States, with its large merchant marine, might enter an alliance with Great Britain. E. Wilson Lyon, *Louisiana in French Diplomacy, 1759–1804* (Norman, 1934); E. Wilson Lyon, "Moustier's Memoir on Louisiana," *Mississippi Valley Historical Review*, Vol. XXII (September, 1935), 251–66; E. Wilson Lyon, "The Directory and the United States," *American Historical Review*, Vol. XLIII (April, 1938), 514–32; and E. Wilson Lyon, "The Franco-American Convention of 1800," *Journal of Modern History*, Vol. XII (September, 1940), 305–33, are drawn from French and other sources and clearly present Talleyrand's tricky diplomacy. Charles E. Martin, *The Policy of the United States as Regards Intervention* (New York, 1921), makes a study of the Hamilton-Jefferson controversy concerning the applicability of the Franco-American treaties at the time Genêt arrived in Philadelphia. Richard K. Murdoch, "Citizen Mangourit and the Projected Attack on East Florida in 1792," *Journal of Southern History*, Vol. XIV (November, 1948), 522–40, gives a well-researched presentation of Maugourit's activities. Louis-Guillaume Otto, *Considérations sur la conduite du government americain envers la France, depuis le commencement de la révolution jusqu'en 1797* (Princeton, 1945), demonstrates how foreign affairs became such an important factor in American party politics. C. M. Thomas, *American Neutrality in 1793* (New York, 1931), is an exhaustive study of the attempt of Washington's administration to establish a neutral course in 1793. Frederick J. Turner, "The Origin of Genet's Projected Attack on Louisiana and the Floridas," *American Historical Review*, Vol. III (July, 1898), 650–71; and Frederick J. Turner, "The Policy of France Toward the Mississippi Valley in the Period of

Washington and Adams," *American Historical Review*, Vol. X (January, 1905), 249–79, discuss the web of intrigue in the Mississippi Valley and the French plan to reacquire the territory eastward to the Allegheny Mountains and thereby render the United States subservient. Arthur P. Whitaker, *Spanish-American Frontier, 1783–1795* (Boston, 1927); Arthur P. Whitaker, *The Mississippi Question, 1795–1803* (New York, 1934); Arthur P. Whitaker, "The Retrocession of Louisiana in Spanish Policy," *American Historical Review*, Vol. XXXIX (April, 1934), 547–76; and Arthur P. Whitaker, "Louisiana in the Treaty of Basle," *Journal of Modern History*, Vol. VIII (March, 1936), 1–26, though based on thorough multiarchival study, make conclusions about Hamilton's Louisiana policy that are open to question.

Farewell Address:

Several of the works listed above deal to some extent with Washington's Farewell Address and Hamilton's assistance in preparing it. Additional works deserve special mention. Samuel Flagg Bemis, "Washington's Farewell Address: A Foreign Policy of Independence," *American Historical Review*, Vol. XXXIX (January, 1934), 250–68, shows that the message was aimed largely at the French effort to undermine American independence. Elbert J. Benton, "The Spirit of Washington's Foreign Policy," *The Review*, Vol. I (October 11, 1919), 469–71, summarizes the attitude of Washington's administration toward foreign policy. Alexander DeConde, "Washington's Farewell, the French Alliance, and the Election of 1796," *Mississippi Valley Historical Review*, Vol. XLIII (March, 1957), 641–58, has enlightening comments regarding the domestic significance of the address. Horace Binney, *An Inquiry into the Formation of Washington's Farewell Address* (Philadelphia, 1859), makes interesting conclusions based on extensive research. Felix Gilbert, *To the Farewell Address: Ideas on Early American Foreign Policy* (Princeton, 1961) is also a helpful summary. The most useful collection of documents, together with extensive editorial comments on the subject, is contained in Victor Hugo Paltsits, *Washington's Farewell Address, in Facsimile, with Transliterations of All the Drafts of Washington, Madison, & Hamilton, Together with Their Correspondence* (New York, 1935).

MISCELLANEOUS SECONDARY WORKS:

John S. Bassett, *The Federalist System, 1789–1801* (New York, 1906), gives a clear statement of the essential facts. Charles A. Beard, *An Economic Interpretation of the Constitution of the United States* (New York, 1913); and Charles A. Beard, *The Idea of National Interest* (New York, 1934), laud Hamilton's honesty and good intentions but picture him as the chosen vessel of a group that sought to use him to advance their own pursuit of power and wealth. Samuel Flagg Bemis, *The Diplomacy of the American Revolution* (New York, 1935), is valuable for the light it casts on the origins of American foreign policy. Edmund C. Burnett, *The Continental Congress* (New York, 1941), emphasizes the importance of Hamilton's foreign policy when he was a member of the Congress. Joseph Charles, *The Origins of the American Party System* (Williamsburg, 1956), is useful for discussion of federalism and republicanism. Arthur Burr Darling, *Our Rising Empire, 1763–1803* (New Haven, 1940), presents valuable information on Hamilton's work. Manning J. Dauer, *The Adams Federalists* (Baltimore, 1953), discusses the economic, geographic, and religious background of the parties. Louise Burnham Dunbar, *A Study of "Monarchical" Tendencies in the United States from 1776 to 1801* (Urbana, Illinois, 1922), refutes the idea that Hamilton was a monarchist and minimizes all "monarchical" moves of that period. T. M. Green, *The Spanish Conspiracy: A Review of Early Spanish Movements in the Southwest* (Cincinnati, 1891), details the intrigues of Spain in the Mississippi region. Charles S. Hyneman, *The First American Neutrality . . . 1792 to 1815* (Urbana, Illinois, 1934), stresses the legal, not the political or diplomatic aspects. H. B. Learned, *The President's Cabinet* (New Haven, 1912), demonstrates Hamilton's influence in establishing the cabinet structure in the national government. Orin Grant Libby, "Political Factions in Washington's Administrations," *University of North Dakota Quarterly Journal*, Vol. III (July, 1913), 293–318, describes the close connection between foreign policy and American party politics. John C. Miller, *Crisis in Freedom: The Alien and Sedition Acts* (Boston, 1951), illustrates the spirit of anxiety, 1798–1799, which resulted in those acts. Allan Nevins, *The Evening Post: A Century of Journalism* (New York, 1922), illustrates Hamilton's influence on the newspaper's editorials.

Albert Sorel, *L'Europe et la Révolution française* (8 vols., Paris, 1885–1904), presents the French Revolution from the Continental point of view. Charles C. Tansill, *The United States and Santo Domingo, 1798–1875* (Baltimore, 1938), describes Hamilton's and Pickering's interest in independence for Santo Domingo. C. H. Van Tyne, *Loyalists in the American Revolution* (New York, 1929), tells the story of the pro-British Americans. Carl Van Doren, *The Great Rehearsal: The Story of the Making and Ratifying of the Constitution of the United States* (New York, 1948), illustrates some of Hamilton's political ideas. Leonard D. White, *The Federalists: A Study in Administrative History* (New York, 1948), and Leonard D. White, *The Jeffersonians . . . 1801–1829* (New York, 1951), a political scientist's evaluation of some of Hamilton's work in the cabinet, occasionally makes interesting comparisons of Federalists and Jeffersonians as administrators. John H. Wolfe, *Jeffersonian Democracy in South*

Carolina (Chapel Hill, 1940), illustrates the regional influence of the Republicans in the South. Henry M. Wriston, "Washington and the Foundation of American Foreign Policy," *Minnesota History*, Vol. VIII (March, 1927), 3–26, effectively refutes some of the adverse criticisms that had been made of the diplomacy of the Washington administration.

Index

The paper on which this book is printed bears the watermark of the University of Oklahoma Press and has an effective life of at least three hundred years.

University of Oklahoma Press

Norman

71
72
74
75
76
77
79
81
83
85
88